ONE HUNDRED YEARS OF
LAND VALUES IN
CHICAGO

THE RELATIONSHIP OF THE GROWTH
OF CHICAGO TO THE RISE OF ITS
LAND VALUES, 1830 - 1933

ONE HUNDRED YEARS OF
LAND VALUES IN
CHICAGO

THE RELATIONSHIP OF THE GROWTH
OF CHICAGO TO THE RISE OF ITS
LAND VALUES, 1830 - 1933

■

HOMER HOYT

BeardBooks
Washington, D.C.

Copyright 1933 by The University of Chicago
Reprinted 2000 by Beard Books, Washington, D.C.
ISBN 1-58798-016-9
Printed in the United States of America

To My Mother

AUTHOR'S PREFACE

This study was undertaken because there seemed to be no comprehensive data available to show the cyclical fluctuations of land values in any American city, and because the knowledge of the past movement of land prices seemed to me to be indispensable for any rational real estate investment policy. The easily accessible land valuations of the tax assessors that are so frequently used, in most cases, either do not adequately show the course of the real estate market as indicated by actual sales or are not available in comparable form for a sufficiently long period of time for this purpose. Accordingly, the most difficult task involved in this study was the computation of land values for the 211-square-mile area within the 1933 corporate limits of Chicago for the period from 1830 to 1933. The records of thousands of sales were examined for this period, which represented the life-span of Chicago from its first subdivision to the present, and these sales were compared with the appraisals and opinions of real estate dealers. During the period 1910–33, the annual land-value maps of George C. Olcott were extensively used to supplement the reports of sales. Even with all the evidence that could be secured from thousands of abstracts in the files of the Chicago Title and Trust Company, from considerations reported in deeds in the files of newspapers, from appraisals, and from tax-assessment records, it was impossible to secure sales or valuation data for every type of land in every square mile in the city for the one-hundred-and-four-year period covered by the study. It was frequently necessary to make interpolations based on the trend of sales data in surrounding sections. Nevertheless it is believed that the results are substantially correct, and that they are as accurate as the nature of the data will permit. Those who have had practical experience with real estate transactions know that the same degree of certainty does not and, perhaps, cannot prevail in the land market as in the stock or commodity markets. During recurring periods of stagnation, there is no active real estate market, and estimates of values at such times can at best be only approximations. I do not pretend that I have charted the final and absolute value of Chicago land for every year, but I have sought to obtain all the evidence that is available and to register in graphic form the records of sales, the opinions, and the current beliefs that made up the Chicago land market.

While assuming sole responsibility for any errors and imperfections in this book, I desire to give credit to those whose aid and co-operation made this study possible. To Professor Chester Whitney Wright, of the University of Chicago, at whose suggestion this investigation was undertaken, and under whose direction it was pursued, I am greatly indebted both for his suggestions in the fundamental plan of the work and for his untiring labor in revising the manuscript. To Professor Harry Alvin Millis, chairman of the Department of Economics of the University of Chicago, I express my deep gratitude for his conscientious criticism and his numerous helpful suggestions. To Professor Simeon E. Leland, of the University of Chicago and of the Illinois State Tax Commission, I am greatly indebted for invaluable constructive criticism during all stages of the work and particularly on the last part of the chapter on the real estate cycle. Professor Garfield V. Cox also gave me many helpful suggestions on the real estate cycle.

Many a member of the real estate profession has contributed a lifetime of effort to gathering information that is presented in these pages. One great organization—the Chicago Title and Trust Company—that is not in the real estate business assisted this publication in many ways. First, it placed at my disposal its invaluable plats, maps, and the abstracts that gave records of sales for over a hundred years. Second, in a time of great financial stringency when real estate was extremely depressed the officials of this Company saw the practical value of a long-range perspective with regard to land values, and they undertook to arouse public interest in this volume. In a series of educational advertisements and booklets they sought to demonstrate that historical research in land values tends to stabilize real estate. Third, the Chicago Title and Trust Company has contributed chiefly to the funds necessary for the cost of publication of this book. This is greatly appreciated. Of course, I am extremely grateful to General Abel Davis, chairman of the Board; Mr. Holman D. Pettibone, president; Mr. Kenneth E. Rice, vice-president; and Mr. Paul P. Pullen, director of publicity, for the benefits that have accrued to me directly as a result of their farsighted policy. I am grateful also to Mr. J. Frank Graf, vice-president of the Chicago Title and Trust Company, for his services in procuring for me the plats and abstracts of his Company, and to Mr. K. L. Van Sickle of the Chicago Title and Trust Company for his invaluable appraisal data. I am greatly indebted also to Mr. Carroll Dean Murphy and Mr. Frank R. Schwengel of the firm of Carroll Dean Murphy, Inc., for their aid in preparing the book for publication.

Other civic groups interested in urban land problems have given me the fullest co-operation. I desire to express my appreciation for the assistance given by Mr. E. L. Bailey, of the Chicago Regional Planning Association, particularly in the case of studies in lots subdivided in the Chicago Metropolitan Area. I also want to thank Mr. Hugh E. Young, of the Chicago Plan Commission, for allowing me to inspect his large maps on the blighted area. Mr. J. V. Sullivan, of the Chicago Surface Lines, furnished me the material for the transportation maps.

The county assessor, Mr. J. L. Jacobs, by whom I have been employed for statistical work in connection with the 1931 assessment of real estate in Cook County, has given me great assistance. In his untiring efforts to make an honest and correct assessment of land and buildings in Cook County in 1931, he secured the co-operation of the leading real estate men in the city and through his efforts I was able to secure the benefits of his voluminous records and also the advice and criticism of men with long experience in the real estate profession. I am particularly indebted also to members of Mr. Jacobs' staff, with whom I have been pleasantly associated: Mr. Walter R. Kuehnle, chief of the Real Estate Division; Mr. F. A. Schepler, chief of the Land Division; Mr. Benjamin Baltzer, chief land assessor for the South Side; Mr. Stanley C. Chadwick, chief land assessor for the North Side; Mr. Roger E. Appleyard, chief land assessor for the West Side; and Mr. H. S. Rosenthal and Mr. A. K. Wyatt of the Industrial Department.

This book would not have been possible without the work of George C. Olcott, who in his lifetime has compiled twenty-two books of Chicago land values, which furnish a reliable annual index of Chicago land values since 1910. There are few, if any, cities that have such a record covering a period of time in which sales data have been difficult to secure. Because of Mr. Olcott's work, Chicago has been selected as a laboratory for land-value analysis by economists and sociologists.

There are many real estate men who have contributed their time and thought to material that has appeared in this book, and among them I should like to express my thanks to Mr. William A. Bond for his appraisals and sales records and to Mr. Clifford R. Bechtel and Mr. John Usher Smyth. Mr. William Scott Bond furnished valuable information on real estate interest rates. Mr. Lyndon Lesch, of the Business Office of the University of Chicago, Mr. Earle Shultz, Mr. John P. Hooker, and Mr. Graham Aldis furnished valuable aid by giving me records of certain buildings. Mr. Edward G. Skindzier, manager of the London Guaranty and Accident Building, furnished me data of great value concerning the central business district of Chicago. Many old residents of the city have aided this work by giving me accounts of the character of the improvements in various sections of the city in the period following the great fire of 1871. I desire particularly to thank Mr. Emil Rudolph, Mr. John E. Cornell, Mr. Frank A. Henshaw, and Mr. William H. Spikings.

The books and monographs of Professor Herbert D. Simpson and John E. Burton of Northwestern University have also proved suggestive and helpful to me in compiling this study.

In the annals of the past, many whose names are unknown to me have furnished invaluable material. The real estate editors of the *Chicago Tribune*, who weekly wrote searching comments upon real estate transactions in the Sunday papers since 1870, the editors of the *Economist*, the editors of the *Real Estate and Building Journal*, have written many lines which reappear in these pages. Mr. Frank Chandler wrote much on early land-value history, and gave me access to his private files before his death.

Mr. Everett Chamberlin, in his book, *Chicago and Its Suburbs* (1874), and Mr. Mark L. Putney, in his *Land Values and Historical Notes of Chicago* (1890, 1900), furnished great assistance. The work of Captain A. T. Andreas on the *History of Chicago* (1886) proved very useful.

In formulating this study I have been greatly stimulated by the ecological studies made by the Departments of Sociology of the University of Chicago and the University of Michigan, and I desire to express my gratitude for helpful suggestions in the works of Professors Robert E. Park, Roderick D. McKenzie, Ernest W. Burgess, and Louis Wirth. Mr. Earl Johnson's studies of the ecology of the central business district of Chicago have been very helpful.

I desire particularly to thank the librarians of the Chicago Historical Society for the use of their books, maps, newspaper files, and

AUTHOR'S PREFACE

manuscript material. Miss Alice Daly, of the Chicago Historical Society, aided me in securing the Ogden letters and other original documents. I am also indebted to the librarians of the University of Chicago, of the Newberry Library, and of the Chicago Public Library for the use of their newspaper files. Mr. Charles Newcomb, of the social-science staff of the University of Chicago, planned the technique of the maps and charts in this book, and Miss Mae Schiffman executed the drawings. To both of them I express my appreciation. I am indebted to Miss Janet Murray for the computations of the trends for the charts on the Chicago real estate cycle. I express my appreciation also to Mr. George S. Wheeler for his careful reading of the manuscript.

Finally, the city of Chicago itself, with all its kaleidoscopic neighborhoods and its babble of tongues, is an inspiration to me. This city, with all its rough edges and its bluntness, is a city with a unique and magnetic urban personality. The land-value changes in such a city reveal the methods of physical growth and the moods of a people in an environment with which I have been intimately associated. Hence, I reluctantly come to the end of a pleasant task, hoping that other citizens of Chicago will have the delight of digging up the facts for histories and studies of other phases of Chicago's many-sided life. For such historical research will make the present Chicago seem more real and vital to us.

HOMER HOYT

CHICAGO, ILLINOIS

FOREWORD

There is a considerable literature on land economics, but in so far as I know Mr. Hoyt's volume presents the results of the first comprehensive study of land values in a large city over a long period of time. It brings together from a great variety of sources the main facts and attempts to explain them in their interrelations. The result is a distinct contribution both to the economic and social history of Chicago and to urban land economics. Most interesting, perhaps, and most suggestive of the several chapters is the final one on the real estate cycle.

The history of land values in Chicago should assist in correcting erroneous notions concerning urban land values. The single tax doctrine that the changes are all gains, large and unearned, might lead us to believe that urban land values rise steadily without any recessions or setbacks. This is not true. Banks, insurance companies, and other investors will find in the volume much to ponder over. Students of taxation will find facts to be taken into consideration when they attempt to develop a properly rounded system of taxation, and those charged with assessing real estate for the purpose of taxation will find detail here and there pointing to matters they should not overlook as they go about their work.

Perhaps this volume could not have been written had not Mr. Hoyt engaged in the "real estate game" in boom and depression, after devoting several years to the study and teaching of economics. His experience in assessing real estate has also been helpful. The volume of data to be collected, studied, and weighed was appalling; the factors to be discovered and held in mind many, interrelated, and confusing. No doubt errors have crept in and remain undetected by the author and by those of us who have read the manuscript. Perhaps there will be difference of opinion as to some of the methods employed. Certainly the volume cannot be regarded as the final word on every phase of the subject discussed. Yet it is a contribution of great value.

H. A. MILLIS

TABLE OF CONTENTS

	PAGE
LIST OF ILLUSTRATIONS	xxiii
LIST OF TABLES	xxvii

PART I. HISTORY OF THE RELATION OF THE GROWTH OF CHICAGO TO THE RISE IN ITS LAND VALUES, 1830–1933

CHAPTER

I. THE CANAL LAND BOOM, 1830–42 3
   A. Introduction: Objectives of the Study 3
   B. Causes of the Early Growth of Chicago 7
      The portage. The fort. The canal. Land trails to Chicago. The growth of Chicago, 1830–32. Chicago in 1833. Chicago in 1834. Chicago in 1835–36.
   C. Land Values in Chicago, 1830–42 23
      The start. The rise begins. Gaining momentum. At full speed. The peak. A survey at the summit. The lull. The forces of depression. The sharp decline. The bottom. A survey at the bottom. The aftermath.

II. THE LAND BOOM OF THE RAILROAD ERA, 1843–62 45
   A. The Period from 1843 to 1848 45
      A new start on the canal. Growth of wagon and lake traffic. The physical growth of Chicago, 1843–48. A slow rise in land values.
   B. The Period from 1848 to 1857; the New Agencies of Transportation and Communication 53
      The canal. The telegraph. The plank roads. The railroads. Grain and lumber trade. Infant industries. The new banks. The new wholesale trade. The physical growth of Chicago, 1848–57. New buildings and public improvements. Chicago's expansion. The rise in land values, 1848–57.
   C. The Period from 1857 to 1862; the Panic of 1857 and the Civil War . . 74
      The panic of 1857. The depression in 1858. The year 1859. The year 1860. The collapse of the state banks of issue, 1861–63. The horse railways. Land values in 1862.

III. THE LAND BOOM THAT FOLLOWED A PANIC, A CIVIL WAR, AND A GREAT FIRE, 1863–77 81
   A. The Later Civil War Period, 1863–65 81
   B. The Post-war Boom, 1865–71 82
      Growth of Chicago's trade and manufactures, 1865–71.

CHAPTER	PAGE
C. Rise in Chicago Land Values, by Use and Occupation Areas, 1865–71	88

The main business district. The fashionable residential areas. The manufacturing centers, 1863–71. The slums, vice areas, and workingmen's quarters, 1863–71. The secondary business streets. The parks, 1865–71. The suburbs. The spread of the speculative land movement, 1868–71.

D. The Great Fire of 1871 and the Period before the Panic of 1873 . . 101

The great fire of October 9, 1871. Increase in the value of outlying lands, 1865–73. A survey of Chicago land values at the peak of 1873.

E. The Panic of 1873 and the Subsequent Depression 117

F. A Survey at the Bottom in 1877–79 125
The silver lining.

IV. THE LAND BOOM OF THE FIRST SKYSCRAPERS AND THE FIRST WORLD'S FAIR, 1878–98 128

A. Recovery in General Business Conditions, 1878–84 128
The effect on the trade, manufactures, and railroads of Chicago. The general effect of improved business conditions upon Chicago land values.

B. The Specific Methods of Recovery of Chicago Land Values, 1878–83 132
1. Bargains in the central business district, 1879–80. 2. The boom on Michigan Boulevard, 1880. 3. The "resurrection" of South Chicago, 1879–83. 4. Pullman. 5. The boom in the new Board of Trade Quarter. 6. The "flat craze." 7. Growth of the outer edges of Chicago. 8. Review of the rise in land values in the Chicago area, 1878–83.

C. The Period from 1884 to 1886 141
The recession in general business activity in 1883.

D. Special Factors in the Movement of Chicago Land Values from 1886 to 1894 142
1. The growth of Chicago railroads and manufactures, 1886–94: (a) The growth of manufacturing. 2. Internal transportation, 1887–94: (a) The cable loops. (b) Projected elevated and surface lines. 3. Steel-frame skyscrapers, 1885–94. 4. Annexation. 5. The World's Fair. 6. Department stores and apartments.

E. The Movement of Land Values in the Chicago Real Estate Market, 1886–94 159
The beginning of a new boom, 1886–88. The boom under way, 1889. Speculation in acre tracts and subdivision activity. The culmination of the boom, 1890. The beginning of the lull, 1891. The onset of the panic, 1893.

F. New Transportation Lines, 1894–98 181

TABLE OF CONTENTS xvii

CHAPTER PAGE
 G. Summary of the Trend of Chicago Land Values, 1877–98 . . . 184
  The central business section. Fashionable residential areas, 1877–95. Outlying business centers. Rise in the value of acre tracts, 1879–92. The rapid population growth of the outlying territories.

V. THE LAND BOOM OF A NEW ERA THAT FOLLOWED A WORLD WAR, 1898–1933 196
 A. Survey of the Causes of the Growth of Chicago, 1830–90 and 1890–1933 196
 B. The Period from 1898 to 1918 200
  Chicago in 1900. Beginning of the recovery in Chicago real estate. New transportation systems. Effect on different sections of the city. The central business district: office buildings. The Loop retail district. Downtown wholesale area. Summary: downtown area. Expanding wholesale and warehouse interests. New manufacturing centers. Value of railroad and manufacturing property. Fashionable residential property. Apartments. Old residential areas. New residential areas. The Chicago land market as a whole, 1900–1908.
  The Period from 1908 to 1918: Central business district. Outlying business centers. Growth of new neighborhoods. Acre and subdivision activity. Fashionable residential areas. Old residential areas. Manufacturing and warehouse districts. Apartments. Review of the market as a whole, 1908–18.
 C. The Period from 1919 to 1933 232
  Survey of the general factors affecting urban land in the United States, 1919–26. The growth of the trade and manufactures of Chicago, 1921–29. The growth in real estate factors, 1919–26. Population increase. The building boom.
  Survey of movement of Chicago land values by regions and types of property: 1. Central business district. 2. The near North Side. 3. Tall apartment buildings. 4. Two- and three-story apartment building areas. 5. Bungalow areas. 6. Old residential areas. 7. Industrial areas. 8. Outlying business centers. 9. Subdivision and acreage tracts.
  The Chicago real estate market as a whole, 1921–29: Chicago land values at the peak.
  The period from 1929 to 1933: Dulness sets in. The stock-market boom and crash. The sharp decline of real estate values in 1931.
  A survey at the bottom, March, 1933: The year 1933: a turning-point.

TABLE OF CONTENTS

PART II. ANALYSIS OF THE RELATION OF THE GROWTH OF CHICAGO TO THE RISE OF ITS LAND VALUES

VI. THE RELATION BETWEEN THE GROWTH OF CHICAGO AND THE RISE OF ITS LAND VALUES 279

   A. The Demand for Chicago Land 279
      1. The swarm of people: (*a*) The growth of Chicago compared with that of other American cities. (*b*) Where did the people come from? (*c*) Why did they come? 2. Increase in the number of buildings: (*a*) Increase in the volume of building space. (*b*) Factors determining the volume of building space. (*c*) Classification of buildings by type of use. (*d*) The average height of buildings in the Chicago area. (*e*) The intensity of land utilization in Chicago.

   B. The Supply of Chicago Land 295
      1. The practical limit to the supply of Chicago urban land: (*a*) Lateral expansion by more rapid transportation. (*b*) The extension into the air.

   C. Causes of Differences in Land Values within Chicago 297
      1. The land-value contour map. 2. Physical causes of land-value variations: (*a*) The effect of the lake. (*b*) The effect of the river. (*c*) The Chicago plain. (*d*) The three sections of the city. 3. The growth of different types of land uses: (*a*) The fashionable residential areas: (1) The decline of Prairie Avenue. (2) The lake front grows in importance. (*b*) Cheap residential areas: (1) Expansion of racial and nationality groups. (*c*) Industrial areas. (*d*) Outlying business centers: (1) Store rents and traffic counts. (*e*) The central business district of Chicago. (*f*) Summary: Chicago land values by types of uses.

   D. The Long-Run Trend of Chicago Land Values 344
      1. Corrections of the land-value data for changes in wholesale prices, wages, and interest rates: (*a*) The change in the interest rate. (*b*) Allowance for the cost of street improvements. 2. Growth of money at compound interest and rise of land values compared. 3. Taxation.

   E. Trend of Population and Land Values by Districts 353
      1. The centrifugal forces affecting population. 2. The effect of population changes on the land-value pattern. 3. The difficulty of developing new areas compared with the difficulty of reclaiming "blighted" areas. 4. The effect of shifting land uses. 5. Speculative exaggeration of possible demand for certain types of uses. 6. The future trend of population and land values.

TABLE OF CONTENTS

CHAPTER	PAGE
VII. THE CHICAGO REAL ESTATE CYCLE	368

A. The Tide of Population 368
B. Definition of the Chicago Real Estate Cycle 369
C. The Effect of Population Growth on the Chicago Real Estate Cycle   372
     1. The initial impulse—a sudden spurt in population growth. 2. The supply of houses cannot be immediately increased. 3. Qualifications as to the influence of population on the real estate cycle: (a) Limitations of the population and land-value data.
D. The Sequence of Events in the Chicago Real Estate Cycle . . . 377
     1. Gross rents begin to rise rapidly. 2. Net rents rise even more rapidly. 3. As a result of the rise in rents, selling prices of existing buildings advance sharply. 4. It pays to erect new buildings. 5. The volume of new construction rises. 6. The volume of building is stimulated by easy credit. 7. "Shoestring" financing swells the number of new structures. 8. The new buildings absorb vacant land: the land boom. 9. Optimistic population forecasts during the boom. 10. The vision of new cities in cornfields: the method of some subdividers. 11. Lavish expenditures for public improvements. 12. All the real estate factors at full tide: the peak. 13. The reverse movement begins: the lull. 14. Foreclosures increase. 15. The stock-market *débâcle* and the onset of the depression in general business. 16. The process of attrition. 17. The banks reverse their boom policy on real estate loans. 18. The period of stagnation and foreclosures. 19. The wreckage is cleared away. 20. Ready for another boom which does not come automatically.
E. Minor Movements of the Individual Real Estate Factors . . . 403
F. Statistical Summary of Sequence of Factors in the Chicago Real Estate Cycle 405
G. The Chicago Real Estate Cycle Compared with the General Business Cycle in the United States 407
     1. The magnitude of the oscillations. 2. Duration of the Chicago real estate and general business cycles: (a) The long periods of depression in Chicago real estate. 3. The relationship of wage and interest rates to the land-value cycle. 4. The sequence of the real estate and the commodity and stock cycles: (a) The valleys coincide but the peaks do not. (b) Commodity, land, and stock speculations do not come together but alternate. (c) The advantage of a source of liquid capital for real estate operators. (d) Speculators tend to stick to the game they know best. (e) The public is swayed by the prevailing crowd psychology. (f) The delayed effects of a great war.
H. Real Estate Cycles May Be a Passing Phase 423

TABLE OF CONTENTS

APPENDIXES

APPENDIX	PAGE
I. THE CHICAGO LAND MARKET	427
A. The Lack of Homogeneity of Chicago Lots	427

1. Layout of the original subdivision lot and block size: depth-rule and corner-influence factors. 2. Differences in the owner's title: (*a*) Guaranty policies of the Chicago Title and Trust Company. (*b*) The Torrens system. (*c*) Differences in mortgages and leasehold interests. (*d*) Differences in financial necessities of the owner. (*e*) Differences in ownership units. (*f*) Differences in the effectiveness of propaganda. 3. Differences in land values due to actions of the community or the state: (*a*) Differences in tax rates and exemptions. (*b*) Differences in foreclosure and other laws relating to land titles. (*c*) Differences in building codes and fire limits.

  B. The Mechanism of the Chicago Land Market 441

1. Buyers and sellers: (*a*) Degree of knowledge of land values. (*b*) Purpose of buying land. (*c*) Residence or occupation of the buyer. (*d*) Race or nationality. 2. Methods of bringing buyers and sellers together. 3. Signing the contract. 4. Terms of sale and methods of financing purchases. 5. Sources of price information. 6. Future relations of the parties. 7. Seasonal elements in the land market.

  C. The Fundamental Basis of Land Values: Capitalization of Net Income 449

1. Necessity of a building to produce income. 2. Suitability of building to location. 3. The residual income. 4. Forecasting future incomes. 5. Factors in determining future ground rent.

  D. Speculative Errors in Calculating Future Chicago Land Income . 456

1. Errors in estimating long-run forces of supply and demand: (*a*) Demand-purchasing power. (*b*) Supply. (*c*) Capitalization rate. (*d*) Wage rates. (*e*) Movement of a leader: human and catastrophic factors. 2. Errors due to the business cycle.

II. METHODS EMPLOYED IN DETERMINING CHICAGO LAND VALUES, 1830–1932 460

  A. The Main Methods Employed in Determining the Value of Chicago Land 460

1. Sources of land-value data—assessments for taxation purposes. 2. Advertised or listed prices. 3. Appraisals and opinions of experts. 4. Sales.

  B. Sources of Sales Data 465

  C. Method of Computing Total Value of Chicago Land from Sample Sales 467

III. STATISTICAL TABLES 470

BIBLIOGRAPHY

BIBLIOGRAPHY 497

INDEX

INDEX 503

LIST OF ILLUSTRATIONS

FIGURE		PAGE
1.	Location of Chicago with Respect to Waterway Systems	8
2.	Land Trails to Chicago	14
3.	Map of Chicago in 1830	16
4.	Subdivision Plat of "Original Town of Chicago," 1830	25
5.	Original Subdivisions, 1830–43	32
6.	Land Values by Square-Mile Sections, 1836	34
7.	Land Values, 1836, Indicated by Sales of Acre Tracts	35
8.	Land Values, 1841–43, Indicated by Sales of Acre Tracts	43
9.	Railroads Entering Chicago in 1854	57
10.	Original Subdivisions, 1844–62	68
11.	Land Values per Front Foot, 1856	71
12.	Land Values by Square-Mile Sections, 1857	72
13.	Land Values, 1856–57, Indicated by Sales of Acre Tracts	73
14.	Land Values, 1860–63, Indicated by Sales of Acre Tracts	79
15.	Chicago Trade and Manufactures, 1840–1931	85
16.	Sewers, Paved Streets, and Bridges, 1873	92
17.	The Burned Area, 1871, and Fire Limits, 1872	105
18.	Extent of Settled Area for the Periods 1834, 1844, 1857, and 1873	106
19.	Original Subdivisions, 1863–79	110
20.	Land Values per Front Foot, 1873	112
21.	Land Values by Square-Mile Sections, 1873	114
22.	Land Values, 1870–73, Indicated by Sales of Acre Tracts	115
23.	Horse-Car Lines in 1880	126
24.	Street-Car Lines in 1891	145
25.	Extension of City Limits by Annexations	154
26.	Land Values per Front Foot, 1892	186
27.	Land Values for Each Square-Mile Section, 1892	187
28.	Land Values, 1890–92, Indicated by Sales of Acre Tracts	194
29.	Extent of the Settled Area in 1899	204
30.	Factors in the Growth of Chicago, 1890–1932	206
31.	Surface and Elevated Lines in 1902	209
32.	Residential Land Values per Front Foot in 1910	220
33.	Land Values for Each Square-Mile Section in 1910	221
34.	Fluctuations in the Net Income of a Chicago Apartment Building, 1907–31	239
35.	Fluctuations in the Net Income of an Office Building in Chicago, 1905–32	240
36.	Distribution of Buildings Seven Stories High or Over, 1933	243
37.	Land Values on Seventy-ninth Street, Stony Island to Crawford, 1910, 1928, 1931	250

LIST OF ILLUSTRATIONS

FIGURE		PAGE
38.	Land Values on Lawrence Avenue, 1910, 1928, 1931	251
39.	Land Values of the Principal Business Corners outside the Loop, 1910	253
40.	Land Values of the Principal Business Corners outside the Loop, 1928	254
41.	Original Subdivisions, 1880–1932	256
42.	Residential Land Values per Front Foot, 1926	259
43.	Land Values for Each Square-Mile Section, 1928	260
44.	Extent of the Settled Area in 1926	262
45.	Increase in Land Values, 1918–28	263
46.	Extensions to Surface and Elevated Lines, 1903–32	264
47.	Residential Land Values per Front Foot, 1931	267
48.	Factors in the Chicago Real Estate Depression, 1926–33	270
49.	The Decline in the Number of Chicago Banks outside the Loop, 1929–33	271
50.	Comparison of Ground Area Occupied by the Houses and Yards of Rich and Poor Families in Chicago, 1886	289
51.	Air Space Occupied by Buildings in Chicago, 1933	293
52.	Extension of Area Occupied by High-Grade Residential or Apartment Buildings, 1833–1933	303
53.	Fluctuations in the Value of Fashionable Residential Land, 1865–1933	305
54.	Land Values in Outlying High-Grade Areas Developed after 1900	306
55.	Residential Land Values, One Block North of Division Street, Lake Michigan to Laramie, 1910 and 1928	308
56.	Residential Land Values, South Side, between Fifty-fifth and Fifty-sixth Streets from Lake Michigan to Crawford Avenue, 1910 and 1928	309
57.	Fluctuations in the Value of Cheap Residential Land, Chicago, 1890–1931	313
58.	Area Occupied by Predominant Racial or Nationality Groups, 1933	315
59.	Land Values in Old Areas Settled before 1873	318
60.	Extension of Area Occupied by Manufacturing and Industrial Buildings, 1833–1933	319
61.	Industrial Land Values, 1931	321
62.	Land Values on State Street, Chicago Avenue to Fifty-fifth Street, 1873, 1910, 1928	323
63.	Land Values on Madison Street, State Street to Central Avenue, 1873, 1910, 1928	324
64.	Land Values on Michigan Avenue, Chicago Avenue to Fifty-fifth Street, 1873, 1910, 1928	325
65.	Land Values on North Clark Street, Roosevelt Road to Lawrence Avenue, 1873, 1910, 1928	326
66.	The Relationship between Store Rents and Pedestrian Traffic Counts	327
67.	Land Values on Cottage Grove, Halsted, and Cicero Avenues, 1928	328
68.	Land Values on Milwaukee Avenue, 1910 and 1928	329
69.	Land Values on Sixty-third and Seventy-ninth Streets, Stony Island to Crawford Avenues, 1928	330

LIST OF ILLUSTRATIONS

FIGURE		PAGE
70.	Air Space Occupied by Buildings in the Central Business District, Chicago, 1836, 1873, 1893, 1923, 1933	332
71.	Maps of Part of the Central Business District of Chicago for the Periods 1830, 1836, 1854–56, and 1870–73	338
72.	Maps of Part of the Central Business District of Chicago for the Periods 1896, 1909–13, 1925–28, and 1931	339
73.	Land Values in the Central Business District of Chicago for the Years 1830, 1836, 1856, 1873	340
74.	Land Values in the Central Business District of Chicago for the Years 1894, 1910, 1928, 1931	341
75.	Land Values in the Central Business District of Chicago for the Years 1910, 1921, 1928, 1931 (Depth of 100 Feet)	342
76.	The Trend of Chicago Land Values, Population, and Manufacturing, 1835–1933	348
77.	Chicago Land Values in Current Dollars and in Values Corrected for Changes in Wholesale Prices, Wages, and Interest Rates	349
78.	The Interest Rate on Improved Real Estate in the Central Business District of Chicago Compared with the Yield on Rail Bonds, 1833–1933	349
79.	Miles of New Pavements Constructed Annually in Chicago, 1855–1932	350
80.	The Rate of Increase of Chicago Land Values, 1830–1933, Compared with the Rate the Total Land Values of Each Peak Period Would Have Increased at 5 Per Cent and 6 Per Cent Compound Interest	352
81.	The Population Growth of Chicago by Two-Mile Zones, 1830–1930	356
82.	Percentage of Increase or Decrease of Population of Chicago by Census Tracts, 1920–30	357
83.	Population per Square Mile in Section from Ashland to Halsted from Fullerton to Pershing Road, 1850–80	358
84.	Population per Square Mile in Sections from Ashland to Halsted from Touhy on North to One Hundred and Twenty-seventh Street on South, 1890, 1910, 1930	359
85.	Residential Land Values, One Block East of Ashland Avenue from Howard Street on North to One Hundred and Twenty-seventh Street on South, 1910 and 1928	359
86.	Population Density per Square Mile for a Zone of Land Extending along the Lake from the Northern to the Southern Limits of Chicago, 1840–1930	360
87.	Land Values per Acre for a Zone of Land Extending along the Lake from the Northern to the Southern Limits of Chicago, 1836–1928	361
88.	Chicago Land Values, 1830–1933 (semi-log. scale)	362
89.	Chicago Land Values, 1830–1933 (natural scale)	363
90.	The Chicago Real Estate Cycle. Fluctuations of Per Capita Land Values, Per Capita Annual New Construction Costs, and Annual Population Increase above and below the Average Figures for the Cycle Period	370

LIST OF ILLUSTRATIONS

FIGURE		PAGE
91.	Population and Residential Land Values in Various Sections of Chicago, 1900–1933	371
92.	The Relation between Increase in Rents per Room and Increase in Operating Expenses in Steam-heated Apartments, Chicago, 1933	380
93.	Volume of New Construction in Chicago, 1854–1932	382
94.	Volume of Subdividing in Chicago, 1830–1932	389
95.	Volume of Real Estate Conveyances in Cook County, Illinois, 1869–1932	396
96.	The Rise in Chicago City Taxes and Special Assessments, 1865–1931	397
97.	The Chicago Real Estate Cycle, 1830–1933 (factors on a semi-log. scale)	406
98.	Chicago Per Capita Land Values Compared with Wholesale Prices, Wages of Unskilled Labor, and Rail Stock Prices in the United States, 1831–1933	410
99.	The Chicago Land-Value and Building Cycles Compared with General Business Activity in the United States, 1830–1933	411
100.	The Chicago Land-Value and Real Estate Transfer Cycles Compared with the Cycle of Chicago Manufacturing, 1866–1933	412
101.	The Chicago Land-Value and Subdivision Cycles Compared with the Cycle of Chicago Bank Clearings, 1830–1933	413
102.	The Chicago Land-Value Cycle Compared with the Cycles of Wholesale Commodity Prices, Canal-Rail Stock Prices, and Industrial Stock Prices, 1830–1933	414
103.	Various Methods of Subdividing a Forty-Acre Tract	431

LIST OF TABLES

TABLE		PAGE
I.	Population of Chicago by Wards, 1837–45	51
II.	Value of New Buildings Erected in Chicago by Years, 1864–70	86
III.	Chicago Land Values by Mile Zones from State and Madison Streets, 1836–79	116
IV.	The Growth of Chicago, 1877–83, as Indicated by Bank Clearings, Number Employed in Manufactures, Total Trade, and Population	129
V.	Value of Chicago Land by Principal Uses, 1876–83	140
VI.	Chicago Manufactures, 1884–93, Showing Number of Wage-Earners, Amount of Wages Paid, and Value of Product	144
VII.	Value of Chicago Land by Principal Uses, 1879–91	175
VIII.	Value of Properties Sold at Judicial Sales in Chicago, 1892–99	181
IX.	Number of Persons over Ten Years of Age in Gainful Occupations in Chicago, 1910–30	200
X.	Rents per Month of Selected Old Houses in Chicago, 1892, 1897, and 1908	216
XI.	Annual Amount of Bank Clearings, Manufactures, Wholesale and Produce Trade in Chicago, 1908–18	222
XII.	Annual Volume of Real Estate Transfers, New Buildings, Lots Subdivided, and Long-Term Leases in Chicago, 1908–18	222
XIII.	Value of New Office Buildings Erected Annually in Chicago Compared with Total New Construction, 1908–15	224
XIV.	Number and Cost of New Apartment Buildings Compared with New Single-Family Residences Constructed in Chicago, 1910–15	231
XV.	Land Values in Apartment Areas in Chicago, 1910–28	246
XVI.	Land Values in Bungalow Areas in Chicago, 1910–28	246
XVII.	Value of Residential Land in Old Settled Areas Occupied by Medium-Grade Homes	247
XVIII.	Value of Land in Industrial Areas, 1910–29	248
XIX.	Value of Land at Principal Outlying Business Corners of Chicago, 1910–29	252
XX.	Average Value of the Land at 425 Street-Car Intersections in Chicago, 1910–29	255

LIST OF TABLES

TABLE		PAGE
XXI.	Value of Land by Principal Areas and Types of Use in Chicago, 1910 and 1928, Compared with Population Growth, 1910 and 1930	261
XXII.	Decline in Pay-Rolls in Chicago Manufacturing Industries by Months from October, 1929, to May, 1933	268
XXIII.	Decline in Employment and in Pay-Rolls in Chicago Manufacturing Industries, 1929–33	269
XXIV.	Average Reduction in Full Value of Land for Assessment Purposes for 1931 as Compared with 1928 Full Value According to the Relative Value of the Land	274
XXV.	Population of Chicago and Other Leading Cities in the Middle West, 1840–1930	280
XXVI.	Population of Chicago and Seaboard Cities, 1840–1930	281
XXVII.	Relative Increase in Population of Eleven Leading American Cities, 1850–1930	281
XXVIII.	Relative Increase in Population of Thirteen Leading American Cities, 1900–1930	282
XXIX.	Population of Some Cities in the Chicago Suburban Area and Population of the Chicago Suburban Area, 1900–1930	282
XXX.	Sources of Increase of Chicago Population, 1830–1930	284
XXXI.	Percentage of Total Increase of Chicago Population Coming from Each Source, 1860–1930	284
XXXII.	Number of Buildings in Chicago Compared with Population at Intervals from 1825 to 1928	286
XXXIII.	Utilization of Land in Chicago, 1850, 1870, 1890, and 1911	290
XXXIV.	Utilization of Land in Chicago in 1923	290
XXXV.	Number of Buildings in Cook County by Principal Types, 1928	291
XXXVI.	Square Feet of Building Space at Various Height Levels in Cook County, 1928	292
XXXVII.	Percentage of Total Rented Homes of Each Group in Chicago Falling within Given Rental Class, 1932	316
XXXVIII.	Percentage of Cubic Feet at Given Heights to Total Cubic Feet in Area (Central Business District)	331
XXXIX.	Percentage of Air Space at Different Heights Occupied by Buildings (Central Business District)	331
XL.	Cubic Feet of Space above the Blocks in the Central Business District of Chicago	331

LIST OF TABLES

TABLE		PAGE
XLI.	Cubic Contents of Buildings in Chicago Central Business District by Age Groups (Including Basement Area)	335
XLII.	Principal Types of Uses of Central Business District of Chicago	336
XLIII.	Land Values in Central Business District and Entire Area of Chicago Compared, 1836–1926	337
XLIV.	Land Values on North-South Streets in the Central Business District of Chicago, 1830–1931	345
XLV.	Value of Land in Chicago by Principal Types of Uses, 1910–33	347
XLVI.	Index Numbers of Chicago Land Values by Principal Types of Uses	347
XLVII.	The Amount to Which the Sales Value of Chicago Land at Different Periods Would Have Grown at 6 Per Cent Compound Interest	354
XLVIII.	The Rise in Chicago Land Values Compared with the Growth of Land Values at 6 Per Cent Compound Interest.	355
XLIX.	Percentage of Increase in the Population of Chicago for Equal Time Intervals in Booms and Depressions	373
L.	Rents of Workingmen's Dwellings and Office Buildings in Chicago	377
LI.	Rate of Population Increase and Rate of Increase in Rents of Office Buildings and Workingmen's Dwellings in Chicago, 1915–33	378
LII.	Gross Income, Total Expense (Including Taxes and Depreciation) and Net Income of a Chicago Office Building, 1918–32	379
LIII.	Seventy-nine Years of Building in Chicago, 1854–1932	384
LIV.	Index Numbers of Population, Office Rents, New Construction, Number of Lots Subdivided, and Aggregate Land Values in Chicago, 1918–27	384
LV.	Index Numbers of Population, Building, Number of Lots Subdivided, and Land Values in Chicago, 1885–93	385
LVI.	The Amount of Money Loaned on Mortgages and Trust Deeds in Cook County, Illinois, 1918–32	386
LVII.	Increase in Annual Cost of Special Assessments in Chicago, 1862–71, for Years Ending April 1	394
LVIII.	Increase in Annual Cost of Special Assessments in Chicago, 1877–92	394
LIX.	Rise in Annual Amounts of Special Assessments in Chicago, 1919–27	395

LIST OF TABLES

TABLE		PAGE
LX.	Decrease in Annual Cost of Special Assessments in Chicago, 1870–77	395
LXI.	Decrease in Annual Cost of Special Assessments in Chicago, 1892–97	395
LXII.	Decrease in Annual Cost of Special Assessments in Chicago, 1927–32	398
LXIII.	Rents, Value of New Buildings, Transfers, Number of Lots Subdivided, Number of Foreclosures, Vacancies in the Central Business District, Land Values in Chicago, 1926–33	399
LXIV.	The Percentage Increase of Factors Affecting Chicago Real Estate in Boom Periods	404
LXV.	The Percentage Decrease of Factors Affecting Chicago Real Estate in Depression Periods	405
LXVI.	Sequence of Factors in the Chicago Real Estate Cycle, as Indicated by Deviations above and below the Normal Trend	408
LXVII.	Average Time Intervals in the Chicago Real Estate Cycle (Years)	409
LXVIII.	A Comparison of Fluctuations of Chicago Real Estate Factors above and below Normal with Fluctuations in General Business Factors	415
LXIX.	Year in Which Major Peaks Occurred in Chicago Land Values Compared with Major Peaks in Wholesale Prices, Canal-Rail Stock Prices, and Industrial Stock Prices	420
LXX.	Year in Which the Maximum Point of Depression Occurred for Chicago Land Values Compared with Maximum Depression Points for Wholesale Prices, Canal-Rail Stock Prices, and Industrial Stock Prices	420
LXXI.	Lot and Block Dimensions of Original Subdivisions in or near the Present Loop	428
LXXII.	Lot and Block Dimensions of Outlying Subdivisions of 1836–37	429
LXXIII.	Aggregate Land Value under Different Subdivision Plans and Depth Rules	430
LXXIV.	Estimated Corner Premiums of Lots in the Central Business District of Chicago	433
LXXV.	Effect of Doubling the Number of Corners upon Aggregate Land Values	433
LXXVI.	Number of Guaranty Orders Taken by the Chicago Title and Trust Company, 1911–33	434

LIST OF TABLES

TABLE		PAGE
LXXVII.	Guaranty Orders of the Chicago Title and Trust Company Compared with Abstract Orders	435
LXXVIII.	Relation between the Rise and Fall of Gross and Net Rents	454
LXXIX.	Land Value Developed on a 50-by-150-Foot Lot in Chicago by Different Types of Residential Uses, 1926	455
LXXX.	Aggregate Value of the 211 Square Miles of Land in the 1933 Corporate Limits of Chicago, 1833–1933	470
LXXXI.	Number of Instruments Recorded in Cook County, 1872–1932	470
LXXXII.	Total Consideration in Deeds Recorded in Cook County, 1868–1902	472
LXXXIII.	Number of Transfers in Cook County, 1901–33	472
LXXXIV.	New Mortgages and Trust Deeds, Cook County, Illinois, 1896–1933	473
LXXXV.	Consideration Stated in Deeds for Transfers of Property More than Seven Miles from the Courthouse Compared with the Total Consideration in All Deeds in Cook County, 1889–1901	473
LXXXVI.	Annual Amount of New Construction in Chicago, 1854–1933	474
LXXXVII.	Number of Different Types of Buildings Erected Annually, 1912–33	476
LXXXVIII.	Index Numbers of Rents of Workingmen's Dwellings in Chicago, 1914–33	476
LXXXIX.	Number of Lots Subdivided Annually in Cook County and the Chicago Metropolitan Area, 1874–1930	477
XC.	Approximate Number of Acres Subdivided Annually in the 1931 City Limits of Chicago, 1830–1932	479
XCI.	Value of Manufactures, Wholesale Trade, Produce Trade, Total Trade of Chicago (Gold), 1850–1931	481
XCII.	Percentage of Vacancies in Chicago Office Buildings, 1926–33	482
XCIII.	Population of Chicago (Present City Limits), 1830–1932	483
XCIV.	Distribution of Chicago Population by Mile Zones, 1860–1916	484
XCV.	Number of Passenger Automobiles, Motor Trucks, and Horse-drawn Vehicles Registered in Chicago, 1910–33	485
XCVI.	Value of Property Placed under Long-Term Leases and Sold at Judicial Sale at the Chicago Real Estate Board Annually, 1890–1928	486
XCVII.	Assessment of Real Estate in Chicago, 1837–1932	487

LIST OF TABLES

TABLE		PAGE
XCVIII.	Chicago Tax Levy, 1837–1931	488
XCIX.	Bank Clearings in Chicago by Years from 1865 to 1933	489
C.	Illinois Bell Telephone Company Stations in Chicago at End of Each Year, 1882–1933	490
CI.	Number of Passengers Carried by Chicago Rapid Transit Company for Years Ending on December 31, 1892–1932	491
CII.	Annual Cost of Special Assessments, 1862–1932	492
CIII.	Electricity Generated and Sold in Chicago by the Commonwealth Edison Company, 1893–1931	493

PART I
HISTORY OF THE RELATION OF THE GROWTH OF CHICAGO TO THE RISE IN ITS LAND VALUES, 1830–1933

CHAPTER I

THE CANAL LAND BOOM, 1830-42

A. INTRODUCTION: OBJECTIVES OF THE STUDY

The growth of Chicago from a hamlet of a dozen log huts in 1830 into an urban agglomeration with a greater population in 211 square miles in 1930 than is contained in 825,000 square miles in eight American states[1] prompts the historian to trace the development of this city from its village embryo. The rise of the ground value of that 211 square miles from a few thousand to five billion dollars—an amount over three hundred times as great as the purchase price of the 375,000,000 acres in the Louisiana purchase in 1803 and slightly more than the aggregate value of all the farm land in twenty-three American states in 1925[2]— invites the student of urban land values to investigate the humble beginnings of this world-metropolis. The very rapidity of the growth and the present magnitude of Chicago induce a searching analysis of the causes for the rise of this city at the juncture of the Chicago River and Lake Michigan.

The uneven character in the rate of growth of the buildings and the land values of Chicago during the dynamic era of the American industrial revolution is, however, of greater significance in the study of economic and social changes than great size or huge land values. Chicago's physical growth in buildings has not proceeded at a steady, even pace through the century, but by fits and starts. Periods of feverish activity

[1] The population of Chicago in 1930 was 3,376, 436. The combined population of Arizona, Idaho, Montana, Nevada, New Mexico, North Dakota, Utah, and Wyoming, with an area of 825,534 square miles was 3,346,843 in 1930 (*U.S. Census, 1930*).

[2] The value in 1925 of 243,330,000 acres—all the farms in the following states was $4,956,206,000: Maine, New Hampshire, Vermont, Massachusetts, Rhode Island, Connecticut, Kentucky, Tennessee, Alabama, Mississippi, Montana, Idaho, Wyoming, Colorado, New Mexico, Arizona, Utah, Nevada, New Jersey, Delaware, Maryland, West Virginia, Virginia. These are the poorest agricultural states. The value of the farm land in these states was only a small part of the value of all farms in the United States, which was $55,000,000,000 in 1920 (*U.S. Census, 1920; Statistical Abstract of the U.S., 1932*, pp. 574-75). The value of all land in the United States in 1922 was estimated at $122,000,000,000 by the Federal Trade Commission (*National Wealth and Income* [69th Cong., 1st sess.; Washington, 1926], Senate Doc. 126, p. 34).

in which the whole city seemed to be possessed with a rage[3] to reconstruct its business center and to cover the adjacent prairie with houses or flats, were followed by periods in which the new growth was so slow as to be almost imperceptible. Similarly, Chicago land values did not rise with the uniform precision of a compound-interest table. Brief intervals of a year when land values in certain quarters advanced 1,000 per cent were succeeded by years of dulness and painfully slow, declining values. These changing moods of the city furnish materials for a research in social psychology, and their analysis also illustrates the actual nature of city growth and the real behavior of an urban land market in a rapidly growing city.

The character, as well as the rate of growth of Chicago, presents startling contrasts. Expanding vertically in taller buildings as well as laterally into the prairie, spreading out solidly from the center and also in gangling lines and in detached settlements flung out in advance of the main body, its physical development was far from uniform. "Chicago is at once a metropolis, a collection of villages and a howling wilderness," said one observer in the eighties.[4] Within the city limits of Chicago in 1933 there are: first, a business center with forty-story skyscrapers beside which old six-story (and smaller) buildings humbly squat; second, an intermediate belt in which old, fashionable residences are found side by side with factories and warehouses, or in which acres of frame hovels are packed closely together; third, a fringe of tall apartment buildings along the Lake Shore; fourth, outlying areas that have independent towns or community centers, some coalescing with one another and others separated by tracts of prairie; and, fifth, square-mile sections covered with grass and lot stakes as reminders of speculative losses in which there is not a solitary inhabitant. In such a variegated urban pattern land values vary in 1933 from $1,000 to $20,000,000 an acre, and there are cases where the range is from $50 to $10,000 a front foot within a distance of 200 feet.

Two processes are the subject matter of this study. The one, the physical growth of the city as measured by new buildings, public improvements, and transportation lines, is visible to the eye. The other, the growth and shifting of the structure of land values, cannot be seen,

[3] Balzac in his novel *Ferragus* describes Paris as a monster with a thousand moods, one of these moods being a rage for building.

[4] Mr. Adler quoted to this effect in the *Chicago Tribune*, February 19, 1888.

but in our society, dominated by the profit motive, it enters into nearly every building project. Except in cases where land is used for signboards or parking space, an income can be derived from an urban site only by erecting a building upon it. Therefore a close relationship might be expected to exist between the physical growth of a city and changes in its land values. The exact character of the kinship between the two sets of forces is not a simple one, and can be determined only by an analysis of their behavior in the past.

The reader may wonder whether a consideration of the unique combination of events that produced Chicago will lead to the formulation of any principles of universal validity. If this fortuitous chain of events is not likely to be repeated in the future, the knowledge of the sequence of these exceptional causes and effects will not give one a physical law, in which a given set of mechanical forces set in motion can be relied upon to produce substantially the same effect. In the history of a city there are elements similar to that found in the biography of a man. An extraordinary combination of hereditary factors, likely never again to be exactly repeated, placed in a historical situation that is also a unique complex of men and events, produces a type of human behavior which may not be duplicated. In the thousands of little communities in a great city, there are local events that have an interest chiefly for those who have passed their lives amid the surroundings described and which have the unique attributes of individual men and women. Land values reflect the influence of factors that are confined to the radius of a block or a precinct in a city ward, and this study therefore necessarily deals with topics that are as narrow in scope as the history of an obscure family or of one of the thousands of commonplace apartment blocks.

A study of an entire city during the whole period of its growth, however, discloses a vision that might escape the glance of one whose horizon was limited by his precinct. The broad sweep of the events of a century reveals recurring cycles in the growth of Chicago in which general moods or similar historical situations are to a certain extent repeated. Each of the five chapters in the first part of this work deals with a complete cycle, which passes through somewhat the same phases. It is possible that this long-run study of one city will lead to the discovery of factors that are characteristic of real estate activity in other cities, if allowances are made for inevitable differences in local histories and local environments. Inasmuch as local forces are at least as important as national or international factors in the determination of the land values of a community, the nature of the urban land market can be learned only by the study of one or more of these local markets for a period of time long enough to cover cycles that are sometimes of thirty-five years' duration. A general survey of a number of cities for a short period of time might conceivably yield less material for the formulation of general laws of urban land values than the investigation of the behavior of land values in one city during the entire period of its history.

For the growth of a city is a cumulative as well as a cyclical process. Each successive building, railroad line, street-car line, or park leaves a permanent impress upon the character of the city. A pattern begins to form at the very outset that with the lapse of time acquires a certain rigidity. The railroad or park system once laid down holds its position through great changes. The physical character of the city is altered by the imposition of new elements, but the effect of the early direction of its growth and of buildings that have long since vanished is never entirely lost. Similarly, the present magnitude and distribution of land values within the city is the summation of a historical process and the final result of a long evolution. In the first part of this book is a description of the manner in which different sections of the city became devoted to certain types of uses, or in which they came to be occupied by certain social classes, races, or nationality groups. In other words, it is an account of how those dominant characteristics of different Chicago neighborhoods which vitally affect land values were themselves determined.

In the second part of this work the principal factors in this one hundred years of growth that can be measured are presented in graphs and charts, and local indices of land values, population growth, trade, and manufactures are compared with one another and with the curves of wholesale prices, stock prices, wages, and interest rates for the entire United States. In this latter section, also, the many different unique and local factors affecting the values of land for the leading types of uses are analyzed from the perspective of a century of dynamic change. Thus the attempt is made to consider the qualitative as well as the quantitative facts of the Chicago land market, and to seek to discover the laws of the behavior of social and economic factors governing urban land values.

B. THE CAUSES OF THE EARLY GROWTH OF CHICAGO

The portage.—The glorious destiny of Chicago was perhaps foreseen by the French explorer, Joliet, when he visited its site, over one hundred and sixty years before its first land boom.[5] The pioneers of empire hunted for such a spot before they had ever seen it, and during the many decades that intervened between its first discovery and its actual settlement the advantages of its site entered into the calculations of ministers in the capitals of Europe. Its location was carefully marked on the maps of North America as a place of strategic importance by those who had never caught a glimpse of the dismal swamp that seemed to belie all promise of future greatness.

The reason for the fortunate position of Chicago could be traced back a million years to the Ice Age when the glaciers scoured out Lake Michigan but did not cut a channel deep enough to turn the waters of the Great Lakes permanently into the Mississippi Valley. The St. Lawrence River and the chain of Great Lakes formed the first highway into the heart of America from the East. The great network of rivers that emptied into the Mississippi was the first road to penetrate the interior of America from the South. Taken together, the two systems formed a huge arc around the English settlements on the Atlantic seaboard, and, if properly fortified, would have formed an insuperable barrier to westward expansion. At one point these two great waterways almost joined, and the land barrier was so slight that it was the route most frequently used for the portage between them. This vital spot was Chicago.

The Desplaines River which flows into the Illinois River, a tributary of the Mississippi, runs parallel to Lake Michigan for a considerable distance not more than ten miles west of it, being separated from it by a low continental divide not over six or eight feet high. The first white explorers, Joliet and Marquette, searching for just such a place, observed in 1673 that even this land passage was shortened at Chicago. There the main channel and the south branch of the Chicago River and

[5] Joliet, in 1673, made a verbal report on the possibility of a canal that would link the Great Lakes with the Mississippi River System, which was reported by Father Dablon as follows: "The fourth remark .... is that we can quite easily go to Florida in boats, and by a very good navigation. There would be only one canal to make by cutting only half a league of prairie to pass from the Lake of Illinois [Lake Michigan] into the St. Louis River [the Desplaines and Illinois]" ("Relations" of Father Dablon, *Historical Magazine*, p. 237, cited in A. T. Andreas, *History of Chicago* [Chicago, 1884], I, 165).

LOCATION OF CHICAGO
WITH RESPECT TO WATER-WAY SYSTEMS

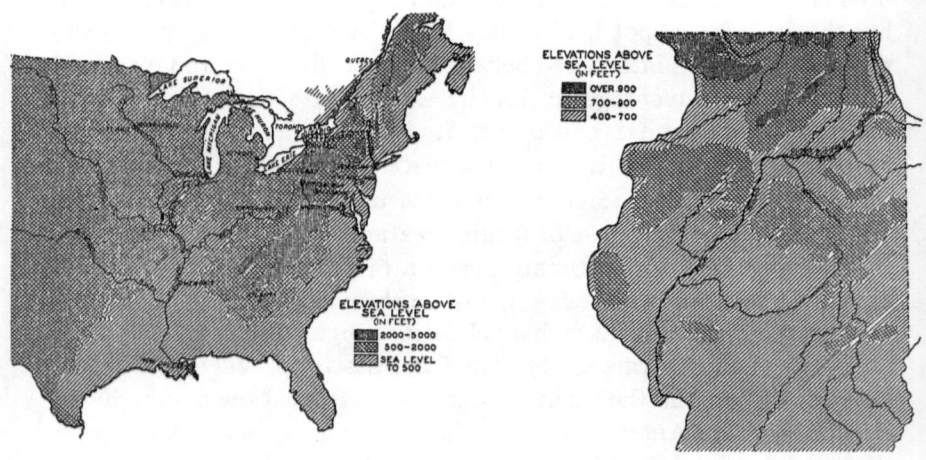

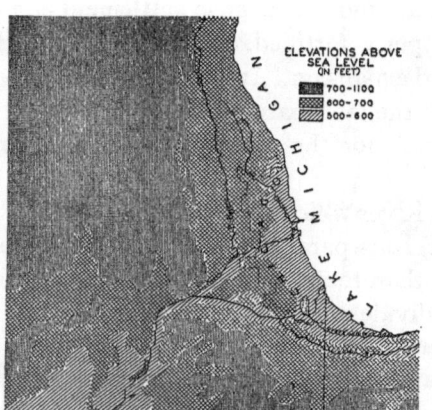

Fig. 1

THE CANAL LAND BOOM

the shallow "Mud Lake" formed during spring freshets a continuous waterway from Lake Michigan to the Desplaines and Illinois rivers.[6] At other seasons the amount of dry ground over which canoes had to be carried varied from one to nine miles.[7] Across this portage Indians traveled in their canoes before the coming of the white man, and here Indians and fur traders met before there was any permanent settlement.[8] The natural advantages of the Chicago portage suggested to the first French explorers two things: first, a fort that would control the point for their own nation; and, second, a canal that would make the temporary waterway of the spring freshets a permanent year-round water route between the Great Lakes and the Gulf of Mexico.

The fort.—In the days when the waterways were the main channels of travel from the seacoast into the interior, a portage such as the one at Chicago was a gateway through which invading armies as well as fur traders were compelled to pass.[9] Its fortification would be the first step of any power seeking the military control of the surrounding region.

[6] Pierre Margry, *Découvertes et établissements des Français dans l'ouest et dans le sud de l'Amérique septentrionale, 1614–1754 mémoires et documents originaux* (6 vols.; Paris, 1876–86), II, 165–67, quoted in Robert Knight and Lucius H. Zeuch, *Location of the Chicago Portage of the 17th Century* (Chicago Historical Society, 1928), pp. 21–22; also in Goodspeed and Healy, *History of Cook County Illinois* (Chicago, 1909), I, 38. Quoting LaSalle in his *Relations:* "This [the Chicago portage] is an isthmus which is 41 degrees, 50 minutes' elevation from the pole [Thirty-third Street and Kedzie Avenue] on the west of the Lake of the Illinois [Lake Michigan] where one goes by a channel [Chicago River] formed by the junction of several streams or gullies of the prairie. It [the Chicago River] is navigable about two leagues to the edge of this prairie. Beyond this at a quarter of a league distant toward the west there is a little lake [Mud Lake] a league and a half in length which is divided in two by a beaver dam. From this lake issues a little stream which after twining in and out among the rushes for half a league falls into the Chicago river [the Desplaines] and from there into the river of the Illinois. When this lake is full either from the great rains in summer or from the floods in the spring, it is discharged also into this channel which leads to the Lake of the Illinois [Lake Michigan] whose surface is seven feet lower than the prairie where is situated this lake.

"The river of Chicago [Desplaines] does the same in the springtime when its channel is full. It discharges by this little lake a part of its water into the Lake of the Illinois, and at this time should one make a little canal of a quarter of a league, says Joliet, from the lake to the basin which leads to the Illinois river, ships could in the summer enter into the river and descend into the sea."

[7] *Jesuit Relations and Allied Documents*, Vol. LIX, n. 41, quoted in Archer Butler Hulbert, *Portage Paths* (Cleveland: Arthur H. Clark, 1903), p. 181.

[8] Milo M. Quaife, *Chicago and the Old Northwest* (Chicago: University of Chicago Press, 1913), p. 21.

[9] The military advantages of portages are discussed by Hulbert in *Historic Highways of America*, Vol. VII; *Portage Paths* (Cleveland, 1903), pp. 51–82.

The Chicago territory was, however, too far removed from the white settlements of the eighteenth century to induce either the French or the British to post a garrison there. General Anthony Wayne quickly saw the vital importance of Chicago in 1795 when he persuaded the United States to acquire from the Indians six square miles at the mouth of the Chicago River.[10] Fort Dearborn was accordingly established there in 1803 to wean away the Indians from the influence of the British outpost at Green Bay. The presence of a garrison of about sixty men at the fort required the annual visit of a ship to bring provisions, which took away on its return trip furs received in trade from the Indians.[11] Accordingly, under the protection of the fort, there was built as early as 1803 a group of five log huts which sheltered the half-breed fur traders.[12] The fort itself was located on the south bank of the Chicago River at what is now Michigan Avenue. After this first fort was destroyed on the eve of the Fort Dearborn Massacre in 1812 and a second fort was built in 1815, there developed by 1818 a village of ten or twelve log huts, characterized by Major Long as "low, filthy and disgusting," and occupied by about sixty half-breeds who were mainly engaged in the fur trade.[13] In 1830 there were still no more than twelve huts, even including three suburban cabins on Madison Street. The fort and trading post were far removed from the course of western emigration, which prior to 1830 had flowed through the Cumberland Gap or down the Ohio Valley and populated in Illinois only the southern portion of the state. Consequently up to this date the growth of Chicago was negligible.

The canal.—The plan for eliminating the Chicago portage by a canal was discussed as early as the project of building a fort to control it, and in determining the destiny of the future town, the canal was by far the more important. The naïve belief that a channel eight or nine miles long from the end of the south branch of the Chicago River to the Desplaines River would provide an adequate ship canal from the lakes to the Gulf of Mexico was quickly dispelled by even the casual observations of travelers. It was soon discovered that the Desplaines River it-

---

[10] Quaife, *op. cit.*, p. 43.

[11] *Ibid.*, p. 154, quoting "Wisconsin Historical Collections," XI, 239–40.

[12] *Chicago: A Book for Strangers and Tourists* (Chicago: Galpin, Hayes, McClure, 1869), p. 20.

[13] Quaife, *op. cit.*, p. 281.

self was but a shallow stream with several rapids, which at times could not be navigated in small boats. The federal engineers who examined the route reported that the construction of a canal for the entire distance of one hundred miles from Chicago to LaSalle would be necessary to insure a continuous waterway for packet boats.

These difficulties which gradually unfolded did not stop attempts to secure state and federal aid to construct a canal. In 1673 Joliet first discussed the canal project. In 1808 Gallatin included it in his program of internal improvements. In 1814 President Madison recommended it to Congress.[14] In 1816 the United States purchased the route from the Indians.[15] Illinois, when admitted as a state in 1818, had its northern boundary extended northward from the southern tip of Lake Michigan for the express purpose of taking in the strip proposed for the canal.[16] In 1817 Major Stephen H. Long surveyed and reported favorably on it.[17] Southern Illinois interests saw in it the possibility of a new way of reaching eastern markets that would free them from dependence on New Orleans. In 1818 Governor Bond of Illinois accordingly urged it in his first message to the legislature.[18] In 1819 Mr. Calhoun, secretary of war, pointing out that the canal would be a vital transportation link in time of war, recommended it as necessary for national self-defense.[19] In 1822 Congress authorized the state of Illinois to survey and take a strip of land ninety feet wide for a canal.[20] In 1823 the Illinois legislature appointed a Board of Canal Commissioners who examined and estimated the cost of five possible routes, the Chicago-Desplaines River route being favored.[21] In January of 1825, the legislature incorporated the Illinois and Michigan Canal Company, a private company with an authorized capital of $1,000,000, to dig the canal.[22] In January of 1826, before this enterprise could get started, the legislature, fearing that federal aid might be jeopardized by its existence, repealed its charter.[23] In 1826 the state petitioned Congress for a land grant to

[14] Knight and Zeuch, *op. cit.*, pp. 4, 16.
[15] Quaife, *op. cit.*, p. 342.
[16] Goodspeed and Healy, *op. cit.*, I, 74.
[17] *Ibid.*, II, 70.
[18] Goodspeed and Healy, *op. cit.*, I, 89.
[19] *Ibid.*, II, 72.
[20] *Public Statutes at Large of the United States* (Boston: Little, Brown & Co., 1854), III, 659–60.
[21] Goodspeed and Healy, *op. cit.*, II, 76.
[22] *Laws of the Fourth General Assembly of Illinois* (1st sess.; Vandalia, 1825), pp. 160–61.
[23] Goodspeed and Healy, *op. cit.*, II, 76.

aid the canal, and, notwithstanding the opposition of New Orleans, the request was granted in 1827. Alternate sections of land for five miles on each side of the route selected were given to the state, but it was provided that unless the canal was started in five years and completed within twenty years after the passage of the act, the money received from the land sales should revert to the United States.[24] In January, 1829, the Illinois legislature, having received this land grant from Congress, appointed three canal commissioners to select the route, to designate which alternate sections were to be taken for the canal, and to sell at $1.25 an acre the land thus chosen. The commissioners picked the Chicago-Desplaines River route, and prepared a list of the sections of land to be granted. This selection was approved by the President of the United States on May 21, 1830. Part of one of these sections of canal lands, three-eighths of a square mile that straddled the forks of the Chicago River, was surveyed and laid out in town lots. This was the original town of Chicago shown in Figure 4. It covered the area from Madison to Kinzie streets, and from State Street to Desplaines Street. The first lots in this first Chicago subdivision were sold on September 4, 1830.

The canal itself was not started until July 4, 1836, and, after a suspension of work in 1842, was finally completed in 1848. Although the canal did not serve as a link in the Lake-to-the-Mississippi transportation route until eighteen years after the first sale of Chicago lots, its importance in directing attention to Chicago and in stimulating the speculative land boom cannot be overemphasized. The success of the Erie Canal immediately after its completion in 1825 and the rapid rise in the land values of the towns along its route led to the extension of the same speculative calculations to Chicago when population began to flow toward it. The first land-buyers in Chicago saw in their minds' eye not the squalid village of log huts on the banks of the Chicago River but the large city that was expected to rise with the completion of the canal. That the canal colored every resident's hopes even in the earliest time is shown by the following account written in 1835:

> There is one improvement to be made, however, in this section of the country, which will greatly influence the permanent value of property in Chicago. I allude to a canal from the head of Lake Michigan to the head of stream navigation on the Illinois River, the route of which has long since been surveyed. The distance to be

[24] *Public Statutes at Large of the United States*, II, 234.

THE CANAL LAND BOOM 13

overcome is something like ninety miles, and when you remember that the head waters of the Illinois rise within eleven miles of the Chicago River, and that a level plain of not more than eight feet elevation is the only intervening obstacle, you can conceive how easy it would be to drain Lake Michigan into the Mississippi by this route. Boats of 18 tons have actually passed over the intervening prairie at high water. Lake Michigan, which is several feet above Lake Erie, is such a never-failing body of water that it would keep steamboats afloat on the route in the driest season. St. Louis would then be brought comparatively near to New York, while two-thirds of the Mississippi Valley would be supplied by this route immediately from the markets of the latter. The canal is the only remaining link wanting to complete the most stupendous chain of inland communications in the world.[25]

Under the caption "The Canal Made Chicago" the importance of the canal is thus summarized by the *Chicago Tribune* of May 13, 1900:

Chicago was then [before 1830] only a military post with an Indian agency attached to it. It didn't have enough taxable property to support a bridge tender, much less build a canal. When the preliminaries to the building of the canal did come about, Chicago immediately leaped into existence as a village. The first plat of Chicago was made by the Canal Commissioners; the first sale of lots of Chicago was made by the Canal Commissioners. Chicago was made by the canal as clearly and as positively as Western towns have been made in recent years and are still being made by the advent of railroads. Chicago was a canal town.

Land trails to Chicago.—In addition to the canal project, the land trails to Chicago were an important factor in its early growth. The paths winding around the lake or following the high ground or the river courses that had been made by buffalo, Indians, and fur traders, on their way to the banks of the Chicago River, were the first highways whose intersection formed the nucleus of a town. Superimposed by the surveyors upon these diagonal and fluctuating routes were the straight section lines, intersecting each other a mile apart, which developed into through highways and carline streets as the city grew, forming a precise checkerboard plan. The early trails, confined to definite lines by the rows of buildings on each side, still survive in those main roads that radiate out from Chicago like the spokes of a wheel. The creation of a hub for this wheel, at which all these routes could meet at a common center, was, however, prevented by the configuration of the Chicago River.

The main channel of the Chicago River and its branches form a Y which divides the Chicago region into three main divisions: the north,

[25] Charles Fenno Hoffman, *A Winter in the Far West* (London, 1835; reprinted by the Fergus Printing Co., Chicago, in 1882), pp. 21–22.

south, and west sides. The Chicago River was the point of entry and departure for the great stream of passengers and merchandise carried on the lake boats, and its banks were the meeting place of land and water commerce. While the boats could unload with almost equal facility on any bank of the river, the land traffic in those days when bridges and

FIG. 2

ferries were crude and few in number generally terminated at the point where a particular land route struck the river. The number and the volume of traffic of the trails entering each division of the city, therefore, had an important bearing on the early relative growth of each of these sections.

The movement of wagons into the south division of the city was from the first by far the greatest. Around the bend of the lake came the

"Chicago Road," the main path by which land emigration from the East poured into Chicago.[26] From the South ran the famous Vincennes trail over which came the caravans of wagons from the Wabash country to bring supplies to Chicago.[27] Southwest along the route of the canal was an old Indian trail, known as the "Road to the Widow Brown's," and later as "Archer Avenue."[28] The "Chicago Road," following the present course of Cottage Grove Avenue, north of Thirty-ninth Street; the Vincennes trail, which fluctuated north of Fifty-first Street between the present line of State Street and Cottage Grove Avenue; the "Road to the Widow Brown's," or present Archer Avenue; and a trail from the west that crossed the south branch at Eighteenth Street[29]—all converged at about Eighteenth and State streets and proceeded from there to Fort Dearborn on the south bank of the main channel at Michigan Avenue.

The North and West Side trails were less important in the beginning, for they led into a territory that contained very few white inhabitants. Terminating on the north bank of the river opposite the fort was the Green Bay trail running northward along the lake shore to Green Bay which had been a British outpost until 1812. It was also used by travelers on their way to Sheboygan, Racine, Kenosha, and Milwaukee when the lake route was not available. The "Little Fort" trail followed the present course of Lincoln Avenue.[30]

On the West Side were trails leading to Galena along the present route of Lake Street and Grand Avenue,[31] the portage trail along what is now Ogden Avenue,[32] and trails running northwesterly on the ridge between the north branch of the Chicago River and the Desplaines River that were later known as Milwaukee and Elston avenues.[33] Most of these trails converged on the west bank of the Chicago River at the forks.

The growth of Chicago, 1830–32.—In 1830 the twelve log cabins that constituted Chicago had two nuclei, the fort and the forks of the river, connected by a road following the course of South Water Street. Three

---

[26] Milo M. Quaife, *Chicago Highways Old and New* (Chicago: D. F. Keller & Co., 1923), pp. 37–46.

[27] *Ibid.*, pp. 54, 58, 60, 69.

[28] *Ibid.*, p. 79.

[29] *Ibid.*, map opposite p. 236.

[30] *Ibid.*, pp. 105–7.

[31] *Ibid.*, pp. 87–88, 91.

[32] *Ibid.*, map opposite p. 236.

[33] *Ibid.*, p. 107.

FIG. 3

THE CANAL LAND BOOM

taverns, one on each bank of the river, faced one another at the forks. One on the South Side, at the corner of Lake and Market streets, was the celebrated Sauganash, opened by Mark Beaubien in 1826. A second on the West Side at Lake and West Water streets was the "Wolf's Point" built by Kinzie in 1828. A third on the North Side at North Water and Orleans Street was established by Samuel Miller in 1828. A ferry connected the taverns in 1831. With its land trails failing to find a common center, the little hamlet faced the river, which was the main avenue of entry from outside.

Chicago did not grow from 1830 to the early part of 1832. There were still only twelve houses in the latter year.[34] The location of these buildings is thus described:

> Besides the fort there were two frame houses on the North Side and the old Kinzie house. On the South Side were two or three small farm houses, and in the West Side the Kinzie store at the forks, and there was Mark Beaubien's tavern on Michigan Avenue.[35]

In these years the tide of western emigration had not yet penetrated the Chicago Region, being partly restrained by fear of the hostile Black Hawk Indians from turning northwestward from the old route down the Ohio Valley.

The way to Chicago was rapidly being made easier and more convenient. The Erie Canal had placed Chicago on a direct line with New York. Steamboats were plying the Great Lakes from Buffalo to Chicago, and the Mississippi River boats from New Orleans and St. Louis had proceeded up the Illinois River as far as Peoria in 1828.[36] Even by 1831 it was found that goods could be brought from New York to St. Louis by way of Chicago one-third cheaper than by New Orleans. Salt, shipped from Syracuse to Chicago by boat, sold for less than the cost of producing salt at Danville, Illinois, and the farmers of the Wabash learned that Chicago was the cheapest market in which to buy eastern wares.

The Black Hawk Indian menace was terminated by an armed force

[34] Andreas, *op. cit.*, I, 119.

[35] *Ibid.* (letter of George W. Hoffman, April 5, 1879). Mark Beaubien's tavern on Michigan Avenue in 1832 was the one he operated after he sold the Sauganash.

[36] No regular line of steamboats was operating on the Illinois River before 1835, but the name of one steamboat running on the river in 1828 is given, and even before this another steamboat of light draft, the "Ottawa," was making trips (Randall Parrish, *Historic Illinois*, p. 427).

under General Scott sent to Chicago in 1832. The soldiers not only rid the country of the Indian peril, but on returning home they spread the news of the wonderful fertility of the Northwest region, while General Scott himself brought a favorable report to Washington about the possibilities of Chicago. The result was that a flow of settlers started toward Chicago in the latter part of 1832. By the end of that year there were thirty buildings and two hundred people in the village. There were two log bridges, one over the south branch near Randolph Street and one over the north branch at Kinzie Street.

Chicago in 1833.—In 1833 there was a row of business houses and cabins on South Water Street between State and Wells Street and this was the principal street of the town.[37] "There was nothing on Lake Street [in 1833]," stated John Bates, a settler of 1832, "except perhaps the Catholic Church begun on the northwest corner of Lake and State."[38] As Rev. Jeremiah Porter said, "The corner of Clark and Lake in 1833 was a lonely spot almost inaccessible on account of surrounding sloughs and bogs."[39] Charles Butler in August, 1833, noticed only a tavern on the West Side and a single building known as the "Block House" on the North Side.[40]

In 1833 the houses began to be constructed of green lumber obtained from a local sawmill on the north branch instead of the logs that had been previously used.[41] Nevertheless, according to Butler, "the houses, with one or two exceptions, were of the cheapest and most primitive character for human habitation, suggestive of the haste with which they had been put up."[42] Charles Latrobe thus describes the building activity of that year:

The interior of the village was one chaos of mud, rubbish and confusion. Frame and clapboard houses were springing up daily under the active axes and hammers of the speculators and piles of lumber announced the preparation of other edifices of equally light character.[43]

[37] Granville T. Sproat, letter to the *Chicago Tribune*, December 12, 1886; letter of Charles Butler, December, 1881, in Andreas, *op. cit.*, I, 129.

[38] Andreas, *op. cit.*, I, 131.   [39] *Ibid.*, p. 300.

[40] *Ibid.*, p. 129 (letter of Charles Butler, December 17, 1881).

[41] Charles Cleaver, *Reminiscences of Chicago during the Forties and Fifties* (Chicago: Fergus Printing Co., 1913), p. 54.

[42] Andreas, *op. cit.*, I, 129 (letter of Charles Butler, December 17, 1881).

[43] *Ibid.*, p. 124.

THE CANAL LAND BOOM

From 150 to 200 new buildings were erected in Chicago in 1833. The number of vessels arriving had increased from 7 in 1831 and 45 in 1832 to 120 in 1833. A newspaper, the *Chicago American*, made its first appearance. A town government was organized by the 350 inhabitants. The federal government appropriated $25,000 for dredging the harbor. The first manufactures—a tannery (1831), Dole's meat-packing plant (1832), a soap factory (1833), and a brick yard (1833)—had started along the banks of the river, chiefly on the North Side.

Chicago in 1834.—The growth of Chicago was particularly rapid during 1834, as its population increased from the 350 of the year before to 2,000. The principal growth of that year was along Lake Street, but the corner of Lake and LaSalle streets was still so far from the center of business that the construction of a four-story brick building at that point was referred to as "Hubbard's Folly." The construction of a drawbridge over the main channel at Dearborn Street in 1834 had the effect of concentrating business near South Water and Dearborn Street. A freshet in the spring of 1834 completed the work of dredging the harbor. Steamboats and larger vessels which had hitherto been compelled to anchor in the lake opposite the bar at the river's mouth could now enter through the main channel into the heart of the business district. The limited extent of the town in 1834 is indicated by the following account:

> Besides the log cabin on the West side kept by Mr. Stiles, there was a blacksmith shop. That was all. On the North side were John Kinzie's house and a few others. On the South side there was one house south of Lake Street. On Lake and South Water streets was the main village. Lake Street boasted one brick block which belonged to Hubbard.[44]

Chicago in 1835–36.—Chicago continued to grow rapidly during 1835 and 1836. The population increased from the 2,000 of 1834 to 3,264 in 1835 and 3,820 in 1836. By 1837 there were 450 buildings as contrasted with 180 in 1833 and 12 at the beginning of 1832.

The main part of the settled area of Chicago in 1836 was on the South Side near the river. As one observer said:

> When the bank was in operation [December, 1835–36], Chicago was confined principally to the vicinity of the river. The dwellings even did not stretch far away from the center. In the spring of 1835 a three-story brick building, probably 117 Lake Street, near LaSalle Street, was erected and finished in the fall. It was

[44] Letter of Enoch Chase, August 2, 1883, in *ibid.*, pp. 138–39.

the general impression that the stand was too far from the center of business and would prove a bad speculation.[45]

The solidly built-up section did not extend south of Randolph Street on the South Side in 1836, according to Mr. Charles C. P. Holden. "It was principally prairie with some timber southerly from Randolph Street, though there were some groups of buildings scattered here and there with small patches of ground inclosed with rail fences."[46] Dearborn Street, near the drawbridge, between Lake and South Water streets, was "the lively street" and the center of activity, for there was located Garrett's auction-room where $1,800,000 worth of real estate was sold in the latter part of 1835 and 1836.[47]

The North Side began to grow rapidly in 1835. When Charles Butler inspected Kinzie's and Wolcott's additions in May of 1835, he gave the following description of the land that lay just north of the main channel of the river. "The property lay there on the north side of the river covered with a coarse growth of oak and underbrush, wet and marshy and muddy from the recent rains."[48] By 1836, however, there was a substantial settlement on the North Side along the river and east of Clark Street, for Mr. Holden said that "the North Side at that time [1836] was very pretentious and there was lots of business done over there, though but a short distance from where we landed was the wild woods of that day."[49] The principal shipping and forwarding business at this time was done on the north side of the river.

The growth of the West Side lagged far behind the other sections in this period. When Charles Cleaver in 1838 put up a building at the corner of Washington and Jefferson streets, which is only three blocks west of the river, he stated that "standing there alone for years, it served as a beacon for many a belated traveller over the ten miles of prairie between the village and the Desplaines River." "At that time," he continued, "it seemed a long way out of town. There was but one shanty between it and the Lake Street bridge, and it really seemed quite a walk over the prairie to reach it." Thereafter, from 1838 to 1843 a house was gradually built here and there between Cleaver's house and the river, but the filling-in process was very slow.[50]

[45] *Chicago Tribune*, July 3, 1887.   [46] *Ibid.*
[47] Letter of J. D. Bonnell, March 15, 1876, cited in Andreas, *op. cit.*, I, 137.
[48] *Ibid.*, p. 131.   [49] *Chicago Tribune*, July 3, 1887.
[50] Cleaver, *op. cit.*, pp. 55–56.

By the close of 1836 Chicago contained some very pretentious structures for that time. The Saloon (Salon) Building, a four-story brick structure at the corner of Clark and Lake streets, contained the finest hall west of Buffalo. The four-story Lake House, built on the corner of Rush and Michigan Street on the North Side at a cost of $100,000 was one of the best hotels in the West. The Ogden House at Rush, Ontario, Cass, and Erie streets, and the Clarke House at Sixteenth and Prairie, standing a mile and a half away from any other house, were the two mansions of that day, whose magnificence surpassed all others. Each of these homes cost $10,000—a large expenditure for that time.

A newspaper correspondent revisiting Chicago in January of 1837 after an absence of two years found that great changes had taken place.

> I can scarcely recognize it as the same spot. Where then I walked over the unbroken prairie, the spacious avenue is now opened, crowded with carts and wagons, and occasionally a showy family rolling and dashing in the hurry of trade, or the pomp of the native "sucker" stumbling as I do, over bales and boxes on the sidewalks, or gaping at the big signs and four-story brick houses.[51]

This scene of activity had a very limited scope, however, for of the 4,179 people in Chicago in 1837, there were only 433 on the entire West Side and only 320 on the North Side west of Clark Street. The limits of the settled area in 1837 were thus defined:

> The inhabited portion of Chicago [in 1837] consisted chiefly of Kinzie Street on the North Side with a few scattered residences on Clark, Dearborn, Wolcott and Rush; on Lake and South Water streets on the South Side; and on those portions of Clark, Dearborn and LaSalle streets between South Water and Washington streets there were small frame houses surrounded by gardens. State and Madison Street was then way out in the country. The West Side was most sparsely settled and plover and snipe abounded from Clinton Street to Union Park.[52]

The concentration of a population of 4,179 into a settled area of only 25 blocks, or 100 acres, when there were boundless tracts of prairie in every direction seems strange. The explanation is to be found in the abnormal age and sex distribution of the population and in the intolerably bad condition of the roads. Over 1,900, or 45 per cent of the total population, consisted of adult males, and there was a large proportion of single men who lived at hotels or boarding-houses or at the stores of their employers.[53] Transient sailors lived on ships; farmers and

[51] Andreas, *op. cit.*, I, 138.
[52] Moses and Kirkland, *History of Chicago*, I, 105.
[53] Wentworth, *Reminiscences of Early Chicago* (Chicago: Lake Side Press, 1912).

emigrants camped in their prairie schooners. Thus, there was an average of over 10 persons to each of the 398 dwellings in the city. The overcrowded condition in Chicago, even in 1834, is thus told:[54]

By the middle of May [1834] there was no room for the constant crowd of incomers, except as buildings were hastily put up for their accommodation, or as sojourners leaving town made room for them. The hotels and boarding houses were always full, and full meant three in a bed sometimes, with the floor covered besides. Many of the emigrants coming in their own wagons had only them or a rude camp, hastily built for home and shelter. All about the outskirts of the settlement was a cordon of prairie schooners, with tethered horses between, interspersed with camp fires, at which the busy housewives were ever preparing meals for the voracious pioneers.

The following description of the early streets of Chicago also explains why people did not venture far out into the prairie but huddled close to the river and the stores: "From the rains the streets of the village soon became deluged with mud. It lay in many places half-leg deep, up to the hubs of carts and wagons in the middle of the street. The smaller children I used to bring to school and take home on my back."[55]

Chicago in 1837 was also abnormally developed with respect to the number of its stores. The 29 dry-goods stores, 5 hardware stores, 45 grocery and provision stores, 10 taverns, and 19 lawyers' offices were far in excess of the requirements of a population of 4,000. Chicago was the trading center of the territory within a radius of 200 miles, however, and as many as 500 farmers' wagons could be counted at one time in their camp in the town. Chicago was also a refitting-point for emigrants, the county seat, and hence the legal center of an area that embraced the present Cook, Lake, McHenry, Will, and DuPage counties, an area of approximately 3,200 square miles. It was the seat of the government land office for the surrounding region, the site of the branch bank of the state, and a distributing-point for the Indian trade. The total volume of business amounted to $1,000,000 in 1836, with one firm on Lake Street reporting sales of $41,000 even in the depression in 1837. At this time the surrounding country was not even self-sufficing, and all the goods sold were imported from the East, the ships going back with sand as ballast.

The North Side was growing faster than the other sections of the city from 1837 to 1840, its population increasing from 1,238 to 1,759, a gain of 41 per cent, while the population of the South Side increased

[54] Andreas, *op. cit.*, I, 134.
[55] *Chicago Tribune*, December 12, 1886 (Granville T. Sproat, the first school-teacher).

only from 2,330 to 2,664, a gain of 14 per cent, and the population of the West Side remained stationary. All the warehouses for receiving farmers' produce were located on the north bank of the river, and as the farmers came from the south, it was necessary for them to cross the Dearborn Street bridge. In 1839 this bridge became unsafe and was demolished, a ferry being substituted for it. About this time property owners on South Water Street began to build warehouses there with the result that the farmers unloaded their produce on the South Side and no longer crossed the river.[56] The North Side interests attempted to regain their old trade by securing the building of a bridge over the main channel at Clark Street in 1840. This move did not bring the trade back to the North Side, but it did aid in the establishment of a new business center at Clark and Lake streets. As William B. Ogden wrote in 1841, "Business is all concentrating on Lake and Clark streets, and every concentration of it makes serious inroads on the little that is left on our [i.e., North Side] side."[57] The North Side never recovered its business prestige, but it held the position, during the forties, of the leading fashionable residential section of Chicago.

Chicago grew slowly during the years of depression, 1837–42. By 1842 it extended three or four blocks in every direction from the river. Mr. Waughop thus characterizes the young city in that year: "In 1842 Chicago had the appearance of an overgrown country town. The limits [i.e., of the settled area] on the north Indiana [Grand], Madison on the South and Jefferson on the West."[58]

Such was the physical growth of Chicago during its first land cycle, which will now be described.

C. LAND VALUES IN CHICAGO, 1830–42

The start.—Although the possibility of a canal from the Chicago to the Desplaines River had been discussed for many years prior to 1830, and the strategic importance of the site of Chicago had long been evident, there was no attempt to buy government land in the Chicago region before 1830. The long nation-wide depression that began in 1819, together with the local financial difficulties that had followed the

[56] Henry Brown, *The Present and Future Prospects of Chicago* (Chicago: Fergus Printing Co., 1876), p. 22.

[57] Letter of William B. Ogden, March 27, 1841 (MS in Chicago Historical Society).

[58] J. W. Waughop in *Chicago Tribune*, September 28, 1884.

collapse of the first attempt at state banking, as well as the lack of population in this region, seem to have prevented any speculative movement from getting started. In 1833 the Pottawatomie Indians sold to the United States 20,000,000 acres near Chicago at the rate of approximately $0.06 an acre.[59] Up to 1830 no part of the Chicago region was considered more valuable than any other government land that was offered for sale throughout the West for a minimum of $1.25 an acre. The value of the 211 square miles in the present city limits of Chicago was, therefore, no more than $800 a square mile, or $168,800, at the beginning of 1830. There were few buyers for it at this price and hence even this valuation for 1830 might be considered excessive. Kinzie did not consider it worth while to exercise his pre-emption rights on the 58 acres lying at the forks of the river.[60] The first sale of lots by the Canal Commissioners in September, 1830, showed only a slight advance over the minimum acre value. The highest price paid for an 80-by-180-foot lot on the river was only $100.

The corners of South Water Street and Lake and Dearborn streets sold for $0.50 a front foot. Back lots sold for as low as $10 for half-acre tracts. The average value of the Original Town could scarcely have exceeded $25 an acre at the time, while land directly adjoining the original townsite on the north side of the river still sold for $1.25 an acre.[61]

The advance in land values from 1830 to 1832 was very slight, for the corner of Lake and Wells (80 feet by 150 feet) sold for only $39 in 1832 and the corner of the same size at South Water and Dearborn for only $78.[62] A corner of Randolph and Dearborn streets sold for only $60 the same year.[63] A visitor to Chicago who saw a sheet of water covering most of the site of the future metropolis said, "I would not give six pence an acre for the whole of it."[64]

The rise begins.—The marked increase in population and building activities during 1833 was reflected in the beginning of a sharp increase in the value of lots in the Original Town in the improved business section on the south side of the river. A lot on South Water Street, just

[59] Andreas, *op. cit.*, I, 125–28.
[60] Quaife, *Chicago Highways Old and New*, p. 19.
[61] *Shortall and Hoard's Abstracts*, Vol. 80, p. 526.
[62] *Ibid.*, Vol. 85, p. 510.   [63] *Ibid.*, Vol. 75, p. 156.
[64] James Parton, article on "Chicago" in *Atlantic Monthly*, March, 1867, p. 326.

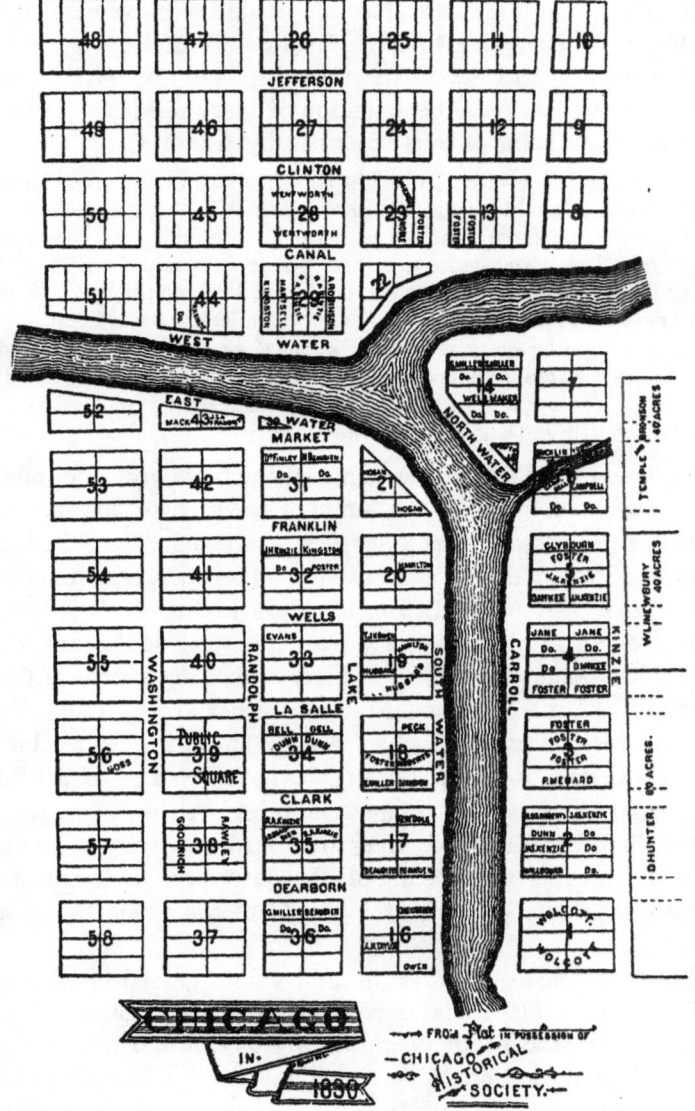

Fig. 4

west of Wells, that sold for $42 in September, 1830, and for only $66 as late as October, 1833, brought $800 on November 30, 1833. The demand for lots for actual use started a speculative movement in which prices advanced from day to day. Real estate activity spread from the center to the periphery of the town, and land operations, at first confined to a few, engaged the attention of every resident. The genesis of this real estate boom is thus described by Andreas:

> At first the purchases were what might be termed legitimate, a lot for cash on which the purchaser would erect a dwelling or a store. The legitimate demand soon absorbed the floating supply and prices began to rise under the competition of anxious buyers. Lots purchased one day for $50.00 were sold the next for $60.00 and resold the next month for $100.00. It did not take long under such circumstances to develop a strong speculative fever, which infected every resident of the town and was caught by every newcomer. At the close of the year 1834 the disease had become fairly seated. Whatever might be the business of a Chicagoan or however profitable, it was not considered a full success except it showed an outside profit on lots bought and sold.[65]

As the demand for lots at the center of the town grew more intense, a new supply of lots beyond the limits of the settled area was put on the market and the scope of activity was broadened. The School Board was prompted to subdivide the School Section—the square mile from State to Halsted streets and from Madison to Roosevelt Road. The 142 blocks of an average size of 3.5–4 acres were sold on October 4, 1833, at the average rate of $60 an acre, or $38,865 for the entire section except the two corners on Madison Street at State and Halsted streets that were reserved for school sites.[66] The advance in value from $1.25 to $60 an acre from 1830 to 1833 was considered quite satisfactory by the School Board at the time of the sale, but they soon regretted their haste in selling this land. Ever afterward they were to be blamed for disposing, for this trifling sum, of what later became the most valuable square mile ever given for the benefit of the education of future generations.

Gaining momentum.—The rise in land values gained momentum in 1834. The entire United States was beginning to engage in feverish land speculation, and people were coming to Chicago with visions of the future city at the mouth of the Illinois and Michigan canal. In June, 1834, the corner of South Water and Clark Street, 80 by 180 feet,

[65] *Op. cit.*, I, 115.
[66] *Ibid.*, p. 133.

sold for $3,500, thirty-five times as much as had been paid for it two years before. A year later it sold for $15,000.[67]

A number of factors contributed to swell the rising tide of Chicago land values in 1835. First, the Illinois legislature on February 14, 1835, authorized the governor to pledge the canal lands and tolls for a loan of $500,000 to start work on digging the canal.[68] Second, the same body chartered a new State Bank of Illinois with a capital of $1,500,000, empowering it to borrow $1,000,000 and reloan it upon Illinois real estate at not more than half its value. It was also permitted to issue notes up to two and a half times its capital to be redeemed in specie under penalty of enforced liquidation.[69] A branch of this bank was established in Chicago in December, 1835, and one of the most potent devices for raising land values, liberal credit to land-buyers, was thereby created. Third, a government land office opened in Chicago on May 5, 1835. This attracted to the city a horde of speculators and real estate agents and created a market in which buyers and sellers were brought into close compass.

Repercussions of speculative forces that were sweeping the entire nation interacted upon these local factors and produced a higher pitch of excitement than these state policies alone could have generated. The bills of the state banks of Michigan, Indiana, and Wisconsin were even more numerous in Chicago than the bills of the State Bank of Illinois. New batches of Michigan bills could be secured almost at will by a law which authorized such notes to be issued in exchange for private obligations secured by mortgages on the lands in that state. The fame of Chicago real estate was so great in New York City that Chicago lots were sold there at public auction. The high prices paid for these lots in the eastern city astonished the local speculators and stimulated fresh advances when the news finally reached the West. The report of a sale by Mr. Hubbard of a half-interest in a tract of eighty acres at the corner of Halsted and Chicago Avenue for $80,000 in New York in 1835, which represented a profit of $77,500 made in a few months, was at first not believed to be true. When confirmed by Mr. Hubbard himself, local landowners revised upward their opinion as to the value of

---

[67] Goodspeed and Healy, *op. cit.*, I, 107; *Shortall and Hoard's Abstracts*, Vol. 40, p. 892.

[68] *Laws of Illinois* (9th General Assembly, 1st sess.; Vandalia, 1835), p. 222.

[69] *Laws of Illinois* (1834–35), p. 7; G. W. Dowrie, *Development of Banking in Illinois, 1817 to 1863* (University of Illinois, 1913), pp. 61–63.

their holdings. Buyers brought money from New York, from the South, and even, in the case of George Smith, from Scotland to invest in Chicago lands. If outsiders were thus so anxious to buy, it is a matter of little surprise that the local residents, who saw the rapid rise in land values which was daily taking place before their eyes, invested all the money they could raise in land, which was making people wealthier in a year than a lifetime of hard labor. The effect upon local sentiment of this outside participation in the Chicago land market is thus described by Andreas:

> The speculative mania was not confined to Chicago or the West. A superabundance of paper money issued under divers state laws had flooded the whole country, in volume far in excess of the requirements of legitimate trade, and was seeking outside investment in all quarters. In the money centers of the East, New York, Boston and Philadelphia, a furore of speculation in all commodities and in real estate was at its height before the Western mania was fairly started. The rumors of fortunes made in a day in Chicago in the purchase of Western lands soon reached New York, where among the capitalists the excitement became but little less than at home. There a new speculative demand grew up which proved an outlet for the avalanche of new towns that were being thrown on the market. But for this the craze might have spent itself sooner; as it was, Eastern capitalists, after once embarked on the trade, became the most reckless and wildest speculators and held the excitement at fever heat until the collapse which began in the East forced them to take an observation, which resulted in a sudden and complete stoppage of monetary supplies from that source.[70]

The supply of subdivided lots in Chicago was constantly being increased to meet the growing demand. Kinzie's Addition, north of the river, east of State Street, had been platted in 1833, Wolcott's and Bushnell's additions, on the North Side from State to Sedgewick streets and from Kinzie to Division Street, were added in 1835. Most of the blocks in the School Section had also been split up into lots by 1835.[71]

At full speed.—Under the influence of these forces, the rise of land values in Chicago in 1835 was extremely rapid. The Tremont House lot at the corner of Lake and Dearborn (80 by 180 feet) that could have been bought for a cord of wood, a pair of boots, and a barrel of whiskey in 1831, 1832, and 1833, respectively, was now valued at a sum of money that would fill a warehouse with such commodities.[72] Dole's cor-

[70] *Op. cit.*, I, 135.
[71] Plats of the Chicago Title and Trust Co.
[72] J. D. Bonnell in Andreas, *op. cit.*, I, 137.

ner, at Dearborn and South Water streets (80 by 180 feet), was sold for $9,000 in March of 1835 and for $25,000 in December. One hundred thousand dollars was offered and refused for Hogan's block at 272 Lake Street.[73]

Lots and blocks in the School Section rose precipitately in value. Block 134 increased from $400 to $2,200 between March 20 and June 6, 1835.[74] Block 137 advanced from $260 in 1933 to $3,500 on December 7, 1835.[75] Block 65 rose from $602 in 1834 to $2,000 in 1835.[76] Other blocks advanced in like proportion. The corner of Clark and South Water streets, 80 by 150 feet, that sold for $2,000 on March 15, 1834, and $3,500 on June 1, 1834, brought $15,000 on June 10, 1835.[77] The effect of the rise was felt as far as six miles from the center of the town. Land at Madison and Kedzie had risen to $10 an acre,[78] at Fullerton and Cicero to $12 an acre,[79] and at Sixty-third and State to $10 an acre[80]—all having made this gain from the base price of $1.25 an acre by the fall of 1835. Land in the southern and northwestern part of the present city, however, could still be bought for $1.25 an acre in 1835.

The peak.—This rise in land values continued during the spring and summer of 1836. The agents of the governor had been unable to obtain a loan of $500,000 at 5 per cent interest, secured only by a pledge of the canal lands and tolls as authorized by the law of 1835, so in January, 1836, a new law was passed authorizing the governor to pledge the general credit of the state for a loan of $500,000 at 6 per cent interest. It also provided for the sale of lots in the Original Town of Chicago and in Fractional Section 15 on June 20, 1836, at prices not less than valuations placed on them beforehand by the Canal Commissioners.[81] The same law also allowed that method of partial payment, known as "canal terms," by which the purchasers of land were required to pay only one-fourth down and the balance in three equal instalments in one, two, and three years, with interest at 6 per cent per annum on the un-

[73] Goodspeed and Healy, *op. cit.*, I, 116.

[74] *Shortall and Hoard's Abstracts*, Vol. 34, pp. 820-21.

[75] *Ibid.*, pp. 320-32.

[76] *Ibid.*, Vol. 39, pp. 114-15.   [77] *Ibid.*, Vol. 40, pp. 892-94.

[78] *Chicago Title and Trust Abstracts*, Vol. 940, p. 569.

[79] *Ibid.*, Vol. 3302, p. 512.   [80] *Ibid.*, Vol. 1078, p. 215.

[81] *Laws of Illinois* (9th General Assembly, 2d sess.; Vandalia, 1836), pp. 145-50, secs. 1, 2, 33.

paid balance.[82] Under the conditions of this law of 1836, a loan of $500,000 was successfully negotiated in New York.[83] The date fixed by legislative fiat for the sale of town lots in Chicago almost coincided with the peak of the real estate market. Consequently, with sales on that day of $1,619,848, of which $400,000 was received in cash,[84] the Canal Commissioners had sufficient funds to start the canal at Chicago on July 4, 1836. At last the preliminary work had begun on the project upon which such great speculative hopes had been founded.

Speculation in Chicago reached fever heat by June and July of 1835. That is was absorbing the attention of nearly everyone in the town is indicated by the following account by Harriet Martineau:

> I never saw a busier place than Chicago was at the time of our arrival [1836]. The streets were crowded with land speculators, hurrying from one sale to another. A negro dressed up in scarlet bearing a scarlet flag and riding a white horse with housings of scarlet announced the time of sale. At every street corner where he stopped the crowd gathered around him; and it seemed as if some prevalent mania infected the whole people. As the gentlemen of our party walked the streets, storekeepers hailed them from their doors with offers of farms and all manner of land lots, advising them to speculate before the price of land rose higher.[85]

Not only Chicago town lots, but the lots of five hundred Illinois towns, many of which never existed except on a plat and are now corn fields, were offered for sale in Chicago.[86] Chicago was "the hatching place of the brood of western towns"; it was the center of a speculative whirlpool whose character and scope is thus vividly described by Joseph N. Balestier:

> But the few miles that composed Chicago formed but a small item among the subjects of speculation. So utterly reckless had the community grown that they chased every bubble that floated in the speculative atmosphere; madness increased in proportion to the foulness of its aliment; the more absurd the project, the more remote the object, the more madly were they pursued. The prairies of Illinois, the forests of Wisconsin and the sand hills of Michigan presented a chain almost unbroken of supposititious villages and cities. The whole land seemed staked out and peopled on paper. If a man were reputed to be fortunate, his touch, like that of Midas, was supposed to turn everything into gold, and the crowd entered blindly

[82] *Ibid.*, p. 150, sec. 35.

[83] James William Putnam, *The Illinois and Michigan Canal* (Chicago, 1918), p. 41.

[84] Moses and Kirkland, *op. cit.*, I, 96.

[85] *Reminiscences of Early Chicago* (1912), pp. 27–28.

[86] William Vipond Pooley, "The Settlement of Illinois from 1830 to 1850," *Bulletin of the University of Wisconsin*, No. 220 (1908), pp. 278–79.

THE CANAL LAND BOOM

into anything he might originate. These worthies would besiege the land offices and purchase town sites at a dollar and a quarter per acre, which in a few days appeared on paper, laid out in the most approved rectangular fashion, emblazoned in glaring colors, and exhibiting the public spirit of the proprietor in the multitude of their public squares, church lots and school lot reservations. Often was a fictitious streamlet seen to wind its romantic course through the heart of an ideal city, thus creating water lots and water privileges. But where a *real* stream, no matter how diminutive, did find its way to the shore of the lake—no matter what was the character of the surrounding country—some wary operator would ride night and day until the place was secured at the government price. Then the miserable waste of sand and fens which lay unconscious of its glory on the shore of the lake was suddenly elevated into a mighty city, with a projected harbor and lighthouse, railroads, and canals, and in a short time the circumjacent lands were sold in lots of 50 by 100 feet, under the name "additions." Not the puniest brook on the shore of Lake Michigan was suffered to remain without a city at its mouth and whoever will travel around that lake shall find many a mighty mart staked out in spots suitable only for the habitations of wild beasts.[87]

Within the present city limits of Chicago, Figure 5 shows town sites were laid out in 1836 at Canalport (Ashland Avenue from Twenty-second to Thirty-first street), Cottage Grove (Thirty-first Street and the lake), Calumet (Ninety-fifth Street and the lake), and Summit (Fifty-first and Harlem Avenue, just outside the present city limits), all of these being either on the Lake or on the route of the proposed canal. The supply of lots near Chicago was increased in 1836 by the subdivision of Fractional Section 15 (from Madison Street to Roosevelt Road, State Street to Michigan Avenue), and by the opening of Carpenter's Addition (northwest corner of Madison and Halsted streets) and Duncan's Addition (northeast corner of Halsted and Roosevelt Road). Fractional shares of unsubdivided lands amounting to as little as one-thirty-second of a quarter-section were bought and sold. "Every man who owned a garden patch stood on his head and imagined himself a millionaire."[88]

The method in which a boom psychology is generated within a close compass by the interaction between minds obsessed with the same beliefs was as well illustrated in 1836 as in later periods of speculative enthusiasm, as the following account shows:

A powerful auxiliary to the speculative spirit was the sale of lands by auction. Where bodies of men, actuated by a common motive, assemble together for a common object, zeal is apt to run to enthusiasm when the common passion is artfully

[87] Andreas, *op. cit.*, I, 135. [88] *Ibid.*, p. 137.

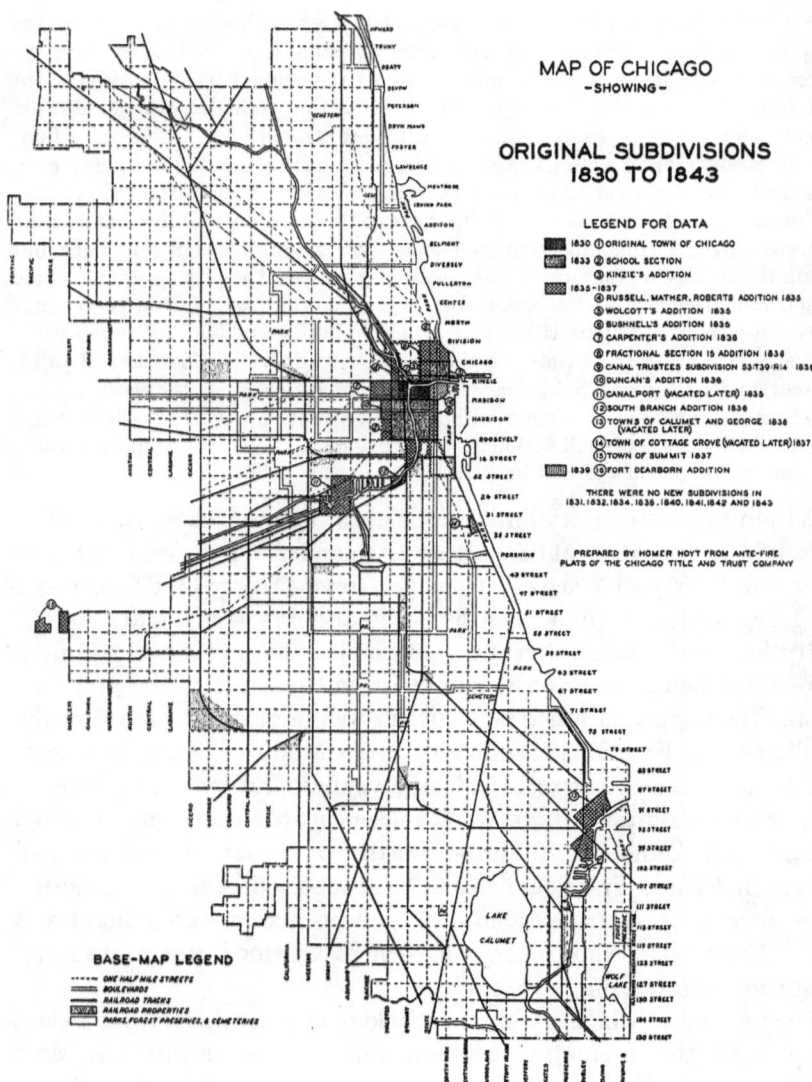

FIG. 5

THE CANAL LAND BOOM   33

inflamed by a skillful orator, enthusiasm becomes fanaticism, and fanaticism, madness. Men who wish to be persuaded are already more than half won over, and an excited imagination will produce almost any anticipated result. Popular delusions have carried away millions at a time, mental epidemics have raged at every period of the world's history and conviction has ever been potent to work miracles. Now the speculating mania was an epidemic of the mind, and every chord struck by the chief performers produced endless vibrations, until the countless tones of the full diapason broke forth into maddening strains of fascination. The auctioneers were the high priests who sacrificed in the Temple of Fortune, through them the speculators spread abroad their spacious representations. Like the Sibyls and Flamens of old they delivered false oracles and made a juggle of omens and auguries.[89]

Thus the dazzling tales of fortunes quickly made, the pyramiding of land profits made possible by the constant emission of state bank notes that created an ever higher structure of land values and the reports of the national speculative mania that were circulated by every traveler were used by skilful auctioners to raise local buyers to the highest pitch of excitement. Figures 6 and 7 show some of the detailed sales of lots and acreage tracts at the peak in 1836. These prices may be compared with the initial prices in 1830 of $100 for the best town lot and $1.25 an acre for quarter-sections adjacent to the present "Loop." To present a picture of the changes in land values in that period for the entire area within the present city limits, an estimate of the total value has been made on the basis of these sample sales.

A survey of the summit.—By the summer of 1836 the total sales value of the land in the present city limits of Chicago had increased from the $168,800 value of 1830 to $10,500,000, a rise of over sixty fold. Of this amount 56 per cent, or 5,900,000, represented the value of the 2.5 square miles within a mile of State and Madison streets. At the prices prevailing on June 20, 1836, the whole of the Original Town alone was worth $2,650,000 and the School Section which had sold for $38,000 in 1833 had advanced in value to $1,200,000.[90] The average advance on these tracts had been a thousand fold since 1830, and the lots along the river had exceeded even this startling rate of increase. The highest values had been reached at South Water and Dearborn, where a 3.5-acre block at the drawbridge over the river had reached an aggregate value of $152,000, and at LaSalle and South Water, where two lots were reported to have sold together for $100,000.[91] Successive blocks

[89] *Ibid.*, p. 135.
[90] See Figs. 71 and 73 for detailed sales and valuations of 1830–36.
[91] Andreas, *op. cit.*, I, 137.

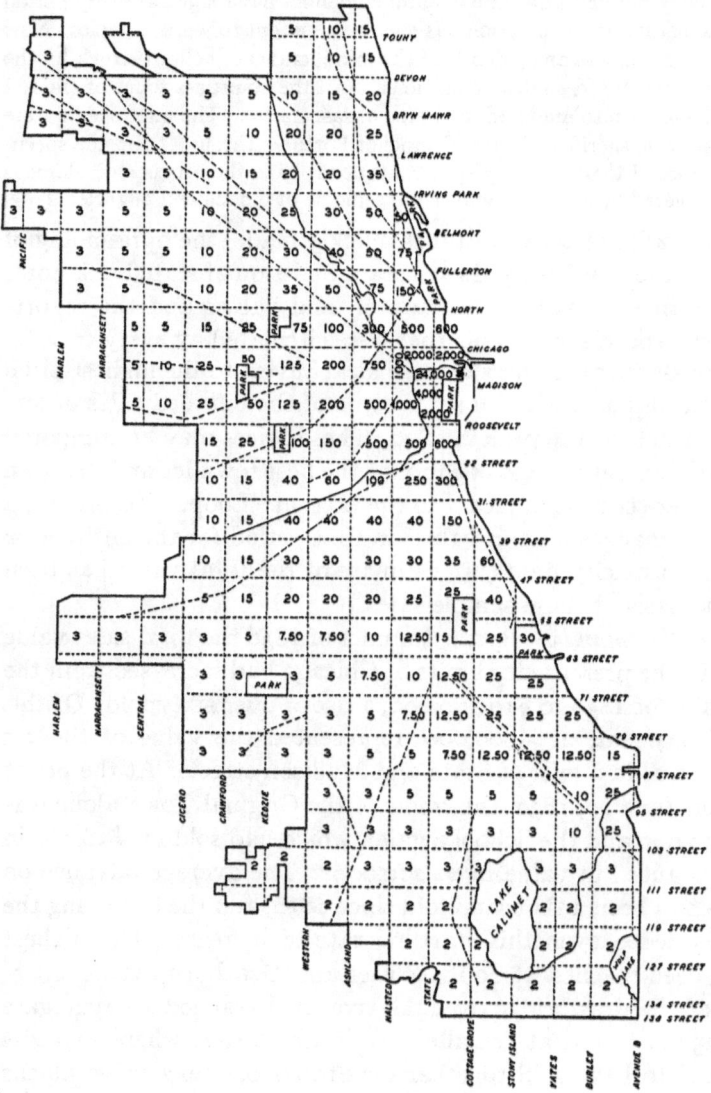

Fig. 6

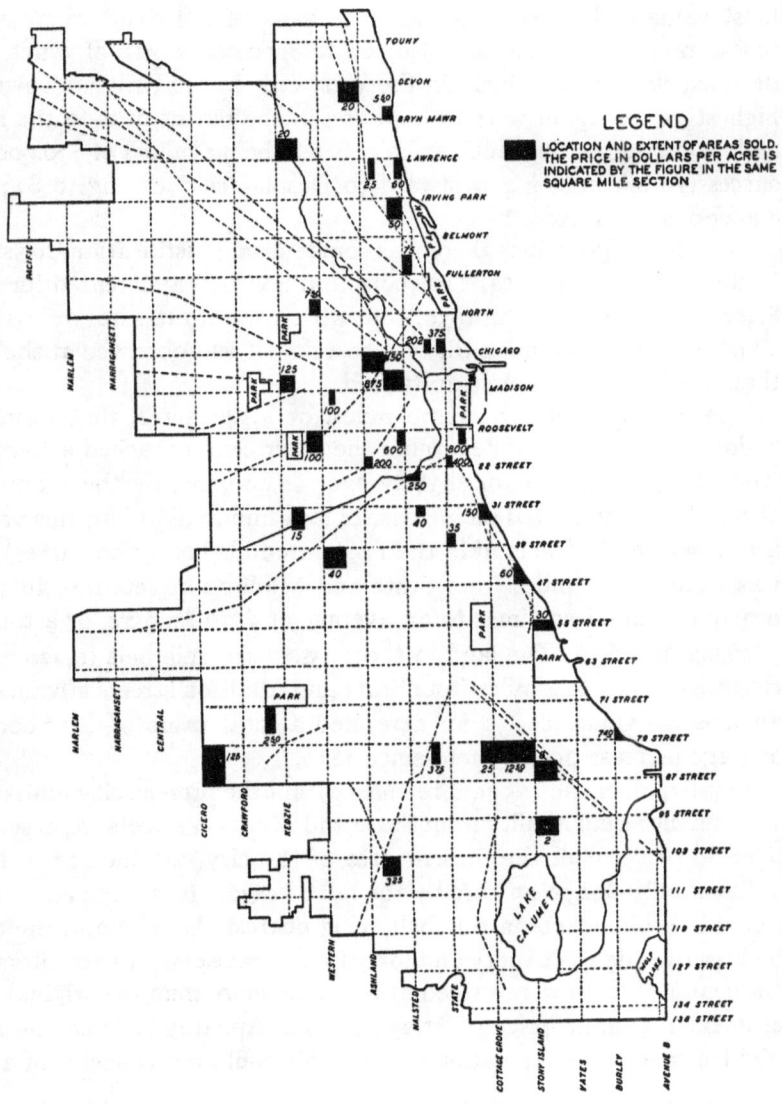

Fig. 7

southward from State and South Water streets had sold at the rate of $100,000 for whole blocks at Randolph, $46,000 at Washington, $23,000 at Madison, and $6,000 at Roosevelt Road. On the North Side the most valuable lots were on the north bank of the river, where entire blocks ranged in value from $50,000 to $100,000, north of which they declined sharply in value. On the West Side in the Original Town the highest values again were to be found in the blocks next to the river, a block on the south branch at Lake Street being valued at $70,000 and successive blocks going westward to Desplaines declining to $29,000, $19,000, and $14,500.[92]

For these high values there was some income justification, for stores in the best locations near Dearborn and South Water rented for from $1,000 to $1,500 a year in 1836,[93] but with interest rates at not less than 10 per cent per annum on the best security, it was observed at the time that this income was overcapitalized.

The next belt of 6.5 square miles, or 4,140 acres, that formed a hollow square a mile wide around the inner center reached an average value of $500 an acre, or slightly over $2,000,000, by the summer of 1836. This represented an increase of four hundred fold for this vacant area since 1830. The land in the 11-square-mile belt (7,000 acres) that was from 2 to 3 miles from State and Madison streets rose in value nearly one hundred times to an average of $116 an acre, or a total of $816,640 by 1836. The land in the 14.5-square-mile belt (9,220 acres) that was from 3 to 4 miles from State and Madison streets advanced to an average value of $50 an acre, and a total value of $416,000, an average increase of forty fold since 1830.

Finally, all of the 175 square miles within the present city limits that were farther than 4 miles from State and Madison streets, representing over 80 per cent of the present area of the city, attained an average value of only $12.50 an acre by the fall of 1836, an average advance of tenfold. While tracts in this belt lying nearest the lake and the town had risen as high as twenty and forty fold, great areas 8 or 10 miles from the center of town were valued at but little more than the original government minimum price of $1.25 an acre. Apparently even the most vivid speculative imagination of that time could not conceive of a city

---

[92] See maps of the Original Town giving sales for lots in each block (Figs. 73 and 74).

[93] *Chicago American*, July 9, 1836.

that would grow so far from the river and the lake that these acres would be needed for urban use. These 112,000 acres, therefore, had a value of only $1,400,000 in 1836, or only 13 per cent of the total land value of Chicago, although they embrace over 80 per cent of its present area.

Thus in the first land boom of 1836, values rose to the peak along the Chicago River and its branches, where land was worth eight to ten times as much as land half a mile back, twenty-five times as much as land a mile away, two hundred times as much as land two miles away, fifteen hundred times as much as land seven miles away, and twenty-five hundred times as much as land ten miles away.

The lull.—The course of prices indicates that the period of most rapid advances in values ended in July of 1836, but that a slow advance was maintained up to the very end of the year.[94] On June 20, 1836, the bids on the lots in the Original Town in most cases exceeded even the high valuation placed upon them by the Canal Commissioners,[95] but on September 5, 1836, the bids on the lots then offered for sale fell short of the Commissioners' appraisals. For some months there was a lull, in which the volume of sales greatly declined, during which speculators sought to perpetuate the high plateau of values that had been established by the last sales. Even on May 26, 1837, William B. Ogden wrote that "my sales this spring thus far amount to over $12,000 at full last year's prices,"[96] indicating that the peak of values was being maintained with difficulty at that time.

The forces of depression.—On the eve of a severe financial crisis, the state of Illinois on February 27, 1837, had recklessly plunged into a program of internal improvements which called for gridironing the state with 1,341 miles of railroads at an estimated cost of $10,250,00 for which state bonds were to be issued. All parts of the state had demanded a share in the benefits which the Illinois and Michigan canal was expected to confer on the Chicago region, with the result that the

---

[94] "Speculation reached its height in the latter part of 1836" (Norris, *Business Directory and Statistics of the City of Chicago, 1846* [reprinted by the Fergus Printing Co., Chicago, in 1883], p. 53).

[95] *Chicago American*, July 23, 1836.

[96] Letter to Frederick Bronson, May 26, 1837 (William B. Ogden, Letter Books, I, 22 [original in the Chicago Historical Society]). In the same letter Ogden also says: "I know of no sales or very few at full prices except some that I now and then make because of being able to suit the purse and give the time that persons applying desire."

success of that undertaking was jeopardized and the credit of the state impaired by a program too great for its existing resources. At first money was borrowed in New York and from the United States Bank in Philadelphia to carry on the scheme, and then when no more bonds could be sold, the legislature increased the capital of the Bank of Illinois of Shawneetown by $1,400,000 and that of the State Bank of Illinois by $2,000,000 and required these banks to exchange this additional capital stock for state bonds. Thus the project of the Illinois and Michigan canal upon which the hopes of Chicago depended became interwoven with a grand plan of internal improvements. The fate of that in turn became involved in the fate of the state banks and the state bonds.

Meanwhile, the existing volume of currency pouring forth from the banks to sustain the expanded structure of land values was greater than could be redeemed in specie. As early as May, 1836, the secretary of the Treasury had issued an order directing the land offices to refuse to accept the bills of non-specie-paying banks in payment for public lands. In the beginning of May, 1837, there was a general tightening of the money market followed by a suspension of specie payments by the banks of New York, which swept southward and westward until it reached St. Louis by May 22.[97] On May 29, 1837, the Illinois banks voted to suspend specie payments for an indefinite period, and the state legislature acquiesced in this suspension by a special act.

Under these conditions it soon became impossible to borrow money on real estate or to renew existing loans. Ogden reported in a letter of May 26, 1837, that "money is very scarce indeed," but by November 23, 1837, he was obliged to write that "I am not aware that a loan of money can be obtained of anyone here or elsewhere at this time at any rate of interest."[98] The sales at the land office in Chicago which had amounted to 370,043 acres in 1835 and 436,992 acres in 1836 dropped to 15,618 acres in 1837.[99] Still there were as yet no distress sales and no drastic declines in land values. In 1838 business improved temporarily and the Illinois banks, after a suspension of thirteen months, resumed specie payments on August 13, 1838.[100] Only 17,640 acres were sold by the Chicago land office in 1838, however, and very few sales were made in Chicago itself.

[97] Dowrie, *op. cit.*, p. 83.

[98] Letter to A. McGregor, November 23, 1837 (Ogden, *op. cit.*, I, 55 [original in the Chicago Historical Society]).

[99] Pease, *op. cit.*, p. 176.   [100] Dowrie, *op. cit.*, p. 87.

The sharp decline.—Another financial crisis swept through the country in the autumn of 1839, however, and after the news of the suspension of banks in the East had reached Springfield, the Illinois banks again suspended specie payments on October 20, 1839.[101] Local conditions in the meantime had grown much worse, for the State Bank of Illinois which had been relied upon to make profits to sustain the credit of the state and to carry on the work of internal improvements had lost $1,000,000 in an attempt to corner the lead market in 1839, and the state, in addition to a $5,000,000 debt incurred in digging the canal, had spent $6,000,000 on its other projects of internal improvements which ultimately yielded it nothing.[102] That real estate values had declined drastically could no longer be concealed by 1839. The extent of the decline was revealed when the government insisted on selling the Fort Dearborn reservation—the land north of Madison Street and east of State Street—in the depressed market of 1839[103] and received from $200 to $500 a lot, or a total of $100,000 for land that would have brought over $900,000 in 1836. Ogden in the latter part of 1839 valued the southwest corner of Dearborn and Randolph, which had sold for $7,800 in 1836, at $350 at a fair valuation and $200 at a forced sale, saying that "I have valued this property hitherto at higher rates than now . . . . but when no one has any money to buy property at any price without reference to what will be its conceded value after a little change in an extreme condition of things, it at least seems questionable as to the propriety of estimating it at the merely nominal price which it will bring at the present moment."[104] In November, 1839, Ogden estimated that the best business property had declined 75 per cent in value since 1836 and that outlying lands had fallen from 90 to 95 per cent from the peak prices.[105]

Except for the Fort Dearborn Addition, arbitrarily dumped on the market by government order, there were no new subdivisions from 1837

---

[101] *Ibid.*   [102] *Ibid.*, p. 88.

[103] Letter of William B. Ogden to Charles Butler, June 17, 1839 (Ogden, *op. cit.*, II, 105): "The very low price at which the Beaubien property [i.e., the Fort Dearborn reservation] has been selling during this and the past week, will for the present stop all sales of other lots except at greatly depressed prices."

[104] Letter to M. J. Williams, January 10, 1840 (*ibid.*, p. 310 [original in the Chicago Historical Society]).

[105] Letter to Charles Butler, June 17, 1839 (*ibid.*, p. 106): "One fourth of 1836 prices can hardly be obtained for much business property at this time and one 10th to a 20th is about all out town property will bring or is worth compared to sales of 1836."

to 1843. The three square miles already cut up into lots provided enough land for at least fifty thousand people when there were only four thousand in the city.[106] "Town lots" became a cry of derision, and the fate of much of this property was pointed out by a reporter who observed:

> In taking a stroll last week up the beautiful avenue, Clark Street beyond the School Section [i.e., south of Roosevelt Road], we observed a considerable portion of the beautiful prairie, which in the eventful days of speculation was staked out and held as thousand dollar city lots without bringing in a cent, is now plowed up for potato patches and purposes of cultivation.[107]

The bottom had not yet been reached, however, nor the extent of the land-buyer's ruin fully realized. It had become increasingly difficult to keep the work on the canal going, the other schemes of internal improvements were breaking down, and the credit of the state and the state banks was sinking lower and lower. In January, 1840, Ogden wrote as follows:

> No satisfactory valuation can be fixed on the three lots at this time because there are no purchases of real estate generally in this vicinity except for immediate use, and a future demand for this property is based chiefly upon the completion of the canal, which is at present of very uncertain result.[108]

Again he writes at about the same time:

> It is not at all the town it was, though the exterior has increased in beauty materially. That buoyancy of feeling and liberal and generous bearing of its people have given way to a close, calculating and care-worn spirit. Its ancient dynasty have mostly fallen and men and families of more recent date seem a good deal in the ascendant. It seems as if there was scarce one left to escape the blight and mildew of 1836. Either as principal or endorser or from confidence unworthily bestowed, all suffer and too often to their ruin.[109]

The bottom.—By 1841 and 1842 the extreme low ebb of state finances and of Chicago land values had been reached. The contractors who were digging the canal accepted checks of the Commissioners bearing 6 per cent interest in lieu of cash, and in 1840 accepted $1,000,000

---

[106] Three square miles or 1,920 acres or 19,200 lots, 25 by 125 feet, would provide residential land enough for nearly 100,000 persons if a family of five lived on each lot. Since there was an average of ten persons to each residential building in Chicago in 1837, and most of the population live on 100 acres of land, this estimate of the number of people that could be housed on the subdivided land is conservative.

[107] *Chicago American*, April 22, 1839.

[108] Letter to J. W. Seaver, January 14, 1840 (Ogden, *op. cit.*, II, 317 [original in the Chicago Historical Society]).

[109] Letter to Captain James Allen, January 15, 1840 (*ibid.*, p. 321).

worth of state bonds at par when they were at a discount of 15 per cent;[110] but when the state failed in May, 1841, to provide any further means for financing the canal, practically all the work came to an end in November, 1841. The State Bank of Illinois failed in February, 1842, and by April, 1842, the value of its notes had fallen from 85 cents to 44 cents on the dollar.[111] The state now owed $14,000,000, and with widespread demands for repudiation of its debt, its bonds dropped by June, 1842, to 18 cents on the dollar,[112] while the bills of the State Bank sold for 34 cents on the dollar at the same time. The Bank of Illinois of Shawneetown also suspended its operations in June, 1842, and soon thereafter the whole program of internal improvements was abandoned.

When the work on the canal stopped, one paper announced, "Speculation has received its deathblow." Foreclosures had constantly increased until the banks of Illinois, which held only $8,296 worth of real estate in 1836 and only $57,138 worth in 1839, had acquired by foreclosure land to the value of $534,421 by 1841, and land worth $1,243,327 by 1843.[113] The buyers of canal lots, unable to meet their payments in 1837, had their time of payment extended by special act of the legislature in 1837. As this relief was of little avail by the time land values had declined drastically, the legislature again came to their relief in 1841, first by deducting one-third from the price they had agreed to pay in 1836, and, second, by allowing them to apply all the money they had paid in toward the full payment of one lot or one portion of a lot, so they received a clear title to at least one piece of land in return for what they had spent.[114]

A survey at the bottom.—The bottom was reached in 1842.[115] The to-

[110] Putnam, *op. cit.*, p. 285.

[111] Dowrie, *op. cit.*, p. 103; *Sangamon Journal*, April 8, 1842

[112] *Chicago Democrat*, June 8, 1842.

[113] *Report of the Comptroller of the Currency* (1876), p. 118.

[114] *Laws of Illinois, 1841* (12th General Assembly; Springfield, 1841), pp. 49–51.

[115] Colbert estimates that they dropped to 5 per cent of the 1836 peak: "The next year [1841] work was suspended on the canal and the situation became more gloomy than ever, real estate being offered at less than 5 per cent of the price paid in 1836" (Colbert and Chamberlin, *Chicago and the Great Conflagration*, p. 1); "In 1842 real estate had but little value, and everybody would have been rid of it but nobody else would take it, and so being obliged to keep what they had, an abundance of people were made rich in spite of themselves" ("Fergus Historical Series," No. 5, Part II, p. 16: "Life of Benj. W. Raymond"); William Bross, *History of Chicago*, p. 17: "Real estate went down to a very low figure, reaching bottom in 1842."

tal land value, according to sales, in the Chicago region had dropped from the $10,000,000 level of 1836 to $1,400,000.[116] Except for the distant land near the present city limits that had hardly risen at all in the boom of 1836, the shrinkage in land values had been remarkably uniform. Land values within the first-mile belt dropped from $5,901,000 to $810,000, in the second-mile belt from $2,070,000 to $207,000, in the third-mile belt from $817,000 to $70,000, in the fourth-mile belt from $461,000 to $46,000, and in the outer belt from $1,400,000 to $269,000.

The value of the best business location in Chicago, on Lake and Clark, did not exceed $100 a front foot in 1842, while most of the land in the present Loop, north of Madison, was worth no more than $10 a front foot and that south of it $2.00 or $3.00 a front foot. As Figure 8 shows, acres within a mile of State and Madison were worth no more than $100 an acre, within two miles they dropped to $10 an acre, and beyond four miles they were worth not over $2.50 an acre.

The aftermath.—The effect of this extreme decline in land values was to ruin most of those who bought land in Chicago prior to 1836. John S. Wright lost all of his land, valued at $200,000 during the boom of 1836, and worth at least $1,000,000 in 1856, because of his inability to meet obligations of $25,000.[117] Philo Carpenter parted with land later worth over $1,000,000 to satisfy a debt of $8,500.[118] Ogden wrote on January 25, 1841:

> As regards Chicago, everything has changed mightily since you left. Property has depreciated monstrously. It often happens that property which sold for hundreds, even thousands, is not now worth even ten dollars. Those too who were the richest when you left are of the poorest now..... Very few of the old stock of '36 are otherwise than deeply embarrassed..... We are all narrowed to picayune operations, and have hard work to make our ends meet and get our daily bread, cheap as it is now. So much for unhallowed speculations.[119]

As the reporter for the *Chicago Journal* stated: "When reverses came upon our business men, it was almost a universal crash and ruin that followed, few old settlers, those who had borne the heat and burden of

[116] Computed by the writer on the basis of sales.

[117] Andreas, *op. cit.*, I, 136, John S. Wright, *Chicago, Past, Present, Future* (Chicago, 1870), p. 290.

[118] *Early Chicago and Illinois* ("Chicago Historical Society's Collection," Vol. IV), p. 119.

[119] Letter to H. Moore, January 25, 1841;(Ogden, *op. cit.*, III, 159 [original in the Chicago Historical Society]).

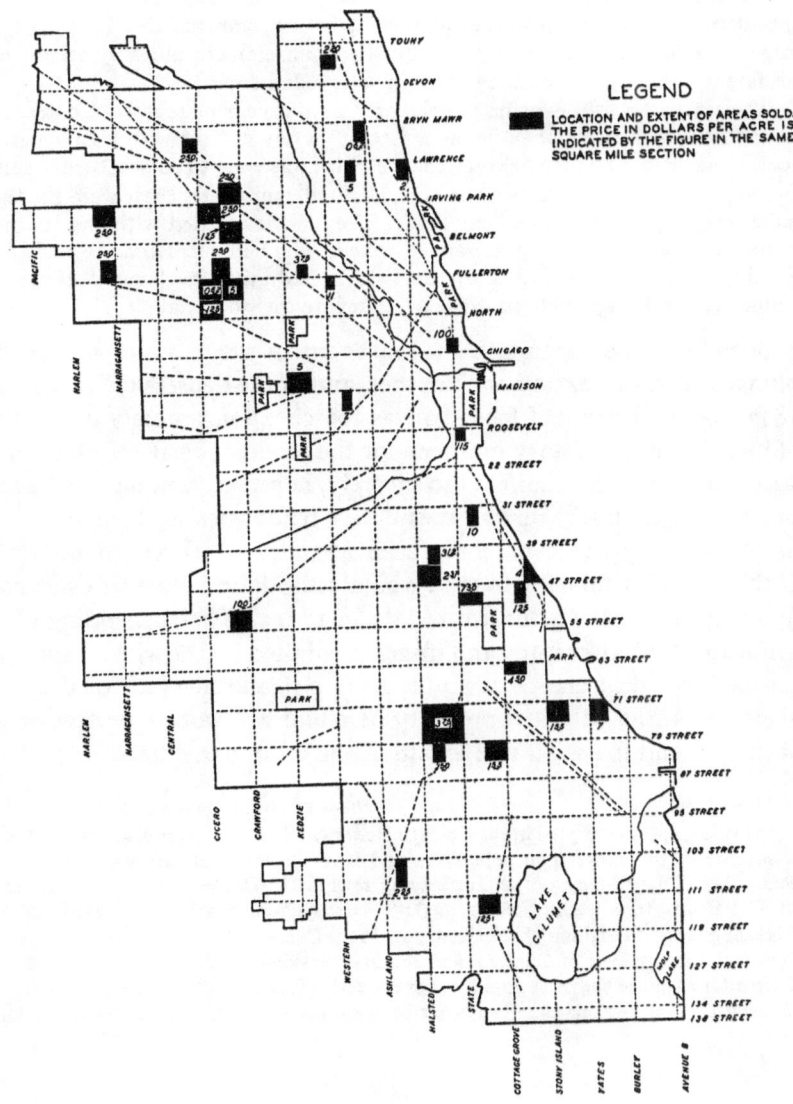

Fig. 8

the day, were enabled to regain themselves."[120] Joseph N. Balestier melodramatically described the *débâcle* in the following words:

> But the day of retribution was at hand, the reaction came—and the professional speculator and his victims were swallowed up in one common ruin. Trusting to the large sums due him, the land operator involved himself more and more deeply, until his fate was more pitiable than that of his defrauded dupes.
>
> The year 1837 will ever be remembered as the year of protested notes..... Misery inscribed its name on many a face but lately radiant with high hopes, despair was stamped on many a countenance which was wont to be wreathed in smiles. Broken fortune, blasted hopes and, aye, blighted characters; these were the legitimate offspring of those pestilent times. The land resounded with the groans of ruined men, and the sobs of defrauded women who had entrusted their all to the greedy speculators. Political events, which had hitherto favored these wild chimeras, now conspired to hasten and aggravate their downfall.[121]

Such was the aftermath of the boom of 1836. Land values had plunged from one extreme to another, and in the depression of 1841 and 1842, the land value of Chicago was too cheap not merely in the light of its subsequent history but even for the modest prospects of a county seat. Those who had suffered so severely, however, would be inclined to put a damper on any further speculative tendencies, and when all hope for completing the canal had been abandoned, there seemed to be nothing to look forward to that would cause land values in Chicago to move upward. As Ogden wrote late in 1841: "The suspending of the canal and the bankruptcy and disgrace entailed by the wicked and wanton legislation of the past winter have put another face of deepened gloom upon the values of property here and will work a perfect dearth of money and make all real estate in the main unavailable."[122]

---

[120] March 27, 1845.   [121] Andreas, *op. cit.*, I, 135.

[122] Ogden, *op. cit.* (original in the Chicago Historical Society). Note also the effect of the suspension of the canal upon population and rents (letter to B. Mager, June 27, 1841 [*ibid.*, III, 326]): "Many people are leaving town..... Houses are vacant." Letter to Dr. U. Parsons, June 7, 1841 (*ibid.*, p. 323): "The suspension of the canal has reduced rents this year greatly." Originals of both letters are in the Chicago Historical Society. William B. Ogden, the first mayor of Chicago, and the first president of the Chicago Northwestern Railroad, was one of the most prominent of the early citizens of Chicago. Ogden, Utah was named after him. At this time he invested large sums of eastern capital in western lands.

CHAPTER II

THE LAND BOOM OF THE RAILROAD ERA, 1843-62

A. THE PERIOD FROM 1843 TO 1848

A new start on the canal.—When the prospect of completing the Illinois and Michigan Canal, apparently involved in the wreck of the state's grandiose scheme of banking and internal improvements, had been abandoned, the death knell of the plans of Chicago to become a great metropolis seemed to have been sounded. The value of its real estate sank to its lowest depths. Of all the projects contemplated by the state, however, the canal, upon which over $7,000,000 had already been spent, was the only one that had been pushed far toward completion. Moreover, it alone possessed in its own right any assets, it still having 230,476 acres of land and 3,491 town lots which had not been sold or mortgaged during the depression.[1] Fortunately for the canal and for Chicago, three different groups found it to their interest to unite to complete the waterway. These were, first, the citizens of Chicago, who fondly expected that the canal would make the city a great emporium; second, the bondholders, who had already sunk their money into the enterprise and who by putting in a little more might recover their entire investment; and, third, the state, which by opening up a profitable market for the products of the Illinois River Valley would enable the farmers to pay the taxes that would enable the state to meet its obligations. It was estimated that the canal could be completed on the shallow-cut plan at an additional cost of $1,600,000, and to procure this sum the state legislature in February, 1843, authorized the governor to borrow that amount on the security of the canal lands and tolls. As an inducement to the old bondholders in London from whom it was hoped to secure most of the money, the law provided that if the holders of the original-canal obligations subscribed to the new loan, the principal and interest of their old obligations would be repaid from the proceeds of the sales of the canal lands and from canal tolls after the princi-

---

[1] James William Putnam, *The Illinois and Michigan Canal, 1918* (Chicago: University of Chicago Press, 1918), p. 58. This is the most authoritative work on the subject of the Illinois and Michigan Canal.

pal and interest of the new loan had been paid. Since nearly everyone believed that the canal lands would appreciate in value after the completion of the canal, the law provided that none of the canal land was to be sold until after the canal was finished, but that thereafter the land was to be offered for sale at least once a year for four years after the canal was opened, at prices not less than those fixed by three disinterested persons in each district.[2] On these overtures from the state, a committee from Baring Brothers, representing the old bondholders, investigated the financial condition of the canal and reported that on January 1, 1844, it had a net debt of $4,847,402 and countervailing assets in the canal itself and its lands and lots of over $9,000,000. They accordingly recommended that the London bondholders advance the sum required to finish it.[3]

Before the complete confidence of these financial interests could be won, however, it was necessary not merely for the state to abandon all its other projects of internal improvements and to begin to reduce its debt by exchanging its stock in the state banks for the state bonds held by the banks, but also to win the fight against repudiation of its obligations by providing in 1845 for a mill tax to pay the interest on its public debt. After these steps had been taken and the credit of the state had rapidly improved in consequence, the new loan for the canal was advanced in 1845. With the joyful shout of the *Chicago Journal*, "Get out your spades and go digging,"[4] the work was resumed. As wages and the price of materials were low as compared with the high levels prevailing in 1836 and 1837, the funds provided proved to be ample. The long-deferred task was now pushed to completion in the scheduled time of two and a half years.

Growth of wagon and lake traffic.—While thus being encouraged by the prospects of better transportation facilities in the future, Chicago was forging slowly ahead as a meeting place of wagon-hauled and lake-borne commerce. Prior to 1837 the territory in the vicinity of Chicago did not raise enough food for its support. That was the first era. Charles Cleaver said:

[2] *Laws of the State of Illinois* (13th General Assembly; Springfield, Ill., 1843), pp. 54–58.

[3] Putnam, "Economic History of the Illinois-Michigan Canal," *Journal of Political Economy*, XVII (1909), 290, quotes Davis and Swift, *Report of the Illinois-Michigan Canal* (1844), p. 134.

[4] March 3, 1845.

From that time to 1842 or 1843 farmers began to raise enough produce for themselves and their neighbors' consumption as well as supplying the citizens of Chicago with all that was necessary, but these years began to show the necessity of having some foreign market to take off the surplus produce, for in the winter of 1842 to 1843 farmers' produce of all kinds was so low it was hardly worth raising. . . . . Gradually all classes of produce were held till spring for shipment round the lakes by vessel to New York; this would end the second era.[5]

As the population of northern Illinois was rapidly increasing and its farm lands were being developed, the best market for farm produce was in Chicago. There the highest prices in the West were paid for wheat that was shipped to the East on lake vessels and there the lowest prices were charged for salt, cook stoves, lumber, and other farm necessities. The relatively lower cost of lake transportation between Chicago and the East made Chicago grain prices only a little less than those in New York and the prices of eastern wares in the Chicago stores only a little more than at the point of their origin. The greatest part of the expense, however, was involved in getting the wheat or produce to Chicago, because it had to be hauled there in wagons over bad roads.

Farmers living on Rock River would take five days to market thirty bushels of wheat, finding when they got home not over ten or twelve dollars left out of the price of their load, but for some purposes they had to have a little cash and so continued to bring it.[6]

Notwithstanding the difficulties involved in this long movement by wagons, the volume of wheat thus brought to Chicago rapidly increased. The export of 78 bushels in 1838 had mounted to 40,000 bushels by 1841 and 587,000 bushels in 1842. Over 1,000,000 bushels were shipped East in 1845 and over 2,000,000 bushels in 1847.[7]

In addition to the farmers hauling in wheat that was mainly exported to the East, there were the farmers from the Wabash country who brought in provisions chiefly for local consumption.

There was also another class of farmers from the south that used in a measure to supply the city with necessaries in the shape of green and dried apples, butter, hams, bacon, feathers, etc. These men would bring their loads two or three hundred miles, camping out on the way. Cooking their rasher of bacon and corn dodgers, and boiling their pot of coffee over the campfire and saving money enough out of their load to purchase a few bags of coffee and the balance in salt—this was the

---

[5] *Reminiscences of Chicago in the Forties and Fifties*, p. 74.

[6] *Ibid.*, p. 75.

[7] *Hunt's Merchants' Magazine*, 1858, p. 422.

invariable return load of all Hoosiers, who used to come in great numbers in their curious shaped covered wagons, known in old times as prairie schooners—I once counted 160 on the corner of State and South Water Street.[8]

One of the most important commodities which the farmers hauled back in their wagons was lumber. White-pine timber from the forests of Michigan was brought in by lake vessels to make good the deficiency of the prairie states. The lumber receipts of Chicago increased from 7,500,000 board feet in 1843 to 19,000,000 board feet in 1844[9] and 32,000,000 board feet in 1847.[10] This incoming lumber traffic and the outgoing wheat shipments as they thus mounted rapidly in volume caused an increase in lake tonnage arriving at Chicago from 117,711 in 1842 to 459,910 in 1844.[11]

Even in the forties when the conditions of land transportation were most difficult, a heavy flow of people and goods passed through Chicago. Not only the movement of farmers' wagons, which increased until 70,000 teams entered Chicago in 1847, an average of 200 a day,[12] but the arrivals and departures of emigrants by stagecoach and steamers brought a large throng of transients into the city. In 1845 it was estimated that four steamboats entering and leaving Chicago every day carried 430 persons or 92,000 during the seven months of navigation, while the eight stages that arrived and departed daily transported 120 persons a day or 43,800 a year.[13]

The purchases of farmers and of emigrants at the stores on Lake Street gave rise to a large volume of retail business in Chicago prior to 1848.

Previous to the opening of the canal, the communication with the country districts was almost altogether by farmers' wagons or prairie schooners. In the fall after the harvest and threshing season, the prairie roads leading to Chicago from all directions were lined with Hoosier, cloth-covered wagons. In the city, Lake Street was the only real business street and that was literally packed with these wagons threading their way in a perfect jam. They came in with wheat, corn, oats and all other farm products and departed with a cook stove, a barrel of salt or a few

---

[8] Cleaver, *op. cit.*, p. 75.

[9] Norris, *City Directory for 1846*, p. 15.

[10] *Hunt's Merchants' Magazine*, 1858, p. 428.   [11] *Ibid.*, p. 421.

[12] *History of the Board of Trade*, ed. Charles H. Taylor (Chicago: Robert O. Law & Co., 1917).

[13] Norris, *Directory for Chicago for 1846*, p. 24.

boards of pine lumber, which could only be had at Chicago. These farmers supplied a very large part of the retail trade of Chicago. Wholesale trade was not then known as such.[14]

The demand of the farmers for commodities not merely increased the retail trade, but in conjunction with lumber imports it also stimulated the growth of such wood manufactures as wagons and agricultural implements, McCormick establishing his reaper works in Chicago in 1847. The flow of grain and live stock into Chicago also caused the development of local flour mills, breweries, packing-houses, soap and tallow plants.

The physical growth of Chicago, 1843-48.—After the population of Chicago had grown from 5,000 in 1841 to 6,000 in 1842 and 8,000 in 1844,[15] the appearance of the city in 1844 was thus described:

> The then mighty city with its "teeming multitudes" of 8,000 people was strung along the banks of the river for half a mile from the lake. It hadn't a paved street or a foot of brick sidewalk. The business part of the town was Lake Street from State to Wells Street, and the residences were scattered along Wabash and Michigan and State to Washington Streets. What is now Madison Street was out of town. South of where the Grand Pacific stands was an unbroken prairie. There was no business and only a few dwellings north of the river, on account of the uncertainties and delays in getting back and forth. There was no sewerage whatever and the water and the surface drainage was the only way to get rid of sewage. The mud is described as having been simply horrible. The low marshy land filled with water like a sponge and the streets were well-nigh impassable for eight months in the year.[16]

An analysis of the place of residence reported by the 2,000 persons whose names appeared in the city directory in 1844 shows that of the 1,200 giving definite addresses, 180 lived in hotels and 275 in boarding-houses or with their employers.[17] Only 5 reported living south of Adams Street, 1 west of Clinton Street, and 7 as far north as Chicago Avenue. There was a concentration of residential population on Randolph and Washington streets, from State to Market Street, on North Water Street from LaSalle to Rush Street, and on the West Side near the Lake Street bridge. Nearly every business house reporting was either on Lake Street or on Clark and Dearborn streets between Lake and South Water streets. There were twenty-five commission mer-

---

[14] I. W. Waughop in *Chicago Tribune*, September 28, 1884.
[15] Charles Colbert in Andreas, *op. cit.*, II, 691.
[16] *Chicago Herald*, September 25, 1882.   [17] Norris, *City Directory for 1844*.

chants on South Water Street. The lumber yards were mainly on the south side of the river, from Wells to Randolph Street.

In 1844, 600 new buildings were erected, and in 1845, 871. The population had increased from 8,000 in 1844 to 12,000 in 1845 and 14,000 in 1846. William Bross painted the following picture of Chicago in 1846:

> The residence portion of it [Chicago in 1846] was mainly between Randolph and Madison Streets, and there were some scattered houses as far south as Van Buren Street in the South Side, four or five blocks north of the river on the North Side, with scattering residences about as far on the West Side. There were, perhaps, half a dozen wooden warehouses along the river on Water Street. The few stores that pretended to be wholesale were on Water Street, and the retail trade was exclusively done on Lake Street.[18]

The growing lumber firms were locating on the west side of the south branch from Lake to Washington Street, as well as on the east side of the south branch as far south as Washington Street. Foundries, sash and door mills, and flour mills were getting started on the West Side by 1846. Wagon works were established on Randolph near Franklin and Market streets. On the North Side was a shipyard near Rush Street, iron foundries on North Water from Clark to Wells, and breweries on the lake front at Illinois Street and Chicago Avenue. The growth of the South Side and the West Side in population was greater than that of the North Side from 1843 to 1845, as Table I shows.[19]

In 1846, according to Norris, three-fourths of the ground within the city limits was more or less built upon, and there were twenty blocks that were compactly occupied with buildings. There were thirty-two large brick buildings three or four stories in height, and numerous blocks of wooden buildings.[20]

The River and Harbor Convention held in Chicago in 1847, which brought delegates from all over the United States to the city, was one of the most important events in its early annals, for it drew the attention of the East to the substantial growth of Chicago within the past decade.

By 1848 the West Side was growing fast as a manufacturing center. "The West Side near the south branch of the canal draws houses, stores, machine shops, planing mills toward it as a magnet draws iron filings," was the statement appearing in the "Gem of the Prairie" in

---

[18] *Chicago Tribune*, June 24, 1876.
[19] Norris, *City Directory for 1846*.   [20] *Ibid.*, p. 5.

1848.[21] The fashionable residential areas were on the North Side on LaSalle and Dearborn streets, Case and Pine streets, and on the South Side on Wabash and Michigan avenues, north of Madison Street. Washington had developed into a street of churches. Madison and Monroe streets in the present "Loop" were occupied by small houses surrounded by gardens. Lake Street was still the main business street. The first slums and vice areas were developing in the "sands" north of the main channel, in "Kilgubbin" at the forks of the north branch, and in the sections west of Wells Street, south of Washington Street to the river.

TABLE I
POPULATION OF CHICAGO BY WARDS, 1837–45

Section of the City	Date			
	1837	1840	1843	1845
South Side, first ward, east of Clark.....	1,021	1,197	1,986	3,238
South Side, second ward, west of Clark...	1,309	1,467	2,231	3,460
West Side, third ward, south of Randolph	195	251	509	1,009
West Side, fourth ward, north of Randolph..........................	238	179	414	830
North Side, fifth ward, west of Clark.....	320	436	600	1,052
North Side, sixth ward, east of Clark....	918	1,323	1,840	2,499
Total..........................	4,170*	4,853	7,580	12,088

* Includes 169 transients not enumerated in ward totals.

At the beginning of 1848 Chicago was still a country town with cows browsing in pastures a mile from the city hall, and occasionally roaming through the main business street. Hogs recently had run wild in the center of town, and wolves had been seen at Wabash and Adams streets. The roads had not been improved in any way, as the following account of "Long John" Wentworth shows:

> I said we had no roads in 1848. The streets were simply thrown up as country roads. In the spring, for weeks portions of them would be impassable. I have at different times seen empty wagons and drays stuck on Lake and Water Streets on every block between Wabash Avenue and the river..... The clerks having little or no business put up signs on mud holes, "no bottom here,"—"the shortest road to China"—or stuck up a figure in effigy with a sign "on his way to the lower regions."[22]

[21] *Chicago Tribune*, July 10, 1887.
[22] Charles Cleaver gives a similar account in *Early Chicago Reminiscences* (Chicago: Fergus Printing Co., 1882), p. 28.

Such was Chicago—a town without pavements, sidewalks, sewers, gas lights, street cars, or railroads on the eve of the influx of a new series of transportation agencies that were to transform it entirely.

A slow rise in land values.—In 1844 began a slow increase in Chicago land values, which was at first confined to the streets close to the main business center. A lot on Randolph Street near State sold for $10 a front foot in 1842, for $15 a foot in 1844, $50 a foot in 1846, and $80 a foot in 1848.[23] Wabash near Van Buren had risen to $18 a foot by 1848,[24] and Clinton Street near Washington Street on the West Side from $1.50 to $11 a foot from 1843 to 1847.[25] Michigan Avenue near South Water (Lot 17, Block 17, Fort Dearborn Addition) advanced in value from $13 a foot in 1840 to $50 a foot in 1848.[26] State Street near Monroe sold for only $30 a foot in 1848, although this was five or six times its value in 1843.[27] In 1848 vacant lots 25 by 150 feet in the business center of Chicago could be rented for $250 a year, and the best four-story brick houses (25 by 100 feet) for $800 a year.[28]

The rise in land values in the outlying acres was in some cases barely perceptible in this period. Land near State and Roosevelt Road had reached only $250 an acre by 1845,[29] and Sixty-third and Stony Island sold for $7.00 an acre in 1847.[30] Roosevelt and Western sold for $50 an acre at the same time (1847),[31] and Sixty-third and Cottage Grove for $4.50 an acre.[32] Irving Park and Narragansett brought only $7.00 an acre in 1849.[33] At Ashland and Lawrence land was only $3.25 an acre in 1847,[34] at Lawrence and the Lake $2.00 an acre in 1847,[35] and at Sixty-third and Halsted streets only $7.00 an acre the same year.[36] Such examples suffice to show that a very low level of values obtained for lands more than a mile from State and Madison prior to the coming of the new transportation factors from 1848 to 1854.

[23] *Shortall and Hoard's Abstracts* (in the files of the Chicago Title and Trust Co.), Vol. 82, pp. 858–67.
[24] *Ibid.*, Vol. 60, p. 848.
[26] *Ibid.*, Vol. 39, pp. 986–88.
[25] *Ibid.*, Vol. 44, pp. 664–67.
[27] *Ibid.*, Vol. 41, p. 962.
[28] M. L. Putney, *Real Estate Values and Historical Notes of Chicago* (1900), p. 121.
[29] *Shortall and Hoard's Abstracts*, Vol. 70, p. 459.
[30] *Ibid.*, Vol. 72, p. 437.
[31] *Chicago Title and Trust Co. Abstracts*, Vol. 1737, p. 704.
[32] *Ibid.*, Vol. 1154, p. 353.
[33] *Ibid.*, Vol. 1588, p. 96.
[35] *Ibid.*, Vol. 2061, p. 61.
[34] *Ibid.*, Vol. 3795, p. 495.
[36] *Ibid.*, Vol. 657, p. 666.

THE RAILROAD ERA

B. THE PERIOD FROM 1848 TO 1857; THE NEW AGENCIES OF TRANSPORTATION AND COMMUNICATION

The canal.—The first of the new transportation agencies was the long-awaited canal, which was opened for traffic in April, 1848.[37] Its almost immediate effect was to turn to Chicago the trade of the Illinois River Valley, which had been tributary to St. Louis.[38] Farmers along the route of the canal now shipped their wheat to Chicago, the canal brought Illinois coal to Chicago that enabled the iron industries to become established, while the canal boats carried return cargoes of lumber that increased from 15,000,000 feet in 1848 to 39,000,000 feet in 1850 and 81,000,000 feet in 1855, thus stimulating the lake-borne lumber trade.[39] St. Louis merchants found that the all-water route by way of the Mississippi-Illinois rivers, the Illinois-Michigan Canal, the Great Lakes from Chicago to Buffalo, the Erie Canal, and the Hudson River was cheaper and quicker than the route by way of the Ohio River, the total freight on a barrel of flour by the Chicago route to New York being $1.48 and the time in transit from twelve to twenty days as compared with thirty to forty days on the Ohio River route.[40] A canal steamboat with room for thirty-five cabin passengers and capable of a speed of six miles an hour began to operate on the canal in 1850,[41] and this service was extensively used by emigrants going westward through Chicago to reach the steamers on the Illinois and Mississippi rivers.

The telegraph.—On January 15, 1848, Speed and Cornell's telegraph line was completed from Chicago to Milwaukee. Shortly afterward O'Reilly's line was opened to St. Louis, thereby giving Chicago telegraphic communication with New York and New Orleans also. In 1850 Snow's line from Laporte to Chicago gave wire connections with Detroit, Toledo, and all of Canada. By 1851 the corner of Clark and Lake streets was the center of four intersecting telegraph lines which put wheat-buyers and wheat-sellers in quick touch with world-markets and facilitated the rise of Chicago as a center of financial control.

The plank roads.—The southwestern plank road was started on Ogden Avenue in 1848 and was completed to Lyons by March, 1849; the

---

[37] Goodspeed and Healy, *op. cit.*, I, 187.

[38] J. W. Putnam, *op. cit.*, p. 102.

[39] *Ibid.*, p. 102; *Hunt's Merchants' Magazine*, XXXIX (1858), 428.

[40] *History of the Board of Trade*, I, 148.

[41] Goodspeed and Healy, *op. cit.*, I, 209.

northwestern plank road on what is now Milwaukee Avenue was started in 1848 and was finished to Desplaines in 1849; and plank roads in the city on Madison and State streets, started in 1848, were heavily used by the wagon caravans bringing wheat to the city before the advent of the railroads. The tolls of the two former roads yielded 10–15 per cent dividends to the private companies that constructed them. Within the city, omnibus lines were quick to take advantage of the plank roads on State and Madison streets, and Peck's line, which operated from the Lake Street bridge to State Street and down State to Twelfth Street in 1852, and the line on Madison Street from State to Ashland Avenue were the forerunners of horse-car lines which later followed these routes.

The railroads.—The chief ultimate importance of the canal, the lake traffic, and the plank roads was that they gave Chicago sufficient advantages to attract the railroads, whose importance in making Chicago a great wholesale and manufacturing center and in causing a tremendous rise in its land values far transcended any other single factor.[42] The railroads finally became an interlocking network of lines covering the entire United States, but in the beginning they were conceived of as merely connecting links between waterways, and hence a city with a large existing canal and lake commerce provided a magnet that was sure to draw them to it. Chicago did not play a prominent rôle, however, in the calculations of the first railway promoters, probably because its lake and canal commerce had not been sufficiently developed. Thus the first plan for the Illinois Central in 1836 and 1837 was for a route between Galena on the Mississippi River, LaSalle, the terminus of the Illinois-Michigan Canal, and Cairo on the Ohio River; the original line of the Rock Island Railroad was to be from the Illinois-Michigan Canal to the Mississippi River at Rock Island; the Michigan Central as first projected was to run from Detroit to St. Joseph on Lake Michigan; and the Galena and Chicago Union was to connect Lake Michigan with the lead mines of Galena. Each state was planning its own railroad system with little regard for its junction with the railroad systems of other states, and hundreds of private companies were planning small lines between neighboring towns. In this welter of projects

[42] "The city of Chicago has built herself up, doubled her trade, trebled the value of her real estate and rendered it saleable by a single act of policy—that of making herself a railroad center" (*Detroit Advertiser*, June, 1853; quoted in Goodspeed and Healy, *op. cit.*, I, 243–44).

THE RAILROAD ERA 55

and of conflicting local systems, there was at first no conception of a great western railroad system with its center at Chicago, and many localities would have combined to fight such a project had it been definitely formulated. The influence of astute eastern capitalists, however, who foresaw the possibilities of Chicago in 1851, compelled the Rock Island to make Chicago its terminus; the branch line of the Illinois Central to Chicago soon became the most important part of its system, and other local lines which started from Chicago, like the Galena, in the end became national systems. What had not even been dreamed of before 1848 had become an accomplished fact six years later. Chicago, without a single mile of railroad in January, 1848, was the railroad center of the West in 1854.

The first railroad at Chicago was the Galena and Chicago Union, which, starting in 1848 with a secondhand locomotive and six old freight cars, began to operate on its ten-mile line to the Desplaines River. Originally it was compelled to stop at the city limits at Halsted and Kinzie, on account of the fears of the retail merchants, who saw in it a menace to the wagon trade. Financed by subscriptions from the "butter-and-egg money" of farmers' wives as well as by eastern capitalists, it pushed westward to Elgin by 1850 and to Freeport by August of 1853, from whence it proceeded to Galena and Dubuque, Iowa, over the recently completed line of the Illinois Central. Into this main line other streams of traffic poured at Geneva Junction: first, the trade of the Fox River Valley coming from the north over the Fox Valley Railroad; second, that of a branch of the Galena running directly west to Fulton, Iowa, on the Mississippi River; and, third, the traffic of the Chicago, Burlington and Quincy Railroad, which was itself a consolidation of several lines built from Aurora to Burlington, Iowa, and which entered Chicago from Geneva over the tracks of the Galena. A success from the very start, the wheat receipts of the Galena Railroad increased to 505,000 bushels in 1852 and 4,500,000 bushels in 1855, and in the same years it shipped out respectively 47,500,000 and 111,000,000 board feet of lumber.[43] Of great importance to the growth of the West Side because of the volume of its traffic, this railroad not only extended its main line to Kinzie and the Chicago River inside the city limits, but in

[43] "The success of the Galena and Chicago Union Railroad is the parent of all subsequent railroad movements in this state. Had that enterprise failed, Chicago would not now count half of its present population" (*Chicago Magazine*, 1857, cited in "Fergus Historical Series," No. 5, Part II, p. 16).

order to secure a still better access to the lake commerce it bought land along the north bank of the main channel of the Chicago River as far east as State Street in 1851, and built a passenger depot at Wells and Kinzie streets at the same time.

In the meantime, the Illinois Central Railroad, conceived as part of the state's great internal improvement program of 1837, had finally in 1850 secured a land grant of 2,500,000 acres from Congress. In 1851 it had become incorporated and with the aid of large loans from abroad had completed by 1852 a line from Mattoon, Illinois, to Kensington (One Hundred and Fifteenth Street). During the early part of 1852 this railroad had been constructing a line along the lake front to Roosevelt Road. From there it was enabled in 1853 by an ordinance of the city council to proceed on piles driven in the shallow waters of the lake to its terminal at Lake Street, east of Michigan Avenue. By 1855 the entire system of 700 miles in Illinois had been completed at a cost of $40,000,000, and it was then the largest railroad system in the world. Its effect on the development of the southern suburban area of Chicago was almost immediate, for in 1856 it began to operate suburban trains to Hyde Park and by 1857 it was running six trains a day in this service.

The Rock Island, with its depot at Sherman and Jackson streets, started from Chicago in 1852 and was completed to Joliet by October of the same year. By 1854 it was completed to Rock Island and the next year crossed the Mississippi River over a new bridge into Iowa. Despite all the efforts of the steamboat interests and the merchants of St. Louis and New Orleans to close the bridge as a menace to navigation, the railroad successfully diverted most of the Iowa trade along its route from St. Louis to Chicago. Its immediate local effect was also important, not merely on the land near its depot, but also on the land near Roosevelt Road where it established carshops and a grain elevator and upon the suburban land all along its route from Roosevelt Road to Englewood and Washington Heights.

The eastern railroads, the Michigan Central and the Michigan Southern, the former entering the city over the tracks of the Illinois Central and the latter over those of the Rock Island, both reached the city from the East in 1852. These new lines proceeded to pour into the city a great flood of emigrants, thereby contributing greatly to increase the permanent and transient population of Chicago in the next few years.

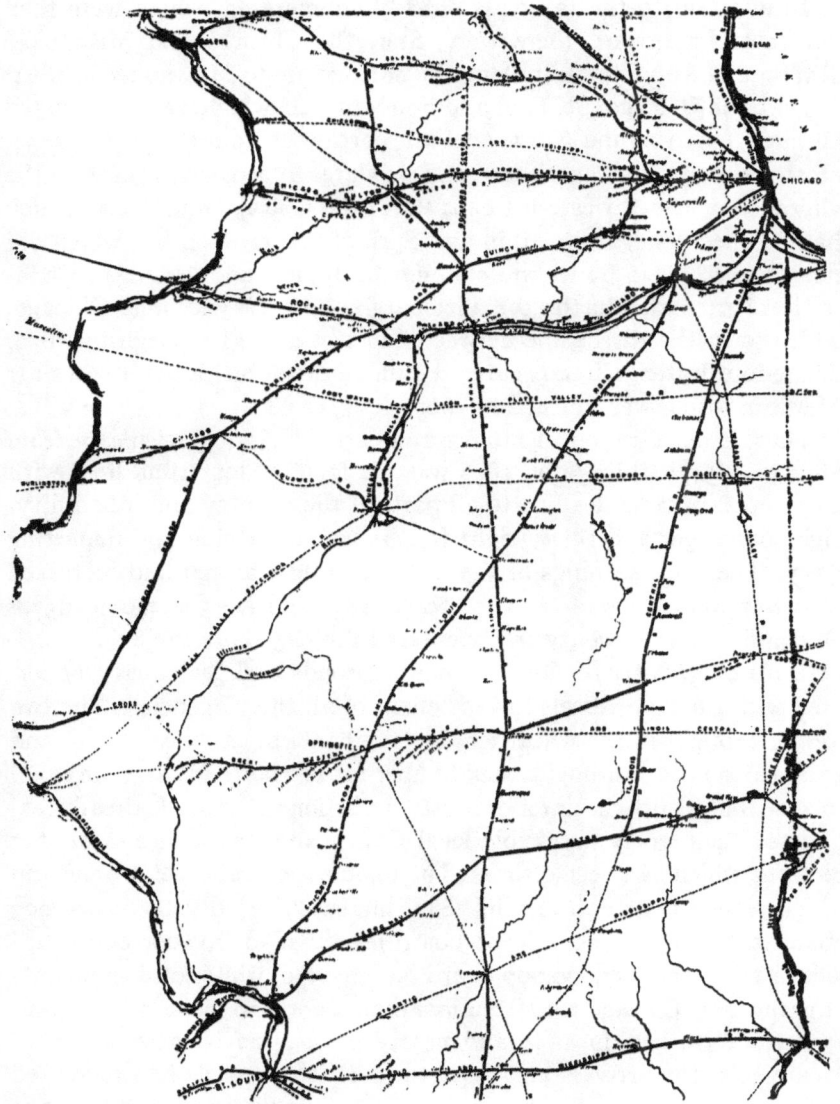

FIG. 9.—Railroads entering Chicago in 1854. Solid line indicates railroad lines actually built in 1854. Dotted line indicates projected railroad lines.

In addition to the railroads already enumerated, which were then the most important, there were, first, the Chicago and Milwaukee Railroad of 81 miles, built along the north shore to Milwaukee in 1854; second, the Chicago, St. Paul and Fond du Lac, which was constructed through Jefferson and Norwood Park northwest from the city in 1854, started suburban villages there, and was later to become the basis of the Chicago and Northwestern Road; third, the Chicago and Alton, which had reached Joliet from Alton and Springfield by 1854, but which did not enter Chicago by its route along the Illinois and Michigan Canal until 1857; and, fourth, the Pittsburgh, Fort Wayne, and Chicago, which formed a direct line between Chicago and Pittsburgh by 1859. These four latter railroads entered a union depot on Canal Street near Madison which was finished in 1860.

Thus, after a period of intense railroad activity, particularly from 1852 to 1854,[44] Chicago by 1856 was the focus of ten trunk lines with 2,933 miles of track leading to all parts of the country and it had fifty-eight passenger and thirty-eight freight trains arriving and departing daily. The total earnings of the lines entering Chicago had increased from $174,000 in 1851 to $10,652,000 in 1855 and $18,590,520 in 1857.[45] One hundred and twenty trains entered the city daily in 1857.

Grain and lumber trade.—The new railroads and the canal co-operated with the lake vessels to the benefit of all three agencies. The two former brought in the wheat for the lake boats to carry eastward, and these ships in turn brought back lumber for the railroads and the canal to distribute into the interior western sections that had already exhausted their easily accessible local timber supplies. Chicago lumber receipts, which had been estimated at 12,000,000 board feet in 1843 and which were 32,000,000 feet in 1847, increased rapidly to 60,000,000 board feet in 1848, 100,000,000 board feet in 1850, 200,000,000 board feet in 1853, and 457,000,000 board feet in 1856, while total shipments of grain from Chicago rose from less than 2,000,000 bushels in 1850 to 13,000,000 bushels in 1854 and nearly 22,000,000 bushels in 1856.[46] Meanwhile, the arrivals and departures of lake vessels had increased from 459,910 tons in 1844 to 1,098,644 tons in 1854 and 1,608,645 tons in 1856. By 1854 Chicago, by virtue of its location and transportation

[44] 1,621 miles in 1854 (Goodspeed and Healy, *op. cit.*, I, 253).
[45] *Hunt's Merchants' Magazine*, XXXVIII (1858), 756; *ibid.*, XXXIX (1858), 424.
[46] Chamberlin, *Chicago and Its Suburbs* (Chicago, 1874), pp. 282, 285.

advantages, had become the leading primary grain and lumber market of the world.

Infant industries.—The teamwork between lake commerce, canal, and railroads further developed a great wholesale trade in groceries, shoes, clothing and hardware, and generated a new manufacturing industry. The eastern railroads brought in a large supply of skilled and unskilled labor; the western railroads widened the market for the wagons and agricultural implements that were already being produced, and they themselves created a new demand for car-repair and car-building shops, boiler works, iron-rail mills, and bridge-building plants. The lake vessels brought iron from as far away as Scotland, and lumber for wagons, agricultural implements, and railroad cars. The canal shipped in Illinois coal for the budding iron industry. The close community between the lake, canal, and railroads, with the Chicago River and its branches serving as a connecting link between them all, was revealed by the tenacity with which the railroad lines clung to the Chicago River where lake and canal commerce met, and by the tendency of the first manufacturing plants to locate near the river and the railroad terminals. Manufacturing was in its infancy, but the foundation of the later enormous increase in volume was being laid. The growth in the number of workers employed in manufacturing from 2,081 in 1850[47] to 10,573 in 1856,[48] and in the value of manufactured products from $2,562,583[47] to $15,513,063,[49] is significant not for the absolute amounts, but for its indication of future growth. The pattern was being formed and the connections being established in this period for the industrial factor that was to be the overshadowing influence in the next few decades.

The new banks.—The new organization of transportation, wholesale trade, and manufacturing urgently called for a new financial system. For nearly a decade Illinois had had no regular banks, and the need for currency had been supplied by George Smith's admirable money, which was always promptly redeemed, other private issues, and the notes of distant banks in other states. In 1851 a new banking law was passed authorizing the organization of banks in Illinois which were allowed to issue their notes against bonds deposited with the state audi-

[47] *U.S. Census* (1950)—figures for all of Cook County.
[48] Local estimate of *Chicago Daily Democrat,* January 1, 1857.
[49] *Ibid.*

tor. A feature of this law, which later became of great significance, was the requirement allowing notes to be issued to the full amount of the bonds only in the case of those obligations that regularly paid 6 per cent interest per annum. This induced the banks to invest largely in the bonds of the southern states, whose 6 per cent bonds were not above par. The effect of this new law, under which nine banks were organized in Chicago by January, 1854, was greatly to increase the ease of borrowing money and, beginning in 1852, this was a pronounced factor in real estate speculation. By 1856 the circulation of all the state banks in Illinois had risen to over twelve million dollars, and while practically no specie reserve was maintained to redeem the notes, on forced liquidation the bonds securing the notes had in every instance before 1860 except one been sold for enough to pay the notes in full. A further important step in market organization was the formation of the Board of Trade in 1848, which was later to have a decisive rôle in determining the location of the financial center. At this time the financial center was on Clark Street near Lake, where the new banks, the old financial houses, and insurance companies were mainly located, and where the telegraph lines had their center.

The new wholesale trade.—The opening of the Illinois and Michigan Canal caused a revolutionary change in the character of Chicago trade with the farmers. Before that event it had been mainly retail. Thereafter it became chiefly wholesale. The manner in which this transformation occurred is thus described:

When the canal was opened all of a sudden, these farmer wagons disappeared and our merchants were greatly astonished and nearly panic-stricken at the wonderful change. The farmers could get for their farm products at the towns on the canal from 30 to 80 miles from Chicago within a cent or two as much per bushel [for their wheat] as in Chicago.

Enterprising grain and provision merchants had pushed out to take the farm products at canal towns, and the merchants sent their goods out to meet the demands of the farmer retail trade. Thus the wholesale trade of the city was inaugurated. The rapid increase in the population of Chicago and the advantages of the wholesale trade soon re-established the business and confidence of the merchants.[50]

The physical growth of Chicago, 1848–57.—After thus briefly describing the forces of transportation that converged upon Chicago and made it in time one of the world's greatest crossroads of commerce, it is neces-

[50] J. W. Waughop in *Chicago Tribune*, September 28, 1884.

THE RAILROAD ERA

sary before discussing the decisive influence of these forces upon the sensational rise of Chicago land values to describe the internal growth of Chicago during these eventful formative years when its future character was being decided.

While the population of Chicago almost doubled from 1847 to 1848, increasing from 10,859 to 20,023, the young city contained, in addition, a large transient population which was constantly passing through it and causing an expansion of its hotels, saloons, and retail stores far beyond the needs of its permanent residents. To the farmers in their prairie schooners, the sailors from the lake vessels, and the emigrants on their way to western farms was now added the throng of "forty-niners" bound for the gold fields of California. The time from New York to Chicago had been reduced from the thirty days of 1836 to seven days in 1849, as a result of the completion of a railroad line from the East to New Buffalo, Michigan, on the opposite side of the lake. Travelers took a steamer at New Buffalo for Chicago, and at Chicago many of them took packet boats on the canal for LaSalle, where they transferred to Mississippi River steamboats. The streets of Chicago were thus places of restless activity even in 1849 before the main development of the railroads. The forces of the new industrialism, then novel and strange, thrilled the local newspaper writers, and they were fascinated by the power of steam and the flow of goods and people that had been rapidly set in motion in this quiet country town.

Our streets present an animated picture. Thronged with laden wagons, filled with busy people, vocal with the rattling of wheels, the rush of steam, the clank of machinery and many voices, goods gaily flaunting from awning posts and store doors, docks piled with boxes, bales and bundles of merchandise, warehouses like so many heart ventricles receiving the grain on one side, and with a single pulsation, pouring it out on the other into waiting vessels and steamers to be borne away on the general circulation, lumber yards heaped with the products of the forest, furnaces and machine shops sending out the exponents of industry and skill, here a drove of horses, there a herd of cattle, those for the Chicago Tattersalls, these for the shambles and the packer—the multitude of strangers whose arrival every packet bugle and locomotive whistle and steamer's bell heralds, all these and more are now pictured upon every observer's eye and swell the diapason of busy life to every listening ear. How different from the listlessness and languor which pervaded the city but two months ago.[51]

Even this tempo was speeded up in 1852 when direct rail communication was opened between Chicago and New York and the time required

[51] *Chicago Daily Journal*, October 18, 1849.

for the trip was reduced from seven days to thirty-six hours. The Irish fleeing from the country stricken by famine in 1845 and 1846 and the Germans emigrating from their homeland because of agricultural depression and the failure of the liberal movement in 1848 could come directly from New York, the main port of entry, into the heart of America. From 1852 to 1853 the population of Chicago increased from 38,754 to 60,666 and half the population in the latter year was foreign born. Most of this increased population was poured into the city by the railroads. Four trains on the Michigan Central Railroad brought in two thousand passengers from the East in one day in 1854. In the five years ending February, 1857, all of the railroads entering or leaving Chicago carried three million passengers. Chicago, however, according to one observer, still presented an unprepossessing appearance even in 1853.

> At that time [October 6, 1853] Chicago was called a city, it is true, but it was a rude, cheaply built and dirty Western town. On the South Side there was beyond Twelfth Street nothing to speak of but one large frame house known as the Clarke House, and the depot of the Michigan Southern Railroad on Clark Street. West of this street there was a broad space of vacant lands on the north and west sides, though there were scattered wooden residences as far west as Bull's Head Tavern in the neighborhood of Union Park. In the center of the city there were some cheap wooden buildings, some on South Water and Lake Streets. A few brick stores stood on Clark and Dearborn Streets north of Randolph. South of Randolph on the same streets, wooden dwellings, houses with now and then an unpretentious church edifice extended southward to 12th Street. The streets of Chicago were at that time execrable, being unpaved, but in the older parts of the city covered with planks, beneath which lay an untold depth of black mud, jets of which were thrown up as wagons passed.[52]

As a result of the heavy volume of European immigrants and homeseekers from the East coming West on the railroads to Chicago, the city grew rapidly in population to 80,000 in 1855, a seven-fold increase in the decade since 1845.[53] The hotels were overcrowded, and notwithstanding the rapid rate of building it was said in 1854 that there was not a house to let in the city. The increased tempo of activity in 1854 is thus described:

> Never in the history of Chicago have the streets of our city given so clear evidence of intense activity as for the past few weeks. Carriages, drays, vehicles of all

[52] Address of Judge John Alexander Jameson, "In Memoriam," *Annals of the American Academy of Political Social Science* (1890).

[53] Chamberlin, *op. cit.*, p. 279.

descriptions fill the streets, the sidewalks are literally crowded with people in a hurry, rushing in all directions. The hotels are crowded to overflowing and those who arrive by the evening trains are fortunate if they find a place to lie down on the parlor floor until morning.[54]

This flow of traffic reached a maximum at the Clark Street bridge, where in one day in 1854 from 6:00 A.M to 7:00 P.M. 24,000 persons and 6,000 teams crossed in both directions, and where from November 13 to 15, 1855, an average of 27,750 persons and 4,909 teams crossed it daily. Next in importance was the Randolph Street bridge from the West Side with an average daily traffic count of 12,660 persons and 2,845 teams in 1855. The Lake, Wells, Madison, and Kinzie Street bridges carried respectively 9,426, 8,836, 7,946, and 6,546 persons daily and 6,587, 1,790, 2,010, and 263 teams daily at the same time. Thus there was a total of 73,164 persons and 18,404 teams daily on all bridges.[55] The incoming passengers on the Michigan Central arrived at the depot of the Illinois Central at Lake Street east of Michigan Avenue; those from the East coming on the Michigan Southern poured in at the station at Van Buren and Sherman streets, while western-bound emigrants left at these depots or at the Wells and Kinzie Street depot of the Galena or the union depot on the West Side.

New buildings and public improvements.—Under the stimulus of increased demand for housing and rising rents, the number of buildings in the city increased from 1,364 in 1842 to 5,798 in 1851 and 9,212 in 1853.[56] In 1854 new buildings and public improvements to a value of $2,438,910 were added, and in the next three years the amounts were respectively $3,735,000, $5,708,624, and $6,423,518, making a total outlay of $18,305,000 for new buildings and public improvements for the four years 1854–57 inclusive.[57] These buildings included not merely thousands of small frame cottages but also four- and five-story brick buildings on Lake and Randolph streets.[58]

[54] *Daily Democratic Press*, November, 1854.

[55] *Ibid.*, December 22, 1855. In 1871, 200,000 a day crossed 27 bridges.

[56] Goodspeed and Healy, *op. cit.*, I, 223, 250. Then in 1851 the number of buildings—1,506 on West Side, 2,742 on South Side, and 1,550 on North Side. There were 7,627 dwellings in 1853.

[57] Moses and Kirkland, *op. cit.*, I, 124.

[58] "A large proportion of the buildings are of brick. Iron has become an article almost indispensable to the builder. A larger quantity of stone has been used during the past than during former years. In finish and design, especially of stores, a greater degree of attention has been paid to taste and style" (*Democrat*, January 5, 6, 1852).

The city was also undergoing a great transformation in regard to its public improvements with the introduction of plank roads, sidewalks, gas lights, sewers, and new bridges. Lake Street was planked as early as 1844; in 1849 nearly 3 miles of planking were laid, and in 1850 6.69 miles of plank roads were constructed in the city, of which 12,667 feet were on State Street, 7,481 feet on West Madison Street, 4,921 feet on Market Street, 4,329 feet on North Clark Street, and a total of 2,930 feet on South Clark, LaSalle, Wells, East Madison, and West Randolph streets.[59] These plank roads contributed greatly to the rise of land values on State, Madison, and North Clark streets, since, as they were planked for considerable distances, they attracted the omnibus lines. By 1856 there were eighteen of these lines making 408 trips daily.[60] Gas lights were first introduced in September, 1850. By 1855 there were 2,000 consumers and by 1856 there were 456 public lamps.[61] The first sewers were constructed in 1851 when 2,987 feet were laid down, and by 1856 there were 6 miles of sewers in Chicago, those east of State emptying into Lake Michigan and those west of it into the river.[62] By 1854, 159 miles of plank sidewalks had been constructed.[63] A new water company was organized in 1851; by 1853 it had completed a crib 600 feet from the shore and by 1857 it was supplying 7,053 buildings with water.[64] Twenty-seven miles of plank road had been laid by 1854, but these soon fell into bad repair, and new pavements of macadam, cobblestones, and finally of wooden blocks were tried, the latter type being used on Wells and Washington streets in 1856 and 1857.[65] Finally, after widening and deepening the main channel of the river in 1855 and 1856, the city, to provide a better grade for drainage, raised the level of the downtown area from 4 to 6 feet during the years from 1856 to 1860.[66] A new iron bridge was constructed over the main channel at Rush Street to connect the Illinois Central and Galena depots in 1856, and new bridges were built in 1857 over the south branch at Polk and over the north branch at Erie and Indiana (or Grand) streets.[67]

[59] *Chicago Daily Journal*, January 4, 1851; Goodspeed and Healy, *op. cit.*, I, 219.
[60] Moses and Kirkland, *op. cit.*, I, 127.
[61] *Ibid.*, p. 124.   [62] Andreas, *op. cit.*, I, 191.
[63] Moses and Kirkland, *op. cit.*, I, 126.
[64] *Ibid.*, p. 125.   [65] *Ibid.*, p. 126.
[66] *Ibid.*, p. 125. The level was raised 10–15 feet altogether, but at this time the level was raised from 4 to 6 feet.
[67] Andreas, *op. cit.*, II, 60; *ibid.*, I, 202.

THE RAILROAD ERA

Chicago's expansion.—During this period from 1848 to 1857, Chicago was building up solidly with four- and five-story brick buildings at its center on Lake Street, and building thousands of frame cottages on the near South, North, and West sides. Lake Street, the main retail street, had by 1856 not a vacant lot from the river on the west to the depot east of Michigan Avenue. South Water Street was rejuvenated from a street of tumble-down shanties into the leading wholesale street. The expansion of business down State, Clark, and Dearborn streets had reached and passed Washington Street, whose churches were beginning to move over to Wabash Avenue. Fashionable homes were being erected on Michigan and Wabash avenues south of Van Buren and Congress streets by 1854. Hotels were springing up around the railroad depots near Michigan and Lake streets, near Van Buren and Sherman and on North Clark streets. Wagon factories were located along Randolph Street just east and west of the south branch, and on Franklin and Market streets; iron foundries and planing mills found sites on Canal and Clinton streets near Randolph and Washington streets; and along the north bank of the river along Kinzie Street were several large industries, including the McCormick reaper works near the mouth of the river. Large grain elevators were along the river near the railway terminals as far south as Roosevelt Road; there were a great many lumber yards on the west bank of the south branch stretching as far south as Twenty-second Street. The largest stock yard in 1856 was at Bull's Head at Madison and Ashland Avenue, but there were other important yards at Eighteenth Street and the south branch, and at Cottage Grove and Twenty-ninth streets. The car-repair shops at the Galena Railroad at Kinzie and Milwaukee, of the Illinois Central south of Roosevelt Road near Michigan Avenue, of the Rock Island near Roosevelt Road and State Street, and the shops of the American Car Company at Twenty-sixth Street and the lake furnished employment for many men and gave rise to workingmen's homes and boarding-houses in their vicinity. To the slum areas along the river, the Kilgubbin, with a notorious population of two thousand in 1858, to the "Sands" north of the river near Lake Michigan, which was raided and burned down by Mayor Wentworth in 1857, and the sailors' resorts on Wells and the streets west of Wells south of Washington were now added such new patches as the forty or fifty acres of shanties on the West Side near Halsted and Twenty-second Street on the south branch;

twenty acres of shacks near Halsted, Desplaines, and Harrison; the Milwaukee and Union Avenue section; the slums on Clark and State near Roosevelt Road and on North Rucker and Kinzie,[68] each of which settlements possessed a peculiar jargon of its own. The floating population brought in by the railroads contributed to the growth of these areas, which were often located near railroad shops and yards.

Of all the sections of the city, the West Side grew fastest in this period from 1848 to 1857.[69] Although in 1851 out of 5,798 buildings in Chicago only 42 were west of Carpenter's Addition (i.e., over one and a half miles west of State and Madison streets) and only 15 were west of Duncan's Addition (i.e., west of Roosevelt Road and Halsted),[70] by December, 1853, the population of the west division was 14,679 and by August, 1856, it had doubled in numbers with a total of 28,250. In the meantime, the population of the North Side increased from 17,859 to 25,524 and that of the South Side from 26,592 to 30,339.[71] The plank roads, the railroads with their terminals and carshops, the lumber yards, and thirty or forty small manufacturing plants on or near the south branch of the river contributed to this growth.

By 1857 Chicago had grown solidly on the west as far as half a mile west of Halsted, as far south as Roosevelt Road, and as far north as Chicago Avenue. There were also patches of growth beyond in all directions. On the West Side a prong of growth extended along Madison to Ashland Avenue. Carville at Twenty-sixth Street and Cottage Grove Avenue, Cleaverville at Thirty-ninth Street and the lake, and Holstein at Western and Fullerton avenues were the satellite industrial towns beyond the main settled area of this period. Other detached settlements had grown up at Clark and Division streets, Division and Clybourn streets, and at Irving Park and Clark streets. Beyond all of these were the embryonic suburban towns just starting along the railroads at Hyde Park, Fifty-third, and the Illinois Central; Englewood, Sixty-third and the Rock Island; Grand Crossing; and a few incipient traces to the north and west. The suburban movement had barely started in this period.[72] Of the 112,000 people living within four miles

[68] Goodspeed and Healy, *op. cit.*, I, 190–91.
[69] *Ibid.*, p. 221.   [70] *Ibid.*, p. 223.
[71] Moses and Kirkland, *op. cit.*, II, 613.

[72] The first settler came to Kenwood in 1856. "In the fall of 1856 there were not more than half a dozen houses in Hyde Park" (Andreas, *op. cit.*, p. 530). There were only three or four shanties at Kensington in 1854 and only a few settlers in Englewood before 1867.

THE RAILROAD ERA   67

of State and Madison in 1860, 79,000, or over 70 per cent, lived within the first two miles.[73]

The rise in land values, 1848–57.—The completion of the canal in 1848 enabled the canal trustees to offer for sale large tracts of canal lands within two or three miles of the main business district of Chicago in ten- and twenty-acre blocks. Then the new boom began to get under way. Increasing business and rising rents in the downtown area slowly raised values there, Lake Street west of LaSalle selling for $225 a foot in 1848, and Madison near State at $120 a foot in 1849. The corner of Clark and Lake sold for $400 a foot in October, 1852.[74] The rise in values from 1852 to 1854 was spectacular, and is but faintly indicated by the increase in the assessed value of real estate from $5,685,965 in 1850 to $8,189,069 in 1852, $13,130,177 in 1853, and $21,637,500 in 1855, large as that was.[75] The ease of borrowing money from the new state banks and sales on easy instalments encouraged real estate speculation in 1852, and the great demand for land for actual use for railroad yards and terminals, for lumber yards, elevator and manufacturing sites, and for hotels, stores, and homes for the expanding population gave a sudden increase to the value of close-in vacant land, while rising rents and taller buildings created a higher value for that already in use. While Lake Street attained an average value of $1,000 a front foot by 1856,[76] the best wholesale streets, such as South Water Street, reached $500 a foot, the best residence sites on Michigan and Wabash near Van Buren $300,[77] and with corners as high as $400 a foot;[78] lots along the river as far south as Eighteenth and as far north as North reached $100 a foot, and other land as far south as Roosevelt Road and as far north as Chicago and as far west as Halsted passed the $100-a-foot level.

By 1856 State and Clark streets near Monroe had sold for $250 a foot,[79] Jackson and Sherman $100 a foot, Clark Street north of Chicago $125 a foot, LaSalle near Oak $200 a foot, Lake near Carpenter $100 a

[73] *Report of Chicago Traction and Subway Commission, 1916*, p. 73.

[74] Goodspeed and Healy, *op. cit.*, I, 239.

[75] Chamberlin, *op. cit.*, p. 201.

[76] *Chicago Democratic Press*, February 5, 1857.

[77] *Ibid.*, November 12, 1855.

[78] Sale of corner of Michigan and Congress for $400 a front foot (*ibid.*, April 17, 1856).

[79] The sale of the southeast corner of State and Van Buren, 160 feet on State by 110 feet on Van Buren, for $32,000 was reported in the *Daily Democratic Press* on December 22, 1855.

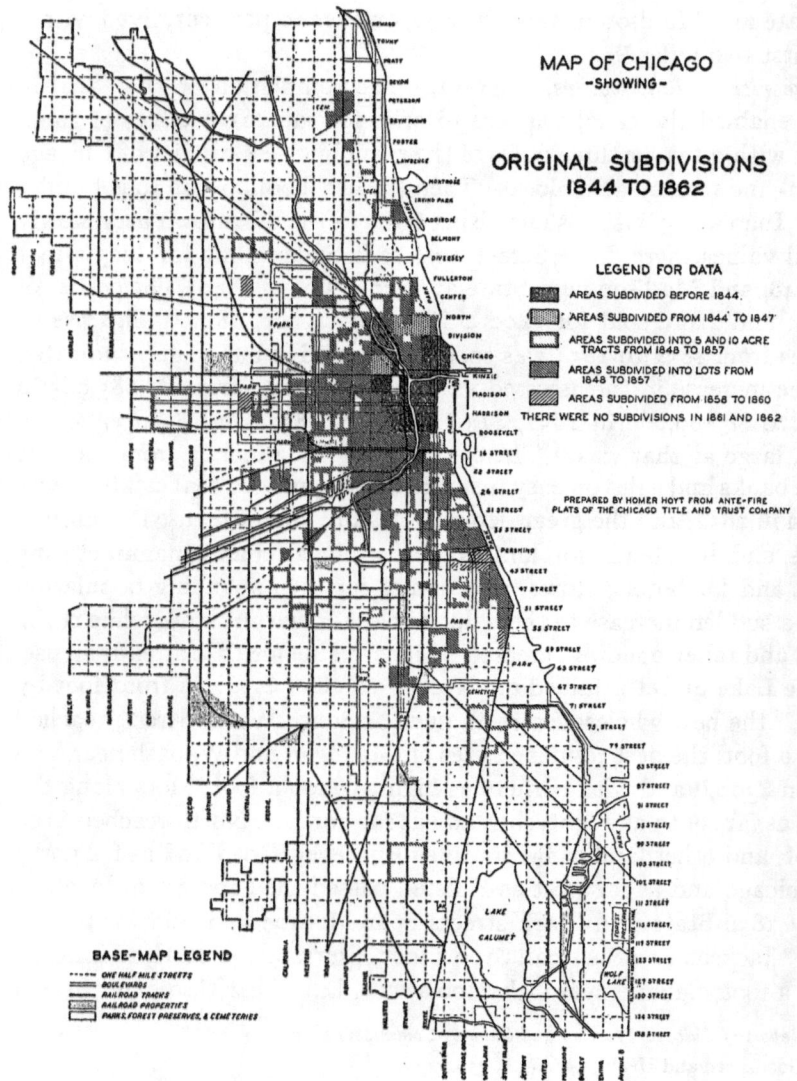

Fig. 10

THE RAILROAD ERA 69

foot, and Lake facing Union Park $100 a foot. Land on Michigan Avenue between Monroe and Adams sold for $325 a foot in 1855.[80] The corner of Lake and Clark reached $1,000 a foot before 1856.[81] Residential property north of Madison and west of Halsted sold for $60 and $70 a foot, but the cheaper property for workingmen's homes was sold for $15 to $20 a foot near Twenty-second and State, Roosevelt and Halsted and on the North Side west of Wells and south of Chicago Avenue, while more distant lots at Holstein at Fullerton and Western, at Bridgeport, Archer, and Ashland, sold for $100 each, or $4.00 a foot.

The rapidity of the increase in the value of land within three or four miles from State and Madison from 1848 to 1856 was astounding.[82] Land near State and Roosevelt Road that was offered for $200 an acre in 1845 sold for from $50 to $150 a foot,[83] or an average of $20,000 an acre in 1856. South of Twenty-second Street, east of State, there were such increases from 1851 to 1856 as from $600 to $10,000 for Block 33; Twenty-fourth and State,[84] $620 to $26,000 for Block 90;[85] and at Thirty-ninth and State (20 acres), from $25 to $1,000 an acre from 1850 to 1857.[86] West of Madison and Ashland, Block 46 in section 7 increased in value from $1,250 in 1848 to $30,000 in 1854, and near State and North Avenue the increase was from $39 to $1,400 an acre from 1848 to 1856.[87] Twelve acres at North, Dearborn, and Clark streets sold for $50 an acre in 1845, and some lots in this tract sold at the rate of $50,000 an acre in 1857.[88]

The land value of the territory within the present city limits of Chicago had increased from an estimated total of $1,400,000 in 1842 to

[80] *Ibid.*, December 22, 1855.

[81] *Chicago Tribune*, February 13, 1891. For land values in the central business district in 1856 see Figs. 71 and 73.

[82] An indication of the extent of the rise by 1853 in the opinion of current observers is this statement in the *Democratic Press* of July 11, 1853: "Five years ago $3,000 would have purchased more land suitable for such purposes [parks] than $500,000 will now."

[83] Sale of 160 by 180 feet on State Street south of Roosevelt Road for $20,000, or $125 a front foot, in 1856 (*Chicago Daily Journal*, December, 8, 1856). Sales on State, Wabash, and Michigan south of Roosevelt Road at from $100 to $124 a front foot at auction (*ibid.*, March 26, 1856).

[84] *Shortall and Hoard's Abstracts*, Vol. 41, p. 356.

[85] *Ibid.*, Vol. 79, p. 141.

[86] *Ibid.*, Vol. 72, p. 904.

[87] *Chicago Title and Trust Abstracts*, Vol. 1605, pp. 627, 630.

[88] Andreas, *op. cit.*, II, 569, in article on Ogden, Sheldon & Co.

$126,000,000 in the latter part of 1856, an increase of over eighty fold in fourteen years, most of the increase occurring in the last five years. The new peak was twelve times as high as the peak of 1836, which for many years afterward had been regarded as fantastic. As the *Chicago Daily Press and Tribune* stated in January of 1859: "The appreciation in Chicago real estate in the last five years has been enormous. Holders of any considerable parcels of property in a comparatively short period found themselves rich."[89]

While the land within the first mile of State and Madison increased in value from $810,000 in 1842 to $50,750,000 in 1856, a gain of over sixty fold, the greatest rate of increase came in the belts from one to four miles from State and Madison. The zone from one to two miles from the center that had been valued at $2,000,000 in 1836 and $200,000 in 1842 had risen to a computed total of $37,000,000, a gain of 185 times over 1842 and of 18 times over 1836. The belt from two to three miles from State and Madison had gained from a computed total of $816,400 in 1836 and $80,000 in 1842 to $18,500,000 in 1856, a gain of 230 times over 1842 and of 22 times over 1836. The zone from three to four miles from State and Madison, valued at $416,000 in 1836 and $40,000 in 1842, had risen to an estimated value of $7,000,000 in 1856, an increase of 175 times over 1842 and 17 times over 1836. The outer belt of 112,000 acres with an estimated value of $12.50 an acre, or $1,400,000, in 1836 and $2.50 an acre, or $280,000, in 1842, had increased in value to $12,000,000 in 1856, a gain of 43 times over 1842 and 9 times over 1836. The land within the first mile of State and Madison, which comprised 56 per cent of the value of all the land in the present city limits in 1836 and in 1842, comprised no more than 40 per cent of that total in 1856.

The railroads had opened up the possibilities of land from one to four miles from the downtown section, and this area was largely subdivided into lots in this period.[90] Twenty-foot stores on Lake Street costing $10,000 to build rented for $4,500 a year, so that a value of $1,000 a foot for the ground was justified even at the prevailing rates of 10 per cent interest per annum. Land even a mile away was in demand for purposes involving the actual use of the ground. The fashionable demand from the newly risen crop of merchant "princes" placed a value of $300 to $400 a foot on the best sites on Michigan and Prairie avenues for $12,000, $15,000, and $25,000 homes. The values of other lands be-

[89] January 6, 1859.   [90] See Fig. 9 on original subdivisions, 1844-62.

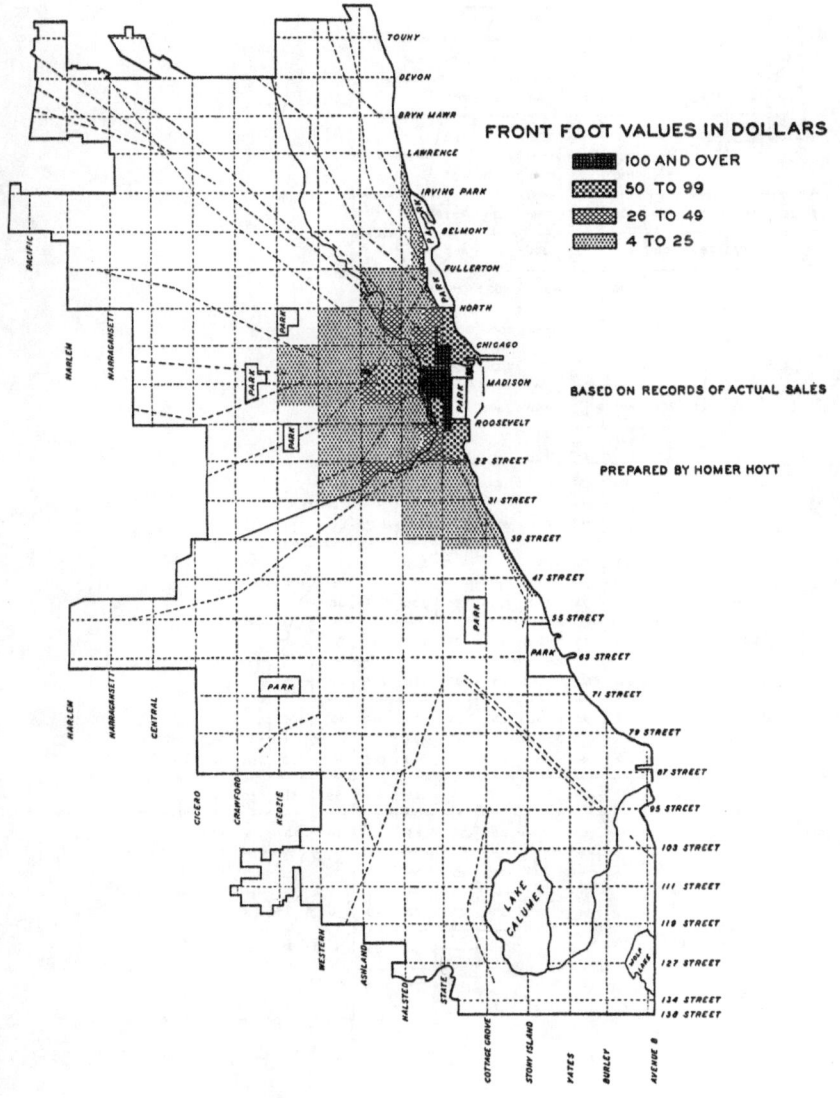

Fig. 11

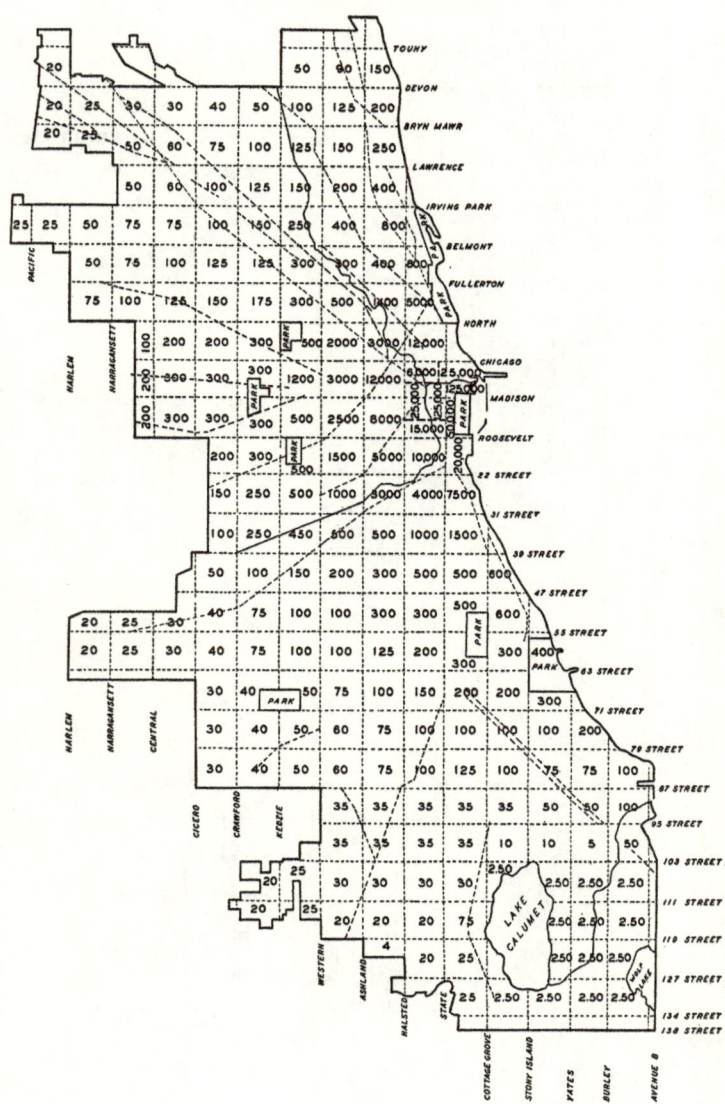

FIG. 12

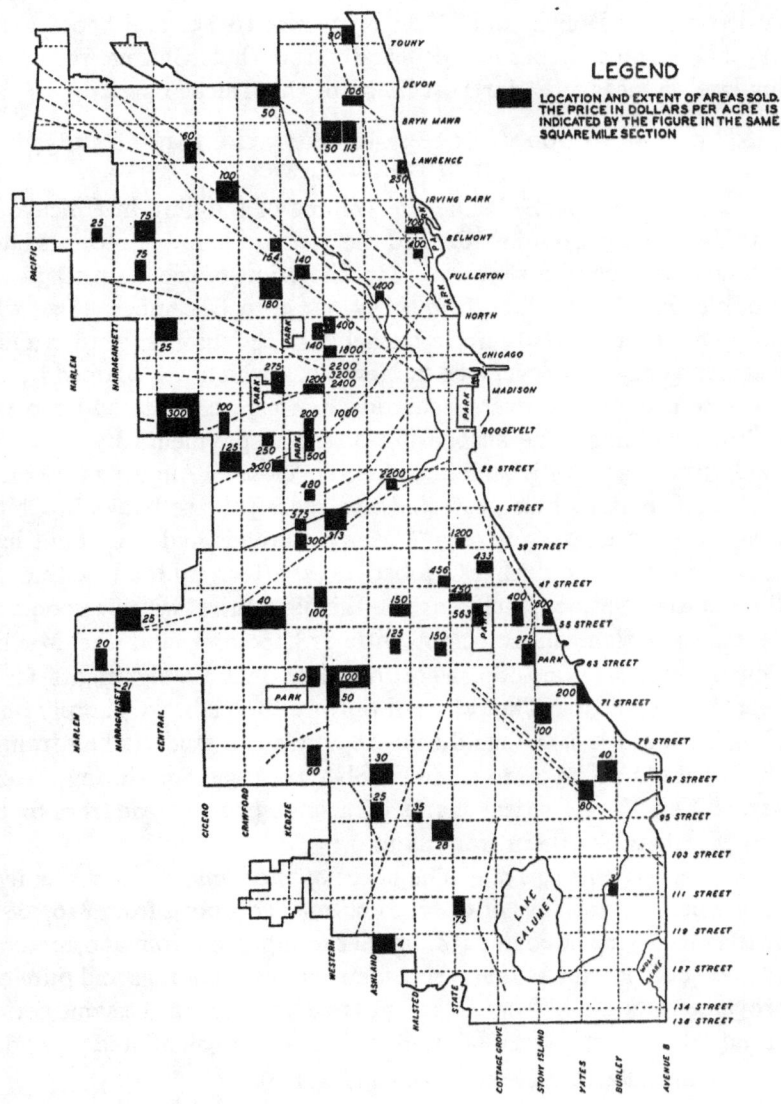

FIG. 13

yond the zone of actual use were based on the expectation of the continued growth of the city. The projection of the trend of the fashionable residential area southward had caused the values of lots at Twenty-second and Prairie and Michigan to rise to $50 and $60 a foot by 1855, and similar hopes had penetrated the whole Chicago region, raising land values to the farthest limits of the Chicago area.[91]

C. THE PERIOD FROM 1857 TO 1862. THE PANIC OF 1857 AND THE CIVIL WAR

The panic of 1857.—While the volume of building in Chicago, the earnings of Chicago railroads, and the grain and lumber receipts had all reached new peaks in 1856 and 1857, the prices of the main staple commodities had been falling from May, 1855, to December, 1856, wheat dropping from $2.00 to $1.00 a bushel.[92] In the summer of 1857 a financial stringency had developed in New York which was blamed by eastern interests on the overspeculation in western lands and too rapid railroad-building. The suspension of specie payments by New York banks forced a private bank in Chicago to close on August 11, 1857, and with their eastern bills protested two more private banks in Chicago closed on September 30, 1857.[93] Many railroads had been built in advance of traffic and during October, 1857, fifteen railroads with obligations of $181,700,000, including the Illinois Central with $24,000,000 in debts, the Michigan Southern with $18,000,000, and the Michigan Central with $14,000,000, were forced to make assignments for the benefit of creditors. The prices of railway shares broke sharply on the New York stock exchange during 1857, Galena stock falling from 119 on December 15, 1856, to 54 on October 12, 1857, and during the same period New York Central shares fell from 93 to 53, Erie from 61 to 8, and Michigan Southern from 88 to 9.[94]

The depression in 1858.—The effect of the panic of 1857 was felt in 1858 when the earnings of Chicago railroads dropped from $16,768,000 in 1857 to $13,062,000 in 1858, lumber receipts fell from 460,000,000 to 279,000,000 board feet, and the volume of new buildings and public improvements declined from $6,423,518 to $3,246,400 in the same period.[95] Hundreds of unemployed laborers in January, 1858, offered to work for

[91] See land-value maps for 1856 (Figs. 10, 11, and 12).
[92] *Democratic Press*, January 1, 1857.   [93] *Chicago Press*, October 1, 1857.
[94] *Democratic Press*, December 15, 1856; *Chicago Press*, October 19, 1857.
[95] For 1858 building volume, *Chicago Daily Press and Tribune*, January 1, 1859.

THE RAILROAD ERA

fifty cents a day and soup kitchens were opened to relieve the distress.[96] In spite of the depression, the work of raising the grade of downtown area was being pushed vigorously forward and the growth of the West Side continued. Eleven hundred new buildings out of a total of 1,872 for the entire city were erected in that section in 1858.[97] Most of the West Side structures were only cheap frame houses. Nevertheless, these figures indicate that new construction had not altogether stopped. The cost of building had fallen at least one-third since 1857 and this stimulated some new projects.[98]

Most of the holders of real estate held firmly during 1858 to the peak prices of 1856 according to the *Chicago Daily Press and Tribune*, which stated in its annual review on January 1, 1859: "Those who are able to hold them [their real estate investments] will not sell below the figures ruling two years ago, and indeed in some parts of the city real estate is held at from 10 to 20 per cent advance upon those figures." It was admitted, however, that the "lame ducks" were being forced to let go of their property at great sacrifices, while the number of newspaper notices of foreclosures and sheriff's sales was greatly increasing.[99]

The year 1859.—There was some improvement in general business conditions in Chicago in 1859, with a slight gain in lumber receipts, a considerable gain in the hog-packing business, and no further appreciable declines in grain shipments or in railway earnings, but the volume of building continued to decline from $3,246,400 in 1858 to $2,044,000 in 1859[100] and land values had by this time fallen sharply. John S. Wright, in a letter of March, 1860, says that "all property but central has depreciated at least one-half since 1857."[101]

The year 1860.—Although the total liabilities involved in failures in Chicago declined from $2,651,000 in 1859 to $1,288,589 in 1860,[102] and the Illinois banks of issue, having successfully weathered the storm of 1857, seemed to be in a highly prosperous condition, the value of new buildings again fell to $1,188,300 in 1860 and rents and land values[103]

[96] Goodspeed and Healy, *op. cit.*, I, 280, 285.
[97] *Chicago Daily Press and Tribune*, January 1, 1859.
[98] *Ibid.*   [99] *Ibid.*
[100] *Chicago Press Tribune*, January 4, 1860.
[101] John S. Wright, *Chicago, Past, Present and Future* (Chicago, 1868), p. 12.
[102] *Chicago Tribune*, January 1, 1861.
[103] "Great numbers of workers left the city for want of employment and those who remained were obliged to go into narrowed quarters to reduce expenses. This caused a great

declined still further. John S. Wright, who was a close observer and inclined to be optimistic rather than the reverse, stated in his circular letter of 1861, "Prices of central lots are reduced nearly one-half and of out-property about three-fourths,"[104] and sample sales bear out this assertion. According to William J. Kerfoot, most of the working people who had bought lots south of Twelfth Street prior to 1857 had forfeited their equities by 1860. According to Colbert:

> The depreciation in the prices of corner lots was great in the winter of 1857, but it was much greater in 1858 and 1859, as payments matured which could not be met. A large proportion of the real estate in the city had been bought on *canal time;* they had depended upon a continual advance in quoted values to meet those payments and found they could not even sell at a ruinous sacrifice.[105]

The collapse of the state banks of issue, 1861–63.—The outbreak of the Civil War revealed the weak spot in the Illinois bank-note circulation of $12,320,964 secured by deposits of $14,000,000 in bonds, of which $9,527,500 were bonds of southern states.[106] By May 15, 1861, Missouri bonds had declined to 35 cents on the dollar, Tennessee bonds to 45 cents, and Virginia bonds to 43 cents,[107] and as the security back of the notes was thus weakening, the state auditor called on the banks for additional bonds, which 17 of the banks affected were unable to furnish. The notes of the state banks soon fell into a chaotic condition, fluctuating daily and ranging in value from 20 cents on the dollar to par. By 1862 the notes of only 3 banks in Illinois were at par, and by 1864, after 98 banks had suspended, only 23 were attempting to maintain an existence.[108] A situation in which there was circulating in the United States 7,000 genuine notes of 1,600 different state banks of issue which were at varying rates of discount, mingled with which were 5,500 varieties of altered and counterfeit notes, was a serious handicap to every type of

---

many residences and stores to be vacated, and brought about a reduction in rents in those still occupied, which impoverished even those who were able to hold on to their property. Many hundreds of lots and houses were abandoned by those who had made only partial payments, and the holders of mortgages needed no snap-judgment to enable them to take possession" (quoted in Chamberlin, *op. cit.*, pp. 201–2).

[104] Wright, *op. cit.*, p. 14.

[105] Colbert and Chamberlin, *Chicago and the Great Conflagration*, pp. 95–96.

[106] Andreas, *op. cit.*, II, 619.

[107] *Financing an Empire: A History of Banking in Illinois* (Chicago: S. J. Clarke Publishing Co., 1926), I, 159.

[108] *Ibid.*

THE RAILROAD ERA 77

business, but fortunately this confusion was all swept away by the new national banking act of 1863 and the later tax on state bank notes.

Meanwhile, notwithstanding the gloom that attended the beginning of the war with the southern states, in which building operations practically came to a standstill, with only $797,800 worth of new buildings in 1861 and $525,000 worth in 1862,[109] the European need for American wheat and the war demands for grain and meat sent Chicago wheat shipments up from 11,000,000 bushels in 1858 to 24,000,000 bushels in 1861, and corn shipments from 4,000,000 to 24,000,000 bushels at the same time, increased the number of hogs packed from 100,000 in 1857–58 to 970,000 in 1862–63, and gave the railroads a profitable business in transporting soldiers and in hauling grain and live stock.[110] The population of the West Side again doubled between 1856 and 1862, increasing from 28,250 to 57,193, while the number of people in the entire city rose from 84,113 to 138,186 in the same time.[111]

The horse railways.—Meanwhile, beginning in 1859, three systems of horse street-car lines were inaugurated, one in each division of the city. The South Side system starting at State and Randolph had a single-track line on State Street as far south as Roosevelt Road by April 25, 1859, and before the end of 1859 had been extended to Twenty-second and State streets, thence east on Twenty-second to Cottage Grove and down Cottage Grove to the Fair Grounds at Thirty-fifth Street.[112] A branch from the State Street line was built down Archer Avenue to Bridgeport near Ashland Avenue in 1864 and 1865, the State Street line was extended from Twenty-second to Thirty-first Street in 1866, and a line was constructed down Indiana Avenue from Twenty-second to Thirty-first in 1864. The State Street line was extremely crowded from the very beginning, because the streets had fallen into such bad repair that it was difficult to drive horses over them.

The West Side system had two main lines running due westward, one on Madison Street and the other on Randolph and Lake streets. Crossing these two lines at right angles was the Halsted Street line, which turned northwest along Milwaukee Avenue and southwest along Blue

[109] *Chicago Tribune*, January 1, 1863.
[110] Moses and Kirkland, *op. cit.*, I, 393.
[111] *Ibid.*, II, 613.
[112] *Ibid.*, pp. 529–30; also letter and map from Mr. Sullivan, assistant to president of Chicago Surface Lines. See maps showing extensions of surface lines (Fig. 23, *supra*).

Island Avenue. All of these lines except the one on Lake Street converged at Madison and Halsted streets and sent their combined traffic load over Madison Street to the central business district. The North Side system began on the north side of the main river. It had its main stem on Clark and Broadway, which was completed by 1863, north to Irving Park Boulevard and thence west to Ashland. In 1859 a short branch was constructed on Chicago Avenue from Clark Street west to the north branch of the river, and in 1865 another branch was built down Division Street to Clybourn and thence to Larrabee Street.[113] An attempt to unite the North Side and South Side systems by laying tracks over the Clark Street bridge was defeated by an injunction in 1860. The horse street-car lines thus followed in the main the principal routes of the omnibus lines; and, while the older system continued to compete with the car lines for a time, it was handicapped by the bad condition of the pavements and the new car lines soon gained most of the traffic.

Land values in 1862.—Notwithstanding the rise of Chicago to the leading position in pork-packing by 1863, the rapid growth of the city, particularly the west division of it, in population, and a big increase in the grain trade, land values in Chicago remained extremely depressed during 1862. Washington Street, east of Clark Street, valued at $500 a foot in 1856, had dropped to $250 a foot by 1861; Madison near Clark and State near Monroe had fallen from $250 and $300 a foot to $150 a foot in the same period. In 1857, $80,000 was offered for the vacant lot, 80 by 180 feet, on the northwest corner of Randolph and Wells. In 1861, when the same land was improved with a $140,000 building, the entire property was sold for the cost of the building alone. A 65-foot vacant lot on Lake Street adjoining the corner of LaSalle could have been sold for $65,000 in 1857. In 1861 it sold for the same price after it had been improved with an $80,000 building.[114] Vacant lands close to the settled areas on the North Side and South Side showed declines of 50 per cent in sales values, while thirty sales of outlying acres showed an average fall of 67 per cent from 1856–57 to 1860–63.[115] The decline on the near West Side, however, was slight, as the continued growth of this section during the depression sustained its values. While the data

[113] See map of transportation lines, 1880 (Fig. 23, p. 126).
[114] *Chicago Tribune*, February 13, 1891.
[115] For sales during 1860 to 1863 see Fig. 14.

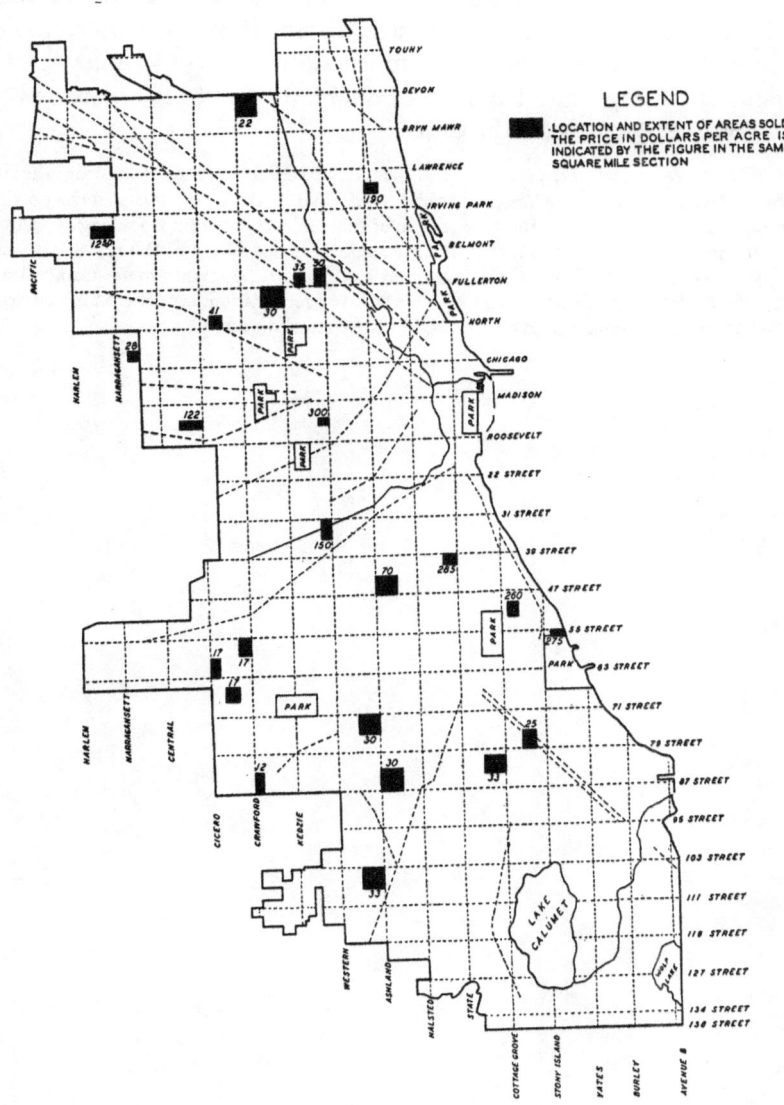

Fig. 14

for the period from 1859 to 1863 are more meager than for any other period, it can be estimated from the basis of the sales available and from the statement of John S. Wright, who had an intimate knowledge of the facts and who, as an enthusiastic real estate promoter, would be inclined to minimize the extent of the decline in land values, that the value of Chicago land had fallen from its total of $126,000,000 in 1856 to not over $60,000,000 in 1861.[116]

[116] Andreas, *op. cit.*, II, 571: "In 1858 the purchases that were made in prior years under speculative influences were largely on time. . . . . The crash of 1857 lessened the possibility of making such payments. In consequence of this difficulty, the unpromising aspect of the future and the depression in prices brought, since their purchase of the realty, the owners very generally relinquished their purchases and lost all payments made on account. In 1859 real estate had a hard struggle to maintain any recognition, except that it was a quicksand wherein all money deposited would only be swallowed up."

CHAPTER III

THE LAND BOOM THAT FOLLOWED A PANIC, A CIVIL WAR, AND A GREAT FIRE, 1863-77

A. THE LATER CIVIL WAR PERIOD, 1863-65

The physical growth of Chicago and the rise of its land values, as indicated in the last chapter, were temporarily checked, first, by the panic of 1857, and, second, by the outbreak of the Civil War. The loss of southern credits, the collapse of the state banks of issue, whose notes were secured largely by the bonds of the seceding states, and the fears that the permanent disruption of the Union would destroy old trade relationships had at first intensified the depression that followed the commercial crisis of 1857. The war that had seemed so disastrous to local business interests in 1861 had, however, assumed an entirely different aspect by the fall of 1862. The western agricultural states that had supplied the cotton-raising states with some of the latter's food found that their southern market connections were severed by war, at the very time when the war requirements of the North and the needs of Europe, now much greater because of poor crops abroad in 1860, 1861, and 1862, were rapidly increasing the eastern market for grain and meat products. As the railroad center of the West and the terminus of the eastern lines, Chicago was the collecting and forwarding point of this suddenly increased flow of foodstuffs from the West to the Atlantic seaboard. From 1860 to 1862 the total grain receipts of Chicago increased from thirty-one million to over fifty-six million bushels.[1] The city became the leading pork-packing center of the world.

Chicago profited by the Civil War in many other ways. The draft, depleting the labor supply on the farms, accelerated the demand for Chicago-built farm machinery. The movements of soldiers and munitions of war gave a heavy volume of profitable business to the Chicago railroads. The imperative war demands for food products, wagons, uniforms, and camp equipment forced a rapid development of local

[1] Chamberlin, *op. cit.*, p. 285.

firms engaged in manufacturing and distributing these essential supplies. Far removed from the seat of actual conflict, Chicago received the influx of capital whose security was endangered in the border states. It was the Mecca of draft dodgers and war profiteers as well. Furthermore, the financial requirements of war had led to the establishment of a national banking system in 1863 and to an inflation of the currency with a resulting rise in prices that presented opportunities for making great profits to the holders of war contracts. Seventeen national banks in Chicago by 1865 attested to the rapid rise of its new financial order. The scale of business operations and the magnitude of profits were lifted by war to an altitude hitherto unknown. During the period of the Civil War, Chicago, as Colbert said, "became the paradise of workers and speculators."[2]

The war-created business and industries of Chicago attracted laborers from Canada and from Europe. Its population increased from 109,263 in 1860 to 187,446 in 1865. The annual value of new construction advanced from the low ebb of $525,000 in 1862 to $2,500,000 in 1863, and $4,700,000 in 1864.[3] By the end of 1864 Chicago was solidly built up for three miles in every direction from its center, with a settled area of eighteen square miles.[4] The purchase of land along the horse-car lines and adjacent to the occupied portions for actual building purposes had raised the value of such close-in vacant land from 10 to 15 per cent during 1864. At the same time rising rents of improved business property in the downtown area had caused a rise of 20 per cent in land values in the business center.[5] Compared with the great advances that had taken place in commodity prices, however, these gains in land values, confined as they were to a few localities, were small.

B. THE POST-WAR BOOM, 1865–71

Growth of Chicago's trade and manufactures, 1865–71.—The transition from war to peace caused marked industrial readjustments. The prices of the leading staple commodities had declined 50 per cent from September, 1864, to May, 1865.[6] The demand for war materials abruptly ceased. Thousands of soldiers had to find places in factories or

---

[2] Colbert and Chamberlin, *op. cit.* (1872), p. 116.
[3] *Chicago Tribune*, January 1, 1865.
[4] Colbert and Chamberlin, *op. cit.*, p. 119.
[5] *Ibid.*, p. 118.   [6] See Fig. 95.

on the farms. The South, prostrated by defeat, with its old slave-owning aristocracy ruined, no longer afforded a profitable market for the products of the North.

In spite of these adverse factors, the North quickly entered into an era of rapid industrial expansion. The introduction of the Bessemer process for making steel and the use of coke for smelting iron ore—both coming into use at the close of the Civil War—caused an enormous growth of bituminous coal mining and of the iron and steel industries. The railroad mileage of the United States doubled from 1865 to 1873, 33,000 miles being constructed in the six years preceding the panic of 1873.

Chicago was in a position, situated as it was between the thick deposits of Illinois coal and the rich iron mines of the Mesabi range, with the Great Lakes connecting the two, to reap exceptional gains from this industrial revolution. Already paramount as a railroad center even before the Civil War, the extension of the railway net westward from the Mississippi River added the rapidly growing West to its hinterland and absorbed portions of the tributary territory of its rivals. The Burlington and Rock Island railroads made Iowa, Kansas, and Nebraska dependent on the Chicago market, and the Chicago and Alton Railroad diverted much of the trade of southern Illinois and eastern Missouri from St. Louis that was at their very door to the city on the lakes.[7] The completion of the Union Pacific and the Central Pacific across the continent in 1869 brought Chicago in contact with the Pacific Coast and the trade of the Orient. Such was the wider market gained for Chicago by the extension of the mileage of its railroads from 4,912 in 1860 to 7,019 in 1869, while the profits to the railroads themselves were shown by an increase in their earnings from $17,609,314 to $48,886,305.[8]

The Chicago wholesale houses took full advantage of the opportunity created by the railroads. Not waiting for business to come to them through the new channels, they sent out "drummers" to the western states to solicit orders—a business policy unknown before the war. As a result of such tactics and the advantages of their position, the wholesale and produce business of Chicago increased from less than $100,000,000 in 1860 to $400,000,000 annually after 1868.[9] Whereas before

[7] Lewis and Smith, *Chicago: A History of Its Reputation*, p. 108.
[8] Moses and Kirkland, *op. cit.*, I, 142. [9] Chamberlin, *op. cit.*, p. 121.

the Civil War there was not a mercantile house in Chicago with an annual volume of sales exceeding $600,000, in 1866 there were twenty-two firms whose sales exceeded $1,000,000 a year. In the one year 1872 one firm alone, Field, Leiter and Company, reported sales of $20,000,000 and a profit of $1,000,000.[10]

Meanwhile, the traffic in the original staple articles of Chicago's commerce, the lake-carried lumber and grain, had been continually growing. The tonnage of lake vessels had increased from 1,931,692 in 1860 to 3,125,400 in 1869. As many as three hundred sailing vessels, loaded with lumber, entered the harbor within twelve hours, passing the drawbridges at the rate of two a minute.[11] Such was the flood of pine lumber that poured into Chicago annually when its volume reached a billion board feet in 1868, a fourfold increase over 1861; and when it required five hundred acres of lumber yards along the south branch of the river for the temporary storage of as many as fifty million boards.[12] Millions of these pine boards from the forests of Michigan were hauled westward on the railroads, and other millions became embodied in the thousands of pine structures that were annually going up in Chicago.

The annual receipts of sixty million bushels of grain were handled with greater facility and dispatch through the medium of the seventeen elevators of 1870 than a million bushels of grain had been marketed by the jostling teamsters on Lake Street in 1847. Warehouse receipts and dealings in futures, inaugurated by government necessities in the Civil War, had transformed the grain market from the dealing in a bulky commodity by actual inspection and delivery of the thing itself to a transfer of the rights of ownership to so many bushels of grain of a given quality stored in an elevator.

Of greater significance, however, to the growth of Chicago in this period than either the wholesale or the grain and lumber trades was the sensational growth of its manufacturing. Whereas before the Civil War the city of Chicago was known as the great "northwestern exchange," a buyer and seller on a great scale, but as a fabricator of but a few articles, by 1867 nearly everything of much bulk used on the railroads, in farming or in the building or furnishing of houses, was made in Chicago. "The prairie world is mowed and reaped by machines made

[10] *Ibid.*, p. 123.
[11] James Parton in *Atlantic Monthly*, March, 1867, p. 335.
[12] Chamberlin, *op. cit.*, p. 282.

A PANIC, A CIVIL WAR, AND A GREAT FIRE 85

in Chicago."[13] In addition to heavy iron, steel, and wood products, shoes, clothing, watches, soap, and distilled liquors were produced in

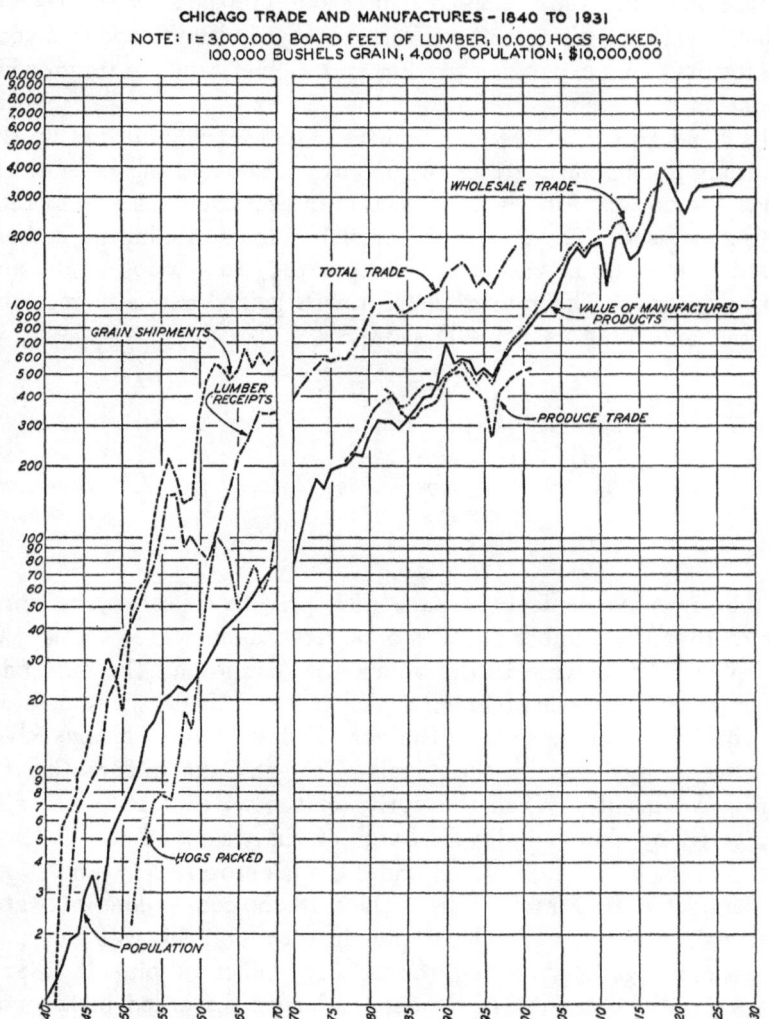

FIG. 15

large quantity. The meat-packing industry, concentrated after 1865 in 375 acres as Thirty-ninth and Halsted streets, with 100 acres of pens,

[13] Parton, *op. cit.*, p. 337.

had secured connections with all the railroads, and continued to hold its leading position. In short, the rise in the value of Chicago's manufactured products from $15,000,000 in 1856 to $176,000,000 in 1873 and the increase in the number of workers employed from 10,000 to 60,000 were results of its expanding market and a chief cause of its growing population.[14]

The rapid growth of the city from 1865 to 1871 is indicated by the increase in its population from 187,000 to 325,000 and the expenditure of over $76,000,000 for new construction in the seven years from 1864 to 1870 inclusive. The total number of buildings in Chicago had increased from 3,742 in 1848 and 19,000 in 1857 to 40,000 in 1868 and 56,000 in 1870.[15] The rate of new growth gained rapid momentum after the Civil War, as Table II shows.[16]

TABLE II
VALUE OF NEW BUILDINGS ERECTED IN CHICAGO BY YEARS, 1864-70

1864	$ 4,700,000	1868	$14,000,000
1865	6,950,000	1869	11,000,000
1866	11,000,000	1870	20,000,000
1867	8,500,000		

Public improvements kept pace with private construction. From 1865 to 1871 the number of miles of sewers was increased from 75 to 151. When the increase in the volume of sewage and the industrial wastes poured into the stagnant Chicago River made the stench almost intolerable in the sixties, the normal flow of the Chicago River was reversed by deepening the Illinois-Michigan Canal in 1871, thereby creating a current.[17] When the purity of the water supply was also endangered by the sporadic discharge of the wastes of the Chicago River into the lake, a new tunnel under the lake to a crib two miles out was completed in March, 1867.[18] Over 18,000,000 gallons of water flowed daily through 154 miles of pipe in 1867, and this was increased to 24,000,000 gallons flowing through 275 miles of pipe in 1871.[19] Meanwhile, the old plank pavements had been discarded in favor of

[14] *Industrial Chicago*, III, 514. [15] Chamberlin, *op. cit.*, p. 67.
[16] Moses and Kirkland, *op. cit.*, I, 142-43; *Chicago Tribune*, December 30, 1865.
[17] Colbert and Chamberlin, *op. cit.*, p. 160.
[18] James W. Sheahan and George P. Upton, *The Great Conflagration* (1872), p. 41.
[19] *Ibid.*, p. 37.

wooden blocks, stone, and macadam, of which the first was the favorite. The number of miles of street paved with wooden blocks increased from 2½ in 1865 to 57 at the beginning of 1871, while 30 other miles were paved with macadam, gravel, cinders, or boulder stones.[20] Notwithstanding this rapid progress in paving, some 446 miles of streets, or 83 per cent of the total, had no paving of any kind. The number of miles of plank sidewalk had increased from 159 in 1854 to 900 in 1871, and the amount of stone sidewalks from 500 feet to 30 miles in the same interval. There were 6,555 lamp posts in 1871 as compared with 2,500 in 1865. Nineteen new bridges had been built in the seven years, and fifteen of these were outside the main business district, serving to connect the outlying West Side with the North and South sides. By 1871 there were six railroad and twenty-seven passenger bridges, costing from $20,000 to $48,000 each, over which 246,015 pedestrians and 45,306 vehicles passed on March 31, 1871, with an additional 7,231 persons and 1,616 vehicles passing through the Washington Street tunnel on the same day.[21] This total of 253,246 persons and 46,922 vehicles in 1871 shows a marked increase over the 73,164 persons and 18,404 vehicles passing over all the bridges of Chicago in a single day in 1855, but this reflected merely a gain in population and not a greater mobility.

The transformation Chicago underwent in the fourteen years from 1853 to 1867 may also be visualized by a comparison of the following description with one previously given for 1853.[22]

In the heart of the town the stranger beholds blocks of stores solid, lofty and in the most recent taste, hotels of great magnificence and public buildings that would be creditable to any city. The streets are as crowded with vehicles as any in New York, and there is nothing exhibited in the windows of New York which may not be seen in those of Chicago. As the visitor passes along he sees at every moment some new evidence that he has arrived in a rich metropolis. Now it is a gorgeous and enormous carpet house that arrests his attention, now a huge dry goods store or a vast depot of groceries. The next moment he finds himself peering into a restaurant as splendid as a steamboat and larger than Taylor's or into a dining room window, where in addition to the delicacies of the season there is a spacious cake of ice covered with naked frogs, reposing picturesquely in parsley. Farther on he pauses before a jeweler's, brilliant with gold, silver, diamonds and pictures, where a single item of last year's business was the sale of 3200 watches.

Along the lake, south of the river for two or three miles extend the beautiful

[20] Colbert and Chamberlin, *op. cit.*, p. 161.
[21] *Ibid.*, p. 160.   [22] See above, chap. ii, p. 62.

avenues which change insensibly into those streets of cottages and gardens which have given Chicago the name of the Garden City. In all Chicago there is not one tenement house. Thrifty workmen own the houses they live in, and the rest can still hire a whole house. Consequently, seven-tenths of Chicago consists of small wooden houses in streets with wooden sidewalks and roads of prairie black.[23]

The appearance of the city had been still further improved by 1871. At that time there were 60,000 buildings, 40,000 of which consisted of wooden houses of an average value of about $1,000 each. In the fashionable avenues of the South Side there were hundreds of marble-front dwellings and ornate homes ranging in value from $8,000 and $10,000 each to $25,000 and $100,000. In the downtown area, with its seventy-nine business blocks built of brick and stone to a height of from four to six stories, there were over sixty stores, hotels, public buildings, churches, depots, and elevators whose value exceeded $100,000 each.[24]

Chicago shared the zeal for public improvements with many other American cities in that post-war decade. It was an era of extravagance and personal display, and people were motivated by a desire to "get rich quick" regardless of the means employed. In 1868 and 1869 there was widespread corruption in municipal and national politics. It was the time of the ugly scandals of the *Crédit Mobilier* in connection with the building of the Union Pacific Railroad, of the wholesale plundering of the Tweed ring in New York City, of Jay Gould's attempt to corner the gold market by political manipulation, of reckless railroad financing, of Boss Murphy in Washington, and of the knavery of the carpetbaggers in the South.[25] In this general let-down of morals, public and private, that followed in the wake of war, Chicago did not escape. Extravagance, lavish expenditures for improvements, and some political corruption were blended in the land boom that culminated in 1873.

C. RISE IN CHICAGO LAND VALUES, BY USE AND OCCUPATION AREAS, 1865–71

The precipitous rise in Chicago land values which began in 1865, after reaching a peak in certain downtown sections in 1869, gained a

---

[23] Parton, *op. cit.*, pp. 338–39.   [24] Colbert and Chamberlin, *op. cit.*, pp. 288–94.

[25] For a contemporary impressionistic account of the land speculation and political corruption of this era see Mark Twain and Charles Dudley Warner, *The Gilded Age* (Hartford: American Publishing Co., 1873), particularly pp. 254–56. For speculation in Paris in 1867 see Emile Zola's novel, *L'argent*.

A PANIC, A CIVIL WAR, AND A GREAT FIRE 89

fresh impetus near the parks and boulevards in 1870 and 1871. After a check and decline caused by the great fire on October 9, 1871, the rise again continued during 1872 and the spring of 1873 in certain spots until the record altitude was reached just before the panic of 1873. The entire movement cannot be described without an account of the changes in the use and occupation of land in certain neighborhoods which accompanied it.

The main business district.—In the post-war period, Chicago not only expanded into the prairie both solidly in long gangling lines and in detached settlements, but it also made a revolutionary shift at its very center. During the Civil War, Lake Street continued to be the leading retail and financial street of the city. The corner of Clark and Lake Street in 1865 was the best business corner in Chicago, and it was valued at $2,000 a front foot. Even at this time the growing financial interests were crowded southward down LaSalle and Clark streets. The retail trades were overflowing along Clark, Dearborn, and State streets toward Madison Street. The enlarged wholesale trades were encroaching on the fashionable residences at the north end of Wabash Avenue. The first important break toward the south came in 1865 when the Board of Trade moved its headquarters from LaSalle and South Water streets to Washington and LaSalle streets. The move was successful, for other financial houses followed the Board of Trade and a new financial center was established that formed a right angle at Washington and LaSalle streets. The value of lots on Washington Street near that point increased from $150 a front foot in 1862 to $1,700 a front foot in 1871. The next southward projection of business was along the line of Clark Street, which had the heaviest traffic on account of the Clark Street bridge over the main channel of the river. Retail business, flowing south on Clark Street, struck a new center of gravity at Madison Street, where it struck the heavy tide of people coming from the west on the Madison Street horse-car lines. In 1869 the corner of Madison and Clark streets, selling at $3,000 a front foot, was acclaimed the leading business corner of Chicago.

Meanwhile, the converging of the street-car traffic from the Cottage Grove, Indiana, State, and Archer lines on State Street to meet the West Side lines at Randolph, Madison, and Van Buren streets, and the southeastward trend of the fashionable residential area were favoring the development of State Street as the leading business center. Potter

Palmer, with a fortune of several million dollars made in speculation in cotton during the Civil War at his disposal, bought three-quarters of a mile of State Street frontage. State Street was at that time a narrow lane between rows of shanties, but Potter Palmer moved back the houses on his lots far enough to allow a hundred-foot street, and he coaxed or frightened his neighboring owners into doing likewise. He then gave the street a new character from Washington to Quincy streets by building a great store on the corner of Washington Street and by replacing the shacks at the southwest corner of State and Quincy streets with a magnificent hotel. The hotel he operated himself, but the store he induced Field, Leiter and Company to rent for $50,000 a year in 1868. The removal of Marshall Field, the recognized leader of the merchants, from Lake Street to State Street was like a word of command to the smaller business men.[26] The exodus from Lake Street was almost a rout. From 1869 to 1871 from thirty to forty marble-front buildings were erected on State Street.[27] The effect of this shift was registered by the sales of land near the corner of State and Madison streets at $300 a front foot in 1860, $500 a front foot in 1866, and $2,000 a front foot in 1869, and by sales of lots on State Street near Madison at the following prices per front foot: $150 in 1862; $300 in 1866; $500 in 1867; $725 in February, 1868; $1,250 in November, 1868; and $2,000 in 1871.[28] All of the downtown streets from Washington to Van Buren streets were sharing in an advance that during 1868 and 1869 was so rapid that it was said to be possible to buy one day and sell at a profit the next.

Meanwhile, the wholesale trades rushed into the vacuum created by the withdrawal of the retail and financial interest from Lake Street, where land values remained stationary at not over $1,000 a front foot. They crowded into Randolph Street and spread down Wabash and Michigan avenues, sending up the value of lots on Wabash and Michigan near Jackson and Van Buren streets from $450 a front foot in July, 1864, to $875 a front foot in August, 1868, and $1,250 a front foot in March, 1869.[29]

The fashionable residential areas.—The value of land along streets made exclusive through their occupancy by the leaders of society is a

---

[26] Frederick Francis Cook, *Bygone Days in Chicago* (Chicago, 1910), pp. 187–89.

[27] Sheahan and Upton, *op. cit.*, p. 51.

[28] *Shortall and Hoard Abstracts*, Vol. 64, pp. 783–85.

[29] *Ibid.*, Vol. 60, pp. 850–54.

direct reflection of the rise of a newly rich class during and after the Civil War and of extravagant tastes on the part of hitherto plain-living American people who had an ambition to live in mansions amid fashionable surroundings. Groups of promoters and politicians combined to secure such public improvements as sewers, water pipes, and woodenblock pavements on the streets they had selected for development as fashionable sections.[30] Most of the improvements installed from 1865 to 1871 were either in the downtown district or in these select areas, as Figure 16 shows. The districts of workingmen's homes had sewers and pavements only on their main business thoroughfares. The upperclass residential streets were located near the lake front on the North and South sides, although not directly on the lake shore, and on the West Side in a belt directly west of the main business section. In every case they were the farthest removed from the open sewer of the Chicago River and the odors of the slaughter-houses, tanneries, and distilleries that lined its banks. They also had the best means of transportation to the downtown area and were most abundantly supplied with such public facilities as sewers, pavements, sidewalks, water, and street lamps. The working population was barred from these exclusive centers by the price of the land, the annual wages of a laborer being insufficient to pay even the interest charges on one of these vacant lots, not to mention the taxes. Whereas a manual laborer could afford to buy or pay rent on a house costing, exclusive of the land, no more than $1,000, and therefore necessarily built of pine on a lot of no greater value than the house, the homesites in these choice avenues cost from $10,000 to $25,000, and upon them were built homes worth from $10,000 to $100,000 or more.

The chief trend of fashionable development in this period was southward. The North Side, with its beautiful trees, some as tall as the spires of churches, had been the first residential center of the social leaders. Dearborn and LaSalle streets, valued at from $150 to $200 a front foot since 1856, still maintained their reputation, but the constant opening of the bridges to permit the passage of an increasing number of ships made the North Side exceedingly difficult of access. Sometimes when unfavorable winds detained vessels in the lake, as many as three hundred were waiting to enter the Chicago River at one time. The description of the following scene, occurring in 1867, shows the conditions prevailing as the ships filed past the open bridges:

[30] Colbert and Chamberlin, *op. cit.*, p. 446.

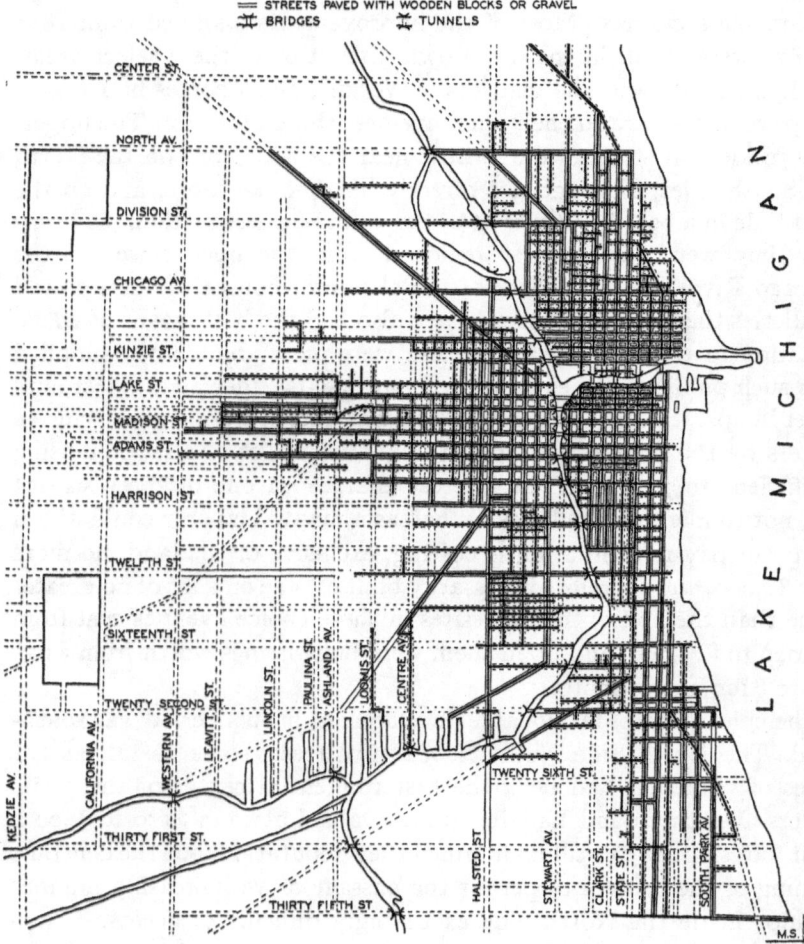

FIG. 16

A PANIC, A CIVIL WAR, AND A GREAT FIRE 93

At all the bridges and on both sides of them crowds of impatient people and long lines of vehicles extending farther back than the eye can reach are waiting. Now and then the bridges can be closed for a short time and there is a tremendous rush to cross. . . . . These are exceptional days and there are other days in which the bridges are seldom opened. But, we are informed that a business man who has any important appointment in any part of town allows one hour for possible detention at the bridges. Omnibuses leaving the hotel for a depot a quarter of a mile distant, but on the other side of the river, start an hour before the departure of the train.[31]

To add to the difficulties, no street cars crossed the bridges from the North Side, while the railroad trains crossing on the grade on the north bank of the river further impeded traffic. The North Side fashionable residential area was further hemmed in between the factories and the slums along the north branch and by the sands along the lake shore, which at times were the habitat of a disreputable element. In view of these obstacles, it is not surprising that business men turned for their homesites from the North to the South Side, which was not separated from the main business section by a water barrier with its bridge uncertainties.

Wabash and Michigan avenues had become high-grade residential streets south of Monroe in the forties and fifties. The southward trend along these streets to Twelfth and Twenty-second streets was hastened by the encroachment of business in the downtown area, by the increase in the number of wealthy men seeking homesites, and by the railroad and street-car transportation that made the more distant area quickly accessible to the main business section. One fine home on Prairie Avenue attracted others,[32] the convenience of Illinois Central Railroad transportation and Cottage Grove Avenue street cars drew the fashionable tide eastward, and *"the* avenues," Indiana, Prairie, Calumet, and South Park, came to be regarded as preferred residential locations. Sales on these thoroughfares near Twenty-second Street that had ranged from $20 to $35 a front foot in 1864, from $100 to $150 a foot in 1867, and from $200 to $500 a foot in 1871, reached their apex on Prairie Avenue near Eighteenth Street where both Marshall Field and Philip D. Armour had their homes after 1873.[33] At this time South Park

[31] Parton, *op. cit.*, pp. 335–36.

[32] Prairie Avenue near Eighteenth Street had acquired prestige since 1837 when Henry Clarke erected a $10,000 house there, which long stood out as a landmark on the prairie, over a mile from any other house.

[33] *Edwards' City Directory* (1873).

Boulevard, with its wooden-block pavement over which 1,500 fine carriages traveled on Sundays to the new parks, had a higher value ($200 a foot to $250 a foot) than the graveled Michigan Avenue. Farther south, east of South Park Avenue, from Thirty-first to Thirty-ninth Street, were streets like Champlain, Forest, and Langley, or the private parks like Groveland, or Ellis Avenue where residential property commanded $100 to $150 a front foot by 1873. Still farther south was fashionable Kenwood at Forty-third and the Illinois Central Railroad that had spread south to Forty-fifth and Greenwood by 1873, and contained property that sold from at $100 to $150 a front foot for its deep lots. Hyde Park, from its center at Fifty-third Street and Lake Park Avenue, was also spreading northward and southward and acquiring a reputation as a fashionable suburb. The avenues near Michigan Avenue had been built up solidly only as far south as Twenty-sixth Street by the latter part of 1871. With the high-grade character of the suburbs to the southward already established, and with the new belt of parks and boulevards lying just beyond, the future growth of the avenues had already been projected by speculators as far south as Sixty-third Street. When the most distant land in the belt from State Street to South Park Boulevard was held at from $60 to $100 a front foot, its high value checked the encircling movement of workers' homes that had filled the land north and west of Fifty-first and State streets.

The West Side had its own fashionable avenues for its merchants, lumber-dealers, and manufacturers. The territory from Lake to Van Buren streets, Halsted to Ashland avenues, was served by a complete network of sewers, wooden-block pavements, on most of the east-west streets by 1871, and horse-car lines on Randolph, Lake, Madison, Van Buren, and Halsted streets, so that it was eligible to become a select neighborhood. Its lots rose in value from $60 to $80 a front foot in 1867 to $150 and $300 a front foot in 1871, with Washington Boulevard the leading east-west residential street. Lots near Union Park, at Washington and Ashland Avenue, had sold for $100 a front foot in 1856, but it was not until 1864 that Ashland Boulevard from Monroe to Harrison Street was developed by Samuel H. Walker. By widening the street, platting deep lots, planting fine shade trees, providing sewers and pavement, and building six expensive homes on six different corners, he made it the most fashionable street on the West Side by 1871.[34] From 1867 to 1871 the value of the best Ashland Ave-

[34] Chamberlin, *op. cit.*, pp. 255–57; Andreas, *op. cit.*, II, 582.

nue lots advanced from $50 a foot to $450 a foot. As on the South Side, the future growth of the West Side fashionable area was projected westward toward the new Central (now Garfield Park, and lots near the park, although then far removed from improvements, sold for from $30 to $50 a foot.

On the North Side, while LaSalle, Dearborn, and the streets east of State Street failed to grow as fast as the South Side avenues, they at least maintained their aristocratic character, with land values ranging from $200 to $300 a front foot, and they secured the most ample public improvements in the form of sewers, water mains, and wooden-block pavements.

Altogether, the 2,500 acres of land within the city limits of 1871 that was reserved for the upper sixth or less of the 325,000 in the city had acquired value of over $100,000,000 while the amount of land outside the city limits that speculators hoped would be occupied by the upper and middle classes exceeded that within the city in both quantity and value.

The manufacturing centers, 1863-71.—By 1871 the railroad arteries had hardened in an iron network around the downtown area. Along the river and its branches in the downtown area were seventeen grain elevators and many warehouses.[35] The McCormick reaper plant, a $600,000 structure, was still on the north bank of the main channel near the harbor. Tanneries, distilleries, flour mills, and some iron-boiler works faced the north branch of the river; large breweries were located on the north side near the waterworks. On the near West Side, from the south branch to Halsted Street, south of Kinzie Street, was a tract of 160 acres devoted to steam-boiler plants and iron- and wood-manufacturing plants. On the West Side, south from Van Buren along the south branch of the river, stretched 500 acres of lumber yards that extended to Twenty-second and Ashland Avenue.[36] West of Twenty-

[35] These seventeen elevators loaded and unloaded wheat by steam power. The facility with which the grain was handled as compared with earlier methods is thus commented upon by James Parton in 1867: "When Chicago exported a few thousands of bushels a year, the business blocked the streets and filled the town with commotion, but now that it exports 50 or 60 million bushels, a person might live a month in Chicago without being aware that there was anything doing in grain" (*op. cit.*, p. 331).

In the grain and lumber commerce were employed 77 steamers, 118 barges, 43 tugs, 33 scows, 613 schooners, or a total of 904 vessels of 218,215 tons, manned by 10,000 sailors.

[36] In 1867, according to an article by James Parton in the *Atlantic Monthly*, there were 614,000,000 board feet of lumber or 50,000,000 pine boards stored in the miles of timber yards along the forks of the river. "The Harbor is choked with arriving timber vessels. Timber trains shoot over the prairie in every direction" (*ibid.*, p. 333).

second and Ashland Avenue a new manufacturing district, the south branch district, was being developed with fourteen miles of docks along the river, and here the new iron industries were locating. South of the canal at Thirty-ninth and Western Avenue, at Brighton, Adam Smith had a chain of small industries. South of the canal at Bridgeport, east of Thirty-first and Ashland Avenue, were other industries, and at Thirty-ninth and Halsted were the new Stock Yards where the entire meat-packing industry was concentrated. Light manufacturing plants, such as clothing and cigar factories, tinsmiths, carpenter shops, and blacksmith shops, were scattered all along the secondary business streets on the horse-car routes of the city. There were other outlying centers such as the Rock Island carshops at Forty-seventh to Fifty-first on Wentworth Avenue; the carshops at Twenty-sixth Street and the Illinois Central Railroad; the Wagon Works at Holstein, Fullerton, and Western avenues; the Watch Factory at Cornell, Seventy-fifth, and Ellis avenues, and the new industrial center that was being prepared at South Chicago by the building of a harbor at Ninety-fifth and the lake and the construction of docks along the Calumet River, which were all pulling workers away from the center of the city. The lower taxes and the cheaper cost of land away from the downtown area were also important factors in the location of new industries. Whereas land values on the north bank of the main channel on Kinzie Street, on the near West Side from Halsted Street to the river, ranged from $300 to $400 a front foot, or over $75,000 an acre, in the new south-branch district at Twenty-second and Ashland Avenue, land with dock frontage was sold for $12,500 an acre, and in the Stock Yards lots with the best facilities were sold at the rate of $4,000 an acre, while in the Calumet region land with river, lake, and rail connections was offered for $1,000 an acre.

The slums, vice areas, and workingmen's quarters, 1863–71.—On the North Side, west of Wells Street, on the West Side, north of Kinzie, south of Harrison Street and west of Ashland Avenue, and on the South Side west of State Street there were in 1871 some 40,000 frame houses of an average value of $1,000 each that were occupied by a population of over 200,000 persons. The rapid increase in the volume of manufacturing which employed 60,000 workers by 1873 had quadrupled the population of the West Side from 1862 to 1872 (57,000–214,000), doubled the population of the North Side from 1862 to 1870 (35,000–70,000), and almost doubled the population of the South Side from 1862 to 1872 (45,500–88,500).[37] The majority of this increased mass of people were workers who crowded into frame cottages, some built on both the front and the rear of lots, near the factories along the river, on streets that had few sewers and practically no pavements. The most densely populated district was that section on the West Side between the south branch of the river, Halsted, Harrison, and Twenty-second streets, and one of the worst spots in this area, Maxwell Street near Halsted Street, is thus described by a current observer.

The street may be singled out of a thousand by the peculiar, intensive stench that arises from pools of thick and inky compound which in many cases is several feet deep and occasionally expands to the width of a small lake. Almost at every step a dead dog, cat or rat may be seen. These unusually sagacious animals had mistaken this for a respectable street because it is very broad and tried to pass through, but with their lives had to pay for their recklessness and foolhardiness. The poor creatures undoubtedly died of asphyxiation.[38]

The vice area was then in that part of the downtown section that lies south of Washington Street and runs west of LaSalle Street to the south branch of the river, with the center of corruption in the notorious Conley's patch at Wells and Monroe streets. The negro population of the city lived chiefly in the section west of State Street just south of Harrison Street until the fire of 1874[39] forced their removal, whereupon they established themselves west of State Street between Twenty-second and Thirty-first streets.

The Irish had a stronghold at Bridgeport, the Swedes and Norwegians were thickly settled west of Wells near Chicago Avenue, and the Germans west of Wells near North Avenue. Other families in the lower-income groups lived over stores in the downtown area or along the secondary business streets. A class midway between the leaders of society on the avenues and the laboring poor next to the factories and the river lived just west of State Street to the Rock Island tracks south of Twenty-second Street, in the section bordering the fashionable North Side streets on the west, or on the Northwest Side along Milwaukee Avenue. The best of this medium range of property was worth $60 a front foot, and the poorest $20 a front foot, though some commanding the higher price was in the worst slum districts, but had acquired its value because of its proximity to the main business section.

[37] Chamberlin, *op. cit.*, p. 279.
[38] *Chicago Tribune*, June 19, 1873.
[39] This fire of 1874 is not to be confused with the great fire of October 9, 1871.

The land occupied by nearly 250,000 persons in Chicago in 1871 did not have a value of over $50,000,000, while the fashionable territory occupied by less than 100,000 had a value over twice that amount. Not mere dense population alone, but a population with a high income gave residential land its highest value.

The secondary business streets.—Chicago grew fastest along the principal streets that had the best pavements and the street-car lines. In the period following the Civil War these horse-car routes, which in turn had followed the main omnibus routes and heavily traveled thoroughfares, began to develop into important business streets. The man who was ridiculed for building stores at Twenty-second Street and Michigan in 1868 reaped a net annual return of from 10 to 15 per cent on his pioneer venture, and by 1871 there had been a rush of business firms towards these arteries of traffic. West Madison Street near Halsted Street became worth $600 a front foot by 1873, and the corner of Madison and Halsted was sold for $1,500 a front foot at the same time, not far below the value of the best corners in the downtown area. Halsted Street from Milwaukee Avenue to Harrison Street also reached front-foot values as high as $500. North Clark Street frontage sold for $1,000 a foot just north of the main channel; it was worth $500 a foot at Chicago Avenue and $250 a foot north of Division Street. Milwaukee Avenue was the main axis of the northwest section in which 25,000 people lived in 1871, and had a value of from $100 to $200 a foot as far north as Division Street. State Street, south of Harrison to Thirty-ninth Street, ranged in value from $500 down to $100 a front foot, passing first through a belt thick with saloons and immoral resorts, and then entering a more respectable territory south of Twenty-second Street. Cottage Grove Avenue, also studded with saloons, reached values of from $100 to $150 a foot, from Twenty-second to Thirty-ninth streets. Lots on Archer Avenue, from State to Ashland Avenue, sold from $60 to $200 a foot; Blue Island Avenue lots from Harrison to Roosevelt Road ranged from $60 to $100 a foot; Twelfth Street (now Roosevelt Road) lots sold for from $150 to $200 a foot near Halsted down to $50 a foot near Kedzie Avenue; and Chicago Avenue east of the north branch ranged from $150 to $300 a foot. Wentworth Avenue was the leading South Side business street west of State Street, with its lots selling for from $60 to $100 a foot, from Twenty-second to Thirty-first Street. North Wells Street was an inferior North Side shopping street, supported by the workers living west of it.

The parks, 1865–71.—The establishment of the outer belt of parks and boulevards in Chicago in 1869 was one of the main factors in the rapid rise in land values just beyond the settled area of the city in this period. Prior to 1866, besides several small parks of a few acres each, the city had only the fifteen-acre Union Park, acquired in 1854, and the part of the present Lincoln Park that was converted from a cemetery in 1865. After the Civil War the fame of Haussman's park and boulevard system in Paris reached the city that was seeking new outlets for fashionable expenditure, and the reports of the rapid rise of land values in the vicinity of Central Park in New York fired the imagination of real estate operators. Paul Cornell conceived the project of a large park on the South Side to be paid for by special assessments, and in February, 1867, he and his associates secured the passage of a bill (to become a law on the approval of the voters) authorizing the establishment of a South Park Board and the purchase of a park site to be located north of Thirty-fifth Street, east of Michigan Avenue, and west of Cottage Grove Avenue, the purchase to be made by the issuance of bonds which were ultimately to be retired by special assessments on the district benefited.[40] This bill was defeated by the voters in April, 1867, but the sponsors of the first bill renewed their efforts at the next session of the legislature and procured the passage of a second bill on February 24, 1869, which definitely fixed the boundaries of the South Side parks and boulevards as they exist today in the present limits of Washington and Jackson parks, the Midway and Drexel, Grand and Garfield boulevards, and authorized a bond issue of two million dollars to purchase the area thus marked out.[41] This bill met the approval of the voters and became a law in March, 1869.[42] Almost simultaneously with the passage of the South Park bill, a bill providing for the West Park Board and the three West Side parks—Humboldt, Garfield, and Douglas parks—was passed by the legislature and approved by the voters,[43] and still another bill provided[44] for the northward extension of Lincoln Park.

[40] *Private Laws of Illinois* (25th General Assembly; Springfield, 1867), II, 472–78.
[41] *Laws of Illinois* (26th General Assembly; Springfield, 1869), I, 358–66.
[42] Chamberlin, *op. cit.*, p. 314.
[43] *Laws of Illinois* (26th General Assembly; Springfield, 1869), I, 342–43.
[44] Chamberlin, *op. cit.*, pp. 337–39.

The South and West Park commissioners sold their bonds and, during 1869 and 1870, bought the 1,100 acres for the south parks and the 600 acres for the west parks. The effect of the purchase of this land, which had hitherto lain dormant a mile beyond the built-up area of the city, was to start a furious speculation in the land facing the parks or in the vicinity of the parks, which reached a high pitch of intensity, particularly near the south parks, just before the great fire of 1871. Since the movement was resumed afterward, the account of this rise in value of lands near the parks will be deferred until after the account of the fire.[45]

The suburbs.—The suburban movement, which did not reach its culmination during this period until after the fire, also began to gain rapid momentum after 1868. The suburbs along the railroads had barely started in 1856 when the panic of 1857 and the Civil War had stopped speculation in suburban lands. In 1866 there were only a few houses in Englewood, notwithstanding three railroad lines. Observers could see only ten houses between the Englewood Depot and the lake. Shortly afterward both Hyde Park and Englewood began to grow rapidly,[46] and in 1868 and 1869 new subdivisions were opened near Hyde Park, Englewood, and, on the northwest side, at Irving Park and Jefferson along the North Western Railroad.[47]

The spread of the speculative land movement, 1868–1871.—Thus the rise in land values which began in 1863 in the downtown business area and in the residential streets near the horse-car lines, where it had increased very rapidly during 1868 and 1869 and then had begun to slow down; spread, after 1869, to land beyond the settled area and to the suburban lands along the railroads. The so-called public participation in land-buying began about 1868 when many cases of large profits made in real estate since 1861 had become common knowledge, and in

---

[45] See pp. ooo ff.

[46] *Real Estate and Building Journal*, August 19, 1871: "As far south as Calumet and Lake townships but a few years ago was one complete swamp, having no particular use but for hunting and fishing. . . . . If building continues at the same rate, the whole section south of the city limits to Englewood will be one dense mass of houses."

[47] *Ibid.*, May 20, 1871: "At Irving Park, at Maplewood, and at points between the latter and Irving Park, men are busy planting trees and shrubbery, laying walks, digging artesian wells and building houses which as a whole will compare favorably with those in any town of the United States. When two years ago there was not a house, a tree, a sidewalk, or even a surveyed street, there are today as handsome villages as can be found elsewhere in the land, numbering each from 20 to 50 as pretty villas as we ever saw."

1871 one writer reports that every other man and every fourth woman in Chicago had an investment in lots. Before the rise in this outlying lands had reached its culmination, however, it was at first interrupted and then stimulated by the great fire October 9, 1871.

D. THE GREAT FIRE OF 1871 AND THE PERIOD BEFORE THE PANIC OF 1873

The great fire of October 9, 1871.—It needed but a flame from an overturned lamp when a southwest wind was blowing with the force of a hurricane over an area of pine shacks and lumber yards that were parched from lack of appreciable rainfall for six weeks to start one of the greatest holocausts in history. The fire started on the West Side near Twelfth and Dekoven streets, but it did small damage there, and under ordinary conditions it would soon have burned itself out when it reached the river and an area that had been cleared by a fire of the night before. The extraordinary gale, however, swept sparks across the river at Harrison Street, where they rapidly started a blaze in the densely packed hovels of that region and, gaining a fresh start, soon generated an intense furnace heat that, sweeping in many columns on the main business district, melted down single five-story brick and stone buildings in five minutes and completely destroyed the principal business blocks, hotels, depots, theaters, banks, newspaper offices, and government buildings of the city. Then in the early morning of the next day the flames leaped the main channel of the river and carried destruction to the North Side, whose factories and beautiful residences were all in ashes before nightfall. Before the fire burnt itself out in the coffins of Lincoln Park, it had swept over 2,100 acres, destroyed 17,450 of the 60,000 buildings in the city, including all of the most valuable, rendered 104,500 persons or one-third of the population homeless, and caused a total loss in buildings, personal property, and merchandise of nearly $200,000,000.[48] The loss had fallen mainly on the central business district and the North Side, the West Side and the new residential sections on the South Side being left almost intact. Nevertheless it was such a blow that many of Chicago's commercial rivals hoped that it would permanently halt the industrial and commercial progress of the city whose growth had amazed the world. Some of its own citizens expected that the obliteration of the downtown buildings would result in

[48] Colbert and Chamberlin, *op. cit.*, pp. 285-87, 301.

the shift of the main business center to a new location. The railroad bands of iron and steel and the trade connections of Chicago, however, were too thoroughly established to permit the happening of either of these events. The fire, nevertheless, had a permanent effect on the growth of the city, although many of its influences accentuated rather than reversed the trends already in evidence before the fire.

Most of the 104,500 persons made homeless by the fire who did not leave the city found refuge on the West Side, whose population increased from 160,000 in 1871 to 214,000 in October, 1872, with the greatest increases taking place on the outer edge of the built-up area. Temporarily, West Madison Street was the most important business thoroughfare in the city, and land values of the near West Side reached a peak immediately after the fire that was not exceeded for many years thereafter. At the same time the value of lots on Wabash Avenue south of Harrison Street increased as ten bankers and the heads of thirty or forty other business firms opened offices in their residences. Marshall Field opened a store at Twentieth and State streets as well as one on the West Side. The fire ended the residential occupancy of the downtown area, where 27,800 persons had lived before; for the shacks in the southwest portion of it were not rebuilt, because of the change to a higher use. The building of temporary business offices in the park along the east side of Michigan Avenue so changed the appearance of that once fashionable street that the former residents sought new quarters in the fashionable avenues to the south.

Meanwhile, land values in the burnt area in the main business district and on the North Side had declined about 30 per cent, on the average,[49] because of the uncertainty as to the future of this land. The owners of the lots bordering the smoking ruins on the south and west were endeavoring, by planning new buildings for its occupancy, to hold permanently the business that had been thrust upon them. The landowners in the downtown area, however, hardly waited for the bricks to cool before measuring the foundations of the ruins for new buildings that were to be more magnificent than the old. In a year of hectic building in which borrowed money from the East, lavishly supplied, enabled Chicago lot-owners to spend over $40,000,000 for new construction, most of which was in the downtown area alone,[50] the retail and financial interests of Chicago were drawn back to the same

[49] *Ibid.*, p. 302.   [50] *Chicago Tribune*, October 9, 1872.

A PANIC, A CIVIL WAR, AND A GREAT FIRE   103

locations in which they had established themselves shortly before the fire. State Street, from Washington to Monroe, as reconstructed, was heralded as the finest retail section in America. Washington Street, near LaSalle Street, had attracted to it seventeen of the national banks.

The land values in the south end of the central business district fully recovered their ante-fire levels. Meanwhile, Wabash Avenue, south of Harrison to Twenty-second Street, was deserted by the banks and business. Its career as a fashionable residential street was ruined by the temporary influx of business, and it assumed a mixed business and residential character as its old mansions were given over to boarding-houses. Its rents declined 30 per cent during 1872. Thus the first tendency of values in the burnt area to decline, and that of land values on the edge of the burnt area to advance, was reversed in less than a year after the fire. The retail and financial interests were more firmly intrenched than ever in the positions they had assumed after the shift from Lake Street.

There were other lasting effects of the fire, however, in addition to those already noted. The fashionable North Side, while largely rebuilt within a year after the fire, had received a setback from which it did not soon recover, and the already pronounced drift to the South Side avenues received additional impetus. The very competition in building between the business section in the burnt area and that on the edge of it had produced a surplus of large stores with a consequent decline in rents in most locations except on State Street, Madison, Washington, and LaSalle streets near the centers of retail trade and finance. The destruction of the shanties of the old vice area south of Washington Street to Harrison Street and west of Wells Street to the river had forced a concentration of the immoral houses into the old territory untouched by the fire that lay south of Harrison Street, west of State Street. The area purified by the fire along Wells, Franklin, and Monroe streets was taken over as a new center for wholesale trade, for lots there could be bought for $500 a front foot as compared with $1,000 a front foot or more demanded on Lake, Randolph, and Wabash Avenue. A further effect of the fire was to hasten other tendencies that were in progress before, for when their buildings were destroyed, part of the inertia that held their occupants to old locations, despite the superior advantages of a new site, was likewise destroyed. McCormick did not rebuild his reaper plant on the expensive ground along the north side of the main channel of the Chicago River, but in the new southbranch manufacturing district near Twenty-second and Western avenue. The last of the banks and retail establishments left Lake Street to occupy new quarters near the new centers of trade and finance. Thus within a year after the fire, the downtown area had been reconstructed with new brick and stone buildings that were predominantly four and five stories high, with three seven-story and six eight-story buildings looming slightly above the rest.[51] In the enthusiasm of the rebuilding and the triumphant emergence of a new city from the ashes of the old, the fire had almost seemed a blessing. While the boom lasted, it was forgotten that the new buildings had been erected at very high costs on borrowed money bearing interest at the rate of 8 per cent per annum that would fall due five years in the future. The outward magnificence of the buildings did not disclose the fact that they were nearly all covered with mortgages.

The fire had also another very important effect in that it accelerated the building of a belt of workingmen's cottages in a semicircle around the outskirts of the city. An ordinance, enacted after the fire, had prohibited the erection of wooden buildings near the center of the city.[52] As the workers could afford to live in no other kind and also found that new carshops, such as those of the North Western Railroad near Crawford and Kinzie street, the iron works, the Stock Yards, and the new McCormick plant, were all being located on the edge of the built-up area, they began to seek homesites outside of the fire limits. The general industrial prosperity and the rush of reconstruction which had raised the wages of skilled mechanics to five dollars and as high as ten dollars a day had given the workers means to buy lots for homes and for speculation. Moreover, the passion to own land that seemed to be the very basis of independence to immigrants who had been oppressed by the landlords of Europe had given them the desire to invest in land. This encircling belt of frame houses that grew rapidly during 1872 started on the North Side at Fullerton Avenue west of Lincoln Avenue, and stretched southward to North Avenue and westward to the north branch. Beginning again west of Milwaukee Avenue, it filled in the space as far west as Western Avenue and as far south as Kinzie Street; then, after a break, it covered the territory from Madison Avenue to Ogden Avenue east of Western Avenue to Roosevelt Road. Com-

[51] *Ibid.*   [52] See map of fire limits in 1873 in Fig. 17.

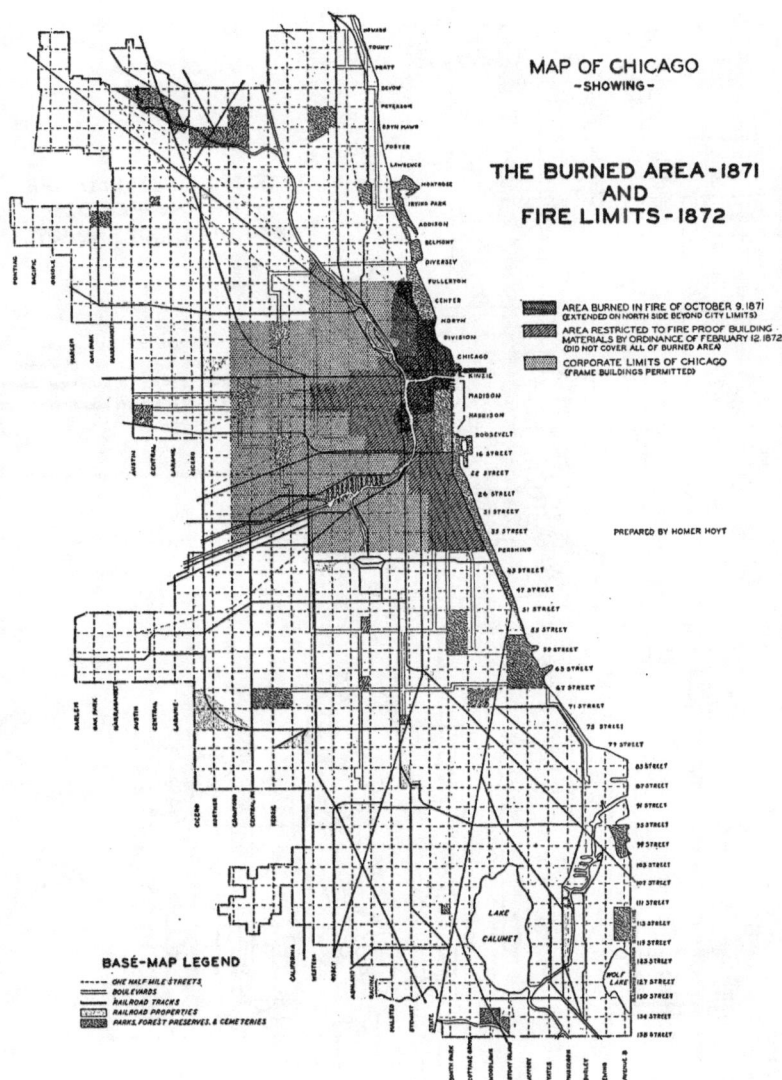

Fig. 17

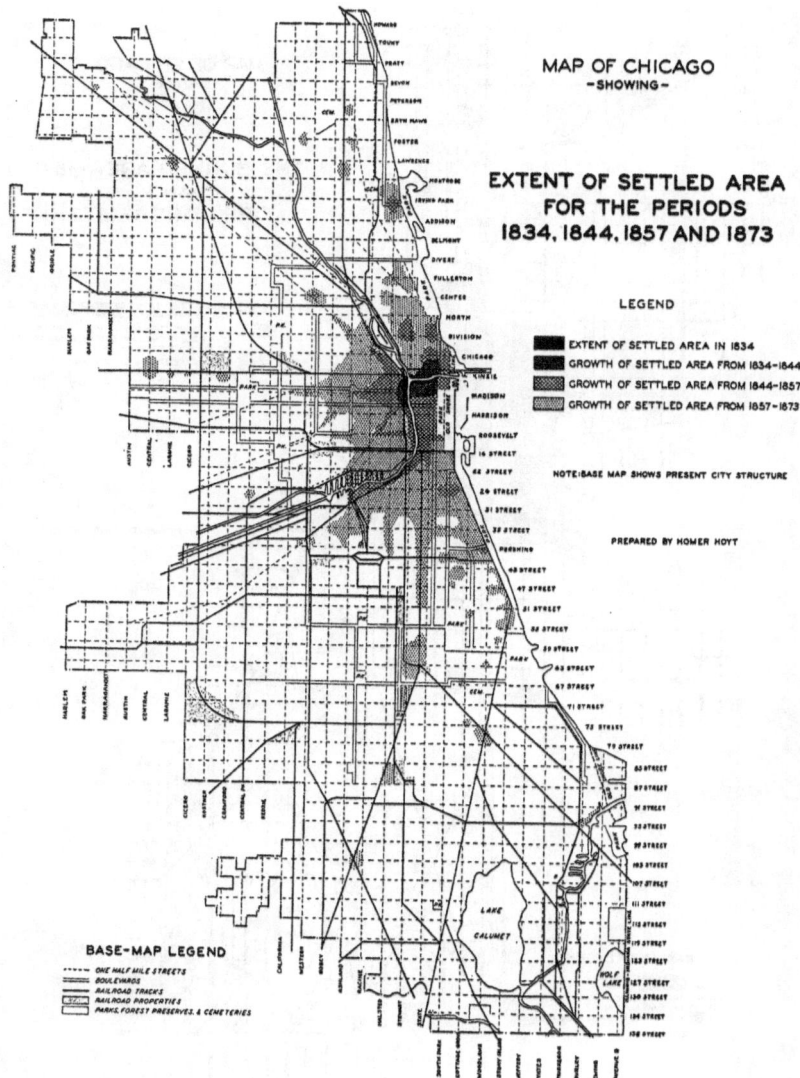

Fig. 18

mencing again south of the Chicago, Burlington and Quincy tracks at Sixteenth Street, it proceeded south to Blue Island Avenue and to Twenty-sixth and California Avenue past the McCormick reaper plant. Crossing the Illinois and Michigan Canal, it began again at Brighton, Thirty-third and Western Avenue, where a number of enterprises were conducted by Adam Smith. Finally, it swung around the Stock Yards to the Rock Island carshops at Fifty-first and Wentworth Avenue, until it came to an end at State Street.[53] In addition to this belt, seven miles long and one mile broad, that adjoined the solid growth of the city, there were streamers of a straggling growth of frame cottages radiating from Englewood along the railroads, northward toward Fifty-fifth Street, southwestward toward South Englewood and Washington Heights, and southeastward toward Grand Crossing and South Chicago.

The great fire temporarily checked but did not stop suburban development. In 1872 and the early part of 1873 this movement raged with greater fervor than ever. The fire hazard and the prohibition of wooden structures inside the fire limits were now added reasons for leaving the close confines of the city. Therefore, the rise in the value of outlying lands near Chicago will be discussed as one continuous movement that lasted from 1865 to 1873.

Increase in the value of outlying lands, 1865–73.—The period from 1865 to 1873 witnessed a remarkable increase in the value of all the land lying from three to eight miles from the center of the city. On the fashionable avenues south of the built-up areas on the South Side, there were such gains from 1866 to 1873 as from $500 to $10,000 an acre at Forty-seventh and State streets,[54] and from $1,000 to $20,000 an acre at Fifty-first and Drexel Boulevard, while some land near the village of Hyde Park is reported to have increased from $100 to $15,000 an acre from 1865 to 1873.[55] Gains almost as great were reported near the West Side parks, as land near Garfield (then Central) Park sold for $275 an acre in 1867 and $4,000 an acre in 1873;[56] near Douglas Park there was a rise in land values of from $500 to $3,500 an acre in the same interval;[57] and near Humboldt Park the gain was from $250 to $5,000

[53] *Chicago Tribune,* May 18, 1873.
[54] Chamberlin, *op. cit.*, p. 309.   [55] *Ibid.*, p. 353.
[56] *Chicago Title and Trust Company Abstracts,* Vol. 5391, p. 638.
[57] *Ibid.*

an acre from 1869 to 1873.⁵⁸ North of Lincoln Park, from Belmont to Fullerton, land values tripled from 1868 to 1872, with lots on Wellington and Barry avenues near the lake selling for $125 a front foot.⁵⁹

The rapid rate of increase was not confined to the fashionable sections. Land west of State Street, near Thirty-fifth Street, rose from $1,000 to nearly $15,000 an acre, and in the Stock Yards, at Thirty-ninth and Halsted streets, sales per acre registered increases thus: $70 in 1863, $250 in 1864, $1,000 in 1868, and $4,000 in 1872.⁶⁰

The growth of the young suburban towns and the birth of new ones were followed by the dazzling transformation of farms that sold for $25 to $100 an acre into staked and platted town lots that brought $400 to $1,000 apiece, although their outward appearance changed but little. Excursion trains carried a thousand people to auction sales of lots at which sales of $500,000 were made in a single day. At Cornell, or Grand Crossing, Mr. Cornell bought land for $25 an acre in 1865 and sold it at $300 a lot, or $3,000 an acre, in 1873. After Hyde Park and Englewood had reported gains in land values ranging from 1,000 to 15,000 per cent in five or six years, the speculative fever spread to more distant suburbs. Washington Heights, along the Rock Island Railroad, from Eighty-seventh to One Hundred and Nineteenth streets, because of its suburban railroad service and a proposed branch line that was to connect it with the industrial section at South Chicago, became the scene of intense activity in the first six months of 1873, when sales to the amount of $2,000,000 were made. The advance in the sales price per acre of one tract near Ninety-fifth and Ashland Avenue is thus recorded: $50, $68, and $100 in 1868; $150 and $250, in 1869; $400 in 1871; $1,000, $1,375, and $1,500 in 1873, as the brokers received over $11,000 in commissions in turning over one forty-acre tract.⁶¹ The Blue Island Land Company which started this ball rolling on a cash outlay of $35,000 had apparent profits of nearly $1,000,000 in 1873. In South Chicago, the Calumet Canal and Dock Company had acquired six thousand acres of land on the Lake and Calumet River at the price of $1.25 to $100 an acre, had secured a government appropriation of $50,000 for a harbor, had built docks, secured railway connections, and platted a new town on the site of the old subdivisions of Calumet and

[58] Chamberlin, *op. cit.*, p. 335.   [59] *Ibid.*, p. 349.
[60] *Chicago Title and Trust Company Abstracts*, Vol. 1830, pp. 522–38.
[61] Chamberlin, *op. cit.*, p. 223.

George that had been abandoned after 1836. In 1874 their holdings were appraised at $5,700,000 or nearly $1,000 an acre, and lots were being sold to workers not only in the close vicinity of Calumet Harbor, but also in the hitherto neglected swamps near Lake Calumet and in distant Riverdale at One Hundred and Thirty-eighth and Indiana Avenue.

West of the downtown area along the Galena division of the North Western Railroad, attracted by the land operations of a syndicate that had bought land for the new carshops west of Crawford Avenue, by the West Side parks, and by the widely heralded advantages of suburban life along the railroads, was another line of new subdivisions that extended far beyond the western limits of the city. Northwestward along the original line of the Chicago and North Western Railroad land worth less than $100 an acre in 1865 was selling at Irving Park, Jefferson, and Norwood Park at from $1,000 to $3,000 an acre in lots. Due north along the Chicago and Milwaukee Railroad were the subdivisions at Ravenswood and Rogers Park in the present city limits and a line of new or rapidly growing suburban towns from Evanston and Wilmette to Lake Forest and Waukegan.

As speculative activities thus extended far along the railroad lines, the spaces in between that were within twelve miles of the center of the city were not neglected. That distant belt of land from Fifty-fifth to Eighty-seventh Street, Kedzie to Cicero Avenue, that is still to a large extent vacant because of the projected Chicago, Danville and Vincennes Railroad along the line of Central Park Avenue, rose in value from $50 an acre in 1868 to $500 and $1,000 an acre in 1873.

The population of Chicago had grown rapidly from 1860 to 1873, and it had spread out until in 1870 the population living from three to five miles from the center of the city numbered 55,000 as compared with 8,000 in 1860. By 1873 the population in this outer belt had increased to nearly 100,000. The increase in the number of inhabitants could not, however, keep pace with the increase in the number of lots that were subdivided and offered for sale in this period. Within the 1873 corporate limits of Chicago were 104,411 lots, of which probably over half were occupied in 1873, and in Cook County outside of Chicago were 120,301 more lots, nearly all of which were vacant. Enough lots had been subdivided from 1868 to 1873 to provide for a total of over 1,000,000 people when the population of the Chicago area was still less than 400,000 in

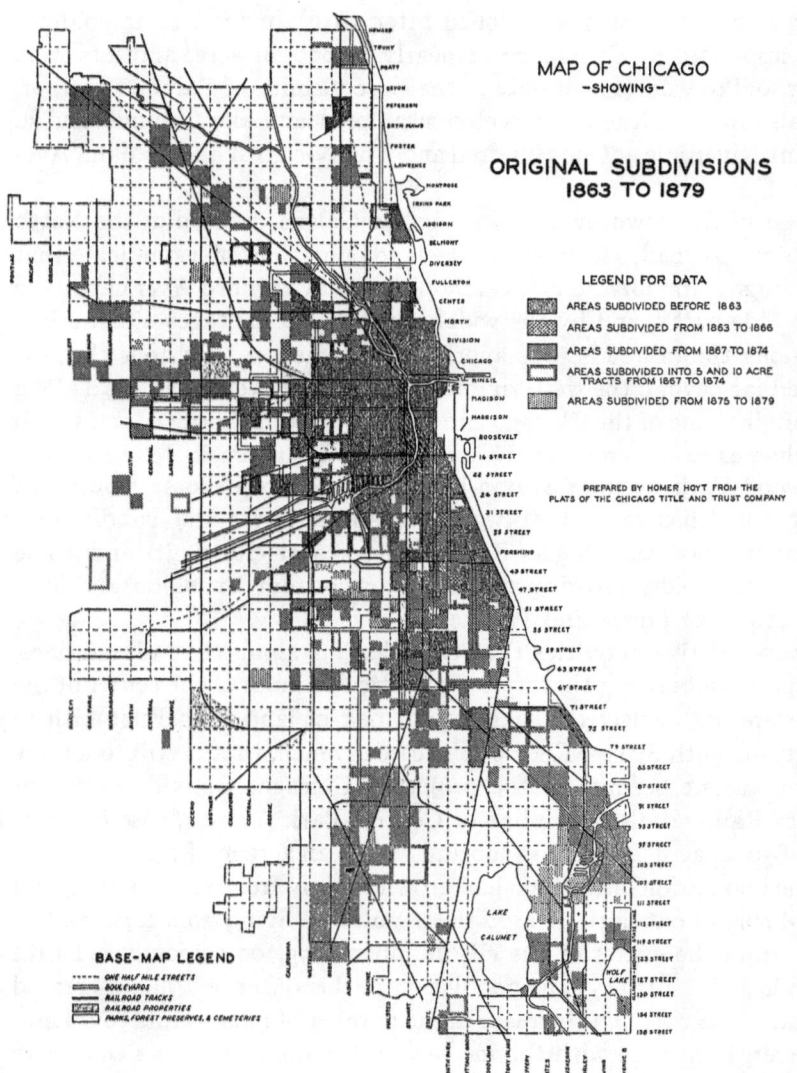

FIG. 19

A PANIC, A CIVIL WAR, AND A GREAT FIRE

1873.[62] The extent of the growth of the straggling suburbs with their scattered houses is not to be overemphasized. In all the 36 square miles of Lake Township there were only 3,360 persons in 1870, and all the territory south of Thirty-ninth Street to One Hundred and Thirty-eighth Street from State Street to the lake contained only 3,644 people in the same year. The growth of the city pushing farthest along the main streets had nearly reached Kedzie Avenue at Madison Street; it had proceeded to Thirty-ninth and Cottage Grove Avenue and Milwaukee and North avenues, but in between there were many gaps and stretches of undeveloped land. The two hundred or more houses within a mile of Englewood in 1873 made an imposing appearance in contrast with the vacant prairie of a few years before,[63] but the population of even such settled areas was sparse in comparison with the compact settlement of the same land at the present time. Not only were there great belts of vacant land such as that from Thirty-fifth to Sixty-third Street, east of State Street, that varied in width from half a mile to over a mile, but the great tract of land on the South Side south of Sixty-seventh Street and west of Ashland Avenue was nearly all vacant, except for the small settlements at Cornell and South Chicago. The land on the North Side north of Fullerton and west of Western Avenue was an almost empty prairie.

A survey of Chicago land values at the peak of 1873.—In the ten years from the autumn of 1862 to the spring of 1873, the total value of the 211 square miles of land in the present city limits of Chicago had increased nearly 500 per cent, or from approximately $60,000,000 to a computed total of $575,000,000 notwithstanding the decline of over 50 per cent in the level of wholesale prices that had occurred after 1864.[64] Compared with the peak of 1856, Chicago land values had increased 360 per cent on the average, although the level of wholesale prices was no more than 20 per cent higher in 1873 than in 1856. The peak values of land by uses in 1873 were $2,000 a front foot for the best inside retail business and financial center lots on State and Washington streets and $2,500 to $3,000 a foot for the best corners on State Street

---

[62] On the basis of a family of five persons for each vacant 50-by-125-foot lot. For the figures as to the number of lots in 1873 see Chamberlin, *op. cit.*, pp. 186–87.

[63] Frontispiece in *Story of Englewood* shows a bird's-eye view of Englewood in 1872.

[64] For detailed prices by sections see Figs. 20, 21, and 22.

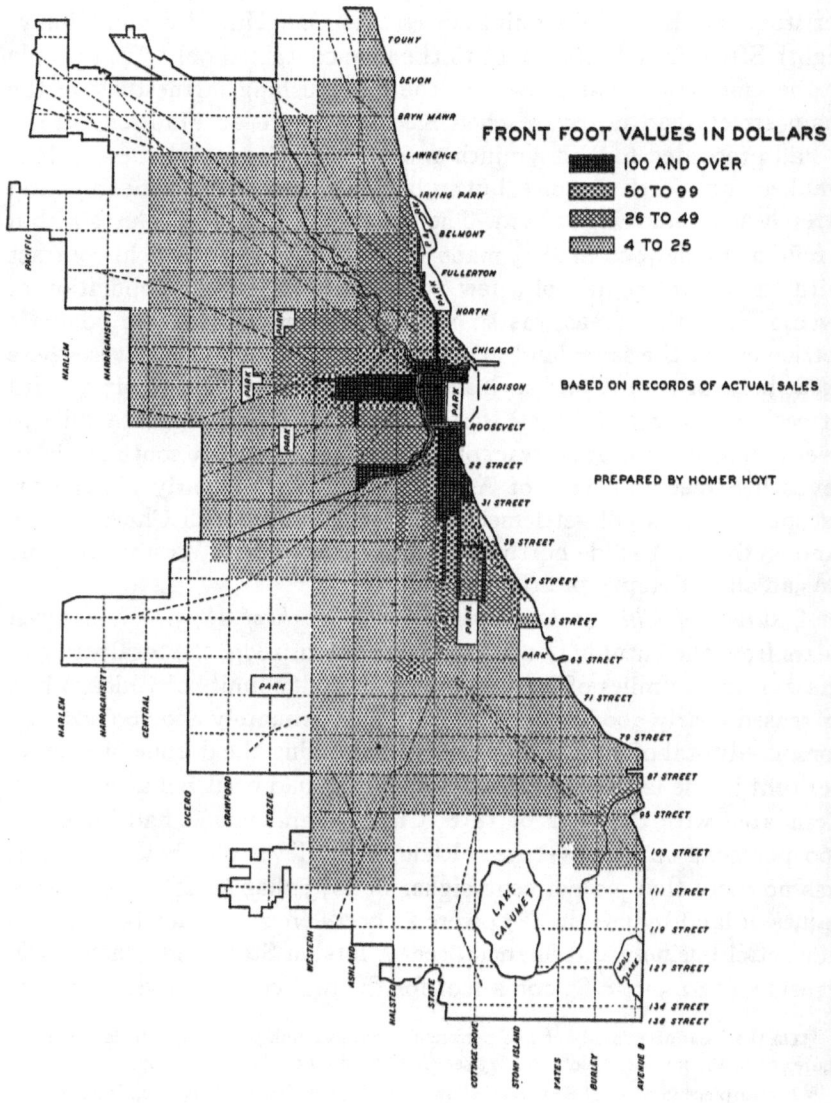

FIG. 20

A PANIC, A CIVIL WAR, AND A GREAT FIRE 113

at Washington, Madison, and Monroe,[65] at Washington and LaSalle and Clark and Madison, $500 to $1,250 a foot for lots in the wholesale section in the downtown area, $300 to $400 a foot for manufacturing sites on the south branch near Western Avenue, $250 to $500 a foot for the most fashionable residence property, $100 to $150 a foot for the middle-class homesites, $20 to $60 a foot for workers' homes, $500 to $1,000 a foot for the best sites on secondary business streets, and $50 to $200 a foot for inferior locations on commercial streets in the poorer quarters, $10 to $100 a foot for suburban lots, and $500 to $2,000 an acre for outlying land near the city. It was contended by current writers that these values were low and that the land in the downtown area, on the basis of capitalized rents, should sell for three times as much as its ruling market price. The optimists, who already predicted that the young city would eventually be the largest in the world, compared the peak price of $30 a square foot for the most expensive Chicago land with the $100 a square foot paid in Boston, the $167 a square foot in New York and the $320 a square foot in London.[66]

The outstanding feature in the rise of Chicago land values in the period from 1862 to 1873 had been the extraordinary advance in the value of the land from three miles to six and eight miles from the center of the city, particularly on the South Side where the fashionable avenues, the aristocratic suburbs, the largest parks, and five of the ten trunk-line railroads combined to send land values south of Thirty-ninth Street upward from a few million dollars in 1862 to $123,000,000 in 1873. While the average gain in value in the area within one mile from State and Madison streets from 1856 to 1873 had been only 150 per cent, with lots on Lake Street and South Water Street actually declining in selling price, and while the belts from one to two miles from State and Madison streets had gained 180 per cent and 332 per cent, respectively, the belt from three to four miles from State and Madison streets had increased in value over 1,000 per cent and the 160 square miles in the present city limits that lie over four miles from State and Madison had appreciated from $12,000,000 to $187,000,000, a gain of over 1,460 per cent. The combined effect of suburban railroads with increasing train service, the horse-car lines, the new belt of parks and boulevards;

[65] For detailed sales in the central business district and other sections of the city, 1870–73, see Chamberlin, *op. cit.*, pp. 298–306, and Figs. 71 and 73.
[66] *Chicago Tribune*, May 31, 1878.

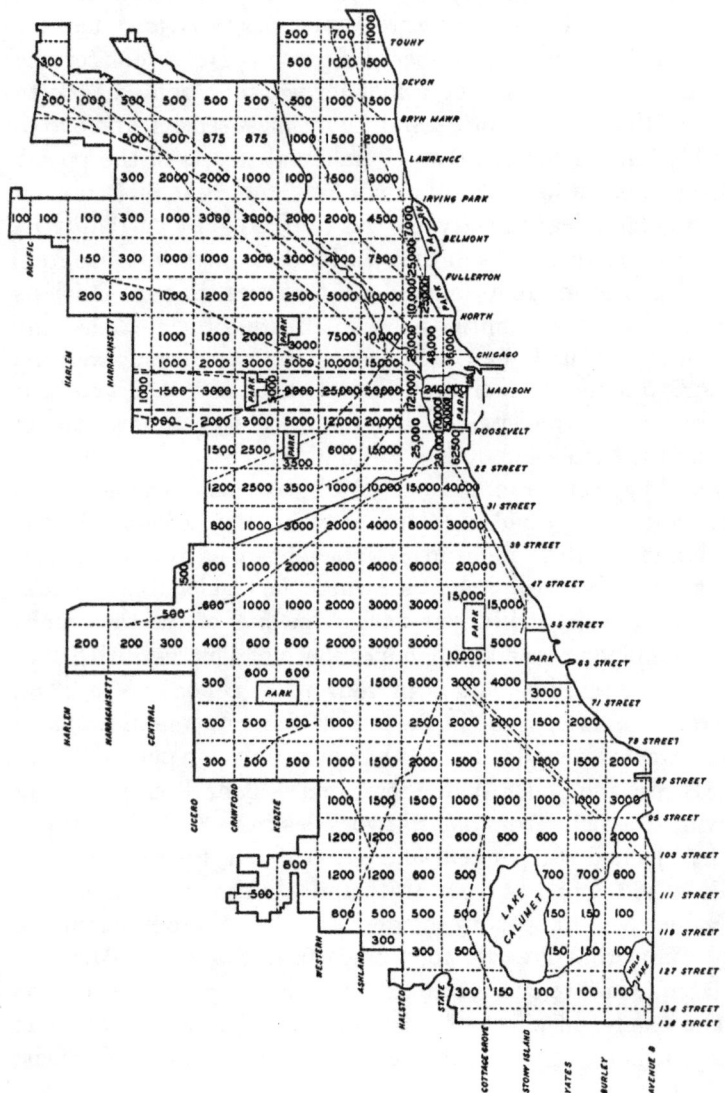

FIG. 21

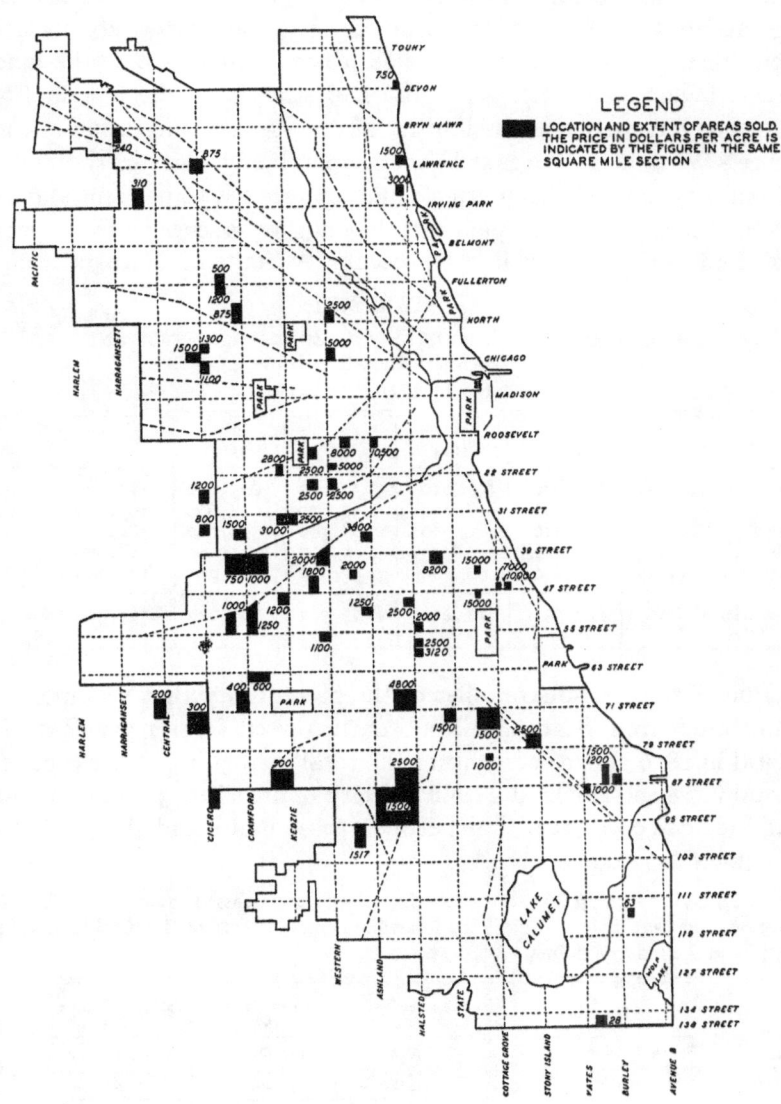

Fig. 22

the fire limits prohibiting wooden buildings near the business center; the lower tax and assessment rates in the suburbs; the removal of industries and carshops to the outer edges of the city; the fear of another great fire; and the desire to escape the noise and odors of streets lacking pavements and sewers had started a heavy migration to the land on the fringe of old settlements and had stimulated the imagination of land-buyers as to the possibilities of even greater migration in the future. Whereas in the first boom of 1836 land values in the first mile from State and Madison streets had represented 56 per cent and in the second boom of 1856 40 per cent, they now represented only 22 per cent of the total land value in the present city limits of Chicago; while the

TABLE III

CHICAGO LAND VALUES BY MILE ZONES FROM STATE AND MADISON STREETS, 1836–79
(In Thousands of Dollars)

Zone in Miles	1836	1843	1856	1861	1873	1879
1	$ 5,900	$ 810	$ 51,000	$25,000	$125,000	$ 60,000
1–2	2,000	200	37,000	18,000	103,000	60,000
2–3	816	80	18,500	10,000	81,700	40,000
3–4	416	40	7,000	3,000	78,600	30,000
Over 4	1,400	280	12,000	4,000	187,000	50,000
Total	$10,532	$1,410	$125,500	$60,000	$575,300	$240,000

value of the 160 square miles of the present city that was more than four miles from State and Madison increased from 7 per cent of the total in 1836 and 10 per cent of the total in 1856 to 33 per cent of the total in 1873. The land within the city limits of 1873 was then valued at $361,000,000,[67] and that between those limits and the present city limits at $214,000,000.

[67] Colbert (*op. cit.*, p. 137) estimates that in 1871 the assessed values of land in Chicago were 60 per cent of true values; the following is his estimate of the total land values in 1871 and the writer's estimate for 1873:

Location	Assessed Value Land Only, 1871	Cash Value, 1871	Estimated Value, 1873
South division	$ 82,609,690	$137,683,000	$161,500,000
West division	65,964,930	109,941,000	155,000,000
North division	28,357,280	47,262,000	44,000,000
Total	$176,931,900	$294,886,000	$360,500,000

In addition to the amount included in Colbert's figures, there was tax-exempt property including land, buildings, and personal property which Colbert estimated had a cash value of

E. THE PANIC OF 1873 AND THE SUBSEQUENT DEPRESSION

The last phase of the boom in the spring of 1873 was a continuation of the rapid rise in land values near the South and West Side parks, in Washington Heights and South Chicago. The selling prices of land in the built-up sections of the city remained practically stationary. In May the market grew dull even in the outlying areas. There was yet no fear of a collapse of the structure of land values that had been reared so high during the last ten years. It was believed that a deflation could be caused only by a catastrophe, and in this category were placed such events as the panic of 1857, the Civil War, and the great fire.

The course of events then regarded as normal had, however, produced a dangerous situation for speculative landholders by the summer of 1873. Municipal extravagance, excessive outlays on magnificent business blocks built at high cost on borrowed money, lavish expenditures on street improvements in sections where they were not required, overexpanded subdivision activity, and a disproportionately large amount of real estate purchases on small down payments—all these had been the result of the extreme optimism of the times. Looking back at the situation "in the cold, gray dawn of the morning after," it was discovered that in city affairs there had been "lavish expenditures, downright thievery on a mammoth scale, and the creation of sinecures for political abettors,"[68] and that "the city [had] acceded to the demand of every real estate speculator who asked for improvements."[69] The value of real estate had, in many instances, been raised on the strength of projected improvements far more than was justified.

> The practice had been [for] the owner to add immediately to his price all that the entire good of the enterprise can bring at its completion. Cases are numerous in this county where thousands of per cent have been added to the prices of lots as soon as some great enterprise was authorized by law.[70]

Reviewing the Chicago real estate market of 1871 to 1873 from the vantage ground of three years afterward, the editor of the *Real Estate and Building Journal* thus described its various moods and tendencies:

$52,951,000 and which he did not include in the foregoing estimate, but the land element of which is included in the writer's estimate. There was also a very marked rise in the value of land on the outer edge of the city within the limits of the city of 1873 on the South and West sides from 1871 to 1873.

[68] *Real Estate and Building Journal*, August, 5, 1876.
[69] *Ibid.*, April 1, 1876.   [70] *Ibid.*, July 22, 1876.

When after the fire everybody was anxious to take advantage of the impoverished condition of the property owners and buy out the ruins of their fortune at a sacrifice, it was very easy to find buyers. The market naturally took on a feverish phase, its pulse beat hot and quick and sales of $2,000,000 a week and over were not exceptional. The great demand almost immediately sent values kiting upwards, and ere two years had passed business lots were bringing twice, thrice, and, in some cases, four times as much as in the date of the city's destruction. Every kind of property, city and suburban, felt the influence of this abnormal inquiry, and followed in a more modest rate, the wake of business property values. Adventurers flocked into the city, laid out supposititious plats and sold to the people who were not too particular to inquire into titles in their anxiety to get hold of lots, blocks or acres in this favored section. Honest men, seeing nothing but a golden future before them—rapid sales and handsome profits—bought heavy interests, paying perhaps one-tenth, perhaps more, of the purchase money down and giving trust deeds for the remainder. Builders were, if possible, even more sanguine and put up magnificent business palaces, running in debt for the site and material to a depth that in the flushest times would hopelessly sink them in adversity and bankruptcy. Subdivisions were laid out every day, new railroads projected and partially carried through and lots went faster than the deeds could be made out. The city authorities found no difficulty in obtaining money to inaugurate improvements on streets and alleys amounting to millions. It made its levies to meet them and for a year or two collected taxes without difficulty.[71]

Such a calm analysis of the land market could not have been made in 1873 when the people were still laboring under the excitement of the boom. In the summer of 1873, the upward movement in land values was nevertheless being halted by a falling-off in the cash resources of prospective buyers. The wages of bricklayers, carpenters, and other skilled building-trade workers had fallen from the five-dollars- to ten-dollars-a-day level of 1872 to three dollars a day, and these laborers who had been heavy purchasers of cheap lots in 1872 no longer had a surplus for such investments. The rents of business blocks in parts of the downtown area had declined and business profits were receding. New surplus funds having dwindled, and lot purchasers finding it difficult to dispose of their earlier investments and being called upon to meet second payments upon the purchases already made as well as taxes, there was a waning in the purchasing power that was necessary for an expanding price level. Moreover, as soon as land values halted in their advance, the desire to purchase land fell off sharply, for nothing so quickly stops an upturn as the belief that a commodity can be bought next month or next year at the same price.

[71] *Ibid.*, May 13, 1876.

A PANIC, A CIVIL WAR, AND A GREAT FIRE

After a lull lasting from May to September, 1873, the landholders, who were waiting for an expected revival of the market in the autumn, were startled by the announcement on September 18 of the failure of Jay Cooke and Company in New York. In quick succession thereafter came the crash on the stock market, the series of bank suspensions, and the commercial failures that characterized the panic of 1873. There was no sudden deflation of Chicago land values, however. Some landowners, hard pressed for cash to meet commercial obligations, found a ready market for their lots on the fashionable avenues at a 20 per cent reduction from the peak prices of 1873. They were aided in this policy by the abundance of loan funds offered to renew mortgages. During 1874, 16,526 real estate loans for a total of $124,000,000 were negotiated to enable landowners to carry their obligations.[72] Land values had shrunk on the average 20 per cent by the spring of 1874, but property could be sold for cash by those who were willing to make this reduction.

The forces of depression were now slowly grinding away. Between 1873 and 1874 the number of workers employed in Chicago manufacturing plants dropped from 60,000 to 52,000 and the wages paid them from $32,000,000 to $26,500,000.[73] The annual value of new construction, after the rush of rebuilding the burnt area, had in the same interval dropped from $25,500,000 to $5,785,000.[74] The wages of common labor had been reduced from $2.00 to $1.00 and even less a day. There were thousands of unemployed men being supported by public charity. House and business rents were declining. While there was a reduction of one-third in the cost of new construction in 1874 as compared with 1872, the effect was to cause a downward revision in the reproduction cost of all buildings previously erected.

Chicago property owners in 1875 were faced with a situation in which their gross incomes from rents were drastically declining, while their expenses in the form of fixed interest charges at the rate of 8–10 per cent per annum and of undiminished tax burdens remained the same. The value of their buildings had fallen as much as 40 per cent because of the lower cost of construction.[75] To escape the resulting loss, they sought to trade their mortgaged property for farms or other property.

[72] *Chicago Tribune*, January 6, 1878.
[73] *Industrial Chicago*, III, 514.   [74] *Ibid.*, I, 149.
[75] *Real Estate and Building Journal*, July 1, 1876.

"During the first quarter of 1875 four-fifths of the sales made were [exchanges] for other property with little if any cash. Nine months exhausted this sort of dicker."[76]

The cash buyers of 1874 had disappeared from the market. The owners of vacant lots, in order to secure an income by any possible means, in certain cases allowed builders to place mortgages on their lots to finance buildings. This frequently resulted in the loss of their entire equity.[77] The majority of the property owners could do nothing to shift their burden, and they waited with growing anxiety for the return of an active market like that of 1872.

Instead of improving conditions, the attrition of the forces of depression continued to wear down the reserve power of the landowners. The number of transfers by deed declined from 64,602 in 1874 to 57,638 in 1875, 50,884 in 1876, and 47,860 in 1877.[78] As the depression continued, more and more of these transfers represented exchanges, foreclosures, or nominal conveyances, so that the number of actual cash sales dropped to a far greater extent than these figures indicate. New loans or renewals of old loans became more difficult to secure, the total advances on new mortgages declining from $124,000,000 in 1874 to $89,000,000 in 1875 and $30,000,000 in 1876. Foreclosures had correspondingly increased from 1,069 in 1874 to 1,166 in 1875, 1,284 in 1876, and 1,803 in 1877.[79] Rents had declined fully 20 per cent on houses and offices by 1876, and by 1877 average rents were 30 per cent lower than in 1873.[80] Houses renting for over $100 a month were a drug on the market.

In 1876 Chicago land values were in a chaotic state, the prices in the same block varying according to the financial condition of the owner.

Prices vary very much. If he [i.e., a prospective buyer] would select such a block, lot or tract as he wishes, and go to the owner and ask his price, he would be answered according to the financial condition of the owner. If he had bought and paid for his property, the advances will all have to come from his side. If, on the contrary, the owner or holder rather has bought in times of flush confidence and made a small payment taking a large risk and finds himself unable to meet it, he will instantly give him the lowest price he can save himself with, and if buyers do not give that, he will let it go under the trustee's hammer.[81]

[76] *Ibid.*, April 8, 1878.
[77] *Chicago Tribune*, November 19, 1876.
[78] *Ibid.*, January 6, 1878.
[79] *Ibid.*
[80] *Real Estate and Building Journal*, March 18, 1876.
[81] *Ibid.*, August 19, 1876.

A PANIC, A CIVIL WAR, AND A GREAT FIRE

Those who were not forced to sell their holdings did not offer them on the market, as they could not realize what they had paid.

Nearly all [holders of acre property] are holding it for a rise in prices and have no intention of selling it for two years at least. Never has there been so little land for sale in this city and county as now.[82]

There is no prospect of uniformity in the values of business property for the reason that much of it has been purchased to hold for a term of years as an interest-yielding investment and it is not for sale at any such price as was last paid for it. One cannot point to a business block, lot or residence sold at a sacrifice in Chicago that was not so heavily encumbered as to make it necessary to dispose of it. Rents in good localities are not so low as not to pay a reasonable interest besides the taxes on the property, and in other places less eligible where they have fallen too low for that, the owners comfort themselves with the belief that though they are losing something, they will stick to their property and make it up in the future advance.[83]

In a land market where some were holding their property at the peak prices of 1873, and others were willing to accept anything above the mortgage, while there were few sales at any price, the current observers of land values confessed the need of some more definite standard of value.

At this time when values are at the lowest ebb, when one can scarcely name a cash price on property, it would be a capital move for a congress of our most experienced and trusted men to convene and arrange a schedule of prices upon property in the city and county, gauging them upon the actual advantages possessed by different tracts. The schedule could be accepted or not by owners, yet it would have a moral influence upon home and outside capital beyond anything else that could be devised. It is doubtful if this could be done. Such is the jealousy of proprietors, and so confirmed the habit of painting every interest in roseate colors, that anything like an amicable agreement on values would perhaps be improbable. But whether definite conclusions could or could not be reached, the discussion would throw light upon the market and enable investors to act more understandingly than is possible under the widely differing representations their inquiry evolves from owners and agents now.[84]

Notwithstanding doubts as to the exact range of prices, there was no question in 1876 but that land values had been steadily declining since 1873, starting first with the depreciation in buildings.

Thus in improved business, the price went down, not at first upon the lots but upon the building. Added to this, heavy incumbrances matured and parties were compelled to sell at any price. Eventually this affected other blocks, not similarly encumbered, and all classes of improved property declined in sympathy.[85]

---

[82] *Ibid.*, June 3, 1876.
[83] *Ibid.*, August 19, 1876.
[84] *Ibid.*, July 22, 1876.
[85] *Ibid.*, July 1, 1876.

The decline had also been accentuated by the burden of taxes for improvements constructed far in advance of their need.

There are miles of gas mains, sewers and water mains, sidewalks and curbing lying along vacant territory which will not need them for years. In many sections needed improvements were left unfinished by the sudden crippling of the money market.[86]

The painfully slow process by which the land-value peaks of 1872 were worn down is thus described:

The land market is at the present time [July, 1876] in a lower condition, as regards transfers, prices and interest felt in it, than it has been in the history of the city since it became a metropolis. The record of sales is extremely light and the inquiry dull in the extreme. Prices have been steadily falling from the fall of 1873 to the just ended spring, and investments were greatly discouraged. Owners and dealers have earnestly watched the decline, unwilling to do anything until it ceased and this very disposition, by almost destroying the demand, accelerated the downfall of prices and made men more and more fearful of buying. If the decline had been a sudden spasm, lasting but a few months and had then suddenly stopped, there would have been good ground for mistrusting the situation and holding back money from real property. Or if it had been precipitate as in some eastern cities and in San Francisco after the bursting of the great mining bubbles, there would then be ample cause for serious alarm and for directing one's attention to other channels for the use of money. But the fall in values had been gradual. The decline in values commenced, continued and ended slowly. Deliberation has marked every circumstance affecting the market. There was no wild scare, no rushing, no jostling. The market, under the weight of a more crushing panic than the thirties, yielded inch by inch, under the influence of maturing notes, national turpitude on the financial problem, local corruption and malappropriation of the public funds, the discouraging of the purchasing of homes by the lowering of rents and various other adverse influences. It was stunned by the shock of tumbling fortunes and exploding schemes. Plans long maturing were at once rendered inoperative and dealers and owners were confused, scarcely knowing which way to turn to save themselves from a ruin that seemed impending over all.[87]

The effect of this declining land market on the individuals involved in it was pathetic.

In the entire history of land dealing there has not been a reverse which has lasted so long or caused such depreciation as the one under which the market has labored for three years—years strewn with the wrecks of fortunes and the destruction of hopes. Indeed it is by no means certain that human minds and lives have not been destroyed under the burden of disappointed expectations and the obloquy which has been cast upon reputations—previously fair and bright—through the inability of persons to meet their promises and carry out their contracts. When a man has

[86] *Ibid.*, April 1, 1876.   [87] *Ibid.*, July 8, 1876.

worked and studied for years in gathering a sum together for investment in something which he believes to be sure to give him respite from toil and enable him to live at ease, if he makes a mistake in judgment and places his funds in some nonproductive property, where because of the panic they must be locked up as completely as if behind impregnable locks so that he cannot use them even for life's necessity, when after waiting patiently and hopefully in vain for better days until he is pressed by his creditors to the wall, when he finds all these expectations so long in being realized, it is not strange if he grows disheartened, hopeless and gloomy, a state of mind favorable to even greater miseries. Some of our dealers have passed away. No one knows how much the reverses of fortune and loss of business may have contributed to the end.[88]

Sad as the year 1876 was to the holders of incumbered property, the year 1877 was to fill their cup of misery to the brim. The bank failures in Chicago that had followed in the wake of the panic of 1873 culminated in 1877 with the failure of the largest savings banks in the city—the Columbian and the Bee Hive—making a total of twenty-one bank failures in four years. Serious labor riots broke out all over the United States, and on July 5, 1877, a pitched battle was fought between the police and a great mob at the Halsted Street bridge over the south branch in which twenty were killed and seventy injured. In this period, when capitalists were frightened by these industrial disturbances, twelve thousand loans for a total of $50,000,000 that had been made by local property owners to finance the rebuilding after the fire fell due.[89] Scant capital was available for refunding these maturing obligations or for buying property at any price. Wealthy men were hoarding their money because currency was constantly appreciating in terms of gold, while lands and commodities had been constantly declining in terms of currency. The holders of property who could not pay off their mortgages were given short shift.[90] In most cases no one attended these sales but the holder of the mortgage. He bid in the property at his own price, sometimes as low as one-fourth of the amount of the mortgage, and secured a deficiency judgment for the balance.[91] The once opulent

[88] *Ibid.*, December 30, 1876.

[89] *Chicago Tribune,* January 28, 1877.

[90] The period of redemption allowed by the laws of Illinois was one year for the mortgagor and an additional three months for creditors, which is the same as at present, but the mortgagees who were residents of other states were allowed to foreclose in the United States district court, which then allowed the mortgagors only one hundred days after the sale in which to redeem.

[91] *Chicago Tribune,* July 28, 1878.

real estate operators in many cases thus not only lost their land but were forced to go into bankruptcy to avoid paying personal judgments on the original purchase price of the land. The fees of courts and lawyers exacted a heavy toll even from the winning side, and these charges, in addition to taxes and special assessments with their penalties of 100 per cent a year for late payment, were added to the costs of holding land. Of the long list of men who were thus reduced from affluence to poverty when "Fickle Fortune, in contrast to her previous smiling visage, threw aside her mask and showed an ugly countenance," may be mentioned Samuel H. Walker, reputed to be worth $15,000,000 in 1873, who had lost all his property by 1877. If the best improved real estate in the central business district of Chicago was thus foreclosed, the fate of vacant land can be imagined. "It first grew dull, then stagnant and then unsaleable." In 1877 the bottom of the real estate market was at last reached. In the wreckage of some real estate fortunes, shrewd capitalists with large cash resources found an opportunity to lay the foundations for huge estates in the future. As in the case of the aftermath of the booms of 1836 and 1856, Chicago land values were not thoroughly deflated until four years after the first shock of the panic. In the absence of short selling in real estate and the lack of any organized market for land in the early period of the depression, the landholders kept their land until the constant attrition of interest charges, taxes, and penalties or the inability to renew mortgages brought foreclosure proceedings that squeezed out the equities above the mortgage. Four or five years seemed to be required to complete this painful process, and it was not until it was over that a definite market for land was established at a lower level of values.

In 1877 and 1878 it had to be mournfully admitted that a quick return to the level of land values prevailing in 1873 was not only not to be expected, but that the values obtaining at that time were the result of a hallucination or a speculative disease. As the real estate editor of the *Chicago Tribune* said in 1878:

> The wills of the wisp [suburban lots] that lured speculators to their financial death in the happy days when there were no panics are extinguished. The water privileges that used to be spoken of with admiration almost too deep for words are now candidly alluded to as swamp lots. The outlying districts that were so handsomely mapped and platted for exhibition in the agents' offices are resignedly if not cheerfully given over to the market gardener and the dairyman.[92]

[92] *Ibid.*, April 14, 1878.

When these lines were published, the corners of Sixty-third and Halsted[93] and Forty-seventh and Ashland were selling for $8.00 and $12 a front foot,[94] land near Twenty-second and Ridgeland in Cicero[95] and One Hundred and Eleventh and Michigan was offered for $100[96] an acre, and Marshall Field was about to buy the present campus of the University of Chicago for $5.00 a front foot.[97]

F. A SURVEY AT THE BOTTOM IN 1877–79

The bottom in land values in the Chicago area for this period was reached in 1877 when there was virtually no market at all, but it is necessary to resort to the sales of 1878 and 1879 and the evidence as to the extent of the decline.

The total land value of the 211 square miles in the present city limits of Chicago declined on the average over 50 per cent from a total of $575,000,000 in 1873 to less than $250,000,000 in 1877.[98] The decline was least on North Dearborn Street; on State Street near Madison; on West Madison Street, which continued to grow during the depression until it was solidly built up to Ashland Avenue; on South Michigan Avenue, which was developing fast south of Thirty-second Street with the growth of the Stock Yards; in the Stock Yards district; on Wabash Avenue north of Monroe Street; and in the medium-grade residential property that was close to the center of the city where the drop varied from 33 to 50 per cent.

The fall in land values was approximately 50 per cent on the fashionable West Side and South Side residential streets except on South Park

[93] *Ibid.*, May 23, 1879. A deed recorded October 5, 1878, showed a consideration of $800 for the northwest corner of Sixty-third and Halsted streets, 75 by 139 feet.

[94] *Ibid.*, November 21, 1878. The southeast corner of Forty-seventh and Ashland, 47 by 121, sold for $600.

[95] *Ibid.*, November 12, 1878.

[96] *Ibid.*, October 5, 1879.

[97] *Ibid.*, August 18, 1879. Marshall Field paid $79,166.67 for $63\frac{1}{3}$ acres between Woodlawn and Egandale (Ellis), Fifty-fifth and Fifty-ninth streets.

[98] *Ibid.*, July 28, 1878: "The prices realized are generally half, often a third, perhaps even less than one-fourth those ruling a few years ago."

"Causes of General Depression," *Labor and Business* (H.R., 46th Cong., 2d sess.; Washington, 1879), Misc. Doc. 5: "1873, Chicago": "CHAIRMAN: What is the average shrinkage in the value of real estate in this city comparing the present time with an average of five years back? MR. CHARLES RANDOLPH [secretary of the Board of Trade]: It would be but a guess on my part, but I should say that the shrinkage between 1873 and today [1879] would be from forty to fifty per cent."

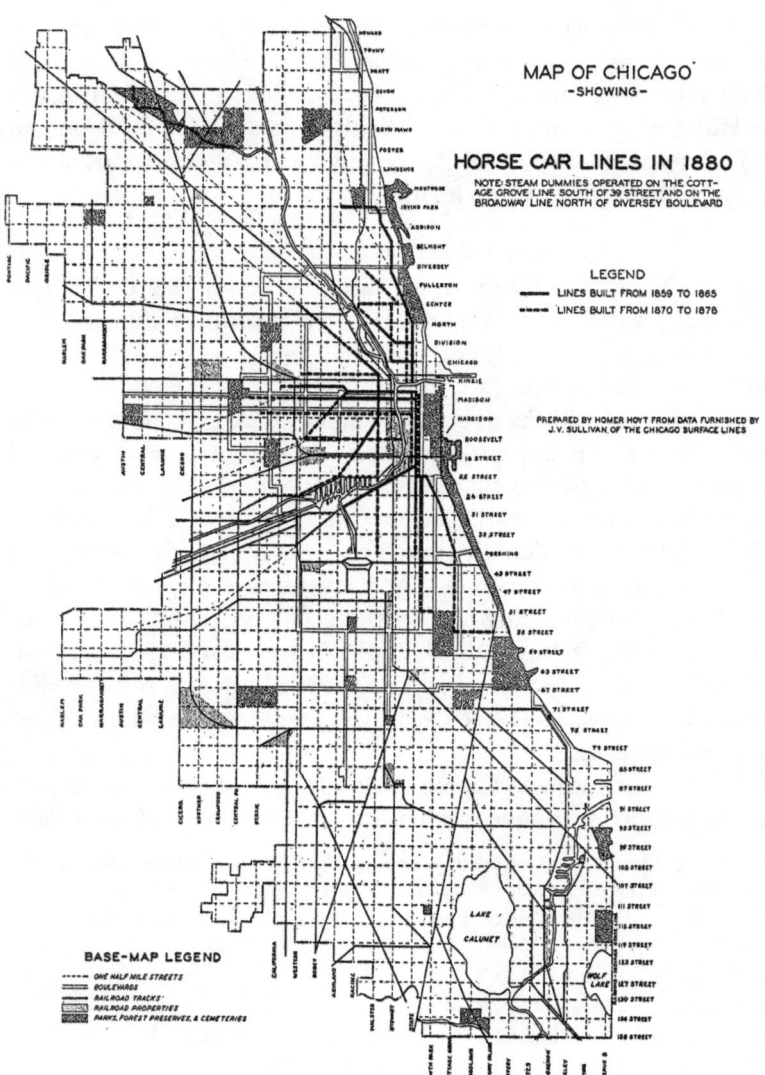

Fig. 23

A PANIC, A CIVIL WAR, AND A GREAT FIRE 127

Avenue where it exceeded 75 per cent, and the deflation was greatest on Wabash and Michigan avenues south of Jackson, on land near the parks and in all suburban and outlying lands where the decline varied from 75 to 90 per cent. For example, Michigan Avenue lots near Jackson sold for $200 a foot compared with $1,000 a foot in 1873, State Street south of Jackson at $500 instead of $1,250 a foot, fashionable residence lots from $75 to $200 a foot instead of from $250 to $500 a foot, acres at Forty-seventh and Drexel at $7,500 instead of $20,000 an acre, a tract at Twenty-fifth and State Street at $5,000 instead of $15,000 an acre, land at Sixty-third and Racine at $500 instead of $2,000 an acre, Forty-eighth and Champlain $2,350 an acre compared with $10,000 an acre, and tracts in Ravenswood at $375 instead of $3,000 an acre.

The silver lining.—It was some consolation to Chicago that the decline in land values in the Central Park district in New York was even greater than the fall of land values in Chicago,[99] for the easterners could not point to Chicago as a horrible example of western boom methods when they were in the same situation. Of far greater significance was the fall in construction costs, the decline in the interest rate on the best real estate security in Chicago from 8 per cent in 1873 to 6 per cent in 1878,[100] which favored a constant annual accretion of thousands of dwellings built at low cost, the number being 875 in 1875, 1,636 in 1876, and 2,698 in 1877—a total of twenty-five miles of frontage for the three years. The packing industry was growing, with Armour and Swift beginning to send chilled beef East in refrigerator cars, while other lines of manufacturing and the wholesale trades were maintaining their volume of business. Representatives of eastern firms were coming to Chicago to establish branch houses. Population was about to catch up with the supply of houses, the resumption of specie payments was not far away, and the motive for hoarding money was disappearing. The telephone had been invented and Edison was about to demonstrate his electric light. The first apartments had appeared in Chicago. While many new factors were thus in the formative stage, the street-car lines on Madison Street, Cottage Grove Avenue, and Milwaukee Avenue were being extended from 1875 to 1877 to the new belt of parks as Figure 23 shows.

[99] *Chicago Tribune*, October 27, 1876.
[100] *Ibid.*, November 17, 1878.

CHAPTER IV

THE LAND BOOM OF THE FIRST SKYSCRAPERS AND THE FIRST WORLD'S FAIR, 1878-98

A. RECOVERY IN GENERAL BUSINESS CONDITIONS, 1878-84

The prelude to the recovery of Chicago land values from the extreme depression of 1877 was the beginning of improvement in general business conditions throughout the United States. The prices of raw materials, the wages of labor, the rents of houses and stores, and the interest rates for capital advances having been reduced to an extremely low level by 1877, it became a favorable time to expand manufacturing operations to replenish depleted stocks. The effect of good crops in 1878 and the confidence engendered by the resumption of specie payments in 1879 gave the new upward movement its initial impetus. Rising prices and profits margins speeded up production, increased employment, and furnished the funds for a brief era of speculation that culminated in 1883. From 1879 to 1883 the railroad mileage of the country increased 50 per cent and the resulting demand for steel rails gave a great impetus to the iron industry. The enlarged demand for labor for railroad construction and for heavy work in factories and mills induced a fresh volume of adult immigrants from abroad. Stimulated by the activity of the agents of steamship companies and frequently by the prepayment of the $22 passage money by friends in America, the tide of this immigration increased in numbers from 130,502 in 1877 to 250,565 in 1879, 593,703 in 1880, 720,045 in 1881, and 730,349 in 1882, a new peak.[1]

The effect on the trade, manufactures, and railroads of Chicago.—Chicago was at a focal point that would benefit to an unusual degree from larger western crops, increased railroad building, and an improved demand for manufactured products. In the three years from 1880 to 1882, inclusive, seven new trunk-line railroads entered Chicago.[2] In the four years from 1878 to 1881, inclusive, Chicago bank clearings in-

[1] *Chicago Tribune*, April 14, 1883.
[2] P. L. Tan, "Belt Railroads of Chicago" (MS thesis, University of Chicago, 1931).

creased from less than $1,000,000,000 to $2,250,000,000.[3] In the five years from 1879 to 1883, inclusive, the number employed in Chicago manufactures increased from 62,948 to 114,457 and the wages paid from $35,000,000 to $59,000,000.[4] In the period from 1877 to 1881 the value of the wholesale and produce trade of Chicago rose from $387,000,000 to $700,000,000.[5] From 1877 to 1883 the population of Chicago advanced from 420,000 to 590,693. A study of Table IV, giving the annual trade indices just referred to, shows a particularly rapid increase in bank clearings and total trade from 1879 to 1881 and a slow gain thereafter to 1883.

TABLE IV

THE GROWTH OF CHICAGO, 1877–83, AS INDICATED BY BANK CLEARINGS, NUMBER EMPLOYED IN MANUFACTURES, TOTAL TRADE, AND POPULATION

Year	Bank Clearings (Millions of Dollars)	Value Manufactures, Wholesale and Produce Trade (Millions of Dollars)	No. Employed in Manufactures	Population
1877	$1,045	$ 595	58,213	420,000
1878	967	650	67,504	436,731
1879	1,258	764	62,948	465,000
1880	1,726	900	80,075	503,298
1881	2,249	1,015	87,900	530,000
1882	2,367	1,045	96,654	560,000
1883	2,526	1,050	114,457	590,693

The general effect of improved business conditions upon Chicago land values.—The effect of the increased volume of trade and manufactures in a market in which selling prices were rising faster than cost prices was greatly to increase the profits of business men. A fund of new capital was thereby coming into existence that was available for investment.[6] To this freshly created surplus there was added by 1879 a large amount of hoarded wealth. Prior to the resumption of specie payments, the steady rise in the value of currency in terms of gold and other commodi-

[3] *Chicago Tribune*, January 1, 1884.
[4] *Industrial Chicago*, III, 194. [5] *Ibid.*
[6] Bank clearings from a typewritten statement of the Chicago Clearing House Association; number employed in manufactures from *ibid.*; the value of manufactures, wholesale and produce trade, from the annual reviews of the *Chicago Tribune* (1878–84), in the issues of January 1 of the years cited.

ties had tempted many rich men to lock their money in strong boxes. As soon as currency reached a parity with gold and general prices began to rise, these funds came from their hiding places. Even during the hard times of 1876 and 1877 the Chicago Stock Yards magnates and the Chicago capitalists who had invested in Leadville mines had accumulated fortunes. With the return of a more prosperous era after 1879, however, a large number of laborers, employed at full time, began to accumulate small amounts of capital. Thus in all ranks of society surplus funds were accumulating or were being made available for investment.

To attract this surplus, Chicago real estate was in an advantageous position. As compared with other forms of investment in 1879 it seemed to offer the highest rate of return compatible with safety. From 1872 to 1880, the net yield of high-grade bonds had fallen from $6\frac{1}{2}$ to 4 per cent per annum.[7] In the same interval the rate of interest on the best real estate mortgages in Chicago had declined from 8 to 6 per cent per annum. The collapse of the Leadville mining boom was over and mining stocks had lost their popularity when many of them became worthless. The failure of practically all the savings banks in Chicago by 1877 had caused the laborers to avoid them as places for depositing their savings.

On the other hand, Chicago real estate in the central business district presented the prospect of increasing rather than declining net income, and of ultimate safety of principal, rather than the final loss of all that was invested. Rents of Chicago improved property ceased their downward movement in 1878, and, as the growth of population and the spreading-out into new quarters of families who had boarded out during the depression proceeded for a time faster than new construction, rents of the houses in the $15- to $40-a-month class advanced 25 per cent in 1879. The advance in house rents and in store rents, particularly on State and South Water streets, continued until in 1882 average rents were 75 per cent higher than in 1878. Meanwhile, the great municipal extravagance that had prevailed prior to 1873 had been sharply checked, with the result that the annual tax bill began to decline after

[7] Yield on high-grade rail bonds as computed by the National Bureau of Economic Research, cited in Philip W. Kniskern, *Real Estate Appraisal and Valuation* (1933), p. 407. For real estate loan rate in Chicago, see Fig. 80, and *Chicago Tribune*, December 28, 1879.

1874. Delinquent taxes had fallen from $500,399, or nearly 25 per cent of the total tax bill, in 1877 to $28,866, or less than 2 per cent of the total tax bill, in 1879. Suburban houses that had been empty for five years were being occupied, heavy masses of brick and masonry were being pushed up to nine stories in one section of the downtown area, and a more intensive and more profitable type of residential building, the apartment, was spreading rapidly.

Thus at this time when the return from improved Chicago real estate was about to show a marked increase, the market value of real estate had been reduced to the lowest point in years. Foreclosure proceedings affecting a considerable proportion of the property in the central business district of Chicago had run their course by 1878 and 1879. Before this process of judicial liquidation had been completed, the transfer of the properties in litigation was very difficult and cumbersome. In addition to the title-holder's equity, there were mortgages due or soon to become due which anyone buying the property had to be prepared to meet in full. Now that the former owner's equity was wiped out and the title vested in the holder of the mortgage, the property was free and clear of all incumbrances. When insurance companies owned such property they were ready to sell it for the amount of the mortgage plus interest and expenses. Thus capitalists with surplus funds for investments found bargains in real estate that would net them from 7 to 15 per cent on their investments even at the low rentals of 1878 and 1879. This high return was entirely consistent with safety, for the insurance companies which had loaned their money on Chicago property in the boom of 1872 finally reported that they had received all their money back, with interest, from the proceeds of foreclosure sales.

Thus as soon as there were surplus funds available for investment, bargains in Chicago real estate were present to attract them. In addition to the demand for income-yielding property, there arose from several sources demands for vacant ground for actual use. Business men who had reaped profits in the rise of stocks or commodities desired palatial homes which required the purchase of boulevard lots. Likewise, mechanics and laborers, whose recent experiences led them to distrust savings banks, invested part of their savings in homesites. Finally, the growth of railroads and manufacturing establishments gave rise to a demand for ground for rights of way and factory buildings.

The theory as to how improved business conditions finally affected real estate was thus stated in 1881 by E. H. Ludlow, who was at that time the oldest real estate broker in New York City:

> Good crops and business activity call for larger stores and warehouses and the rise in rents of such buildings increases their value. Then the men engaged in business want, as they make money, to live better, to move from small houses in downtown streets into their own houses in more fashionable locations. This makes a demand first for small up-town residences, then for larger ones, then for palaces. This starts the builders and their demand for vacant land increases the price for vacant land where the street improvements are completed, and this finally starts the value of land not yet ready for building and speculation follows.

The flow of the surplus profits of industry and trade into Chicago real estate for actual use and as the most attractive form of investment of funds was the first phase in the recovery of Chicago land values after the depression of 1877. The purchase and removal from the market of the most attractive offerings of central business property had the effect of raising land values to the level of the lowest asking prices of the owners who had not been forced to sell. After the chaotic and confused conditions of 1877, in which there was hardly a market for real estate at any price, there developed a cash market for "bargains" from 1878 to 1880. After the bargains resulting from foreclosure sales had been disposed of, a market developed from 1881 to 1883 with a narrower range between bid and asked prices and fewer discrepancies between properties in similar income classes or in similar locations.

B. THE SPECIFIC METHODS OF RECOVERY OF CHICAGO LAND VALUES, 1878 TO 1883

The general forces already discussed by no means diffused themselves evenly over the Chicago land area, but their influence was concentrated on certain spots, producing increases in land values in the favored localities and passing by other sections altogether. To discuss the specific mode of operation of this recovery in land values it is accordingly necessary to skip from point to point and to consider (1) the picking-up of bargains in the central business district, (2) the rise in values on Michigan Boulevard, (3) the "resurrection" of South Chicago, (4) Pullman, (5) the boom in the new Board of Trade quarter, and (6) the growth of Hyde Park, Englewood, and the outer edges of the North and West sides.

1. *Bargains in the central business district, 1879–80.*—The purchase of land on Michigan Avenue from Jackson Street to Washington Street at from $200 to $250 a front foot in 1879,[8] or 75 per cent less than the values of 1873, would seem to be no evidence of a recovery in land values. Sales made in 1879 at the rate of $333 to $400 a front foot on Wabash Avenue from Jackson to Monroe Street, of the corner of State and Madison at $1,150 a foot, and of the corner of Adams and Wells at $250 a front foot were lower than any recorded since 1873.[9] The very fact that sales were made, however, is an indication of improvement, as in the worst period of the depression in 1877 scarcely any property could be sold, so that the worst depths of the depression could not be measured. The effect of purchasing and taking from the market the greatest bargains was to raise the level of values to the next lowest stratum of offers.

2. *The boom on Michigan Boulevard, 1880.*—The parade of fashionable carriages, the feminine occupants of which were taking the opportunity to show off their expensive gowns and jewelry, proceeding slowly down the boulevards to the south parks and the Washington Park race track, was a marked feature of social life in the eighties. On one summer afternoon in 1881, 4,700 carriages moved south on Grand Boulevard.[10] Consequently when Michigan Avenue was made a boulevard in 1880 from Jackson Street to Thirty-fifth Street, it became the cynosure of all eyes. The Stock Yards magnates, who had prospered even during the depression of the seventies, found it a most convenient place to live. The bidding for Michigan Boulevard lots for fashionable homesites by 1881 sent up the front-foot values south of Twenty-sixth Street to higher prices than had been reached in the boom of 1873. The corner of Twenty-ninth and Michigan Avenue, for instance, which had sold for $330 a foot in 1874,[11] and dropped to $200 a foot in 1879,[12] had been bid up to $500 a foot in 1881 and $600 a foot in 1883,[13] while sales of inside frontage from Twenty-second Street to Thirty-seventh Street were being made at from $250 to $400 a foot in 1881.[14]

While Michigan Boulevard was thus rising in the social scale, Potter

[8] *Chicago Tribune*, June 18, 1879.
[9] *Ibid.*, September 28, 1879; October 17, 1879.
[10] *Real Estate and Building Journal*, May 12, 1883.
[11] *Chicago Tribune*, December 20, 1874.
[12] *Ibid.*, April 5, 1879.   [13] *Ibid.*   [14] *Ibid.*

Palmer, in 1882, was filling in a frog pond on the North Side and planning in 1884 to erect a mansion costing $250,000 on what was soon to be known as the Lake Shore Drive. The conversion of Washington Street into a boulevard west of Ashland Avenue had doubled its value. Prairie Avenue near Eighteenth Street, the home of the great financial and social leaders of Chicago, Marshall Field, Philip Armour, and George Pullman, still held the hegemony, as land near its $200,000 mansions reached a new high level of $700 a foot in 1882; but its supremacy was already being threatened.

3. *The "resurrection" of South Chicago, 1879–83.*—The possibilities of South Chicago and the Calumet region, first, as a canal and shipping center, and, second, as a great railroad and manufacturing center, had produced booms in that territory in 1836 and in 1873. Nothing had been done in 1836 except to plat a townsite that was later vacated; but in the boom of 1873, a harbor and docks had been constructed, the Baltimore and Ohio shops erected (1874), and a number of small industries and lumber yards had been induced to locate on the Calumet River. The revival of railroad-building suddenly gave new life to these old plans. The Chicago and Western Indiana railroad (or its corporate predecessors) was a short line that succeeded in forcing its way from the Indiana state line to Polk and Dearborn streets in Chicago; and this new line provided terminal facilities in the central business district for four new trunk railroads in the period from 1880 to 1882, namely, the Grand Trunk (1880), the Chicago and Eastern Illinois (1881), the Chicago, Indiana, and Louisville (1882), and the Erie (1882). The entry of these new lines through the Calumet region, and the entry of three other trunk lines, making a total of seven trunk lines from 1880 to 1882, stimulated plans for a belt-line railroad that would begin at East Chicago, Indiana, and circle Chicago. The wealth of transportation facilities in South Chicago and its strategic location as a meeting place of lake-borne iron ore and railroad-shipped coal from Illinois mines induced two large rolling mills to locate in South Chicago in 1880. In 1881 the Calumet and Chicago Canal and Dock Company, which owned 6,000 acres in the South Chicago region, but was unable to sell small tracts because of a $2,000,000 blanket mortgage which covered its entire holding, succeeded in paying off this mortgage by a sale of preferred stock. Its land was then put on the market in whatever sized tracts were desired for actual use. The Chicago Belt Line

Company, organized to build a great belt line around Chicago and with plans for a manufacturing city, bought the Forsythe tract of 8,000 acres around the present site of East Chicago for $1,000,000, one-third of which was paid down.[15] These schemes naturally had the effect of stimulating speculation in acre tracts throughout the Calumet region in 1881 and 1882 until some tracts were held as high as $1,000 an acre. But the belt-line scheme collapsed and the Forsythes took back their tract of land. This put a damper on the option trading and the speculative fever. A solid and substantial growth nevertheless continued. The United States Rolling Stock Company founded the town of Hegewisch in 1883. By 1883 the South Chicago region, including Hegewisch and Pullman, which had less than 2,000 population in 1880, had, as a result of the location of these new industries, a population of 16,000.

4. *Pullman.*—George Pullman, deciding in 1880 to locate his great carworks near Chicago, was followed wherever he went by a crowd of brokers and newspaper men, but he threw them off the scent by publicly inspecting land near Austin, while secretly buying 3,500 acres of land near One Hundred and Eleventh Street and Lake Calumet at from $75 to $200 an acre. In 1883, after the new works had been built, this land had risen in value to from $1,000 to $3,000 an acre. The model town of Pullman, with its own gasworks, waterworks, and sewage disposal plant, was then, as it still is, an independent center in the Chicago area, being surrounded on all sides by vacant land of lower value.

5. *The boom in the new Board of Trade Quarter.*—The decision of the Board of Trade in 1881 to move from the corner of LaSalle and Washington streets to a neglected section left vacant since the great fire of 1871 in the vicinity of Jackson and LaSalle streets had the effect of shifting the financial center of Chicago to the new region. From 1881 to 1883 the value of land on Jackson, Van Buren, Wells, and LaSalle streets near the Board of Trade advanced from $200 and $400 a front foot to from $1,500 to $2,000 a front foot, and the value of land on some of the side streets, like Sherman and Pacific, increased in an even greater ratio, from less than $200 to over $2,000 a front foot.[16] In this new quarter the best office buildings in the city were constructed from 1883

---

[15] *Real Estate and Building Journal*, August 28, 1881. Where there had not been a single house in 1880, there were 1,000 houses and a population of 5,000 in 1882.

[16] *Chicago Tribune*, July 23, 1881.

to 1885. Among the new buildings, with a total value of $7,000,000, were heavy stone and masonry structures nine stories high. One of them, the Home Insurance Building at the corner of Adams and LaSalle streets, erected in 1885, has lately been pronounced to be the first steel skeleton skyscraper, although it did not embrace all the features of such construction.[17] The era of the "skyscraper" had not quite arrived by 1885, however, for the tenants avoided the upper stories of the new buildings and revolutionary significance of the tall building was not yet realized.

The total increase in the value of land and buildings within half a mile from the Board of Trade from 1881 to 1885 was estimated by current observers at from $20,000,000 to $40,000,000. To offset this gain, however, there was a temporary decline in the rents and the land values of the old quarter at Washington and LaSalle that had been abandoned by the Board of Trade. The exodus from the old section was caused not merely by the desire to follow the Board of Trade, but by the superior type of officers and the better elevator service offered in the new financial center.

6. *The "flat craze."*—From 1881 to 1883 the tendency to live in apartments began to grow so rapidly that it was called the "flat fever" or the "flat craze." In 1883, 1,142 flat buldings, many of them poorly constructed, divided into two parts with a front parlor and a rear consisting of darkened rooms and a kitchen, were built.[18] Some of the better ones had steam heat, gas light, and porcelain bath tubs. While these flat buildings were attacked on the ground that the noises of neighboring apartments could be heard throughout the entire building, and that they were lacking in light, air, and yard space, they appealed to many housewives because of the convenience of living on one floor, the fewer servants and less furniture required, and the comfort of having the furnace cared for by the janitor. At any rate, flats were profitable to their early builders as they yielded 10 per cent net on the investment. Their coming signified a more intensive use of residential land and made possible a higher value for it. The invasion of fashionable residential districts by the apartment building, however, lowered the value of such districts for high-grade homes, and property owners in such sections frequently made private agreements to exclude them. The first apartments were built along car-line streets like Cottage

[17] *Ibid.*, October 28, 1883.   [18] *Ibid.*, December 9, 1883.

Grove Avenue, or on parts of fashionable residential streets that had begun to decline, or on medium residential streets that were in close proximity to fine homes.

7. *Growth of the outer edges of Chicago.*—Outside the city limits of the Chicago of 1880, but within the present city limits or adjacent to them, were sixty suburban towns, and villages with populations ranging from 500 to 2,000 at that time. The feature of the decade from 1880 to 1890 was the rapid growth of these small centers, as well as the growth of the city outward south of Thirty-ninth Street, west of Western Avenue to the West Side parks, and north of North Avenue until many of these independent centers became merged in a continuous line of settlement.

Of all sections, however, the growth of the South Side in population and land values was most marked. Its transportation facilities to the downtown business district were far superior to those of the North or West sides. It was not handicapped by the opening and closing of the bridges over the Chicago River, which delayed traffic crossing the river so frequently as to be a source of constant complaint. It not only had the best suburban railway service in the Illinois Central, the Rock Island, and the Michigan Southern, but to this group was added the Chicago and Eastern Illinois in 1881. Its horse-car lines had been the most numerous and had provided the fastest service, yet in 1882 its trunk State Street and Cottage Grove Avenue car lines were converted into cable lines as far south as Thirty-ninth Street, with the result that it required no more time to go to Thirty-ninth Street than was formerly needed to reach Twenty-second Street. In addition to these advantages of quick transit, there was the appeal of the fashionable avenues that led out to aristocratic Kenwood and Hyde Park and the great South Park system. The way to the better residential districts of the West Side lay through a rough and turbulent quarter teeming with uncouth foreigners, while the South Side east of State Street presented an inviting aspect all the way from the downtown district to the parks. Furthermore, the effect of the rapid growth of Pullman, South Chicago, and Hegewisch as industrial centers exerted a pull toward the South. Thus the boom on Michigan Avenue, at Pullman, and at South Chicago diffused itself over wider areas of the South Side. Stores and apartment buildings in considerable number were constructed along the Cottage Grove and State Street cable lines in the eighties and land values on these streets had doubled by 1883. Kenwood and Hyde Park were pushing north and south. Englewood was growing fast, and its business center was shifting from Wentworth Avenue to Sixty-third Street. Woodlawn at Sixty-third Street and the Illinois Central tracks, a country hamlet in 1880, was beginning to acquire stores and houses. The population of the twenty separate communities in the 48-square-mile village of Hyde Park increased from 15,000 in 1880 to 45,000 in 1883.[19]

8. *Review of the rise in land values in the Chicago area, 1878–83.*—The accumulation of new capital from the profits of trade had been invested first in 1879 and 1880 in "bargains" in central business property, offered as a result of foreclosure proceedings, and then in homesites for actual use along the boulevards. Purchases of land for railroad yards and rights of way and for new manufacturing centers had caused a remarkable increase in land values in a few locations by 1881. The shifting of the Board of Trade to new quarters had caused a sensational advance in the southwest corner of the downtown area. The purchase of homesites by laborers and speculative purchases had diffused the advances that had begun in a few spots over a wider area. By 1883 Chicago land values had been stabilized on a basis that on the average was thought to be approximately equal to the peak prices of 1873 for land within the city limits, with an average recovery of about 40 per cent in value from the depression of 1877. It was admitted that the value of suburban lands, except in a few favored localities, was still far below the prices of ten years before. In fact, within the old city itself, while there were some sections, as in the case of Michigan Boulevard, the new Board of Trade quarters, and portions of the South and North sides, where the land values of 1883 exceeded the 1873 peaks, there were other sections that had deteriorated. In particular, that part of the West Side from Fulton to Madison Street, west of Halsted Street to Ashland Avenue, was on the downgrade because of its poor improvements and its nondescript population. The northern and eastern parts of the central business district had not recovered the values of 1873. The favorite scenes of speculation of the decade before—the land near the south and west parks—still languished dismally.

Real estate brokers and landowners in 1883, however, were disposed to view the situation with equanimity. After all the storms they had passed through and after all the gyrations of land values it seemed that

[19] *Ibid.*, January 6, 1884.

values had reached a normal level. Some seventeen hundred of the obsolete types of houses were vacant; there was an oversupply of the poorer types of flats; the purchasers of suburban lots and acres had been taught a lesson they would not soon forget, and most of the owners of downtown business property who had mortgaged it heavily to erect a fine building in 1872 now possessed neither land nor buildings. The new owners found the situation satisfactory. Most property was clear of all incumbrances. The interest rate on the best mortgages had fallen to 5 per cent by 1881.[20] The best income property yielded 10-30 per cent net on the investment. Under no pressure to sell, these holders could view the extreme fluctuations of the last ten years as evidence of mental disturbances which would be avoided as men learned the true principles of land valuation. Thus the editor of the *Real Estate and Building Journal* described the past:

> Real estate has had for the past decade a fitful history—the feeling changing from dismay amid the ash heaps to furious speculation and back again [to dismay], then softening into apprehension, then into half belief and finally into full confidence. Any individual who should successively exhibit these grades of feeling with half the force with which they were felt by the public at large would be sent to a lunatic asylum. During the prevalence of them real estate went to the bow-wows. But as the land itself remained fixed, without a change of countenance (except for the better in its improvement by buildings and lawns) the market worked around all right again. We are of the opinion that it is more than a lucid interval. It is a graduation to fixed and downright common sense in land dealing and history has made a good deal of literature which can be profitably used as a text for dealers to consult in the future.[21]

Again he comments on the return to normal:

> If the statistics were published of the rise and downfall of prices and their latest return to a just value, a panorama of the emotions and acts it caused would prove perplexing but interesting. There would be found a good deal of romance, considerable fiction, something of libel, immensity of imagination, bottomless depths of despondency, astronomic altitudes of enthusiasm and general derangement of system and precedent.[22]

During this period of "stability," in the latter part of 1882, Mr. J. G. Cozzens of the Citizens' Association, after a tabulation of sales of land in all parts of the city, concluded that the average value of the 121,002 lots in the city limits was $3,168 or a total value of $383,328,000 for all

---

[20] *Ibid.*, August 13, 1881.

[21] *Real Estate and Building Journal*, November 20, 1880.

[22] *Ibid.*, November 13, 1880.

the land within the city limits.[23] This would indicate at least a full recovery of land values within the city limits to the peak values of 1873, if contrasted with the writer's own estimate of $360,000,000 for the same area in 1873. The recovery in land values outside the city limits of 1883 and inside the present city limits had not exceeded 50 per cent

TABLE V

VALUE OF CHICAGO LAND BY PRINCIPAL USES, 1876–83
(In Dollars per Front Foot)

CLASS OF PROPERTY	DATE			SAMPLE LOCATION (STREETS)
	Jan. 1, 1876	Jan. 1, 1879	Jan. 1, 1883	
First-class retail.............	$2,000	$1,500	$3,000	State
Banks and offices...........	1,250	1,100	2,000	LaSalle, Washington
Wholesale business..........	700	600	1,500	Wabash, Franklin
Second-class retail..........	500	400	600	N. Clark, W. Madison
Local business...............	400	300	400	Twenty-second
Local business...............	200	150	250	Cottage Grove, Thirty-fifth, Thirty-ninth
Aristocratic residence.......	350	250	600	Michigan, Prairie, Calumet
First-class residence........	200	200	300	Dearborn, Indiana
First-class residence, West Side	....	150	200	Ashland, Washington
First-class residence, 3 miles out...................	150	150	150	Avenues near Twenty-ninth
First-class residence, 3½ miles out...................	125	125	125	Avenues near Thirty-first
First-class residence, 4 miles out...................	100	90	100	Avenues near Thirty-fifth
First-class residence, 4½ miles out...................	90	75	85	Langley, Vincennes
Medium residence...........	65	50	65	All divisions
Mechanics' residences.......	50	40	50	All divisions
Laborers' residences.........	30	20	40	All divisions
Laborers' cheap residences...	12	10	20	All divisions
Fashionable suburban.......	60	45	60	Hyde Park, Evanston
Genteel suburban...........	20	15	30	Englewood

of the 1873 values, and the total value of this outer belt was not over $100,000,000 in 1883. The total land value of the area within the present city limits of Chicago was therefore approximately $485,000,000 in 1883 as compared with $575,000,000 in 1873. The value of different types of property per front foot at the beginning of 1883 was indicated as shown in Table V by Frank R. Chandler.[24]

[23] *Ibid.*, September 30, 1882.
[24] *Ibid.*, January, 1883.

THE FIRST SKYSCRAPERS AND THE WORLD'S FAIR 141

C. THE PERIOD FROM 1884 TO 1886

The recession in general business activity in 1883.—The upward movement in the volume of production and in wholesale prices that had been in progress since 1879 was checked in 1883 when a reverse movement began. The prices of staple commodities like wheat and pig iron declined. The value of the 145 most active stocks on the New York Stock market—mostly railroad securities—fell from three to two billion dollars during 1883.[25] Thousands of "lambs" who had been dabbling in stocks lost their small savings. New railroad construction was sharply contracted.

The effect on Chicago trade and manufactures was shown by the decline in the number employed in manufactures from 114,457 in 1883 to 105,725 in 1884 and in the fall in the combined value of manufactures, wholesale, and produce trade from $1,050,000,000 in 1883 to $933,000,000 in 1884.[26]

The effect on the real estate market of this recession in general business activity was to check any further advance in house and store rents, which had climbed steadily from 1879 to 1882, and to put a damper for the time on any further upward tendencies in land values. Labor troubles also seemed to furnish a disquieting element. A bricklayers' strike in the spring of 1883 slightly checked building activity. The more serious Haymarket riot of 1886 evoked considerable mistrust among eastern capitalists.

The volume of real estate sales and of new construction dropped only slightly in 1884, however, and during the sharp decline that occurred in commodities and stocks. Chicago land values remained firm without any recorded decline. The real estate market, while sensitive to changing business conditions, does not fluctuate as rapidly as the more volatile stocks.

While land booms were being generated in Los Angeles, Seattle, Kansas City, Omaha, Duluth, Minneapolis, and many other cities which reached their peaks in 1887, the Chicago land market was slowly increasing its volume as the result of a steady growth of population and a continuous demand for lots on the edge of the built-up area. There were few evidences of speculation and only moderate increases in land values during this quiet period.

[25] *Chicago Tribune,* January 1, 1884.
[26] *Ibid.,* January 1, 1885; *Industrial Chicago,* III, 194.

D. SPECIAL FACTORS IN THE MOVEMENT OF CHICAGO LAND VALUES FROM 1886 TO 1894

The Chicago land market from 1886 to 1894 was influenced to a remarkable degree by a series of special factors, which will be discussed separately for the sake of clarity, before their combined effect is described in the tone and temper of the market itself. The reasons for the extraordinary growth in land values during this period in the central business district and the South Side, while land values in the old intermediate residential belt were stagnant and while the value of suburban acres on the west and northwest sides were rising only moderately, can best be explained by a consideration of the following forces: (1) the growth of Chicago railroads and manufactures, 1886–94; (2) the growth of internal transportation systems, 1886–94; (3) steel-frame skyscrapers, 1885–94; (4) annexation, 1889; (5) the World's Columbian Exposition, 1887–94; and (6) department stores and apartments.

1. *The growth of Chicago railroads and manufactures, 1886–94.*—From 1886 to 1889, inclusive, five trunk railroad lines—the Wisconsin Central (1886), the Sante Fe (1887), the Chicago Great Western (1887), the Illinois Central (West) (1888), and the Cleveland, Cincinnati, Chicago and St. Louis (Big Four) (1889)—entered Chicago.[27] In the two decades from 1870 to 1890 the mileage of railroads entering Chicago had increased 370 per cent; their tonnage 490 per cent. These railroads affected land values in a variety of ways. First, their direct demand for land for rights of way, freight yards, shops, and terminals gave a cash value to some land that had long lain dormant, and changed the character of the use of other tracts. Thus the purchase of land for freight yards by the Santa Fe in 1887 doubled the value of land in the vicinity of Thirty-fifth and Central Park Avenue, and its purchase of land along State Street from Sixteenth to Polk Street, to gain additional terminal facilities, completed the conversion of that old vice and slum area into railroad land. It thereby hastened the shift of the vice area southward. Second, new railroads furnishing a suburban service greatly increased the value of land along that portion of their route that was within commuting distance from the city. The building of the Wisconsin Central in 1886 through the territory of Douglas Park greatly increased the population and land values of that territory in the next few years. Third, the entry of so many railroads into Chicago

[27] *Tan*, op. cit.

THE FIRST SKYSCRAPERS AND THE WORLD'S FAIR 143

made the problem of transferring freight between them an increasingly important one. To solve this problem a plan was proposed for the construction of a great clearing yard on a 1,200-acre tract about 10 miles southwest of the city. The land in this so-called Stickney tract was purchased by a syndicate in 1887. Nothing was actually done on this project during the period under discussion (1887-94), but its existence led to many rumors and the possibilities of its exploitation as a site for factories, mills, and packing plants was the chief cause of wild speculation in acre tracts in that vicinity in 1889 and 1890. In addition to the Stickney plan, many other belt-line projects were formulated in this period. These belt lines were usually projected to start at the lake front in the Calumet region and to swing from thence in a circle around Chicago. The Chicago and Calumet Terminal Railroad was organized on July 2, 1886, and the Elgin, Joliet and Eastern Railroad, the outer belt, was chartered on March 18, 1887. The latter road traced a wide arc around Chicago passing through Porter, Dyer, Joliet, and Waukegan. Fourth, the chief significance of these belt-line railroads from the land-value standpoint was the fact that they were linked up with the establishment of new manufacturing projects. At this time there was a rush of manufacturing concerns to locate in the Chicago area to obtain the advantage of its superior terminal facilities and favorable railroad rates. The promoters of the belt lines not only contracted to buy huge tracts, like the Forsythe tract of 8,000 acres at East Chicago and 2,000 acres near Tolleston, Indiana, but they made deals with the manufacturers to locate on sites to be selected by them. Farm land far from any transportation was bought at farm-land prices, belt lines projected through the site selected, manufacturing plants projected along the projected belt, townsites platted and lots sold to clerks in the city. Schemes for belt lines and manufacturing towns were one of the most prominent features of the acre and lot sales of 1889 and 1890. They contributed toward the direction of speculative activity to the suburbs and to new towns as far as forty miles from Chicago.

a) The growth of manufacturing.—The growth of manufacturing in the Chicago area was exceptional, the number of employees and the value of manufactured products almost doubling from 1884 to 1890, as Table VI shows.[28] The census figures for 1890 are not strictly comparable with the statistics for the other years collected by local authorities,

[28] *Industrial Chicago*, III, 194.

as the census figures included many small firms not previously counted. A peak was unquestionably reached in 1890, however, that was higher than the returns for 1891, even with the products of small firms deducted. The rapid increase in the number employed and the wages paid from 1885 to 1890 as indicated by Table VI accounts to a great extent for the rapid increase in "cheap" lot sales in this period, for it is when workers are fully employed that they accumulate small surplus funds for investment.

TABLE VI

CHICAGO MANUFACTURES 1884–93, SHOWING NUMBER OF WAGE-EARNERS, AMOUNT OF WAGES PAID, AND VALUE OF PRODUCT

Year	No. Employed in Manufactures	Wages Paid (Millions of Dollars)	Value of Product (Millions of Dollars)
1884	105,725	$ 48.1	$292.2
1885	109,625	51.2	316.9
1886	126,430	67.7	349.7
1887	134,615	74.6	403.1
1888	132,016	73.4	401.2
1889	151,070	84.5	452.2
1890	210,336	124.0	664.6
1891	180,870	104.9	567.0
1892	186,085	114.3	586.3
1893	171,700	99.2	574.5

2. *Internal transportation, 1887–94.*—A succession of devices for faster means of local transportation followed each other rapidly in this period, enabling people to skip the intermediate areas partially filled with obsolete houses occupied by the poorer classes and seek homesites where the houses were new and the neighborhood had not acquired an adverse character. These devices were (1) cable lines, (2) elevated steam railroads, and (3) electric surface lines.[29]

The South Side again led the way until the end of this period. By 1882 it had cables on its main trunk lines of travel, State and Cottage Grove Avenue, and in 1887 before cable lines had been put in operation on either the North or the West sides, the State Street cable was extended to Sixty-third Street and the Cottage Grove cable was extended to Sixty-seventh Street, with a branch running down Fifty-fifth Street

[29] See maps of the Chicago street-car lines in 1891 (Fig. 24).

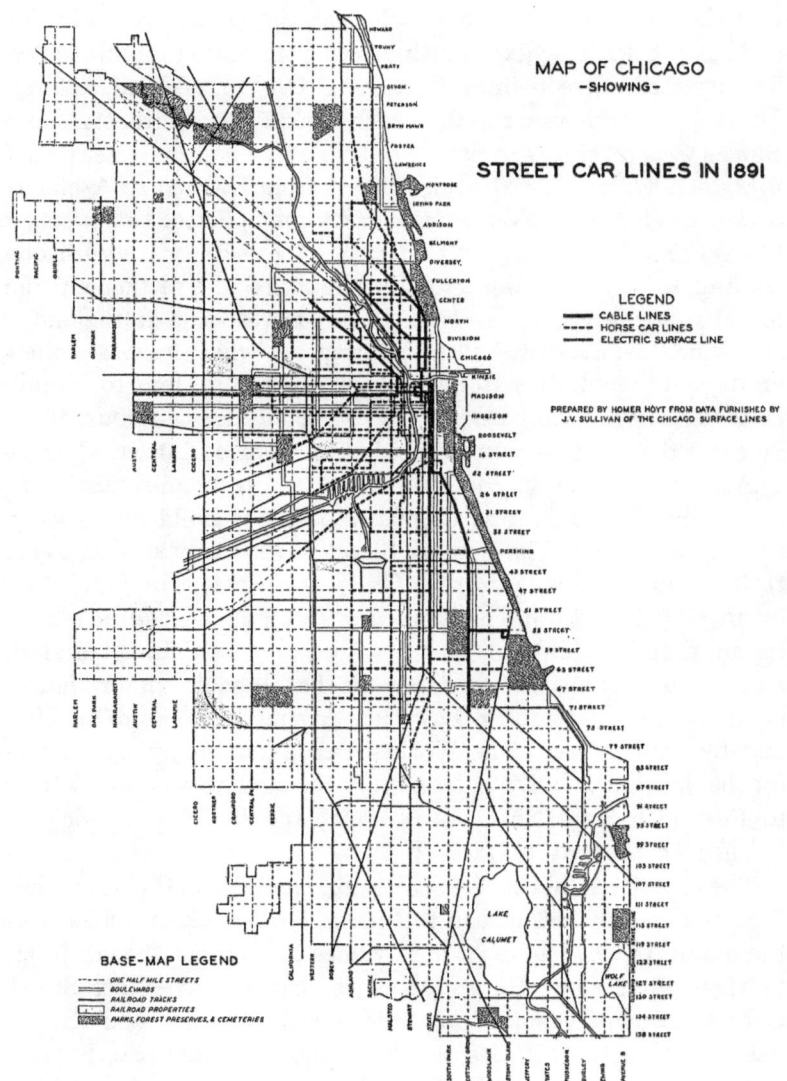

Fig. 24

to Lake Park Avenue. To supplement the cable, horse-car lines on cross-streets such as Sixty-ninth Street from State to Ashland Avenue, Twenty-sixth Street from Cottage Grove to Halsted, Thirty-fifth Street from State Street to the South Fork, Forty-third Street from the Illinois Central tracks to State Street, Forty-seventh Street from State to Ashland Avenue, Sixty-third Street from Halsted to Ashland Avenue, and Vincennes Avenue from Sixty-ninth Street to Seventy-ninth Street, were built from 1887 to 1889. A five-cent fare with one free transfer to any cross-line greatly stimulated the settlement and rise in value of the vacant lands on the southwest side at the end of the cross-lines. Not satisfied with this progress, which increased the speed on its main trunk lines from the horse-car rate of four to six miles an hour to the cable-car rate of nine to twelve miles an hour, the South Side was the first to secure elevated steam transportation, which moved express trains at a speed of fourteen to fifteen miles an hour. The South Side Rapid Transit Company began to build its structure between Twelfth and Thirty-ninth Street in 1890, and started to operate trains from Congress Street to Thirty-ninth Street in June, 1892. Its future course south of Thirty-ninth Street was decided in 1891 to the extent that it would run in the alley between Calumet and Prairie avenues, but for a time it was thought that its southern terminus would be at Seventy-first and St. Lawrence Avenue or even at One Hundred and Eleventh Street. The World's Fair undoubtedly was responsible for the decision to build to Jackson Park. Its line was completed south to Fifty-fifth Street in October, 1892, and by May 1, 1893, it was finished all the way to Jackson Park.

The superiority of the transportation facilities on the South Side and their steady improvement in this period are among the chief causes of the uninterrupted rise in its land values throughout the era from 1882 to 1890. First, along the routes of the cable lines—State Street and Cottage Grove Avenue—there were steady building and rise of land values during the eighties; second, along the horse-car lines, which acted as feeders for the cable lines, values rose as virgin acre tracts were open for settlement; and, third, along the route of the "Alley L" and near its stations on cross-town streets land values rose rapidly in this period. "Transfer corners," or corners where two street-car lines intersected, first acquired a high value for business purposes, as the corners of Thirty-fifth and Thirty-ninth and Cottage Grove Avenue and

Thirty-first and Indiana Avenue attained peaks not before reached outside the central business district.

The North and West sides were lagging far behind the South Side at this time in transit facilities. They were both handicapped by the bridge evil at first as both the LaSalle and the Washington Street tunnels were not kept in repair for horse-vehicle or pedestrian traffic.[30] The North Side improved its service by building its first cable lines on Clark Street from Diversey to the downtown section, and on Wells Street from Illinois Street to Lincoln Park, in 1888. These cable lines entered the main business district through the LaSalle Street tunnel. Additional North Side cable lines were constructed on Lincoln Avenue from Center to Fullerton and on Clybourn Avenue from Division to Fullerton Avenue in 1890. A further improvement in transportation was furnished by the building of the Chicago and Evanston Railroad along the north shore near the lake. Land values along the North Side advanced along the routes of these new transit lines, but the service of the North Side cable, on account of frequent breakages, was said to be greatly inferior to that of the South Side cable. Furthermore, the North Side could not match the frequent suburban train service of the South Side.

The West Side had the poorest transportation service of all at this time. Its horse-car lines running east and west, to and from the main business district, were the slowest in the city, the Harrison Street line barely making four miles an hour and cross-lines running north and south being almost wholly lacking. It was not until 1890 that a cable line was completed on Madison Street from the downtown area west to Crawford Avenue. By 1891, however, cable lines were completed on Milwaukee to Armitage, and on Halsted Street and Blue Island Avenue. These cable lines entered the main business district through the Washington Street tunnel. In 1890 an electric surface line, the Cicero and Proviso Electric, was completed from the end of the Madison Street cable line on Madison Street to Harlem Avenue, and this line caused a rise in land values along its route. The building of the Wisconsin Central Railroad in 1886 had raised land values in the vicinity of Douglas Park. An ordinance for an elevated line on Lake Street had been passed on December 18, 1888; but the company building it went

---

[30] The Washington Street tunnel was completed January 1, 1869, and the LaSalle Street tunnel was opened July 4, 1871 (Moses and Kirkland, *op. cit.*, I, 145).

through many vicissitudes and it was not until November 6, 1893, that it was in operation from Market and Madison streets to Lake and California Avenue. Meanwhile, a comprehensive scheme for West Side elevated transportation was formulated in the Metropolitan Elevated Company, but this project did not become an actuality until 1895.

a) The cable loops.—By 1890 three separate cable systems, from the South, North, and West sides, respectively, after collecting the passengers from their tributary horse-car lines and ancillary cable systems, carried them through three separate gateways to the main business section and deposited them along a brief loop which each cable line transcribed in the central area.[31] Long before the elevated loop became an accomplished fact, downtown business men were taught the value of a traffic loop which deposited the passengers gathered from a wide residential area into a limited business area. The oldest loop, formed by the South Side cables in 1882, inclosed the section between State Street, Wabash Avenue, Lake Street, and Madison Street. It contributed greatly to the rise of business frontage values at State and Madison streets. The loop made by the North Side cables in 1888 was formed by the North Side cable lines turning from Clark to LaSalle Street at Illinois Street, thence running south on LaSalle Street to Monroe Street, east on Monroe Street to Dearborn Street, north on Dearborn Street to Randolph Street and west on Randolph Street to LaSalle Street. This loop was one of the chief causes for the sudden rise of Dearborn Street from a place of obscurity to one of the most prominent office streets of Chicago in 1889, as it was also the cause of the decline in the value of North Clark Street south of Illinois Street where the cable line turned from Clark Street. The West Side cables, entering the central business district through the Washington Street tunnel, formed a loop around the section from Randolph to Madison streets and Wells to LaSalle streets. The cable lines on Randolph Street and LaSalle Street that were built from 1888 to 1890 were undoubtedly a factor in prompting the location of a number of new skyscrapers on these streets, reversing the southward flow of business that had begun with the migration of the Board of Trade.

b) Projected elevated and surface lines.—Not merely the lines that were actually constructed, but visionary lines that were projected by promoters but never built had a great influence on the speculative real

[31] See Fig. 24 for a map of transportation lines in 1891.

THE FIRST SKYSCRAPERS AND THE WORLD'S FAIR 149

estate market of 1889 and 1890. In the welter of projects that were discussed or that were started but could not overcome all the obstacles to obtaining the consent of property owners, securing an ordinance from the city council, and raising the necessary capital, it was difficult for the average lot-buyer to decide which transportation lines would succeed and which would fail. Even in the case of lines already partly constructed, it was often not known where the termini would finally be located. Nearly every subdivision was sold under the assurance that an elevated line or electric street-car line would run directly past the buyer's lot, or as close as it would be desirable to have it run. Had all the projected lines been actually constructed, the city and its suburbs would have been gridironed with elevated and electric lines. As these transportation schemes by their number and variety confused land-buyers, and as some of these illusions had more effect on the market of 1889 and 1890 than the actual construction of lines did on the market of 1896, it may be well to mention some of them. There were abortive elevated lines like the Chicago, Cook County Passenger and Dummy Railroad, which secured the consent of the majority of the owners for an elevated line along Milwaukee Avenue; the Milwaukee Alley Elevated Company; and North Side elevated lines that were to run from the downtown business district to Evanston, such as the Chicago and Evanston Elevated Railrod and Transit Company, the Cass Street, Lake View and Evanston Railroad Company, the Chicago Transit, and the Citizen's Rapid Transit Company. There were South Side schemes like the Calumet Transportation Company (from Blue Island to Chicago), the proposed elevation of the Rock Island Railroad, the Forsythe Elevated Railroad Company (to run from the Indiana state line to Chicago), a State Street elevated line, and an elevated line that was to run on Sixty-third Street and southwest through Englewood. Again there was the Chicago North and South Elevated Railroad Company that was to run north and south from city limits to city limits on Halsted Street. All these plans, vividly set forth by their promoters and acted upon as almost certain of realization in 1890, had died a natural death by 1891.[32]

3. *Steel-frame skyscrapers, 1885–94.*—Before 1880 there were few buildings in Chicago exceeding six stories in height, and none higher than eight stories. Crude elevators, worked by hand power, imposed

[32] *Chicago Tribune*, April 12, 1892.

the first limitation on vertical expansion. As elevators were improved by the use of water, steam, and electric power, it was found that the increased weight of the stone and masonry on the ground floor that was necessary to support additional stories curtailed the valuable first-floor space. Furthermore, not only did the expense of the foundations increase at a disproportionate rate for each additional story added, but an absolute limit to height was soon reached when the base, no matter how massive, would support no more weight. Even with these handicaps, there was the expanding demand for floor space in a limited area which exerted a strong pressure from 1881 to 1885 to raise the height of buildings in the new Board of Trade quarters. The height limit on five buildings was pushed up to nine stories and, finally, by 1884 and 1885, to eleven and twelve stories. One of these buildings, the Home Insurance Building, started in 1884 at the corner of LaSalle and Adams streets, had a steel frame. While not generally recognized at the time, its architects had hit upon a principle that was to revolutionize office-building construction. The weight of the upper floors was no longer to rest upon the first floor, but a steel frame like a basket supported each floor at its own level, so that the masonry on the top of the steel frame could be built first if desired. The chief limitation to the height to which buildings could not be pushed upward was imposed by the increasing space needed for elevators.

The Home Insurance Building was somewhat of a compromise between the old and the new types of construction, so that the full possibilities of the new method were not at first recognized or appreciated. In fact, the upper floors of these nine-story buildings were at first avoided by tenants, and there was a period of hesitation in which new buildings were planned with foundation strong enough to support nine stories, but which were first to be carried only to a height of only seven stories. With the completion of so many new office buildings in the Board of Trade quarters, some of which were only partially filled, there seemed, moreover, no pressing need for more and higher buildings.

The tide turned in favor of the skyscraper in 1888 and 1889 when the Tacoma Building at the northeast corner of Madison and LaSalle Street, a thirteen-story building of out-and-out steel-skeleton type, was started and finished. The popularity of the upper floors on account of the abundance of air and light had been conclusively demonstrated. The success of the first tall buildings, made possible by their scarcity, by the prestige of having an office in them, and by the fact that the sites for them had been purchased at values based on the income of six-story buildings, started a craze to put up skyscrapers that was not to be explained by economic considerations of net income alone. While the prospectus of these buildings always presented an attractive income set-up on the assumption that all the offices would be rented, which would probably have provided incentive enough in the gullible days of 1889, other non-commercial motives played an important part. There had been no general advance in office rents and, in fact, a decline in the Board of Trade quarters. It was estimated in 1885 that seven-hundred new offices were required annually, but in the period from 1885 to 1888, thirty-three hundred new offices had been built, of which five hundred were vacant.[33]

In spite of this apparent lack of need for more office space, great structures were erected. The Auditorium, finished in 1889, had been built as a civic enterprise by a stock subscription of wealthy men to provide a hall for national political conventions. The eighteen-story Masonic Temple was financed by the sale of stock to Masons on the plea that it would not only be profitable but would provide lodge halls and be a monument to their order. The Medinah Temple was a similar lodge enterprise. A projected thirty-four-story Odd Fellows Temple, however, proved to be a castle in the air. The example of the Auditorium was followed in the case of many other buildings. In this period a total of twenty-one buildings was constructed out of the proceeds of the sale of stocks and bonds—$15,500,000 in stocks, and $6,000,000 in bonds—to wealthy men. As ninety-nine-year leases had become popular and it was possible to make loans upon them, some of these buildings were constructed by promoters with very little cash capital.

The financial success of these new skyscrapers was, until the end of the World's Fair in 1893, greater than might have been anticipated. Tenants poured out of the old buildings, now rapidly becoming obsolete, into the new and more modern quarters that had better elevator service, more ornate fixtures, and more light and air.[34] This exodus was facilitated in many cases by the assumption of old leases by the agents

[33] *Ibid.*, March 25, 1888.

[34] For an impression by a contemporary writer of the prestige attached to an office in a skyscraper see Henry Blake Fuller's novel, *The Cliff-Dwellers* (New York: Harper & Bros., 1893).

of the new buildings. A large demand for office space sprang up from the new manufacturing concerns that were locating in or near Chicago at this time. Other tenants were secured from the increasing numbers of people who were entering the real estate business, and from promoters of enterprises for the World's Fair, who sought to enhance their prestige by having an office in these popular skyscrapers. Doctors and dentists found that it paid to have an office in high buildings near the State Street stores. Department stores discovered that people preferred to ascend in elevators rather than walk a block to a side street. Thus vertical rather than lateral expansion became the order of the day, and some of these structures paid handsome returns, for a time, even on their common stock.

The high buildings were well distributed over the downtown area. There was a group at the south end of the business district mainly on Dearborn Street, such as the sixteen-story Monadnock Building (1891), sixteen-story Manhattan Building (1893), the Old Colony Building (1893), the Ellsworth Building (1893), the Marquette Building (1894), the Great Northern Hotel (1893), and the Hartford Building (1894). There was another group along LaSalle Street such as the Stock Exchange Building, the Y.M.C.A. Building, and the New York Life Building. Still another group was located at the north end of the central business district on Randolph and Washington streets, such as the eighteen-story Masonic Temple (1891), the Ashland Block (1891), the German Theater Building (1891), the Cook County Abstract (now Chicago Title and Trust) Building (1891), and the Unity Building (now American Bond and Mortgage Building) (1891) on Dearborn Street near Randolph. The Columbus Memorial Building, the Reliance Building, and the Champlain Building were erected on State Street from Washington to Madison streets. These buildings were regarded as so many anchors to hold trade in their vicinity, and the large number of tenants concentrated in these structures did have a tendency to enhance the value of surrounding business property.

The advent of the skyscraper was responsible for a marked increase in ground values in the central business district of Chicago from 1889 to 1891. Although the twenty-five or thirty buildings from twelve to sixteen stories in height erected from 1889 to 1894 if bunched together would not have occupied more than three solid blocks, or 7 per cent of the main business district, all land in that area was revalued on the basis of what it would produce if occupied by a sixteen-story building. "Tear down that old rat trap and erect a sixteen-story building" became the slogan of 1889, and if the owner of the land did not actually erect one himself, he constructed a hypothetical sixteen-story building on his land to determine what his land would be worth to someone who did want to put up such a building. Had all these lots in the downtown area been covered with skyscrapers, there would, of course, have been a vast oversupply of offices which would have caused a reduction in rents to a point that would have nullified these calculations. The result of revaluing the ground on the basis of what it would yield if improved to the best advantage was that the income on old buildings dropped to 2 per cent on the higher land value. Stories were added to buildings whose foundations were strong enough to stand it, and other old structures were remodeled and modernized to enable them to hold their tenants in the face of the new competition. Skyscrapers thus increased the potential floor space that could be obtained from the same ground area. It was, however, the more intensive use of the ground floor areas due to the increased number of shoppers rather than the taller buildings that was responsible for higher land values in the retail shopping centers on State Street.

Opposition to the skyscraper had begun to develop even in 1889. It came first from the owners of property on the edge of the main business district and on secondary business streets who wanted business to expand laterally rather than vertically. Second, it came from the owners of some skyscrapers already erected who wanted to enjoy a monopoly advantage. Third, it came from owners of old buildings who objected to the assessment of their land for taxation on the basis of its use for a tall building. These various interests were successful in securing the passage of an ordinance in 1893, limiting the height of buildings to 130 feet, or virtually ten stories. A few taller buildings were put up afterward under special permits secured before the passage of the ordinance. As there was an oversupply of high office buildings by 1894, this ordinance did not have a pronounced restrictive tendency of itself, as other forces were coinciding with it to check further skyscraper construction.

4. *Annexation.*—On June 29, 1889, by an affirmative popular vote of both the city and the townships affected, a territory of 120 square miles was annexed to Chicago. By the addition of the townships of

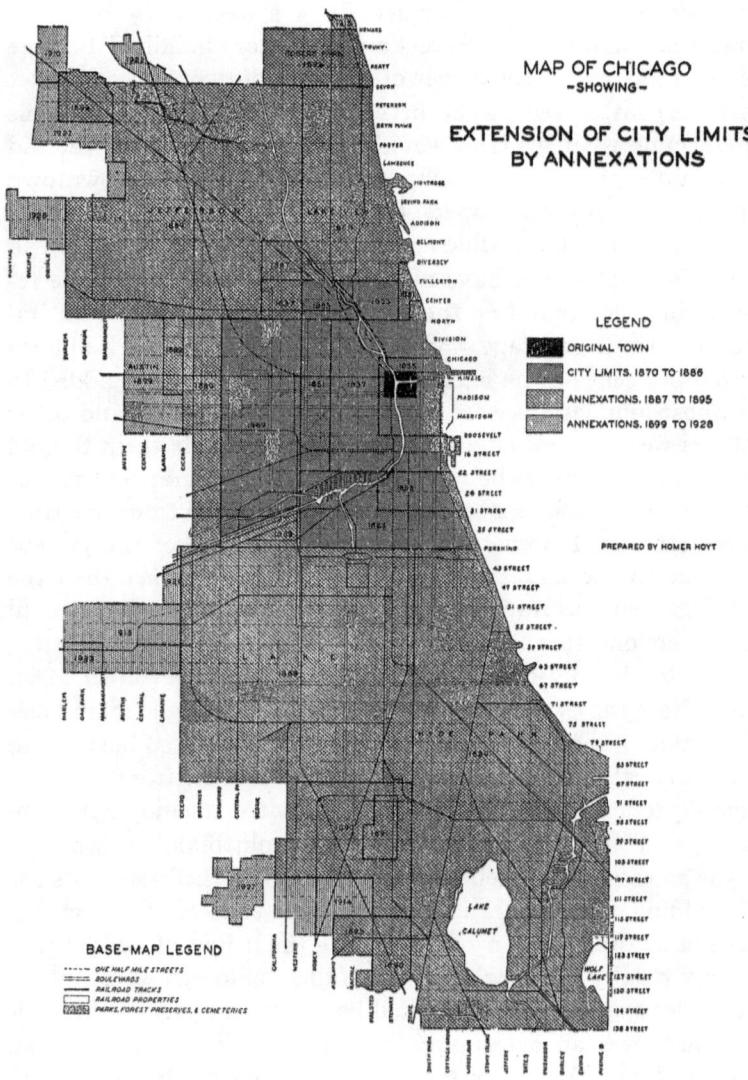

FIG. 25

THE FIRST SKYSCRAPERS AND THE WORLD'S FAIR 155

Hyde Park, Lake, Lake View, Jefferson, and part of Cicero, the area within the city limits was increased from 36 to 169 square miles.[35] With the addition of over two hundred thousand people in the new territory, Chicago had over a million population and became the second largest city in the United States.

The actual effect of annexation could easily be overestimated. The annexed territory had long been closely associated with Chicago. The formal extension of the city limits did, it is true, exert an important influence in enabling the outlying territory to secure city water service, sewers, pavements, and police and fire protection, which were most important factors in securing a favorable vote.[36] The psychological effect of the announcement that Chicago was a city of over a million people, however, coming at a time when other cities were using every possible method to swell their population figures by adding suburban areas and even padding the census figures, drew the particular attention of the nation to the remarkable growth of Chicago in sixty years and aided it in securing the World's Fair. From a subdivider's standpoint, a great expanse of prairie had been brought inside the city limits, to which city water, sewers, and pavements might be extended or projected and which could be platted and sold as Chicago city lots.

5. *The World's Fair.*—The fact that a World's Fair to celebrate the four-hundredth anniversary of the voyage of Christopher Columbus would probably be held somewhere in the United States in 1892 led to anticipations as early as 1887 that Chicago would be selected as the site. The Chicago members of Congress worked with such astuteness to effect political combinations to bring this about that by 1889 Chicago was considered the probable choice of Congress. Although New York was a serious contender for the honor, with St. Louis and Washington as other candidates, Chicago received the majority vote of Congress on February 25, 1890. This favorable action had already been largely anticipated by local real estate men, but non-resident owners of Chicago property were so surprised that they advanced the

---

[35] For details as to area annexed at this time, and as to other smaller areas annexed shortly afterward, see Fig. 25.

[36] This was particularly important in the township of Jefferson according to a statement made to the writer in September, 1933, by William H. Spikings, an old resident. These advantages were not so great in the case of that part of Hyde Park near Fifty-third Street and Lake Park Avenue which had its own waterworks. Here there was strong opposition to annexation, according to John E. Cornell, a son of Paul Cornell, the founder of Hyde Park.

prices of their holdings 25 per cent or withdrew them from the market altogether.

After Chicago had been selected as a site, there was a baffling delay of over six months before it was decided in what part or parts of the city the Fair would be held. At first there were proposals for dividing the Fair into two sections, giving part to the South Side and part to the West or North sides. A united Fair was next decided upon, and the first location picked for it was on the lake front near the downtown area on two hundred acres of ground to be made on the lake front for that purpose. In spite of a majority decision in favor of the lake-front site, a minority, led by Lyman J. Gage, influenced partly by the fear that the manufacture of so much new land would lower the value of central business property, induced the World's Fair Commission to select Jackson Park as the main site of the Fair.[37] The lake front, however, was to be retained as the gateway to the Fair. West Side politicians then attempted some machinations with the state legislature that would put Jackson Park out of the running. The South Park Commissioners had sought permission to issue bonds to drain Jackson Park, the cost of which was to be borne by the people as part of the permanent expense of improving the park, for it was believed that those promoting the Fair would not incur this cost when other sites already improved were available. Those favoring the West Side parks as a site for the Fair sought to prevent a law authorizing this South Park bond issue from being passed. This indirect attack failed, however, and the West and North sides were eliminated as possibilities. The exact location of the Fair was not yet settled. The idea of extending the Fair along the lake front north of Jackson Park was abandoned and the consent to use the Midway in addition to Jackson Park was obtained from the South Park Commissioners. The request made in September, 1890, for the use of Washington Park also started a wild boom in lots along Cottage Grove Avenue from Forty-ninth to Sixtieth streets, but this movement collapsed when the South Park Commissioners refused permission. After many months of vacillation, the selection of Jackson Park and the Midway as the only site of the Fair was finally made.

The expectation that Jackson Park would be the final choice as the site of the Fair had already caused land values near by to rise to what

[37] *Chicago Tribune*, September 13, 1890.

the real estate editor of the *Chicago Tribune* called "crack-brained altitudes." The chances of the West and North sides had always seemed so remote that they never had an appreciable land boom on the possibility of securing the Fair. The imagination of the times alternated from speculation about the site of the Fair to the actual content of the Fair itself. Some of the bizarre and grandiose conceptions of projected World's Fair towers may give the readers an idea of the extravagant fancies of a boom era.[38]

The effect of the World's Fair on land values in the vicinity of Jackson Park and the Midway had been almost fully discounted before the end of 1890, nearly three years before the Fair opened its gates. In the meantime, during 1891 and 1892 landowners in that vicinity sought to realize something on their investment in land which they were unable to sell at a profit by building World's Fair hotels and apartments. Many of these were built along Fifty-fifth Street and near Jackson Park. The extravagant hopes that were entertained as to the possible income to be derived from World's Fair guests were doomed to grievous disappointment. The crowds were slow in coming, the full peak of attendance lasted only a short time, and soon after the close of the Fair most of these projects were in the hands of receivers. The low rents at which the vacant apartments were offered in the winter of 1893–94 attracted tenants from all parts of the city to this section.

The Fair proved to be a great disappointment to the hopes of real estate owners. While its construction was going on, many potential buyers waited for the reaction in land values which was expected to take place after it closed. While it was open and attracting the greatest

[38] The following were some of the proposed projects submitted by various people in 1890: "Buildings 50 stories high, amphitheatres to hold 100,000 people, a building 1000 feet high in the form of an eagle, a rotating coliseum, a building six stories high resting on metal replicas of the animals mentioned in Revelations, a building with 42 towers representing each of the states, a collection of vast halls under a single roof, a combined park and opera house, a Tower of Babel 40 stories high with a different language spoken on each floor, a tower on rollers, a tower half a mile high surmounted by a globe and the statue of Columbus, five floating islands turning on a central pivot, an aerial island supported by six balloons, the construction of all buildings on floats with viaducts between them, a colossal globe with two theaters on the interior, a ground map of the United States covering 750 acres, the hanging gardens of Babylon reproduced, a mountain 1000 feet high with a glass palace on the summit, a replica of Dante's Hell, a telescope on a tower powerful enough to discover animals on the planets, a monument to Lincoln 1000 feet high, a replica of Niagara Falls worked by steam power, a pyramid 1200 feet square at the base and 1200 feet high and a reproduction of the seven wonders of the ancient world" (editorial, *ibid.*, June 15, 1890).

crowds, it engendered a holiday spirit that was not conducive to the purchase of real estate. When it was closed, amid a financial depression, leaving empty flats and apartments in its vicinity, a deeper gloom set in than had been anticipated. The World's Fair, however, was unjustly made the scapegoat by the generation that succeeded for all the ills that followed the falling-off in real estate activity after 1890 and the panic of 1893. Its specific influence was confined to a few square miles near Jackson Park, and it was but one of a number of factors contributing to the boom of 1890. Had it occurred at another time, the effect it exerted on land values might have been altogether different.

6. *Department stores and apartments.*—Large stores with many departments under one roof were an innovation of this period that made heavy inroads on the business of the small store. These stores advertised extensively in the newspapers and offered "bargains" to the housewife as well as a variety of goods that the small stores could not match. The improved transit facilities to the downtown area facilitated the rise of these large emporiums, and their popularity in turn was a contributing cause of the rise of land values in the central business district, as it was likewise a factor in depressing the values of certain streets such as West Madison Street, Milwaukee Avenue, and Cottage Grove Avenue.

The increasing demand for apartments as a result of the improved types of apartment construction and room layout was tending to raise the value of land suitable for apartment sites and to lessen the tendency to spread out into the suburbs.

The aggregate effect of the factors just described was to concentrate business in the downtown area, to depopulate the intermediate belt of old wooden houses, and to build up virgin land on the edge of settlement. Such was the specific effect of the swifter transportation afforded by cable, steam, elevated, and electric lines that enable people to hurry past the decaying areas built up by the transit lines of the former generation. It was the effect of the skyscrapers and department stores in concentrating business in a small downtown area, and it was the effect of manufacturers and belt-line railroads, of annexation, of the World's Fair, and of new suburban transit lines to spread out the residential area over new tracts that were not stigmatized by obsolete buildings or an immigrant population. Many half-built-up tracts close to the heart of the city were skipped over in this exodus to new unde-

THE FIRST SKYSCRAPERS AND THE WORLD'S FAIR 159

veloped tracts. In 1889 an observer estimated that the population within the old city limits could be doubled if it were compactly settled.

The factors just considered have had a most potent effect in determining the extent of the variation between land-value peaks and valleys and in fixing the location of the high points on the land-value maps. It would be a mistake, however, to suppose that such forces would have produced the same effect operating in a vacuum or apart from the general market conditions that prevailed from 1887 to 1894 in Chicago. The tone of the land-value market itself and the psychology it generated determined to a considerable extent what weight and bearing these factors would immediately have on land values. It is therefore necessary now to describe this market as a complex entity.

E. THE MOVEMENT OF LAND VALUES IN THE CHICAGO REAL ESTATE MARKET, 1886–94

The beginning of a new boom, 1886–88.—The new equilibrium of Chicago land values in which the land within the city limits had regained by 1883 the peak level of ten years before was maintained with little change, despite the decline in general business activity, during 1884 and 1885. In 1886 there was a marked gain in the volume of manufacturing and of real estate transfers as compared with the preceding year, the total value of real estate sales increasing from fifty-seven to eighty-seven million dollars.[39] Subdivision activity was still restricted. The 4,135 new lots platted in Cook County in 1886 showed an increase over the 3,210 laid out in 1885, but both these amounts were relatively low compared with the peak figures of 1873. Land values in Hyde Park and Englewood were advancing.[40] The construction of the Wisconsin Central Railroad through the territory west of Douglas Park was arousing hopes on the part of those owners who were nearly worn out by the payment of interest and taxes since the boom of 1873 that they might soon get their money back.[41] Property in the downtown section was firm and values were slowly advancing, although property subject to long-term leases could still be bought at prices that would net 7 or 8 per cent to the owner.[42]

In 1887 a number of new factors appeared to enliven the real estate

---

[39] *Real Estate and Building Journal*, January 2, 1892.
[40] *Chicago Tribune*, August 8, 1886.
[41] *Ibid.*, September 5, 1886.   [42] *Ibid.*, October 31, 1886.

market. The Santa Fe Railroad bought land for its yards and right of way into Chicago.[43] The Stickney tract was purchased. The South Side cable lines were extended from Thirty-ninth to Sixty-third and Sixty-seventh streets. The first rumors of the coming World's Fair were being discussed.[44] The Calumet Canal and Improvement Company bought the Forsythe tract of 8,000 acres at East Chicago, Indiana, for a manufacturing center. People were vacating houses in the city to go to the suburbs. New belt-line companies were being organized. There was talk of new cable lines and of elevated railroads.[45] The yield on the best improved properties had fallen to 6 per cent as compared with the 8 or 9 per cent yield of a few years before.[46] The number of new lots subdivided increased from 4,135 in 1886 to 13,714 in 1887. In the fall, as the land booms in Kansas City, Omaha, and Minneapolis began to wane, veteran operators from those cities began to come to Chicago and to marvel at the cheapness of its acre tracts.[47] Chicago investors still remembered the losses they had sustained in acre property bought in the boom of 1873, but the newcomers had more confidence and bought acres on the Southwest Side that the natives would not touch.

The succession of favorable factors continued in 1888. The cable on North Clark Street was completed from Lincoln Park to the main business section.[48] The South Side Elevated Company obtained the consent of a majority of the property owners along its proposed route and secured an ordinance from the city council permitting it to construct its line. The suburbs were building up rapidly. Extensive growth was taking place over a wide area within the city. New stores and flats were going up along Cottage Grove Avenue as far south as Fifty-fifth Street.[49] The population of Englewood had increased to 20,000. The territory northwest of Milwaukee and Armitage avenues was being settled.[50] The Polish quarter at Chicago, bounded by Ashland, Clybourn, and Carpenter streets, had gained a population of 30,000, principally since 1886.[51] In aristocratic Edgewater there were

[43] *Ibid.*, May 22, 1887.
[44] *Ibid.*, August 21, 1887.　　　　　[46] *Ibid.*, April 29, 1887.
[45] *Ibid.*, May 22, 1887.　　　　　　[47] *Ibid.*, January 15, 1888.
[48] Statement of J. V. Sullivan, assistant to the president of the Chicago Surface Lines, to the writer in 1932.
[49] *Chicago Tribune*, August 4, 1888.
[50] *Ibid.*, September 16, 1888.　　　　[51] *Ibid.*, November 4, 1888.

THE FIRST SKYSCRAPERS AND THE WORLD'S FAIR 161

200 people where there had been none in 1886.[52] In the vicinity of Douglas and Garfield parks, in the neighborhood of Halsted Street between Fifty-fifth and Sixty-ninth streets,[53] in the territory along Fifty-fifth Street east of Cottage Grove, in the area along Sixty-third Street near the Illinois Central tracts and near the Rock Island tracts in Englewood, many buildings were being erected in 1888. The belt of growth was on the outer edge of the old city. The belt of wooden houses built after the fire of 1871 was now passed by for the zone of new growth. West Side landowners in particular complained of the decay of the region from Grand Avenue to Madison Street and from Halsted to Ashland Avenue and of the increasing number of vacant houses close to the city. Optimism on the whole prevailed at the close of 1888. "Everyone is a bull on real estate" expressed the tone of the market in November, 1888.[54] The value of downtown property, notwithstanding stationary rents and interest rates, had risen because it was now capitalized on a 5 per cent basis, instead of the 7 or 8 per cent basis of 1885 and the 10 per cent basis of 1873.[55] The number of new lots subdivided in Cook County had increased from 13,714 in 1887 to 18,813 in 1888 and acre values were rising. In the downtown area there was an eager demand for property situated north of Madison Street and east of Wells Street, particularly on Dearborn Street. Except for South Water Street, which had a monopoly of the commission-merchant business, there was less demand in 1888 for business frontage north of Madison Street than for that south of it. The heavy hardware firms were moving from Lake Street to the West Side in the section on Canal Street from Randolph Street to Madison Street.[56]

As credit conditions were favorable, and as the decline in railroad stocks and bonds and the lull in the booms in real estate in other cities had turned the attention of speculators to Chicago real estate, the stage was set late in 1888 for a boom.

The boom under way, 1889.—The mood of the market of 1889 was one that was ready to respond quickly to new developments or even to the rumors of coming projects. Consequently the effect of the announcement of new electric lines, manufacturing towns, skyscrapers, a larger city with over a million population, and a coming World's Fair regarded

[52] *Ibid.*, October 28, 1888.
[53] *Ibid.*, August 5, 1888.
[54] *Ibid.*, November 18, 1888.
[55] *Economist*, October 19, 1889.
[56] *Chicago Tribune*, June 22, 1888.

as probable stimulated the imagination of every class of people in Chicago and attracted investors and speculators from all over the United States. The earnings of local business men had been favorable, the number employed in manufacturing industries in Chicago had increased from 132,000 to 151,000 in a year, people were bringing their savings and speculative profits from other cities, and immigrants recently arrived in Chicago had hoards they would not trust to the banks. Tales of profits in real estate already made by their neighbors circulated among the residents of local communities and aroused their desire to use these accumulating funds for the purchase of Chicago land. This desire was artificially enhanced by professional promoters and subdividers.

This demand, in the main, divided itself into an inquiry for central business property, on the one hand, and for outlying acre tracts and suburban lots, on the other. The large investor was interested in both, but wage-earners and clerks were restricted by their purchasing power to the cheap-lot market, unless they banded together to form syndicates.

The scenes of speculative excitement were first in the territory along Madison Street west of Crawford Avenue where the reports of the new Cicero and Proviso Electric Line project aroused sudden interest in a territory that had been dormant for sixteen years. Then, in the downtown area, Dearborn Street which had long been an obscure and neglected thoroughfare because it had not been cut through south of Monroe Street, received the benefit of the North Side cable loop, and under expert pool manipulation made sensational gains in value. The climax came when the 20-by-40-foot corner of Madison and Dearborn, called "the diamond on the shirt front" because it was at the point of maximum value, sold for $150,000, or at the rate of $7,500 a front foot, the highest price ever paid up to that time in Chicago. The effect of this sale was to break the customary level of values, and to convince many Chicago owners of central property that they had hitherto undervalued their property. The increasing demand for space on State Street within two blocks of Madison Street was also pushing values upward there. Meanwhile, the rapid growth of the outer edges of the city had created a strong demand for acres for subdivision purposes, particularly on the Southwest Side, and out of this situation grew up a demand for acres on the part of one group of speculators to sell to another group of speculators.

THE FIRST SKYSCRAPERS AND THE WORLD'S FAIR 163

Speculation in acre tracts and subdivision activity.—The most characteristic feature of a real estate boom is the speculation in acre tracts and the sale of lots in subdivisions to small investors. A description of this phase of the market indicates the widespread interest of all classes of people in Chicago lots in 1889, and it also illustrates the unique qualities of land valuations based on such sales.

The prices of acre tracts close enough to the city to be suitable for subdivision fluctuated from farm-land values to the aggregate value they would bring if sold out in lots. Since the marketing of lots in a subdivision required an organized sales campaign on the part of a professional subdivider, whose propaganda was chiefly responsible for the high level of prices obtained for the lots, as will presently be shown, there was usually a wide margin between the selling prices of the land in large tracts and the aggregate retail value of the lots which were obtained by subdividing it. Often the ratio was three to one and sometimes it was as high as ten to one.[57] The possibility of a sale to a subdivider at a price low enough to pay him to undertake the work of dividing into lots and selling the lots was supposed to set the limit of value of an acre tract. As both the suitability of the land for subdivision and the retail prices of the lots were determined by no fixed rules, acre tracts were in fact subject to extreme fluctuations in values in a short time. Sometimes in the excitement of speculation their values were carried as high as lots were selling at retail. There being no way of calculating their value on an income basis, and as their possible future use varied from that of farm land to that of intensive residential or industrial use, there was such a wide range of possibilities that the Valuation Committee of the Chicago Real Estate Board refused to appraise them at all.

Into this speculative field of acre tracts there rushed in 1889 and 1890 several classes of buyers: (1) the subdivider buying for the purpose of cutting the tract into lots and selling the lots at retail; (2) professional acre speculators purchasing for the purpose of selling at a profit to other acre speculators, to subdividers, or to syndicates of amateur speculators; (3) groups of professional men or clerks who were buying tracts for actual use as homesites; and (4) syndicates of clerks who had pooled their savings to buy acre tracts for a resale as a whole or in lots at a profit.

[57] This is the increase in the price obtained by the retail sale of a tract over the price prevailing in large units and does not include the cost of any street improvements.

There were acre tracts available even in 1889 that would have proved profitable investments to any of these classes of buyers. The majority of buyers, however, ran in crowds to the spot where the most rapid rises were taking place and where land values where highest;[58] and that meant in five cases out of six that they purchased on the South or Southwest sides instead of on the neglected Northwest Side, where land equally distant from the city was only one-third as high. They were influenced by the rumors that were circulating everywhere. As the real estate editor of the *Chicago Tribune* phrased it:

> The air is filled with the music of coming improvements. Something important is about to happen all around. Almost every quarter section that is between six and nine miles of the court house has its remarkable development just ahead. One is to be the site of a big manufacturing plant, another is to have car shops, another is to have a new railroad, another has all but got the world's fair.[59]

What had been regarded as farm land on the Southwest Side was now valued as the potential site of factories or railroad yards.

> Land that a year ago was valued according to its ability to produce crops of corn, oats and potatoes is now considered with reference to its location to the Calumet terminal, the Stickney tract, the proposed Stock Yards, or any of the other schemes to be located in this section. Some say the values are justified by the future prospects, while others deny that the prices are in any way warranted.[60]

The buying of these acre tracts in 1889, even in the opinion of current observers, was frequently reckless and indiscriminate:

> When men, tempted by the reports of advancing prices and not knowing whether the advance is genuine and substantial or merely the result of manipulation, rush to a map and pick out something for their broker to buy, they are gambling and are introducing an unnatural and unhealthy stimulus into the market. Few people, for instance, appear to know just what is to be the outcome of the famous Stickney purchase southwest of the city, yet because a few people do appear to know and have paid high prices in that quarter buyers are rushing thither and making bids which would have been grounds months ago for appointment of a commission de lunatico inquirendo.[61]

A majority of the purchases were made with a down payment of not over one-fourth of the total price, the buyer expecting to sell before he was called on for his second payment. The purchasers of acre tracts that "had no other qualifications than that it occupied so much space on a map of Northern Illinois" and that were far removed from trans-

---

[58] *Chicago Tribune*, March 17, 1889.
[59] *Ibid.*, November 17, 1889.
[60] *Ibid.*, August 24, 1890.
[61] *Ibid.*, November 24, 1889.

portation facilities, as well as the buyers of better-located acres who were paying the greatly increased prices, were warned that the whole process must finally stop.

It is perhaps more than likely, whatever the purchase price and whatever the property, a market could be found in the next two years which would give the purchaser of today [May, 1890] a profit. But will that last purchaser be croaking to the next generation about the way he was caught back in '93?[62]

Again it was pointed out that it was a dangerous game to pay far more than the intrinsic value of the property in the expectation that someone else could be found who would pay still more.

In the ruins of all collapsed booms is to be found the work of men who bought property at prices they knew perfectly well were fictitious, but who were willing to pay such prices simply because they knew that some still greater fool could be depended upon to take the property off their hands and leave them a profit.[63]

Such booms in acre property could collapse as quickly as they were generated. In the fall of 1889 there was a lull in the acre market. It was declared that "acre values are so full of wind that if any more is pumped in the blue arch of heaven will have to be lifted to make room for their expansion" and that "present values will not stand the test of subdivision."[64] The holders of acre tracts at these inflated values anxiously waited for the spring of 1890 to see whether the furious speculation would be revived on a larger scale or whether that fatal dulness had begun which would render their property unmarketable. To their great joy, once more the merry dance of speculation carried the value of their holdings to new heights.

If speculating in acre tracts was a hazardous game for the professional operator who "had cut his eyeteeth" in the booms in Kansas City or Minneapolis two years before, it was particularly dangerous for amateurs. Early in 1889 thousands of laborers and clerks pooled their savings and formed syndicates to purchase suburban acre tracts. "Even servant girls, seamstresses and woman clerks have caught the fever, put their savings into a lump and become joint owners of suburban property. Kindled by stories of large profits, they believe it is impossible to pay too much."[65]

Their judgment of values was faulty and they were extremely gullible. "Amateur acre speculators see millions in swamp lands and cab-

[62] *Ibid.*, May 4, 1890.
[63] *Ibid.*, April 13, 1890.
[64] *Ibid.*, November 24, 1890.
[65] *Ibid.*, April 21, 1889.

bage fields a mile away from a railroad track."[66] They were easily imposed upon by professional operators, not knowing that the asking prices were far above what the property could be secured for by shrewd bargainers; and they were easily led to believe they could quickly resell the property at a large profit to other speculators or that they could subdivide the property and easily obtain the same prices for the lots that the big firms received. The real estate editor of the *Chicago Tribune* commented on their inexperience: "It takes the green buyer of acres some time to learn that all is considered fair in real estate as in love and war,"[67] and on the fact that they paid too much for their property, "if syndicates pay retail prices for ten or twenty acre tracts none but a professional boomer can figure out a profit for them."[68]

Having thus been led to pay too much for their holdings, even in terms of the inflated boom prices, when the amateur acre syndicates turned to the one-time optimistic operators who had sold them their tracts and who had assured them the land could quickly be disposed of at a profit, they found that these wily men had now changed their tune. The real estate operators who had before expressed such willingness to take the acres off their hands at an advance in price had suddenly become extremely pessimistic about the value of their tracts and gave them not the slightest encouragement.[69] When the amateurs next sought to convert their land into lots and to realize the same prices that were apparently so easily gathered in by the big subdividers, they suddenly found that "lots did not sell themselves"; that it required great ingenuity, as well as the use of brass bands, fireworks displays, large advertisements, excursion trains, and an organized sales campaign "to work off" the lots at retail prices. It was not enough to attract customers to offer their lots at lower prices with more improvements:

A small dealer, who has a few hundred lots in a steady going suburb, complains that people pass him by and make purchases in Messrs. Whoopla and Bangs new prairie subdivision paying $15 a foot for land at a distance from all improvements, although his lots, with houses all around them, with sewers and gas and water pipes in, were offered at $12 a foot. He can't understand such conduct except on the hypothesis that people have lost their heads and are accepting for gospel truth everything a dealer tells them so that the biggest liar gets all the trade.[70]

It is little wonder that the amateur syndicates sold very few lots in competition with old established firms like S. E. Gross, who had sub-

[66] *Ibid.*, November 17, 1889.   [68] *Ibid.*, April 21, 1889.
[67] *Ibid.*, October 6, 1889.   [69] *Ibid.*   [70] *Ibid.*, July 14, 1889.

THE FIRST SKYSCRAPERS AND THE WORLD'S FAIR 167

divided sixteen towns and who had attracted an extensive clientèle of investors, many of whom had reaped large profits from his earlier subdivisions. When it is considered that in addition he and other large subdividers like E. A. Cummings regularly ran half- or quarter-page advertisements in the newspapers, that they operated free excursion trains to their properties, gave free lunches, band concerts, fireworks displays, and bicycle races to entertain crowds which in the boom days of 1889 and 1890 were counted by thousands, it is a matter of no surprise that concerns operating without these attractions should have failed. Nor were the foregoing methods the sole or even the chief resource of the large subdivider:

> The successful dealers employ devices and methods unsuspected by the uninitiated. They do not merely erect a shanty in the subdivision, a branch office with a manager on the grounds, put an advertisement in the Sunday papers and wait for buyers to come to them. They build the branch office and do the advertising but that is only the beginning of their work. They enlist an army of drummers who canvass the city, giving them $5 to $10 commission for every lot sold. These drummers, among whom are many women, go diligently through stores, shops and factories and they tell wonderful stories about values. Sometimes they profess to be selling lots at $100 in neighborhoods where buyers of six months ago are re-selling at $200 —just to close out the subdivision and because the owner is satisfied with a reasonable profit. These lot canvassers are the most polite and insidious drummers in the field, and have a great advantage over book agents and miscellaneous peddlers. They carry no suspicious bundle and easily gain admittance where an ordinary peddler would be snubbed. It is through them that the largest number of lots is sold.[71]

As a result of these tactics the lion's share of the small savings set aside to be invested in lots was captured by the large and experienced dealer who "blew his trumpet loudly." Nevertheless, the large subdividers regarded the amateur acre syndicates with animosity, not because they were successful in selling lots, but because the members of the syndicate would have bought lots of the subdivider if they had not entered the syndicate.

The end linked in this speculative chain, the final consumer, was the buyer of lots in the subdivision. High as the value of acre tracts was carried in the boom, the purchaser of a 25-foot lot at retail paid for his one-tenth of an acre a price that was frequently from three to ten times as high as the wholesale price in acres, and in addition he usually paid for most of the improvements. "Land in a well known suburb cost

[71] *Ibid.*, August 25, 1889.

the owner $200 an acre, he spent as much more on improvements, so that the lots cost him $50 each and he sold them for $150 to $300 each ($1,500 to $3,000 an acre) easily."[72]

In the earlier stages of the rising land market, prior to 1889, a considerable proportion of these lots was brought for actual use as homesites, in which cases the saving in rent offset the interest lost on the capital invested; but in the height of the activity of 1889 and 1890, less than 10 per cent of the lots purchased were built upon and the main object of the buyer was to sell again at a profit.

The heavy sales of lots in subdivisions in 1889 and 1890 were due to the fact that prosperous times and full employment had placed small accumulations of capital in the hands of thousands of persons, and that these persons were led by the boom psychology of the period and the persuasive tactics of the subdividers to buy a lot on easy payments. "North, south, and west the opportunities offered a poor man to buy a lot are simply bewildering."[73] Under the urge to buy something, and without the experience necessary to appraise the differences between different sections of the suburban area, he fell in with the suggestion of the professional "boomer" that he could not make a mistake if he bought a lot anywhere around Chicago.

All lots about Chicago are good things to buy, some being merely a little better than others. This rosy view of lot investments is shared by a large percentage of the public, by business men, by clerks, by bank employees, by servant girls, and by wage earners generally. They have heard that it is advancing, have seen their fellows make profitable deals in the last year or so and are convinced that he who buys is sure to win.[74]

Consequently the prospective lot purchaser was ready to buy whatever was offered by a personal friend or by any dealer who induced him to attend an excursion at the right moment.

The average lot buyer is sadly in need of a counsellor. He buys because a friend has bought or because a dealer has treated him to a picnic and assured him that prices would be raised all around within a week or because he has suddenly resolved to save $5 a week and has often heard it said that nobody makes a mistake when he puts money into Chicago dirt.[75]

The result was that he frequently was "danced or whooped into the purchase of lots for $10 a foot which current observers predicted would

[72] *Ibid.*
[73] *Ibid.*, November 24, 1889.
[74] *Ibid.*, July 7, 1889.　　　　[75] *Ibid.*, June 30, 1889.

THE FIRST SKYSCRAPERS AND THE WORLD'S FAIR 169

not support for ten years any improvements more valuable than those made by the hoe and spading fork."[76]

The probable aftermath was already being forecast in 1889:

> Conservative men shake their heads and declare that these boom methods will be followed by an injurious reaction. People will either find their lots under water next spring or discover that they promised to pay more than a fair market price and will stop further payments in disgust. Having been bitten once, they will not only fight shy of real estate dealers in the future but will warn their friends to beware of suburban lots.[77]

In addition to a belated discovery that he had paid too much for his lot, this small land-buyer was frequently confronted by a special assessment bill for $300 or $400 to be paid in one lump sum on a lot which he was being taxed to the utmost to pay for at the rate of $5.00 or $10 a month.[78] If he managed to pay all these sudden charges for improvements, for which there was no present need, and which were installed without his knowledge or consent by some contractor who had received a permit from the City Council, the amateur land speculator sometimes next discovered that on the completion of his final payment to the subdivider he could not get a clear and unincumbered lot because the subdivider had failed to retire out of the proceeds of his sales a blanket mortgage covering the entire subdivision.

Land in substantially the same locations was thus sold in 1889, as it had been before and since, at different prices according to the experience or lack of experience of the buyer. It should by no means be inferred that all or even a majority of all the lots sold in the boom of 1889 or 1890 were disposed of in the manner above indicated, nor even that all the lots sold by subdividers, even those under water, proved to be eventually unprofitable to the buyers. Lots sold in old subdivisions through brokerage offices had a more standard and stabilized price, and it was this type of lot that was usually bought by business men of greater experience and larger resources than the clerical or laboring classes. Moreover, some of the lots in new subdivisions contiguous to the city proved bonanzas. The dangers of such wild and indiscriminate buying of lots to the stability of the land market will, however, be disclosed in the aftermath of the boom or in the period after 1894.

As the land boom had thus spread to acre tracts and suburban lots during 1889, it had also seized upon central business property. Invest-

[76] *Ibid.*, July 7, 1889.   [77] *Ibid.*   [78] *Ibid.*, April 13, 1890.

ors by the score were bidding for downtown property,[79] but asking prices were constantly being advanced to keep ahead of the advancing offers and late in September it was stated that 75 per cent of the property in the heart of the city was out of the market.[80]

Buyers far outnumber sellers. A buyer wastes time if he goes around trying to purchase property at prices asked last spring, last summer or last month. Owners' ideas of values are apt to change each week and their ideas are always moving upward. Owners have been approached by so many brokers with bids and with proposals for leases that they feel independent, perfectly confident of their ability to sell at terms which would have seemed impossible a year ago. The enthusiasm of buyers has made owners optimistic in the highest degree, and negotiations for large pieces are dragging in consequence of bids always being a little under asking prices.[81]

Since business and office rents had not advanced, there seemed to be no basis for such increased values. "It is generally admitted that pieces of real estate have sold this year for amounts much above what is warranted by the present income received from them, and in several cases above what they can be made to yield immediately by the best possible impovements."[82]

Buyers in the immediate past who had bought central business property without stopping to reason about it, however, had profited, while those who had made careful calculations had failed to gain, so headlong and unreasoning optimism seemed the better policy. "Buyers have banked on the future of Chicago. This has been a safe and paying thing to do during the last half dozen years."[83]

The entire Chicago area, however, did not participate in this upward movement, as it did in the case of the earlier booms. "The amount of Chicago property is too great to be stirred by any speculative whirlwind. Chicago still has its booms, but they are confined to districts, to special classes of property, to limited areas."[84]

Residential property in old sections of the city, for instance, was a drug on the market.[85] The near West Side was not only not having a boom, but its land values in the region west of Halsted Street to Ashland Avenue from Grand Avenue to Madison Street were lower than they were twenty years before. Acre tracts on the North and Northwest sides had advanced only moderately in price, and were being

[79] *Ibid.*, September 29, 1889.
[80] *Ibid.*, September 22, 1889.
[81] *Ibid.*, October 13, 1889.
[82] *Ibid.*, August 18, 1889.
[83] *Ibid.*
[84] *Ibid.*, September 8, 1889.
[85] *Ibid.*, September 29, 1889.

offered for sale at what a few years later were regarded as bargain rates.

Ignoring these dead spots, the year 1889 closed with a rush of business that was carried over into the usually dull Christmas holiday season.[86] The aggregate sales of real estate as shown by the recorded transfers—$135,800,000[87]—had broken all previous records; and even this figure understated the case, for it did not include the large volume of sales of subdivision lots made on instalment contracts. The number of lots subdivided in Cook County—39,997—also set a new record. Projected skyscrapers, elevated railroads, belt lines, manufacturing towns, and the World's Fair took shape in the minds of the public and gave a rosy tint to their hopes.

The culmination of the boom, 1890.—The year 1890 fulfilled at its peak period the most fervent hopes of the land speculators. The World's Fair was awarded to Chicago by Congress on February 25, 1890. Land values near Jackson Park advanced as much as 1,000 per cent in the year, as tracts partly under water south of the park were bid up from $600 to $6,000 and even $15,000 an acre.[88] The acre speculation around the Stickney tract and from Forty-seventh to Ninety-fifth Street from Western to Harlem avenues carried acre tracts to double and triple their former apparently inflated values. The sale of lots surpassed all previous records. S. E. Gross was selling as many as five hundred lots a week, and on one of his free excursions to his subdivision Grossdale, west of Chicago, twenty-seven coaches pulled by two engines were required to transport the three thousand people who were eager to buy lots.[89] Five times as many manufacturers located in Chicago in 1890 as in any single year before, and the sale of acres and lots near the site of actual or projected factories was at fever heat. The "Alley Elevated" road was being constructed between State and Wabash Avenue with the result that the value of State Street frontage from Twenty-second to Sixty-third streets increased several hundred per cent in a few months. Projects for hotels and apartments for the World's Fair were sending up the value not only of Michigan Avenue near Twenty-second Street but of property all over the South Side. "It is a poor neglected corner of the South Side that does not have its hotel scheme."[90] The skyscrapers planned for the downtown office sec-

[86] *Ibid.*, December 29, 1889. [88] *Ibid.*, May 25, 1890.
[87] *Ibid.*, January 1, 1890. [89] *Ibid.*, June 15, 1890. [90] *Ibid.*, April 9, 1890.

tions, and sales or leases for projected buildings, kept values jumping. State Street, with seventy-five hundred people passing hourly from Madison to Monroe Street, was at a greater premium than ever before, and those who had a store within two blocks of State and Madison Street found that the very force of their location inevitably attracted a great trade, while those who moved away in the hope that their customers would follow them into the next block were glad to pay a bonus to get back. The owners of Wabash Avenue property were looking to the South Side Elevated Railroad, then having its projected terminus at Wabash and Congress street, as "the Moses that would lead them out of the wilderness." Property along Michigan Avenue south of Madison Street had come into great demand for hotel purposes, especially after the completion of the Auditorium in 1889, because of its freedom from the heavy traffic of the downtown area, and its values had risen to an amazing degree. The wholesale quarter southwest of Jackson and Wells Street was building up rapidly. On the West Side speculators were buying land west of Halsted and Jackson streets in the expectation that the light manufacturing district would spread westward. The new cable line on Madison Street to Crawford was infusing some activity into that street. Northward, the rise of the Lake Shore Drive and the streets adjacent to it to a position of social eminence and of high land values was now an accomplished fact. The completion of the new Sheridan Road to Waukegan had also stimulated activity along the North Shore.

In the general rush and feverish scramble in so many sections of the city and the surrounding suburbs, the seven thousand vacant houses in the near West Side were lightly passed by. In the favorite scenes of speculative activity, sales were made so fast that half-a-dozen transfers of contracts to purchase were sometimes made before one deed was recorded. Buyers were in such a hurry to get the property that they neglected many formalities of title examination. In the general excitement there was much sharp dealing bordering on actual fraud. Taking advantage of the faith and confidence of the public in the accuracy of the considerations expressed in the deeds of conveyance which were recorded and published in the newspapers, sales were made in many cases at fictitious considerations to dummy buyers for the purpose of creating the impression of activity and advancing prices. The ruse was frequently successful, as buyers rushed to any spot that appeared to be going up in value. Again there were many cases of "scalping" unnoticed at the time but the details of which came out in the aftermath of the boom. Some of the unscrupulous "curbstone" brokers, who had been attracted to Chicago by the boom, sometimes contrived to make more than a regular commission by selling the property intrusted to them at a higher price than was paid to the owner and by keeping the difference. Again there were cases of property being sold at an abnormally high price on the strength of a fictitious lease, by which an irresponsible confederate of the seller agreed to pay an unusually high rent for the property.

Such were the components of the real estate market of Chicago of 1890. Good and bad elements were hopelessly mixed together and anyone was regarded as a traitor to Chicago who questioned any part of the process that was making so many people rich. The apex of the boom was reached in June, July, and August, when the volume of weekly and monthly sales broke all past records. At last, in early September, there came the report that Washington Park might be used for the World's Fair, whereupon buyers on options and most slender margins undertook to boost the prices of Cottage Grove Avenue frontage from Forty-ninth to Sixtieth streets from $100 to $200 to $300 to $500 a front foot.

This proved to be the last phase of the boom. The failure of the Baring Brothers in London precipitated a serious financial stringency in September. The banks suddenly refused to make loans for the purpose of purchasing real estate, although the borrower was allowed funds for other uses. "The blandishments of real estate agents fall pointless against a stringent money market," was the current comment in September. By November there was a financial panic. The Washington Park boom had collapsed in October and the effect of a fall of "300 per cent" in values there, as one naïve statistician put it, had a chilling effect on the hitherto confident belief that the boom values would not decline. By December there was no active real estate market in the sense that speculation was active. "Sales have come to a sharp halt. Negotiations even are silenced."[91]

At the close of the year, the situation was reviewed in which annual sales in Cook County had reached the record-breaking total of $237,831,000,[92] in which 40,000 lots[93] had been subdivided and a considerable

[91] *Ibid.*, December 7, 1890.   [92] *Ibid.*, January 1, 1891.   [93] *Ibid.*, September 21, 1890.

proportion of them sold in the first six months of the year, in which single firms like Snow and Dickinson had sold $7,500,000 worth of property, and in which all brokers, even those of the curbstone variety, had made money. The fortunes made by some read like romances. Notwithstanding the sharp check in operations beginning in September, there was still a confident belief that activity would revive in the spring of 1891. If general business conditions did not improve, Chicago at least, on account of its coming World's Fair, was expected to be a bright exception to conditions elsewhere.[94] Great store was placed on remarks by Chauncey Depew as to the vast amount of money the Fair would put in circulation in Chicago. Consequently, while considerable anxiety was felt by the purchasers of tracts aggregating thousands of acres as to whether they would be able to sell their holdings before the next payment came due,[95] there were no reductions in asking prices, and holders of improved property were even more confident.

The gains in land value from the beginning of 1889 to the beginning of 1891 had been far greater than in the preceding six years, particularly in the case of central business property and first-class residential property made accessible by fast transportation, but the value of land occupied by cheap homes had declined because of the increased competition of suburban land. Table VII, the data for which were prepared by Frank R. Chandler, indicates the percentage of change for different types of property.[96]

It will be seen that cheap houses are cheaper now than ten years ago. So they are, because more land has been brought into requisition, also that property under the head of office buildings is as high as the best retail business. This is the result of high buildings mainly. First class residence property 4½ miles out is just as desirable as property three miles out. This is due to improved transit facilities and the rapid growth and extension of the business districts. The average increase in values since 1889 approximately given is from 100 to 200 per cent and in exceptional cases an increase of 300 to 400 per cent has been made.

The beginning of the lull, 1891.—The real estate speculators discovered in 1891 that checking the boom of 1890 in mid-career had changed the temper of the market and that the one-time buoyant optimism could not be revived.

[94] *Ibid.*, December 7, 1890. [95] *Ibid.*, September 14, 1890.

[96] *Real Estate and Building Journal*, April 4, 1891. Since the figures for 1879 are average and not maximum values, the lower figures for 1891 are taken in computing the percentage of increase. This minimizes the extent of the actual advance.

THE FIRST SKYSCRAPERS AND THE WORLD'S FAIR

No train of transactions will be brought to an absolute halt by unfavorable events as quickly as real estate transactions. The financial disturbances of last fall stopped almost completely for a time these speculative operations. The influence of that crisis has nearly departed, but it left the country in a far different temper from that of a year ago. The sanguine optimists have become conservative. So long as there is a speedy turning over of property at advancing values the speculative real estate operator has little thought of the point prices have reached. When that movement has stopped for a time and holders of property whose equity is represented by only a narrow margin have exhausted themselves in searching for a buyer, it is not only discouraging to see how slow it is to market a piece of realty, but their fate warns other men.[97]

TABLE VII
VALUE OF CHICAGO LAND BY PRINCIPAL USES, 1879–91

CLASS OF PROPERTY	DOLLARS PER FRONT FOOT				PERCENTAGE OF INCREASE 1879–91
	Jan. 1, 1891	Jan. 1, 1889	Jan. 1, 1883	Jan. 1, 1879	
First-class retail, central.......	$7,000–$10,000	$4,000	$1,500	$1,500	367
Banks and offices.............	7,000– 10,000	3,000	2,000	1,100	536
Wholesale business...........	2,000– 5,000	2,000	1,500	600	233
Local business centers........	600– 1,000	600	400	300	100
Aristocratic residence, South Side...................	800– 1,000	800	600	250	220
First-class residence, South Side, 3 miles.............	250– 400	200	150	95	163
First-class residence, South Side, 3½ miles............	250– 400	175	125	70	257
First-class residence, South Side, 4 miles.............	250– 400	150	100	75	233
First-class residence, South Side, 4½ miles............	125– 300	125	80	60	108
First-class residence, West Side	450– 600	250	200	100	350
Aristocratic residence, North Side...................	350– 450	500	400	250	40
Cheap homes................	7– 20	25	20	10	decrease
Fashionable suburban.........	75– 100	85	60	40	90

Farming lands, Cook and DuPage counties, $200–$1,000 and $2,000 an acre.

A large number of people had now purchased real estate which they could not sell, and that required further outlay on their part to keep up the payments of principal and interest as well as of taxes and assessments. The funds available for purchasing more property were thus curtailed, and they were further reduced by a decline in the number employed in manufactures and the falling-off in business profits. Potential buyers, seeing that land near the World's Fair ground and the

[97] *Chicago Tribune*, May 17, 1891.

Alley Elevated that people rushed to buy in 1890 could still be bought at no material advance, were now in no hurry to make commitments.[98] Announcements of new projects and even the completion of many enterprises had lost their potency to stampede the buyers. "The announcement of enterprises and negotiations under way which would have caused a sensation during the summer of 1890 was received in 1891 without causing the slightest stir in realty circles."[99] Buyers now took more time in examining abstracts, and they were careful to look into all phases of the deal, as the buyers of 1890 were indulging in recriminations and complaints about scalping and imperfections in their titles. Land values were nominally higher than ever, and the volume of recorded sales was not far below the peak level of 1890, but this appearance was deceptive. There were many exchanges of property at inflated considerations in which two parties, unable to sell their holdings for cash, traded with each other at abnormally high considerations on both sides. It was further estimated that as much as half of the deeds recorded in 1891 were the result of deals made in 1890 which involved the carrying-out of contracts made in the earlier year.[100]

As yet there were few signs of actual decline in values. The purchasers of acres and lots were still struggling to keep up their payments, and if they could not pay these sums promptly, they found their creditors lenient; for the former owners did not want the property back, and they knew that under the foreclosure law it would take them eighteen months to secure the title and to wipe out the equity of the mortgagor.[101]

Some of the speculative bubbles had already been pricked. The Stickney acres were in ill repute; the projected removal of the packing plants to Tolleston was now referred to as a fiasco.[102] Acre tracts were a drug on the market, an inquiry for one such tract bringing in eighty replies and offering a total of 2,500 acres, half of which was located in new manufacturing towns such as Harvey, Hammond, Stickney, Chicago Heights, South Chicago, and Wireton Park.[103] The sale of lots in subdivisions had decreased drastically. S. E. Gross sold only 129 lots during the week ending July 26, 1891, as compared with 529 for the same week a year before.[104] In one case where a dozen carloads of

[98] *Ibid.*, June 28, 1891.
[99] *Ibid.*, July 30, 1893.
[100] *Ibid.*, June 7, 1891.
[101] *Ibid.*, May 3, 1891.
[102] *Ibid.*, August 23, 1891.
[103] *Ibid.*, July 26, 1891.
[104] *Ibid.*

THE FIRST SKYSCRAPERS AND THE WORLD'S FAIR 177

prospective purchasers were taken to a South Side subdivision under conditions that would have insured the sale of hundreds of lots in 1890, only a few lots were sold.[105] There were too many agents trying to make deals, with the result that the commissions were split up among too many to be profitable to any one. Many negotiations were broken off because "a friend of one of the parties" to a deal who was in the real estate business advised against it in order to promote a sale of his own.[106]

Notwithstanding these drawbacks, many sales were negotiated in 1891, but they were for actual use rather than for speculative resale. Purchases were made downtown for sites for sixteen-story buildings, and on the South Side for apartment or hotel sites.

Despite the decline in the sales of subdivision lots, the number of lots subdivided in 1891 in Cook County far exceeded all previous records with a total of 111,000.[107] Only a small percentage of this number was sold. The volume of building activity, augmented by the erection of skyscrapers and the building of apartments and hotels on the South Side for the World's Fair, also reached a new peak, having increased from a total of $25,000,000 in 1889 to over $47,000,000 in 1890 and $54,000,000 in 1891. Those who had purchased land at high valuations were persuaded to build in order to earn something on their investment. Others were induced to erect buildings under the most extravagant notions as to the income they would yield during the World's Fair. One advertisement contained the assuring estimate that four rooms in an ordinary six-room house would earn $5,760 in the six months of the Fair.[108]

This building activity reached a new peak in 1892, when the total volume amounted to $63,463,400.[109] Wages and materials costs were forced upward 20–25 per cent[110] under this intense demand combined with the demand created by the construction of the Fair buildings, so that the buildings of this year were erected at an abnormally high cost.

[105] *Ibid.*, July 5, 1891.   [106] *Ibid.*, July 19, 1891.

[107] Computation of the editor of the *Real Estate and Building Journal*, June 9, 1894. Another authority gave a total of 79,803 for Cook County and 115,892 for the Chicago Metropolitan Region in 1891.

[108] *Chicago Tribune*, April 11, 1891. Advertisement of E. A. Cummings of house at Forty-first and Ellis Avenue.

[109] Annual reviews of the *Economist* (1891–97).

[110] *Chicago Tribune*, November 13, 1892.

Speculation in ninety-nine-year leases as a prelude to the erection of skyscrapers and hotels also reached a peak in 1892, the value of property so leased amounting to $12,000,000 as compared with $10,000,000 in 1890 and $8,700,000 in 1891.[111]

The market of 1892 was thus partly sustained by record-breaking building activity, by speculation in downtown leases in which certain operators leased whole floors and sublet them at a profit, by the construction of the Alley Elevated Railroad, and by the plans for the Metropolitan Elevated Railroad on the West Side. The organization of the University of Chicago also exerted an influence on the real estate market: first, because the section selected by the professors for their homes was expected to create a choice residential center that would be fashionable because of its aristocracy of learning;[112] and, second, because the announced plan of the trustees to invest part of the endowment of the University in property in the central business district enhanced the investment prestige of that territory.[113] On the whole, however, even with these favorable factors, land values in the centers that had been whirlwinds of activity in 1890 were drifting toward complete stagnation.[114] The collapse of the cheap-lot market and the failure of the great schemes for railroad yards and manufacturing plants had almost destroyed the cash market for acre tracts.[115] The number of lots subdivided fell from 110,000 in 1891 to 65,000 in 1892. In the downtown section the supply of office space was being increased faster than the demand. Foreclosures, while still few, were increasing in number.

The onset of the panic, 1893.—The year when the World's Fair opened was also the year of the panic of 1893. The prospect at the beginning of the year was none too bright, but when the belated World's Fair guests failed to fill the hotels that were built for their reception and when they failed to respond to invitations to inspect real estate, the Chicago land market was in the dumps even when the Midway and the Court of Honor were packed with dense throngs. The peak values were still maintained, and there was no break in prices because a scaling-down of prices did not attract many buyers.[116] There was a great difference between the bid and asked prices, the owners not being inclined to

[111] *Ibid.*
[112] *Ibid.*, October 30, 1892.
[113] *Ibid.*, December 4, 1892.
[114] *Ibid.*, September 25, 1892.
[115] *Ibid.*
[116] *Ibid.*, July 30, 1893.

make sacrifices and the purchasers looking for bargains.[117] "The whole city practically is for sale but not at bargain counter prices."[118]

The last six months of 1893 were far worse than the first half of the year. When the World's Fair crowds departed, the almost empty flats and hotels near the grounds quickly passed into the hands of receivers, and as rents were cut sharply to attract tenants, the overbuilt condition of the city as regards flats was emphasized. The rapid increase in unemployment, as factories curtailed operations and as the volume of building dropped from over sixty-three to twenty-eight million dollars, forced people to double up in their living quarters. The termination of World Fair projects, and the contraction of firms into smaller quarters reduced the demand for office space at the very time when its supply was being greatly increased by the completion of a number of new skyscrapers.

There were bright spots in the picture, however. Store rents on State Street near Madison had trebled since 1889 and land values throughout the central business district showed no inclination to decline. While the prices of lots on Grand and Drexel boulevards from Thirty-ninth to Fifty-first Street were cut in a few instances to raise cash during the panic, this reaction was but temporary; and, under the influence of the building of many fine homes along these thoroughfares, land values had increased from 25 to 75 per cent over 1890 prices by 1895. The North and Northwest sides scarcely felt the depression, for their boom was only about to begin. The depression particularly affected those portions of the South and Southwest sides where speculation had been most intense in 1890. The panic of 1893 marked the beginning of the passing of the South Side as the leader of fashion and of real estate speculation.

The condition of the scenes of speculative excitement of 1890 steadily grew worse from 1894 to 1898. In 1894 the first drastic cuts in real estate selling prices were made when weak holders accepted a 30 per cent reduction from the prices of 1890 for lots on South Side avenues.[119] Real estate values were apparently being maintained in 1895 when there was a brief recovery in general business conditions, but a majority of the recorded transfers were said to be masters' sales or

[117] *Ibid.*, July 9, 1893.
[118] *Ibid.*, July 2, 1893.
[119] *Real Estate and Building Journal*, August 25, 1894.

sales to avoid foreclosure.[120] However, another panic on the stock market late in 1895 intensified the depression in real estate by 1896, particularly that in vacant lots. At last there were no more excursions to take prospective lot-buyers to subdivisions.[121] "The demand for vacant property is at the lowest ebb in the history of the city. Nine out of the dealers in suburban property said there was absolutely nothing doing and there was no indication of a demand for vacant lots."[122] By this time a majority of the buyers of lots on easy payments had lost their holdings and had nothing to show for their investment. "Other real estate dealers said that in some localities two-thirds and perhaps three-fourths of the lots sold in good times had been sold on foreclosure and that nine-tenth of the cheap lots sold on easy payments had been sold for taxes and special assessments."[123]

In 1896 taxes had been increased 33–50 per cent[124] and this burden was most inequitably distributed as between persons and districts, assessed values varying from 4 to 64 per cent of true value in the central business district[125] and in other cases ranging from 1 to 100 per cent of true value. The method of allowing contractors to instal improvements to be paid for by special assessments in any territory in which they could secure the consent of the City Council had resulted in evils that were a constant source of complaint. Sidewalks were built where there was no one to walk on them, and water pipes were extended to sections where there were only one or two families to the mile.[126] A thousand boulevard lamps were erected in the swamps of the Calumet region. It is little wonder that the weight of such burdens had crushed the small-lot purchasers and that the number of lots subdivided declined from 111,000 in 1891 to 3,500 in 1898.

By 1896 real estate was in such a dull and disorganized condition that land values were difficult if not impossible to determine in many cases. "In the absence of sales enough to show a demand for real estate, the market must be a mere matter of opinion and when it gets so dull that a majority of the agents say that they cannot even hazard an

[120] *Ibid.*, November 16, 1895.
[121] *Ibid.*, June 6, 1896.
[122] *Ibid.*, November 21, 1896.   [123] *Ibid.*
[124] *Ibid.*, May 30, 1896.
[125] *Ibid.*, May 9, 1896 (Mayor Swift's Tax Commission report).
[126] *Ibid.*, August 1, 1896.

THE FIRST SKYSCRAPERS AND THE WORLD'S FAIR 181

opinion, it is certainly very quiet."[127] The morale of the once optimistic real estate brokers had declined to a very low ebb and their talk now discouraged prospective customers. "By far the most hurtful of all are the depressed feeling and discouraging talk of the brokers. Many of them are disheartened and some of them are in straightened circumstances."[128] The volume of recorded sales did not indicate that there was any real activity in the market, for "some estimate that not more than one-third of the transfers reported are entitled to be considered as a result of a demand for real estate, the other two-thirds being credited to exchanges, liquidations of debts, etc."[129]

The worst point in the depression was not reached in 1896, however, for in 1897 it was said that "real estate is a liability instead of an asset" and that it had declined 25 per cent in value during the year.[130] Foreclosures as indicated by the judicial sales at the Chicago Real Estate Board were increasing every year and did not reach their peak until 1898, as the Table VIII shows.[131]

TABLE VIII
VALUE OF PROPERTIES SOLD AT JUDICIAL SALES IN CHICAGO, 1892–99

1892 (beginning May 1)..	$2,537,262	1896..................	$10,697,288
1893..................	4,182,603	1897..................	13,380,240
1894..................	6,967,192	1898..................	13,609,858
1895..................	8,256,527	1899..................	11,821,711

During this very period of intense depression, however, an improvement was taking place in the transit facilities of the central business district and of the West and North sides that was to have both an immediate and an ultimate effect on their land values. These influences must now be considered.

F. NEW TRANSPORTATION LINES, 1894–98

The period from 1894 to 1898 was marked by the building of many new transportation lines, both elevated railroads and electric surface lines, on the North and West sides. The Lake Street elevated railroad, which had begun operation on the West Side late in 1893, was extended from Market Street to State Street in October, 1894. The Metropolitan elevated made rapid progress in 1895, the Garfield Park branch being

[127] *Ibid.*
[128] *Ibid.*, May 16, 1896.
[129] *Ibid.*
[130] *Ibid.*, June 12, 1897.
[131] Annual review in the *Economist* (1900).

completed from Franklin to Cicero Avenue, the Logan Square branch finished to Logan Square, the Humboldt Park branch built to Lawndale Avenue, and the Douglas Park branch constructed to Eighteenth Street.[132] The route of the Northwestern Elevated Railroad line was surveyed to Wilson Avenue in 1893 and construction was begun in 1896.[133] In 1895 and 1896 many new electric surface lines were built on the North and Northwest sides, particularly on Belmont, Irving Park, and Lawrence avenues, and territory that had the worst transportation before now secured the best. A rapid conversion of horse-car lines into electric-trolley systems was also taking place in these years until in 1897 the South Side surface lines had only 7.5 miles of horse-car lines compared with 141.5 miles of electric and 30 miles of cable lines, and the West Side lines had only 6.5 miles of horse-car lines compared with 165.5 miles of electric and 30 miles of cable lines.[134] The promises of improved transportation made in the boom of 1890 had been fulfilled, but the actual construction of the new lines did not produce the effect on land values in the depressed market from 1894 to 1898 that the mere promises of such facilities had exerted on the excited land market of 1890. Mr. Yerkes, who was promoting the North Side lines, was however, even in 1895, forming syndicates to purchase land along the route of the new electric surface lines; and the new means of electric transit—both surface and elevated—were to exert a marked influence on the rise in land values on the North and Northwest sides in the next few decades.

Meanwhile, the location of the downtown termini of the three elevated lines already constructed—the South Side elevated line, the Metropolitan elevated, the Lake Street elevated, and the projected Northwestern elevated—was in 1895 exerting a powerful influence on the values of land in the central business district. The new elevated roads were carrying passengers into the downtown area to shop who had formerly patronized stores on West Madison Street, Twenty-second Street, and Milwaukee Avenue. Rents of stores on these streets were

[132] Statement of J. V. Sullivan, assistant to the president, Chicago Surface Lines, to the writer in 1932.

[133] Emil Rudolph, who surveyed the route, in a statement to the writer in August, 1933, said that he was instrumental in selecting the route that was followed, as he persuaded Lauderback not to construct the line to Lincoln Park but to tap the territory farther west that lacked transportation facilities.

[134] Statement of J. V. Sullivan to the writer in 1932.

lower in 1895 than in 1889 while on State Street near Madison Street business rents had tripled. The exact route of each of these lines into the downtown area was a matter of great concern to owners of land on the various streets in that section. When the Lake Street elevated was finally extended to State Street, it was found that the thirty to forty thousand passengers poured daily from the stations at Wells, Clark, and State streets greatly increased the business of the stores on these streets running at right angles to Lake Street, but that they did not stop at all at the inside stores on Lake Street, which were therefore injured by the noise of the elevated structure without receiving any benefit in return.[135] Some of the owners of the Wabash Avenue property were therefore inclined to oppose the extension of the South Side elevated lines from Congress Street north to Lake Street, but there were others at the north end of Wabash Avenue who were anxious to secure the benefit of the traffic that was poured out at Congress Street, so the consent of the property owners was finally obtained. Instead of each elevated line constructing its own loop in the downtown area, as was first proposed, plans for a union loop were considered in 1895. Several possible routes were discussed, some contemplating elevated lines as far east as Michigan Avenue and as far west as Franklin Street. The building of lines that could be used for two sides of the Loop on Lake Street and Wabash Avenue was followed by the construction of the Van Buren and Wells Street sides. On October 12, 1897, the Union Loop was opened. The benefit was so pronounced to the property lying within the Loop that "the Loop" became a synonym for the high-value zone or the central business district of Chicago, while property owners outside the golden circle cursed the Loop as a Chinese Wall that stopped the natural expansion of the central business area. Meanwhile, a cable line on Blue Island Avenue that entered the downtown area through a tunnel on Van Buren Street had after 1894 been a large factor in promoting activity in the south end of the central business district.

The construction of the new elevated lines and the completion of the Union Loop so increased the business of retail merchants on State Street that there was no decline but even a slight advance in land values along State Street during this period of otherwise extreme depression. In fact, a new high record for land values was made in 1896 when the corner of

[135] *Real Estate and Building Journal,* December 7, 1895.

State and Madison was leased for $50,000 a year—only slightly less than was paid for the entire corner seventeen years before. This sale established a value of $18,000 a front foot for this peak-value corner of Chicago.

While land values in all parts of the central business districts were firmly maintained, the effect of the depression was felt here as well as in the suburban areas of the South Side. Most of the speculators in business leases were forced into bankruptcy by 1897, for they had contracted to pay higher rent than the stores could be made to pay. The "fad" of constructing high office buildings was overdone by 1894. A considerable number of the new skyscrapers started in prosperous times were not ready for occupancy until after the panic of 1893. Office rents were greatly reduced, agents scoured the streets for tenants, tenants were allowed to stay who were unable to pay their rents, and still a considerable proportion of the space in the new buildings remained vacant.[136] Under these conditions, many of these buildings did not yield enough income to pay their operating expenses, fixed charges, and ground rent, and new capital for erecting more skyscrapers was not available.[137] Instead of the urge to erect new tall buildings, the emphasis was now placed on the science of successful management of those already erected.[138]

G. SUMMARY OF THE TREND OF CHICAGO LAND VALUES, 1877–98

The aggregate value of the land in the 211 square miles of the present city limits of Chicago having declined from $575,000,000 in the peak reached before the panic of 1873 to approximately $250,000,000 in 1877, the brisk recovery beginning in 1879 had brought this aggregate back to $485,000,000 by the end of 1882. A period of equilibrium then followed in which land values remained almost stationary until 1886, when they began to rise slowly, until by the end of 1888 this aggregate amounted to approximately $650,000,000. In the extraordinary boom of 1889 and 1890, in spite of the failure of land values to advance in the residential belt of the old city, and only a moderate increase in land prices on the Northwest Side, the rise in values on the South Side and the central business district was so great that the average gain for the entire city was over 100 per cent in less than two years, bringing the

---

[136] *Chicago Tribune*, February 4, 1894.

[137] *Ibid.*, April 15, 1894.   [138] *Ibid.*, April 22, 1894.

THE FIRST SKYSCRAPERS AND THE WORLD'S FAIR 185

aggregate value of the 211 square miles in the present city limits of Chicago to $1,500,000,000. In the period of dulness that began in 1891 and the drastic depression that ensued after the panic of 1893, this aggregate declined to only $1,000,000,000 by 1898, a smaller percentage of decline than in any previous depression, because land values on the North Side and the central business district were holding firm or advancing during the deflation on the South Side. The South Side, where the value of land south of Twelfth Street, east and south of the Chicago River, and the Illinois-Michigan Canal had in 1890 surpassed that of the North and West sides combined, was rapidly losing its lead to the North Side from 1893 to 1897 because of the after-the-Fair reaction, the beginning of the shift in the fashionable residence section northward to the Lake Shore Drive, and the rapid improvement of the transit facilities of the North and Northwest sides.

The central business section.—Average front-foot land values in the section bounded by the lake, the main and south branches of the Chicago River, and Van Buren Street increased from $1,000 in 1873 and $500 in 1877 to $4,000 in 1891–92. The aggregate land value of $288,000,000 for the 72,000 front feet in this district obtained from actual sales is corroborated by the report of the Tax Commission in 1896.[139] Their valuations, made separately for each parcel in the central business district except tax-exempt property, when added together with an estimated value for the exempt tracts give practically the same result. Since there were no appreciable changes in average land values in the central business district from 1892 to 1896, a rise of 700 per cent in downtown land values from 1877 to 1892 is clearly indicated. This remarkable gain in property that was yielding an income all the time in most cases was due to a number of factors, most important of which were the skyscrapers, permitting a more intensive use of office-building sites, the increased volume of trade brought to the downtown area by the cable and elevated loops which in turn greatly increased the rents on the best retail streets, particularly State Street near Madison Street, and a decline in interest and capitalization rates until central business property which yielded a net return of from 10 to 30 per cent on the selling value of 1872 yielded only from 2 to 5 per cent on the selling values of 1892.

[139] See *Economist*, May 16, 1896, supplement. See Figs. 72 and 74 for land values in the central business district of Chicago for 1894–96.

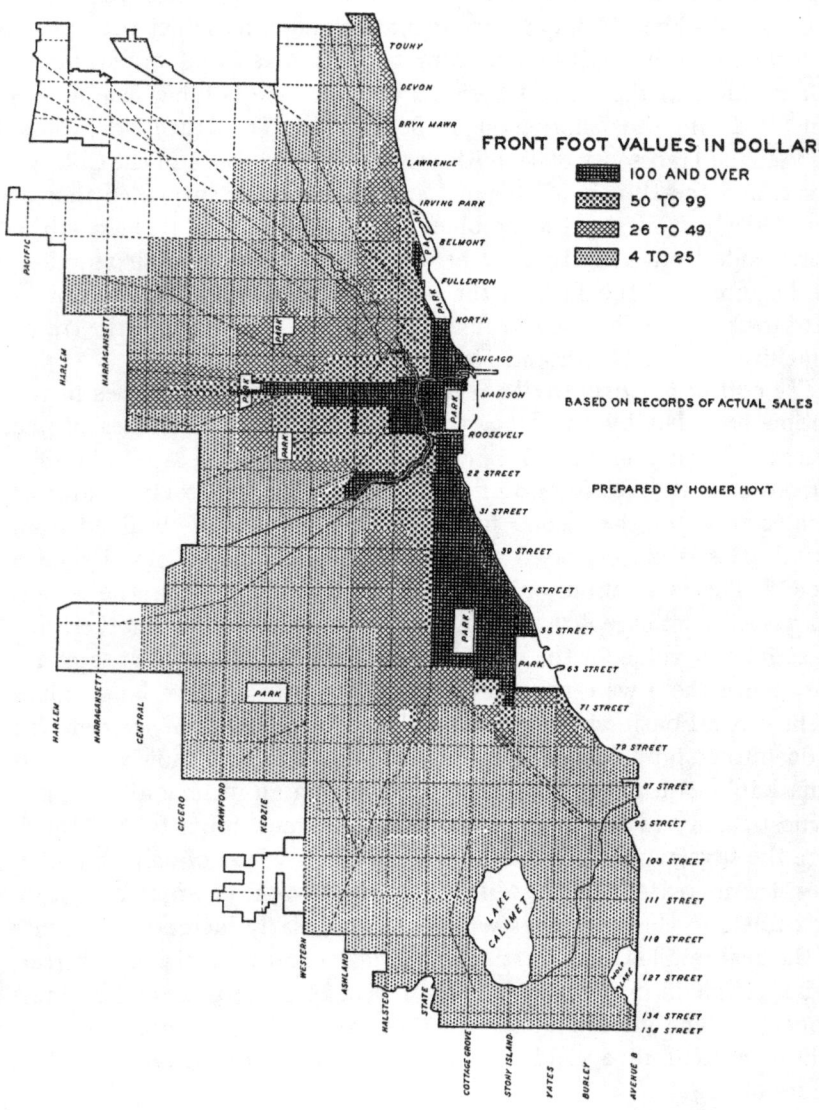

Fig. 26

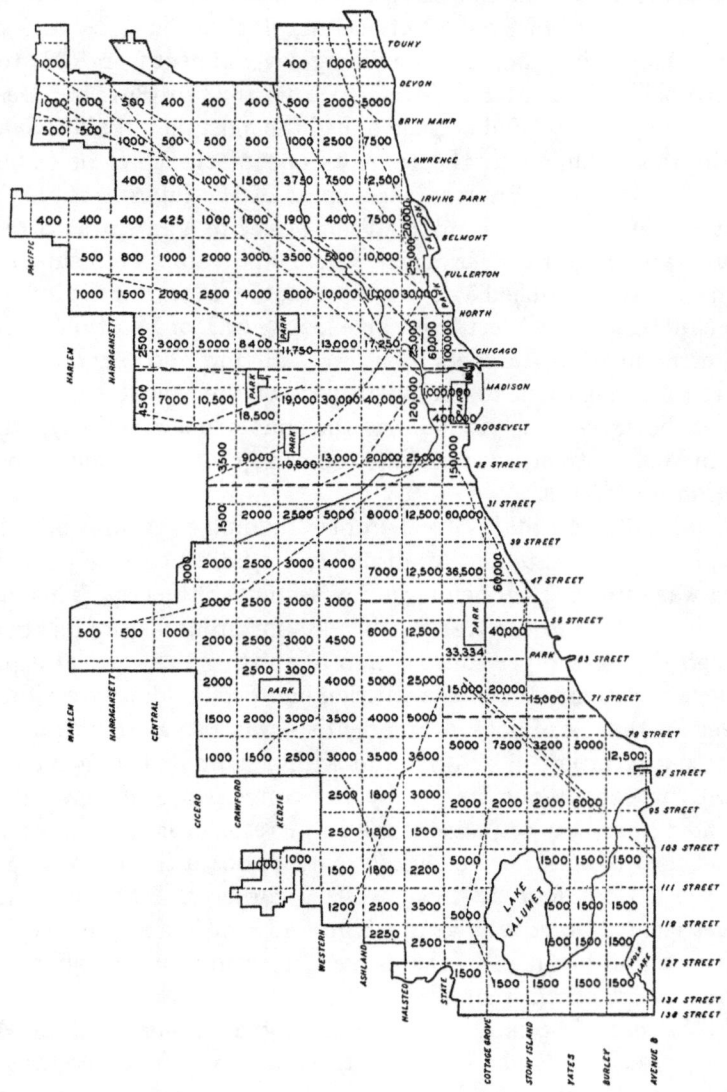

Fig. 27

The rise of land values in the central business district was by no means uniformly distributed, however, and there were eddies and crosscurrents of value shifts as buyers now rushed to this spot and now to that. The Board of Trade section near Jackson and LaSalle streets, having had its land boom and building development from 1881 to 1885, lagged behind in the later movement from 1888 to 1891; but Dearborn Street, long obscure and neglected, had the most remarkable advance of all in 1889, coming to the front as one of the chief office-building streets in the city. Prior to 1890, most of the interest of the buyers centered in the region from Madison Street to Van Buren Street and from State Street to Wells Street, where land values for inside frontage on most streets reached $7,000 a front foot by 1892; but the influence of the North Side and West Side cable loops north of Madison Street and the erection of skyscrapers along Washington and Randolph streets caused a swing back to the north part of the downtown area. Lake Street, however, was now outside the zone of main activity, although South Water Street was in greater demand than ever among the commission merchants.

Land values on State Street from Randolph to Adams Street, with the pinnacle at State and Madison streets, rose to a new peak, higher than was ever reached before in any section of the city. This increase was due mainly to the trebling of rents for ground-store locations, although the skyscraper construction permitting the vertical expansion of department stores and the erection of office buildings over the retail stores for the use of doctors and dentists was also an important factor. The concentration of retail trade within a limited area on a single street, brought about largely by the convergence of new cable and elevated lines, was responsible for an increase of land values on State Street near Madison from slightly over $1,000 a front foot in 1877 to $11,500 a front foot by 1896; while a corner of State and Madison Street yielded practically as much ground rent in a single year in 1896 as it was sold for in 1877, the increase in front-foot values being from $1,000 to $18,000 in that time.

In the meantime, land values on Michigan Avenue south of Monroe Street, which in 1879 had dropped to $200 a front foot, had, as a result of the completion of the Auditorium Hotel at Congress Street and the building and planning of other hotels to occupy half the ground from Monroe to Congress streets, advanced to $3,000 and $5,000 a front foot by 1892. Wabash Avenue, also, while hopelessly falling behind State Street as a retail shopping street, had become the center of the trade in musical instruments, and had been benefited by the completion of the South Side elevated line so that its land values from Monroe to Jackson streets had risen from $400 a front foot in 1879 to $6,000 a front foot in 1892.

Fashionable residential areas, 1877–95.—Medium-class houses, seven thousand of which were vacant in the West Side alone in 1890, were in such poor demand in the old sections of the city, as a result of the exodus to the suburbs and the growing popularity of apartments with gas, steam heat, and janitor service, that middle-class as well as poor-class residential land remained stationary or declined in this period.

Land in the fashionable residential sections in the old city or in the suburban districts, on the other hand, advanced rapidly, particularly in certain new locations. The value of fashionable residential land did not depend upon its income, for mansions costing from $25,000 to $200,000 could not be rented for enough to pay 2 per cent income on the investment; but upon the number of wealthy men in Chicago, the prevailing social customs of the time, which required the rich to maintain elaborate homes, and the desire of the social élite to congregate on certain streets on which circulated fashionable carriages and along which were arrayed the palaces whose massive exteriors and profuse decorations proclaimed the wealth and social standing of their occupants. The use of such land as a fashionable consumption good could change quickly with the whims and caprices of fashion. In that event, not only did the land lose its value for that purpose, but the mansions themselves were abandoned and frequently left as derelicts to be looted by vandals.

Prairie Avenue from Eighteenth to Twenty-second streets had been the center of Chicago's social world in the seventies. The land values even in that choice spot had declined to as low as $250 a foot in 1879, but there was a quick recovery to $700 a front foot in 1882. Thereafter the advance was slow, although the $1,000 a front foot offered for the corner of Twentieth and Prairie Avenue in 1889 was the highest price ever bid for residential land in Chicago up to that time. Meanwhile, the Lake Shore Drive, reclaimed from a frog pond by Potter Palmer, constructed along the lake by filling in the ground, and crowned by the erection of a $150,000 home for the leader of the "400," had risen in value near Burton Place from $160 a front foot in 1882 to $800 a front foot in 1892. As the old Prairie Avenue neighborhood, encroached upon by the vice area at Twenty-second and State streets, rapidly lost its prestige after 1893, the new "Gold Coast" of the North Side rose into prominence, until it became the chief center of fashionable society.

Michigan Avenue, converted into a boulevard for fashionable carriages, had had, meanwhile, a remarkable rise in its land values south of Twenty-sixth Street by 1881, and this rise slowly continued until by 1888 the corner of Twenty-ninth and Michigan Avenue sold for $700 a front foot. The land along Michigan Avenue as far south as Twenty-sixth Street had acquired a new value, because of its use for apartment hotels for the World's Fair, so that its land values near Eighteenth Street rose from $225 a front foot in 1879 to $1,500 a front foot in 1891.

The most rapid rises in high-grade residential property in the period from 1885 to 1890, however, were in the territory south of Thirty-ninth Street. Drexel and Grand boulevards from Thirty-ninth to Fifty-first streets were building up rapidly with fine homes from 1885 to 1895, Drexel Boulevard lots from Forty-seventh to Fifty-first streets rising from $100 to $600 a foot in that interval, and Grand Boulevard lots near Forty-seventh Street rising from $75 to $350 a foot from 1879 to 1893. The fashionable Kenwood and Hyde Park district was also expanding rapidly, with the result that land values on Woodlawn, Ellis, and Greenwood from Thirty-ninth to Fifty-first streets rose from $25 and $50 a foot in the early eighties to $200 a foot by 1891, while lots on Kimbark, Blackstone, and Lake Park avenues in the same region rose to $300 a foot. Farther south, from Fifty-first to Sixty-third streets on Harper, Blackstone, and Dorchester avenues, the rapid growth of apartment buildings in preparation for the World's Fair added to the increase in population that was taking place as a result of other forces and caused land values to rise from $20 and $50 a front foot to from $200 to $350 a front foot from 1882 to 1892. The building of the South Side elevated line had given a great impetus to land values along Prairie, Calumet, Indiana, and Wabash avenues from Thirty-ninth to Sixty-third streets, and their land values had risen from $10 to $20 a front foot in 1879 to $125 to $150 a front foot by 1891. Englewood, also, had its fashionable residence district on Yale, Harvard, and Normal avenues, where land values had increased from $25 to $150 a front foot from 1880 to 1890.

THE FIRST SKYSCRAPERS AND THE WORLD'S FAIR 191

On the West Side the conversion of Washington Street into a boulevard from Ashland Avenue to Garfield Park had doubled the value of its frontage in the late eighties, until its lots sold for from $250 to $300 a front foot by 1892.

Outlying business centers.—The effect of new transportation lines on cross-town streets intersecting transit lines running to the central business district had given relatively high value to transfer corners that were becoming neighborhood shopping centers from 1880 to 1890. The corner of Thirty-first and Indiana Avenue was leased on a $2,000-a-front-foot valuation in 1892, the highest value paid up to that time outside the central business district. The corner of Thirty-ninth and Cottage Grove Avenue, where the Cottage Grove horse-car line, the Thirty-ninth Street horse-car line, and the Hyde Park dummy lines had their terminal transfer points in 1875, grew into the most important neighborhood shopping center for a wide range of territory, its land value increasing from $220 a front foot in 1881 to $1,500 a front foot in 1889. The State Street and Cottage Grove Avenue cable lines, completed to Thirty-ninth Street in 1882 and to Sixty-third Street in 1887, had greatly enhanced land values along both those streets, the average front-foot values of State Street from Fifty-first to Sixty-third streets increasing from $15 to $160 from 1879 to 1892, and of Cottage Grove Avenue between the same streets for the same interval from $10 to $250 a front foot. The importance of Twenty-second, Thirty-first, Thirty-fifth, and Thirty-ninth streets as cross-town streets connecting with the downtown lines on State Street and Cottage Grove Avenue, crossing the main boulevards on the South Side, and leading to the Illinois Central Railroad stations, led to the speculative activity on Forty-third Street in 1891, where land values ranged from $200 to $300 a front foot.

Meanwhile, Sixty-third Street from the Illinois Central Station to Cottage Grove Avenue, which had been an unimproved country road in 1880, had begun to expand near that station as a result of the suburban railroad service in the early eighties. Its straggling shops had received a great accession of business when the cable line was completed on Cottage Grove Avenue to Sixty-third Street in 1887 and a horse-car line constructed east on Sixty-third Street in 1888. The coming of the World's Fair to Jackson Park and the completion of the South Side elevated line down Sixty-third Street in 1893 capped the climax. Land values of Sixty-third Street in this section rose from $20 to $30 a front foot in 1883 to $250 and $300 a front foot in 1891, with the corner off Sixty-third and Cottage Grove selling for $400 a front foot.

In Englewood the business center had been shifting from Wentworth Avenue from Fifty-ninth to Sixty-third streets to Sixty-third Street west of Wentworth Avenue, and the growth of this community had been so great from 1880 to 1890 that the best locations along Sixty-third Street in Englewood were valued at over $400 a front foot in 1891. In South Chicago, Ninety-second and Commercial Avenue had become the main business center of that community during 1890 with inside lots on Ninety-second near the corner of Commercial valued at $600 a front foot in 1891.[140] At the old center of the village of Hyde Park, Fifty-third and Lake Park Avenue, land values had reached $1,000 a front foot in 1891, while during the boom on Cottage Grove Avenue near Washington Park in the latter part of 1890 the northeast corner of Fifty-first and Cottage Grove Avenue that had sold for $60 a front foot in 1879 brought $750 a front foot.

On the West Side, Madison Street west of Crawford Avenue was particularly benefited by the cable line on Madison Street to the central business district, completed in 1890, and the new Cicero and Proviso electric line, built to Harlem Avenue along Madison Street in 1891. On the North Side, the corner of North and California had developed as a business center by 1895. Cable lines on Milwaukee Avenue, Clark Street, and Blue Island Avenue also aided business volume at the outer limits of development on these streets.

Notwithstanding the growth of outlying business centers at a considerable distance from the main business center during this period, the effect of swift transportation, afforded first by the cable lines, then by the elevated railroads and the electric surface lines, was to cause shoppers to pass by the stores in the old sections on Cottage Grove Avenue north of Thirty-ninth Street, Madison Street, Milwaukee Avenue, Blue Island, and Clark Street, and to come directly to the downtown area where the conveniences and bargains offered by the big State Street department stores held a magnetic attraction for them. Consequently, the speculative possibilities of the development of outlying business centers just beyond the settled area did not attract much attention at this time, and corners that a few decades later commanded values almost as high as downtown land were sold at very low prices even during the boom of 1890.

[140] *Economist*, May 16, 1891.

THE FIRST SKYSCRAPERS AND THE WORLD'S FAIR 193

Rise in the value of acre tracts, 1879-92.—The rise in the value of South Side acre tracts, that in many cases exceeded 1,000 per cent in ten years, was one of the most marked features of the real estate market from 1888 to 1890, as has already been noted. The extent and character of that movement can be best illustrated by a few representative sales. Thus land at Forty-eighth and Grand Avenue sold for $4,000 an acre in 1881 brought $32,500 an acre in 1892. The old Washington Park race track at Sixty-third and Cottage Grove Avenue, bought for $2,000 an acre in 1883, was valued at $20,000 an acre in 1893. Land south of Jackson Park advanced from $1,000 to $15,000 an acre from 1879 to 1893. Acre tracts at Eighty-seventh and Stony Island Avenue that were worth $500 an acre in 1881 sold for $5,600 an acre in 1891. The ground from Seventy-fourth to Seventy-fifth, State to Stewart Avenue in Englewood, that sold for $1,000 an acre in 1886 brought $15,880 an acre in 1891. The corner of Sixtieth and State advanced in value from $1,000 an acre in 1883 to $24,000 an acre in 1891. Land at Fifty-fifth and Ashland Avenue rose from $500 to $4,500 an acre from 1880 to 1891, and at at Eighty-seventh and Ashland Avenue there was a tract which sold for $90 an acre in 1880 which had sold for $1,800 an acre in 1890. The influence of Stickney tract speculation sent up the values of acres at Seventy-first and Western Avenue from $600 to $3,000 an acre from 1888 to 1890, and at Sixty-third and Crawford Avenue from $600 to $2,500 an acre from 1888 to 1891. Thus an extremely rapid advance in land values in this decade occurred throughout the entire South and Southwest sides of Chicago.

The advance in the value of acre tracts at the west city limits was also noteworthy, although not so extreme as on the South Side. Land at the corner of Madison and Oak Park avenues rose in value from $400 an acre in 1881 to $3,000 an acre in 1890, and the tract at Twelfth and Cicero Avenue from $800 to $3,000 an acre in the same period.

Along the North Shore at Lawrence Avenue and in Rogers Park, there was a rise in land values to $5,000 and $7,500 an acre in this period, and land near North and California avenues at Humboldt Park was also showing a marked increase in value, but the gain in prices on most of the Northwest Side was very moderate before 1890. Acre tracts along Crawford from North to Fullerton avenues gained in value from $800 to $3,000 an acre from 1882 to 1890, but much land within the northwestern part of the city could still be bought for $500 an acre in 1895. In no cases were there advances comparable to the ten-year increases of 1,000

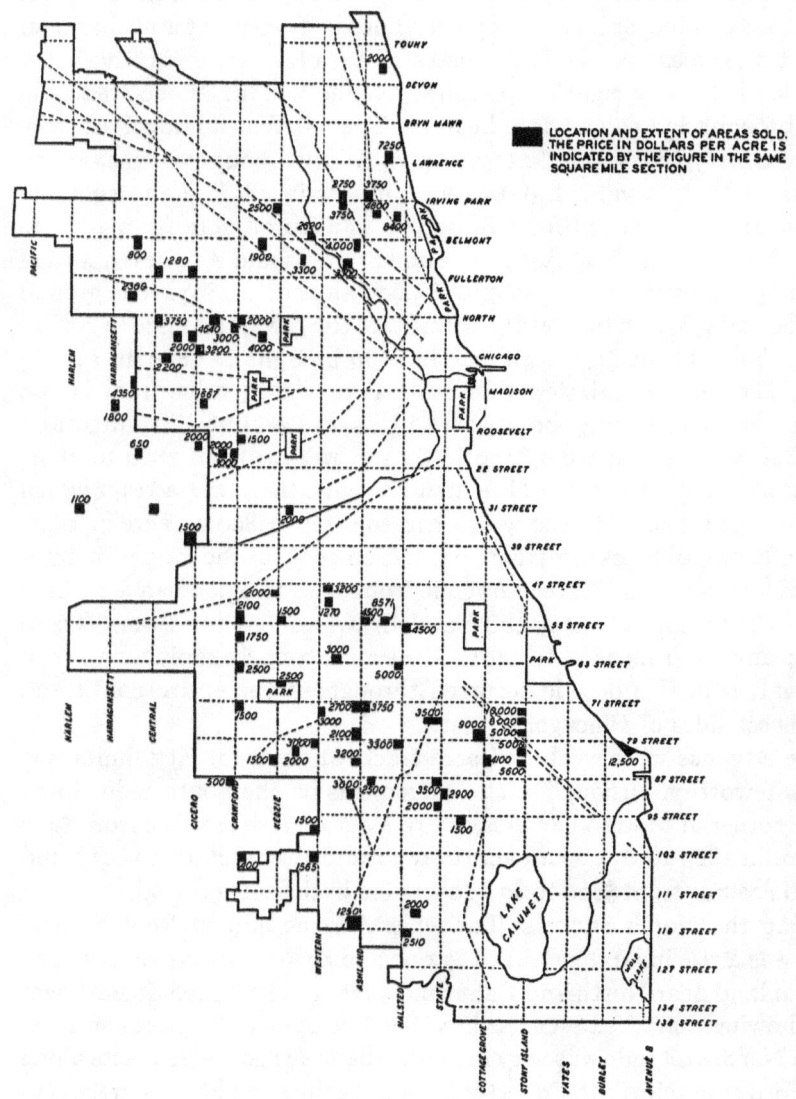

FIG. 28

THE FIRST SKYSCRAPERS AND THE WORLD'S FAIR

and 2,000 per cent shown in many instances by sales on the South Side.

Thus the rise in land values that culminated in 1890 or shortly afterward was distributed throughout the Chicago area in a widely varying manner. In fact, in some sections of the near West Side there was an actual decline in land values during this period, and in most of the cheap residential sections of the old city there was little if any rise in ground values. Even in the downtown area, the rise in land values on Lake Street was very slight. The land values of close-in secondary business streets, such as West Madison, Clark Street, Halsted Street, Blue Island Avenue, Milwaukee Avenue, Twenty-second Street, and Cottage Grove Avenue north of Thirty-first Street, affected adversely by competition of downtown stores, remained stationary or had only slight gains. Acre tracts on the Northwest Side that were not over six or eight miles from the city hall had been affected little by the boom that raged elsewhere. Notwithstanding the dead weight of these inert sections, there were enough centers of speculative excitement in and around Chicago to absorb funds from a considerable part of the people of Chicago and to create a furor of real estate activity that pervaded the entire community. Gains of 700 to 1,000 per cent in land values in ten years on the South Side and in the central business district were the main factors in the total aggregate advance for the city as a whole.

The rapid population growth of the outlying territories.—The rapid rise in land values in the decade from 1880 to 1890 in the territory just beyond the old city limits of 1888 was accompanied, and to a large extent caused, by an extraordinary population growth of the new areas annexed to the city in this same decade. Thus the population of the township of Lake increased from 18,380 to 100,223 from 1880 to 1890, or a gain of 550 per cent; the number of people in Lake View rose from 6,505 to 52,273, or a gain of 800 per cent; and the population of Hyde Park increased from 15,716 to 133,496, or a gain of 850 per cent, in the same decade. While the population in the old city limits increased from 503,145 to 792,377, or 57 per cent in the decade, the population of the main portion of the annexed territory advanced from 40,601 to 308,123, a gain of 650 per cent.[141] The demand for vacant land on the fringe of settlement for the actual use of this rapidly growing population had caused the first steady rise in land values which developed into a wild speculative boom in 1889 and 1890.

[141] *Ibid.*, July 19, 1890; U.S. Census for 1890.

CHAPTER V

THE LAND BOOM OF A NEW ERA THAT FOLLOWED
A WORLD WAR, 1898-1933

A. SURVEY OF THE CAUSES OF THE GROWTH OF CHICAGO,
1830-90 AND 1890-1933

Chicago's growth from the hamlet of a dozen log cabins in the swamps around Fort Dearborn in 1830 to the metropolis with over a million population at the time of the opening of the World's Columbian Exposition in 1893 was attained by the constant accession of new functions and new sources of power which reinforced the earlier forces before they began to wane. The inherent advantages of its situation were but dimly realized when it was a military and fur trading post prior to 1833 because its hinterland was then almost uninhabited. As the migration to the Northwest gained in volume, with the increase in the population of Illinois from 157,445 in 1830 to 851,470 in 1850, and a gain in the population of all the North Central states[1] from 1,610,473 to 5,403,595 in the same interval, the young city by the lake became the retail center of trade carried on by wagon caravans that had a radius of two hundred miles. From 1841 to 1848 Chicago developed a rapidly expanding commerce that was based on the imports of timber from the white-pine forests of Michigan, which were easily accessible to lake vessels, and the exports of grain brought in over dirt roads by horse-drawn vehicles. The completion of the canal in 1848 facilitated the shipments of grain and lumber, and the coming of the railroads from the East in 1852 and their extension westward to the Mississippi River and beyond extended Chicago's trading area enormously. While the population of the East North Central states was increasing from 4,523,260 in 1850 to 9,124,517 in 1870 and the population of the West North Central states was rising from 880,335 to 3,856,594, the railroads from Chicago were penetrating this rapidly filling area and developing for Chicago

[1] Ohio, Indiana, Illinois, Michigan, Wisconsin, Minnesota, Iowa, Missouri, North Dakota, South Dakota, Nebraska, and Kansas are the states in the North Central group. The first five of these states are listed in the East North Central group and the last seven in the West North Central classification.

A NEW ERA THAT FOLLOWED A WORLD WAR 197

merchants a great wholesale trade. For the spreading of the railroad net disclosed the fact that Chicago was the main transportation gateway between the East and the West, for it was located on the southern tip of Lake Michigan on a direct line with New York City and the Mohawk Pass which provided the only break in the Appalachian Mountain chain. The settlement of the Middle West led to the discovery that it was one of the richest agricultural valleys in the world, for the soil was fertile and the rainfall sufficient to insure maximum crops. Within a radius of six hundred miles from Chicago is the area that contains most of the improved land in crops in the United States, for the soil to the south and east of this belt is poorer and the rainfall to the west of it is far less abundant.[2]

From 1870 to 1890 the mileage of Chicago's railroads continued to increase, and the population of the East North Central states rose from 9,124,517 to 13,478,305 and that of the West North Central states from 3,856,594 to 8,932,112. To its position as a trading center for forest and farm products Chicago now added the manufacturing and industrial functions. Situated in the midst of agricultural resources of unsurpassed fertility that enabled bountiful crops of wheat and corn to be produced and that supported great numbers of hogs and cattle, it was in a natural position to supply this prairie world with manufactured products. In addition to all of these advantages, it occupied a location that was of paramount importance with respect to coal and iron—the basic materials for modern industrial growth. Chicago at the southern tip of Lake Michigan is close to the Illinois coal fields. In Minnesota, on the Mesabi Range, are iron-ore reserves hundreds of feet thick which run as high as 65 per cent iron and which can be worked from the surface with steam shovels. These iron deposits, the richest and most abundant in the United States, are within easy access of Lake Superior. Since it long required above two tons of coal to smelt one ton of iron, iron tended to be transported to coal rather than the reverse. The Great Lakes furnished a water highway on which specialized ore steamers carried the iron ore at the lowest ton-mile cost in the world, and Chicago was a natural meeting place of Minnesota iron and Illinois coal. The opening of the Minnesota iron mines in 1884 gave a further

[2] Maps of improved land in crops, and value of all farm crops (U.S. Census [1910, 1920]). Also see J. Paul Goode, *The Geographic Background of Chicago* (1926), for a discussion of all of these factors.

tremendous impetus to the growth of Chicago and to the further development of its trades and manufactures.

The growth of Chicago, however, did not stop in 1890, for from 1890 to 1930 its population tripled. Although the forces responsible for the early growth had begun to wane, as the lumber trade declined with the exhaustion of the pine forests of Michigan and as primary grain shipments fell off when grain was diverted to northern lake or southern gulf ports, some of the old forces continued with undiminished vigor and new factors appeared to reinforce the original ones.

As the pig-iron production of the United States increased eightfold from 1885 to 1916, and as its coal production increased twelvefold in the same interval and the young republic became the largest industrial nation in the world, Chicago gained a more than proportionate share in this expansion. For the center of population continued to move westward until in 1920 it was in Indiana almost due south of Chicago, as the population of the East North Central states increased from 13,478,305 to 25,297,185 between 1890 and 1930. The basic steel industries in the Chicago region grew and expanded as East Chicago and Gary were developed at the tip of the lake. Oil refineries rose in Whiting as trunk pipe lines were constructed from the producing fields in Kansas and Oklahoma to Chicago.

Even the remarkable expansion of such basic industries were not enough to sustain the upward curve of Chicago land values and population in the last four decades. Power resources were multiplied, the mobility of the population greatly increased, and the banking strength enhanced by a series of inventions and financial devices which came to full fruition in this period. The steam power, which, applied to lake and river vessels, had brought the tide of population from all parts of the United States and Europe to Chicago, and which, applied to the wheels of factories, had enabled this population to be supported, was supplemented by electric and auto-motive power. Chicago became the center of a great power pool or a generating point of electricity from which energy was transmitted over high-tension wires to hundreds of small communities. It became a part of a national telephone network and the principal manufacturing center of telephone equipment, as the telephone ceased to be regarded as a toy or a luxury and came into general use in the United States. With the advent of the mail-order house, the city soon assumed the position of dominance as a distribut-

A NEW ERA THAT FOLLOWED A WORLD WAR

ing center for Sears, Roebuck and Company and Montgomery Ward and Company, for it was located close to the population center of the United States. With the growth of the automobile industry from its humble start in 1900 to its overshadowing position by 1929, Chicago failed to become an important manufacturing center, but the 260,000 private garages in Cook County, the thousands of filling stations, public garages, and automobile showrooms that sprang up within the city attested to the importance of the automobile in altering the city's physical structure. The paving of most of the alleys in the city after 1910, the building of hundreds of miles of concrete highways in the city's environs, the widening of a number of the principal streets, and the erection of many new bridges over the Chicago River and its branches were likewise the result of the omnipresent automobile. The radio, which rose from nothing to almost the saturation point of possible demand with a set in nearly every home, gave rise to radio-manufacturing industries within Chicago and to a multiplication of retail outlets. The airplane furnished a demand for large landing fields on the outskirts of the city, and gave the maximum possibility of speed in the movement of people.

With the increased speed of transportation and communication, there was a surge of population outward from the center of the city to vacant prairie tracts where new homes with all modern improvements could be built. As a result there was a great increase in the demand for plumbing supplies and bathroom fixtures, as well as for new furniture that was in keeping with the new surroundings. Manufacturing plants and retail stores were kept busy in supplying this demand.

Still all this was not enough to keep up the constant expansion of the numbers of the people who could find employment in Chicago and to sustain the rising curve of land values. The banking and financial power of Chicago must likewise be expanded. The great Loop banks gained primacy in the Middle West, as they came to hold the deposits of seven thousand correspondent banks in smaller cities and country towns. In addition, there was a remarkable growth of banks in the outlying neighborhoods of Chicago, which attracted the savings of their own communities and reinvested them in local enterprises. Finally, in that grand multiplication of debt which occurred in the United States from 1914 to 1931, in which long-term obligations increased from $38,-000,000,000 to $134,000,000,000, there was a vast outpouring of accumulated savings upon real estate bonds in Chicago and upon the grandiose financial empire of Insull.

As Table IX shows, the growth of Chicago's population was not sustained in the last few decades so much by increased opportunities for employment in manufacturing as it was by the various types of services that were rendered in non-material form. The increase in the number of salesmen, school-teachers, beauty-parlor operators, advertising men, and clerks became a striking feature of the generation of this

TABLE IX*

NUMBER OF PERSONS OVER TEN YEARS OF AGE IN GAINFUL OCCUPATIONS IN CHICAGO, 1910–30

OCCUPATION	AGGREGATE NUMBERS			INDEX NUMBERS 1910 = 100		
	1910	1920	1930	1910	1920	1930
Manufacturing and mechanical...	421,740	489,001	563,750	100	166	133
Transportation...	98,649	110,521	143,553	100	112	145
Trade...	163,124	206,975	264,817	100	125	163
Public service...	15,960	23,110	28,329	100	145	177
Professional...	51,899	71,191	115,970	100	137	223
Domestic and personal.	119,374	116,102	191,570	100	98	165
Clerical...	120,247	210,537	255,495	100	175	213
Total...	996,589	1,231,434	1,658,858	100	124	166

* "Occupational Statistics, Illinois," *Fifteenth Census of U.S.* (1930), Table III, p. 6.

new era which sought to avoid physical exertion, to get rich by speculation, to create values by advertising, to appear beautiful, well groomed, and youthful at all costs, and to rise to positions of power and dominance through the magic potency of a formal education ending with a college degree. Thus the employees in manufacturing increased 33 per cent from 1910 to 1930, while employees in all other lines increased 90 per cent in the same interval.

B. THE PERIOD FROM 1898 TO 1918

Chicago in 1900.—The Chicago of 1900 presented a picture that may be contrasted with the appearance of the city in 1873 and in 1933. In the central business district, the elevated loop had just been completed. Above the skyline of the five- and six-story buildings erected after the fire of October 9, 1871, rose the first crop of skyscrapers—the twenty

A NEW ERA THAT FOLLOWED A WORLD WAR

buildings from twelve to nineteen stories high that were the marvel of the nineties. State Street department stores were just attaining their first exuberant expansion, and as the elevated lines brought people downtown, these multiple stores were bitterly attacked by the small local merchants, even as the chain stores are today. The banks and theaters were practically all concentrated in the central business area, so that the Chicago "Loop" had become the place where the people in the Metropolitan Area congregated for the purpose of making most retail purchases, except foodstuffs, for transacting financial business and for entertainment. For this reason, land values in the central business district had advanced greatly even from the boom prices of 1873, and the gain had been maintained even during the depression following the panic of 1893.

The belt of land extending for three miles from the Loop on the South, West, and North sides, which was an area of new and vigorous growth in 1873 and an obsolete and blighted area in 1933, contained a strange conglomeration of social and economic forces in 1900. A considerable proportion of all the factories and industries in the city still hugged the banks of the Chicago River and its branches on the near West, North, and South sides. Close to the workshops of the West Side in the 1 square mile from Twelfth to Twenty-second streets and from Halsted to Ashland avenues were packed 73,400 people, or twice as many as lived in 88 square miles inside the outer edges of the city limits. The influx of a steady stream of Italians, Poles, and Russian Jews into the old residential areas of the city kept up a demand for this cheaper type of property. The older Irish and German elements sold out to new immigrants and used the proceeds to buy homes along the new elevated or electric lines. Industries were also beginning to expand into the old residential sections, so that owners of such property felt that there was a prospective demand from this source also. The colored race, confined within the narrow limits of a belt from Twenty-sixth to Thirty-ninth streets, from State to LaSalle streets, also paid high rents for the shacks within those boundaries. Likewise, the Chinese segregated on South Clark Street, and the Jews, hemmed in by the invisible wall of their West Side ghetto, paid high rents for obsolete buildings because of the social barriers against their movements. The wide-open "red light" district, with its two hundred and sixty houses of prostitution on State and Dearborn streets from Eighteen to Twenty-second street, also paid high returns to the owners for their immoral use. A more intensive use of land for apartment buildings along business streets and in close proximity to fashionable residential areas also had supported land values in these sections to some extent. Where other opportunities did not present themselves, the once fashionable residences on the near North and South sides were converted into boardinghouses.

Thus land in what is now known as the blighted area yielded an income and had prospects of enhancement in value due to absorption by industry that it does not have in 1933. Even in 1900, however, the returns from this class of property were capitalized at a high rate, so that the land values as a whole had ceased to advance. Moreover, the close proximity of the vice section, the colored belt, and of the advancing line of industries and warehouses to the fashionable residential section on Prairie Avenue had already started its decline. Similarly, Ashland Avenue, Jackson Boulevard on the West Side, and Dearborn and La-Salle streets on the North Side were sliding downward and losing their social prestige.

The intrusion of the races of the new immigration, of factories and warehouses, and of vice elements was thus pushing the older immigrants and the higher-income classes into a zone of new growth. The new areas being built upon in 1900 were chiefly located along the new elevated lines, such as at the terminus of the Northwestern elevated line at Wilson Avenue, southeast of Sixty-third and Cottage Grove Avenue, along the Metropolitan elevated line from Cicero to Crawford avenues and from Madison to Harrison streets. It was the era when the two-apartment building was gaining rapid popularity and when rows and rows of such structures were being erected. Other areas of rapid growth at the beginning of this century were the Kenwood district; Englewood; Milwaukee Avenue from Chicago to North Avenue, where a colony of Poles was expanding rapidly; and the district east of Humboldt Park, which was being settled by Germans.

Beyond this ring of new growth that was being added to the solid nucleus of the old city were detached settlements that varied in size from hamlets to cities of fifty thousand population. The largest of these planetary urban bodies was South Chicago, which had become a great iron and steel center as the commerce on the Calumet River was about to surpass the waning traffic on the Chicago River. Other industrial

A NEW ERA THAT FOLLOWED A WORLD WAR

towns inside the city limits of Chicago, but separated by tracts of prairie from the main body, were Hegewisch, Pullman, Kensington, and Riverdale on the South Side. Southwestward was the pleasant suburb of Morgan Park. Beyond the city limits to the north and west communities were being settled by the office workers in Chicago. These included Oak Park and LaGrange to the west and Evanston, Wilmette, Winnetka, and Lake Forest along the North Shore. These outlying settlements within and without the city limits of Chicago ran the entire gamut of the social scale from the squalid quarters in South Chicago, where fifty-thousand inhabitants were "hemmed in by stretches of railroad tracks and ugly buildings" and "where scores of towering smoke stacks and furnaces pour out smoke and dust day and night," to the spacious estates of the millionaires of Lake Forest.[3]

As Figure 29 shows, beyond the main body of the settled area of Chicago and between the detached settlements there were thus wide stretches of vacant land within the city limits of Chicago on both the North and the South sides. The Northwest Side, west of Western Avenue and north of North Avenue, was mostly vacant, except for the 2 square miles from Western to Kedzie and from Belmont to North avenues. In the area thus defined, excluding these 2 square miles, there were 32 square miles, and in it there lived only 39,131 people in 1900. Even though the population of this area had increased from 3,000 in 1880 and 10,734 in 1890 to this number, not more than one-fourth of this territory had buildings on it and one-third of it was farm land that had never been subdivided. There were parts of it that were 2 or 3 miles from a street-car line or a paved street. Less than 6 per cent of the streets was paved and no alleys had been improved. The population was clustered around many small centers such as Bowmanville, where there was a pickle factory; Cragin, a small Polish manufacturing town; Dunning, the county infirmary; Hermosa; Hanson Park; and stations on the Northwestern Railroad at Avondale, Irving Park, Montclaire, Jefferson, and Norwood Park.[4]

Chicago in 1900 thus presented a series of startling contrasts: wide-open prairies and densely crowded, sunless, ill-ventilated tenements without gardens, shade trees, or grass in their vicinity;[5] houses in the

[3] "Report of the South Park Commission on Small Parks, 1902" (an unpublished report).
[4] *Chicago Tribune*, August 24, 1900.
[5] "Report of the South Park Commission."

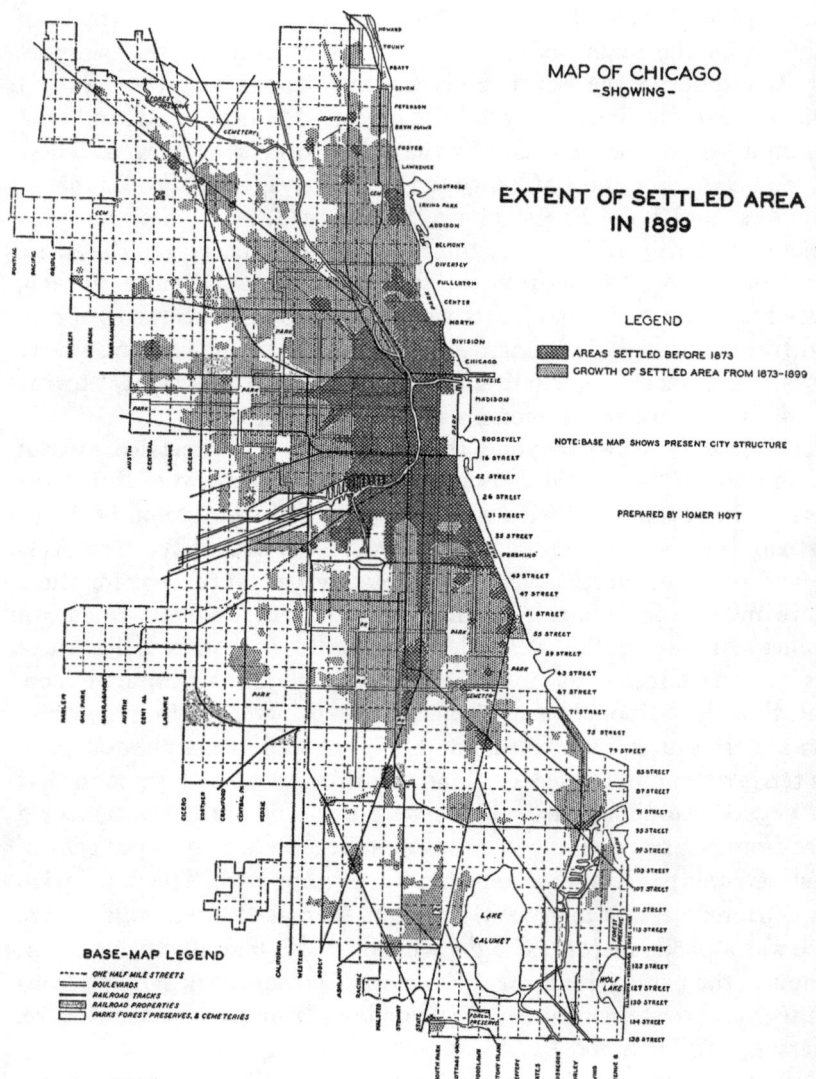

FIG. 29

A NEW ERA THAT FOLLOWED A WORLD WAR

"red light" district a few blocks from the mansions of millionaires; sixteen-story office buildings next to three-story obsolete buildings; large local-option districts without a single saloon and the Stock Yards district with 500 saloons in a few blocks. In all, there were 6,373 saloons occupying 31 miles of street frontage in Chicago, and it was estimated that the 153,477,900 gallons of intoxicating liquors consumed annually would completely immerse the Masonic Temple.[6]

The period of twenty years from 1898 to 1918 was one of remarkable physical growth, as Figure 30 shows. The city of Chicago added a million to its population from 1900 to 1920, an increase of 60 per cent. Bank clearings rose from $5,517,335,477 in 1898 to $16,198,985,175 in 1915, or a gain of 194 per cent.[7]

The value of Chicago's manufactured products more than tripled between 1896 to 1915, rising from $483,000,000 in the former to $1,723,700,000, or 357 per cent in the latter year.[8] Traffic on the elevated lines increased from 55,204,936 passengers in 1898 to 197,440,107 in 1918,[9] or a rise of 258 per cent. The gains registered in the new industries were far more sensational. The number of automobiles in Chicago in 1908 was multiplied by seventeen before the end of 1920 as the number rose from 5,000 to 86,500.[10] The number of telephones installed in Chicago increased from 11,680 in 1895 to 575,840 in 1920—a gain of nearly fifty fold.[11] Electricity generated for Chicago consumers mounted one hundred and thirty-four fold in the same period from 1895 to 1920, with an increase from 13,720,000 to 1,831,628,000 kilowatt-hours.[12] These gains were accomplished during a period of slowly rising wholesale prices in the United States, but the increase was moderate, so that the wholesale price level of 1915 was only 25 per cent above that of 1900.

Notwithstanding this marked growth of Chicago in the first two decades of the twentieth century, there was no general land boom in which values took a sudden spurt in these years. It is true that the

[6] *Chicago Tribune*, September 8, 1900.   [7] Annual reviews in *ibid*.
[8] Typewritten statement from the Chicago Clearing House Association published in the early part of January of each year.
[9] Letter to the author from the receiver of the Chicago Transit Lines.
[10] Report of the License Department of the city of Chicago.
[11] Letter to the author from the statistician of the Illinois Bell Telephone Co.
[12] *Commonwealth Edison Company Chicago Year Book* (1931), p. 31.

annual volume of new building more than tripled from 1900 to 1916,[13] that the annual number of transfers of real estate and the number of lots subdivided quadrupled in the same time interval, and that land

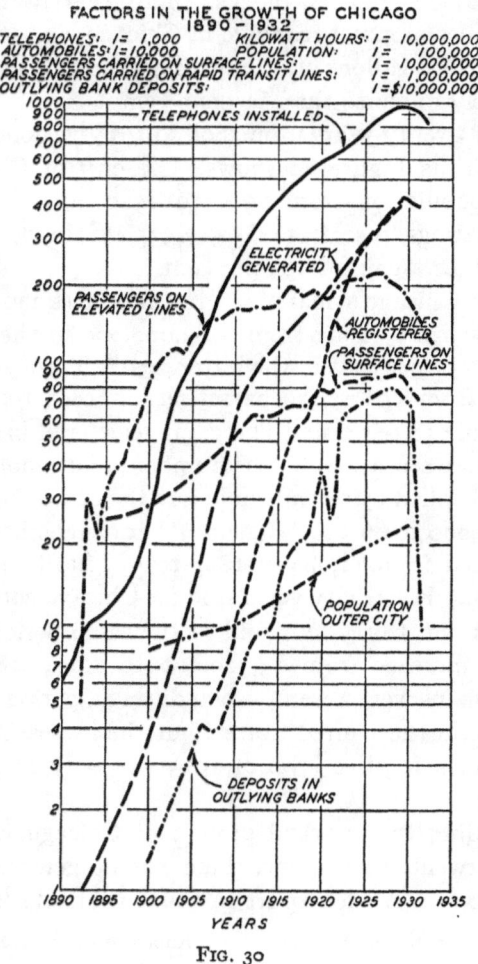

FIG. 30

values of the city of Chicago doubled in these sixteen years, but the growth was gradual. There was no wild excitement and no widespread public participation in the real estate market. Land values advanced

[13] Measured by the number of buildings or by street frontage occupied by new buildings. The value of new construction was $20,000,000 in 1900 and $112,000,000 in 1916.

A NEW ERA THAT FOLLOWED A WORLD WAR

steadily in the Loop, the North and Northwest sides, along the newly extended elevated lines, and in the rising outlying industrial and business centers, but the painful remembrance of the aftermath of the boom of 1890 checked any tendency toward reckless speculation. While St. Louis, New York, Seattle, and the cities of the Canadian Northwest had the experience of real estate booms from 1904 to 1915, the Chicago land market remained quiet and unruffled.

The narration of the changes in land values in Chicago in the period from the beginning of the twentieth century to the end of the World War lacks the stirring and dramatic episode of the periods that preceded and followed it. The character of the growth of the city and the nature of the land market in the pre-war days nevertheless deserves careful study, for it presents the picture of a market in which there was a steady occupation for those engaged in the real estate business. After the hectic experiences of a boom and a depression many of those plunged from wealth to poverty sigh for a return of the "good old days when a modest competence could be earned by all brokers."

The leading features in the Chicago real estate market for the period beginning in 1898 may now be considered.

Beginning of the recovery in Chicago real estate.—In 1898 the Chicago real estate market was at its lowest ebb of activity. Foreclosures and judicial sales were at their peak. Rents, the number of lots subdivided, and the volume of real estate transfers were at their lowest points since 1892. There was an oversupply of office buildings in the central business district, of old houses in the intermediate belt, and of apartments in the vicinity of the World's Fair grounds. Vacancies meant a total loss of income, while rents of occupied buildings were not only low but in many cases were not promptly paid. The landlords not only accumulated a load of bad debts, but they were forced to accede to the demands of tenants for extensive repairs. Many apartment buildings and downtown skyscrapers were in the hands of receivers or in more favorable cases barely paid 2 per cent on the investment. Such conditions were not conducive to the sale of improved property, which was further demoralized by the load of foreclosure sales hanging over the market. For vacant lots in most localities there was scarcely any demand at all. Subdivision activity, as measured by the number of new lots platted in the Chicago Metropolitan Region, had declined in 1899 to 4 per cent of the peak volume of 1891.

Even in this trough of the depression there were some favorable factors. Interest rates on mortgages in the central business district had declined to 4 and even $3\frac{1}{2}$ per cent,[14] with the result that long-term leaseholds were capitalized on a 4 instead of a 5 per cent basis. This alone would tend to raise downtown land values 25 per cent, and although its effect did not immediately show itself in such a blanket increase, the lowering of the capitalization rate was now operating to increase valuations. Moreover, even in 1898 apartment buildings were being built along the line of the South Side elevated system, and houses were going up along the tracks of the Northwestern elevated railroad, which was then in process of construction.

In 1899 there was a general improvement in business conditions. Wages advanced 5 and 10 per cent.[15] There were not one-fourth as many vacant flats in the spring of 1899 as in the spring of 1898.[16] Office rents were lower,[17] but rents elsewhere ceased to decline and were more promptly paid.[18] Capitalists began to buy property at foreclosure sales.[19]

New transportation systems.—One of the factors that was of the greatest aid in the renewal of real estate activity was the improvement in transportation. From 1890 to 1900 there had been a revolutionary change in the internal transportation system of Chicago. Elevated lines had been constructed on the South Side, the West Side, and finally on the North Side, and these were at last linked together in a union loop in the central business district in 1900, which thereafter became known as the "Loop." Of even greater importance was the substitution of electric power for steam and horse power in the elevated and surface lines. From 1895 to 1897 many new street-car lines were laid in the northwest section of the city, and these new lines were being operated by electric power. In addition, horse-car lines, the slowest parts of the transportation system, were being rapidly electrified at this time, and, finally, electric power was installed in the cable trunk lines.[20]

Effect on different sections of the city.—Prior to 1893 the South Side had by far the best transportation facilities, with four railroads providing good suburban service. The North and West sides not only had fewer

[14] *Chicago Tribune*, August 14 and September 4, 1898.
[15] *Ibid.*, March 4, 1899.
[16] *Ibid.*, March 12, 1899.
[17] *Ibid.*, January 29, 1899.
[18] *Ibid.*, December 31, 1899.
[19] *Ibid.*, March 5, 1899.
[20] See Fig. 31.

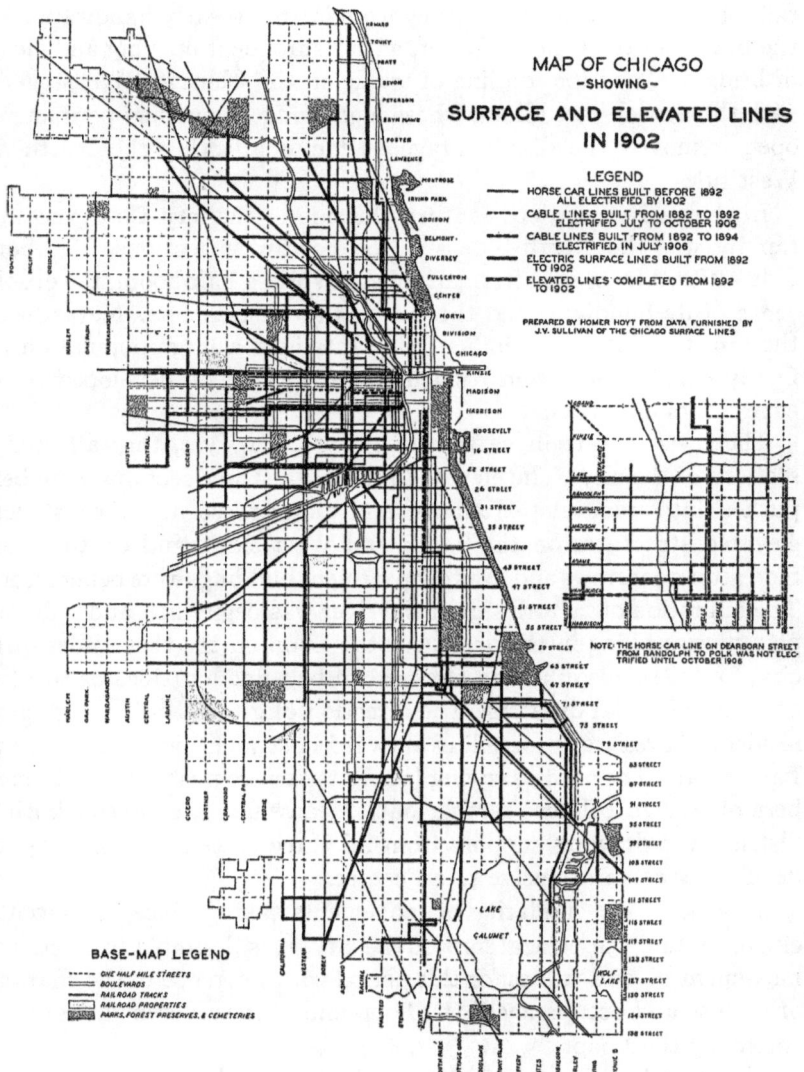

FIG. 31

railroads and cable lines, but they were further greatly handicapped by the barrier of the Chicago River, with its frequent opening and closing of bridges. The rapid decline of traffic on the Chicago River, together with the new elevated lines, whose high bridges remained permanently open, removed the disadvantageous factor affecting the North and West sides.

In the early twentieth century the side of the city that grew most rapidly was the North Side and the northwest sections. The South Side suffered from the aftermath of the World's Fair boom, the obsolescence of its buildings, and the spread of vice elements. Nevertheless, the growth of its great industrial plants held a large population and finally enabled new high residential sections to be developed on the edges of its old areas.

There was a certain pattern of growth, however, that affected all sections of the city. The elevated lines in the three sections were being pushed into undeveloped tracts, and along these newly constructed elevated structures on the South and West sides, and on the North Side after 1900, rows and rows of apartment buildings were being erected. The migration of factories from the river was beginning, and industrial plants were filling in the area near the Loop on the three sides of the city, and were also moving outward to belt-line locations or to newly created industrial districts. The direction of growth of the high-grade residential area was proceeding outward in straight lines and along the Lake Shore. The newly arriving immigrants were pushing the old members of foreign colonies farther out. Meanwhile, the central business district was drawing support from all three sections of the city and developing as an exclusive retail center.

Because of the similarity of movements taking place in concentric circles around the central hub of the city, it is desirable to discuss the movement of land values for this period with reference to the character of the use and occupancy of the Loop and of the different belts of land encircling the Loop.

The central business district: office buildings.—With the cessation of the construction of new office buildings, the large supply of vacant offices existing in 1900 had been almost entirely absorbed by 1902. Rents were advanced 15 per cent in 1902.[21] Plans for the erection of eighteen new buildings to cost over $10,000,000[22] caused the City Coun-

[21] *Economist*, May 15, 1902.   [22] *Ibid.*, January 25, 1902.

A NEW ERA THAT FOLLOWED A WORLD WAR

cil to remove the old limit of 130 feet on the height of buildings and to establish a new maximum height of 260 feet.[23] In 1903 office rents were again advanced 15 per cent, and buildings, such as the Monon and the Caxton, were fully rented for the first time.[24] Downtown office property was thus once more a profitable investment.

The Loop retail district.—The completion of the Northwestern elevated lines to Wilson Avenue in 1900 and the growing traffic on all the elevated roads had greatly increased the throng of shoppers in the Loop retail district. Locations on State Street, the "Main Street" of two million people, were in greater demand than ever before. The value of lots on State Street from Washington to Van Buren streets reached levels by 1904 "that would not have been dreamed of a few years ago, not even in the boom times preceding the World's Fair,"[25] and in 1906 the *Economist* declared that "there was nothing in the world so valuable as State Street frontage."[26] Advancing business rents made possible by a larger volume of sales at higher prices and a decline in the capitalization rate from 5 to 4 per cent had raised the peak prices of State Street frontage in 1890 to levels that were two and three times as high. In 1903 the southwest corner of State and Adams streets was leased on a basis of $20,731 a front foot.[27] In 1905 frontage on State Street between Washington and Madison streets was leased on a valuation of $22,500 a front foot,[28] and a lease on the basis of $15,300 a front foot was refused for a lot on State Street south of Jackson Boulevard.[29] In 1906 the corner of State and Quincy streets was capitalized at $26,114 a front foot, and State Street north of Madison Street at $24,419 a front foot.[30] Ten years before, $10,000 a front foot had been regarded as a top price.

Retail trades were expanding until by 1907 they occupied the ground floors of the entire Loop area.[31] Firms that could not afford to pay the high rents demanded on State Street moved to Wabash Avenue or to Dearborn, Clark, and Wells streets, or to the east-west thoroughfares. Lots on Wabash Avenue, as a result of the change from wholesale to retail use, reached the highest prices in their history. Michigan Avenue, evolving as a hotel center, also had a remarkable transformation. In

[23] *Ibid.*, March 1, 1902.
[24] *Ibid.*, February 7, 1903.
[25] *Ibid.*, December 31, 1904.
[26] *Ibid.*, March 24, 1906.
[27] *Ibid.*, May 23, 1903.
[28] *Ibid.*, October 7, 1905.
[29] *Ibid.*, September 30, 1905.
[30] *Ibid.*, March 10, 1906.
[31] *Ibid.*, August 24, 1907.

1902 a lot on Michigan Avenue south of Jackson was leased on a basis of $5,707 a front foot.[32]

Downtown wholesale area.—The wholesale firms in the area south of Monroe Street and west of Wells Street had recovered from the panic of 1893 within four years. A remarkable expansion of business had by 1902 filled all the available space at advancing rents. Ten new buildings, with a total of 1,063,000 square feet of floor space, were erected during 1903 and 1904, creating a temporary oversupply of over 1,000,000 square feet in 1904, which was, however, entirely absorbed during 1905.[33]

Summary: downtown area.—Thus nearly the whole of the downtown area profited from the growing retail and wholesale businesses and the enlarged demand for office space. In addition, the prosperity of the financial interests caused the erection of new bank buildings on LaSalle Street. Buyers sought old run-down properties yielding a low return on the investment which with modern improvements and superior management could be made to yield 8–12 per cent on their original cost.[34] Leases made in the preceding decade were sold at large premiums. Central business property had become concentrated in fewer owners and tied up to an increasing extent under long-term leases, so that sales of land, free from leases, were less frequent.

Expanding wholesale and warehouse interests.—The expansion of the retail area in the Loop district and the higher land values resulting therefrom forced the warehouses and wholesale houses that were formerly located on Wabash, Wells, and on other streets adjacent to the Loop to move into the old residential area near the Loop that had long been dormant. On the near South Side, Clark at Sixteenth Street,[35] Indiana at Sixteenth Street,[36] and Wabash near Twenty-third Street[37] began to develop as warehouse centers in 1903. On the near North Side on Illinois and Erie streets east of St. Clair Street, a section of reclaimed land was sold for warehouse purposes in 1907.[38] In 1902 the first automobile shop was leased on Michigan Avenue near Fourteenth Street.[39] In 1903 a new furniture center was established at Twelfth and Michigan

[32] *Ibid.*, November 22, 1902.
[33] *Ibid.*, November 19, 1904; September 2, 1905.
[34] *Ibid.*, June 27, 1903.
[35] *Ibid.*, September 19, 1903.
[36] *Ibid.*, October 10, 1903.
[37] *Ibid.*, March 10, 1906.
[38] *Ibid.*, October 19, 1907.
[39] *Ibid.*, January 11, 1902.

A NEW ERA THAT FOLLOWED A WORLD WAR

and at Sixteenth and Indiana Avenue. At this point 623 agencies out of a total of 4,000 in the United States sold over $40,000,000 worth of furniture in 1903.[40]

Other large mail-order and wholesale firms moved north and west from their old locations near the Loop. In 1904 Sears, Roebuck and Company left their building at Canal and Washington streets to go to a huge new building at Kedzie Avenue near Twelfth Street.[41] In 1906 Montgomery Ward, Sprague-Warner, and the Edward Hines Lumber Company moved to the north branch at Chicago Avenue.[42]

New manufacturing centers.—Old manufacturing centers near the Loop continued to grow in this period. New boot and shoe manufacturing plants were located on the district from Grand to Chicago avenues, west of Wells Street to the river, while refrigerating plants for fruits and vegetables were expanding on Illinois and Michigan east of State Street. On the near West Side, machinery houses were growing in the area on Canal and Clinton streets between Washington and Randolph streets, and south of Adams Street high-class manufacturing plants were pushing toward Roosevelt Road.

The most important manufacturing developments, however, were in regions farther from the Loop. The Western Electric Company moved from Clinton and Congress streets six miles southwestward to Twenty-second and Cicero Avenue on the Chicago Belt Line in 1903.[43] The Central Manufacturing district, from Thirty-fifth to Thirty-ninth streets, Ashland to Morgan Street, starting in 1902 with the purchase of the ground for $900,000, had developed rapidly from 1904 to 1906 when twenty-five manufacturing plants were located there.[44] Pullman was growing as an industrial center. The Corn Products Company bought 140 acres for their new plant at Summit in 1906.[45] The Clearing railroad yards were built and factories began to be erected near them. Two new plants were built at the Stock Yards.[46]

The most remarkable growth of manufacturing plants, however, took place in the Calumet region. The commerce of the Calumet River which had been only one-tenth of that of the Chicago River in 1889 had steadily advanced as that of the Chicago River declined. In 1906 the

[40] *Ibid.*, November 7, 1903.
[41] *Ibid.*, December 24, 1904.
[42] *Ibid.*, March 24, 1906.
[43] *Ibid.*, October 24, 1903.
[44] *Ibid.*, September 21, 1907.
[45] *Ibid.*, December 1, 1906.
[46] *Ibid.*, December 17, 1904.

commerce of the two rivers was equal in value. In 1916 the traffic on the Calumet was five times as great as that on the Chicago River.[47] The iron and steel industries were leading factors in this growth, although grain and lumber were scarcely less important. There were sixty grain elevators in South Chicago in 1907.[48] The development of this region was not confined within the city limits of Chicago, although the benefit of Chicago railroad rates aided the new cities growing beyond its boundaries. Indiana Harbor, Indiana, was being boomed in 1903.[49] Gary was founded in 1906.

Value of railroad and manufacturing property.—The lower value of manufacturing sites at a distance from the central business district was one of the reasons for the more rapid growth of the outer manufacturing districts. Land on the South Side adjacent to the Loop sold for not less than $20 a square foot. On the West Side, at Madison and Clinton, the Northwestern Railroad paid $10 a square foot for its depot site. A little farther out from the center of the city, at Sixteenth and Indiana Avenue, Twenty-second and Dearborn streets, and at Chicago Avenue and the north branch of the river, the value was only $2.00 a square foot. On the West Side, the value of land along the Chicago River ranged from $10 a square foot at Madison Street to $5.00 a square foot at Harrison Street, $1.25 a square foot at Twenty-second Street, and 5 cents a square foot at Crawford in the period from 1905 to 1908. Land at St. Clair and Illinois streets sold as low as 60 cents a square foot in 1907, in the Central Manufacturing District at from 25 to 60 cents a square foot, at Arthington and Kedzie avenues 30 cents a square foot in 1904, at Lake Michigan and the Calumet River 45 cents a square foot in 1905, and at Twenty-second and Cicero Avenue at 5 cents a square foot in 1906.

Fashionable residential property.—The Lake Shore Drive, from Division to North Avenue, valued at from $1,000 to $1,500 a front foot, was the center of fashion after 1900. The building of new high-class residences had practically ceased from 1900 to 1908, because old mansions on Michigan and Prairie avenues could be bought at prices far below their original cost. The residence at 1922 Calumet which cost $100,000 was sold with 100 feet of ground for $33,500 in 1908.[50] The

---

[47] *Chicago Tribune*, December 30, 1916.

[48] *Economist*, February 9, 1907.

[49] *Ibid.*   [50] *Ibid.*, October 24, 1908.

A NEW ERA THAT FOLLOWED A WORLD WAR 215

John W. Gates's mansion at 2944 Michigan Avenue that cost $300,000 was sold with 145 feet of ground, valued at $1,000 a front foot in the eighties, for $65,500 in the same year.[51] As fine homes were being abandoned for apartments, $40,000–$60,000 houses were offered for rent at $200 a month. Kenwood was the preferred residential section of the South Side at this time, with deep lots on Woodlawn, Ellis, and Greenwood avenues from Forty-fifth to Fifty-first streets selling for only $200 a front foot. Grand and Drexel boulevards were selected as locations for high-grade apartments, and their lots were valued at from $200 to $300 a front foot.

Apartments.—There was a rush to apartment construction at this time. Even during the extreme depression of 1897 and 1898, speculative builders had erected apartments along the line of the South Side elevated road. By the fall of 1901, the excess of apartment space built during the World's Fair boom had been largely filled.[52] In 1902 apartment rents advanced 10 per cent.[53] Of 9,200 apartments and houses in the hands of leading agents in 1903, only 131 were for rent.[54] Apartments varied in size and quality from the modest two flats of the West Side to the *de luxe* apartments erected by Potter Palmer on the Lake Shore Drive to rent for $1,000 a month.[55] Fine apartments renting for from $100 to $300 a month were being built on Grand and Drexel boulevards, on Michigan Avenue near Garfield Boulevard, on Cornell and East End avenues near Fifty-fourth Street, and on Hyde Park Boulevard.

Old residential areas.—Rents of old houses, although more promptly paid than in 1897, were lower in 1908 with steam heat added than in 1897, and of course were far below the peak levels of 1892, as Table X shows.[56]

The increase in immigration and the growth of the negro section was causing an expansion of some of these old areas. The ghetto was overflowing westward and a new ghetto was forming between Harrison and Fourteenth streets, Racine and Robey streets, by 1903.[57] The colored belt had burst the boundaries that had prior to 1900 confined it between State and Federal streets from Twenty-second and Thirty-

[51] *Ibid.*, May 23, 1908.
[52] *Ibid.*, September 7, 1901.
[53] *Ibid.*, January 3, 1903.
[54] *Ibid.*, October 10, 1903.
[55] *Ibid.*, February 1, 1902.
[56] *Ibid.*, April 11, 1908.
[57] *Ibid.*, May 17, 1903.

ninth streets where negroes had paid 8 per cent higher rents than were paid for far better houses east of State Street. By 1908 the colored people had occupied Wabash Avenue solidly from Twenty-sixth to Thirty-ninth Street, had taken possession of many houses on Vernon and Calumet avenues in the same limits, and had placed thirty-two of their race on Groveland Avenue from Twenty-ninth to Thirty-third Street. An organization of white property owners endeavored to halt the advance east of Wabash Avenue by an agreement not to rent or sell to colored people. The effect of the appearance of the first colored family in a neighborhood was thus described: "The first colored man to move into

TABLE X

RENTS PER MONTH OF SELECTED OLD HOUSES IN CHICAGO, 1892, 1897, AND 1908

Location	1892	1897	1908
South Park near Thirty-third Street...................	$75	$40	$35
South Park near Thirty-third Street...................	65	35	25
Lake Park–Oakwood Boulevard.	....	40	35–37.50
Vernon near Forty-third Street..	....	70	45*
Wabash–Twentieth Street......	....	50	40
348 North Clark Street........	....	60	50
Elm–Dearborn Street..........	....	83.33	60*
Elm–Dearborn Street..........	....	65	65*
Elm–Dearborn Street..........	....	75	50*
Elm–Dearborn Street..........	....	50	50*

* Steam heat added.

a community of this character is compelled to pay higher rent but as soon as he is discovered, rents throughout the entire section go down, and it is with difficulty that any one is secured to occupy adjoining flats or houses."[58]

New residential areas.—In 1907 the branch of the South Side elevated road was completed to Englewood, and the branch of the Northwestern elevated line was finished to Ravenswood. In 1908 the Northwestern elevated line was extended from Wilson Avenue to Evanston. The most rapid growth took place at the termini of these extensions. By 1908 there was a population of 100,000 around the Wilson Avenue station. Sixty-third and Halsted streets and Lawrence and Kimball avenues were developing rapidly as important outlying business cen-

[58] *Ibid.*, August 8, 1908.

ters as a result of these elevated lines. The Douglas Park branch of the Metropolitan elevated line was being extended along Twenty-second Street to carry the employees of the Western Electric plant to and from their work.

The Chicago land market as a whole, 1900–1908.—The foregoing account shows that in certain spots, as in the central business district, in the Calumet region, and along the new elevated extensions, land values were constantly making new high records from 1900 to 1908. It was by no means true, however, that land values were advancing generally or that real estate activity was distributed throughout the entire Chicago area. In fact, notwithstanding the improvement in general conditions, land values in many sections continued to decline in this period. It was not that real estate conditions grew worse, but that landholders, finding that the market for certain kinds of property did not improve, at least reluctantly accepted a lower price than their asking price in 1900. Thus sixty-seven parcels of property scattered all over Chicago were valued by George C. Olcott at 20 per cent less in 1910 than they were appraised at by William A. Bond in 1898 and 1899.[59]

Several times in this period it was thought that the turn of the tide had come. Thus in March, 1902, the editor of the *Economist* said:

> Events now known to everybody prove conclusively that the market has started on a career of greater activity. Nor can it be said any longer that the downtown area is the only one where large business is being done. All the localities are coming in, notably the north shore, the west side, the vacant properties of the southwest, the Calumet district and other areas.
>
> The ebb has certainly been long enough and trying enough to the brokerage fraternity and the owners of property, beginning as it did in 1893 and continuing to about the close of the year 1900. We are not entirely through all the phenomena of a depressed market for there are always some remnants of insolvency and bad luck after the market has taken a turn for the better.[60]

In spite of this hope that the market for vacant property would soon revive, over two years later at the end of 1904 the following pessimistic accounts were given:

> From month to month and from year to year they [holders of outlying vacant property] have been looking forward hopefully to a revival in the speculative inter-

---

[59] From the records of William A. Bond & Co. There is, of course, the possibility that the two appraisers had different standards of valuation, so that this comparison taken alone is not conclusive.

[60] *Economist*, March 1, 1902.

est which would encourage subdividing. The speculative interest in outlying property is entirely absent, nor is there any inquiry for any property of this kind except for immediate development.[61]

The basic reason for the pessimistic view has been that vacant lots no longer are sold in any appreciable amount, nor will constant offering and continuous advertising induce the sale of such lots. There is in Chicago today within the corporate limits enough of vacant subdivided property to hold double the number of inhabitants Chicago contains at the present.[62]

Again in 1905 when the demand for State Street frontage was extraordinary, forty acres south of Jackson Park on Jeffery Avenue for which $10,000 an acre was offered in 1893 was sold for $3,125 an acre. At the same time, the depressed condition of the market for vacant land was shown by the following account:

There are a large number of acre tracts in all sections to be purchased at prices far below anything that has prevailed for years. Instances can be cited where acre property can now be purchased at as low a figure as it sold for 25 years ago, but it is the uncertainty of a favoring gale creating a popular demand in one particular section for lots for improvement which makes buyers hesitate. One thing is quite certain and that is, that the kind of cheap lot trade which Chicago enjoyed prior to the World's Fair will not soon be duplicated in this section.[63]

Again after the panic of 1907 W. D. Kerfoot said:

Ever since the panic of 1893, real estate has declined. . . . . Whether real estate will show a decline depends upon affairs in the financial and commercial world in the next few months, but I do not look for any material change in conditions. The fact of the matter is that real estate is at about as low a figure now as it is possible for it to be.[64]

The condition of Chicago real estate was made but little worse by the panic of 1907, for it had been in a depressed condition in most localities for years, as the following account shows:

Prices of real estate in any direction, with the exception of the North Shore and central business property, were higher fifteen years ago than now, while the population has increased by over a million people. It will thus be seen that there has been no active general market in any section such as characterized the period prior to 1893. This is a favorite time for the small investors in the various specialties. If he wishes to buy acres, they can be had within a short distance of the heart of the city at one-third to one-fourth the prices prevailing fifteen years ago and as for single lots and houses, there never was a more opportune time. Acre and half acre lots in almost any direction are selling at about what a lot 25 by 125 feet [*note:* there are

[61] *Ibid.*, November 26, 1904.
[62] *Ibid.*, December 17, 1904: letter of Aaron McKay.
[63] *Ibid.*, July 29, 1905.   [64] *Ibid.*, December 14, 1907.

ten such lots in an acre] sold for years ago, with all the improvements in and with more convenient transportation. As to improved residence property in the older sections, many houses are for sale at a little more than the value of the land, and these can be bought on favorable terms. It should not be thought that these conditions are the result of the distress of the money market. They have prevailed for years; only the present seems a more favorable time to avail one's self of them.[65]

In this period subdividers could only sell vacant lots by building houses or apartments on them and selling land and building together. Although seventeen years had passed since the peak of 1890, there was no general boom in 1907, as there has been at seventeen-year intervals prior to 1890. Either the excesses of the boom of 1890 had produced an unusually long aftermath or else land values had not kept pace with the growth of the city. Figures 32 and 33 indicate the land values of Chicago in 1910.

THE PERIOD FROM 1908 TO 1918

In the period from 1908 to 1918, while the physical volume of production in the United States increased 50 per cent, the dollar value of manufacturers, wholesale trade, and bank clearings in Chicago doubled, as Table XI shows.

At the same time, the indices of Chicago real estate activity (Table XII) indicate a high volume of building until 1917, a peak of transfers in 1916, and a peak of subdivision activity in 1914. Compared with 1890, however, these were only minor peaks.

In 1909 Chicago land values were on the whole lower than in 1890 when the city was only half as large, and, according to William E. Harmon, they were no higher than other cities with half the population. Current writers gave their explanations as to why the prices of land fluctuated above and below what was warranted by the normal growth of the city. Thus W. L. Bonney said:

> Under existing conditions, the market prices of all commodities including real estate moves by a series of violent advances and reactions. This seems illogical but it is the process of price-making in any investment market. A quiet, steady, lady-like movement is unknown in commercial systems. This fact gives the speculator his trade and the investor his opportunity. In real estate this systole and diastole covers long periods, a decline continuing for many years and an advance running sometimes four or five years. The last decline in Chicago has persisted since 1893 and has carried prices down to a point as low as prices in Cleveland, Baltimore, Pittsburgh or Detroit.[66]

[65] *Ibid.*, November 16, 1907.   [66] *Ibid.*, August 28, 1909.

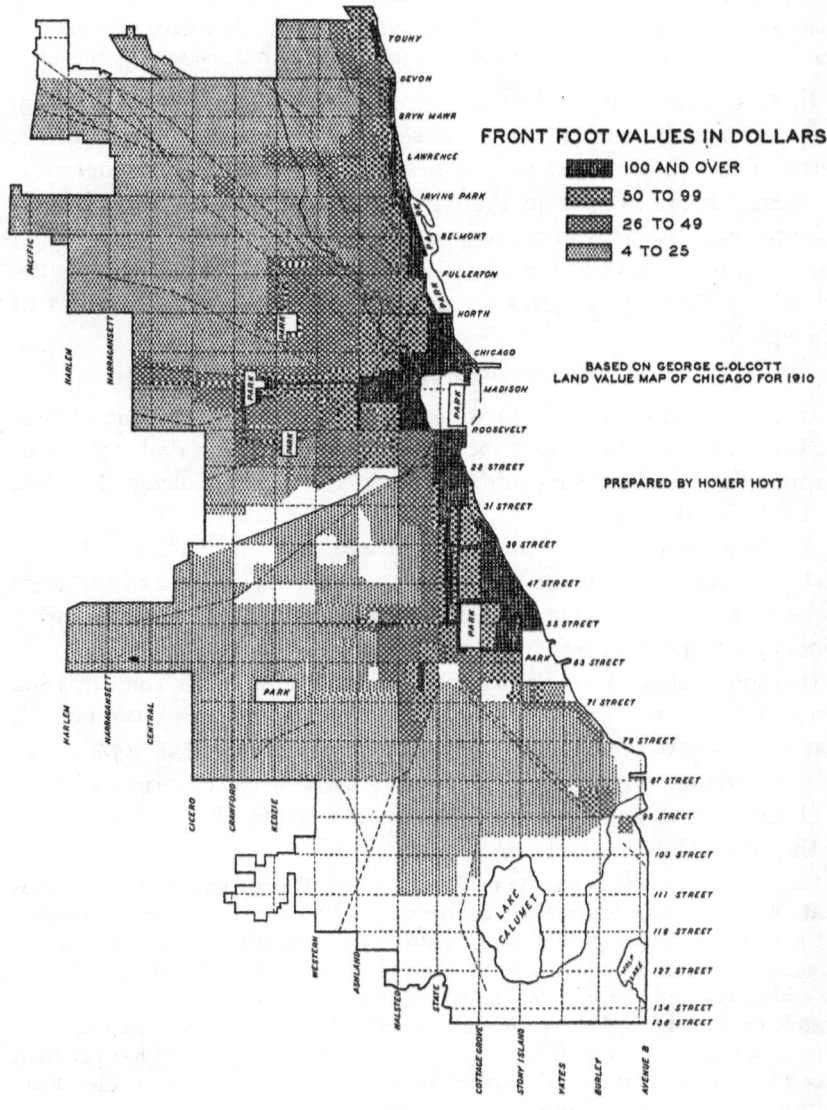

Fig. 32

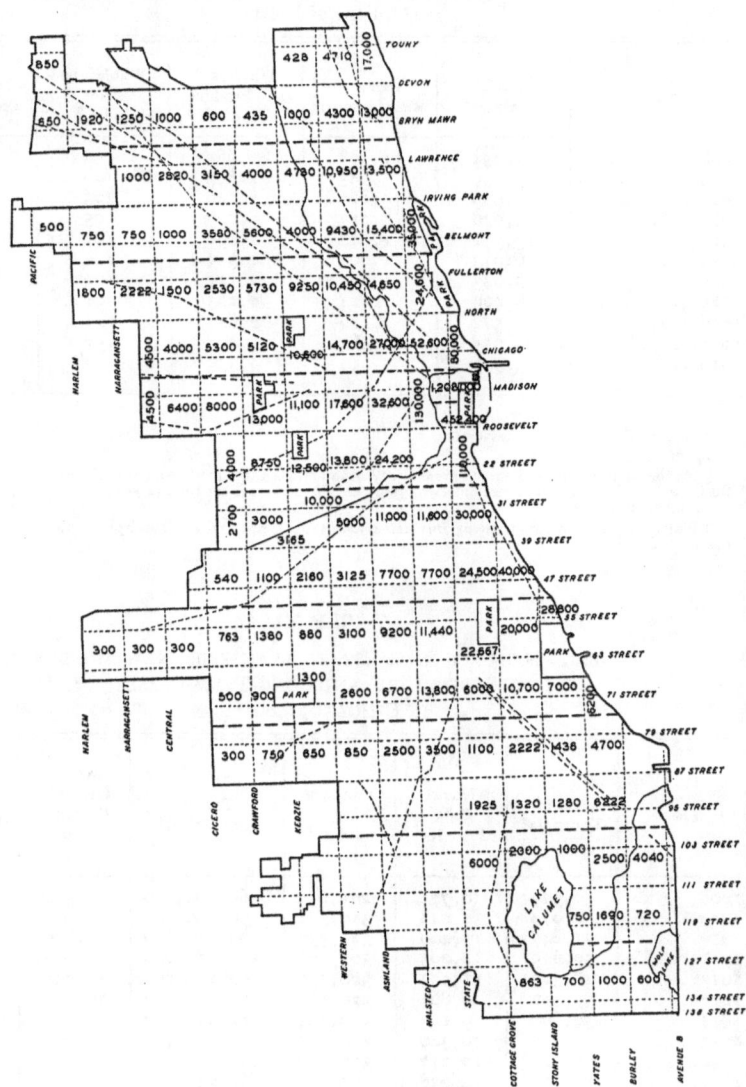

Fig. 33

TABLE XI

ANNUAL AMOUNT OF BANK CLEARINGS, MANUFACTURES, WHOLESALE
AND PRODUCE TRADE IN CHICAGO, 1908–18

(Millions of Dollars)

Year	Bank Clearings*	Value of Manufactures†	Wholesale and Produce Trades‡	Wholesale-Price Index§	Index U.S. Production‖
1908	$11,854	$1,598	$1,685	92	94
1909	13,939	1,783	1,893	99	106
1910	13,930	1,867	2,046	103	110
1911	13,926	1,213	2,027	95	105
1912	15,381	1,978	2,296	101	122
1913	16,073	1,999	2,334	102	120
1914	15,693	1,660	2,122	100	119
1915	16,199	1,724	2,283	101	130
1916	20,542	2,112	2,841	125	139
1917	24,975	2,483	3,200	155	143
1918	25,930	3,944	3,338	183	142

* *Economist*, annual reviews.
† *Chicago Tribune*, annual reviews.
‡ *Ibid.*
§ Wholesale-price index of Professors G. F. Warren and F. A. Pearson, from the Cleveland Trust Co. chart, "Business Activity and Four Price Series, 1831–1932." The average for the five years from 1910 to 1914, inclusive, is taken as 100.
‖ Warren M. Persons, *Forecasting Business Cycles* (1931), pp. 137–47. Total production for 1905 is taken as 100.

TABLE XII

ANNUAL VOLUME OF REAL ESTATE TRANSFERS, NEW BUILDINGS,
LOTS SUBDIVIDED, AND LONG-TERM LEASES
IN CHICAGO, 1908–18

Year	No. of Transfers*	No. of Bldg. Permits*	Frontage New Bldgs.*	Cost of New Bldgs.*	No. of Lots Subdivided in Cook County	Long-Term Leases (Millions of Dollars)
1908	30,327	10,771	291,655	$ 66,204,080	5,560	$ 7.4
1909	34,074	11,241	310,351	90,509,580	7,061	16.6
1910	31,847	11,409	327,350	96,932,700	11,870	9.8
1911	39,629	11,203	305,326	105,489,600	9,844	31.0
1912	48,529	11,153	320,357	88,190,800	10,235	15.0
1913	57,489	10,867	320,889	89,150,200	19,173	13.7
1914	59,660	9,163	290,494	82,947,200	20,231	8.6
1915	56,882	10,340	318,011	97,301,480	12,705	3.2
1916	60,520	10,277	327,496	112,835,150	12,937	9.1
1917	54,677	4,938	161,698	64,244,150	6,962	5.9
1918	46,883	2,529	85,630	34,791,850	2,939	3.4

* *Chicago Daily News Almanac.*

A NEW ERA THAT FOLLOWED A WORLD WAR

Again he said:

Another upward movement in the early nineties carried values some ten years ahead of real conditions. The city began rapidly to overtake these values while the values themselves began to fall back to meet real conditions. This process has gone on now for fifteen years. Since the World's Fair a new city has been added to each of the three sides of the river, wealth has accumulated, public improvements have been made, every token which goes to make a great metropolis has come into evidence, but the real estate pendulum has only begun to swing upward.[67]

William B. Harmon explained the process in these words:

Land values as distinguished from land prices grow almost exactly as population increases, for they are determined by the economic returns in rents when improved, while real estate prices are not determined by intrinsic values, but largely by sentiment, so that prices and values do not necessarily, in fact, rarely mean the same thing. In 1889 everybody thought real estate prices would never stop going up, while now they are just as firmly convinced that they will never stop going down, and the facts in the case are that prices are actually beginning to recover, although within the past month we have bought real estate in your city at about one-half of what we would have paid for property with equal facilities in transportation and city improvements twenty years ago. Now economic realty values are way above the prevailing market. A lot of land in Chicago, properly improved, will return a net income double the amount of the income from property of equal cost in New York, Boston or the average American city. Conditions which apply in one part of the country do not apply in another. Real estate booms are local and reactions from booms are local. Land may be on a speculative basis in one city and far below its intrinsic value in another. Chicago has now entirely recovered from the wild speculation of the early nineties, and if nothing whatever was done to attract attention to real estate in your city, a buying movement would soon set in of its own accord which would bring about a renewed period of real estate activity.[68]

There were, of course, a few bright spots in this dark picture. Michigan Avenue from Randolph Street to Roosevelt Road took on a new aspect in the summer and fall of 1909 with the completion of the Blackstone Hotel, the McCormick Building, the People's Gas Building, and the Harvester Building.[69] Southward, on Michigan Avenue, the automobile center was growing fast. Land values had doubled in the five years ending in 1909 along the line of the Northwestern elevated road from Wilson Avenue to Evanston.[70] Business corners in outlying neighborhoods such as Sixty-third and Halsted streets were reaching higher peaks than ever before. Office buildings were crowded to capacity. The West Side land near Madison and Halsted had reached the

[67] *Ibid.*, July 24, 1909.
[68] *Ibid.*, April 24, 1909.
[69] *Ibid.*, November 27, 1909.
[70] *Ibid.*, March 13, 1909.

highest values in its history. Twenty-five houses had been built in the Kenwood district in four years. Factories continued to expand in the Calumet region. Such was the view in 1909.

Central business district.—By 1910 there was a lull in transactions in retail property in the Loop, the asking prices based upon leasing valuations being regarded as too high.[71] The rise in the interest rate from 4 to 4½ per cent on downtown fees also tended to lower valuations based on 4 per cent capitalization rate. Rents for stores and offices were continuing to rise, however.

TABLE XIII*

VALUE OF NEW OFFICE BUILDINGS ERECTED ANNUALLY IN CHICAGO COMPARED WITH TOTAL NEW CONSTRUCTION, 1908–15

Year	No.	Cost	Per Cent Total New Construction	Value of Property Long Leases
1908				$ 7,400,000
1909				16,600,000
1910	45	$16,461,500	17.0	9,800,000
1911	48	23,101,000	21.9	31,000,000
1912	49	4,571,000	5.1	15,000,000
1913	76	2,706,400	3.0	13,000,000
1914	72	2,520,400	3.0	8,649,800
1915	45	4,200,000	4.4	3,230,000

* *Economist*, June 3, 1916. The value of new construction as shown by permits from the records of the City Building Department of Chicago.

In 1910 and 1911 there was a wave of office building in the Loop, which reached larger proportions than the skyscraper boom from 1890 to 1892. From 1909 to 1914, inclusive, property of a value of over $94,000,000 was placed under long-term leases, a considerable part of which was due to office-building activity. Table XIII shows the extent of these operations which fell off greatly after 1911.[72]

The rush to erect office buildings in 1911 was partly due to an ordinance passed in January limiting the height of buildings to 200 feet after September 1.[73] The result of this office-building boom was to create another oversupply of space, and there were many vacant offices by the spring of 1913.[74]

[71] *Ibid.*, July 2, 1910.
[72] *Ibid.*, June 3, 1916.
[73] *Ibid.*, January 7, 1911.
[74] *Ibid.*, April 19, 1913.

A NEW ERA THAT FOLLOWED A WORLD WAR

Land values on some of the streets that hitherto had been outside the main retail district reached peaks far exceeding the prices of 1890. Thus on Michigan Avenue at Congress Street was a lot under the Auditorium Hotel that had been leased on a basis of $1,150 a front foot in 1886 that was leased for $15,000 a front foot in 1916.[75] Frontage on Wabash Avenue south of Madison Street that sold for $5,000 a front foot in 1899 was valued at $11,000 a front foot in 1912.[76] The southward trend of business had become so pronounced in 1911 that frontage on State Street south of Van Buren sold for $7,300 a front foot.[77] The corner of State and Madison Street itself was valued at $300 a square foot in 1912, or over three times its value in 1890.[78]

South Water Street continued to be the congested produce market with 154 firms between State and Lake Street requiring 800 teams to do their hauling, but there were several plans for a removal of this market to a new locality.[79] Plans for the widening of Roosevelt Road, for the new Field Museum, and for the Michigan Avenue link bridge were being discussed in 1915 and 1916, but the war intervened before they were started.

The elevated lines were consolidated in 1911, and continued with the surface lines to pour a heavy volume of shoppers into the stores on State Street. In 1911 it was estimated that 1,350,000 passengers went in and out of the Loop daily on the surface and elevated lines, 1,000,000 of these riding on the surface lines.[80]

Outlying business centers.—At this time outlying transfer corners, or points where street-car lines intersected, came into prominence. A movement away from the retail stores in the central business district was inaugurated by the development of a new automobile center on Michigan Avenue south of Twenty-second Street where by 1911 there were twenty-six automobile showrooms between Twenty-second and Twenty-fifth streets.[81] Lots on Michigan Avenue near Twenty-second Street advanced from $200 a front foot in 1907 to $2,000 a front foot in 1910 as a result.[82]

Of greater significance than this overflow from the Loop southward was the establishment of new community centers at points where

[75] *Ibid.*, August 19, 1916.
[76] *Ibid.*, March 16, 1912.
[77] *Ibid.*, October 14, 1911.
[78] *Ibid.*, April 6, 1912.
[79] *Ibid.*, February 27, 1915.
[80] *Ibid.*, January 7, 1911.
[81] *Ibid.*, January 7, 1911.
[82] *Ibid.*, July 2, 1910.

street-car lines intersected or near elevated railway stations. Several factors contributed to the establishment of many small business centers outside the central nucleus in the Loop. The first was the movement on the part of chain stores to seek retail outlets near where the consumers lived. Forty outlying stores could be rented at the same cost as one store on State Street. In 1910 the Columbia drug stores leased twenty-five transfer corners, which of course commanded a higher rental than the ordinary neighborhood store.[83] The Atlantic and Pacific Tea Company, the United Cigar Store, and other chain organizations also began to establish stores in every neighborhood. The second factor was the building of theaters outside the Loop. At first vaudeville houses, whose performances were inferior to the Loop theaters, and then showings of moving pictures that were the same as those displayed downtown induced people to seek their entertainment near their homes. The third factor was the growth of neighborhood banks. Prior to the World's Fair there had been only one bank outside the Loop, that at the Stock Yards, but at this time many banks were organized to do business in the new community centers. The fourth factor was the moving of manufacturing plants and wholesale houses away from the downtown area, with the result that new communities formed near them. Even when the factories or plants did not move, as in the case of the Stock Yards, the higher class of employees sought to get away from the noise and odors of the industrial district as well as from the old neighborhoods occupied by unskilled laborers of the new immigration or of the colored race. The fifth factor was the character of the transportation system. As the population moved farther out and away from the railroads and elevated lines, more reliance was placed upon the surface cars. While these street cars were adequate to carry people to and from outlying factories and neighborhood centers, they were a slow medium for reaching the Loop. Thus, as a result of a drift of population away from the downtown area, neighborhood centers with their own stores, banks, and theaters began to develop at this time. Within another decade the movement reached its apex.

The growth of these community business centers was reflected in the rise of land values at transfer corners. The corner of Sixty-third and Cottage Grove Avenue, valued at no more than $400 a front foot at the peak of the World's Fair boom, was sold for $640 a front foot in 1906

[83] *Ibid.*, June 11, 1910.

and leased for $1,400 a front foot in 1909, and for $3,398 a front foot in 1912.[84] The corner of Sixty-third and Halsted Street was leased for $2,873 a front foot in 1913[85] as compared with $1,754 a front foot in 1910.[86] The corner of Lawrence and Kimball increased in value from $52 to $300 a front foot from 1909 to 1912, and by 1918 it sold for $606 a front foot.[87] Triple intersections along Milwaukee Avenue acquired a high value. The corner of Lincoln, Robey, and Irving Park, bought for $25 a front foot in 1904, was leased for $900 a front foot in 1912.[88] The corner of Milwaukee, Western, and Armitage was leased for $9.00 a square foot in 1910.[89] Corners beyond the settled area, if at the intersection of two actual or potential car lines, began to acquire a speculative value. The corner of Sixty-third and Western Avenue was sold for $282 a front foot in 1911.[90] The corner of Sixty-third and Kedzie Avenue sold for $400 a front foot in 1913.[91] At the same time the corner of Devon and Western was bought for $177 a front foot and that of Belmont and Cicero for $50 a front foot, both representing great advances over previous acre values.[92] The corner of Madison and Crawford was leased for $972 a front foot in 1913.[93] The corner of Lawrence and Kedzie rose in value from $53 a front foot in 1911 to $433 a front foot in 1915.[94] Lincoln Avenue between Leland and Lawrence increased from $100 a front foot in 1909 to $1,000 a front foot in 1915.[95] Seventy-ninth and Halsted corner advanced from $530 a front foot in 1911 to $924 in 1912. The first fervor of transfer corner speculation began to abate in 1913 and it was not renewed generally until after 1919.

Growth of new neighborhoods.—New neighborhoods were being built in all sections of the city. The Washington Park race track, from Sixty-first to Sixty-third streets, Cottage Grove to South Park Avenue, closed as a result of the anti-betting law of 1905, was subdivided and built up almost solidly from 1908 to 1912.[96] Near Seventy-ninth and Racine 150 new houses had been built from 1906 to 1910.[97] In Avalon highlands,

[84] *Ibid.*, April 3, 1909; December 31, 1912.
[85] *Ibid.*, April 19, 1913.
[86] *Ibid.*, July 9, 1910.
[87] *Ibid.*, April 6, 1912; April 20, 1918.
[88] *Ibid.*, July 6, 1912.
[89] *Ibid.*, November 19, 1910.
[90] *Ibid.*, October 14, 1911.
[91] *Ibid.*, October 11, 1913.
[92] *Ibid.*, November 8, 1913.
[93] *Ibid.*, September 20, 1913.
[94] *Ibid.*, January 2, 1915.
[95] *Ibid.*, April 17, 1915.
[96] *Ibid.*, February 1, 1913.
[97] *Ibid.*, November 19, 1910.

southeast of Seventy-ninth and Cottage Grove Avenue, 150 houses had been built from 1911 to 1915.[98] In 1915 a new city was being built south of Jackson Park east of Stony Island Avenue.[99] The region near Archer and Kedzie was being settled in 1914 as a result of the establishment of the Crane plant near there,[100] and land values tripled in the two years from 1913 to 1915.[101] A new residence section was being developed north of Diversey to Belmont on the Lake Shore Drive in 1915.[102] The entire North and Northwest sides were growing fast. The relatively rapid growth in the outer zone of the city from 1906 to 1916 is shown by the increase in the number of telephones. While the number in the Loop increased from 33,000 to 83,000 and in the inner zone from 27,659 to 54,538, the number in the outer zone rose from 50,240 to 274,147. The increase was greatest in Irving Park, Rogers Park, and Edgewater, with advances of 907, 346, and 343 per cent, respectively.[103] In the period from 1910 to 1916, while the population within the first four miles of the corner of State and Madison Street remained almost stationary at slightly more than 1,000,000, the population from four to seven miles from this center increased from 460,000 to 1,076,000. In the same interval the population in the belt from seven to ten miles from the center increased from 180,000 to 332,000.[104]

Acre and subdivision activity.—In the beginning of this period, subdivision activity, notwithstanding the doubling in the population of the city from 1890 to 1910, had not recovered from the aftermath of 1890. In 1910 sales of acre tracts on the South Side were made at prices far below the levels of 1890. The accompanying tabulation shows the level of values in 1910, with the corresponding values for 1890.

	1910	1890
Devon–Western	$800 an acre	$1,000
Sixty-third–Cicero	600	2,000
Seventy-ninth–Racine	900	3,500
Belmont–Laramie	550	750
Forty-seventh–Crawford	350	2,000

The very fact that sales were made indicated an awakening of activity. Acre tracts on the North Side began to advance in value. By 1913 land at Devon and Kedzie sold for $3,125 an acre, an advance of 300

---

[98] *Ibid.*, April 3, 1915.
[99] *Ibid.* (annual review), 1915.
[100] *Ibid.*, November 28, 1914.
[101] *Ibid.*, March 27, 1915.
[102] *Ibid.*, February 6, 1915.
[103] *Ibid.*, April 6, 1916.
[104] *Report of the Chicago Traction and Subway Commission* (1916), p. 73.

A NEW ERA THAT FOLLOWED A WORLD WAR

per cent in three years.[105] Elston Avenue south of Diversey had sold for $5,000 an acre in 1897, but it brought $21,000 an acre in 1912.[106] Subdivision activity increased. Frederick H. Bartlett bought 1,727 acres in the Clearing district in 1910 for $500 an acre,[107] and in this tract he sold 800 lots for $100,000 in one day.[108] Lots were being sold at Sixty-third and Western Avenue, sales of $300,000 being made in a short time during 1912.[109] In 1914 lots were being sold south of Jackson Park, at Seventy-ninth and Cottage Grove, at Archer and Kedzie avenues, and on the Northwest Side. In the fall of 1914, at the southwest corner of Seventy-ninth and Cottage Grove in the new subdivision called "Chatham Fields," 894 lots out of a total of 1,146 were sold in five weeks for $994,000.[110] Subdivision activity declined after 1914, but in 1917 Frederick H. Bartlett sold 2,694 out of 2,994 lots in "Greater Chicago" at One Hundred and Third Street and the Illinois Central Railroad, and he reported total sales for the year of over $6,000,000.[111] William Britigan sold 2,629 lots of a value of $4,187,621 in 1917, but to make these sales it was necessary for his 53 employees to make 169,456 telephone calls, to make 5,000 automobile trips, and to use 1,399,835 pieces of advertising.[112] The automobile, the telephone, and widespread advertising were means now used by trained sales organizations to sell lots. Only a few large firms were successful in stimulating an interest in buying lots, and even their efforts were almost suspended by the outbreak of war. Prior to 1918 speculation in lots and acre tracts had only a mild revival that was not comparable as a whole to the activity in 1890. There had, however, been slow and persistent gains year after year on the North Side since 1900 and spectacular rises in values at transfer corners.

Fashionable residential areas.—The ultra-fashionable residential area was extending northward along the Lake Shore Drive from Diversey to Belmont Avenue in 1915. The Lake Shore Drive near Division Street had reached values of over $2,000 a front foot, and the spread of fine homes to Astor Street had raised its values in a few years from $200 to over $1,000 a front foot.[113]

[105] *Economist,* January 22, 1910.
[106] *Ibid.,* May 14, 1910.
[107] *Ibid.,* September 3, 1910.
[108] *Ibid.,* June 28, 1910.
[109] *Ibid.,* June 22, 1912.
[110] *Ibid.,* September 19, 1914.
[111] *Ibid.,* February 2, 1918.
[112] *Ibid.,* January 5, 1918.
[113] *Ibid.,* November 14, 1914.

Meanwhile, the old mansions on Prairie Avenue continued to be sold at a fraction of their original cost. A house near Eighteenth and Prairie Avenue that cost $200,000 was sold with 81 feet of ground for $25,000. A home at Twenty-third and Calumet Avenue that cost $150,000 and was the finest in the city in 1870 was sold with 120 feet of ground for $36,000. This was in 1909.[114] The old homes on Ashland Boulevard on the West Side met the same fate. These commodious houses were too large to be maintained when the servant problem became acute, and it was becoming the fashion to live in apartments and not to imitate the castles of the feudal barons.

Old residential areas.—Old houses near the Loop were used for boarding-houses or torn down to make way for warehouses. The old "red light" district at Twenty-second and State Street was abolished in 1912, and with it went the exceptionally high rents paid for the use of the property for immoral purposes. The expansion of warehouses soon gave it a prospective commercial value as high as that for the old use, however.

Manufacturing and warehouse districts.—Manufacturing districts were growing and increasing in value in this period. The land in the Central Manufacturing District bought for $900,000 in 1900 was valued at $15,000,000 in 1915.[115] The Clearing district, where the railroad transfer yards saved a day getting freight in and out of Chicago, was acquiring new factories. The Crane plant moved from Roosevelt and Canal streets to Kedzie near Thirty-ninth Street in 1912,[116] and as it gave employment to fifty-seven hundred men, it created a new settlement in that prairie region. The Kenwood manufacturing district was established at Forty-seventh and Kedzie Avenue. The industries of the Calumet region and of South Chicago continued to grow as the traffic on the Calumet River became the main stream of water-borne commerce entering Chicago by 1916. Iron, steel, chemicals, beds, cements, tile, railroad equipment, musical instruments, corn products, spirits, oil, and food products were all manufactured there.

Apartments.—Apartment building was the leading type of new construction in 1915, as Table XIV shows. As a result of this extensive building of apartments, thirty thousand houses and apartments were reported vacant in 1912,[117] and apartment rents declined in 1913. Nev-

[114] *Ibid.*, November 20, 1909.
[115] *Ibid.*, April 24, 1915.
[116] *Ibid.*, November 23, 1912.
[117] *Ibid.*, September 13, 1913.

ertheless, a new peak of apartment building was reached in 1915 when apartments with sun parlors became the vogue. The one-room apartment made its début in the Wilson Avenue district in 1916.[118]

Review of the market as a whole, 1908–18.—In 1910, notwithstanding record high values in the Loop, at Michigan Avenue near Twenty-second Street, along the North Shore, and at certain street-car intersections, the prices of outlying acre tracts were lower than they were twenty years before. A large volume of property sold at bankruptcy

TABLE XIV*

NUMBER AND COST OF NEW APARTMENT BUILDINGS COMPARED WITH NEW SINGLE-FAMILY RESIDENCES CONSTRUCTED IN CHICAGO, 1910–15

YEAR	APARTMENT BUILDINGS			SINGLE-FAMILY RESIDENCES	
	No.	Cost	Per Cent Total Construction	Cost	Per Cent Total Construction
1910	4,362	$34,372,500	34.4	$ 8,379,300	8.5
1911	4,599	36,401,000	34.8	8,535,500	8.0
1912	4,767	43,619,000	49.0	8,198,000	9.3
1913	5,034	39,565,800	44.0	9,159,500	10.2
1914	4,729	40,632,000	48.8	10,862,500	12.0
1915	4,470	59,567,750	61.2	10,500,000	10.8

* *Economist*, June 3, 1916. From records of the Building Department of Chicago.

and foreclosure sales could still be bought at bargain prices. High office rents stimulated a large volume of new construction in the Loop in 1910 and 1911. Apartment construction continued in large volume from 1910 to 1916, although there were many vacant apartments in 1916. Transfer corners rose sharply in value from 1909 to 1913, when the movement slackened for the time being. From 1911 to 1917 subdivision activity revived to a moderate extent. Land south of Jackson Park began to rise in value after 1915, and throughout this period there was a steady gain in land values north and northwest. From 1910 to 1918 the average land values of Chicago rose 50 per cent,[119] but there was nothing resembling a boom. After 1916 rents remained stationary

[118] *Ibid.*, April 1, 1916.

[119] Herbert D. Simpson, *The Influence of Public Improvements on Land Values*, Annals of American Academy (March, 1930), p. 128.

while operating costs advanced with prices. The outbreak of war reduced building activities to a low ebb.

C. THE PERIOD FROM 1919 TO 1933

Survey of the general factors affecting urban land in the United States, 1919–26.—In each of the preceding chapters of this study there was presented a spectacle of an exuberant and rapid rise of land values during which the energies and hopes of the entire population of the city were raised to the highest pitch, followed by the painful decline in the same values that checked this ardent activity and brought disillusionment and despair to great masses of people in Chicago. The newly created wealth in the form of higher land values, which seemed so solid and substantial when it was buttressed by bank loans and when it was readily convertible into cash, was seen first to lose its liquidity and then much of its value in each of these successive land cycles of the past. As a result of the continued remarkable growth of the metropolis by the lake, a recovery in the real estate market after every depression carried land values as a whole to higher peaks with each successive boom and caused later generations to overlook the preceding valleys in which their fathers and grandfathers had floundered. In this last period, the facts as to the rise and fall of Chicago land values since the end of the World War are still too recent to be forgotten. Those who have witnessed the fifth act of this century-long drama almost doubt the evidence of their senses. It seems impossible that such changes could have occurred in so short a time, and if people had not seen with their own eyes what has occurred, they would not have believed it.

The United States has just passed through a period similar in many respects to that "gilded age" following the Civil War. There was that same striving for sudden wealth on the part of the masses of the people, and that same financial manipulation on a grand scale by men like Krueger and Insull. Men were dazzled by the rising skyscrapers and the new comforts of living. It seemed to be a new era in which poverty in the United States was to be forever banished. Then the whole structure toppled down like a house of cards, and today we look back on it as a bubble or a mirage.

Wealth in the form of land or buildings which seemingly rests on so secure a physical foundation in fact depends on the ability of landlords to maintain gross rents above operating costs for long periods in the

A NEW ERA THAT FOLLOWED A WORLD WAR 233

future. When a combination of circumstances increases the net income of landlords for a short time, however, people seem always to proceed immediately to the conclusion that this profitable situation will endure for years to come. Land values are capitalized not merely on the new basis, but even on the assumption that the profit margin of landlords will continue to increase. Taxes are levied, bank loans are made, and long-time commitments are entered into on this new basis, until the whole financial structure of society is involved in the support of the newly created land values. This situation is brought about not merely because of the increase of the spread between gross rents and operating costs which makes land at least temporarily a profitable investment, but also because of the pressure of funds seeking investment. When the banks are able to expand their loans with ease and wage-earners are accumulating surplus funds in large volume, if opportunities for employment of such savings do not exist, they tend to be created. Instead of the rate of interest being forced down by the large supply of capital, it is sustained by the manufacture of new enterprises which appear to be much safer than they really are. Money that was ostensibly being poured out for investment purposes with the expectation of an annual interest payment was used to pay wages, financing costs, commissions, brokers' fees, etc., on so high a basis that future rents could not possibly be high enough to yield a return on this inflated load of costs.

The fortuitous circumstances that operated to raise and lower the value of urban and rural land in the United States since the beginning of the World War will now be described. Land, together with the buildings upon it, represented in 1922 over one-half of our total national wealth.[120] Therefore the fluctuations in so important a species of property could not fail to affect our entire financial and industrial structure.

Urban land in the United States was generally depressed during the World War. The depression of 1914 had slowed down a mild revival in Chicago real estate and had cut short land booms in the cities of the Canadian Northwest and in New York City. The war turned world-demand away from housing to the production of munitions and foodstuffs to supply the armies in the field. While the prices of American farm products more than doubled from 1914 to 1918, average house rents in the United States rose only 9 per cent. The result was that the value of American farm land, which had doubled from 1900 to 1910

[120] *U.S. Census of Wealth, Debt and Taxation* (1922).

as a result of slowly rising prices of agricultural products, doubled again from 1910 to 1920, reaching a total value in the latter year of $55,000,000,000.[121] In Iowa, in the heart of the corn belt, the boom in farm lands carried sales prices to $500 an acre by 1920.

Then came the remarkable reversal in the relative position of urban and rural real estate. Whereas in 1920 all the urban land in cities over 30,000 in the United States had a value of scarcely over $25,000,000,000, or half that of the value of farm land, by 1926 the value of all farm land had dropped from $55,000,000,000 to $37,000,000,000, while the value of urban land in American cities over 30,000 population had risen from $25,000,000,000 to over $50,000,000,000. The area of land within these cities was only one-fifth of 1 per cent of all the land in the United States, and yet it was valued in 1926 at 33 per cent more than that of all the farm land in the United States, whose area was two hundred times as great.[122] The cause of this great shift was due to a double set of forces, one acting to depress the value of farm lands and the other to elevate the value of urban lands.

American agriculture and American farm-land values were depressed as a result of the disappearance of the extraordinary combination of factors, behind the war-time demand for American foodstuffs. Australian wheat, mainly unavailable during the war because of the long route

---

[121] *U.S. Census* (1910, 1920).

[122] The value of urban lands within the corporate limits of cities of 30,000 population and over in the United States is an approximation computed by the writer by two independent methods. The first method is based on per capita land values. Zangerle found that the average per capita land value in nine cities in 1921 was $756 (John A. Zangerle, *Principles of Real Estate Appraising* [Cleveland, 1924], p. 229). These nine cities were New York, Boston, Pittsburgh, Cleveland, San Francisco, Cincinnati, Baltimore, Milwaukee, and Detroit. The population of all American cities over 30,000 in 1920 was 36,705,911. Applying the average per capita land value in the nine cities to the entire urban population would give a total urban land value of $27,750,000,000. It may be objected to this method that per capita land values are higher in the larger than in the smaller cities, and that applying the average for these large cities to the smaller ones would result in too high a figure. It will be observed, however, that some very large cities were not included in the nine cities taken by Zangerle, and that Chicago, Philadelphia, Los Angeles, St. Louis, New Orleans, Minneapolis, St. Paul, Kansas City, Atlanta, Washington (D.C.), Seattle, Portland (Ore.), Columbus, Toledo, Louisville, Newark, Jersey City, Indianapolis, Akron, Denver, Birmingham, and many other large cities were omitted. The twenty-one cities specifically mentioned that were omitted had a population of approximately 10,800,000 in 1920, or about the same population as the nine cities taken by Zangerle.

To check this method another one is employed. The U.S. Federal Trade Commission in their estimate of the national wealth in 1922 do not give a separate estimate for urban

through the submarine zone, and Argentine wheat, withheld for lack of ships, were again poured into the markets of Europe. Continental European countries, with the war veterans back on the farms, needed to import less. It was discovered that large surplus stocks of many commodities were piled up in warehouses at the close of the war, and there was a sudden and sharp decline of commodity prices in 1920. The agri-

---

land, but they do give a total figure for all land apart from buildings of $122,000,000,000. By a process of elimination, an estimate may be made for urban land. The following items are subtracted from the total to give the urban land only in 1920:

		Source
Improved farm land (est. in 1922)............	$40,000,000,000	U.S. Census for 1920
Land owned by public utilities...............	6,000,000,000	Federal Trade Commission*
City streets................................	9,000,000,000	Federal Trade Commission*
Forest land, 493,000,000 acres, $20 an acre......	10,000,000,000	Writer's estimate
Arid land, pasture land, rocky peaks, country roads, not included above, 400,000,000 acres at $10 an acre.............................	4,000,000,000	Writer's estimate
	$69,000,000,000	

    * 1922 figures of the Federal Trade Commission.

Subtracting the $69,000,000,000 from the total of $122,000,000,000 would leave $53,000,000,000 for all the land in all the villages, cities, and towns in the United States. If one-half of this value is assigned to the value of land in cities and towns over 30,000 in population, and to any other possible forms of land wealth omitted in these deductions, a figure of approximately $26,000,000,000 would be derived for the value of land in cities over 30,000 population. This would seem to be an extremely high figure to be deducted but the estimate for urban land value here presented is believed to be ultra-conservative and to err on the side of understatement rather than overstatement.

So much for the method of arriving at the urban land values for 1921. Using another method, it was found by the writer that the sales value of land in Chicago in 1926 was $1,500 per capita. In New York City the assessed value of $8,000,000,000 for the land alone in 1926 is $1,250 per capita, and this was probably below the sales value. It is believed that $1,200 per capita would have been a conservative value for all the land in cities over 30,000 population in the United States in 1927. The population on July 1, 1929, in such cities was 44,318,900. On the basis of a population of 42,000,000 for these cities in 1927, the value of this urban land would have been slightly over $50,000,000,000.

The foregoing computation is far in excess of the estimate of the value of urban land in the United States in 1920 made by W. R. Ingalls in his *Wealth and Income of the American People*, who put the amount at only $13,800,000,000. This estimate did not include vacant urban land, but, even so, it seems far too low. The basis of calculation seems to be wrong, for the author arrives at it by first computing the value of urban buildings at $65,100,000,000 by a very rough method of calculation and then by assuming that land under those buildings represents one-fifth of the value of the building alone. It is true that a 5 to 1 ratio between buildings and land has frequently been assumed as a normal ratio, but lots under stores and at the business centers of our great cities are frequently valued as high as the buildings. There are also large areas occupied by old and obsolete buildings where the value of the land is higher than that of the buildings. In the 1928 assessment of land and buildings in Cook County, land and buildings were assessed at equal value. It is true that the land

cultural depression began in 1921 and, as farm-land values declined, many banks failed in rural sections, particularly in Iowa where the farm-land boom had been most intense.

On the other hand, the return of five million soldiers and sailors from army camps and ships to their homes and opportunities for employment in large urban centers caused an increase from 1920 to 1930 of nearly nine million in the population of American cities of over thirty thousand population. The pent-up demand for luxuries after the rigors of war started a revival of manufacturing and wholesale trade. There was also a great increase in the demand for personal service, for real estate brokers and bond salesmen, for operators of beauty parlors and attendants at gasoline filling stations, and for advertising and insurance agencies. The center of the demand was in the large cities. As the flood of migration came from the war camps and the country districts to the urban centers, which as a result of the war-time restrictions on building and the high prices of building materials had had practically no residential building in 1917 and 1918, an acute housing shortage developed. As a result of this population pressure, apartment rents in most American cities doubled from 1919 to 1924. Meanwhile, average construction costs in the United States had dropped from 270 in 1919 to 165 in 1921 and the cost of operating buildings had increased but slightly. The first result was that the net income of the owners of existing buildings greatly increased; and as the buildings could no longer be reproduced at their pre-war cost, the capitalized value of the income of existing urban buildings, their reproduction cost, and their sales value all rose sharply. The second result was that it became very profitable by 1921, as a result of rising rents and falling construction costs to erect new buildings. The absorption of vacant land for buildings and the higher net return left to the owners of land under existing buildings caused urban land

---

figure included much vacant land, but this land is on the average of far less value than that under buildings.

That Ingall's estimate is far too low is also indicated by the study of the Federal Trade Commission and the *U.S. Census of Wealth, Debt and Taxation*. After deducting known items of the value of land represented by farms, there is still a large amount left, which can hardly be accounted for except on the assumption that it is mostly urban land. Furthermore, Zangerle computed the land value of nine cities with a population of 11,300,000 to be $8,550,869,757 in 1921. If Ingall's estimate were correct, there would be left only $5,300,000,000 plus the value of the vacant land in the nine cities to represent the value of the urban land in all the other cities and towns in the United States. It could hardly have been that low.

A NEW ERA THAT FOLLOWED A WORLD WAR 237

values in the United States to double between 1919 and 1926. A widespread sale of real estate bonds, based on these higher values to a public educated to buy bonds by the Liberty Bond campaigns, resulted in a sale of ten billion dollars' worth of such securities by 1929. Such was the general situation in the United States which existed during the period of the last real estate boom in Chicago.

The growth of the trade and manufactures of Chicago, 1921–29.—The trade and manufactures of Chicago had a substantial but not a remarkable rate of growth from 1921 to 1929. In these eight years of relatively stable wholesale prices, the dollar value of manufactured products and of bank clearings increased 50 per cent.[123] In the period from 1921 to 1926, surface and elevated traffic increased 25 per cent while the number of new telephones installed and the dollar value of the wholesale trade increased 50 per cent.[124] Truly spectacular gains, however, were registered by the radio industry, the motion-picture industry, and the automobile trade. From 1920 to 1930 the number of automobiles in Chicago increased 400 per cent.[125] In the same period the amount of electricity generated for Chicago consumers increased 133 per cent.[126]

The growth in real estate factors, 1919–26.—Outstripping the rate of growth of manufactures, banking, transportation, and the wholesale trades in this last period was the growth of population, building, subdivision activity, and land values. From 1918 to 1926 the population of Chicago increased 35 per cent, the land values increased 150 per cent, the value of new buildings as indicated by permits increased 1,000 per cent, and the number of lots subdivided in the Chicago Metropolitan Region increased 3,000 per cent.[127]

---

[123] "Chicago Manufactures," *U.S. Census;* Chicago bank clearings from a typewritten statement prepared by the Chicago Clearing House Association.

[124] Elevated traffic from a letter from the receiver of the Chicago Rapid Transit Co.; surface-line traffic from the eighteenth annual report of the president of the Chicago Surface Lines for the year ending January 31, 1932; telephones installed from a letter dated July 23, 1932, from the statistician of the Illinois Bell Telephone Co.; wholesale trade—value in 1918 from *Chicago Tribune Annual Review of Business* given at $3,338,175,100, value in 1926 given as $4,484,761,000 by Mr. Scott of Carson, Pirie & Scott as coming from the *Census of Distribution.*

[125] Figures furnished by the City License Department of Chicago.

[126] *Year Book* (Chicago: Commonwealth Edison Co., 1931).

[127] Land-value increase as computed by the writer; the value of new buildings as indicated by permits issued by the Building Department of the city of Chicago.

Population increase.—The first of these phenomena to show its effect was the increase in population. The population of Chicago, according to estimates based on the enrolment in the grade schools, had remained almost stationary from 1916 to 1917.[128] Then a population tide, composed of the influx of negro workers from the south, returning soldiers and sailors, and white workers from smaller cities or rural sections, poured into Chicago, until, with the increase of births over deaths, there was a total gain of 910,000 persons from 1917 to 1927. All of this increased population and in addition 150,000 persons who left the old residential areas within four miles of State and Madison Street, or a total of 1,060,000 persons, settled in the outer belt beyond the limits of the territory settled by 1880. The entire effect of the population increase was felt by the new areas, whose population increased from 1,552,500 to 2,670,000 from 1917 to 1927, while the inner territory declined from 848,500 to 700,000 in the same period.[129] In this old area outside the Loop and the near North Side, there was practically no new construction in these years, but in the new expanding territory from 1919 to 1929, inclusive, there were erected buildings with a street frontage of 730 miles, which would fill a solid area of 25 square miles, if allowance were made for streets and alleys and back yards.

The building boom.—The remarkable migration of population then caused a building spurt that began in 1919 and continued to a peak in 1926, from which it tapered down gradually to 1928 and then began a precipitous decline. This feverish spurt of new construction was caused by the doubling of Chicago apartment rents from 1919 to 1924, the increase of 80 per cent in office rents,[130] and the rise in retail store rents from 100 to 1,000 per cent at the same time that operating costs were

[128] The method employed is that described by Earle Young, *American Journal of Sociology*, February, 1933. The number of pupils enrolled in the grade schools of June of each year is taken from the records of the Board of Education. The ratio between the total population of Chicago according to the U.S. Census in 1910, 1920, and 1930 and the number so enrolled in the grade schools was respectively 7.84 to 1, 7.708 to 1, and 7.638 to 1. The ratios for the intercensus years are derived by interpolating on the straight-line method, and the ratios so obtained are multiplied by the school enrolment in the grade schools in June of each year to give the population. As there is no great change in the ratio for these three census periods, it is believed that this method will produce fairly reliable results for this period. The results seem to agree with facts derived from general observation.

[129] The area of this map is defined as the area which declined in population from 1920 to 1930 (see Fig. 82, p. 357).

[130] Earl Shultz, "*What of the Future*" in *Proceedings of National Association of Building Owners and Managers* (1931), p. 521.

rising only 10 per cent.[131] The curve of gross income and operating costs, which had begun to come close together in 1919, sprang far apart, as Figures 34 and 35 show.[132] With rapidly advancing rents, practically no vacancies, and almost stationary operating costs, the owner of an apartment building in Chicago had a bonanza from 1920 to 1929. The value of old two-apartment buildings in all sections of Chicago that

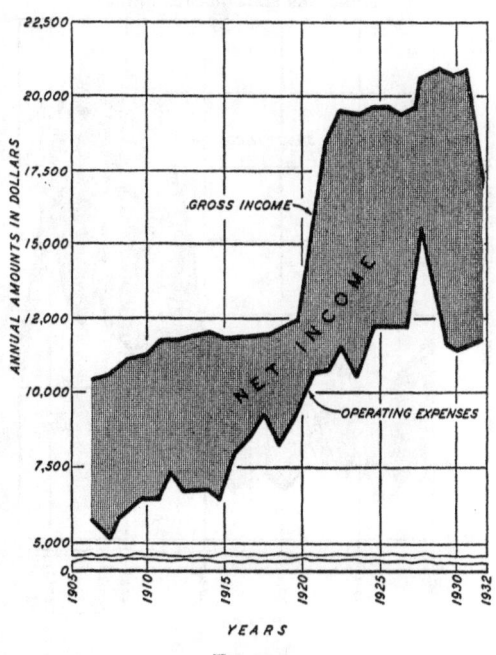

FIG. 34

sold for $6,000 in 1918 readily sold for from $12,000 to $15,000 in 1926. The Chicago index of building costs declined from 258 in 1920 to 210 in 1922.[133] New buildings were nearly always sold at a substantial profit above the land and building cost. Bungalows costing $5,000 to con-

[131] Rise in store rents taken from records of McKey & Poague for Sixty-third Street near Cottage Grove.

[132] Chart based on the records in the office of the Business Manager of the University of Chicago. Operating expenses include taxes.

[133] *Holabird and Root Index*, on basis of 1888 = 100.

struct sold for $7,500. Profits of $25,000 and $50,000 were made on single multiple-apartment buildings. Since the entire cost of the building could often be borrowed, it is little wonder that there was a rush into the building field analogous to a Klondike gold rush.

The rapid absorption of vacant land by new buildings and the high earnings of existing buildings made possible by the purchasing power

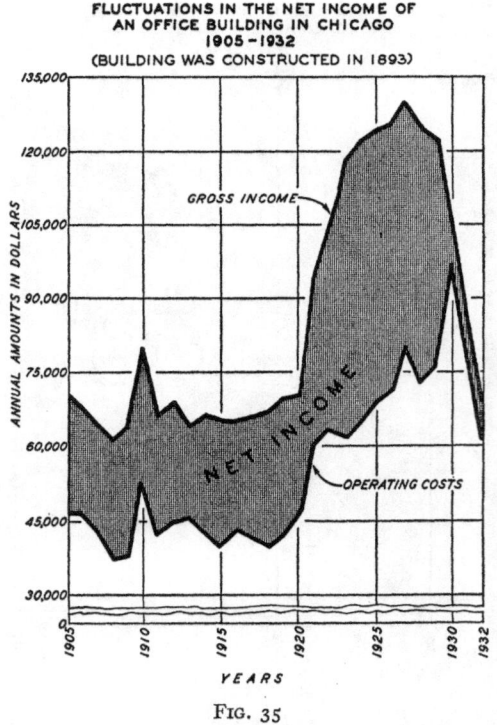

FIG. 35

of post-war urban labor, which was reflected in high apartment rents and high store rents, caused a boom in vacant land. This reached its most hectic phase in 1925 and the early part of 1926.

SURVEY OF MOVEMENT OF CHICAGO LAND VALUES BY REGIONS AND TYPES OF PROPERTY

Such are some of the broad and general factors behind the movement of Chicago land values from 1919 to 1926. It is now necessary to describe that movement by regions and by types of property. The ensuing discussion will concern itself, first, with the central business district of Chicago; second, with the near North Side; third, with the old area settled before 1880; fourth, with the outlying business centers; fifth, with new tall apartment buildings along the lake; sixth, with areas occupied by three-story apartment buildings; seventh, with bungalow and small-home areas; eighth, with outlying industrial property; and, ninth, with subdivision vacant land and outlying acreage.

1. *Central business district.*—In the building boom from 1924 to 1929, the central business district of Chicago expanded both vertically and laterally. The limitation on the height of buildings was raised in 1923 to permit the erection of towers. Above the old twenty-two-story plateau of the Loop, nearly a score of new pinnacles of from thirty-five to forty-six stories formed a new skyline. Notwithstanding the monumental appearance of these tower buildings when viewed from the ground, the floor area in this upper stratum above the twenty-two-story level was in 1933 only 2 per cent of the entire floor area in the Loop.

At the same time that the central business district of Chicago was making its pioneer ventures into the layers of air ranging from 264 feet to 560 feet above the city datum, it was sending outposts beyond the orbit of its iron-bound circuit of elevated lines. The commission houses along the south bank of the main channel of the Chicago River were cleared away, and the entire frontage along this new double-decked Wacker Drive was made available for the raising of a new crop of skyscrapers westward. On the bank of the south branch of the river was completed in 1930 the huge Civic Opera Building. Southward on Michigan Avenue beyond Harrison Street was erected in 1928 the Stevens Hotel, which, with its three thousand rooms and three thousand baths, is the largest hotel in the world. Northward, across the river at Wolf's Point, the gargantuan Merchandise Mart, occupying two city blocks of air-right property over the railroad tracks, achieved the distinction in 1930 of being the largest building yet erected by man. Eastward, near the site of old Fort Dearborn, several towering office buildings arose, and the plans for a huge colossus that was intended to bestride the tracks of the Illinois Central Railroad and to rise to a height of forty stories was only blocked by the inability to secure a special ordinance authorizing such a behemoth. Thus in the optimistic days of that "new era" which came to an end on October 24, 1929, the Chicago

Loop surged upward and outward, and the air castles of promoters and the dreams of architects became realities in steel and stone.

The spreading-out of the central business district in this period tended to prevent the extreme rise in land values which might have occurred if the new office buildings had been concentrated in a small area. The average increase in Loop land values from 1910 to 1928 was only 62 per cent, a moderate gain compared with that registered by the outlying sections of the city. Extraordinary prices were indeed paid under leasehold agreements for certain corners in the Loop, but such transactions were not regarded as fair criteria of the market value even at the time. The promoters agreed to lease a corner at extravagant figures, because they could float a bond issue and erect a building on the strength of their leasehold without any cash investment of their own. The subsequent forfeiture of the twenty-two-story building at the southwest corner of Clark and Madison streets for failure to pay the ground rent indicated that the leasing value of $50,000 a front foot for this corner was far too high.

2. *The near North Side.*—The central business district of Chicago, which in previous booms had been pulled southward by the influence of fashionable homes on Prairie, Calumet, and Michigan avenues, received a powerful tug from the North Side when the center of fashion shifted to the Lake Shore Drive. The effect was slow to manifest itself, however. The growth of the Gold Coast on the North Side had proceeded far by 1900, but the northward thrust of the Loop did not come until the Michigan Avenue bridge was opened on May 14, 1920. Michigan Avenue on the South Side, which had hitherto come to an end in the maze of wagons on South Water Street, was opened through to the North Side and a new thoroughfare was carved through the middle of the old boarding-house section on the near North Side. The new double-decked Michigan Boulevard became the busiest automobile highway in Chicago. While the last vestiges of obsolete houses fronted the lower level of the street, the newest and finest examples of skyscraper architecture presented themselves to the fashionable throngs passing along the upper deck of the new avenue. The rise in land values that followed this almost magical transformation of a decadent rooming-house district into an annex of the central business district was sensational, increases of from two to twenty-five dollars a square foot in land values in two years being common.

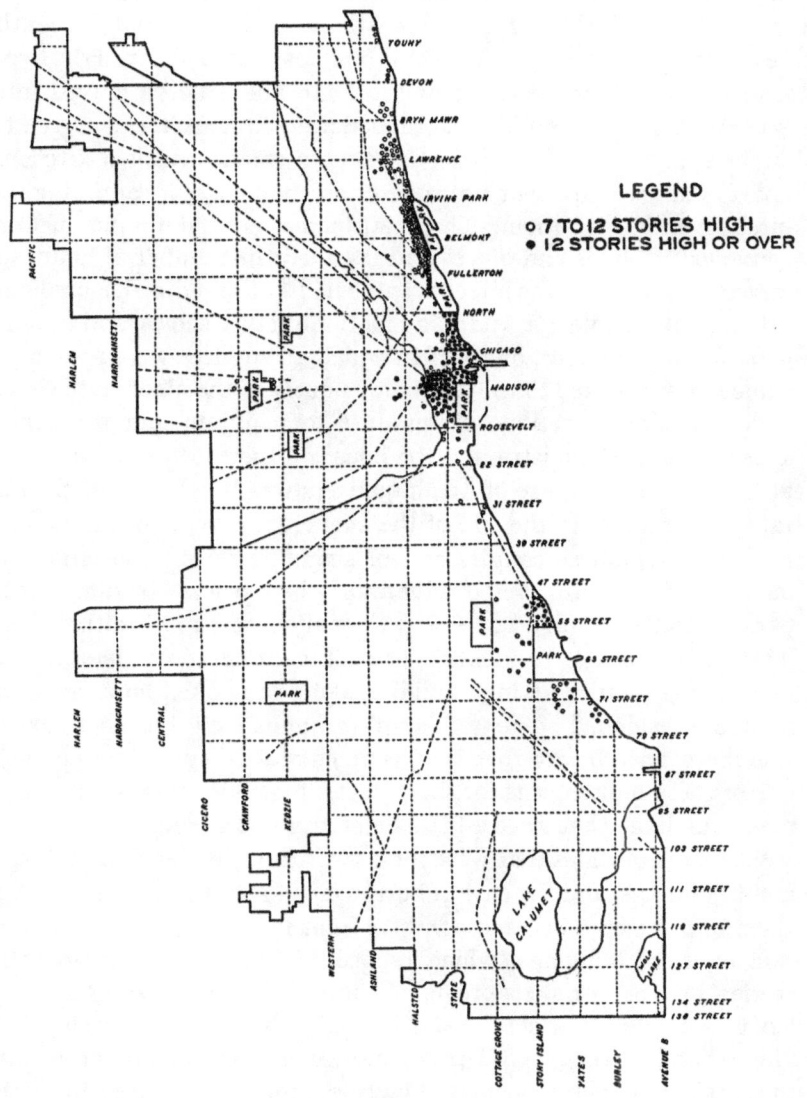

Fig. 36

3. *Tall apartment buildings.*—In this period from 1922 to 1929, a fringe of tall apartment buildings from seven to twenty-two stories high grew up along the lake front on the North Side, and on the South Side from Fiftieth to Fifty-sixth streets and from Sixty-seventh to Seventy-ninth streets.[134] Wealthy families who had formerly lived in mansions on Prairie Avenue or the Lake Shore Drive moved into *de luxe* apartments. People in more moderate circumstances moved from larger apartments of the older types into small furnished kitchenette apartments, where one or two rooms were made to serve as dining-room, kitchen, and living-room. The great increase in the number of women employed in shops and offices had lessened the number of hours spent at home, as had also the increase in the habit of spending leisure hours in driving automobiles, in attending motion-picture shows, and in playing golf. Small, compact, quarters in which all services were provided for came to be preferred to the old roomy houses of the nineteenth century, which required a retinue of servants to maintain and the constant supervision of the mistress of the house. Other powerful factors operating to reduce the size of living quarters was the decline of the birth-rate, the decrease in the size of the average family, and the increasing number of childless couples and of single persons. The large apartment buildings also offered advantages in the form of dining-rooms, parlors, and swimming pools, and they afforded opportunities of social intercourse for the residents. Thus it became convenient and also fashionable to live in a high building along the Lake Shore rather than in an old-fashioned home with ample grounds, and to such an extreme was this carried before 1929 that as much rent was paid for one room in one of these buildings as for six or seven rooms in steam-heated apartment buildings that were a little older and not so tall.

The large incomes that were for a short time derived from tall apartment buildings, and the ease of borrowing money to build them, caused them to be erected in large numbers from 1922 to 1929. The construction of these buildings, which ranged in height from six to twenty stories, in neighborhoods previously occupied by three-story structures led to a revaluation of all land in the vicinity on the basis of this "higher and better use." The percentage of the total land occupied by these tall buildings was small, however, and did not exceed one-third

[134] See Fig. 36 on distribution of buildings seven stories or more in height.

A NEW ERA THAT FOLLOWED A WORLD WAR

of the eligible ground area in the immediate vicinity even in the case of the Belmont Harbor district.

4. *Two- and three-story apartment building areas.*—Encircling the old settled areas of the city, and filling in vacant prairie tracts between the communities along the railroads, there arose in this period thousands of apartment buildings two and three stories high. These varied in size from the "two-flat" building to the court or corridor building that contained forty-two or more separate apartments. The distinguishing characteristic of the entire class was the lack of elevators and of the steel and concrete fireproof construction which were required in taller buildings. The principal subclasses were the "two-flat," designed to be sold to individuals who desired a home and an income, and who provided janitor service to their single tenant; the "three-flat," which required a slightly heavier initial investment by the purchaser; the "six-flat"; the "twelve-flat," on a fifty-foot corner lot; and the larger apartment buildings containing eighteen, twenty-four, thirty-six, or forty-two living units. Apartment buildings containing less than twelve apartments were considered as semi-investments, as the maintenance and building cost per room were higher in buildings where one steam boiler served only two apartments than where it provided heat for forty residential units.

The more intensive use of land for apartment buildings caused a rapid rise in land values in outlying residential areas between 1921 and 1926. Vacant prairie tracts, such as Devon and Western avenues, the Windsor Park golf course, Chatham Fields, Avalon highlands, Lawrence and Kimball, and North Avenue and Austin, were covered with rows of new buildings in a few years. Table XV shows the rise in land values that took place in some of the new apartment areas between 1910 and 1928.[135]

5. *Bungalow areas.*—In the period following the World War, one hundred thousand bungalows were erected in Cook County on the cheaper land beyond the apartment areas. Land in bungalow areas did not reach as high a level as that in apartment districts, but the gain in the new areas was nevertheless large, as Table XVI shows.

6. *Old residential areas.*—Outside of the central business district of Chicago is a belt of old houses in which population is declining and

[135] Computed by George C. Olcott from his *Land Values Blue Books of Chicago*.

vice and delinquency increasing. This so-called "blighted area" has had practically no new residential buildings for thirty or forty years, and land values rose but slightly in the boom that culminated in 1926, as Table XVII shows.

TABLE XV

LAND VALUES IN APARTMENT AREAS IN CHICAGO, 1910–28

BOUNDARIES OF AREA	FRONT-FOOT VALUE OF INSIDE RESIDENTIAL LOTS				
	1910	1915	1920	1925	1928
Howard–Devon, Lake Michigan–Ashland..................	$47.20	$97.00	$141.00	$377.50	$466.25
Devon–Foster, Western–Kedzie...	5.00	14.00	21.12	70.50	118.00
Foster–Irving Park, Kedzie–Crawford.......................	14.95	21.28	30.80	107.35	151.95
Kinzie–Roosevelt Road, Cicero–Central.....................	23.25	37.35	43.40	143.05	243.65
Seventy-fifth–Eighty-seventh, State–Cottage...............	6.25	15.45	19.60	50.30	116.55
Seventy-fifth–Eighty-seventh, Brandon–Yates...............	16.35	18.00	30.30	73.45	153.00

TABLE XVI*

LAND VALUES IN BUNGALOW AREAS IN CHICAGO, 1910–28

BOUNDARIES OF THE AREA	FRONT-FOOT VALUE OF INSIDE LOTS				
	1910	1915	1920	1925	1928
Diversey–North, Crawford–Cicero	$11.65	$20.80	$25.60	$51.90	$71.30
Roosevelt–Twenty-sixth, Central–Ridgeland...................	7.75	12.50	20.00	51.75	75.90
Fifty-first–Sixty-third, Western–Kedzie.......................	3.35	17.40	24.15	44.80	73.45
Eighty-seventh–Ninety-ninth, Halsted–Ashland.................	8.65	12.90	13.00	27.20	66.28

* Computed by George C. Olcott from his *Land Values Blue Books of Chicago.*

7. *Industrial areas.*—The period following the World War was featured by the continuation of the shift of factories and industrial plants away from the territory adjacent to the Loop to new specialized industrial districts along belt-line railroads such as the Clearing, the Kenwood, and the Healy districts. The advantage of cheaper land, which in turn permitted one-story construction with continuity of

TABLE XVII

VALUE OF RESIDENTIAL LAND IN OLD SETTLED AREAS OCCUPIED BY MEDIUM-GRADE HOMES
(Dollars per Front Foot)

Location—Street	1890*	1910†	1915†	1929†	1931‡
South Side:					
Broad n. Archer	$ 65	$ 15	$ 15	$ 20	$ 20
Buffalo s. Eighty-eighth	40	40	40	55	25
Carpenter s. Fifty-sixth	26	40	35	60	35
Green Bay n. Ninety-first	40	20	25	25	12
Justine s. Forty-ninth	48	20	22	32	20
Langley s. Forty-seventh	85	70	50	55	40
Paulina n. Thirty-fifth	62	25	30	45	25
Shields n. Thirty-second	44	50	35	60	25
Thirty-fifth e. Auburn	40	25	50	40	20
Thirty-sixth e. Gage	26	25	25	50	20
Thirty-sixth w. California	56	12	18	20	25
Thirty-seventh e. Archer	68	48	45	75	60
Thirty-seventh e. Parnell	54	20	30	32	20
Twenty-third w. Wentworth	56	45	70	75	40
Twenty-seventh w. La Salle	67	40	40	40	25
Twenty-ninth w. Stewart	48	35	30	40	35
Vernon s. Thirty-seventh	40	60	45	50	25
Wallace s. Thirtieth	48	40	30	50	40
Wallace s. Twenty-ninth	52	40	30	50	40
Wood s. Fifty-first	23	20	28	45	25
Average	$ 49.40	$ 34.50	$ 34.60	$ 45.40	$ 28.85
North Side:					
Blackhawk w. Larrabee	$ 93	$ 60	$ 55	$ 80	$ 35
Bissell s. Clay	44	40	45	50	40
Chatham n. Hobbie	30	45	40	70	20
Evergreen s. Milwaukee	35	60	60	80	65
Front (Fry) w. Sangamon	60	50	65	70	40
Holt n. Blanche	56	40	40	40	40
Hoyne s. Thomas	50	40	40	75	70
Huron e. Paulina	60	40	45	55	35
Huron e. Hoyne	41	40	40	50	35
Grand e. Robey	76	60	60	60	40
Iowa w. Rockwell	30	35	40	70	60
Lyndale w. Robey	30	35	30	40	30
Lill e. Perry (Greenview)	56	25	30	50	40
Noble n. Ohio	62	60	70	65	50
Ohio w. Robey	46	36	40	45	35
Ohio w. Union	80	100	125	125	80
Robey n. Grand	60	40	45	45	40
Sangamon s. Austin	65	80	125	100	60
Sheffield n. Clay	50	40	50	70	70
Smith cor. Blackhawk	60	55	66	100	100
Washtenaw cor. Iowa	27	38	38	70	82
Willow w. Burling	77	50	80	90	50
Wood s. Thomas	48	40	45	60	45
Wrightwood e. Racine	55	55	55	100	55
Average	$ 52.70	$ 48.50	$ 55.40	$ 70	$ 50.20
West Side:					
Fifteenth e. Wood	$ 50	$ 30	$ 35	$ 40	$ 35
Fifteenth e. Union	50	40	50	80	35
Eighteenth e. Western	70	30	35	40	50
Fisk s. Sixteenth	92	40	50	65	40
Flournoy e. Francisco	40	32	40	65	45
Fourteenth cor. Lincoln	27	33	38	60	44
Laflin s. Polk	83	60	70	70	60
Leavitt s. Nineteenth	51	40	40	45	45

* The 1890 figures are from sales tabulated by M. L. Putney, *Land Values and Historical Notes of Chicago* (1890).

† The figures for 1910, 1915, and 1929 are from George C. Olcott, *Land Values Blue Books of Chicago* (1910, 1915, 1929).

‡ The figures for 1931 are from the assessed value of land in Cook County for 1931.

TABLE XVII—*Continued*

Location—Street	1890*	1910†	1915†	1929†	1931‡
West Side (continued)					
May s. Eighteenth	$ 44	$ 60	$ 60	$ 60	$ 40
Nineteenth e. Western	44	40	40	45	40
Nutt (Loeffler) s. Sixteenth	70	35	45	70	40
Park (Maypole) w. Western	60	35	30	70	35
Sixteenth e. California	48	30	45	50	45
Sixteenth e. Wood	66	30	25	40	40
Thirteenth w. Robey	64	40	40	45	30
Thirteenth w. Paulina	60	40	50	45	30
Throop s. Nineteenth	83	60	60	65	40
Troy n. Twenty-fifth	48	25	40	55	30
Twentieth e. Albany	27	20	35	50	35
Twentieth w. Lincoln	48	50	50	40	40
Twentieth w. May	63	60	60	60	40
Twenty-first e. Paulina	64	45	40	50	75
Twenty-first w. May	60	40	40	70	75
Washtenaw near Fourteenth	30	30	35	45	35
Washtenaw s. Fulton	33	30	35	65	30
Spring s. Canalport	51	40	60	70	25
Average	$ 55	$ 40	$ 44.40	$ 56.50	$ 41.50

plant operation, lower taxes, direct freight-car service into the plant, a better lot layout for industrial purposes, and closer contacts with associated and complementary industries, favored the growth of these outlying industrial areas. As a result, land values of industrial tracts rose faster in these newly developed tracts than in the old districts near the Loop. This is shown by Table XVIII.

TABLE XVIII

VALUE OF LAND IN INDUSTRIAL AREAS, 1910–29
(Per Square Foot Except as Otherwise Indicated)

Boundaries of Areas	1910	1915	1918	1921	1925	1929
	New Districts					
Healy manufacturing district–Fullerton–Crawford	$ 0.03	$ 0.10	$ 0.30	$ 0.65	$ 0.85	$ 1.25
Clearing, Sixty-fifth–Seventy-first–Cicero to Harlem	600*	800*	1,000*	1,000*	1,500*	3,500*
Central manufacturing district–Thirty-ninth–Ashland, sw. cor	0.25	0.60	1.25	1.25	1.35	3.00
	0.03	0.10	0.12	1.00	1.00	1.00
Kenwood–Forty-seventh and Kedzie	0.15	0.30	0.40	0.40	0.65	0.80
Cicero–Division	0.05	0.25	0.40	1.10	1.00	1.00
Forty-seventh–Western, ne. cor						
	Old Districts					
Jackson–Monroe, Halsted–Morgan	$250†	$440†	$ 425†	$ 425†	$ 430†	$ 500†
Calumet River, Ninety-ninth–One hundred and sixth		0.30		0.25	0.25	0.30
North Branch, east bank Kinzie–Chicago	4.33	5.33	5.67	6.00	6.67	7.00
South Branch at Morgan	0.90	1.00	1.00	1.10	1.20	1.20
State–Sixteenth	10.00	8.00	8.00	5.00	6.00	6.00
South Branch, Roosevelt–Sixteenth	5.00	5.00	5.00	5.00	5.00	5.00

* Per acre. † Per front foot.

8. *Outlying business centers.*—As Table XX shows, the average value of outlying business corners doubled between 1910 and 1915, and then, as the rising prices of building materials and the war halted new construction, remained stationary from 1915 to 1921. The rapid growth of population in the outlying areas from 1921 to 1927, however, caused the upward course of values to be resumed until the sales prices of the major corners tripled on the average between 1921 and 1928. Not only did an increase of population of one million in these newly developed territories, combined with employment at high wages, furnish added consumer purchasing for local stores, but a number of factors tended to divert much of this shopping away from the Loop to these community centers. The rapid growth of outlying banks furnished depositories for local funds and collected neighborhood savings for reinvestment in local building projects. The new palatial motion-picture houses furnished the same entertainment that was afforded in the Loop. The Walgreen Drug Store, the Woolworth or Kresge Store, or the Goldblatt or Wieboldt Department Store offered a wide choice of merchandise. Hence the residents in these new areas, finding it increasingly difficult to park their automobiles in the downtown area, came to prefer to do their banking, shopping, and to seek their entertainment close to home.

As a result, store rents in some of the major outlying centers increased 1,000 per cent from 1915 to 1928. The gain in land values on the full section line streets that were traversed by car lines and that were zoned for business or upon the radial streets that were main thoroughfares exceeded the increase of any other type of property. The intersection of two full section lines, where two street-car lines usually crossed, produced a peak of land values because these so-called double-section or transfer corners commanded exceptionally high rents as locations for drug stores, cigar stores, and banks. The competition among rival department-store chain organizations for good locations as a means of swelling their volume of sales and thereby to enable them to sell more of their securities caused rents to advance above what other lessees could afford to pay. The bidding of rival banks, drug stores, and cigar stores for corners was likewise keen, and in several instances transfer corners were leased by one organization for the purpose of keeping them out of the hands of a rival concern. In the prosperous times prior to 1929, many clerks set themselves up in business and for a while did a profitable trade. All of these factors caused business areas to expand and store rents to rise. Large office buildings were erected on some of the outlying corners, so that the development was intensive as well as extensive.

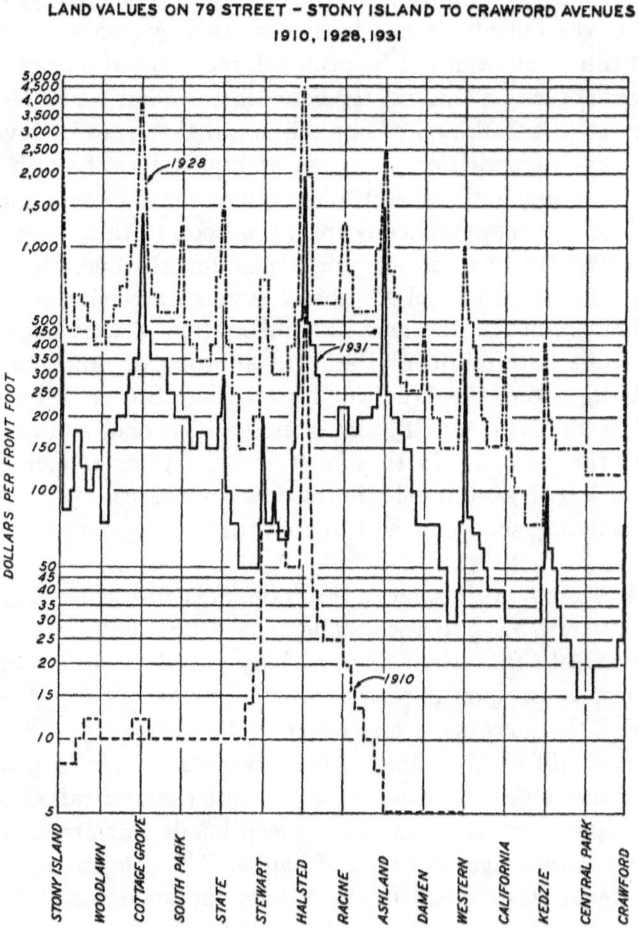

FIG. 37

Lawrence Avenue on the North Side and Seventy-ninth Street on the South Side ran through the center of zones of maximum population increase, and the rise in land values for the entire length of these streets shown in Figures 37 and 38 probably exceeded that of any other streets in the city. Hundreds of outlying corners, however, rose into the thousand-dollar-a-front-foot class in the boom from 1921 to 1926. Table XIX shows the course of land values on a number of prominent

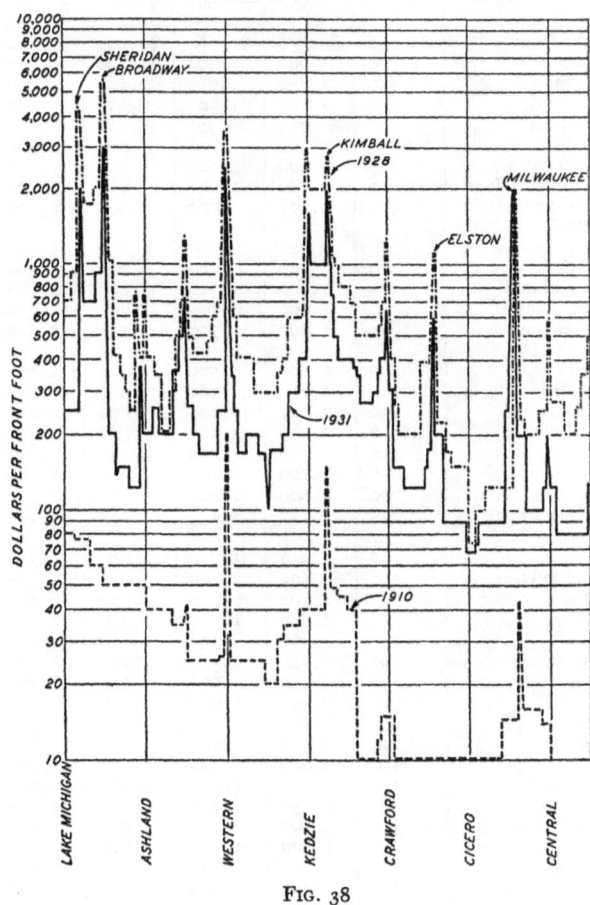

Fig. 38

corners. Figures 39 and 40 indicate graphically the increase in the value of such corners between 1910 and 1928. Table XX gives the average value of 1,700 outlying business corners at 425 different streetcar intersections, showing the increases from 1910 to 1929. In 1910

TABLE XIX*
VALUE OF LAND AT PRINCIPAL OUTLYING BUSINESS CORNERS OF CHICAGO, 1910–29
(Dollars per Front Foot)

Location	1910	1915	1918	1921	1925	1929
South Side:						
Fifty-third–Lake Park	$ 250	$ 750	$ 750	$1,000	$1,500	$ 2,750
Sixty-third–Halsted	1,500	5,000	5,000	4,000	9,000	10,000
Sixty-third–Cottage	750	1,750	1,750	2,000	5,000	7,000
Sixty-third–Ashland	750	1,500	1,500	1,350	2,000	3,000
Sixty-third–Western	100	750	900	800	1,750	2,500
Sixty-third–Kedzie	75	400	700	600	1,500	2,000
Seventy-first–Jeffery	100	100	500	400	1,300	2,250
Sixty-seventh–Stony Island	100	750	1,000	900	3,000	4,000
Ninety-second–Commercial	450	1,500	1,500	1,500	2,500	4,000
One Hundred and Eleventh–Michigan	....	700	700	800	2,000	4,000
Seventy-ninth–Cottage	20	300	300	200	1,500	3,750
Seventy-ninth–Halsted	600	1,000	1,000	1,000	2,500	4,500
Seventy-ninth–Ashland	10	400	500	400	1,250	2,500
Forty-seventh–Ashland	800	1,500	1,750	1,750	3,000	4,000
West Side:						
Madison–Kedzie	500	2,000	1,500	1,750	2,500	3,500
Madison–Crawford	500	1,000	1,100	1,250	2,250	7,000
Madison–Cicero	250	1,200	1,000	800	2,000	2,500
Roosevelt–Halsted	2,000	2,500	2,500	2,500	3,000	5,000
Roosevelt–Kedzie	500	1,500	1,500	1,750	2,500	4,000
Roosevelt–Crawford	600	1,000	1,000	1,000	1,500	2,500
Madison–Ashland	700	1,000	1,000	800	1,500	2,500
Lake–Marion, Oak Park	175	175	175	200	1,000	2,250
North Side:						
Chicago–Ashland	100	750	1,000	1,000	1,750	3,000
Milwaukee–Division	1,200	3,500	3,000	4,000	5,000	5,000
North–California	150	1,500	1,250	1,000	2,000	2,500
North–Milwaukee	500	1,500	1,500	1,750	2,000	2,000
Clark–Center	150	300	300	500	2,000	2,250
Milwaukee–Western	200	1,250	1,250	1,250	2,000	2,250
Logan Square	150	600	600	750	800	1,750
North–Crawford	60	1,250	1,000	1,000	2,000	3,000
Grand–Harlem	....	150	200	200	600	1,250
Broadway–Clark	500	500	800	900	2,000	3,000
Lincoln–Belmont	750	2,000	2,500	2,250	4,000	6,000
Milwaukee–Cicero	250	1,000	1,000	1,100	1,750	3,750
Lawrence–Broadway	100	1,250	1,750	2,000	4,000	5,500
Broadway–Wilson	300	2,000	2,250	2,750	6,000	5,500
Wilson–Sheridan	150	1,500	1,750	2,500	6,000	5,500
Lawrence–Sheridan	125	375	675	1,000	2,500	4,250
Lawrence–Western	200	800	800	900	1,700	3,500
Lawrence–Kedzie	50	500	750	1,000	2,000	3,000
Lawrence–Kimball	150	700	700	700	1,500	2,750
Lawrence–Milwaukee	60	500	500	450	1,200	2,000
Devon–Sheridan	200	750	750	600	2,000	3,000
Devon–Western	....	100	150	250	1,000	2,000
Howard–Paulina	40	90	250	225	1,000	2,500

* George C. Olcott, *Land Values Blue Books of Chicago* (1910, 1915, 1918, 1920, 1925, and 1929).

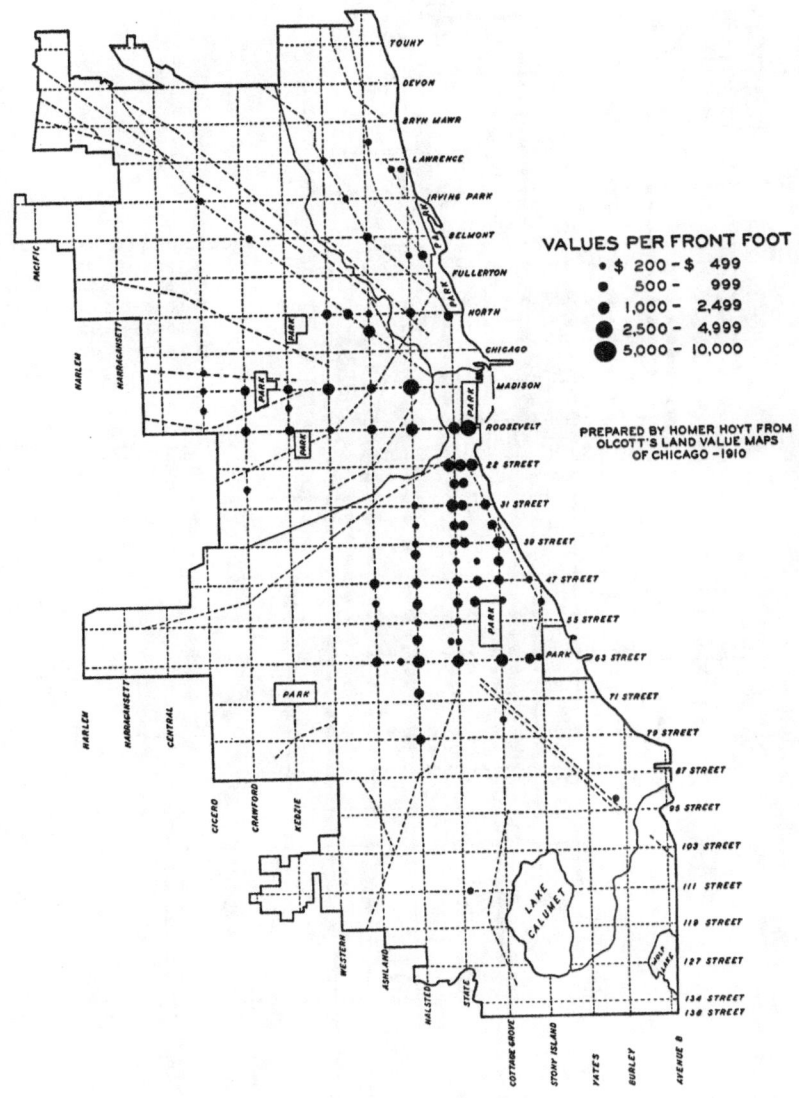

Fig. 39

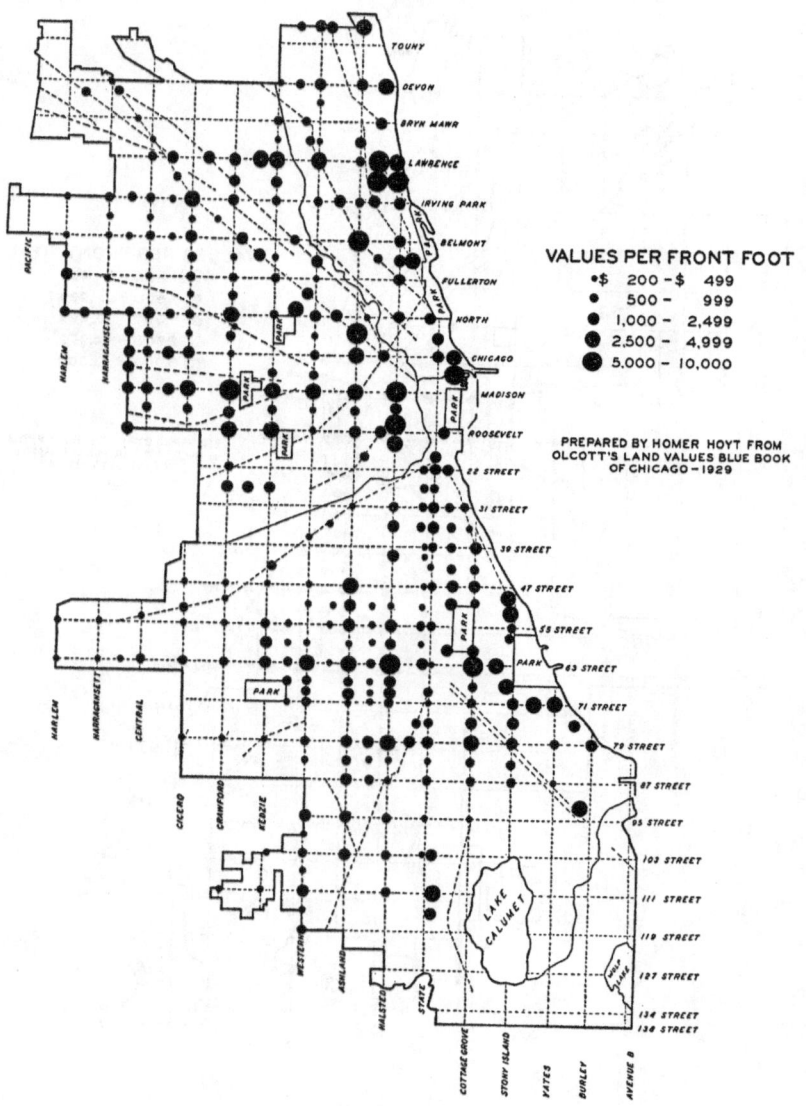

FIG. 40

only 52 corners at 13 different street-car intersections were valued at one thousand dollars or more a foot, but by 1929 the number of one-thousand-dollars-a-foot corners had increased to 816 at 204 different intersections.

9. *Subdivision and acreage tracts.*—Prior to the boom of 1925, most of the land within the city limits of Chicago had been subdivided as Figure 41 shows. In this last boom, however, nearly all of the remaining areas that were not industrial were converted into lots. The far northwest and the far southwest corners of the city limits and the Calu-

TABLE XX*

AVERAGE VALUE OF THE LAND AT 425 STREET-CAR INTERSECTIONS IN CHICAGO, 1910–29

Year	Per Front Foot Average	Index Numbers 1910 = 100
1910	$ 222	100
1915	444	200
1920	444	200
1925	880	400
1929	1,292	582

* George C. Olcott, *Land Values Blue Books of Chicago* (1910, 1915, 1920, 1925, and 1929).

met region were platted and offered to lot-buyers. The boom did not stop with the city limits, however, but went far beyond them. When the extension of the rapid transit system to Niles Center and the Skokie Valley was announced in 1925, the prices of acre tracts jumped from $500 to $3,000 an acre overnight. A belt of land three miles wide was subdivided along the North Shore for forty miles to Waukegan and even to the Wisconsin State line. The uninterrupted advance of the North Shore since 1900 make this territory the most fruitful of all for the subdivider. Other sections were not neglected, however. A line of new subdivisions was opened along the line of the Chicago & Northwestern Railroad past Arlington Heights to Barrington and Lake Geneva. The extension of the rapid transit lines to Westchester and the growth of the western suburbs led to the opening of new subdivisions along Roosevelt Road and the new electric line as far west as Wheaton. Southward, the electrification of the Illinois Central Rail-

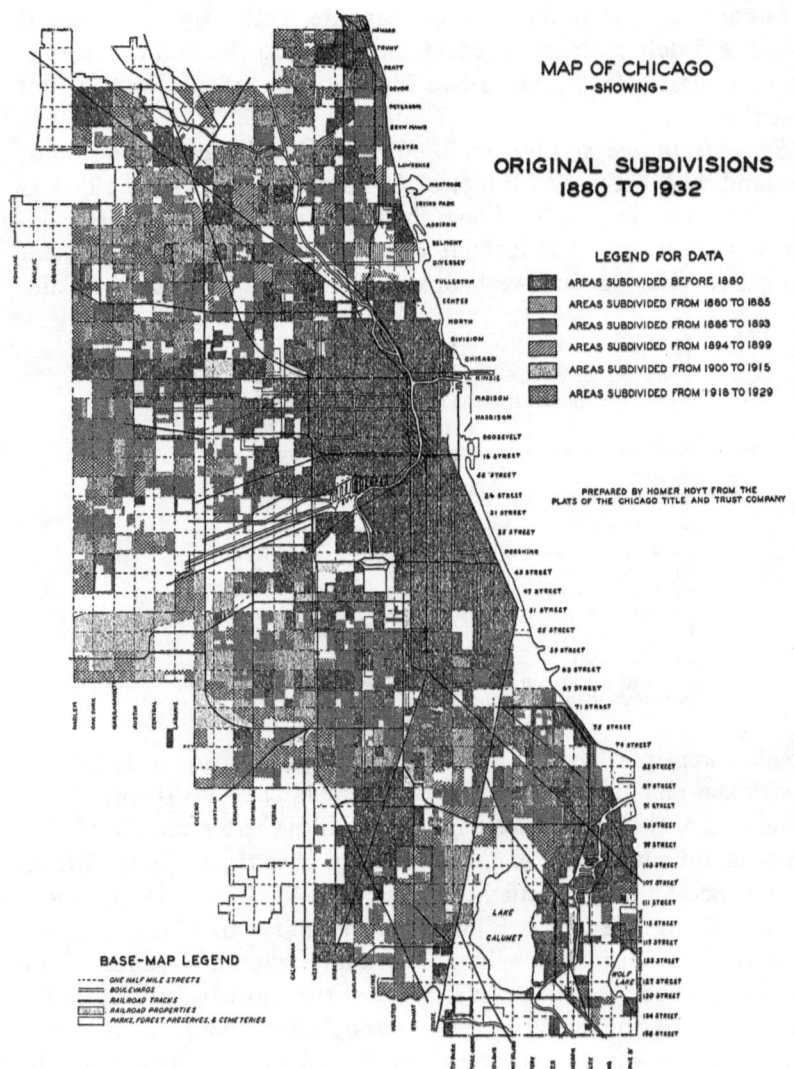

FIG. 41

A NEW ERA THAT FOLLOWED A WORLD WAR 257

road to Matteson caused developments at Ivanhoe, Flossmoor, and as far south as Two Hundredth Street. Southeastward, a new rapid transit line to Michigan City and South Bend paved the way for developments of several thousand acres along the lake near Michigan City. Southwestward, the new automobile highways opened up new tracts as far away as One Hundred and Twenty-seventh and Harlem Avenue.

The supply of lots that was thus thrown upon the market in 1925 and 1926 quickly exceeded any possible demand, but great organizations employing systematic tactics realized over $100,000,000 from the sale of lots in 1925 alone. The public was canvassed by telephone men who called nearly every person listed in the telephone directory and sought to make an appointment with a salesman. Salesmen were hired to make sales among the circle of their acquaintances. Free train rides and free lunches lured the prospect to the property where promises of a safe investment coupled with a great speculative profit led many people of small means to invest their life-savings. The prices obtained for these lots, on down payments varying from 20 to 33 per cent of the purchase price, were from three to ten times the current boom price for large tracts of land, and frequently two to three times as high as the current price of subdivided lots adjoining the new subdivision, but purchasers in this artificial market were afforded little time to make comparisons.

The sale of lots by subdividers did create a speculative market for acreage tracts. Farms were bought to sell to subdividers or to other speculators on the basis of what the land would sell for if subdivided less the cost of marketing it. Thus the suburban area for forty miles or so from Chicago felt the stimulus of the speculative boom.

In these subdivisions, "business corners" sold for high prices, and an unduly high percentage of land was designated as business land or apartment or high-grade residential land, for it was evident that these more intensive uses afforded greater opportunities of profit-making.

THE CHICAGO REAL ESTATE MARKET AS A WHOLE, 1921-29

In the Chicago real estate market as a whole, these various factors just described interacted or furnished a succession of stimuli to landbuyers. Different types of properties and different sections of the city and suburbs competed for the favor of purchasers, and some territories lay dormant while other areas were enjoying booms.

The advance in real estate began with the rise in the value of old apartment buildings, which, as a result of rising rents and higher building costs, more than doubled in value from 1919 to 1926. As an example of the general upward movement, two-apartment buildings that sold for $7,000 in 1919 brought $15,000 in 1926.[136] The movement spread to the building of stores and apartment buildings of the walk-up type, in which great profits were made by speculative builders from 1921 to 1925. A rapid rise in business and apartment lots ready for building then began. By the spring of 1925 a great subdivision and acreage boom was under way and real estate was most active in all its phases—building, subdivision, acreage sales, business leases—in all sections from the Loop to the forty-mile suburban radius. In the fall of 1926 the collapse of the Florida boom helped to put a damper on the excessive subdivision and speculative activities in vacant land. The building of large office and apartment buildings continued with undiminished ardor in 1927 and 1928, however, and the competition of chain stores for space caused land values to rise in established business centers like Sixty-third and Halsted Street and Madison and Crawford. The general market was growing dull, however, and while there were no recessions in asking prices, it was becoming more and more difficult to sell for cash, and a general trading in equities began.[137] Lot-buyers began to default on their contracts and second-mortgage holders to foreclose in 1928 and the early part of 1929. The last business sections to enjoy booms were the Davis-Orrington section in Evanston, where the advance continued to the fall of 1929, and the Lake-Marion section in Oak Park where it continued even into 1930. On October 24, 1929, however, a great crash in the stock market terminated the "new era" of uninterrupted profits and unchecked speculative advance.

Chicago land values at the peak.—The sales value of the land in the city limits of Chicago increased from two billion dollars in 1921 to five billion dollars by 1928.[138] This increase in the site value of the city was

---

[136] According to sales reported by Chicago real estate brokers.

[137] According to the statements of numerous real estate brokers.

[138] Computed on the basis of the values in George C. Olcott, *op. cit*. The correctness of this computation is checked by another method. The 1928 assessment of land in the city of Chicago was $3,710,000,000 full value. According to estimates made by Professor Herbert Simpson in his book, *Tax Racket and Tax Reform*, and also by the writer, this assessment was approximately 75 per cent of the full sales value, which would give the sales value as five billion dollars for 1928.

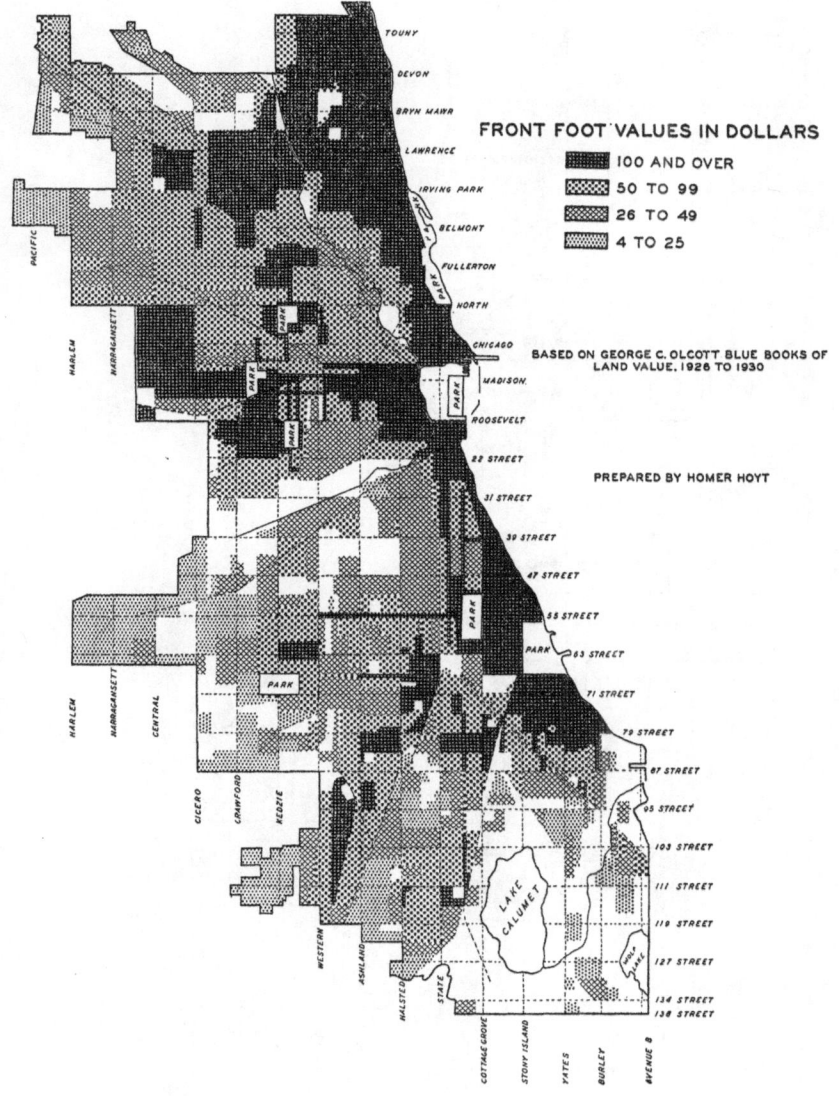

Fig. 42

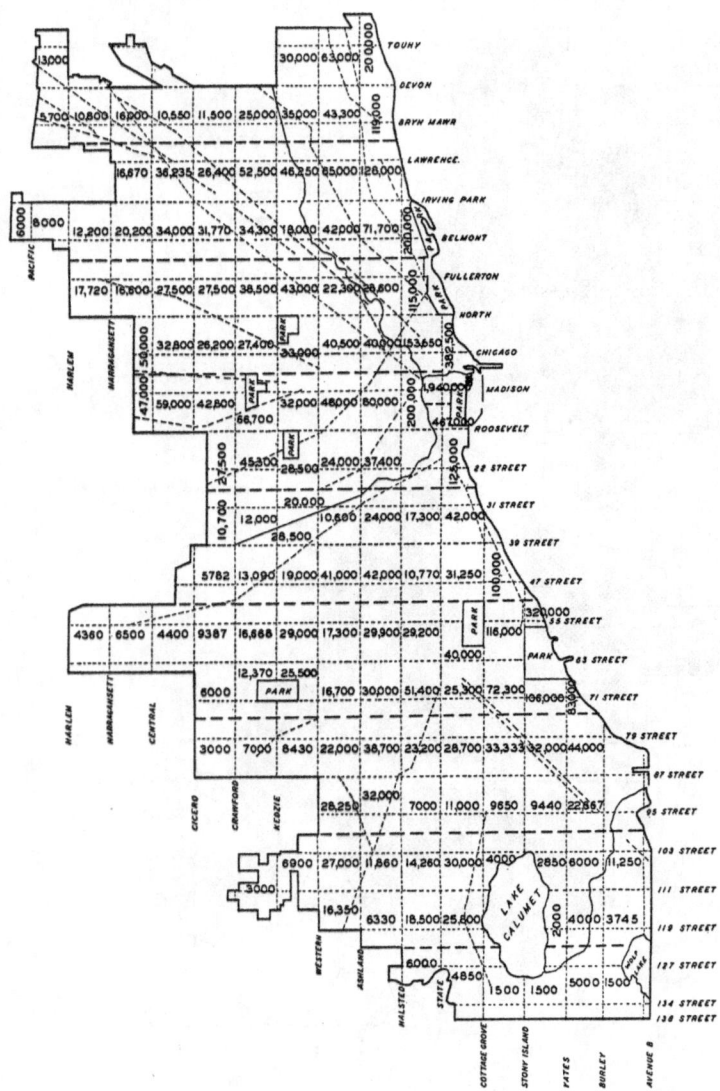

Fig. 43

A NEW ERA THAT FOLLOWED A WORLD WAR 261

by no means equally distributed by regions or types of property, as Table XXI shows.

As Figure 45 shows, the increase in land values was greatest in two semicircular belts, north and south, that traced arcs around the old blighted area where population declined between 1920 and 1930 and

TABLE XXI

VALUE OF LAND BY PRINCIPAL AREAS AND TYPES OF USE IN CHICAGO, 1910 AND 1928, COMPARED WITH POPULATION GROWTH, 1910 AND 1930

	LAND VALUE (MILLIONS OF DOLLARS)		POPULATION (THOUSANDS)	
	1910	1928	1910	1930
Area:				
The Loop..................	$600	$1,000	....	....
Area bounded by Belmont, Kedzie, Pershing, outside the Loop................	400	1,000	731	720
Area in 1933 city limits north of Belmont, west of Kedzie, and south of Pershing Road	500	3,000	967	2,656
	By Uses		Percentage Increase	
Type of use:				
Residential................	$500	$2,267	353	
Industrial.................	200	400	100	
Outlying business..........	200	1,333	566	
Central business...........	600	1,000	67	
	Average 15 Districts in Outlying Areas			
Residential................	$ 37	$ 316	760	
Outlying business..........	29	390	1,247	

where the population that remained consisted of races or nationalities that were lowest in the economic and social scale. It was in this area that was largely settled between 1899 and 1926, as Figure 44 shows, that the largest increases in land values occurred. The extension of transportation facilities into these areas; as Figure 46 indicates, had likewise facilitated the process of settlement and the rise in land values.

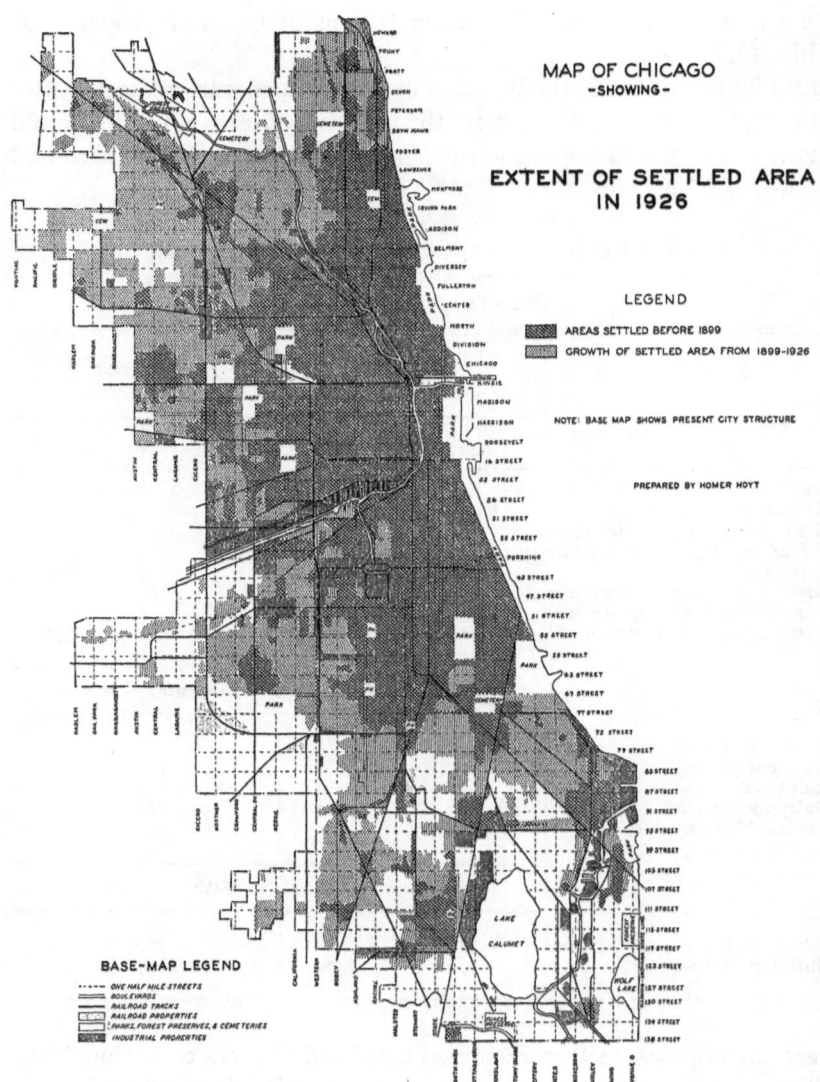

Fig. 44

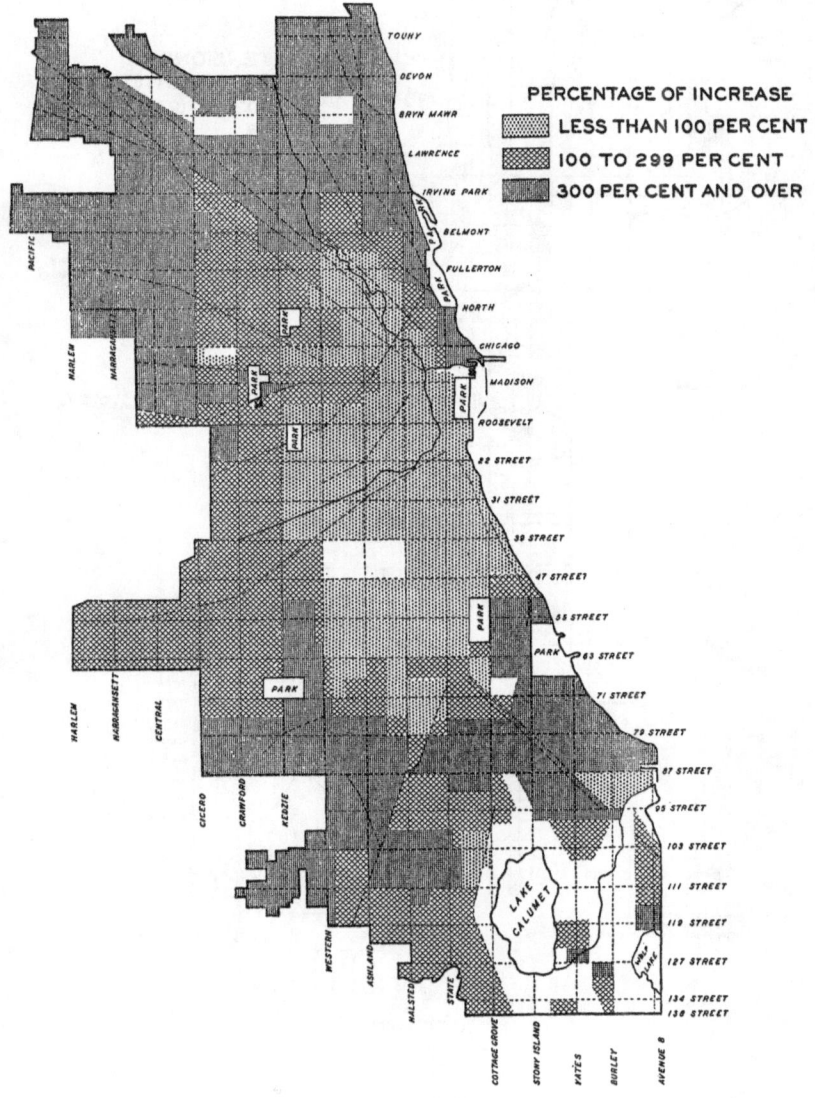

FIG. 45

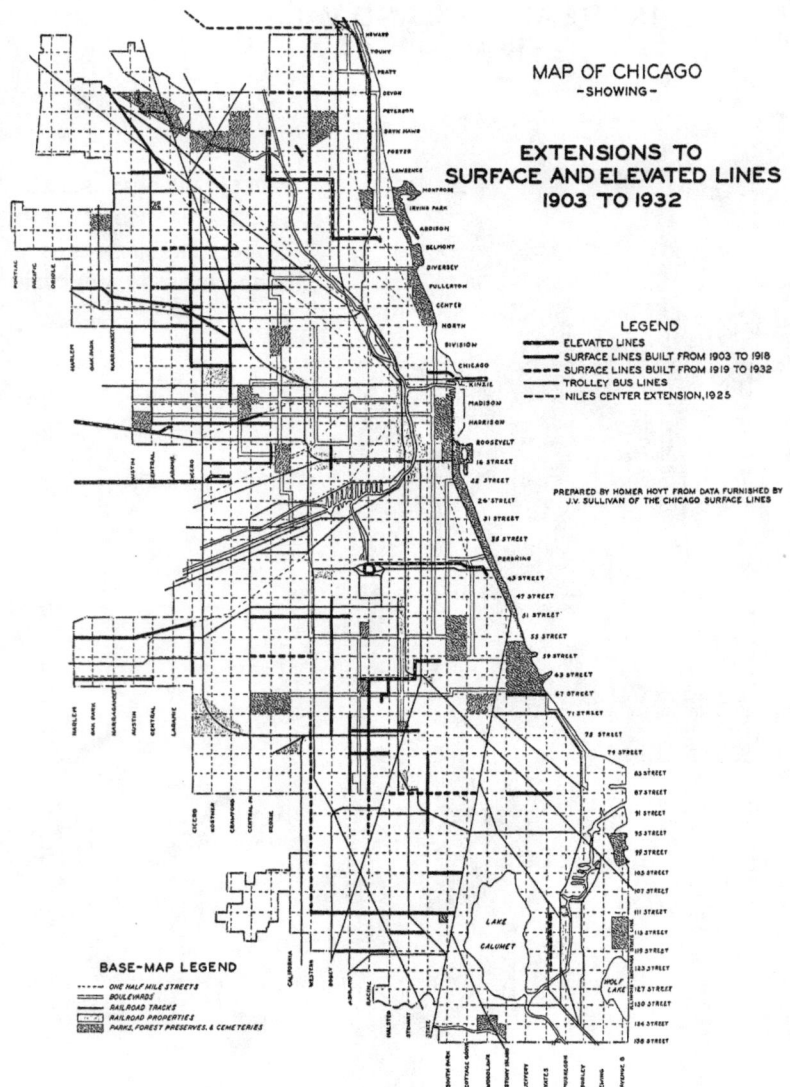

FIG. 46

THE PERIOD FROM 1929 TO 1933

Dulness sets in.—The Chicago real estate market had begun to grow dull as early as 1927. A decline in the volume of transfers, of new buildings, and of lots subdivided had indicated that the feverish activity of 1925 and 1926 was subsiding, while a slight increase in the number of foreclosures was a barometer of approaching financial storms. The underlying reason for this slackening of the pace of speculation had been the falling-off in the rate of population growth in the Chicago area after 1927[139] while the supply of residential accommodations was being greatly increased. As a result, apartment rents ceased to advance, while operating costs commenced to creep upward. The demand of builders for vacant lots began to abate, and the buyers of subdivision lots had already discovered that they could rarely resell their holdings at a profit.

While the land market was thus losing its buoyancy, in 1927 and 1928, there were no recessions in values. In fact, asking prices of properties continued to advance slowly. Cash transactions were becoming less frequent, however, and the illusion of a rising market was sustained by trades of one type of property for another, in which the price was padded by both parties.[140] The high level of values was also supported by first-and second-mortgage loans, so that owners could borrow up to 80 per cent of the peak value of their property, even when they could not sell their entire equity. The market for real estate "gold" bonds was still so good that huge Loop office buildings and large apartment hotels could be financed on the proverbial shoestring. In many cases it was possible for a promoter to borrow enough money on a bond issue to buy a lot, erect a twelve-story building, and pay himself a cash profit besides. Some operators negotiated leases of Loop corners at high figures, put out a bond issue on the security of the leasehold, and then proceeded to erect a skyscraper, to which they held title, without having made any substantial investment.

The stock-market boom and crash.—Notwithstanding these efforts to prop up real estate values from 1927 to 1929, the speculative public was forsaking real estate for the stock market. Land purchases no longer

[139] See the computations of the writer based on the school enrolment.

[140] The prevailing practices of this time are illustrated by the story of the lady who had a dog, which she insisted was worth $10,000. One day she triumphantly announced to a friend that she had sold the dog for $10,000. "Did you get cash?" inquired the friend incredulously. "No, not exactly," said the lady, "but I got two $5,000 cats for him."

yielded quick cash profits, and real estate ceased to lure the crowds of new buyers who were being attracted by the fortunes that were being made in securities. Consequently, many real estate operators viewed the stock-market crash of October 24, 1929, with ill-concealed satisfaction. The public would be taught not to dabble in margin accounts, they thought, and would return to land-buying as the safest form of investment.

It was soon discovered, however, that the financial collapse was not confined to the stock market, and that the readjustment of values could not fail to affect the entire American economic structure. The decline in real estate activity continued in 1929 and 1930. The number of transfers in Cook County declined from 102,239 in 1927 to 67,770 in 1930.[141] The value of new construction in Chicago, as shown by permits, fell off even more drastically from $315,800,000 in 1928 to $79,613,400 in 1930.[142] Subdivision activity came to a complete standstill. The number of foreclosures in Cook County increased from 3,148 in 1928 to 5,818 in 1930,[143] and the second-mortgage holders, who had been the first to foreclose, were now themselves being forced out by the holders of the underlying liens. Loans on new mortgages and trust deeds dropped from over $1,000,000,000 in 1928 to $425,000,000 in 1930.[144]

Up to 1930, however, there had been only a moderate recession in rents, in wages, and in employment. The majority of real estate owners were grimly hanging on, hoping for a revival that would restore the prosperous days of 1926.

The sharp decline of real estate values in 1931.—In 1931 came the collapse of the peak values of 1928. Chicago real estate received a series of shocks which forced reluctant owners to admit that a drastic decline had occurred. Sharp reductions in employment and in wage rates, as wages paid by American manufacturing industries dropped from $11,500,000,000 in 1929 to $7,000,000,000 in 1931, forced store and apartment rents downward.

As Tables XXII and XXIII show, the decline in employment and payrolls in Chicago manufacturing industries beginning in Novem-

[141] *Reports of the Recorder of Deeds of Cook County.*
[142] *Reports of the Building Department of the City of Chicago.*
[143] Computed by the Chicago Title and Trust Co.
[144] Annual reviews of the *Economist.*

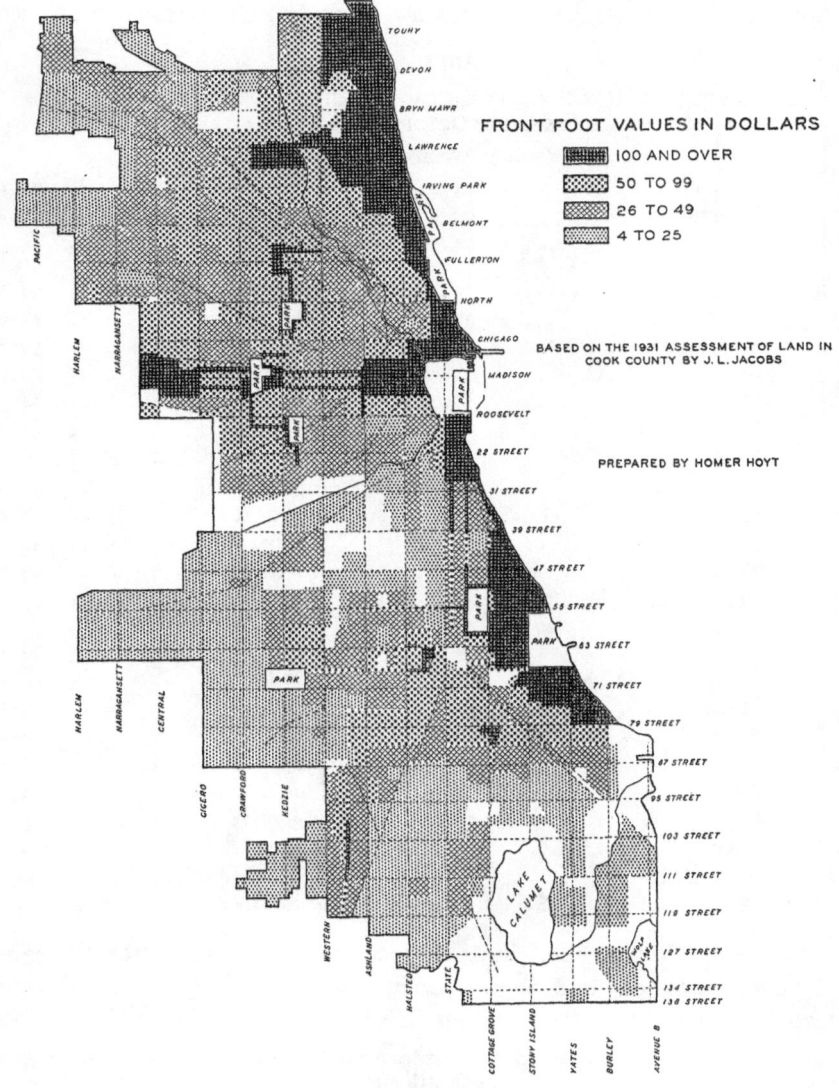

FIG. 47

ber, 1929, continued steadily almost without any upturn until March, 1933.[145]

In June, 1931, began the *débâcle* of the outlying banks, loaded with non-liquid real estate, as thirty banks, including the Bain chain, closed

TABLE XXII*

DECLINE IN PAY-ROLLS IN CHICAGO MANUFACTURING INDUSTRIES
BY MONTHS FROM OCTOBER, 1929, TO MAY, 1933

(Monthly Average, 1925–27 = 100)

1929—	October	103.9	1931—October	46.8
	November	99.4	November	42.4
	December	94.5	December	44.3
1930—	January	89.5	1932—January	42.8
	February	92.3	February	41.6
	March	88.4	March	39.8
	April	87.4	April	36.9
	May	84.9	May	34.9
	June	80.7	June	33.5
	July	73.2	July	28.9
	August	71.9	August	31.0
	September	70.1	September	31.8
	October	67.7	October	32.1
	November	62.8	November	29.7
	December	62.2	December	29.1
1931—	January	59.6	1933—January	28.4
	February	61.6	February	28.6
	March	61.7	March	25.7
	April	60.0	April	26.4
	May	58.2	May	29.3
	June	55.5	June	32.2
	July	53.6	July	35.2
	August	52.9	August	39.5
	September	49.4	September	39.9

* Illinois Department of Labor, *Labor Bulletin*, p. 143. Releases, February 19–October 20, 1933.

their doors. Meanwhile, the total local tax levy had increased from $65,000,000 in 1915 to $290,000,000 in 1930. More city taxes had been levied in the eight years ending in 1931 than in the entire period

[145] Employment in manufacturing industries for the United States as a whole declined slightly more than the average for all industries from 1929 to the first four months of 1933, the decline for manufacturing being 42.8 per cent and for all industries 40.7 per cent. ("Employment during the Depression," *National Bureau of Economic Research Bull.* 47 [June 30, 1933]).

before 1923, and taxes levied for the year 1930 alone exceeded the total amount collected from 1830 to 1893. Most of the burden of local taxes fell upon real estate, and, to make matters worse, the collection of the 1928 taxes had to be postponed, as a result of the gross errors in the original assessment, from a period of prosperity to one of depression. Foreclosures were mounting rapidly, the number increasing from 5,818 in 1930 to 10,075 in 1931 and the total value of the trust deeds in which suits were brought rising from $244,246,577 to $457,268,689.[146] Vacancies and delinquencies in collections were likewise increasing rapidly, as Figure 48 shows.

TABLE XXIII*

DECLINE IN EMPLOYMENT AND IN PAY-ROLLS IN CHICAGO MANUFACTURING INDUSTRIES, 1929–33

(Figures for the Month of April of Each Year; Monthly Average, 1925–27 = 100)

Year	Employment	Pay-Rolls
1927	100.9	99.0
1928	93.3	88.9
1929	97.8	100.5
1930	90.9	86.0
1931	74.3	59.8
1932	56.5	35.9
1933	49.3	26.4

* Illinois Department of Labor, *Labor Bulletin*, XII, No. 7 (January, 1933), 143. Release, May 18, 1933.

The forces of depression dealt even harder blows to Chicago real estate in 1932 than they had in 1931. The continued decline in wages and employment until 170,000 families in Chicago were supported by charity, and the inability of the local governments to pay their employees, reduced the public buying power. By December, 1932, pay-rolls in Chicago manufacturing industries had declined to 29 per cent of the level of November, 1929. Store and apartment rents continued to decline throughout the year, and there was an increase in vacancies and in delinquencies in collections. It is estimated that 40,000 families "doubled up" or occupied apartments jointly and many thousands left the city. The population of Chicago certainly failed to gain, and it probably received a setback. As gross rents of all types of properties

[146] Computed by Quinlan & Tyson, a prominent real estate firm.

were falling faster than operating expenses, the net incomes of landlords was reduced almost to the vanishing-point, particularly in the case of kitchenette apartments requiring heavy maintenance costs. Meanwhile, the shock of outlying bank failures continued until March, 1933, when a total of 163 banks, whose locations are indicated on Figure 49, had been closed in Chicago. This had a particularly depressing effect on outlying real estate, where the gains in land values had been

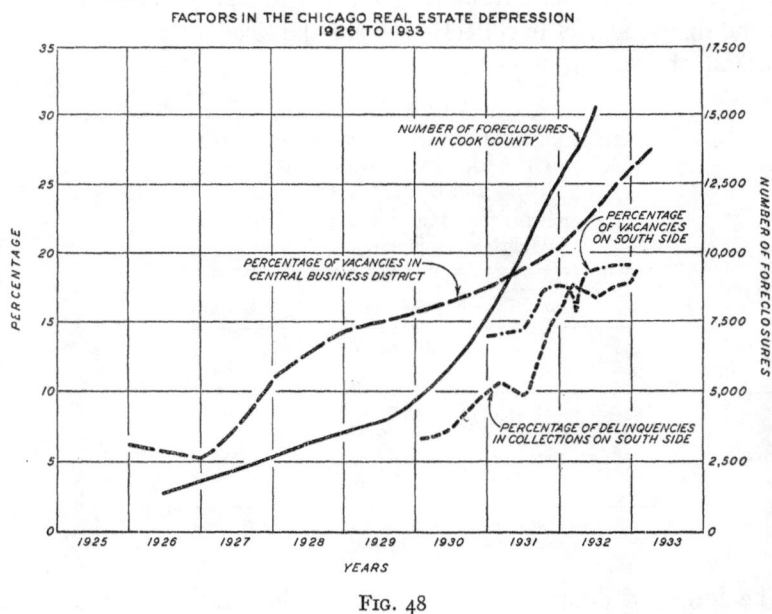

FIG. 48

greatest, because it meant the destruction of the local institutions that had hitherto made loans upon neighborhood real estate and that had financed local merchants. In communities where all the banks had failed, the loss of confidence and the decline in land values were particularly severe. Meanwhile, foreclosures reached a new peak in 1932, rising from 10,075 to 15,201 in number and from $457,268,689 to $574,589,646 in amount.[147] Trust deeds to the amount of $2,000,000,000 had been involved in foreclosure suits by the end of 1932, and if allowance be made for deeds that were given by equity holders to avoid fore-

[147] The number of foreclosures was computed by the Chicago Title and Trust Co., the amount of trust deeds foreclosed upon by Quinlan & Tyson.

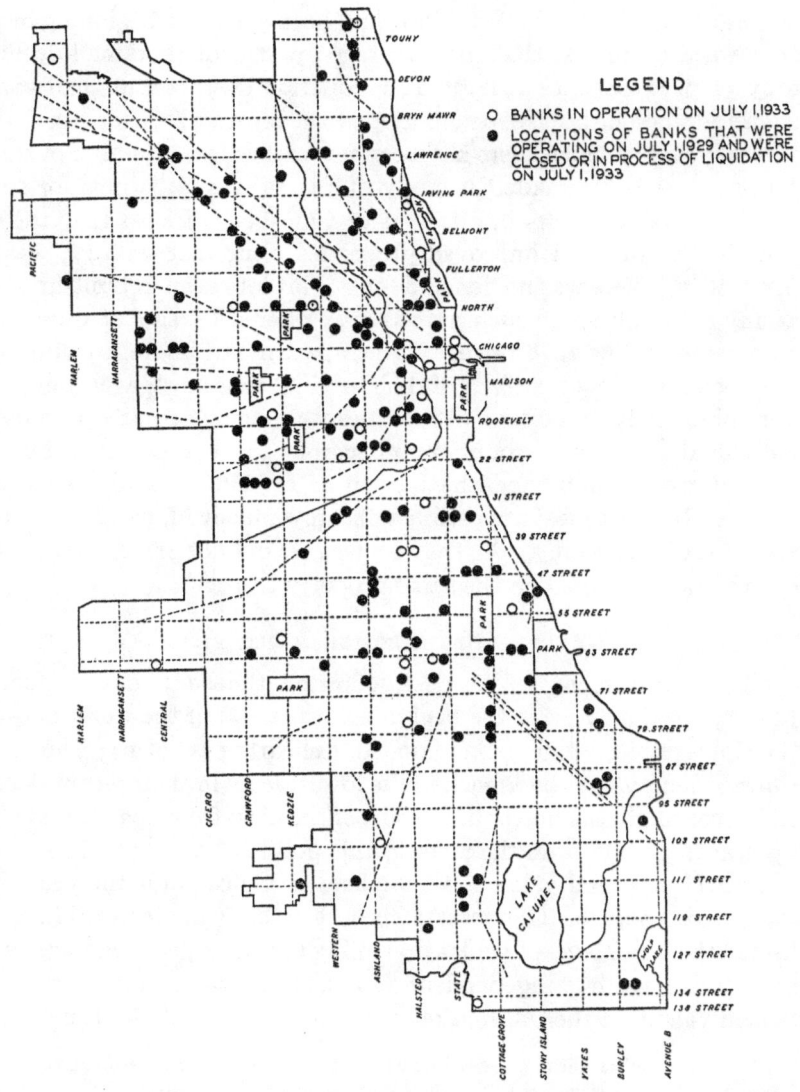

Fig. 49

closure, it is probable that half of the property in Cook County will pass into the hands of mortgage holders before the end of the depression.

At the beginning of the bank moratorium in March, 1933, Chicago real estate was at the lowest ebb it had been since the beginning of the downward trend. At that time average apartment rents had declined fully 50 per cent since 1928.[148] The reduction in store rents had varied from 40 to 90 per cent, depending upon the location. After a period of several years in which there had been few cash sales, a number of transactions were being made. A study of 127 sales and listings for small homes and apartments in all parts of Chicago indicated that the decline in the value of improved properties from 1928 to 1933 was 50 per cent.[149] There was no demand for vacant lots even in built-up areas at any price, although such parcels were offered for sale at from 75 to 90 per cent below 1928 prices. Large apartment buildings could have been bought at less than half of their original first mortgages, but there were practically no buyers. Properties were being acquired by buying individual bonds at discounts ranging from 50 to 90 per cent, but the evils of receiverships and the burden of unpaid taxes deterred purchasers. It was almost impossible to borrow money on new trust deeds, and where loans were made, they sometimes did not exceed 10 per cent of the amount loaned on the same property in 1928.

A SURVEY AT THE BOTTOM, MARCH, 1933

The improvement in business following the bank moratorium in March, 1933, may mark the beginning of the end of the worst phase of the Chicago real estate depression. In the early part of 1933, however, Chicago land values had reached the lowest level in their recent decline and accordingly the maximum extent of the drop from 1928 is indicated by drawing a line from the peak to this point.

The full assessed value of all the land in Chicago for the year 1931 was $2,500,000,000. This assessment was actually made in 1932 and reflected the lower level of values prevailing at that time. Compared with twenty-five hundred independent appraisals, this assessment seemed to be equivalent to the full market value of the land at the time it was

[148] This is based on the average reduction reported by leading brokers in all sections of Chicago in an unpublished report to the county assessor, J. L. Jacobs.

[149] A study made for the county assessor, J. L. Jacobs.

A NEW ERA THAT FOLLOWED A WORLD WAR 273

made.[150] Hence the decline in Chicago land values from the $5,000,-000,000 level of 1928 to the $2,500,000,000 level for the early part of 1932 was 50 per cent. From the spring of 1932 to the spring of 1933 it is estimated that a further decline of 20 per cent has occurred, so that the value of Chicago land at the beginning of 1933 was $2,000,000,000.

The reduction in land values was by no means uniform. It was greatest in the case of business property and in high-grade apartment property in which there had been the greatest advances, and least in the case of cheap residential land. It was recognized that far more land was zoned for business and tall apartment buildings than could be used in the near future, and that land values that reflected conversion to such uses could not be justified. The greatest reductions in the 1931 assessment as compared with the 1928 assessment were made in these classes of land, and it is believed that this represented the true market situation. Table XXIV, therefore, indicates the extent of the relative decline in different types of land, although the full extent of the decline would have been even greater, as the 1928 assessed values were about 25 per cent below the sales prices of that time.[151]

In business properties, however, the decline varied greatly between different locations. There was a contraction of the profitable business area in each outlying center, and the best locations in the center of a district maintained themselves far better than sites on the fringes. Thus rents at the southwest corner of Sixty-third and Halsted Street declined only 40 per cent from 1928 to 1933, while the reduction in rents on Halsted Street north of Sixty-first Street or South of Sixty-fifth Street ranged from 80 to 90 per cent.[152] Similarly, on the west side of Commercial Street, from Ninety-first to Ninety-second Street, the string of chain stores held the throngs and maintained values, but there was a collapse of rents on the opposite side of the street and on Ninety-second Street. In the Loop, also, there was a retreat from the outer fringes to the center. The Stevens Hotel was too far south to be profitable while the Civic Opera Building was too far west. The Wacker

---

[150] Of these 2,500 appraisals, approximately one-half were made by the Chicago Title and Trust Co. and one-half by Harry Cutmore & Associates. The appraisals were made in the latter part of 1931 and early part of 1932.

[151] As indicated by the study of Herbert D. Simpson, *Tax Racket and Tax Reform in Chicago*, and by the analysis of 127 properties made by the writer.

[152] Based on local survey of rents by writer.

Drive development was regarded as premature and North Michigan Avenue as overboomed. The wholesale district west of Wells Street was adversely affected by the depression and by the completion of the Mer-

TABLE XXIV*

AVERAGE REDUCTION IN FULL VALUE OF LAND FOR ASSESSMENT PURPOSES FOR 1931 AS COMPARED WITH 1928 FULL VALUE ACCORDING TO THE RELATIVE VALUE OF THE LAND

(Taking Average Values for Entire Maps)

Range in Value 1928 Assessment	No. Maps	Per Cent, 1931 as Compared with 1928	Per Cent Reduction
Residential Land			
$4–$25 front foot.............	23	85	15
$25.01–$50 front foot..........	32	82	18
$50.01–$100 front foot.........	40	75	25
$100.01–$500 front foot........	31	62	38
$500 and up..................	4	59	41
Average all residential.....	....	74.7	25.3
Business Land			
Under $50 front foot..........	6	58	42
$50.01–$100 front foot.........	22	63	37
$100.01–$200 front foot........	22	63.5	36.5
$200.01–$500 front foot........	61	60	40
$500.01–$1,200 front foot......	12	55	45
Loop—retail area.............	1	70	30
Loop—wholesale area..........	1	60	40
Average all business outside Loop..................	....	60.6	39.4
Average including Loop.....	....	63	37.5
Average all types of Land..	....	69	31

* Unpublished study made by the writer for the county assessor, J. L. Jacobs, based on the comparison of 1928 and 1931 front-foot values for the entire city. The typical unit, or "map" is an area 1 mile wide and 1½ miles long, containing 960 acres with streets and alleys. Some maps contain a smaller area than this. The maps correspond exactly to the pages in George C. Olcott's *Land Values Blue Books of Chicago* as well as to pages in the land-value maps in the assessor's office.

chandise Mart, which drew away some of its best tenants. So land values on the outer edges of the Loop declined from 40 to 50 per cent, while the center of it dropped only 25 to 30 per cent.

Outlying business centers were affected in some cases not only by the depression but by the growth of rival centers. The establishment of branches of Loop department stores at Lake and Marion streets in Oak Park and at Davis and Orrington streets in Evanston tapped the trade of adjacent Chicago areas. The Madison-Crawford and Madison-Kedzie districts were unfavorably affected on the west and the Wilson Avenue and Howard Avenue districts on the north. Instead of attracting trade from the suburbs, the suburbs in their new satellite loops attracted trade away from the outer edges of Chicago. The cancellation of chain-store leases by bankrupt concerns, the failure of banks that had supported local merchants, the great reduction in public buying power as a result of unemployment, and chain-store competition that bore severely upon the independent merchant—all combined to demoralize the rents of commercial property. A great many vacant stores were to be seen on leading business streets, and there was a widespread delinquency in rent collections. Landlords were satisfied to accept in many cases whatever rent the tenant offered, regardless of the amount stipulated in the lease, for it was considered better to have the store occupied at a nominal rent rather than to have it empty.

The depression was by no means confined to store property. Home-owners had been prevailed upon to assume heavy mortgages, and when these came due, many, notwithstanding heavy sacrifices, could not pay any part of the principal. Thousands of small home-owners lost their properties after having invested their life-savings to acquire a shelter. By March, 1933, the depression had driven down the value of bungalows until there was in most cases no equity left above the mortgage.

The decline of values went even farther in the case of large properties. Not only was the equity of the owner and the lien of the second mortgage successively made valueless, but finally the interest of the scattered bondholders, racked by receivers and burdened with tax charges and foreclosure fees, was reduced in value to one-third or one-half of the original obligation.

After the bank moratorium in March, 1933, there was a rapid rise in the price of wheat, corn, and securities in the United States, and a marked improvement in general business conditions. While the influence of inflation had been but faintly reflected in real estate values if at all by the summer of 1933, there was a decline in vacancy rates for apartment buildings in many sections of the city, which is usually the first step in the recovery.

The year 1933: a turning point.—The year 1933 may not only mark the turning-point of one cycle in real estate; it may be the year of transition from a century-old American policy of almost uncontrolled individualism to one of planned economy. Whatever may be the course of the future events that are hidden from the eyes of the present writer, the history of Chicago land values from 1830 to 1933 must be regarded as an example of the doctrine of laissez faire applied to American conditions. Here was exhibited an energy that at times reached an unusual pitch of intensity, and which produced in a century a city covering six times the ground area of Paris and rising in towers and pinnacles nearly as high as the Eiffel Tower. Here there was a mingling of races and a mobility of the population with but few parallels in the history of the world. Its growth, however, was accomplished at great social cost. Its exuberant periods of building, subdividing, and land speculation were followed by the inevitable aftermath of foreclosures, bankruptcies, bank failures, and losses of savings that affected not only the speculators but the entire community. Cheaply constructed and poorly planned buildings, a helter-skelter development of dwellings and industries, and subdivided tracts with sidewalks overgrown with weeds were the products of this unbridled individualism. Great public works were indeed undertaken and plans for the improvement of the city formulated which bore fruit in such magnificent achievements as the Michigan Avenue and Wacker Drive developments and the construction of the Outer Drive on land pumped out of the lake, but most of the Chicago lots were subdivided and the Chicago buildings erected solely under the guidance of a speculative profit motive. In this method of its growth, Chicago was not unique. Such were the characteristic traits of American development during the period of rapid expansion in the past century.

PART II
ANALYSIS OF THE RELATION OF THE GROWTH OF CHICAGO TO THE RISE OF ITS LAND VALUES, 1830–1933

CHAPTER VI

THE RELATION BETWEEN THE GROWTH OF CHICAGO AND THE RISE OF ITS LAND VALUES

In the first part of this work, the factors affecting Chicago land values were presented in their historical setting, and the emphasis was placed upon the current background and the qualitative differences between the five major periods in Chicago's real estate history. In this part, the broad sweep of these forces through the century will be reviewed, and their behavior as revealed by statistical records analyzed. From this point on, the quantitative measurement of the various factors will be stressed.

A. THE DEMAND FOR CHICAGO LAND

1. *The swarm of people.*—One of the chief requisites for the growth in the volume of buildings in any urban community is an increase in the number of people dwelling on or near the site. As the growth in the number of persons living in a city thus has a direct bearing upon the increase in land values, the increase in the population of Chicago is of fundamental importance in this study.

The growth of Chicago in the nineteenth century has been paralleled by that of no other great city of a million population or over in either ancient or modern times.[1] In the one hundred years that represent the life-span of Chicago, its population increased from 50 to 3,376,438. It compressed within a single century the population growth of Paris for twenty centuries. From 1840 to 1890, the rapidity of its development outstripped that of every other city in the world. An insignificant town in 1840, Chicago forged ahead of its older rivals in the Middle West before 1880, as Table XXV shows, and by 1890 it was the second city in point of numbers in the United States. In 1930 only London, New York and Berlin—all much older—contained more people. Nevertheless, the relative growth of the population of Chicago since 1900 has not been materially greater than that of a number of other American cities, and

[1] Maurice Halbwachs, "Chicago, experiénce ethnique," *Annales d'histoire économique et sociale*, IV (January 31, 1932), 10-11.

it has been far surpassed by that of Detroit and Los Angeles.[2] The growth of some of the suburbs of Chicago in the twentieth century, however, has been comparable to that of even those two rapidly growing cities.[3]

a) The growth of Chicago compared with that of other American cities.—The population growth of Chicago may be compared first with that of its older rivals in the Middle West—St. Louis, Cincinnati, and New Orleans—that were mainly supported by the commerce of the Mississippi River and its branches. Table XXV shows how rapidly Chicago outstripped these competing cities after the railroads entering Chicago

TABLE XXV

POPULATION OF CHICAGO AND OTHER LEADING CITIES IN THE MIDDLE WEST, 1840–1930

YEAR	Chicago	RIVER CITIES				LAKE CITIES	
		New Orleans	St. Louis	Cincinnati	Pittsburgh	Cleveland	Detroit
1840	4,479	102,193	16,469	46,338	31,201	6,071	9,102
1850	29,963	116,375	77,860	115,435	67,863	17,034	21,019
1860	109,206	168,675	160,780	161,044	77,923	43,417	45,619
1870	298,977	191,418	310,864	216,239	139,256	92,829	79,577
1880	503,298	216,090	350,518	255,139	235,071	160,146	116,340
1890	1,098,570	242,039	451,770	296,908	343,904	261,353	205,876
1900	1,698,575	287,104	575,238	325,902	451,512	381,768	285,704
1910	2,185,283	339,075	687,029	363,591	533,905	560,663	465,706
1920	2,701,705	387,219	772,897	401,247	588,343	796,841	993,678
1930	3,376,438	458,762	821,960	451,160	669,817	900,429	1,568,662

diverted traffic from the river ports. The same table also shows the more rapid growth of the lake cities, such as Detroit and Cleveland, as compared with the river towns. Again the increase in the population of Chicago may be contrasted with that of the cities on the Atlantic seaboard and the Pacific Coast. Chicago, as Tables XXVI and XXVII indicate, is seen to grow at a much more rapid rate than the eastern cities, as the tide of population shifted westward, but as Tables XXVI and XXVII show also, its population gain since 1900 has been far less than that of Los Angeles on the Pacific Coast and Detroit on the Great Lakes. The growth of Chicago has not been at the expense of all of its rivals, for the direct water and rail connections between New York and

[2] See Table XXVIII.   [3] See Table XXIX.

Chicago have been a primary factor in the rise of New York City in its struggle with Boston and Philadelphia.

b) *Where did the people come from?*—Where did all these people come from and how were they brought to a spot which a century ago was a

TABLE XXVI

POPULATION OF CHICAGO AND SEABOARD CITIES, 1840–1930

YEAR	CHICAGO	ATLANTIC SEABOARD				PACIFIC COAST		
		New York*	Philadelphia	Boston	Baltimore	San Francisco	Los Angeles	Seattle
1840	4,479	391,114	†	93,383	102,313			
1850	29,963	696,115	†	136,881	169,054		1,610	
1860	109,206	1,174,799	565,529	177,840	212,418	56,802	4,385	
1870	298,977	1,478,103	674,022	250,526	267,354	149,473	5,728	1,107
1880	503,298	1,911,698	847,170	362,839	332,313	233,959	11,183	3,533
1890	1,098,570	2,507,414	1,046,964	448,477	434,439	298,997	50,395	42,837
1900	1,698,575	3,437,202	1,293,697	560,892	508,957	342,782	102,479	80,671
1910	2,185,283	4,766,883	1,549,008	670,585	558,485	416,912	319,198	237,194
1920	2,701,705	5,620,048	1,823,779	748,060	733,826	506,676	576,673	315,312
1930	3,376,438	6,930,446	1,950,961	781,188	804,878	634,394	1,238,048	365,583

* Corporate limits of 1930.
† Population of 1840 did not include a large area annexed prior to 1850.

TABLE XXVII

RELATIVE INCREASE IN POPULATION OF ELEVEN LEADING AMERICAN CITIES, 1850–1930

(1850 = 100)

Year	Chicago*	New York†	Detroit	Los Angeles	Cleveland	St. Louis	Baltimore	Boston	Pittsburgh	Cincinnati	New Orleans
1850	100	100	100	100	100	100	100	100	100	100	100
1860	356	169	214	270	254	206	126	130	115	140	145
1870	939	216	390	358	546	400	158	180	205	191	165
1880	1,680	276	554	700	941	449	199	266	345	222	186
1890	3,370	360	980	3,130	1,537	579	257	327	506	259	209
1900	5,158	492	1,360	6,362	2,246	737	300	410	664	282	247
1910	6,640	671	2,217	20,000	3,300	881	330	490	789	316	293
1920	8,188	800	4,540	35,818	4,700	990	433	546	716	350	333
1930	10,231	993	7,470	76,900	5,300	1,054	476	570	985	392	370

* Population within 1933 corporate limits.
† Population within 1930 corporate limits.

dismal swamp far removed from the path of settlement? The natural rate of increase of the population could not account for so prodigious a rate of growth in the earlier period. An analysis of the sources of the supply of population of Chicago shows that the extraordinary rate of gain in the number of persons residing within its limits was the combined result of three main factors: immigration from Europe, migration from other

TABLE XXVIII

RELATIVE INCREASE IN POPULATION OF THIRTEEN LEADING AMERICAN CITIES, 1900–1930

(1900 = 100)

Year	Chicago	New York	Philadelphia	Detroit	Los Angeles	Cleveland	St. Louis	Baltimore	Boston	Pittsburgh	San Francisco	Cincinnati	New Orleans
1900	100	100	100	100	100	100	100	100	100	100	100	100	100
1910	129	139	120	163	311	147	119	110	119	118	122	111	118
1920	159	164	140	349	562	210	133	144	133	130	148	123	135
1930	198	203	151	550	1,208	233	143	158	139	148	185	139	160

TABLE XXIX

POPULATION OF SOME CITIES IN THE CHICAGO SUBURBAN AREA AND POPULATION OF THE CHICAGO SUBURBAN AREA, 1900–1930

City or Town	1900	1910	1920	1930
Cicero	16,310	14,557	44,995	66,602
Evanston	19,259	24,978	37,234	63,338
Highland Park	2,806	4,209	6,167	12,203
LaGrange	3,969	5,282	6,525	10,102
Maywood	4,532	8,033	12,072	25,829
Park Ridge	1,340	2,009	3,383	10,417
Wilmette	2,300	4,943	7,814	15,233
Winnetka	1,833	3,168	6,694	12,166
Gary		16,802	55,378	100,426
East Chicago	3,411	19,098	35,967	54,784
Suburban area*	242,652	393,214	630,594	1,065,310
	Relative Number 1900 = 100			
Cicero	100	89	276	408
Evanston	100	130	193	329
Highland Park	100	150	220	435
LaGrange	100	133	164	255
Maywood	100	177	266	560
Park Ridge	100	150	252	777
Wilmette	100	215	340	662
Winnetka	100	173	365	664
East Chicago	100	560	1,054	1,606
Suburban area*	100	162	260	439

* Cook County outside of Chicago, Lake, and DuPage counties, Illinois, and Lake County, Indiana.

parts of the United States, and the excess of Chicago births over deaths. Only a succession of improved transportation devices, combined with the stimulation of the flow of migration, settled so many people upon this prairie site in so short a time. Lake steamers and prairie schooners brought the advance guard of the thirties and forties, but combined ocean steamers and the newly completed railroads poured in the great stream of Irish and German immigrants of the fifties, sixties, and seventies, and the same agencies of transportation opened up the floodgates of southern European immigration beginning in the eighties.

When the European sources of supply of adult man power began to fail altogether after the outbreak of the World War and the subsequent passage by the United States of drastically restrictive immigration laws, the shortage was made good by a migration of negroes from the rural South, immigration from Mexico, and an increased flow of white families into Chicago from other parts of the United States. In the meantime, the growth of the resident population from migration had provided an increasing parent-stock to provide for a substantial gain by natural increase and the decline in the city birth-rate from 27 to 17 per thousand population was partly offset by a decline in the death-rate from 15 to 11 per thousand for the period from 1898 to 1931 so that a substantial part of the city's growth came from the excess of births over deaths within the city. Tables XXX and XXXI show the relative amount contributed by each factor to the city's growth in population.

c) *Why did they come?*—Such being the sources of the Chicago population, why did the people come to that particular spot? The opportunity to earn a living in trade, manufactures, banking, transportation, and professional and personal service was of course the reason. The advantage of the site of Chicago as a meeting place first of lake, river, canal, and wagon transportation, and then of lake and rail carriers in turn, made it the principal distributing and manufacturing center for a valley containing the richest combination of agricultural and mineral resources of the world that was being exploited for the first time. Higher wages could be paid at such a strategic site than at other less favored places, and the concerns located there could still undersell their competitors by virtue of lower shipping charges. Packing plants, agricultural implement works, stove factories, steel mills, electrical generating plants, gigantic mail-order houses, railroad shops, clothing shops, wholesale houses, banking institutions, and interval transportation lines—these were some of the magnets that pulled this great population to Chicago. In addition to these industries there were the retail stores, the theaters, the local building trades, the schools, and the local governmental agencies that supplied the needs of the resident population. The

TABLE XXX*

SOURCES OF INCREASE OF CHICAGO POPULATION, 1830–1930

Decade	Total Increase in Population	Increase in Foreign-born Population	Increase in Colored Population	Increase in White Population from Other Parts of U.S.	Increase in Births over Deaths
1830–40	4,429	†	†		400
1840–50	25,484	†	†		2,000
1850–60	79,243	†	†		10,000
1860–70	188,717	90,133		63,000	30,000
1870–80	205,108	60,302		95,000	50,000
1880–90	496,665	244,769	7,791	144,106	100,000
1890–1900	588,725	137,584	15,879	265,262	170,000
1900–1910	468,708	194,105	13,953	48,650	212,000
1910–20	525,422	24,165	65,000	236,257	200,000
1920–30	674,733	36,575	146,000	259,158	233,000

* Total population increase, increase in foreign-born, and increase in colored population are from the U.S. Census figures. Increase in births over deaths computed from actual birth and death statistics since 1900. Figures for earlier periods estimated on basis of death-rates published since 1867 and estimated birth-rate. Increase in number of white persons coming from other parts of the United States computed by subtracting other factors from total population increase. The figures for increase of births over deaths assume that persons born in Chicago remain there for at least a decade.

† Before 1860 no accurate date is available for increase in foreign-born population. Increase in colored population in this period was negligible.

TABLE XXXI

PERCENTAGE OF TOTAL INCREASE OF CHICAGO POPULATION COMING FROM EACH SOURCE, 1860–1930

Decade	Total Increase in Population	Increase in Foreign-born Population	Increase in Colored Population	Increase in White Population from U.S.	Increase in Births over Deaths
1860–70	100	47.8		33.4	15.9
1870–80	100	29.4		46.3	24.4
1880–90	100	49.3	1.6	29.0	20.1
1890–1900	100	23.4	2.7	45.0	28.9
1900–1910	100	41.4	3.0	10.4	24.2
1910–20	100	4.6	12.4	45.0	38.0
1920–30	100	5.4	21.7	38.4	34.5

magnitude of the population was but the measure of the strength of the economic advantages of the site of Chicago, and of the economic resources of its hinterland—the Upper Mississippi Valley.

GROWTH OF CHICAGO AND ITS LAND VALUES

2. *Increase in the number of the buildings.*—The physical body of the growing city was the buildings connected with transportation lines, sewers, pavements, and water pipes that began to spread over the prairie as the number of the people grew. Such structures were erected, of course, only because the population in its need for housing, stores, and workshops paid rent at least high enough to cover the operating costs, taxes, depreciation, and interest on the cost of construction. In fact, the superior sites yielded an income not merely enough to amortize the cost of the improvement, but they also returned a surplus income to the owner of the land, which formed the basis for its value. The absorption of vacant land in the Chicago region for building purposes therefore enabled hitherto unused plots of prairie to pay ground rent to their owners. The prospect for the continued growth of the settled area gave a speculative value to all the nearby vacant land. Hence the rate of growth of new construction and the amount of vacant land required for the houses, stores, factories, and schools of Chicago are the measures of the aggregate demand for vacant land on the edge of the built-up area and the source of its value. Corresponding to the growth of the population of Chicago, therefore, is the growth of the number of its buildings.

The hamlet with twelve log cabins in 1831 had grown to a metropolis with 400,000 buildings in 1928, as Table XXXII shows.[4]

The buildings in Chicago in 1933, exclusive of garages, vary in size from a small cottage of 400 square feet to a structure with nearly 4,000,000 square feet or 50 acres of floor space. They vary in height from low one-story bungalows to the Board of Trade Building in the central business district that rises to the height of 612 feet above the street level.[5]

[4] See Putney, *op. cit.*, for the years 1825, 1831–37, 1868, 1890; Goodspeed and Healy, *op. cit.*, I, 223, for the years 1842, 1851, 1853; Chamberlin, *op. cit.*, p. 69, for the years 1848 and 1857. J. L. Jacobs (*Journal of the Proceedings of the Board of Commissioners of Cook County*, April, 1928, pp. 1379–80) gives the result of the tabulation of all the buildings assessed in Cook County in 1928. Exclusive of sheds and garages, there was a total of 360,250 buildings in townships wholly within Chicago and 44,329 buildings in townships partially within Chicago. Most of the buildings in townships partially in Chicago were in Chicago and there were some tax-exempt buildings. The estimate of 400,000 is made by the writer.

[5] The height of the tallest buildings in Chicago, measured from the sidewalk level to the top of the highest pinnacle, is as follows:

Board of Trade	612	Mather	519	Furniture Mart	474
Chicago Temple	569	Carbide	500	Medinah Athletic Club	471
Pittsfield	557	LaSalle Wacker	491	Palmolive	468
20 N. Wacker	555	State Bank of Chicago	479	Steuben	465
One N. LaSalle	530	Bankers	476	Tribune	462
Morrison Hotel	526	Straus	475	Roanoke Tower	452
Pure Oil	523			Willoughby	448

They differ in material and type of construction from the frame stove-heated houses to the brick and stone elevator apartments with steel frames. They vary in age from structures antedating the Chicago fire of 1871 to buildings a year old. For tax-assessment purposes, this conglomeration of buildings is grouped into 48 major divisions with a total of 288 different subgroups.[6]

a) *Increase in the volume of building space.*—Ignoring the number of separate structures and considering merely the cubic contents of the

TABLE XXXII

NUMBER OF BUILDINGS IN CHICAGO COMPARED WITH POPULATION AT INTERVALS FROM 1825 TO 1928

Year	No. of Buildings	Population	Buildings per 1,000 Inhabitants
1825	14		
1831	12	100	120
1832	30	200	150
1833	180*	350*	
1836	450	3,820	118
1837	516	4,170	124
1842	1,361	6,000	227
1848	3,742	20,023	187
1851	5,798	34,000	170
1853	9,212	59,130	156
1857	19,008	93,000	204
1868	39,366	252,054	142
1869	43,920	272,043	161
1870	52,610	298,977	176
1871	61,000	325,000	186
1890	127,871	1,098,570	116
1928	400,000	3,402,296	118

* Population, early part of 1833; buildings, latter part of 1833.

entire mass of buildings, the space inclosed between walls and roofs of major buildings in Cook County increased from less than 200,000 cubic feet in 1830 to an estimated 22,000,000,000 cubic feet in 1930.[7] Of approximately 500,000 buildings erected within the present city limits of Chicago since 1830, nearly 400,000 are still standing.[8] The replacement of buildings has been small in relation to the volume of new construction. The buildings in Cook County in the latter year had a floor area

[6] *Assessor's Manual, Cook County, Illinois, 1930.*

[7] Estimated from the number of buildings at each period with the average cubic content of each estimated from the records of the assessor's office.

[8] This figure is obtained by adding the total number of building permits issued since 1872 to the number of buildings in existence in 1870.

GROWTH OF CHICAGO AND ITS LAND VALUES 287

of approximately 1,600,000,000 square feet, which would cover 57 square miles to a height of one story. If streets and alleys are allowed for, this quantity of construction would solidly fill all the lots in 83 square miles, and if the rear half of the lots were kept vacant, as is usually the case, it would spread over 166 square miles on a one-story level. On the other hand, all of this building space could be put into one forty-story building $1\frac{1}{2}$ miles square or into one solid twenty-story building 3 miles square. Such a building, with no space allowed for light courts or air shafts, would of course never be built, but the example illustrates the possible range in ground area that might be covered by the existing buildings in Cook County.

b) Factors determining the volume of building space.—Neither the aggregate number of people living on an urban site nor the aggregate floor space in the buildings is sufficient to determine the ground area covered by structures. The demand for land for urban use is the aggregate demand of the population for a variety of uses such as for streets, parks, homesites, factory sites, stores, churches, schools, governmental buildings, cemeteries, and railroad rights-of-way. The amount of space required for the principal uses enumerated is subject to wide variations. Thus the amount of floor space required to house the population is much less when there is a large proportion of single men in the city who sleep in the rear of stores, or fourteen to a room, as they did in 1836 in Chicago. The amount of space for residential purposes contracts in periods of depression when families "double up," live in a single room in an apartment and share dining-room and kitchen in common, and it expands when these families on the return of prosperity take separate apartments. The amount of space required for dwellings is greater when people live in large rooms with high ceilings than when they live in one-room kitchenette apartments with disappearing beds and gas ranges, where the one room has the efficiency of three. Less space is required for a population of childless couples than for one with children, and smaller quarters are needed when all the children sleep in one room than when the custom becomes established of having a separate bedroom for each child. The amount of space required for stores and factories also varies with the concentration of the business. A heavy volume of trade or work spread out over a long period of time with day and night shifts requires less store space than a smaller volume scattered over a wider area during a shorter time interval. The demand for space for governmental buildings increases with the complexity of governmental functions, and the need for space for cemeteries increases with enlargement of the city's total population and the increase in the number in the older age groups; although this demand might cease almost entirely if the practice of cremation became common. The space taken for parks varies in different cities, and the amount of ground needed for railroads depends upon the importance of a city as a railroad center. The area taken for streets and alleys is far less in urban communities where the only thoroughfares are narrow lanes than it is in cities where the streets are wide or have parkways in the center and where the blocks are short and cross-streets frequent.

The number of persons who live within a given inclosed building space thus varies with the habits, customs, and standards of living of the people. The amount of ground occupied by a given amount of floor space or used in conjunction with a given building also varies greatly. The motto of Chicago, *"Urbs in horto"* ("City in a Garden"), once meant—in the forties and fifties—that nearly every family had a garden plot next to the house, and for that a lot 50 by 125 feet was required. Near the central business district, however, by 1858 frame shacks were crowded together and built on both the front and the rear of the lot. A mansion of a millionaire of the eighties, even in the city, would contain yard space enough to provide sites for from ten to twenty of these cottages of the poor.[9] The small cottage or bungalow today, however, rarely occupies more than one-third of a lot, while the large apartment building occupies from 75 to 90 per cent of the ground space on which it stands. Similarly, the small store usually occupies no more than the front half of the lot, because for most purposes, except for laundries, restaurants, chain department stores, banks, or theaters, the deep store no longer pays the cost of maintaining the rear half. The large department store in the Loop, however, covers the entire block, even the alleys, to a height of from twelve to sixteen stories and to a depth of two or three basements.

Not only does the percentage of the lot occupied by the building range from 20 to 100 per cent, but the number of floors superimposed on each lot varies from one to twenty-two before the tower setback requirement lessens the floor area of the space from the twenty-third to

[9] See Fig. 50 for an illustration of this point.

the forty-fourth floors. In the case of tall kitchenette apartments, all the factors of concentrated land use are combined. The ground area is fully occupied, the height is carried to twenty-two stories, and the apartments are of the one-room Pullman type. This makes it possible for as many as one hundred families to live on the ground where one family lived in a cottage.

The intensity of utilization, not only of the lot but also of the block or of the neighborhood, also fluctuates within a considerable range. Thirty per cent of all the lots inside the city limits of Chicago were still

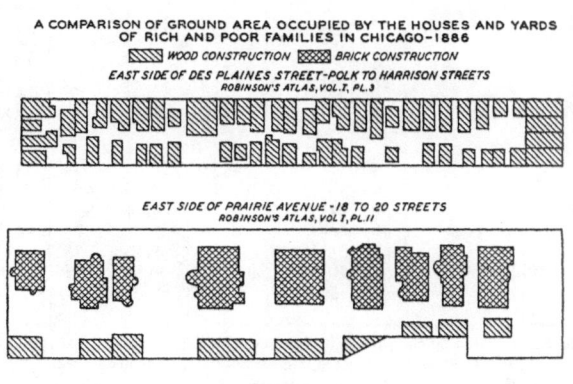

Fig. 50

vacant in 1928, and there was in 1933 a gradation from blocks with only one or two houses to those which are solidly built up.[10]

c) *Classification of buildings by type of use.*—The percentage of the land area of Chicago used for the various purposes from 1850 to 1911, according to statistics gathered by the Bureau of statistics and the Chicago Municipal Reference Library, is indicated in Table XXXIII.[11] In Table XXXIV is shown the utilization of land in Chicago in 1923.

d) *The average height of buildings in the Chicago area.*—The building space in Cook County in 1928 was distributed over approximately the

---

[10] In Chicago in 1928 there were 517,086 improved lots and 223,126 vacant lots (Herbert D. Simpson and John E. Burton, *The Valuation of Vacant Land in Suburban Areas: Chicago Area* [Chicago: Northwestern University, 1931], p. 14).

[11] This table is reproduced from Dorau and Hinman, *Urban Land Economics* (New York: Macmillan Co., 1928), p. 146.

TABLE XXXIII*
UTILIZATION OF LAND IN CHICAGO, 1850, 1870, 1890, AND 1911

Class of Utilization	1911 Acres	1911 Per Cent	1890 Acres	1890 Per Cent	1870 Acres	1870 Per Cent	1850 Acres	1850 Per Cent
Total area...............	124,448	100.0	115,520	100.0	22,463†	100.0	8,966	100.0
Water area...............	4,215	3.4	3,290	2.9	385	1.7	170	1.9
Land area................	120,233	96.6	112,230	97.1	22,078	98.3	8,796	98.1
Vacant land..............	37,334	30.0	64,142	55.5	9,409	42.6	6,338	70.7
Utilized land.............	82,899	70.0	48,088	44.5	12,669	57.4	2,458	29.3
Publicly utilized.........	30,968	37.4	23,531	48.9	5,835	46.1	1,682	68.4
Streets and alleys........	26,368	31.8	20,721	43.0	4,725	37.3	1,630	66.3
Recreational lands.......	4,500	5.4	2,735	5.7	1,096	8.7	50	2.1
Other Public uses‡.......	100	0.2	75	0.2	14		2	
Privately utilized.........	51,931	62.6	24,557	51.1	6,834	53.9	776	31.6
Residential..............	30,138	36.4	11,008	22.9	3,481	27.5	465	18.9
Manufacturing...........	9,672	11.7	6,146	12.8	1,330	10.5	135	5.5
Steam railroads..........	6,904	8.4	4,501	9.4	1,373	10.8	50	2.1
Business§...............	3,252	3.9	1,722	3.6	525	4.1	33	1.3
Education and religious‖..	850	1.0	375	0.8	125	1.0	28	1.1
Cemeteries..............	5	1.2	805	1.3			65	2.7

* Based on statistics gathered by the Bureau of Statistics and Chicago Municipal Reference Library.
† Area reported for 1870 was 22,823, but total of items is only 22,463, as here given.
‡ Does not include utilization for public education or conduct of corporate business.
§ Includes a small amount of publicly utilized land.
‖ Includes land utilized for public education, etc.

TABLE XXXIV*
UTILIZATION OF LAND IN CHICAGO IN 1923

	No. of Acres	Per Cent of Total Land Area
Total land area..........	120,000	100.0
Vacant................	30,000	25.0
Utilized...............	90,000	75.0
Utilized:		
Streets................	30,000	25.0
Residential...........	30,000†	25.0
Manufacturing........	16,640	13.8
Business..............	5,568	4.6
All other uses.........	7,792	6.5

* *Chicago Zoning Commission Report* (1923).
† This figure of 30,000 acres of residential land in 1923 is not consistent with the figure of 30,138 acres given in Table XXXIII for the year 1911, as there was a large amount of vacant land absorbed for residential use between 1911 and 1923. The two tables were either computed in a different manner or else the figure for 1911 is too high.

height levels shown in Table XXXVI.[12] The actual ground space occupied by buildings in Cook County is thus 18,400 acres, or 3 per cent of its total land area.

TABLE XXXV*

NUMBER OF BUILDINGS IN COOK COUNTY
BY PRINCIPAL TYPES, 1928

Type of Building	No.
Residential:	
One-family dwellings...................	240,540
Two-family dwellings...................	145,171
Multi-family dwellings..................	40,249
Dwellings with stores or offices..........	41,517
Hotels................................	513
Club and lodge buildings...............	129
Total...........................	468,119
Commercial buildings:	
Stores................................	8,963
Office buildings.......................	808
Theaters..............................	345
Public garages........................	3,359
Service stations.......................	1,608
Hospitals.............................	72
Miscellaneous commercial...............	1,920
Total...........................	17,075
Industrial and farm buildings:	
Factories and loft buildings.............	7,130
Warehouses...........................	286
Farm buildings........................	1,280
Total...........................	8,696
Grand total......................	493,890
Private garages........................	260,567
Sheds, barns, and fences................	126,768
Miscellaneous.........................	53,170
Total...........................	440,505
Grand total......................	934,395

* J. L. Jacobs, *Journal of the Proceedings of the Board of Commissioners of Cook County* (April 28, 1931), p. 1380.

[12] This was computed in the following manner: The number of buildings in each of the 48 classes of the *Assessor's Manual* was determined by the actual count of J. L. Jacobs already referred to. One-, two-, and three-story buildings are separately given in this classification. The average number of square feet in each class was determined by taking the measurements of a number of buildings in each class from the records of the county assessor's office. The total number of square feet for each class was estimated by multiplying this average for each building by the total number of buildings.

Figure 51 indicates how the Chicago buildings are distributed as to height. Most of the tall buildings are along the lake front, and the height tends to decline as one proceeds west.

e) The intensity of land utilization in Chicago.—As regards the intensity of utilization of land for its residential buildings, Chicago occupies a middle ground between European and smaller American cities. On the one hand, it does not possess the tenements or the dense apartment areas of Berlin, Paris, and New York, in which the poorer families are crowded into a limited space. On the other hand, it is, relative to population, not spread out as much as the smaller American cities, where the majority of the people reside in single-family dwellings. One

TABLE XXXVI
SQUARE FEET OF BUILDING SPACE AT VARIOUS HEIGHT LEVELS IN COOK COUNTY, 1928

Height	Square Feet	Acres	Per Cent
First story..................	800,000,000	18,400	50
Second story................	480,000,000	11,000	30
Third story.................	180,000,000	4,000	11
Fourth story and higher......	140,000,000	3,400	9
Total..................	1,600,000,000	36,800	100

striking characteristic of Chicago is the two-apartment building, or the "two flat," in which one-third of the population dwelt in 1930. As compared with 30 per cent of the Chicago population occupying "two flats," in sixteen self-contained American cities with an aggregate population of 1,583,187, only 10.44 per cent of the population lived in two-family dwellings in 1930.[13] In these smaller cities, on the other hand, 78.6 per cent[14] of the people occupied single-family residences as compared with 19.4 per cent for Chicago.[15] Finally, in the smaller

[13] Figures for smaller American cities: Harland Bartholomew, *Urban Land Uses* (Cambridge: Harvard University Press, 1932), pp. 38, 60. The smaller cities were Knoxville, Tenn.; Vancouver, B.C.; San Angelo, Tex.; Fort Worth, Tex.; Cape Girardeau, Mo.; Sacramento, Calif;. San José, Calif; Springfield, Mo.; Cedar Rapids, Iowa; Tulsa, Okla.; Louisville, Ky.; Peoria, Ill.; Jefferson City, Mo.; San Antonio, Tex.; Troy, Ohio; and Binghamton, N.Y.

[14] *Ibid.*, pp. 28, 60.

[15] Chicago Association of Commerce, *Survey of Business Research Bureau* (January 1, 1931). This figure included 625,000 living in single-family homes, 37,500 living in single-family homes in the rear of stores, and 6,500 living in single-family homes over stores.

GROWTH OF CHICAGO AND ITS LAND VALUES

cities, only 7.6 per cent of the people lived in multi-family buildings[16] compared with 48.4 per cent for Chicago.[17] The average population density of Chicago within areas occupied for residential uses was 100

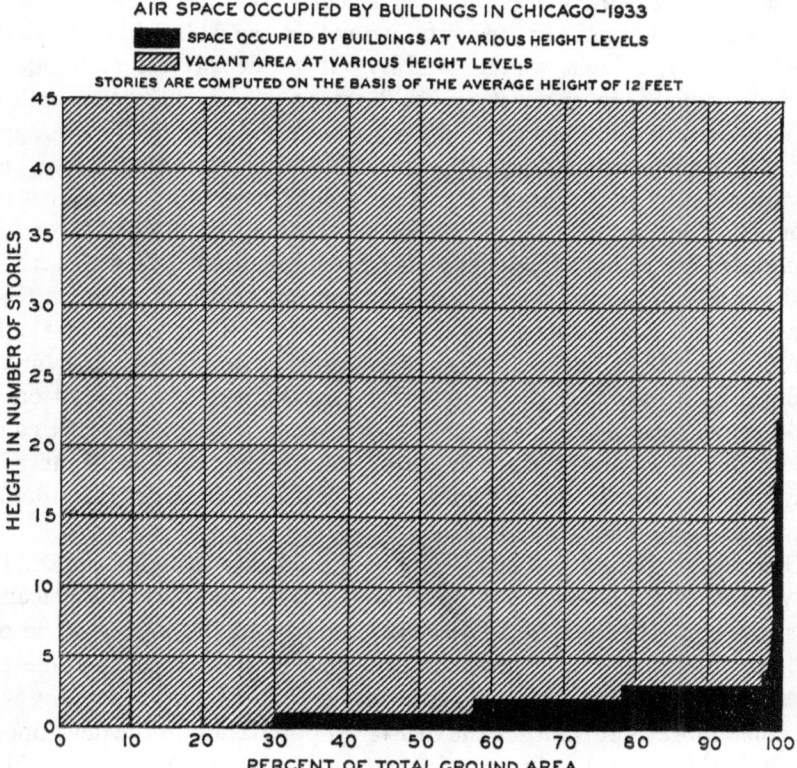

FIG. 51

per acre in 1923;[18] the average population density of the residential land in the smaller American cities in 1930 was 34.4 per acre.[19]

The area of Chicago, however, is widely extended in proportion to its

[16] *Ibid.*, pp. 44, 60.

[17] Chicago Association of Commerce, *op. cit.* This included 500,000 persons living in three-flat buildings, 800,000 in apartment buildings larger than three-flat buildings, 325,000 living in apartments over stores, and 36,000 living in apartments in the rear of stores.

[18] On the basis of the *Chicago Zoning Report* estimating 30,000 acres used for residential purposes in 1923 and the writer's estimate of 3,000,000 for the population of Chicago in 1923.

[19] Bartholomew, *op. cit.*, p. 61.

population as compared with other metropolitan cities of similar size. If its people were distributed evenly over its land surface, there would be only 28 persons to the acre. Paris occupies only 15 per cent as much ground, and its density of population is nearly six times as great as that of Chicago.[20] Thus the space contained within the walls of buildings in Cook County, Illinois, which could be put in one forty-story building $1\frac{1}{2}$ miles square, or in six-story buildings occupying 28 square miles, or in one-story buildings covering 166 square miles, actually averages two stories in height. Allowing for streets and alleys and for yard spaces covering half the lot, these buildings would use 83 square miles of ground. The intensity of utilization of the land by buildings varies from the Loop, where the average height of buildings is eleven stories, and where the ground occupying less than one-tenth of 1 per cent of the area of Cook County has 6 per cent of the floor space of Cook County, to the bungalow areas where only 27 per cent of the lot is utilized by a residence that is one story in height.[21] Finally, not only were 30 per cent of the lots in Chicago vacant in 1928, but another considerable area was occupied by parks, cemeteries, railroad rights-of-way, school grounds, and airports, where but a small part of the ground area was occupied by buildings.

The corporate limits of a city may be extended to include wide tracts of vacant ground and even of farm lands. The amount of the vacant area between the main settled area of a city and the invisible line of the city limits that in modern cities is marked by no wall or line of fortifications has little bearing upon the density of urban population. Of much more importance is the density of population in the developed tracts or the amount of intervening vacant land between houses within the main settled areas. Chicago has not grown in a compact body, because new transportation lines made it possible to pass over old areas that were partly built up in favor of virgin tracts that were not marred by obsolete buildings, and because the cupidity of owners frequently caused them to raise prices of land adjoining new improvements to prohibitive figures. Rather than pay such advanced prices for land, builders tended to jump several blocks ahead into another area.[22]

[20] Halbwachs, *op. cit.*, p. 15.

[21] The average bungalow contains 1,000 square feet of floor space and occupies a lot with 3,750 square feet of ground (records of the assessor's office of Cook County).

[22] Clifford Bechtel in an interview with the writer stated that this was the cause of the scattered nature of the development on Wabash Avenue south of Roosevelt Road.

B. THE SUPPLY OF CHICAGO LAND

1. *The practical limit to the supply of Chicago urban land.*—The increase in the number of people living in Chicago and in the amount of building space occupied by them thus required the utilization of increasing amounts of land for building sites. What has been the amount of ground surface in the Chicago area that has been available to meet this demand for additional ground-floor area? The total ground surface of the United States is, of course, almost absolutely fixed by nature. The entire area of the land within the city limits of all the cities in the United States of over 30,000 population in which over 45,000,000 people resided in 1930 is, however, only one-fifth of 1 per cent of the land area of the United States. Even after allowing for indispensable farm land and for land not easily accessible to existing cities, it is apparent that the upper limit imposed by the physical surface of the United States is a very distant one when the possibilities of urban expansion are being considered. The practical limit to the supply of urban land is set not by the total land surface of America but by the amount which is accessible to people working at a certain strategic spot. The supply of the urban land area and of the air space above the ground in Chicago has, in fact, been greatly increased in the past century by projection of rapid-transit facilities outward from the center and the upward extension of steel-frame skyscrapers. The time and expense required to go from the center of the city outward or upward, and not physical extension, determines the effective supply of urban land.

a) Lateral expansion by more rapid transportation.—Accessible building space in Chicago in 1833 was the ground and the layer of air above the ground to a height of about 50 feet, within walking distance over dirt roads to the main channel of the Chicago River. Outward extension began with plank roads and street railway lines. Omnibuses and horse cars which traveled at a rate of 6 miles an hour instead of a walking pace of 3 miles an hour doubled the radius of settlement. Cable cars in the eighties, with a speed of 12 miles an hour, doubled the radius again along trunk lines. Suburban steam railroads and elevated electric lines, traveling at from 25 to 30 miles an hour, again doubled the radius of settlement along their routes.

The universal adoption of the automobile with a possible speed on superhighways of 60 miles an hour has enabled the worker to go twenty times farther from his factory to his home in an hour than he could in

1836. The airplane extends the possible range from home to office to 150 or 200 miles, although the location as well as the expense of landing fields greatly limits the general use of the air as a means of suburban transportation.

The effect of doubling the radius of the settled area, if the settlement is carried to a full circle, is not merely to double but to quadruple the original area, for the area of a circle is obtained by multiplying a constant factor π by the square of its radius. This rate of increase of area applies as well to a half-circle as to a full circle. Therefore as the increased speed of transportation has tapped a widening area on the outer edge of the city, the amount of land made available has increased at a rate greater than the increase in the length of track. The amount of new land has not increased by the square of the distance added by the new lines, because the supply of land so added has been confined to belts along the lines themselves and there are intervening spaces between these radial lines that are less accessible. The supply of available ground sites in Chicago has been further limited by the lake on the east, which prevented the development of Chicago in a full circle from the center, and caused the city to expand farther to the west and south than it would otherwise have grown.

b) The extension into the air.—In addition to this extension outward, there has been an extension upward and downward. While the ground area of the city increased twenty fold from 1833 to 1933, the possible air space that could be occupied by buildings increased tenfold. The elevator and steel-frame skyscraper rising successively from nine, twelve, sixteen, twenty-two, to forty-four stories tapped the horizontal layers of air 100, 150, 250, and over 500 feet above the ground level.[23] At the same time the raising of the level of the central business district of Chicago from 15 to 20 feet prior to 1859 enabled basements to be built. Taller buildings called for deeper foundations and deeper basements until today in the Chicago Loop there is an average of over one floor underground. The supply of land available for Chicago has been further increased by accretions along the lake shore. The Municipal

[23] The zoning law of 1923, which permitted the construction of towers above the twenty-two-story level, fixes no absolute height limit but provides that the tower part shall occupy not over one-fourth of the lot and that the space contained in it shall not exceed one-sixth of the entire building. On a lot large enough a one-hundred-and fifty-story tower would be possible, but the size of the lots so far utilized in the Loop have limited buildings to a height of forty-five or forty-six stories (Chicago Zoning Ordinance, par. 21*d*).

Pier, the land in Streeterville, Grant Park, the Outer Drive, have all been "made" by filling in along the lake shore. Finally, the legal concept of horizontal layers of air which could be separated from the title to the ground has created a great volume of building space over railroad tracks. Supported by piers over such railroad yards is the Merchandise Mart, the largest building in the world. A few more such gargantuan buildings could house the entire wholesale business of Chicago. A further large potential supply of land would be made available by rebuilding the blighted areas.

Thus the supply of urban ground and air space that could be reached within an hour's ride or by prevailing construction methods in Chicago has so increased in the past century that there is no scarcity of air space for skyscrapers. If built up to the limits permitted by the present zoning regulations, it is estimated that the entire population of the United States could be housed in the city limits of Chicago.[24] Such intensive utilization of land would, however, require, the erection of steel-frame apartment skyscrapers in all the areas zoned for such use, and the added construction expense of so tapping these higher air levels is the cost of acquiring this increased supply of space.

C. CAUSES OF DIFFERENCES IN LAND VALUES WITHIN CHICAGO

1. *The land-value contour map.*—Up to this point, the factors affecting the aggregate demand for Chicago building sites have been considered without reference to the distribution of different types of uses and of different degrees of intensity of each use within the city. Even if the total land value of an urban region be determined by the population mass and by the combined rent roll, the distribution of that aggregate land value between the different areas of the city is still unknown. If the land values in Chicago were shown in the form of a relief map, in which the elevations represented high land value, a picture of startling contrasts would be disclosed. In the center would be the Himalaya Mountain peaks of the Loop, but on all sides except along a high ridge running north along the lake there would be a descent into the deep valleys of the blighted areas. Gradually, as one went farther from the center, the elevation would begin to rise. Along the lake, both north and south, would be a high ridge which slopes down sharply as

[24] Estimate made in an unpublished study by the Chicago Regional Planning Association.

one goes west. Beginning 5 or 6 miles from the center of the city, there would be a plateau several miles wide encircling the city that is up-tilted toward the lake, on top of which were high ridges a mile apart that culminated in towering pinnacles at each intersection. If a dollar a front foot in land value were represented by 1 foot in height on this map, the changes in elevation within the 211 square miles of Chicago's area would be greater than the differences in physical elevation of any part of the land surface of the globe, for the variation would be the same as from 5 to 50,000 feet above sea-level. Within a little over a mile one might drop from an altitude of 50,000 feet to one of 50 feet,[25] and within a short block a person could fall from an elevation of 4,000 feet to one of 25 feet.[26] What is the explanation of this unusually abrupt change? Why is it that when one passes from one street to the next land values rise or fall precipitously in some cases, while in other areas there are wide plains of substantially equal land values?

The land-value pattern of a city that is illustrated throughout this book by land-value maps and by numerous charts is naturally of the greatest importance, particularly in a city like Chicago where such tremendous differences in land values exist. To explain the land-value structure of a city and the causes of the variations in value, it is necessary to go back to the beginning of the history of a city, to trace the manner in which each section of the city started to develop, and to show the direction of growth of different types of uses. That was one of the main purposes of the first part of this book. It is now necessary to bring the threads of that discussion together, and to illustrate by a series of charts and maps the course of progression during the entire century of the major factors causing differences in land values between different sections of the city in order that the separate effect of each factor may be demonstrated.

When Chicago was a marshy plain entirely unimproved, who could tell which spot would sometime be passed by several hundred thousand people daily and which one would be in the heart of a slum? On that lot where a cow is grazing a forty-story building will rise. There where that pig is rooting will be a huge bank building. Go a short distance away from this magic spot and the soil is just as good, the grass just as green, but the ground the cows trod on there is doomed to pro-

[25] From State and Madison Street to Townsend Street near Chicago Avenue.
[26] From Forty-seventh and Ashland Avenue to Forty-sixth and Laflin.

duce nothing but shacks, gangsters, and land values that do not cover the cost of the street improvements. Miles farther away from the heart of the city there is land on which men will shoot snipe and plover for many decades after the city is founded that will surpass in value this ground that is so close to the city's center. What establishes the lines of cleavage between areas of intensive utilization and high land values and those less favored districts that will be thinly settled and used for purposes that yield low returns? Where will the main retail shopping area be located? What tracts will be selected for high-grade residential use or tall apartment buildings? What corners will be the center of an outlying business subcenter? What regions will command a premium for factory sites? These are the grand prizes. The person who could select these spots in advance will reap a fortune. The other areas—the tracts occupied by the poor and middle classes, the low-grade outlying business locations, and the poorer industrial land—will yield a profit to those who first develop them from farm land. Once such districts are improved with mediocre dwellings and filled with tenants who rank low in purchasing power, and there is little hope for a further rise in land value. Owners of vacant farm land on the city's edge have then a far better chance to reap the "unearned increment."

In tracing the causes of the great differences in land values between different sections of the city, some of the main factors to be considered are the topography of Chicago, the origin and direction of movement of different types of uses, the points of settlement and lines of expansion of different races and nationalities, and the extent of vertical as contrasted with lateral expansion of high land-value areas.

2. *Physical causes of land-value variations.*—Three main factors in the topography of Chicago have affected the pattern of its land values: the lake on the east; the Chicago River and its two branches, forming a Y with its base on the lake, and a broad level plain west of the lake that interposes no barriers to lateral expansion.

a) The effect of the lake.—As has been noted, Chicago is situated on the west side of Lake Michigan near its southern tip. The lake prevented any appreciable growth on the east, and forced Chicago to expand more to the north, south, and west than it would otherwise have done. As the lake curves toward the east as it proceeds southward from the northern to the southern limits of Chicago, the area available for settlement likewise expands as one goes south, so that the lake cuts off less than half of the arc of a full circle with a radius of eight miles from the center of the city. The lake also prevents the entry of highways and railroads directly from the east, but compels them to come into Chicago from the south around the bend of the lake. The lake finally provides what has lately come to be regarded as the "front yard" of Chicago, and land facing the lake has acquired the highest value for residential purposes. In the pre-railroad era, the lake was one of the principal avenues of approach to the city.

b) The effect of the river.—The Chicago River and its branches divide Chicago into its three main divisions—the North, South, and West sides—and thus sets up a barrier that caused the somewhat independent development of each section. At the same time, by affording a meeting place of lake, river, canal, and railroad traffic, it provided during the first part of the city's history the medium for binding together the separate parts of the city's commercial and industrial life. Both sides of the Chicago River were lined with elevators, factories, warehouses, and lumber yards; and from the point of view of water commerce, it mattered little in which division of the city a factory on the river bank happened to be. The difficulties of crossing the river in early days, first, because of the scarcity of bridges and, later, because of their frequent opening and closing, proved to be very serious obstacles to the unity of the three sections of Chicago. The separation of the three sections was further accentuated by the mode of development of the transportation systems. From the time of the first horse-car lines in 1859 to the cable lines of 1881 and the elevated lines of 1892–1900, each section of the city virtually had an independent system of transportation leading to the central business district, with no transfer points or encircling connecting system outside the downtown area. Hence each section has had a different rate of growth and a different land-value history.

c) The Chicago plain.—The Chicago plain affords practically unlimited room for urban growth to the west, south, and north. The few slight elevations that rise above it are at a premium for residential use, and there are no bluffs, steep hills, or ravines to prevent the even spreading of new buildings over the prairie. If the three sections of Chicago that are caused by the configurations of the Chicago River are considered, however, the amount of land available for use as one proceeds in square-mile belts from the center of the city varies considerably. Thus in the south division, the south branch of the Chicago River which

GROWTH OF CHICAGO AND ITS LAND VALUES

splits off from the main channel less than a mile west of the lake curves eastward for its first two miles, forming a narrow bottle neck at Eighteenth and State streets and limiting the available land area on the South Side within two miles from State and Madison streets to about one square mile. As the south branch and the Illinois-Michigan and Drainage canals turn southwesterly beyond Twenty-second Street, the South Side broadens out to cover an ever increasing territory. The area of the North Side is confined by the north channel of the river to a strip from two to three miles along the lake shore, and the land available for settlement within the first two miles from State and Madison streets was only about two square miles. On the West Side, however, the land area widens out both north and south, and within the first two miles from the center of the city, over five square miles were available for occupation. Hence the West Side provided the space for the greatest expansion of population when horse-car transportation limited the radius of city growth to a few miles from the center.

d) The three sections of the city.—The growth of the three sections of the city has proceeded at different rates in the various periods. The south division had the advantage in the fact that the land trails, railroads, and highways from the centers of population in the East and South entered the city through that section, and from the first it attracted the central business section. In the forties and fifties, the North Side, in the district south of Chicago Avenue near the present Michigan Boulevard, contained some of the finest homes, but in the period following the Civil War, the growth of the fashionable sections on the South Side was rapid. The West Side developed early as an industrial and manufacturing area, and as factory workers settled near their places of employment, its population growth prior to 1873 exceeded that of other sections. From the great fire of 1871 to the World's Fair of 1893, the development and rise of land values on the South Side outstripped that of the other divisions of the city, but after the panic of 1893 it went into an eclipse, and shortly thereafter the North Side and the north-shore suburbs attracted the leaders of fashion. From 1900 to 1929 the North and Northwest sides as a whole recorded more rapid gains in land values than any other entire section of the city. After 1873 the old West Side east of Ashland Avenue and south of Chicago Avenue languished as a residential area, although the expansion of industry absorbed part of its space.

3. *The growth of different types of land uses.*—In all three sections of the city, however, areas devoted to the different types of uses developed near the common junction point of the divisions and grew away from this center in direct lines south, west, and north.

a) The fashionable residential areas.—Fashionable or high-grade residential areas were started with the building of large homes or mansions on ample grounds, with carriage and servant quarters in the rear. These sections were located on the avenues adjacent to the best transportation lines leading directly to the central business district, and in the beginning they were located within a few blocks of the principal shops and stores. Thus, as Figure 52 shows, on the North Side the finest residential section in the forties and fifties was on Cass and Rush streets near Ontario Street, on the West Side it was on Washington Street east of Halsted Street, and on the South Side it was first on Washington Street and then on Wabash and Michigan avenues within the confines of the present Loop. From 1860 to 1873, with the first horse-car lines in all sections and the first suburban railroad service on the South Side, the North Side fashionable area shifted to Dearborn and LaSalle streets and expanded from Chicago Avenue to Lincoln Park along those streets. The West Side high-grade area grew westward along Washington Street to Union Park at Ashland Boulevard, and the development also proceeded westward along Monroe, Adams, and Jackson streets to Ashland Boulevard. Ashland Boulevard was laid out as a fashionable street and the first homes were erected on it at this time. On the South Side the fashionable growth had proceeded south from Washington Street along Wabash and Michigan avenues, and at Eighteenth Street had swung eastward to Indiana, Prairie, and Calumet avenues and was projected southward along these avenues as far as Twenty-sixth Street. Thus by 1873 three main bands of fashionable growth, four to six blocks wide, had been developed like spokes of a half-wheel. The vacant lots on these avenues for several miles beyond the settled portions had acquired values which reflected the anticipated high-grade residential use. The continuation of the fashionable areas in straight-line projections along these avenues was favored by the placing of a belt of large parks in the direct path of growth, several miles beyond the fashionable settled area, and the development of boulevards leading from the high-grade areas to these parks. A vanguard of fashionable suburban settlements, like Kenwood on the South Side and Pine Grove

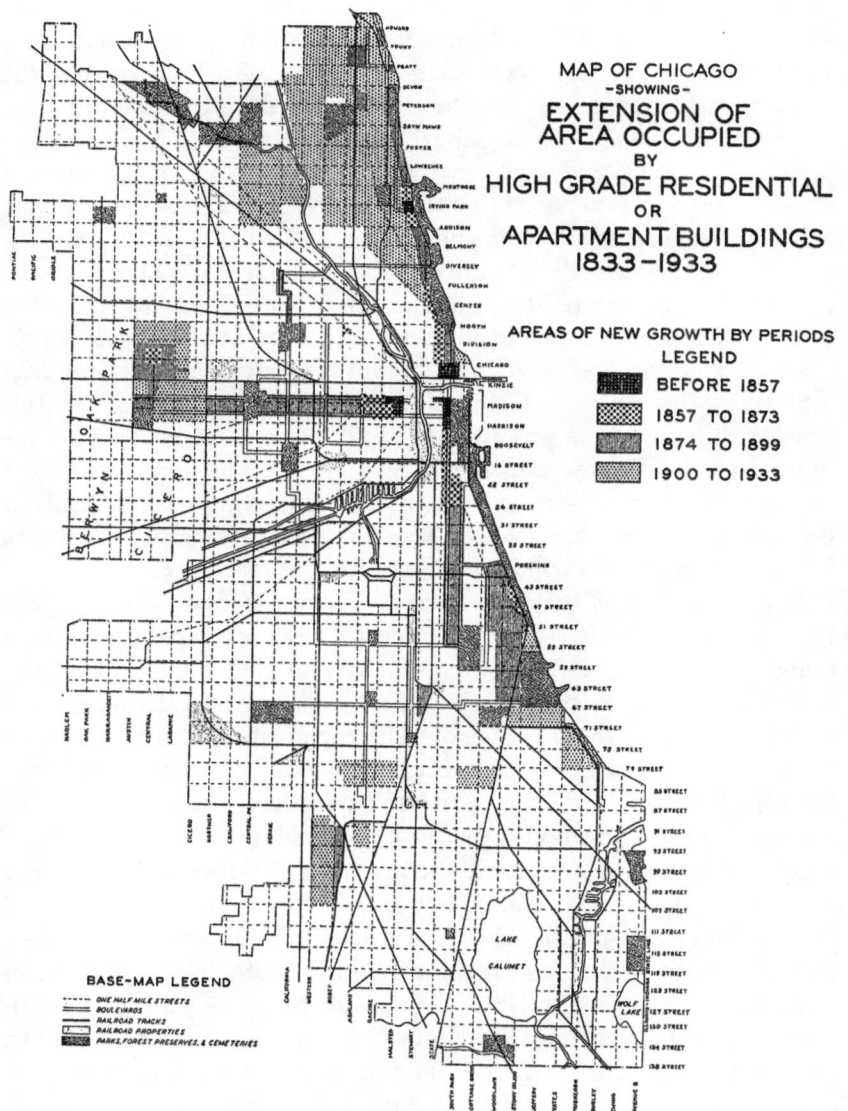

Fig. 52

on the North Side, also guarded areas beyond from the intrusion of undesirable elements. The exclusion of saloons from these chosen spots also preserved their high-grade character. Pushed by the growth of the business of the city from the rear and attracted by the lure of parks, boulevards, and fashionable suburbs ahead, rows of fine homes were built north, south, and west down the "avenues" in ever lengthening lines. In each section of the city there was a sharp line of demarcation between the fashionable belt and the slums that almost directly adjoined it. On the North Side the dividing line was Wells Street, on the South Side it was State Street, and on the West Side it was Randolph Street or Lake Street on the north and Harrison Street on the south.

In the eighties, Prairie Avenue between Eighteenth and Twentieth Street was the center of Chicago's most aristocratic homes. At this time Michigan Avenue was growing rapidly as a place of residence for Stock Yards magnates. On the West Side, Ashland Boulevard from Madison to Harrison streets, and Jackson Boulevard east of Ashland Boulevard, were in their heyday. The Lake Shore Drive, then known as "Potter Palmer's frog pond," was just beginning to develop.

(1) *The decline of Prairie Avenue.*—After the first World's Fair, Prairie Avenue on the South Side began to decline rapidly in importance, as the segregated vice area was by that time only a few blocks west of it. On the North Side the movement away from Dearborn and LaSalle streets to the Lake Shore Drive gained momentum and the North Shore "Gold Coast" began to emerge as the social capital. On the West Side, Ashland Boulevard had passed its peak, and the growth of fine homes was now taking place along Washington Boulevard in the vicinity of Garfield Park. On the South Side those social leaders who did not migrate to the North Side moved farther out to Grand and Drexel boulevards and the Kenwood district. There was thus an eastward shift of the fashionable home area of the South Side. The avenues from State Street east to Grand Boulevard began to be filled in with apartment buildings which gave a more intensive use to the land, but did not cause its value to rise beyond the values already anticipated because of the expected extension of the fashionable-home area. The land-value changes of these different areas are shown in Figure 53.

(2) *The lake front grows in importance.*—Finally, in the twentieth century, and particularly after the World War, the relative value of land along the lake shore compared with land away from the lake great-

ly increased. At first, land fronting on the lake was not considered so attractive because of the lake storms that sent spray dashing across the streets, because of the undeveloped nature of the sandy wastes along

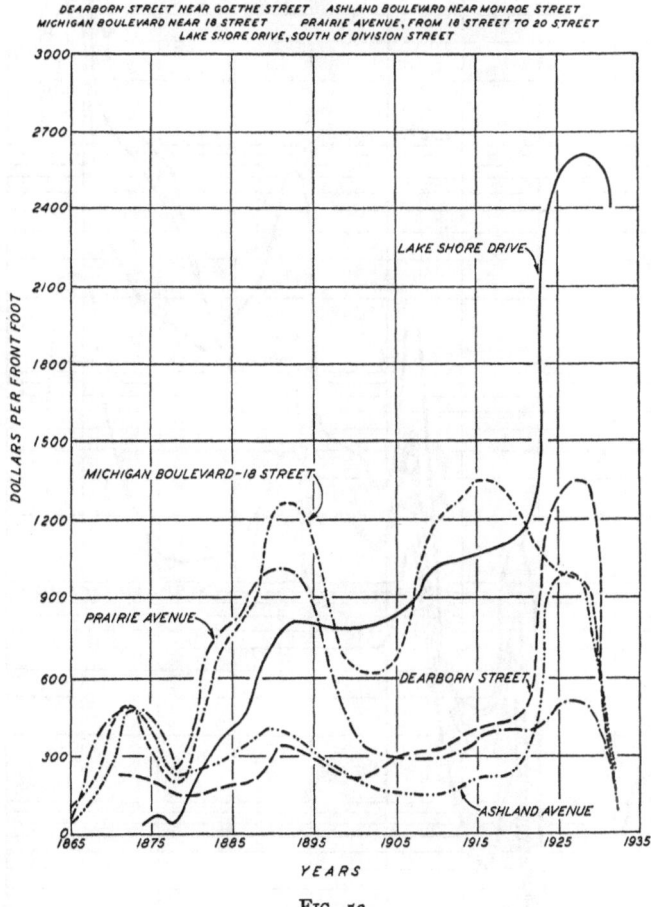

Fig. 53

the lake front, and because sewage was dumped directly into the lake. While Michigan Avenue within the present Loop was occupied by fashionable homes in the forties and fifties, Wabash Avenue in the same vicinity was preferred to Michigan Avenue because it did not face the

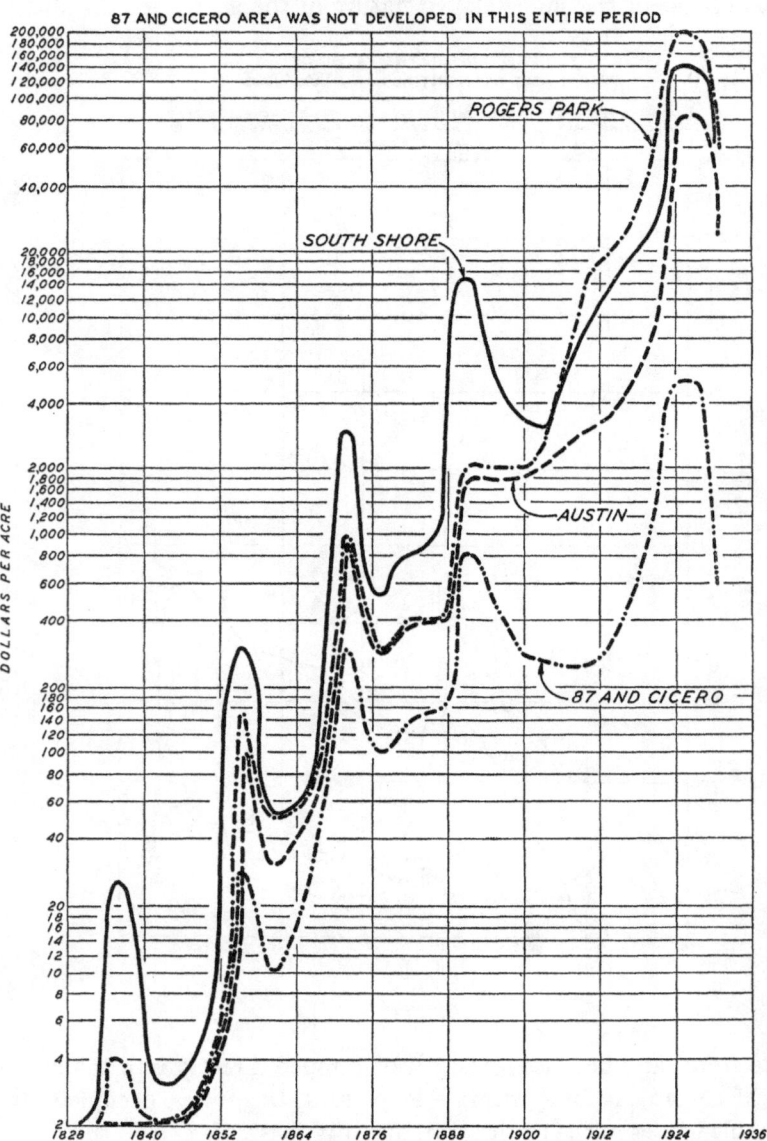

Fig. 54

GROWTH OF CHICAGO AND ITS LAND VALUES 307

lake storms, and as the expansion of the area proceeded southward on a straight line, it grew farther from the lake. On the North Side, land on the lake shore south of Chicago Avenue was occupied first by the settlement occupied by disorderly persons known as the "Sands" and later it became the precinct of Captain Streeter, the celebrated squatter. The growth of the fashionable north-shore towns along the lake, beginning even in the sixties, and the building of Sheridan Road and of North Side elevated lines had caused the North Side fashionable development to get started along the lake front at many points. On the South Side the colored influx into the old fashionable area in the avenues from State Street east to Grand Boulevard and farther east to Cottage Grove Avenue forced the fashionable settlement to turn eastward to the lake front. On the South Side, also, the advantages of Jackson Park and the Illinois Central suburban transportation along the lake front, which was considered the best in the city, also gave higher value to the lake-front lots. Not the least in importance, however, was the turning of sewage away from the lake, the development of bathing beaches, and the completion of outer drives, which permitted automobiles to speed along the lake front without stopping for cross-streets. Automobile traffic reaches its heaviest concentration along the lake shore and this is both a cause and effect of high land values for residential purposes, for it has a maximum of transportation advantages. Finally, in the era from 1922 to 1929, fringes of tall apartment buildings were erected along the lake shore on the North Side from Chicago to Howard Avenue and on the South Side from Fifty-first to Seventy-fifth streets. This intensive land use made possible high land values. As Figure 36[27] shows, practically all of the tall apartment buildings in Chicago are along the lake shore, and those along Michigan and Cottage Grove avenues not so located were built in the boom of 1890 to 1892. Thus, as illustrated by Figures 55 and 56, a cross-section of residential land values from the lake westward indicates that not only do land values slope upward toward the lake, but that the differential between the value of land near the lake and that farther away greatly increased from 1910 and 1928.[28] The reason for these higher land values is to be sought not merely in the more intensive use of land as evidenced by tall apartment buildings, but also in the higher rents paid for the

[27] See pp. 308–9.
[28] Based on George C. Olcott's *Land Values Blue Books of Chicago* (1910 and 1928).

same space. In 1933 apartments on the Gold Coast on the north shore of the lake rented for fifty dollars a month per room, while apartments away from the lake rented for as low as five dollars a month per room.

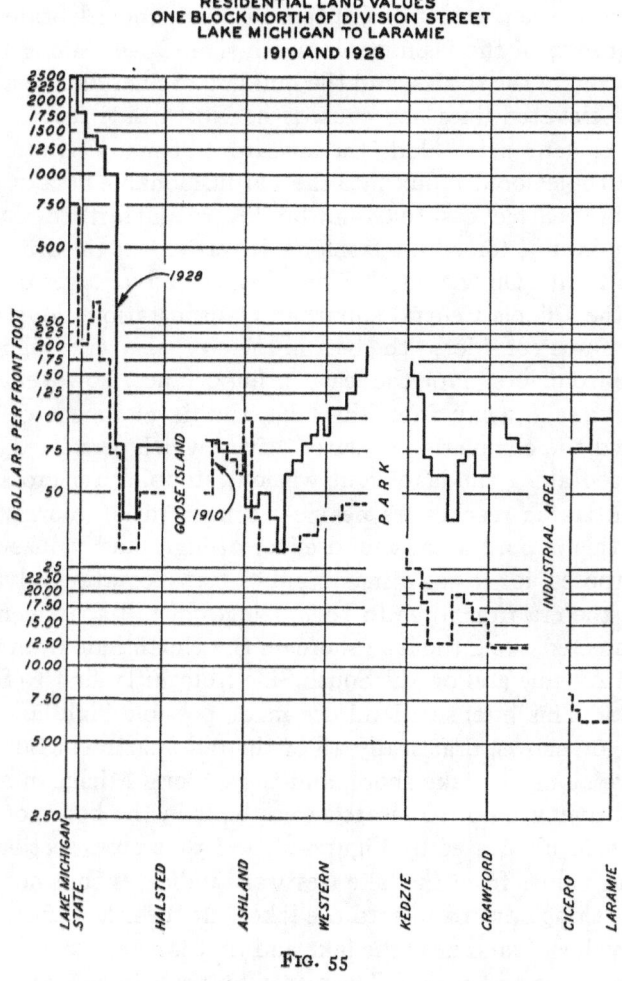

Fig. 55

While there is a considerable difference in the quality of construction in the two cases, this would by no means account for the tenfold difference in rents.

The land along the lake shore in Chicago has thus come to be utilized

GROWTH OF CHICAGO AND ITS LAND VALUES

for the highest and most intensive residential types of development. The fringe of land on the eastern edge of Chicago was held at too high a price and was too limited in amount to provide space for the two- and

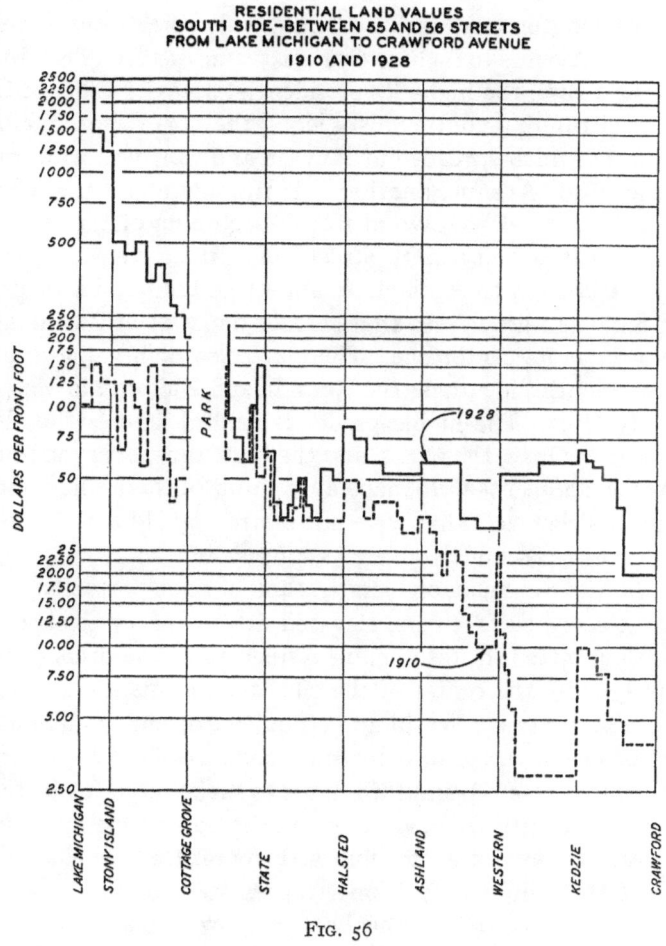

FIG. 56

three-story apartment buildings known as "walk-ups" because they have no elevators, which house over half of the population of Chicago. Accordingly, these apartment districts spread westward from the lake just beyond the old settled areas in the period from 1910 to 1928 and they filled in vacant tracts between old suburban towns along the railroads. The two major axes of these developments were Lawrence Avenue on the North Side and Seventy-ninth Street on the South Side, which were the business streets of a rapidly growing area contiguous to them. At the same time, on the West Side, the old high-grade belt between Washington and Jackson boulevards spread out fan-shaped west of Cicero Avenue to include Oak Park and Austin. Thus by 1933, as Figure 52 shows, the high-class residential areas of Chicago include a belt of land running continuously along the north shore far beyond the city limits, which spreads out fanwise and runs westward on both sides of Lawrence Avenue, another belt running along the lake front from Fifty-first Street southward to the beginning of the factories at South Chicago at Seventy-ninth Street, where it curves westward along Seventy-ninth Street to Ashland Avenue (see land-value maps), and the West Side high-grade area that spreads out west of Cicero Avenue, with Madison as its center line. There are also high-value residential areas on the South Side along the Rock Island Railroad in Englewood and Beverly Hills. The higher-grade residential land is thus located not only near the lake, the parks, and the best transportation lines, but when new developments were made away from the lake, they tended to take virgin prairie tracts that were not marred by old and obsolete improvements or by an undesirable class of people.

While the development of faster means of transportation, such as cross-town electric surface cars, elevated extensions, or electrified railroads, thus permitted the fashionable residential neighborhoods to push farther away from the center of the city, the old mansions on Prairie Avenue, LaSalle Street, Washington Boulevard, and Ashland Boulevard were being converted into boarding-houses or light manufacturing establishments, or were being torn down to make room for factories or warehouses. Michigan Boulevard lots on the South Side for a time acquired a value for use for automobile showrooms that even exceeded at some points the values they formerly possessed for fashionable residential use, the expansion of the Loop northward gave a speculative market for old boarding-house property on the near North Side which raised it above the former peaks, and the growth of factories westward from the Chicago River revived the values of old residential areas there. As Figure 53, shows, however, the decline of these once fashionable residential areas, when their mansions become obsolete, is not necessarily followed by a new type of use that restores the former value.

b) Cheap residential areas.—Land areas in Chicago occupied by the unskilled and semi-skilled laboring classes must necessarily comprise a greater amount of ground than those sites used for the abodes of the wealthy or middle classes, because the poorer groups in society are more numerous and because, in Chicago, they tend to live in cottages or two-apartment buildings rather than in tenements. While in the eighties and nineties the rich occupied with their mansions lots that would hold ten or twenty houses of the poor, today the reverse is true. The rich live in tall elevator apartments, and the poor tend to occupy a small house with yard space. Nevertheless, prior to 1929 the wealth and income of all classes in American society had so increased that the cheapest residential land, or that less than fifty dollars a front foot, while comprising a considerable area,[29] was worth in the aggregate far less than the higher-grade residential or business land.

Like the fashionable areas, these poorer areas had their points of origin and their lines of progression. Workingmen's cottages tended to grow up in all sections of the city between the belts of fashionable land and the industries and factories along the Chicago River. They filled in the spaces not wanted for industries or for high-grade residences. The tracts they occupied were close to the noise and dust of factories but not directly contiguous to water or rail transportation. Such sites were poorly provided with street improvements and with surface-car transportation. The people who remained in such neighborhoods were the lowest in economic status, intelligence, and ambition since the more progressive elements tended to move to better neighborhoods as soon as possible. Located often near railroad yards or terminals, they suffered from proximity to the vagrant population of tramps and homeless men. Foreign colonies tended to locate in such sections, because they were nearest to the railroad stations at which they first arrived in the city, because they found their fellow-countrymen there, and because the quarters there were the cheapest and no worse than those to which many of them were accustomed in Europe. The buildings in such areas are seldom replaced, because when the cheap character of a residential neighborhood is once thoroughly established, builders prefer to invest their labor and materials in sections that have not yet acquired an adverse character. Consequently, as the survey of the Chicago Plan Commission, based on the insurance atlases, shows, prac-

[29] See land-value maps for the different periods.

tically all of the buildings in these so-called blighted areas were forty or more years old in 1933.

The manner in which the cheaper residential areas were extended, and in which acre tracts in advance of them reflected the cheap use to which they would ultimately be put, has a history as well as the mode of growth of the fashionable avenues. On the North Side patches of shacks early developed west of Wells Street near the industrial plants along the river. The factories and carshops on the West Side caused workingmen's boarding-houses to spring up along Lake Street near Halsted. The factories and lumber yards along the river resulted in workingmen's settlements in the near West Side, down Roosevelt Road and Blue Island Avenue. On the South Side, Irish laborers settled at Bridgeport in 1848 after working on the canal. The section in the downtown area west of Wells Street and south of Madison Street was a vice area in the fifties and sixties, and when it was cleared out by the fire of 1871, these elements of the population established a new center of saloons and vice dens west of State Street and south of Harrison. A colored population in this same area moved after a fire in 1874 to Dearborn and Federal streets south of Twenty-second Street. Between then and 1915 the colored belt had extended down to Thirty-ninth Street, but it was confined in the region west of State Street to the Rock Island tracks. Meanwhile, the segregated vice area after 1893 became concentrated in the vicinity of Eighteenth to Twenty-second street, from State Street to Dearborn, where it remained until 1912, when it was abolished by a reform movement.

Thus the cheaper and poorer residential sections moved in lines of progression from the downtown areas even as did the fashionable areas. Another factor entered into the situation after the great fire of 1871. This was the tendency of the working classes to build wooden houses—the only kind they could afford—in a belt around the settled parts of the city just beyond the fire limits. This belt was broken at those points where it came into contact with the bands of fashionable residential land, however, for the high speculative values at which these tracts were held precluded their use as homes for unskilled laborers.

(1) *Expansion of racial and nationality groups.*—From 1900 to 1929 there began an expansion of racial and national groups in these old areas. The new immigration from Poland, Russia, Italy, and Czechoslovakia had displaced the older Irish, German, and Scandinavian ele-

GROWTH OF CHICAGO AND ITS LAND VALUES

ments in the sections near the present Loop even by 1900, and they had formed close, compact colonies near the downtown area. An expansion of these races now began to take place along definite paths. The Jews from their ghetto east of Halsted Street on Maxwell moved westward between Roosevelt Road and Sixteenth Street to Douglas Park and beyond. The Italians north of Roosevelt Road and east of Halsted Street expanded westward between Harrison and Roosevelt

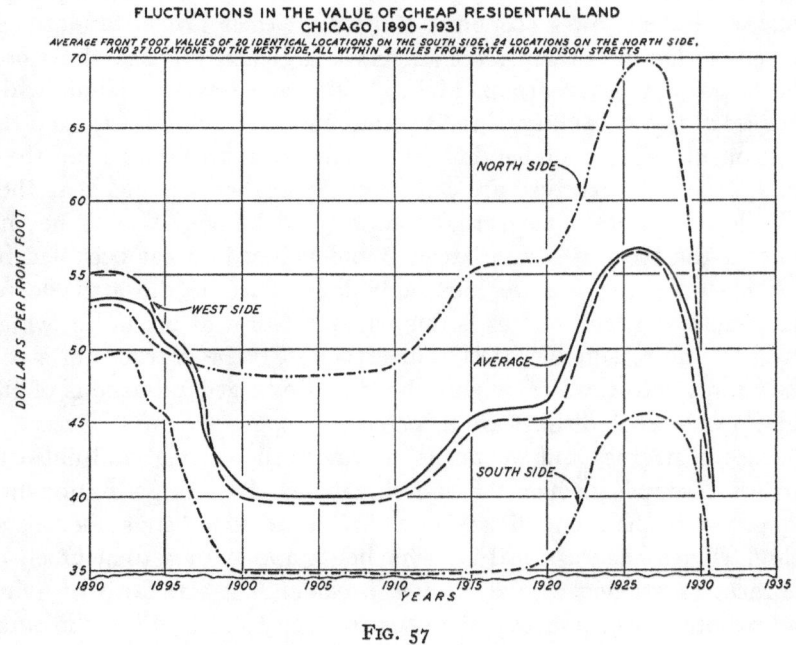

FIG. 57

Road to Cicero Avenue and beyond, and another colony of Italians near Grand Avenue east of the north channel of the river proceeded westward along Grand Avenue. The Poles on the North Side moved from their original base near Chicago and Milwaukee avenue along the line of Milwaukee Avenue to Irving Park Boulevard, and the Poles on the South Side expanded their section southwest from the Stock Yards. The Czechoslovakians, who had originally settled near Eighteenth and Blue Island Avenue, moved down Blue Island Avenue to Twenty-second Street and thence west on that thoroughfare to Cicero and Berwyn. Meanwhile, a great influx of colored workers from the South, beginning during the World War, had burst the barrier that confined their race west of State Street and filled the territory to Cottage Grove Avenue on the east and Sixty-seventh Street on the south. Another segment of colored people penetrated the old area along Lake Street as far west as Western Avenue. Figure 58 shows the extent of the area occupied by these groups in 1933.[30]

The significance of these racial and national movements upon Chicago land values lies in the fact that certain racial and national groups, because of their lower economic status and their lower standards of living, pay less rent themselves and cause a greater physical deterioration of property than groups higher in the social and economic scale. Because of the instability of the tenants, high collection losses, and the aversion of persons higher in the social order to living near these classes, the rents received are capitalized at higher rates, so that they yield lower capital values than property yielding the same net income in the most desirable areas. Land values in areas occupied by such classes are therefore inevitably low. Part of the attitude reflected in lower land values is due entirely to racial prejudice, which may have no reasonable basis. Nevertheless, if the entrance of a colored family into a white neighborhood causes a general exodus of the white people, such dislikes are reflected in property values.[31] Except in the case of negroes and Mexicans, however, these racial and national barriers disappear when the individuals in the foreign nationality groups rise in the economic scale or conform to American standards of living. Hence, the classification given below applies only to members of the races mentioned who are living in colonies at standards of living below those to which most Americans are accustomed. While the ranking given below may be scientifically wrong from the standpoint of inherent racial characteristics, it registers an opinion or prejudice that is reflected in land values; it is the ranking of races and nationalities with respect to their beneficial effect upon land values. Those having the

[30] This map is based on U.S. Census tracts and reports of real estate rental agents. See map by Halbwachs, *op. cit.*

[31] This phenomenon seems strange to a foreign observer. "Il s'est produit alors un phénomène très curieux. Dès que les nègres ont réussi à prendre pied dans quelques maisons, alors, dans toute la rue, sur une longueur de 4 ou 5 km., quelquefois de 7 ou de 8, les maisons vident, les appartements deviennent vacants, les blancs disparaissent, cédant la place aux nouveaux venus" (*ibid.*, p. 22).

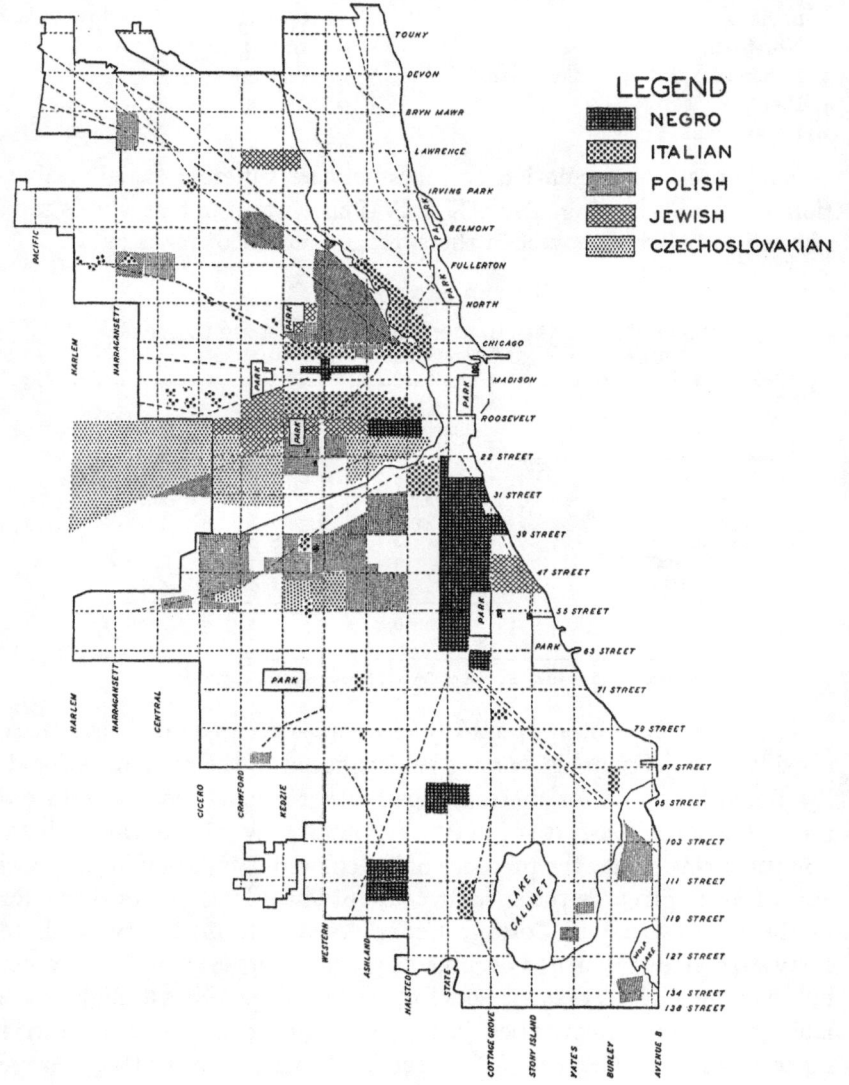

Fig. 58

most favorable come first in the list and those exerting the most detrimental effect appear last.[32]

1. English, Germans, Scotch, Irish, Scandinavians
2. North Italians
3. Bohemians or Czechoslovakians
4. Poles
5. Lithuanians
6. Greeks
7. Russian Jews of the lower class
8. South Italians
9. Negroes
10. Mexicans

While precise information on rents between different racial and national groups is lacking, Table XXXVII shows that native whites rank highest and negroes lowest in the average amount of rents paid.

TABLE XXXVII*

PERCENTAGE OF TOTAL RENTED HOMES OF EACH GROUP IN CHICAGO FALLING WITHIN GIVEN RENTAL CLASS, 1932

Rent	Native White	Foreign-born White	Negro
Under $30	15.7	32.7	36.2
$30–$49	24.3	26.8	29.3
$50–$74	37.6	27.3	25.5
$75–$99	13.2	8.0	6.1
$100 or over	7.2	3.7	0.8
Not reporting	2.0	1.5	2.1
Total	100.0	100.0	100.0

* Department of Commerce, Bureau of Census, release, September 7, 1932.

The entire effect of low land values in areas occupied by these races, considered objectionable, cannot be attributed to the race or nationality alone, however, for these groups have frequently moved into old areas that were in a state of deterioration already. There can be little doubt, however, that the presence of the colored population in the areas east of State Street is the specific cause of lower land values there, for in the district east of Cottage Grove Avenue from Thirty-ninth to Fifty-first Street, which is occupied by white persons, the land values in the opinion of the tax assessors for 1931 are three times as high as the land values in the colored belt just west of Cottage Grove from Thirty-ninth to Fifty-first Street. While the land just east of Cottage Grove Avenue has better improvements and is a little closer to the lake and

[32] The list was prepared chiefly by John Usher Smyth, West Side real estate broker.

would bear a higher value on that account, it also suffers from proximity to the colored section, so that a considerable part of the difference in land values is due to the difference in the race of the tenants. In many cases, however, the undesirable racial factor is so merged with other unattractive features, such as proximity to factories, poor transportation, old and obsolete buildings, poor street improvements, and the presence of criminal or vice elements, that the separate effect of race cannot be disentangled.

The expansion of these racial and national groups has perhaps had a greater effect in promoting a rise in the values of land in the outer areas of the city than it has had upon the older areas, for it has forced or stimulated the old American stock to seek new neighborhoods and has caused them to migrate from their old homes. Even these races themselves have pushed farther from the center of the city, leaving behind an area to be occupied by the least desirable members of their own race. As new immigration from Europe has almost ceased, and as industrial expansion in these near-in areas has come to an end, there is now very little demand for these areas for any purpose, and the problem of the blighted area, or the ring of land between the central business districts and the outer areas of new growth, has become more acute. As Figures 57 and 59 show, land values in these old areas have increased but slightly since 1890.

In addition to the old cheap residential areas near the Loop, there are newly developed areas occupied by cottages and bungalows on the fringes of the city. As the space just beyond the old settled areas has been occupied by the new apartment buildings, as already noted, the bungalow and small-home areas have been forced still farther out. On the South Side west of Western Avenue and south of Eighty-seventh Street, and on the North Side west of Crawford Avenue, are great areas of bungalows—the modern cottage for the family of moderate means. This land, developed from raw acreage, had phenomenal increases in value from 1918 to 1928, despite its lack of intensive use, but any further advance is definitely limited by its small-home use.

c) Industrial areas.—As Figure 60 shows, the industrial areas of Chicago spread northward and southward along the branches of the Chicago River during the days when lake and river commerce were of paramount importance, and with the emergence of belt-line railroads and of specialized manufacturing districts with switch-track connec-

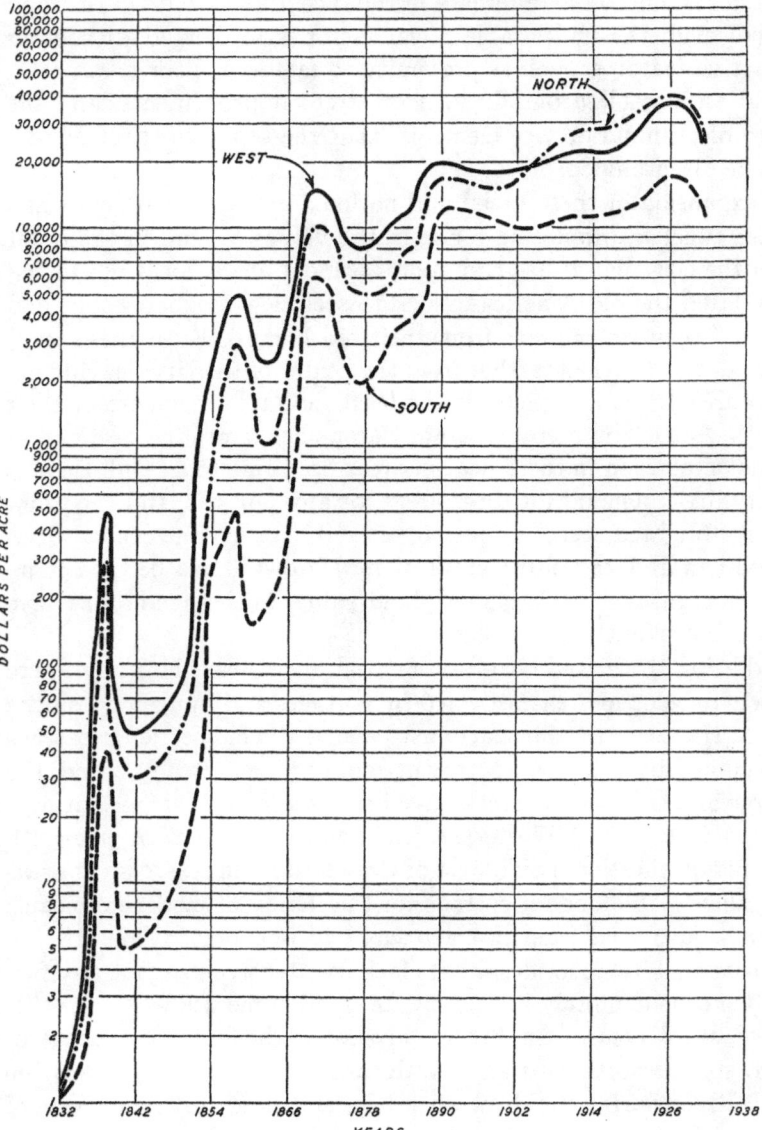

Fig. 59

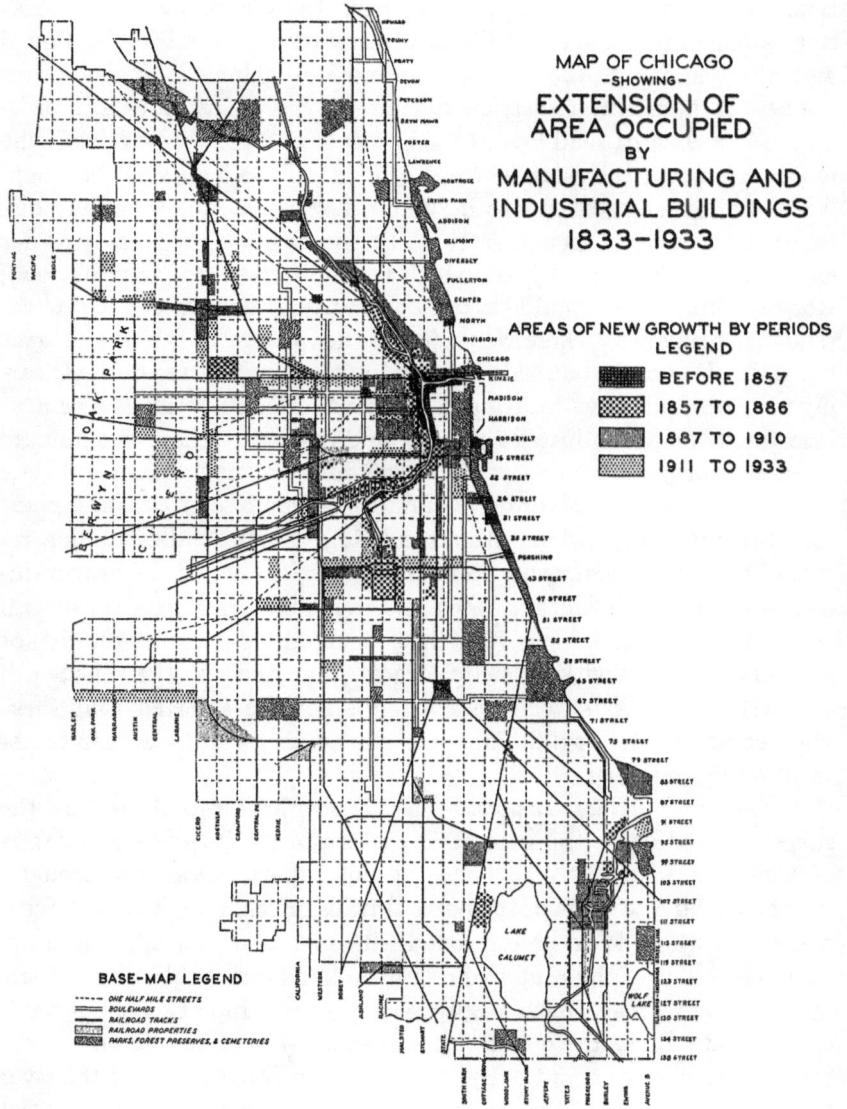

FIG. 60

tions, factories began to move away from the Chicago River to locations along switch tracks. A direct connection with a railroad siding is a great advantage in the quick and economical shipment of goods, and the new manufacturing districts offered services of freight cars in picking up less than carload lots at factory doors. With the advent of the motor truck and the establishment of freight depots outside the Loop, it was no longer necessary to be within horse-and-wagon hauling distance of a downtown freight station. By moving out, the factory owner could obtain cheaper land, on which he could afford to construct one-story buildings that would permit continuity of operation with its attendant economies. There was a further advantage in savings in taxes when the site was just outside the city limits, as in the case of the Clearing district. Industries locating in industrial districts could also be near associated or allied industries which would unite with them to eliminate objections property owners adjoining might file against them, and they could also secure the advantages of flexible layouts of ground and plant that permitted expansion without crossing streets or alleys. As a result of this movement away from the center, the values of near-in industrial land on the Chicago River have remained stationary for several decades, and there is now very little demand for most of the five-or six-story buildings without switch-track connections on the near South or West sides. Consequently, it cannot now be asserted that these blighted areas are in a state of transition or are awaiting a definite absorption by industry.

d) Outlying business centers.—The section lines established by the surveyors laid down the geometric pattern of the business subcenters of Chicago. These straight lines, a mile apart, became "through" streets, as did also some of the natural trails or radial highways.[33] Such roads were the first to be improved with planks or macadam and became successively the routes of omnibus, horse-car, cable, and electric lines. Taverns, blacksmith shops, grocery stores, and other shops tended to locate along these streets because they provided access to the greatest number of people. By 1873 Madison Street, west of the river to Racine; Clark Street, north of the river to Lincoln Park; State Street and Cottage Grove at Twenty-second Street—all had become leading local business streets. Other streets passing through poorer neighbor-

[33] For the impression which the rigid checkerboard pattern of Chicago made upon a French observer, see Halbwachs, *op. cit.*, p. 44.

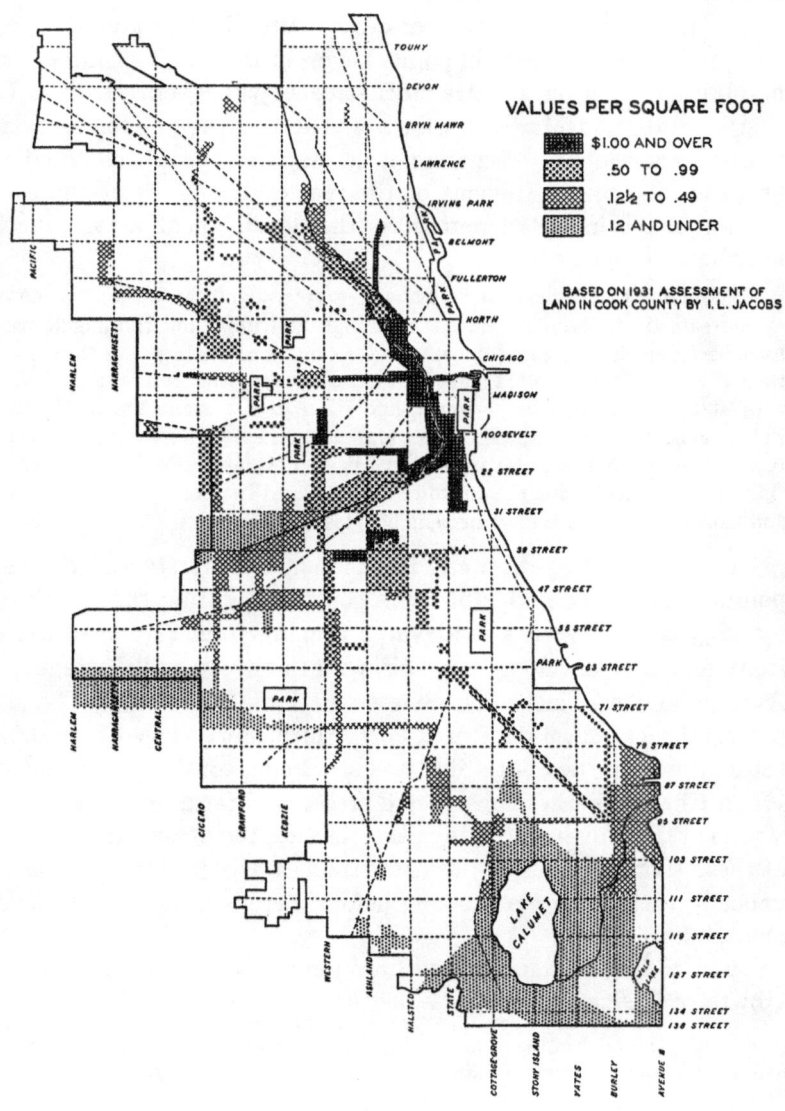

FIG. 61

hoods, such as Halsted Street, Blue Island Avenue, Milwaukee Avenue, North Wells Street, and Archer Avenue, were second-grade business streets, or the "rialtos of the slums."

The intersection of main horse-car routes had produced, even by 1873, peak values at certain points beyond the central business district, notably at Madison and Halsted streets—values only a little below that of State and Madison streets.[34] The tendency of the section-line streets to develop into commercial thoroughfares had been noted early, and the following statement of the real estate editor of the *Chicago Tribune* made in 1884 summarizes the development as one that had long been recognized.

> The section and division streets have a greater significance than the surveyors ever dreamed of. Being in all cases through and unbroken thoroughfares, they have become, with few exceptions, business centers of the localities through which they pass. Thus the streets running east and west, Madison, 12th, 16th, 22nd, 35th and 39th streets on the south, and Chicago, Division, North, Centre, and Fullerton on the north, contain stores and markets supplying local neighborhoods. North and south the same is true of Halsted, Center (Racine) and Western. Oblique cross streets such as Lincoln, Clybourn, Milwaukee, Blue Island, Archer, and Cottage Grove also have become business streets.[35]

The growth of stores along full section-line streets and at transfer points of horse-car and cable lines continued during the eighties, and by 1893 corners with a land value ranging from $1,000 to $1,500 a front foot had developed at Thirty-ninth Street and Cottage Grove Avenue, and at Thirty-first Street and Indiana Avenue. The anticipated business development of Forty-third, Forty-seventh, and Sixty-third streets on the South Side was also being considered at that time. When Charles Yerkes constructed street-car tracks in the section-line streets of the Northwest Side in the nineties, the prospective utilization of these thoroughfares as business streets was reflected in a sharp advance in their selling prices long before there was any actual development.[36]

The building of the elevated lines gave a setback to the continued growth of business subcenters—as the new lines carried people to the

[34] In 1873 the value of the corners of Madison and Halsted streets was $1,500 per front foot and that of the corners of State and Madison streets $2,500 a front foot.

[35] *Chicago Tribune*, August 23, 1884.

[36] Statement of Alonzo H. Hill, a director in some of the Yerkes traction lines, made to the writer in September, 1933.

rising Loop department stores. In 1910, as Figures 62, 63, 64, and 65 show, land values sloped sharply downward away from the central business district along Madison, State, Clark, and Michigan streets.

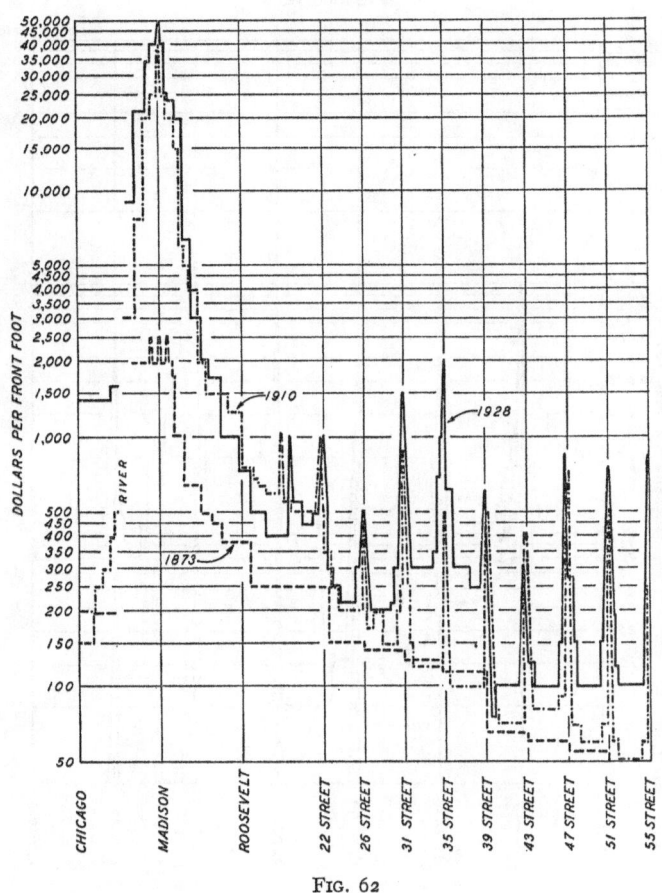

FIG. 62

The number of outlying business corners in 1910, as Figure 39 shows,[37] was relatively small in the light of later development. Then from 1910 to 1915, and from 1921 to 1928, came those remarkable spurts of out-

[37] See above, p. 253.

lying business centers until, as Figure 40 shows,[38] the number of valuable corners outside the Loop had by 1928 greatly increased.

In the boom following the World War, enough land—5,000,000 front feet—was zoned for business in Chicago to support a population

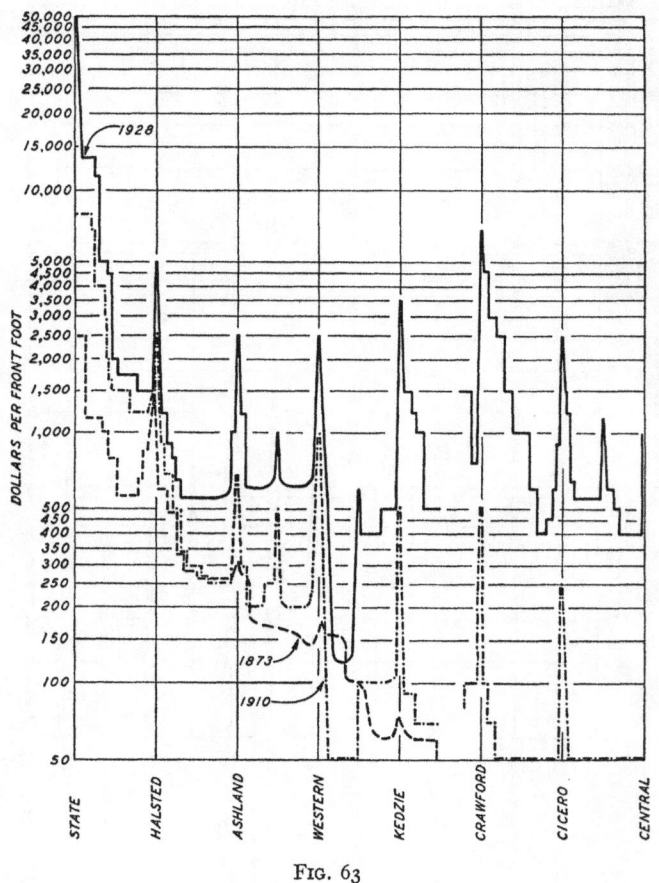

FIG. 63

of 10,000,000 while miles of business frontage were laid out on all the highways leading into Chicago. The value of the business land in Chicago exceeded in 1928 that of all other land.

[38] See above, p. 254.

Figures 67, 68, and 69 show the pattern of these business land values on major outlying streets. Since nearly every street falling on a full-section or half-section line was zoned for business, the lines along which business development might take place were known in advance, and the

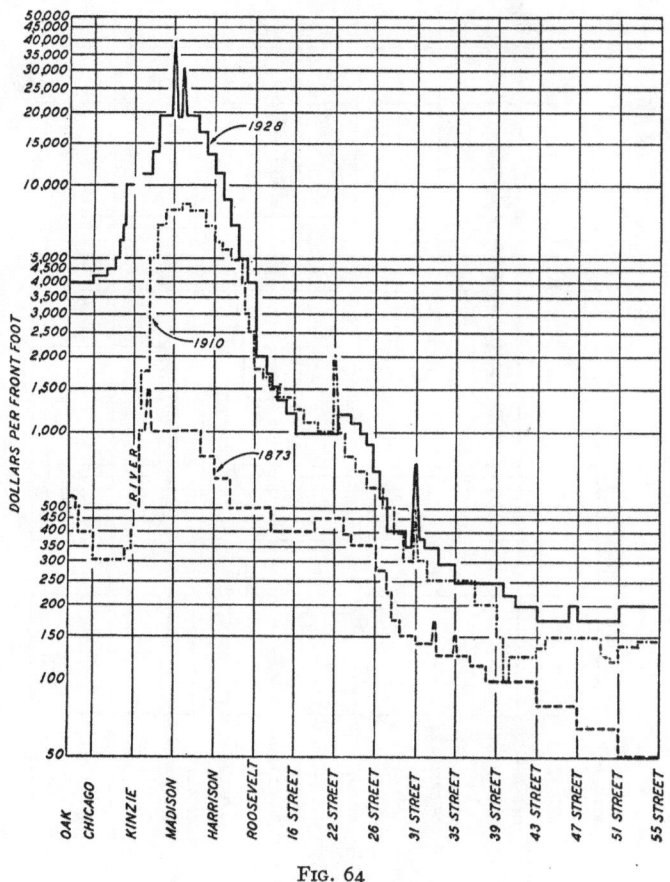

FIG. 64

optimistic hopes of speculators made it appear that every street zoned for business would actually be so occupied. It will be noted how regularly land values reach peaks at section-line intersections or transfer points. Such peak values were partly sustained by the competition of drug stores, banks, and chain stores for locations. In many cases, however, the values were based on hypothetical projections of the rate of growth of the business area based on the records of the few years be-

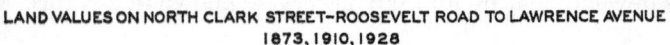

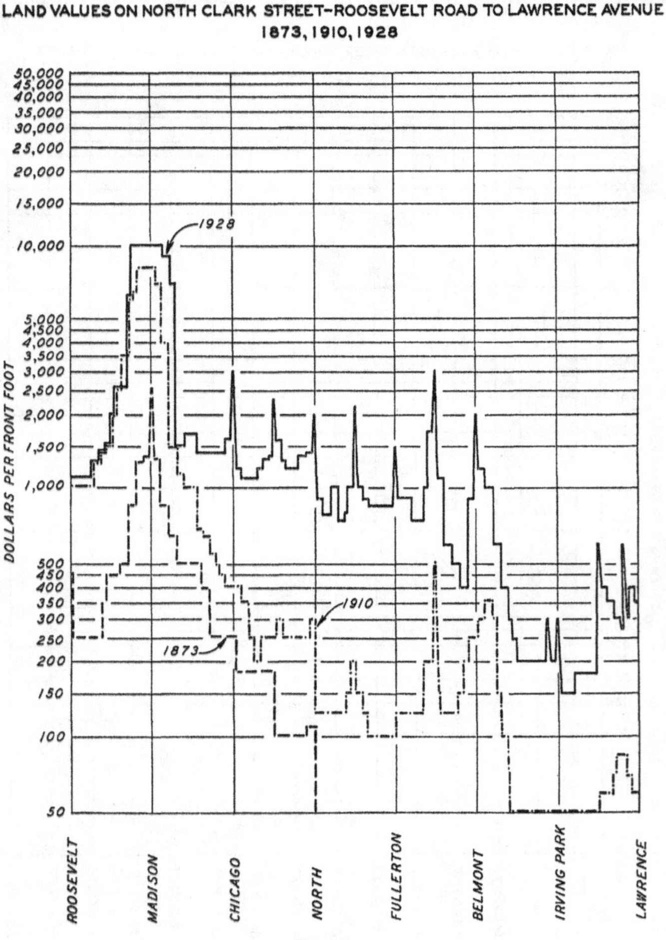

LAND VALUES ON NORTH CLARK STREET—ROOSEVELT ROAD TO LAWRENCE AVENUE
1873, 1910, 1928

FIG. 65

fore. Any land near a double-section corner sold for a high price, regardless of the actual business done or the volume of traffic passing the point.

(1) *Store rents and traffic counts.*—In the depression of 1932, it was found, however, that in certain locations there was a great difference

between the flow of pedestrian traffic and of potential purchasing power between the two sides of a street at a transfer corner and also that there was a sharp drop in the flow of traffic in a short distance. The gradation of actual rents paid was found to correspond very closely with this flow of traffic as Figure 66 shows, which is sometimes subject to sudden

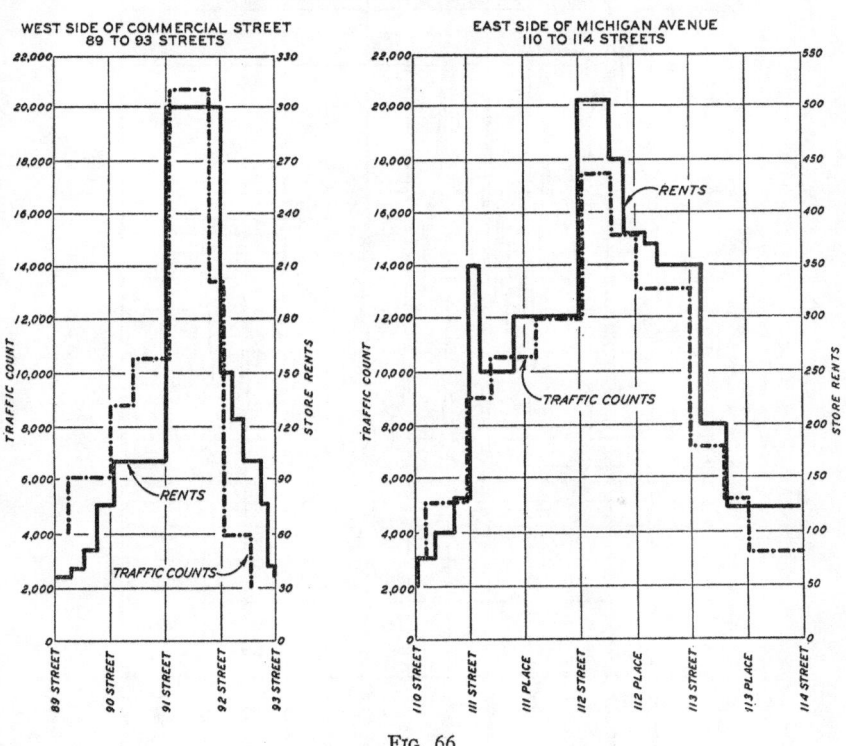

Fig. 66

and capricious changes, so that land values may depend in the future more closely upon a study of the actual potential purchasing power represented by the people passing a store and less upon a graduated chart rising and falling at regular intervals.

e) The central business district of Chicago.—Although the population of Chicago moved farther away from the central business district, and the area immediately contiguous to it began to decay, the Chicago downtown district maintained steadily rising land values. The Chicago transportation systems were so routed as to pour the residents of the three sections of the city successively by omnibuses, steam railroads,

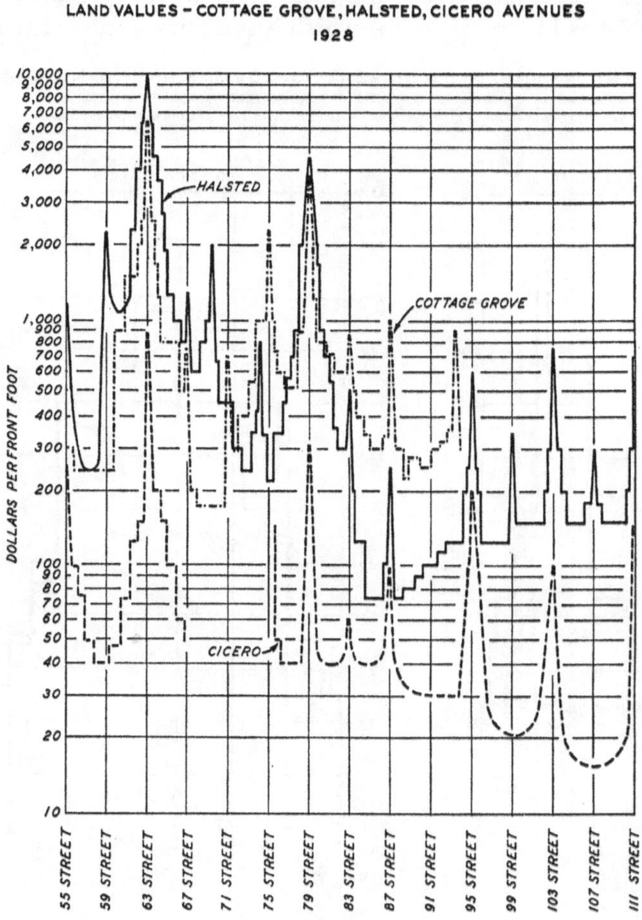

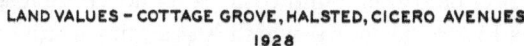

LAND VALUES – COTTAGE GROVE, HALSTED, CICERO AVENUES
1928

FIG. 67

horse cars, cable cars, elevated lines, electric surface lines, electrified railroads, and automobiles into the central business district. No outer belt of passenger transport lines encircled the city. Until the last few decades at least, it was necessary to pass through the downtown area to go from one part of the city to another. Even today that is usually the most convenient way.

Tables XXXVIII, XXXIX, and XL show how the Chicago Loop buildings under the pressure of expanding business confined to a limited area have tapped successively higher layers of air. By 1893

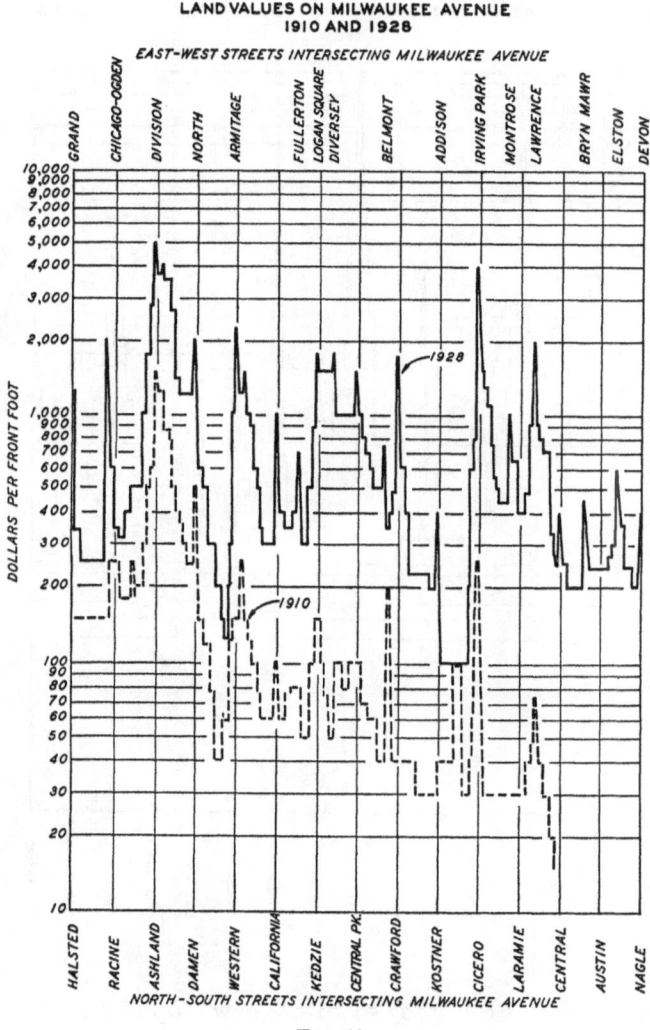

FIG. 68

over 10 per cent of the air layer from seven to twelve stories had been filled with buildings, and the highest towers extended to sixteen stories. By 1923, when the new zoning law permitted tower buildings that contained as many as forty-four stories, 37 per cent of the area from seven to twelve stories had been occupied, 17 per cent of that between twelve and sixteen stories, and over 6 per cent of that between sixteen and

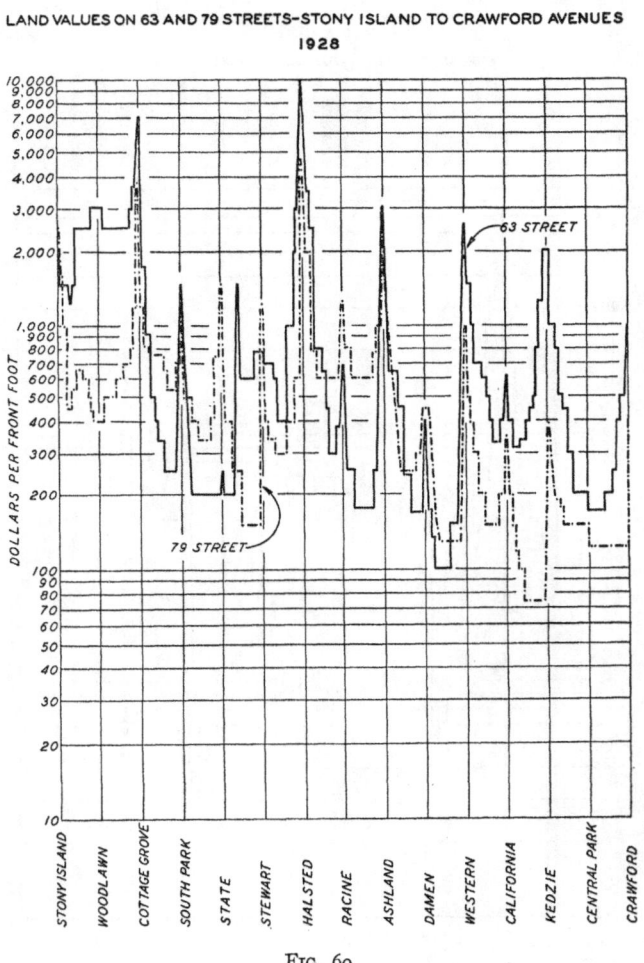

Fig. 69

twenty-two stories. From 1923 to 1930 a new crop of a score of tower buildings arose in Chicago, which created a new skyline and tapped the layer of air that contained as much cubic air space as all of that which buildings had previously penetrated. Yet, as Figure 70 shows, these

GROWTH OF CHICAGO AND ITS LAND VALUES

TABLE XXXVIII
PERCENTAGE OF CUBIC FEET AT GIVEN HEIGHTS TO TOTAL CUBIC FEET IN AREA (CENTRAL BUSINESS DISTRICT)

Building Height in Stories	1836	1856	1873	1893	1923	1933
Ground–6	100.0	100.0	99.7	84.3	60.2	46.2
7–12	0.0	0.0	0.3	12.5	26.7	28.1
13–16	0.0	0.0	0.0	3.0	8.3	13.7
17–22	0.0	0.0	0.0	0.2	4.8	9.8
23–44	0.0	0.0	0.0	0.0	0.0	2.2
Total	100.0	100.0	100.0	100.0	100.0	100.0

TABLE XXXIX
PERCENTAGE OF AIR SPACE AT DIFFERENT HEIGHTS OCCUPIED BY BUILDINGS (CENTRAL BUSINESS DISTRICT)

Building Height in Stories	1836	1856	1873	1893	1923	1933
Ground–6	0.2	30.0	40.0	61.0	85.0	82.4
7–12	0.0	0.0	1.0	10.3	37.2	50.1
13–16	0.0	0.0	0.0	3.3	17.0	36.7
17–22	0.0	0.0	0.0	0.2	6.3	17.4
23–44	0.0	0.0	0.0	0.0	0.0	1.07

TABLE XL
CUBIC FEET OF SPACE ABOVE THE BLOCKS IN THE CENTRAL BUSINESS DISTRICT OF CHICAGO

BUILDING HEIGHT IN STORIES	TOTAL CU. FT. AIR SPACE	NO. OF CU. FT. OCCUPIED BY BUILDINGS			
		1873	1893	1923	1933
Basement area					101,200,000
First 6 stories (0–72 ft.)	416,520,000	150,000,000	290,000,000	350,000,000	343,000,000
7–12 stories (73–144 ft.)	416,520,000	500,000	43,000,000	155,000,000	209,000,000
13–16 stories (145–92 ft.)	277,680,000		10,000,000	48,250,000	102,000,000
17–22 stories (193–264 ft.)	416,520,000		800,000	27,500,000	72,500,000
23–44 stories (265–528 ft.)	1,522,220,000				16,200,000
Total above basements	3,042,440,000	150,500,000	343,800,000	580,750,000	742,700,000

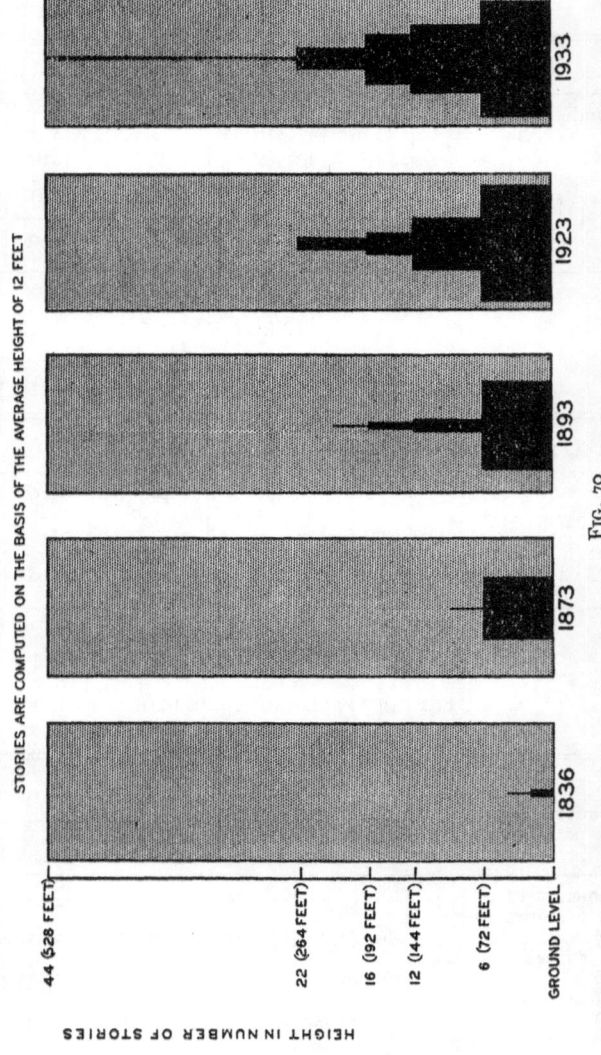

Fig. 70

new towers filled only 1 per cent of the air layer into which they jutted, and the space in these towers represented only 2 per cent of all the space in the buildings in the central business district.[39]

This vertical expansion of the Loop was made possible and necessary by the completion of elevated lines on the South, West, and North sides, which were routed to pour their traffic into the limited iron-bound circuit known as the "Loop." A different system of transportation, such as that of the subways, might have spread this development out in a longer line, or a different routing of the elevated system might have developed a concentration point elsewhere; but the Loop land-value pattern as it developed was the inevitable result of the laying-down of a transportation system which intensified the natural advantages of the Loop area.

The rapid development of the north shore and the Gold Coast after 1900, the great increase in the number of automobiles after 1910, and the opening of the Michigan Avenue link bridge did, however, combine to break the iron bands of the Loop after 1920. The new double-decked Michigan Avenue opened a channel across the river for the flow of automobile traffic to the Gold Coast and the north shore. The fashionable carriage trade that had developed South Michigan Avenue now spread northward.

[39] This computation and those following showing the air space occupied by buildings in the Loop at different periods were made in the following manner: The calculations were first made for the year 1933. The height of every building in the central business district of Chicago in the area north of the middle of Van Buren Street to the river on the north and west and to Grant Park and Beaubien Court on the east was determined by actual inspection. The number of cubic feet in every building in this area was obtained from the measurement made by the assessor for taxation purposes in 1931. The cubic feet in basements given in these same measurements were subtracted from the totals, which included the basement areas. For each building the total cubical content above the ground was divided by the number of stories to obtain the average cubic content of each floor. The total space in towers in each building is separately given by the assessor's measurements. Allowances were also made for setbacks in buildings or unusual variations between the cubic content of different floors in each building. The averages for each floor thus determined were multiplied by the number of floors in each building falling within the height limits shown in the chart. It is important to note that the chart shows only the cubic content of each class taken as a total. Thus the content of the air space occupied by the first six stories contains one-, two-, three-, four-, and five-story buildings. The vacant air space up to the six-story level includes not merely vacant ground, but the air space above buildings lower than six stories.

Having thus determined the air space occupied by Loop buildings in 1933, the age of all buildings standing in the Loop was ascertained from the records of the county assessor's

In the last boom from 1923 to 1929, the central business district expanded laterally as well as vertically. Skyscrapers were erected outside the circuit of the elevated lines on North Michigan Avenue, on the new Wacker Drive along the south bank of the river, on South Michigan Avenue south of Van Buren Street, and on Madison Street at the south branch of the river. On the North Side at the forks of the river was completed in 1930 the huge Merchandise Mart. Thus the amount of cubic air space in which it was sought to project buildings was increased by doubling the ground area laterally and by doubling the air layers vertically. Such expansion, made possible by the reckless bond financing of the neo-gilded age, could not be maintained. Already there has been a tendency to contract from the outposts of the Stevens Hotel and the Civic Opera Building, which are too far from the main center of business to be profitable at the present time.

The area occupied for retail uses in Chicago expanded following the completion of the elevated Loop, so that the wholesale trades were pushed out of Wabash and Michigan avenues by 1910. The removal of the South Water Street market in 1922 and the completion of the Wacker Drive likewise expelled the wholesale trades from the north end of the central business district. The wholesale district is now chiefly confined to the area west of Wells Street to the river, from Madison to Harrison Street, and this area has suffered since 1930 from the competition of the Merchandise Mart on the north bank of the river. The financial center along LaSalle Street has expanded vertically rather than

---

office. The height distribution of the cubic content of existing buildings that were also standing at the periods shown in the chart was then computed. To this were added computations for buildings torn down, estimates of the cubic content for which were obtained from the records of the *Economist*. This carried the record back to 1872.

Estimates for the periods prior to the fire of October 9, 1871, which destroyed all buildings in the present Loop, were made from computations from photographs of the city showing the character of buildings in the area.

The accuracy of the foregoing chart and tables is therefore greatest for the recent periods; the margin of error is greatest for the early periods. Some of these early figures, however, are highly accurate, as it was known, for instance, that in 1836 and in 1856 there were no buildings in Chicago over six stories in height, and that in 1873 there were very few such buildings.

In these calculations, spires of churches, monuments, and flagpoles on the tops of tall buildings have been ignored, as the purpose has been not to show maximum heights established by such objects, but to indicate the rentable building space at different height levels. The total number of cubic feet of air space over the Loop does not include that over streets and alleys.

GROWTH OF CHICAGO AND ITS LAND VALUES 335

laterally, a succession of new buildings on the same sites providing the needed growth. These buildings fronting on LaSalle Street or Jackson Street near LaSalle have, however, been extended to cover entire blocks and thereby carried over the influence of the main financial street to the adjoining streets.

The continual growth of the central business district of Chicago for a century has required successive crops of buildings on the same site to meet the demands of different or more intensive uses. Since 1830 at least six different structures have occupied the southeast corner of Washington and LaSalle streets, each of which in turn was expected to

TABLE XLI

CUBIC CONTENTS OF BUILDINGS IN CHICAGO CENTRAL BUSINESS DISTRICT BY AGE GROUPS (INCLUDING BASEMENT AREA)

Classification According to Date of Erection	No. Buildings	Percentage Total Number	Cubic Content	Percentage Total (Cubic Content)	Percentage Average Depreciation in 1928
1871–87.....	230	37.91	97,109,713	11.47	63.0
1888–1900...	168	27.69	160,657,824	19.01	47.5
1901–20.....	125	20.60	353,544,243	41.80	23.0
1921–33.....	84	13.80	234,458,055	27.72	9.0
Total...	607	100.0	845,759,835	100.00	22.0

endure for many years. There are probably few spots in the downtown district which have not been occupied by at least three, if not four, sets of buildings. Along LaSalle Street, where the replacement has occurred more frequently than on any other street, thirteen-story skyscrapers with a structural life of a century or more have been torn down to give room for twenty-two- or forty-four-story tower buildings. The age of the buildings in the Loop as given in Table XLI shows, however, that a great many of the buildings erected just after the fire of 1871 still survive. Yet, in cubic content, these buildings are of far less importance than the ground area covered by them would indicate. Most of the sites occupied by them are awaiting conversion to a higher and better use. Table XLI shows the number of cubic feet by age groups, including basement space, of the buildings standing in 1933 in the area bounded by the lake, the river, and the center line of Van Buren Street.[40]

Thus, as Table XLI shows, approximately 70 per cent of the cubic

[40] From the property record cards of the county assessor of Cook County, Illinois.

space in the present Loop has been built since 1900. The heart wood of the organic Chicago is constantly replacing old tissues with new ones, in marked contrast with the static condition of the belt of dead wood around the Loop known as the "blighted area" which has ceased to grow.

Tall buildings do not necessarily develop high land values, for the returns may not pay for the added building costs. Some of the highest land values on State Street, as, for instance, the Woolworth Store south of Washington Street, are derived from business mainly conducted on the first floor and in the basement.

It is difficult to classify the uses of the central business district by cubic space because there is some overlapping. Table XLII indicates, however, the major classifications.

TABLE XLII

PRINCIPAL TYPES OF USES OF CENTRAL BUSINESS
DISTRICT OF CHICAGO

Type of Building	Cubic Ft. Occupied
Department stores	105,000,000
Hotels	65,000,000
Theaters	15,000,000
Office buildings	350,000,000

Of these uses, department stores have been static for a decade, as have also legitimate theaters. The numerous bank consolidations have left a dozen vacant bank floors in the Loop, which it is difficult to convert to any other use. There was, before the opening of the World's Fair, at least a temporary surplus of hotel space.

The fact that the central business district of Chicago has not moved out of the square mile of land surrounding State and Madison streets in a century and after 1882 almost ceased to spread has caused the intense utilization and the tremendous increase of land values in that area. As Table XLIII shows, the value of the land in a district that represented only one-tenth of 1 per cent of the land area within the 1933 corporate limits of Chicago has varied from one-eighth to two-fifths of the value of a territory approximately one thousand times as large. The relative importance of the land value in this concentrated area as compared with the rest of the land in the city, however, has risen and fallen. The early importance of this district in 1836, when it contained most of the set-

GROWTH OF CHICAGO AND ITS LAND VALUES 337

tled area of Chicago, and in 1856, when it had within its boundaries a retail and wholesale area that had risen rapidly in value, had declined with reference to the rest of the city by 1873 as a result of a suburban movement stimulated by horse-car lines, steam railroads, and the parks. At that time fashionable residential land on Prairie Avenue was worth nearly half as much as land on the best retail shopping streets in the downtown area. The coming of the elevated lines, skyscrapers, and the State Street department stores caused a strong centralizing movement, and from 1873 to 1910 land values in the central business district rose

TABLE XLIII
LAND VALUES IN CENTRAL BUSINESS DISTRICT AND
ENTIRE AREA OF CHICAGO COMPARED, 1836–1926
(Millions of Dollars)

Year	Loop Land Value	Percentage of Value of Land for the Entire City
1836	$ 2	20.0
1856	35	28.0
1873	72	12.5
1892	350	23.3
1910	600	40.0
1926	1,000	20.0

from 12.5 to 40 per cent of the aggregate values for the entire city. After 1921 the centrifugal forces again gained the ascendancy with the rise of the outlying neighborhood centers and the shift of population outward, and the proportion of Loop land values to aggregate land values for the city dropped from 40 to 20 per cent when Loop values rose only 67 per cent from 1910 to 1928 compared with a rise of 233 per cent for the city as a whole.

In view of the high percentage of the entire land value of the city that is represented by the value of this limited area, and in view of the great differences in values between different parts of this Loop, it has been considered desirable to show the land values of this section block by block for important peak and valley years. Accordingly, in Figures 71, 72, 73, 74, and 75 value data that will tend to establish the contours and elevations of these Himalaya Mountain peaks of Chicago land values for a century are given.

FIG. 71. MAPS OF PART OF THE CENTRAL BUSINESS DISTRICT OF CHICAGO — SHOWING — VALUATIONS OF INDIVIDUAL LOTS FOR THE PERIODS 1830, 1836, 1854–1856 AND 1870–1873

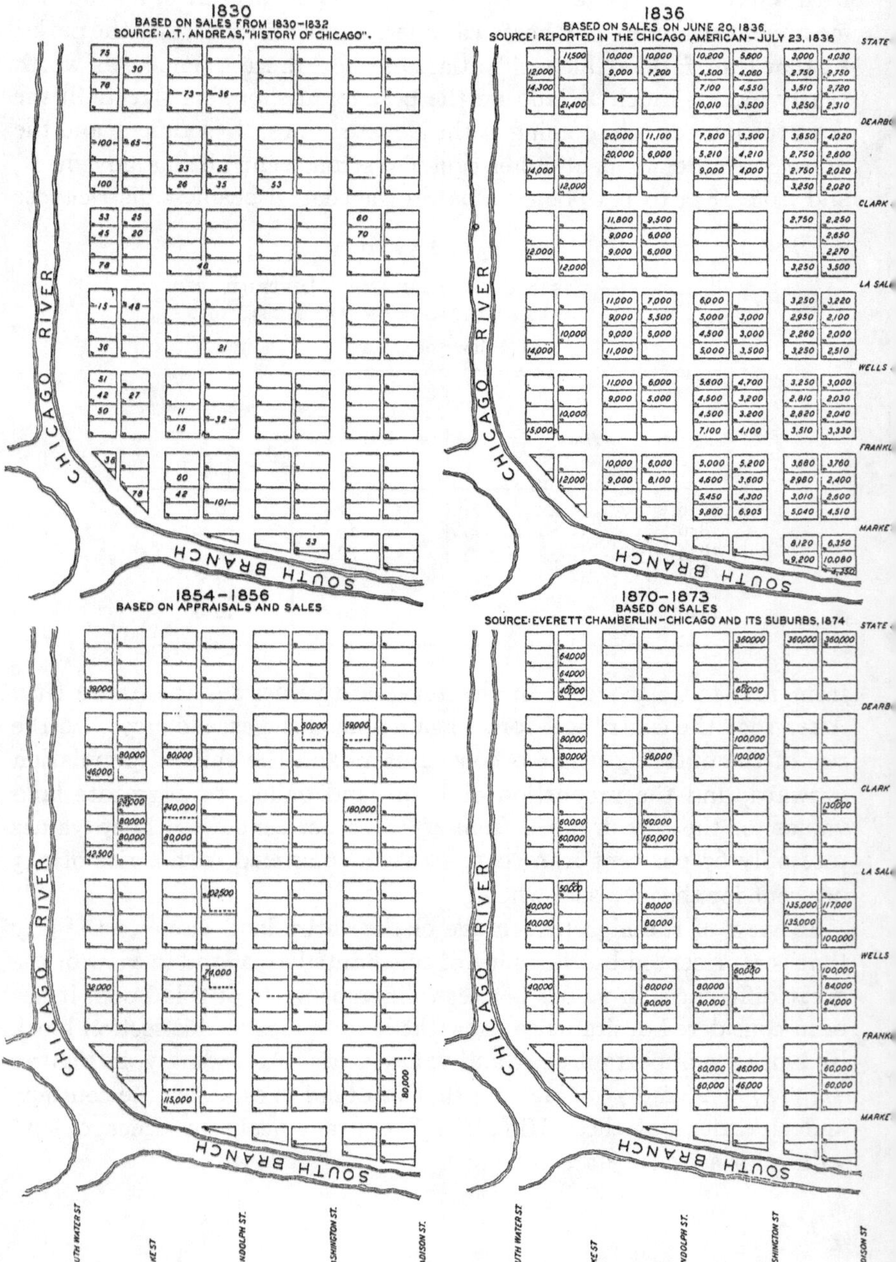

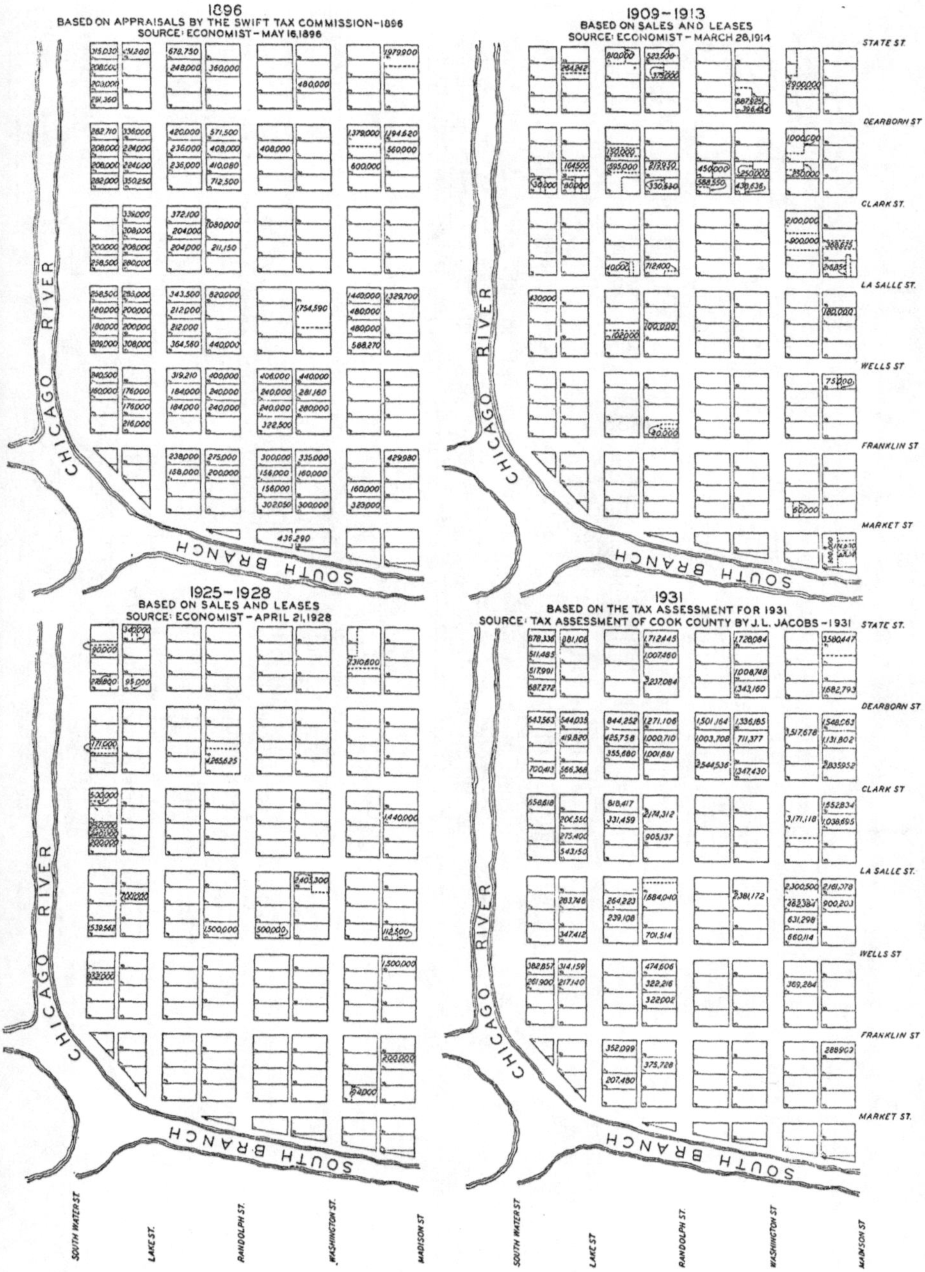

FIG. 72

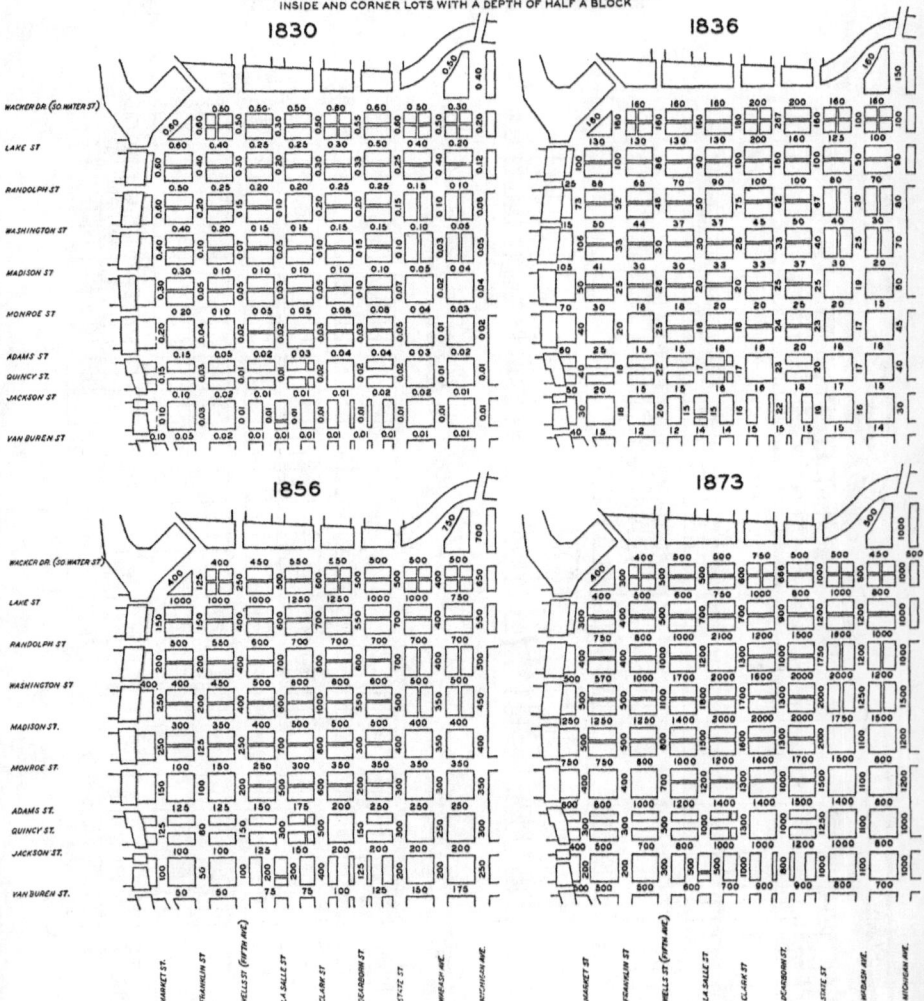

Fig. 73

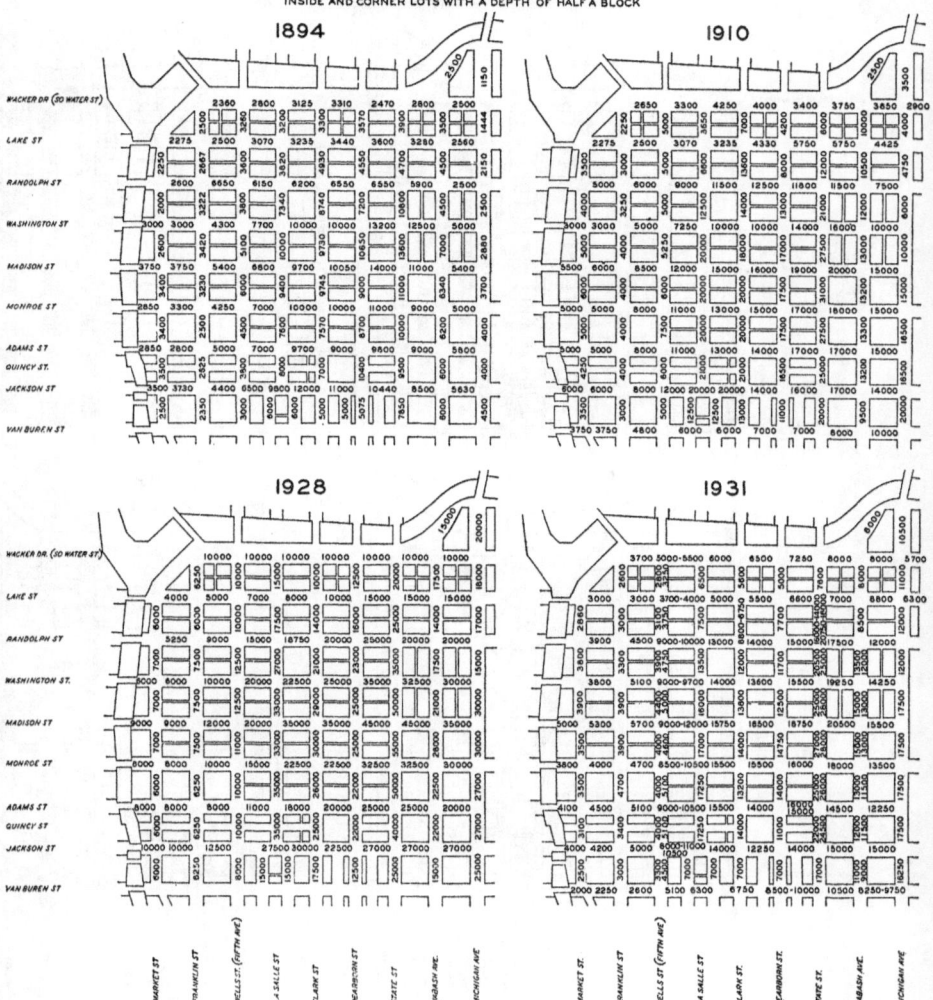

Fig. 74

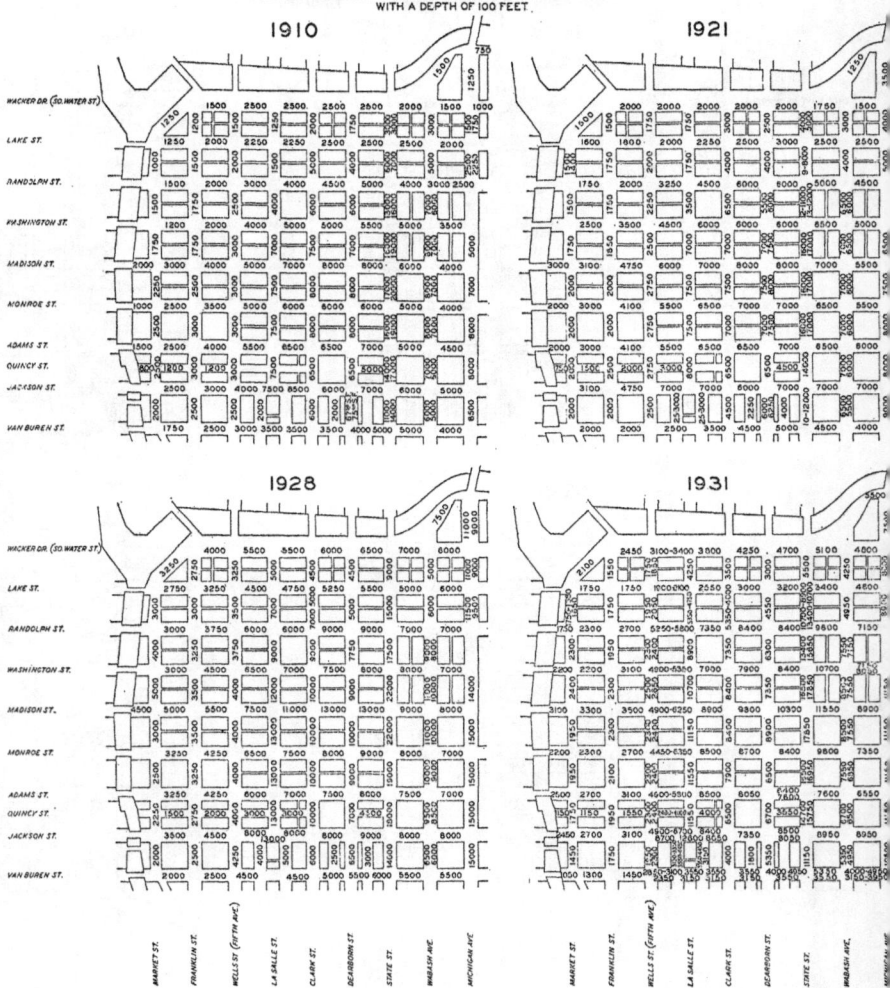
Fig. 75

GROWTH OF CHICAGO AND ITS LAND VALUES

In Figures 71 and 72 sale prices or valuations of entire lots or parcels in part of the central business district are shown, and in Figures 73, 74, and 75 computed front-foot values are presented. In the earlier periods up to 1873, when whole lots were sold and when the differences between corners and inside lots were not so great, the problem of land values in the central business district was relatively simple. Since 1890, however, the computation of values in the Loop has become far more complex because of the splitting of the original lots into smaller holdings or the combination of several lots into larger plots of irregular size and the increasing importance of corner influence and depth factors. Valuations by George C. Olcott and by the tax assessors since 1910 have been on the basis of a standard front foot in the middle of the block with a depth of 100 feet. As this has become a familiar and somewhat customary standard for purposes of comparing recent Loop land-value trends, valuations made on this basis by Olcott for 1910, 1921, 1928, and by the tax assessor for 1931 are presented in Figure 75.

Since lots in the central business district as originally platted were from 160 to 190 feet in depth, and early sales were made on that basis, it is evident that front-foot valuations with a depth running to the middle of the block cannot be compared with later valuations applying to a front foot with a depth of 100 feet. Since modern depth rules could not be correctly applied to earlier conditions to reduce the earlier values to a 100-foot depth basis, valuations have been prepared showing recent Loop land values on a basis of a front foot running to the middle of the block, and also on the basis of an average front foot for the entire block including corners. The earlier land-value maps were computed on the same basis, so that the eight land-value maps in Figures 73 and 74 are strictly comparable.

Inasmuch as an increase of depth from 100 to 180 feet adds 43.2 per cent to the front-foot value and corner premiums add as high as 60 per cent to the front-foot value according to the rule applied by the tax assessor in 1931, such a method of computation adds considerably to front-foot values given on a 100-foot basis. The values in Figure 74, which are based on sales and leases, show amounts that are considerably higher for 1910 and 1928 than the Olcott figures, even after the addition to Olcott's value is made for depth- and corner-influence factors. This is due to the method employed by the writer consistently in this book of registering the sales value of properties and not conservative appraisals. Some extremely high leases were disregarded in computing the front-foot values shown in Figure 74, but the writer did not deem it proper to discount Loop leases or to ignore speculative sales in the central business district, when they entered into valuations made elsewhere.

In Figures 71 and 72 sales data and tax valuations are presented for parcels actually sold or valued, so that the reader may make his own comparisons as to increases in land values for part of the Loop area for the period of the century.

In Table XLIV the land values per front foot for the north-south streets in the central business district are presented for both boom and depression years in each cycle from 1830 to 1931.

f) Summary: Chicago land values by types of uses.—Tables XLV and XLVI summarize the movement of land values in Chicago from 1910 to 1933 by principal types of uses.[41]

D. THE LONG-RUN TREND OF CHICAGO LAND VALUES

So far Chicago land values have been discussed in terms of current dollars and no adjustments have been made for changes in the level of either prices, wages, or interest rates. In order to measure the gain in land values that would have occurred had the price level, wage, and interest rates been stationary, Fig. 77. has been prepared. Since Chicago land values rose after the first great declines in the level of wholesale prices in the Civil War and World War periods, and since the rise in prices prior to 1836 and 1857 was moderate while that prior to 1890 was negligible, the correction of the current dollar figure of Chicago land values for changes in wholesale prices does not greatly affect the rise of land values in boom periods. Because of the long-run upward tendency of prices, particularly since 1900, however, the deflation for changes in the purchasing power of the dollar does lower the height of the last peak in 1926–28 as compared with earlier peaks.

1. *Corrections of the land-value data for changes in wholesale prices, wages, and interest rates.*—It is questionable as to whether or not correction on the basis of the wholesale price index, including the prices of many raw materials and of farm products, is the appropriate method of deflation for urban real estate. In the city, the cost of urban goods and

[41] Based on the writer's computations of the data in Olcott, *op. cit.* (1910, 1929, and 1933).

GROWTH OF CHICAGO AND ITS LAND VALUES

TABLE XLIV

LAND VALUES ON NORTH-SOUTH STREETS IN THE CENTRAL BUSINESS DISTRICT OF CHICAGO, 1830–1931

(In Dollars per Front Foot for an Average Front Foot, Including Corners Running to the Middle of the Block)

Block	Depth E.F.	Depth W.F.	1830	1836	1841	1856	1861	1873	1877	1894	1910	1928	1931
\multicolumn{13}{c}{State Street, 5,856 Feet}
Wack.–Lake......	160	171	0.60	160	(12)	(500)	(200)	1,000	500	3,900	6,000	20,000	7,600*
Lake–Rand.......	160	113	0.25	100	(12)	(550)	(250)	1,200	800	4,700	12,000	25,000	18,350*
Rand.–Wash......	160	151	0.15	67	0	(400)	(200)	1,750	1,200	10,800	21,000	35,000	25,000*
Wash.–Mad......	160	151	0.10	40	7	300	200	2,000	1,000	13,600	27,500	50,000	28,000*
Mad.–Mon.......	160	143	(0.07)	25	(6)	300	200	1,750	1,000	11,000	31,000	55,000	28,000*
Mon.–Adams.....	160	147	(0.05)	23	(5)	250	(150)	1,500	800	10,800	27,300	50,000	26,000*
Adams–Jack......	160	144	(0.02)	20	(4)	150	(100)	1,250	600	9,500	25,000	40,000	24,500*
Jack.–Van B......	100	145	(0.01)	19	(3)	(100)	(100)	1,000	500	7,850	20,000	25,000	17,000*
\multicolumn{13}{c}{Michigan Avenue, 4,472 Feet}
Wack.–S. Water...	112	62	(0.50)	(150)	5	700	(350)	1,000	(400)	1,150	3,500	20,000	10,500
Water–Lake......	132	70	(0.20)	(100)	2	650	(300)	1,000	(300)	1,444	4,000	18,000	11,000
Lake–Rand.......	129	70	(0.12)	(90)	2	550	(250)	1,000	(300)	2,150	4,750	17,500	12,000
Rand.–Wash......	163		(0.08)	(80)	2	(500)	(200)	1,000	(300)	2,500	6,000	15,000	12,000
Wash.–Mad......	163		(0.05)	(70)	2	(450)	(175)	1,500	300	2,880	10,000	30,000	17,500
Mad.–Mon.......	163		(0.04)	60	2	(400)	(150)	1,200	400	3,700	15,000	30,000	17,500
Mon.–Adams.....	163		(0.02)	45	2	(350)	(125)	1,200	300	4,000	16,500	27,000	17,500
Adams–Jack......	163		(0.01)	40	2	(300)	(100)	1,000	250	4,000	16,500	27,000	17,500
Jack.–Van B......	163		(0.01)	30	2	(250)	(100)	1,000	250	4,500	20,000	25,000	16,250
\multicolumn{13}{c}{Wabash Avenue, 5,837 Feet}
Wack.–Lake......	171	216	(0.50)	(100)	3	(400)	(200)	800	(400)	3,500	10,000	17,500	8,000†
Lake–Rand.......	206	220	(0.40)	(50)	2	400	(200)	1,200	(500)	4,500	10,500	14,000	8,500†
Rand.–Wash......	151	163	(0.10)	(30)	2	(400)	(200)	1,000	(500)	4,500	12,000	17,500	13,500†
Wash.–Mad......	151	163	(0.03)	(25)	2	(350)	(175)	1,250	(500)	7,000	13,000	21,000	15,000†
Mad.–Mon.......	170	171	(0.02)	19	2	(350)	(175)	1,100	(400)	6,340	13,200	28,000	15,000†
Mon.–Adams.....	174	170	(0.01)	17	2	(300)	(150)	1,100	400	6,200	13,300	22,500	13,000†
Adams–Jack......	171	171	(0.01)	17	2	(250)	(125)	1,100	500	6,000	13,200	22,000	12,000†
Jack.–Van B......	120	163	(0.01)	16	3	(200)	(100)	1,100	(400)	6,000	9,500	15,000	11,000†
\multicolumn{13}{c}{Dearborn Street, 6,531 Feet (Including Plymouth–Federal)}
Wack.–Lake......	160	160	0.55	267	(50)	500	(250)	666	(350)	3,570	4,200	12,500	5,000
Lake–Rand.......	160	160	0.33	160	(25)	550	(275)	900	(450)	4,550	8,000	16,000	7,700
Rand.–Wash......	160	160	(0.20)	62	(7)	600	(300)	1,000	(500)	7,200	13,000	23,000	11,700
Wash.–Mad......	160	160	(0.15)	33	(3)	550	(275)	1,300	(650)	10,650	17,500	25,000	12,500
Mad.–Mon.......	160	160	(0.10)	25	(2)	(300)	(150)	1,300	(650)	9,000	17,500	25,000	14,750
Mon.–Adams.....	160	160	(0.03)	24	(2)	(150)	(100)	1,000	(500)	8,700	17,500	22,000	14,000
Adams–Jack......	160	160	(0.02)	(23)	(2)	(100)	50	1,000	(500)	10,440	16,500	22,000	11,000
Jack.–Van B......	66	70	(0.01)	(22)	(1)	(100)	50	800	(400)	5,075	11,000	12,500	7,000
\multicolumn{13}{c}{Clark Street, 5,898 Feet}
Wack.–Lake......	160	160	0.50	180	(50)	600	(300)	600	(300)	3,300	7,000	10,000	5,600
Lake–Rand.......	160	160	0.30	100	(40)	700	(350)	700	(350)	4,930	13,500	14,000	7,800
Rand.–Wash......	160	160	0.20	75	(10)	800	(400)	1,300	(650)	8,740	14,000	21,000	12,000
Wash.–Mad......	160	160	0.10	28	(3)	1,000	(300)	1,700	(750)	9,730	18,000	29,000	13,800
Mad.–Mon.......	160	160	0.05	25	(2)	800	(100)	1,600	(800)	9,745	20,000	30,000	14,000
Mon.–Adams.....	160	160	0.03	(18)	(2)	600	(100)	1,300	(600)	9,570	20,000	26,000	13,200
Adams–Jack......	125	160	0.02	(17)	(2)	500	(100)	1,300	(600)	7,000	21,000	25,000	14,000
Jack.–Van B......	107	103	0.01	(16)	(1)	1,000	(100)	1,000	(500)	5,000	13,500	17,500	7,000

* East side of street.   † West side of street.

TABLE XLIV—Continued

Block	Depth E.F.	Depth W.F.	1830	1836	1841	1856	1861	1873	1877	1894	1910	1928	1931
LaSalle Street, 6,466 Feet (Including Sherman Street)												
Wack.–Lake	160	160	0.30	160	(30)	500	(250)	500	300	3,200	3,650	15,000	6,500
Lake–Rand	160	160	0.20	90	(20)	600	(300)	700	350	3,820	6,600	17,500	7,500
Rand.–Wash	160	160	0.10	50	(5)	700	(350)	1,200	400	7,340	12,500	27,000	13,500
Wash.–Mad	160	160	0.05	30	(2)	800	(400)	1,800	(500)	10,000	20,000	33,000	16,000
Mad.–Mon	160	160	(0.03)	(20)	(2)	(700)	(350)	1,500	(400)	9,400	20,000	33,000	17,000
Mon.–Adams	160	160	(0.02)	(18)	(2)	(500)	(250)	1,200	(300)	7,600	20,000	35,000	17,250
Adams–Jack	160	177	(0.01)	(17)	(1)	(300)	(150)	1,000	(200)	8,000	21,000	35,000	17,250
Jack.–Van B	87	105	(0.01)	(16)	(1)	(200)	(100)	500	(150)	6,000	12,500	15,000	7,000
Sherman	100	87	(0.01)	(15)	(1)	(200)	(100)	500	(100)	6,000	12,500	15,000	7,000

Block	1830	1836	1841	1856	1861	1873	1877	1894	1910	1928	1931
Wells (Fifth Avenue) Street, 5722 Feet											
Wack.–Lake	0.50	160	(20)	250	150	500	(250)	3,260	5,000	10,000	3,250*
Lake–Rand	(0.30)	86	(10)	400	200	500	(250)	3,600	5,000	10,000	3,750*
Rand.–Wash	(0.15)	48	(3)	400	225	1,000	(500)	3,800	5,000	12,500	4,750*
Wash.–Mad	(0.07)	30	(2)	400	225	1,100	(550)	5,100	5,250	12,500	5,000*
Mad.–Mon	(0.05)	(28)	(1)	250	175	800	(400)	6,000	6,000	11,000	4,600*
Mon.–Adams	(0.02)	(25)	(1)	200	100	700	350	4,500	7,500	10,000	5,100*
Adams–Jack	(0.01)	(22)	(1)	150	75	500	250	3,800	6,000	10,000	5,100*
Jack.–Van B	(0.01)	(20)	(1)	100	50	300	150	3,000	5,000	8,000	4,500*
Franklin Street, 5721 Feet											
Wack.–Lake	(0.60)	160	(15)	125	50	300	200	2,500	2,250	6,250	2,600
Lake–Rand	(0.40)	100	(8)	150	75	400	250	2,667	3,600	6,000	3,000
Rand.–Wash	(0.20)	52	(3)	200	90	400	300	3,222	3,250	7,500	3,300
Wash.–Mad	(0.10)	33	(2)	200	90	500	350	3,420	4,000	7,500	3,900
Mad.–Mon	(0.05)	(25)	(1)	125	60	500	350	3,230	4,000	7,500	3,900
Mon.–Adams	(0.04)	(20)	(1)	100	50	400	275	2,500	4,000	6,250	4,700
Adams–Jack	(0.03)	(18)	(1)	80	40	300	200	2,625	4,000	6,250	3,400
Jack.–Van B	(0.03)	(16)	(1)	50	25	200	100	2,350	3,000	6,250	3,000
Market Street, 5241 Feet											
Lake–Rand	(0.60)	(100)	(20)	(150)	(75)	300	200	2,250	3,500	6,000	2,800
Rand.–Wash	(0.50)	73	(10)	(200)	(100)	400	250	2,000	4,000	7,000	3,800
Wash.–Mad	(0.40)	106	(7)	(250)	(125)	500	300	2,600	5,000	7,000	3,900
Mad.–Mon	(0.30)	(50)	(5)	(250)	(125)	500	350	3,400	6,000	7,000	3,500
Mon.–Adams	(0.20)	(40)	(5)	(150)	(75)	400	275	3,400	5,000	6,000	3,500
Adams–Jack	(0.15)	(40)	(4)	(125)	(60)	300	200	3,500	4,250	6,000	3,100
Jack.–Van B	(0.10)	(35)	(4)	(100)	(50)	200	100	2,500	3,500	6,000	2,500

* East side of street.

services has mounted more rapidly than the prices of farm products, and it is believed that an index based on the current wages of unskilled factory labor would be as good if not a better means of correcting the current dollar value of Chicago land. Accordingly, Figure 77 shows the number of days of unskilled labor required to purchase the site of Chicago at different periods. Inasmuch as wages of unskilled labor have hitherto held a considerable part of the gains made on each violent upswing in the price level and unskilled wages in 1926 stood five times as

GROWTH OF CHICAGO AND ITS LAND VALUES

high as in 1840, such a method of correcting the aggregate land values of the city greatly reduces such values. In fact, even including the areas that have registered the greatest increases and not singling out the blighted areas, the increase in the number of labor days required to purchase the site of Chicago increased but slightly from 1892 to 1926.

TABLE XLV

VALUE OF LAND IN CHICAGO BY PRINCIPAL TYPES OF USES, 1910–33
(Millions of Dollars)

Year	Outlying Business	Loop	Industrial	Residential	Total
1910	200	600	200	500	1,500
1928	1,333	1,000	400	2,267	5,000
1933	300	500	200	1,000	2,000

a) The change in the interest rate.—Another factor of the greatest importance has been the change in the long-term interest and capitalization rates in Chicago. As Figure 78 shows, interest rates on Chicago real estate have changed greatly in a century. In 1856 the interest rate

TABLE XLVI

INDEX NUMBERS OF CHICAGO LAND VALUES BY PRINCIPAL TYPES OF USES
(1910=100)

Year	Outlying Business	Loop	Industrial	Residential	Total
1910	100	100	100	100	100
1928	667	167	215	453	353
1933	150	83	100	200	143

on the best mortgages in the central business district was 10 per cent, by 1873 it was 8 per cent, and from there it dropped to 5 per cent in 1881 and to 4 per cent by 1897. From 1873 to 1897 central business land values would have doubled even if the income had remained the same, because the same income would have been capitalized at half the former rate. Accordingly, it has seemed proper to construct a curve of land values on the supposition that the 8 per cent rate of 1873 had continued to prevail and to show how much change in land values has occurred independent of the changes in interest rates. This irons out much of the rise from 1879 to 1890.

b) Allowance for the cost of street improvements.—A deduction must likewise be made from aggregate Chicago land values for the cost of

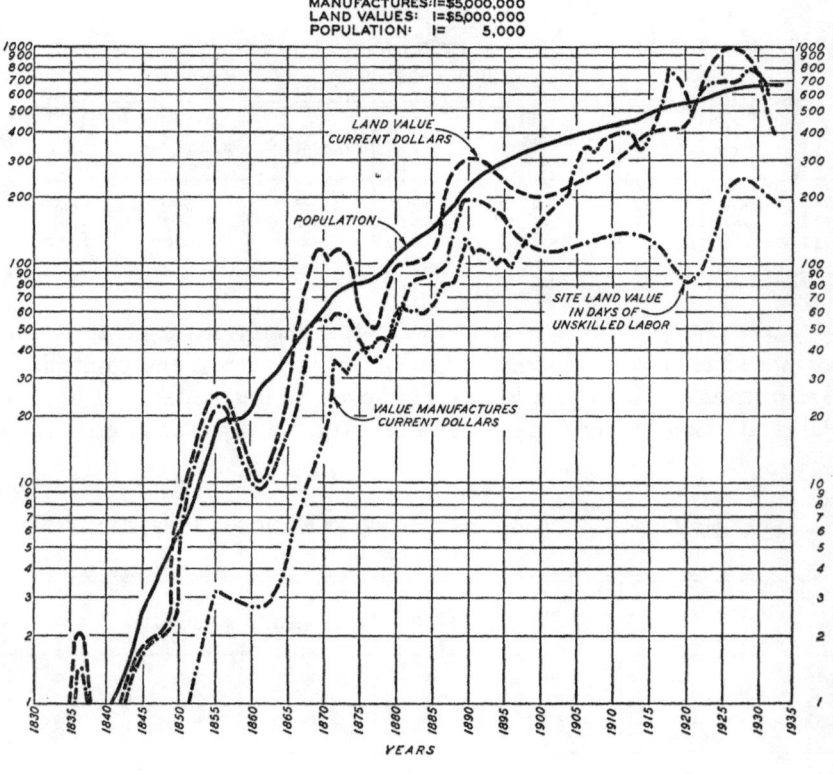

Fig. 76

street pavements, sewers, sidewalks, and other improvements, the cost of which has been chiefly paid for by special assessments against the property affected, if one desires to obtain the net site value of the land. The total amount so spent in the entire period of the century has amounted to approximately $600,000,000. Current prices of lots include all street improvements installed and paid for but are usually subject to unpaid assessments. In deducting the cumulative amount of the

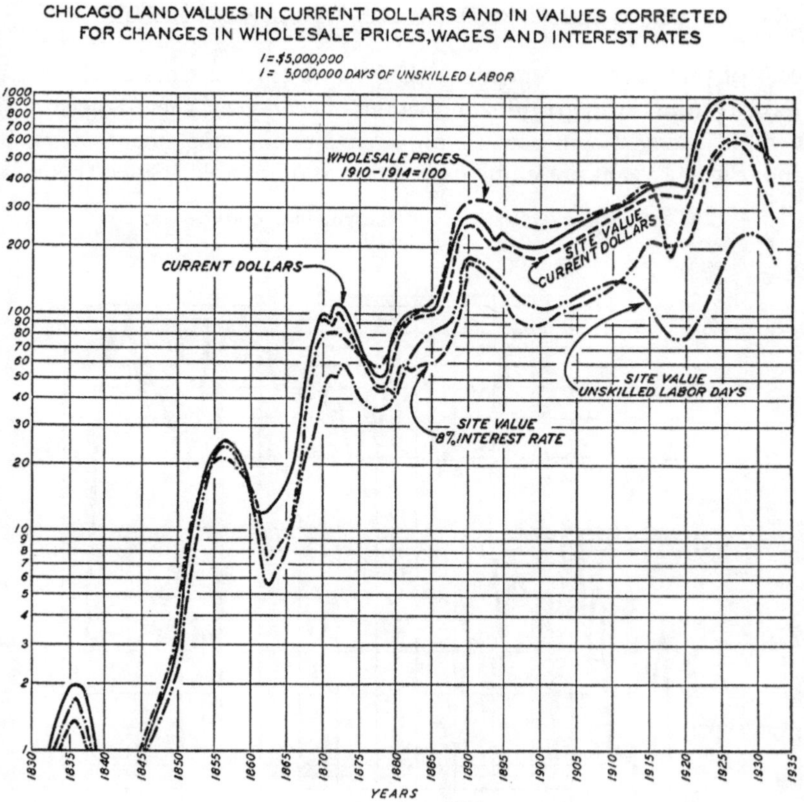

CHICAGO LAND VALUES IN CURRENT DOLLARS AND IN VALUES CORRECTED FOR CHANGES IN WHOLESALE PRICES, WAGES AND INTEREST RATES
1 = $5,000,000
1 = 5,000,000 DAYS OF UNSKILLED LABOR
WHOLESALE PRICES 1910-1914=100
CURRENT DOLLARS
SITE VALUE CURRENT DOLLARS
SITE VALUE UNSKILLED LABOR DAYS
SITE VALUE 8% INTEREST RATE
YEARS

Fig. 77

THE INTEREST RATE ON IMPROVED REAL ESTATE IN THE CENTRAL BUSINESS DISTRICT OF CHICAGO COMPARED WITH THE YIELD ON RAIL BONDS 1833-1933
PERCENT
CHICAGO REAL ESTATE INTEREST RATE
UNITED STATES NOT ON GOLD STANDARD
RAIL BOND YIELD
YEARS

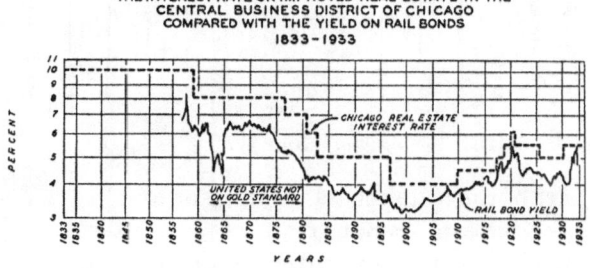

Fig. 78

cost of public improvements in Chicago from the time of the earliest records from the aggregate land values of each year, there is accordingly a slight exaggeration because only parts of the assessments of each of the last few years are immediately due and payable. Since this affects

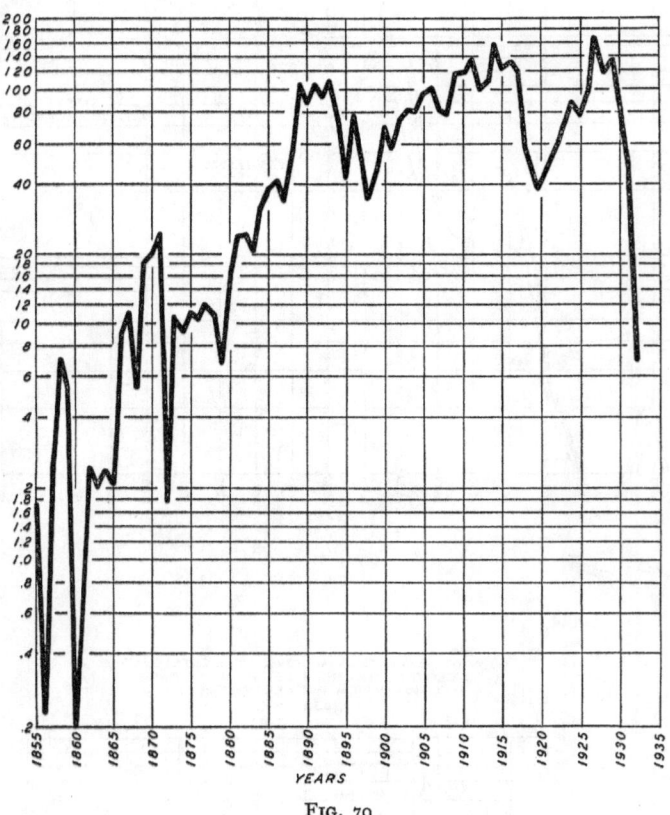

Fig. 79

only the part of the instalments for three or four years, and not for the entire period, the error is not great.

If Chicago land values are corrected for these various factors, it will be noted that land values so deflated have failed to keep pace with the increase of population. It would appear, therefore, that if inflationary elements are eliminated from land values, population growth must not only continue to sustain rising land values, but it must continue at a faster pace than at certain past periods, if a real increase in aggregate land values is to be maintained. If the blighted area of declining population be reduced to the number of days of unskilled labor required to purchase it, a sharp decline in its labor day value occurred from 1892 to 1928.

2. *Growth of money at compound interest and rise of land values compared.*—A further comparison may now be made between the rate of growth of money at compound interest and the rate of increase of Chicago land values. In Tables XLVII and XLVIII, and in Figure 80, the aggregate values of Chicago land at peak and valley periods at different dates have been put at compound interest at 6 per cent per annum. It will be noted that even the peak land value of 1836 would have amounted by 1933 to the land value actually prevailing in that year, while later peak values would have amounted to much greater sums. In regard to such comparisons, two qualifications, however, must be made. The first is that such computations could only be fairly applied to vacant land, inasmuch as improved land in most cases earns its interest, so that any increase in capital value is a net gain. The second observation is that it would have been extremely difficult if not impossible to have selected investments that have yielded a net return of 5 or even 6 per cent per annum for the period covered by this study.

3. *Taxation.*—During the century of the rise of Chicago land values, aggregate taxes have been constantly increasing, as Figure 96 shows. The actual assessment of taxes prior to 1928 favored outlying vacant land at the expense of the Loop and of developed property, so this increase in the tax rate did not bear so heavily on the sections in which land values rose so greatly from 1921 to 1926.[42] The reassessment in 1928 shifted the burden from the Loop to the outer sections.[43] Taxes continued to increase until the Chicago tax levy for school and corporate purposes for the eight years ending in 1931 was greater than the entire tax levy for the ninety-three years before 1923.[44] The per capita tax

[42] Herbert D. Simpson, *Tax Racket and Tax Reform in Chicago* (1930).

[43] According to investigations made by the writer, the tax bills for most of the Loop were lower in 1928 than in 1927, while for nearly all other property they were much higher.

[44] The aggregate Chicago city and school tax levy for the eight years 1924–31, inclusive, was $1,061,100,362. The aggregate Chicago city and school tax levy for the eighty-six years from 1837 to 1922, inclusive, was $1,020,561,853. As the taxes for the seven years 1830–36 were insignificant, being only $5,906 in 1837, there can be no doubt but that the

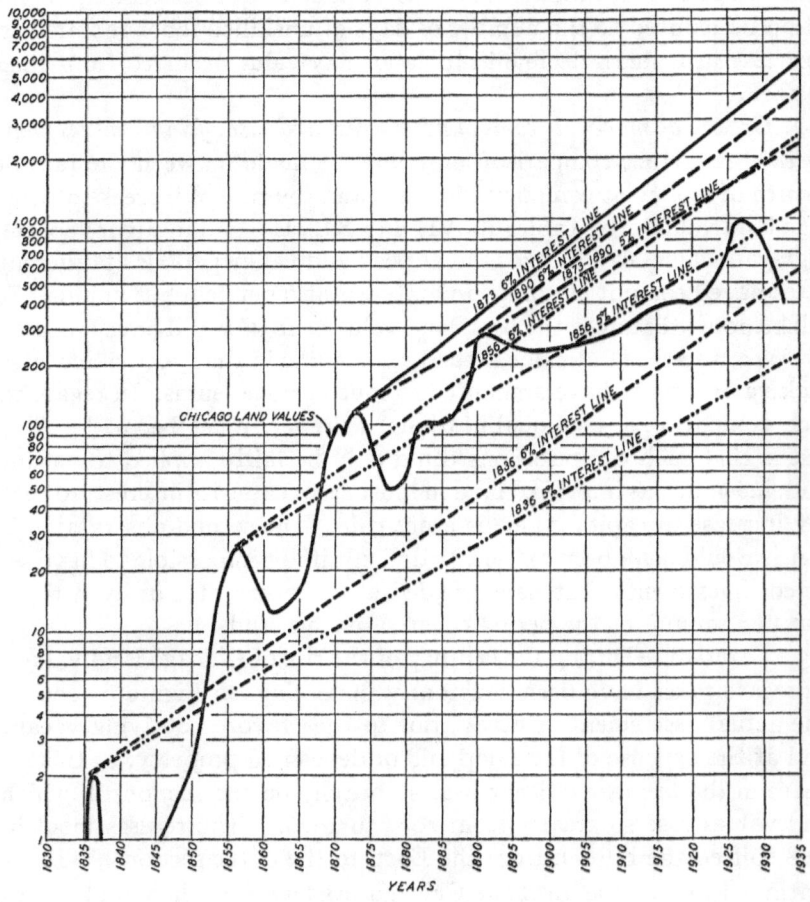

Fig. 80

taxes for the ninety-three years from 1830 to 1922, inclusive, were less than for the eight years ending in 1931. Of course, the growth of the city in area, population, and in the number and complexity of its governmental agencies must be taken into account in considering the absolute increase in taxes. Moreover, it is important in connection with tax policy to note that expenditures on such improvements as school buildings may favorably affect real estate values (*Report of the Comptroller of the City of Chicago* [1931], p. 173, for the figures from 1837 to 1930, inclusive; figures for 1931 from unpublished records of the City Comptroller's office).

GROWTH OF CHICAGO AND ITS LAND VALUES   353

for city and school purposes increased from approximately one dollar in 1840 to fifty dollars in 1930, a rise of fifty fold. The Chicago tax levy for the year 1930 alone was greater than the corresponding city and school levy for the entire period from the founding of the city to the first World's Fair.[45] The continuing heavy tax load in 1930, when real estate net incomes had sharply declined and when several years' taxes had accumulated, was another blow to land speculation.

E. TREND OF POPULATION AND LAND VALUES BY DISTRICTS

In considering the trend of aggregate or average Chicago land values, there is a danger in overlooking the vast differences in value that exist at the same time between different tracts of land within the city. The numerous charts and graphs showing land values by types of uses and by square-mile sections should have made the reader familiar with these land-value variations. In this concluding section of this chapter, space prevents the repetition of this mass of detail, and only a broad view of the relationship between population shifts of land values within the city can be presented.

1. *The centrifugal forces affecting population.*—The population of Chicago was at first concentrated near the center of the city and the density curve resembled a cone with the sides sloping sharply downward.[46] As population increased and transportation facilities improved, the base of this cone widened and the rate of most rapid population increase passed to successive belts of land, each one in turn farther from the main business district.[47] After 1870 the height of the population pyramid rose only slowly but the base widened rapidly. In the twentieth century the number of people living within the areas that once contained the entire city stopped advancing and began to decline.[48] Between 1920 and 1930 the remarkable change in the distribution of the population of Chicago is made strikingly evident by Figures 82 and 86. A large crater has appeared near the heart of the city, and there is no

[45] The aggregate Chicago city and school taxes from 1837 up to and including 1893 were $155,977,669. The Chicago city and school tax for 1930 alone was $168,606,720. Same references as in note 44.

[46] See Figs. 85 and 86. Population by square-mile areas from 1840 to 1890 based on the study by R. G. Callahan based on returns from election precincts. For the periods 1900–1920 the figures of the Chicago Surface Lines are used, and for the year 1930 the square-mile totals are derived from U.S. Census tracts.

[47] See Fig. 83.   [48] See Fig. 84.

TABLE XLVII

THE AMOUNT TO WHICH THE SALES VALUE OF CHICAGO LAND AT DIFFERENT PERIODS WOULD HAVE GROWN AT 6 PER CENT COMPOUND INTEREST

(Thousands of Dollars)

Year	Original Amount	1836	1841	1856	1861	1873	1879	1892	1900	1910	1926	1933
1830	$ 160	$ 227	$ 304	$ 728	$ 1,024	$ 1,900	$ 2,780	$ 4,820	$ 9,452	$ 16,928	$ 43,012	$ 64,602
1836	10,000	10,000	13,382	32,071	42,919	81,473	122,504	261,293	416,462	745,820	1,894,645	2,848,846
1841	1,400		1,400	3,355	4,490	9,035	12,815	27,336	43,568	78,025	198,211	302,035
1856	125,000			125,000	167,250	336,600	477,470	1,018,400	1,623,140	2,657,000	7,384,500	11,103,500
1861	60,000				60,000	120,732	171,260	365,280	582,210	1,042,650	2,648,700	3,982,662
1873	575,000					575,000	971,451	1,739,720	2,772,849	4,965,752	12,614,751	18,968,180
1879	250,000						250,000	533,200	1,205,600	2,157,200	3,866,500	5,664,000
1892	1,500,000							1,500,000	2,390,872	4,281,508	10,876,537	16,354,291
1900	1,000,000								1,000,000	1,790,848	4,549,383	6,840,590
1910	1,500,000									1,500,000	3,810,528	5,195,304
1920	2,000,000										2,837,000	4,265,856
1926	5,000,000										5,000,000	7,518,150
1933	2,000,000											2,000,000

longer any population cone, for as one goes northward along the lake the population density does not show a downward slope. This is demonstrated again by Figure 84, which shows how the population curve drawn through the area extending north and south for a mile east of Ashland Avenue had flattened out by 1930. This great shift of population from close proximity to the center of the city to new districts on what had once been the outer edges of Chicago was made possible by the elevated lines, the automobile, and the telephone, which quickened the speed of transportation and communication. The attractions of

TABLE XLVIII

THE RISE IN CHICAGO LAND VALUES COMPARED WITH THE GROWTH OF LAND VALUES AT 6 PER CENT COMPOUND INTEREST

(Per Cent of Sales Value at Respective Periods of Original Investment Was Put on Compound Interest at 6 Per Cent)

Year	Original Amount (Thousands)	1836	1841	1856	1861	1873	1879	1892	1900	1910	1920	1926	1933
1830	$ 160	2.27	21.7	0.58	1.7	0.34	1.1	0.32	0.94	1.1	1.5	0.86	3.2
1836	10,000	100.0	947.0	24.8	70.0	14.0	48.8	17.4	41.6	53.3	66.7	38.0	142.4
1841	1,400		100.0	2.7	7.5	1.5	5.1	1.9	4.4	5.2	3.9	4.0	15.1
1856	125,000			100.0	280.0	58.5	191.0	67.9	162.3	190.0	260.0	148.0	555.2
1861	60,000				100.0	21.0	68.5	24.4	58.2	74.4	93.3	53.0	199.1
1873	575,000					100.0	388.6	116.0	277.3	355.0	313.5	252.3	948.4
1879	250,000						100.0	35.6	120.6	154.0	136.2	77.3	283.2
1892	1,500,000							100.0	239.0	305.0	383.0	217.5	817.7
1900	1,000,000								100.0	128.0	160.4	90.6	342.0
1910	1,500,000									100.0	100.0	76.2	255.0
1920	2,000,000										100.0	56.7	213.3
1926	5,000,000											100.0	375.9
1933	2,000,000												100.0

modern buildings and of motion-picture places, banks, and chain stores in these newly settled communities were the centrifugal forces that whirled people from their old abodes into the new bright-light areas. In their wake, between the Loop and the new sections were left the "blighted areas."

The difference in land values between these old and new areas is not measured by the number of people alone, for the races, nationalities, and classes dwelling in these "blighted areas" are the lowest in the social and economic scale. As people are not concentrated in large tenements in these poor areas, but are thinly spread over these districts in single-family dwellings or small apartment buildings, their low individual purchasing power is not overcome by their aggregate mass. Consequently, a low level of rents and a high percentage of loss in collecting that small amount, a heavy rate of physical deterioration of property caused by waste, neglect, and acts of vandalism, reduce land values in these sections occupied by "hobos," seasonal workers, and criminals of

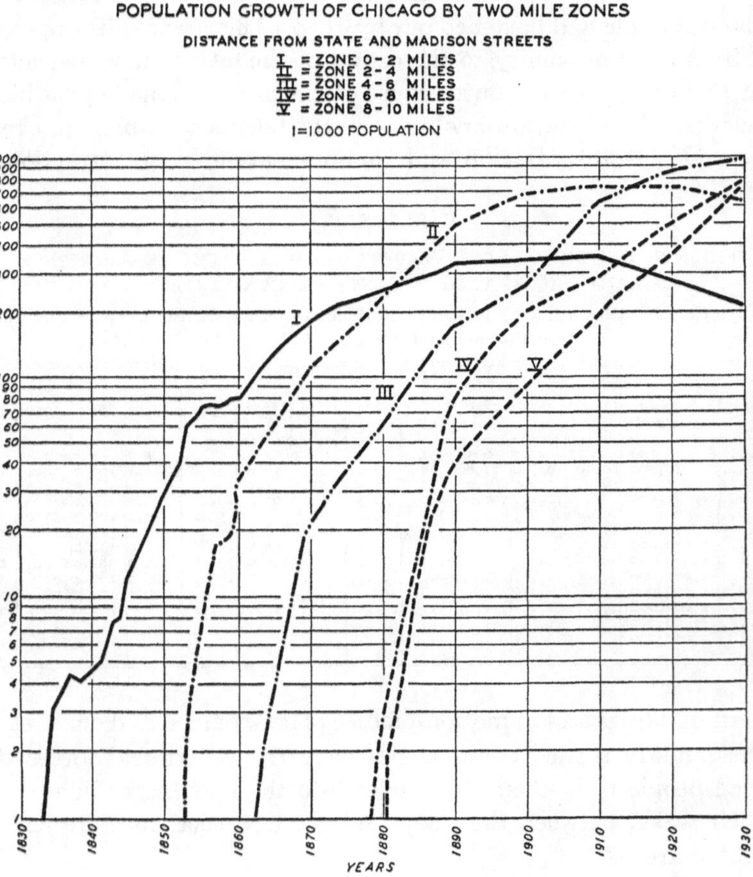

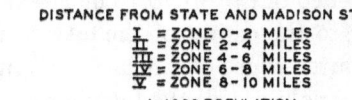

FIG. 81

native American stock and by the lowest classes of Mexicans, negroes, and South Italians to a very low point.[49] There is now a valley in the land-value curve between the Loop and the outer residential areas that indicates the location of these sections where the buildings are mostly

[49] See Fig. 86.

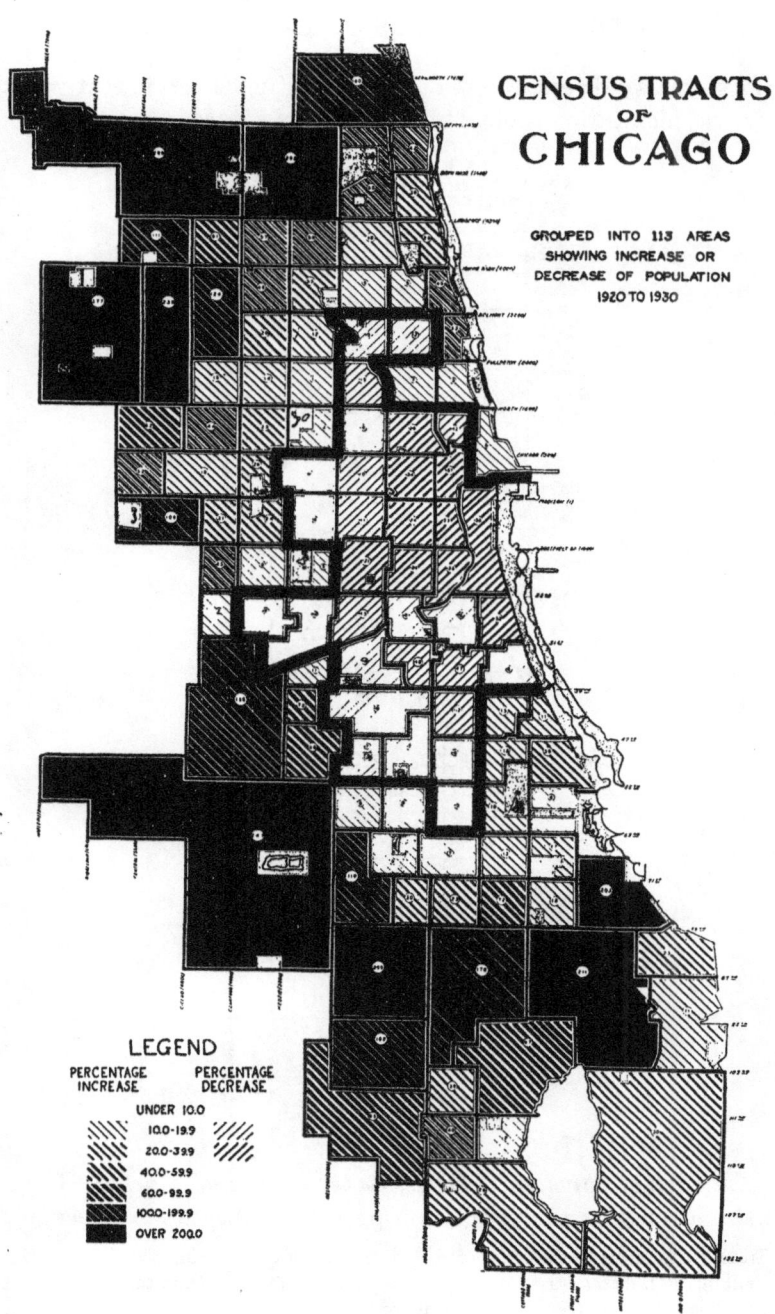

FIG. 82.—Area inclosed by broad black band is the territory in which the population declined from 1920 to 1930.

over forty years old[50] and where the residents rank lowest in rent-paying ability and highest in criminal activity.[51]

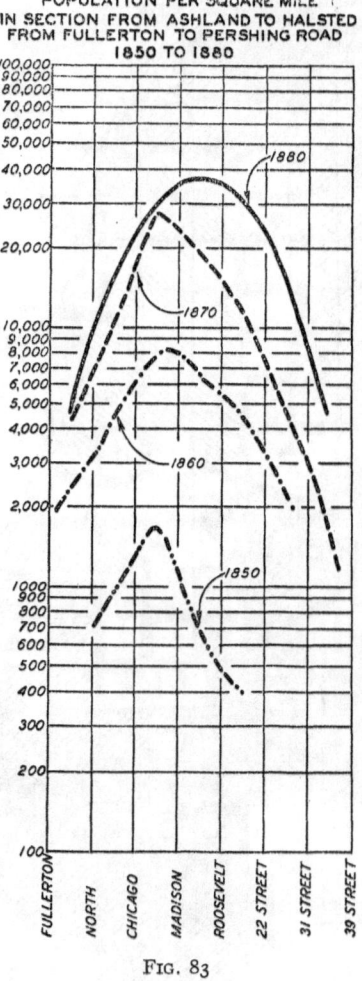

FIG. 83

2. *The effect of population changes on the land-value pattern.*—The remarkable change in the population pattern of the city between 1920

[50] From a large map in the office of the Chicago Plan Commission showing the age of every building in the area from Belmont to Sixty-third Street and from the lake to Kedzie Avenue. This study was based on the Sanborn insurance atlases.

[51] Clifford R. Shaw, *Delinquency Areas* (Chicago: University of Chicago Press, 1929).

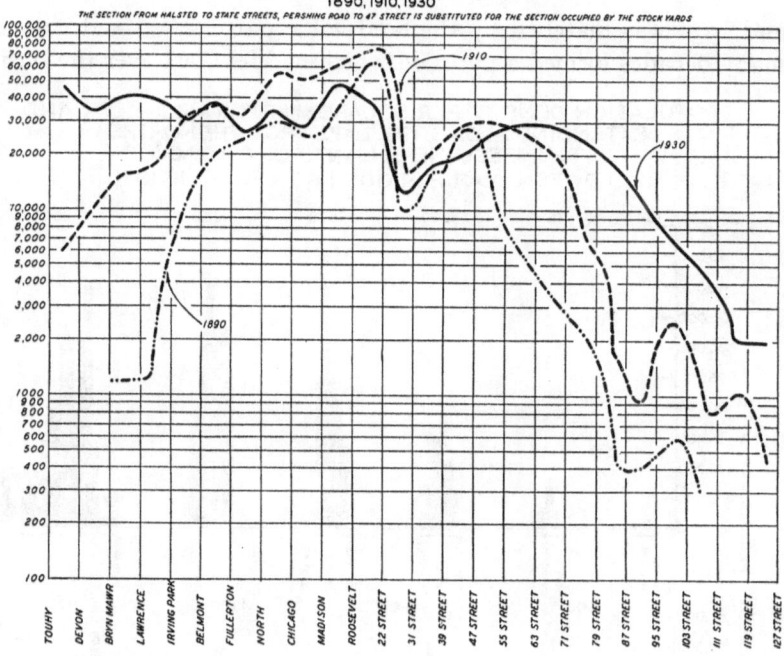

Fig. 84

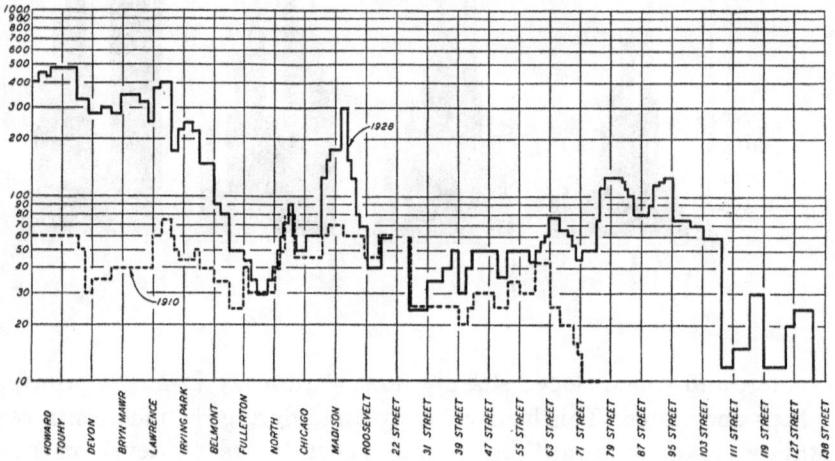

Fig. 85

and 1930 was matched by the land-value pattern.[52] Land values for many decades formed a pyramid which had its apex over the business

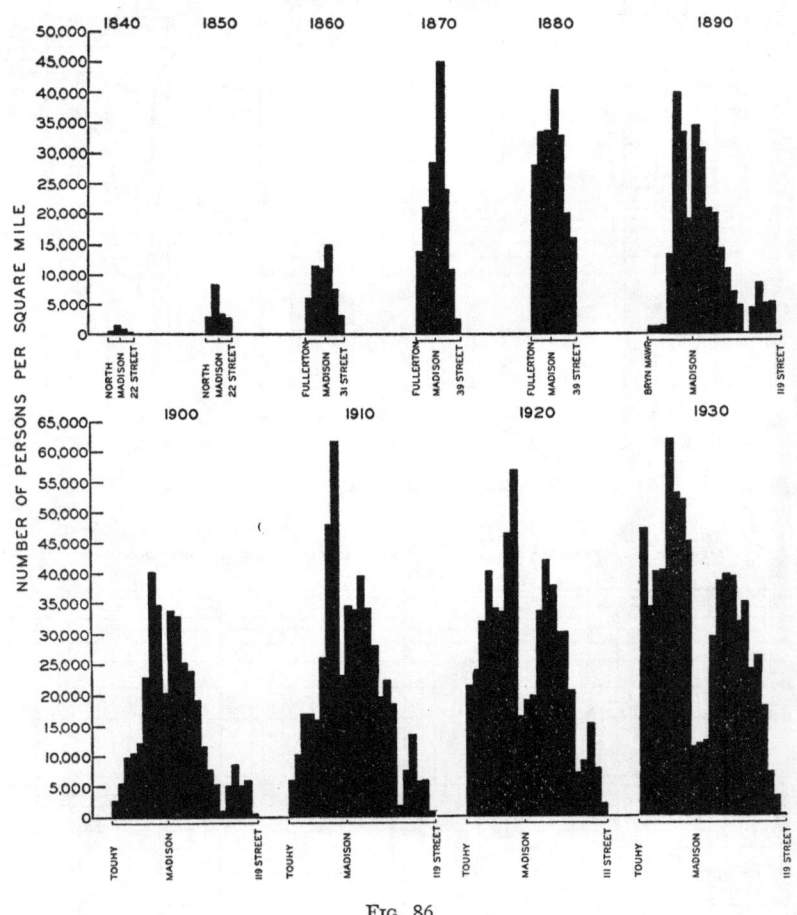

Fig. 86

center, and which sloped sharply downward away from the principal shops and stores. This land-value pyramid during the nineteenth century was skewed toward the south to reflect the greater development of

[52] See Fig. 87.

that side of the city, but since 1900 it has become skewed to a far greater degree toward the north. Even more startling than the shift from south to north was the raising of a great plateau northward to correspond with that of population, and the disappearance of the pyramid pattern of land values.[53] The uplifting of land values in the outlying sections until they were equal to or greater than the values of sections near the Loop was the consequence of the rise in land values of the

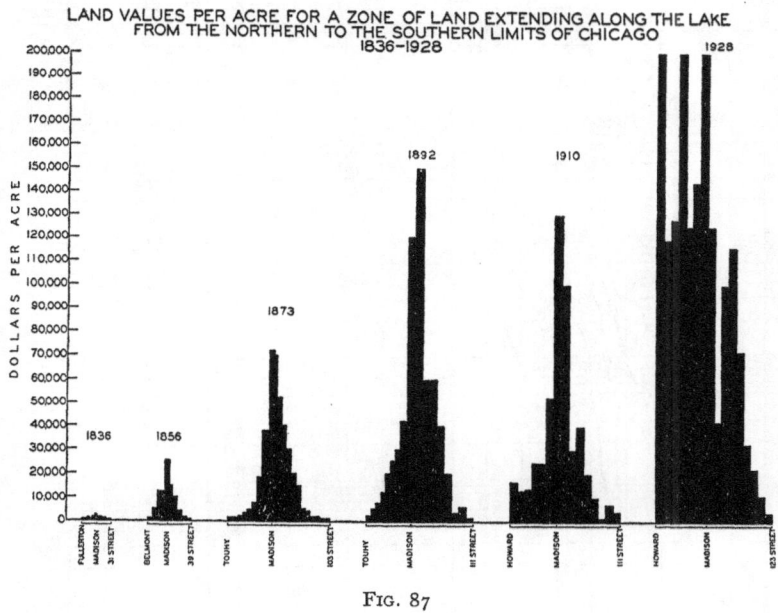

FIG. 87

"outer city" or the area north of Belmont Avenue, west of Kedzie Avenue, and south of Thirty-ninth Street at a much more rapid rate than that of the "inner city."[54]

3. *The difficulty of developing new areas compared with the difficulty of reclaiming "blighted areas."*—The change in the pattern of the distribu-

[53] Land values for the area extending north and south along the lake shore omitting the Loop. From Kinzie Street to Roosevelt Road, the area west of the south branch of the Chicago River to Halsted Street was taken. Loop land values were omitted because they bear no relationship to the population residing in the Loop, and because they are too great in magnitude to be shown on the same scale in the later years. Loop land values would rise like a flagpole in the center of each of the pyramids in Fig. 87.

[54] See Figs. 88 and 89; also Fig. 45 on p. 263.

tion of population and of land values within Chicago during the last few decades indicates that the friction imposed by transportation to an expanding population was less than that of obsolete improvements and diversified ownership. There being no physical barriers to the expansion of Chicago save that imposed by the lake on the east, it was easier

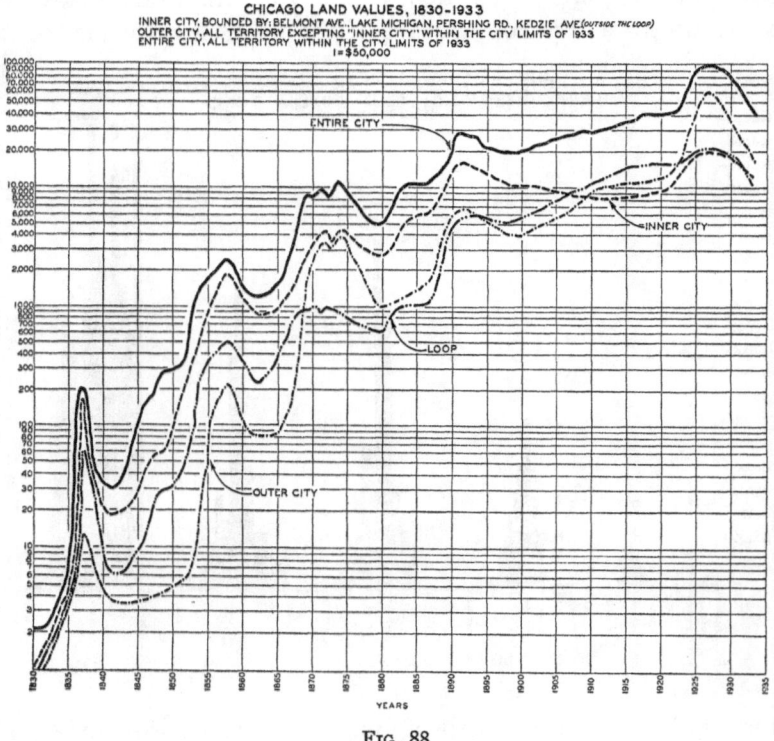

Fig. 88

in most cases to build new communities on tracts of virgin prairie by electric elevated or surface lines, or by automobile or by electrified railroad, than it was to remake an old settled area and to give it a new character. That a renaissance of old areas is not impossible, however, is indicated by the transformation of the near North Side after 1920, but there the creation of a new double-decked street, which became the busiest auto highway in Chicago, the proximity of this section not only to the Loop but to the lake shore and the Lake Shore Drive, combined to give this area advantages which most other old sections did not possess. The once fashionable area of the near South Side near the lake shore may be redeemed, for the strip of land east of Cottage Grove Avenue from Twenty-second Street to Thirty-ninth Street has many advantages, with both the lake and the Illinois Central suburban trans-

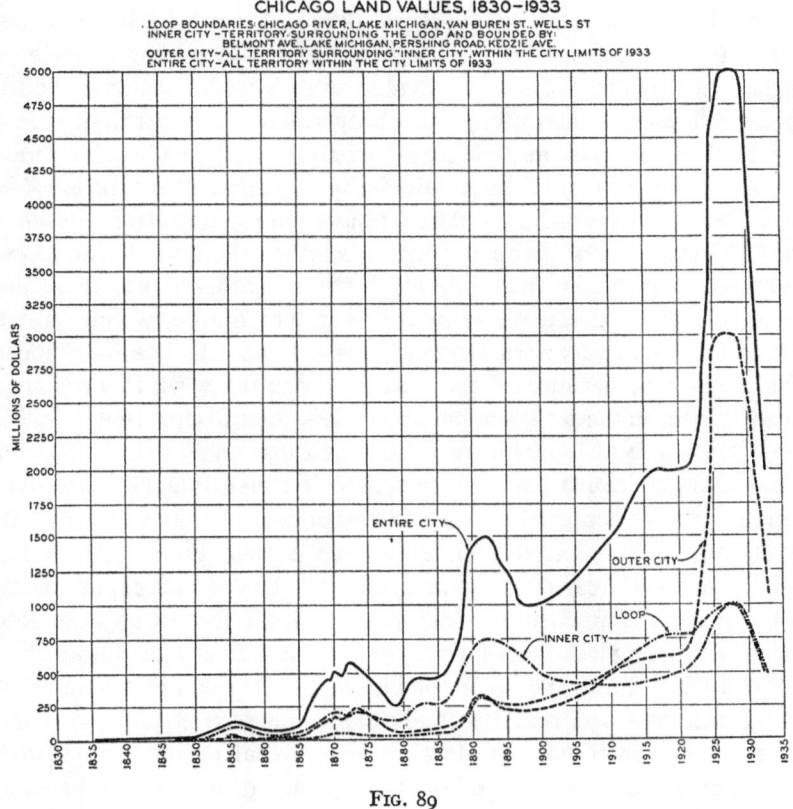

Fig. 89

portation close at hand. There are large sections near the packing plants on the South Side, west of Wells Street on the North Side, and south of Harrison Street on the near West Side that seem to offer few attractions for residential development, unless reclamation of the blighted areas is to be attempted on a grand scale. In the early twentieth century, when wholesale houses and manufacturing plants were expanding in the vicinity of the Loop, it seemed possible that much of this area would be absorbed for industrial uses, but in view of the tendency of factories to move farther out to locations along belt lines, it now seems to be the consensus of opinion that most of this low-grade residential area has little chance of being converted into a higher-value industrial use.[55]

4. *The effect of shifting land uses.*—The land values in different sections of the city have followed several different trends. The areas developed for workingmen's homes that were close to the central business district later acquired a high land value as sites for banks, office buildings, warehouses, or factories. The cheap residential sites that were a little farther away, as at Bridgeport or that were on Grand Avenue west of Halsted Street, never acquired any higher value except in a few cases. Land values in those old areas have tended to flatten out since 1890.[56] This tendency became pronounced when the Loop began to expand vertically rather than laterally. On the other hand, there are fashionable districts like those in the near North Side, which after a period of brilliance as sites for mansions decline into boarding-house areas, and then, because of the natural advantages which originally favored them, make a "come-back" as sites for tall apartment buildings. Other once-fashionable areas such as those on Prairie Avenue or on Ashland Boulevard partially regain their former values when they become partially occupied with industrial or commercial buildings, but they never attain their former land-value peaks. Finally, there are newly developed areas on the outskirts of the city, which remained almost entirely vacant until the last few decades, but whose values rose in each succeeding land boom, until they reached their apex for all time prior to 1929.[57] From the foregoing discussion, it becomes evident that it is difficult to assert that the land-value cycle of a given section follows a definite pattern. In general, a section that becomes filled with cottages or bungalows has reached the "ceiling" or limit of its development, as it is easier to move to a new, unoccupied area than it is to wreck the existing structures. Land values in such a section will tend to decline as the buildings grow older and the original community migrates or is replaced by a lower economic or social class. Areas in specially advantageous locations such as along the lake shore, however,

---

[55] Clifford Bechtel, chairman of the Committee of the Chicago Real Estate Board, working on the problem of the blighted area, has expressed this opinion in public addresses.

[56] See Fig. 59 on p. 318.

[57] See Fig. 54 on p. 306.

that were first developed as home sections later acquired high land values as sites for kitchenette-apartment buildings.

5. *Speculative exaggeration of possible demand for certain types of uses.*
—In each successive land boom there is a speculative exaggeration of the trend of the period, until an inevitable reaction follows. In 1836 there was overspeculation in land fronting on rivers and lakes; in 1856 excessive emphasis was placed on lots for cheap homes; in 1873 there was an inflation in the amount and the ground values of land suitable for mansions and suburban residences; in 1890 wild-cat speculation prevailed in projected manufacturing townsites or in lots along proposed elevated routes or near the World's Fair; and in the boom prior to 1929 there was an unprecedented rise in the values of apartment-building land and of outlying business sites. The movement of population outward from the center of the city produced even greater changes in speculative land values than the situation warranted, so that even if the migration of people toward the suburbs continues in the future, it can hardly exceed the expectations of 1926. On the other hand, the proposals to reclaim the blighted areas set up the prospect of a possible reversal of the movement away from the center in favor of living within walking distance of the Loop.

6. *The future trend of population and land values.*—The future population and land-value patterns of Chicago depend upon a sequence of factors. If the population of the entire United States, with immigration curtailed and birth-control practices on the increase, reaches a static equilibrium of 155,000,000 by 1955 and then begins to decline, as Professor William F. Ogburn suggests,[58] the rate of growth of Chicago in the nineteenth and early twentieth centuries which was supported by heavy immigration from abroad as well as by the natural increase of the resident population can hardly be maintained. If the proportion of people dwelling in cities diminishes instead of increasing as it has in the past century, the possibilities for the further rapid growth of Chicago will likewise be limited. It will finally also be a question of what proportion of all the urban residents in the United States the industries located in Chicago can attract and support in competition with the producing concerns in other cities. In the past century Chicago, by its favorable situation, has been able to attract industries that could draw to the city and support a rapidly growing population that increased

[58] Lecture delivered at the University of Chicago in 1933.

faster than the urban population of the nation as a whole, which in turn was increasing much faster than the number of people in the entire United States, which aggregate population in turn was growing faster than that of most of the older countries of Europe. From 1830 to 1930 the growth of Chicago was helped by the strong current of population increase for the United States and for American industrial and trading cities, but if this current slackens or reverses itself, it is hard to believe that Chicago will make as rapid progress against this current as it did with it. This is of course to a large extent speculative.

Moreover, if a changed national policy should open the doors to another tide of European immigration, and if the demand for increasing manpower to defend the nation from foreign aggression, added to the condemnation of birth control by some of the churches, leads again to the rearing of large families, then the population of the United States may continue to grow until it reaches a total of 200,000,000 or more. Again, it is possible that, without any such rate of increase in the number of people in the country, sensational gains in the amount of crops harvested per acre may reduce still further the number of persons required to till the soil, and will enable an even greater proportion of the population to live in the cities. Chicago itself may continue its remarkable growth, even if other urban centers decline. New and startling inventions such as occurred during the first hundred years of Chicago's development may continue during the second century of its history, and these may bring about in the Chicago region the greatest concentration of people the world has ever known. Finally, the shift in emphasis from heavy manufacturing industry to trade, finance, and professional service may well redound to the advantage of Chicago, whose location as a site for a trading and financial metropolis is unsurpassed.

If the aggregate population of Chicago be determined as a result of the foregoing factors, the distribution of that population within the city's metropolitan area will depend upon the strength of the desire to live in the suburbs or in new neighborhoods far from the Loop, compared to the intensity of the demand for residences in apartments near the business center in reclaimed blighted areas. The effect of the population distribution upon land values will likewise depend upon whether people prefer to live in small homes or in large apartment buildings, which will depend in turn upon the size of the average family and upon social habits and customs. The effect of the population upon land values will likewise depend upon the distribution of purchasing power between the members of that population and the proportion of their income that is available for rent. While an expanding population is compelled to pay for the added quarters, rents high enough at the outset to pay operating expenses, and a normal return on building costs, a stationary or declining population might not find it necessary to maintain such charges on existing buildings. Rents might then be determined as they are in depression periods by the amount of money available for rent payments after food requirements were met.

Land values will likewise be affected in the future by the aggregate amount of the tax burden and by the proportion of it that is levied on real estate and by the rate of interest on real estate mortgages and the rate for capitalizing net rents. Such factors will affect the long-run trend of land values as measured in dollars of constant purchasing power.

It is obvious from the preceding discussion, however, that land values in terms of market prices rise far above the capitalized long-term net-income value in a boom and fall below it in a depression. A land-value forecaster would have to determine not only the future trends of population, rents, operating expenses, taxes, and capitalization rates, but he would have to estimate to what extent these movements will be exaggerated by speculative manias or be underrated in the period when foreclosures of trust deeds are at their peak. Finally, an estimate must be made for changes in the purchasing power of the dollar, particularly when rapid changes in the gold value of the dollar are imminent.

In view of the complex nature of the foregoing factors, and the almost unlimited number of combinations of ways in which they could interact upon each other, it would be foolhardy, indeed, to predict the future aggregate trend of Chicago land values. If, as asserted by students of the population problem,[59] the trends of growth of the past century are not likely to be repeated, then it seems probable that the land-value curve of Chicago of the past century will not be duplicated.

[59] R. K. Whelpton, *American Journal of Sociology*, May, 1933, pp. 825–34.

CHAPTER VII

THE CHICAGO REAL ESTATE CYCLE

A. THE TIDE OF POPULATION

The causes of land booms in American urban sites in the past century could usually be traced to factors which led speculators to expect an extraordinary increase in the population of the locality within a relatively short time, or the expectation of its development for commercial and industrial purposes. The anticipated population growth was itself due to deep-seated forces, operating over the entire area of Western industrial civilization. There was a rapid growth of the population of all of the leading nations of Europe and America by natural increase that was made possible by the new machine technique and the opening of new continents to settlement. In addition, there was a great westward migration of people from Europe to America, and from the eastern to the western part of the United States. The individual components of this human tide were attracted by the lure of cheap land and were carried to these hitherto sparsely settled regions by the new steam transportation. This great population stream, consisting largely of young people with high potential powers of natural increase, spread out over the land or collected in pools at certain strategic spots as it flowed westward. The number of persons which any one townsite could attract from this current of people and hold for itself depended upon its natural advantages for trade, commerce, and manufactures. Therefore the particular factors contributing to the mercantile, financial, and industrial growth of Chicago that were described in the first five chapters of this work are of fundamental importance in explaining why so many people settled there. So necessary to the population growth of an urban center is the growth of its factories, transportation lines, banks, wholesale houses, and stores, which in turn depend upon the extent of its trading hinterland and its advantages for manufacturing plants, that land speculators seldom fail to stress these factors in describing the possibilities of further growth and the rise of land values of any city.

The expectations of the population growth of American townsites in the nineteenth and early twentieth centuries were thus partly based on a great actual movement of people and the rapid growth of the cities in the territories first occupied. During periods of optimism throughout the United States, as in 1836 and in 1925 and 1926, or in particular sections of the nation as in the North following the Civil War or in the Middle West in the fifties and late eighties, the possibility of population growth was magnified to undue proportions. More townsites were laid out in Illinois in 1836 than could be filled even by the present population, and within the vicinity of Chicago itself more lots were subdivided in each successive boom than were needed for several generations to come.

Therefore, there is no exact relationship between the increase in the number of people at an urban site and the increase of land values, because speculative influences may magnify the expected future increase beyond all reasonable possibilities. Nevertheless, land booms in Chicago have generally been sustained and carried to their peaks partly by a sudden and extraordinary rate of increase in actual population growth which persisted for a few years,[1] helped to foment speculative excitement, and led to even more extravagant hopes for future population increase. This increase in the rate of population growth was one of the factors that led to an increase in rents, building activity, and subdivision activity, each of which in turn was carried to speculative excess, and each of which interacted upon the other and upon land values to generate and maintain the boom psychology. There is thus a chain of events communicating with each other which quickened or retarded the pace of all the activities connected with real estate. The description of the sequence of certain of these phenomena, which can be measured, is one of the best ways of defining the Chicago real estate cycle. In the following account it must be constantly borne in mind that the definite quantitative factors are but symbols of the broad range of forces discussed in detail in Part I.

B. DEFINITION OF THE CHICAGO REAL ESTATE CYCLE

The Chicago real estate cycle is a term used here to describe the composite effect of the cyclical movements of a series of forces that are to a certain degree independent and yet which communicate impulses to each other in a time sequence, so that when the initial or primary factor appears it tends to set the others in motion in a definite order. Accord-

[1] See Figs. 90 and 91.

THE CHICAGO REAL ESTATE CYCLE

FLUCTUATIONS OF PER CAPITA LAND VALUES, PER CAPITA ANNUAL NEW CONSTRUCTION COST AND ANNUAL POPULATION INCREASE ABOVE AND BELOW THE AVERAGE FIGURES FOR THE CYCLE PERIOD

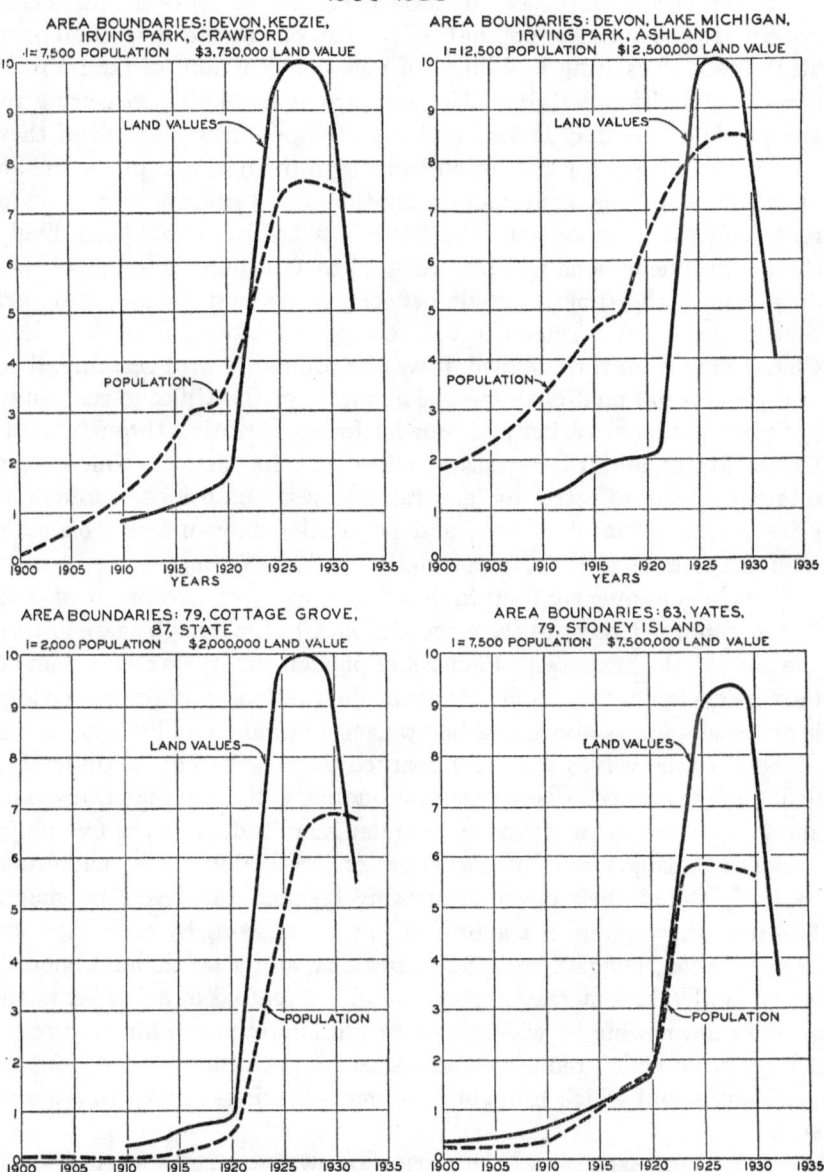

Fig. 91

ing to the view here presented, these cycles in the order in which they appear are the cycles of population growth, of the rent levels and operating costs of existing buildings, of new construction, of land values, and of subdivision activity. The data are available for measuring the amplitude of the fluctuations and the time periodicity for all of these factors in Chicago for the period from 1830 to 1933, except for the annual volume of new construction for the period prior to 1854 and for rents and the costs of operating buildings before 1900. Accordingly, these local phenomena will be measured to ascertain the range of their fluctuations, the time intervals between peaks and valleys, and their time sequence with reference to each other. After the local cycle in Chicago has been thus defined, it will be compared with certain indices of a general national character. The forces of the Chicago real estate cycle are but local variants of broader forces operating throughout the United States, and it is necessary to keep in mind that the Chicago real estate cycle is affected by general business conditions, commodity price levels, value of money, and population movements within the United States as well as by peculiarly local conditions.

A cycle is frequently used to describe a wavelike movement of some factor from the trough to the crest and back to the trough again or from one crest to the next crest. Each set of phenomena by its own action defines its cycle, for the amplitude of the fluctuations of different economic and social forces above and below their normal trend line and the interval between waves vary to a marked degree. It may be difficult to define a cycle in the case of those economic activities that trace short and choppy waves or waves of irregular amplitude, but the five major cycles of Chicago real estate, which were like tidal waves in magnitude, have registered their effect in striking fashion. All five movements, Figure 90 shows, were characterized on their upswing by rapid increases in population, feverish building operations, and a hectic land boom in which land values increased from twofold to tenfold in a few years and on their downswing by widespread declines in rents and foreclosures on a large scale which reduced land values 50 per cent or more from the peak levels and which brought building operations almost to a standstill.

C. THE EFFECT OF POPULATION GROWTH ON THE CHICAGO REAL ESTATE CYCLE

The explanation of the exceptional spurt in real estate activity that is followed by almost complete stagnation is to be found in the forces

THE CHICAGO REAL ESTATE CYCLE 373

which cause alternately an acceleration and a slackening in the demand for land and buildings. One of the important factors is the change in the rate of population growth. A stationary population would require no additional houses or stores except those needed to replace obsolete or depreciated structures or those destroyed by fire, earthquake, or tornado, or except as changing habits and customs or new inventions gave rise to new types of buildings such as garages. A population increasing at a constant rate with constant per capita residential requirements could keep a building force employed with a fair degree of regu-

TABLE XLIX

PERCENTAGE OF INCREASE IN THE POPULATION OF CHICAGO FOR EQUAL TIME INTERVALS IN BOOMS AND DEPRESSIONS

No. Years	On the Upswing	No. Years	On the Downswing
2, 1833–35	933	2, 1837–39	0.7
2, 1852–54	70		
2, 1854–56	28	2, 1857–59	2
3, 1864–67	37		
3, 1867–70	36	3, 1873–76	7
3, 1870–73	27		
3, 1888–91	24	3, 1894–97	11
6, 1919–25	26	6, 1927–33	No increase*

* According to computations by the writer on the basis of grade-school enrolment. Other estimates, such as by the Chicago Association of Commerce, show an increase in population in this period.

larity in erecting new housing facilities, and the rate of land absorption could be so calculated in advance that the value of potential building sites would increase at the regular rate of a compound-interest table as the time grew near for their utilization.

In the case of Chicago, however, there were sudden changes in population growth that accompanied sudden changes in land values. As Table XLIX shows, the population of Chicago has not increased at an even annual rate.

1. *The initial impulse—a sudden spurt in population growth.*—During the early stages in a revival in general business conditions, exceptional economic opportunities attracted a tide of people to Chicago. Sometimes a barrier has dammed up this flow of human beings, so that it has come in a rushing flood. Thus the Black Hawk War of 1832 kept back

the early settlers, but within a year after the removal of that menace the population of Chicago increased from 200 to 2,000. Again the lack of direct rail connections with the East diverted part of the west-bound migration from Chicago, but within three years, from 1852 to 1855, the population of Chicago had increased from 39,000 to 80,000. The panic of 1857 momentarily checked the population flow, but the industrial expansion of the city during and after the Civil War caused the number of its inhabitants to increase from 120,000 to 380,000 between 1861 and 1873. The panic of 1873 caused a slackening in the rate of increase, but in the decade from 1880 to 1890 the opportunities for employment in Chicago factories and on the expanding railway system enabled the population within the present city limits to grow from 550,000 to 1,-100,000. Finally, after several decades of steady population growth, the outbreak of the World War, calling for enlistment of able-bodied young men in the army and navy, held back the increase of population for a time. The return of the soldiers and sailors to their homes and the migration from the rural centers in response to the industrial attractions of Chicago caused its population to increase from 2,500,000 to 3,400,000 between 1918 and 1927. In each of these five major cycles the sudden increase in population preceded the rapid upturn in new construction and in land values.[2]

2. *The supply of houses cannot be immediately increased.*—The new arrivals in Chicago in these periods required housing facilities. They could not ship their old homes to their new abode as they could transport food and furniture. A mere shift in population from one place to another therefore increases the aggregate demand for new residential buildings, because the vacant space left behind cannot be transferred to the city to which the people are flocking.[3] This unexpected need for more dwelling units cannot be supplied at once, as the time required to select a building site, to examine the title to the ground, to draw plans for the structure, to arrange for financing, to order the materials, and to perform the work of construction from foundation to roof would amount to from six months to a year. As the work must be done out of doors, the loss of time in winter months and on rainy days further

[2] See Fig. 90.

[3] It is true that this increase in the local demand for housing in the localities attracting population is counterbalanced by a falling-off in the demand in the places of origin. Since the vacant space left behind cannot be transferred, there is a net increase in demand for new buildings caused by the shift.

lengthens the process. Thus this sudden increase in the number of people in Chicago, which was greater than anticipated by local builders and for which they were not prepared, put a premium upon quarters that happened to be in existence at the time. As people crowd into all the available space, vacancies virtually disappear and the rents of old buildings rise. The newcomers have to live on the spot in order to share the economic opportunities, and they have either accumulated funds or present employment that affords them the means to pay higher rents.

3. *Qualifications as to the influence of population on the real estate cycle.*—The effect of population growth on land values must not be overemphasized, however. A spurt in the rate of population increase does not of itself always cause a land boom, on the one hand, nor does the lack of such a sudden growth in the number of people in a city prevent a rapid rise in land values. Thus, according to available population data, there was a marked increase in the rate of population growth of Chicago in 1845, 1862, 1897, 1898, 1909, and 1910 without any exceptional rise in land values. On the other hand, while there was a steady growth of the population of the city prior to the land booms culminating in 1873 and in 1892, there was no exceptional flood of people entering the city in any one year.[4]

The effect of population growth upon land values depends partly upon the condition of real estate and of general business at the particular time. Speculators may anticipate a growth of population that has not yet taken place, or after population has increased rapidly for a number of years they may suddenly awake to the realization of what has occurred. If a manufacturing concern announces that it will erect a large plant in some sparsely settled region, there will often be a land boom before any of the expected workers arrive on the scene. Conversely, a large number of people entering the city during a depression when there is a large supply of vacant houses and when the resident population is painfully aware of the collapse of the last land boom will not have the same apparent effect upon rents and land values as in an influx of people coming in a period of expanding business and of general optimism. The coming of these people into the city at such times may, however, prevent rents and land values from falling still further.

Not only is there no exact relationship between the population

[4] See Table XCIII in Appendix III.

growth of Chicago and the rise in its land values that have been influenced by speculative moods, but there is no perfect correlation between a mere increase, or lack of increase, in the number of people and the gross and net rents that determine the investment value of land over long periods of time. For, on the one hand, there may be a rise in rents without any sudden increase in the rate of population growth, if new construction activities have been suspended for some time. On the return of prosperity giving employment to more people at higher wages, a population that has "doubled up" may spread out and create a demand for more residential units. Or as the standard of living rises in either short or long periods, a stationary population might vacate old or obsolete houses, leaving them empty, and move into new buildings with all modern improvements, thereby causing a rise in rents for structures of the improved type. The demand for more housing space may be caused likewise by a sudden increase in the marriage rate, resulting in the establishment of more new households for the time being than old households that were dissolved by death or other causes.

Thus a demand for more building space may spring up from a stationary or slowly expanding population, so that a sudden spurt in population growth is not indispensable to a rise in rents. On the other hand, a rapid increase in population, if it consists of a class of people with low earning power or low standards of living, may not lead to an increase either in rents or in speculative values. Immigrants may crowd closely together in poor quarters without raising the rent level of their own area, and the influx of negroes into a district in Chicago usually causes its property values to decline.

a) Limitations of the population and land-value data.—There is further need for caution in dealing with the relationship of population to land values because of the fact that both land-value data and the annual figures for population are only approximations at best. The various methods of computing the population for intercensus years do not produce the same results, and in the past the results obtained in the school census varied widely from the United States Census returns. Because of the rapid rate of growth of Chicago, more annual census data were taken by city, state, and school authorities than in most other communities; but the fact that the early population estimates between census years were made by different organizations, probably using different methods, subject to varying margins of error, prevents their use for purposes re-

THE CHICAGO REAL ESTATE CYCLE

quiring superfine accuracy. Accordingly, the figures of annual population have been used in this study only to show broad and striking conclusions that would not be affected materially, even if there was a considerable margin of error in the figures.

Finally, even if the annual increments of population could be measured exactly, that would merely register the effect of the manufacturing

TABLE L

RENTS OF WORKINGMEN'S DWELLINGS AND
OFFICE BUILDINGS IN CHICAGO
Relative Numbers (1915 = 100)

Year	Office Buildings*	Dwellings†
1915	100	100.0
1916	101	99.9
1917	102	100.7
1918	104	101.4
1919	108	108.0
1920	126	135.1
1921	149	178.2
1922	167	187.4
1923	176	192.1
1924	183	204.4
1925	183	205.6
1926	186	199.5
1927	188	193.9
1928	190	186.8
1929	180	180.3
1930	174	175.1
1931	163	164.4
1932	....	138.8
1933	....	108.7

* Earle Shultz, "What of the Future?" *Proceedings of the 24th Annual Convention of the National Association of Building Owners and Managers* (1931), pp. 523–24. The base was changed by the writer from 1910 to 1915. Average rents for ten Chicago Office buildings.

† U.S. Department of Labor, *Retail Prices and Cost of Living* (December, 1932), p. 16; *Monthly Labor Review*, XXIX, No. 2 (August, 1929), p. 20. Figures are for June of each year from 1919 to 1933, inclusive, except for 1921, when the figure is for May. The figures for 1915–18, inclusive, are averages of figures for December of the year preceding and following.

and commercial opportunities of Chicago that made it possible to support that many people on its site. As already pointed out, population itself is not a final cause, but a symbol, for a complex combination of other forces.

D. THE SEQUENCE OF EVENTS IN THE CHICAGO REAL ESTATE CYCLE

With these various qualifications as to the use of annual population data, Figure 90 tends to show that the land booms in Chicago were preceded by a spurt followed by a slackening in the rate of population growth and Table LI presents evidence for the last cycle tending to indicate that the increase in this population growth was one of the factors leading to a rapid rise in rents.

1. *Gross rents begin to rise rapidly.*—It will be noted from Table XLIV that notwithstanding the rise in commodity prices of 100 per

TABLE LI

RATE OF POPULATION INCREASE AND RATE OF INCREASE IN RENTS OF OFFICE BUILDINGS AND WORKINGMEN'S DWELLINGS IN CHICAGO, 1915–33

YEAR	TOTAL POPULATION*	PERCENTAGE INCREASE OVER PRECEDING YEAR		
		Population	Office Rents†	House Rents†
1915	2,448,426	....	....	....
1916	2,492,204	1.8	1.0	0.0
1917	2,492,200	0.0	1.0	0.7
1918	2,546,144	2.2	2.0	0.7
1919	2,599,502	2.1	4.0	6.5
1920	2,701,705	3.9	16.7	26.4
1921	2,820,992	4.4	18.3	31.9
1922	2,901,507	2.9	12.1	4.2
1923	3,010,850	3.8	5.4	2.5
1924	3,155,843	4.8	4.0	6.4
1925	3,263,196	3.4	0.0	0.6
1926	3,296,679	1.0	1.7	3.0‡
1927	3,402,296	3.2	1.1	3.3‡
1928	3,397,067	0.1‡	1.1	3.7‡
1929	3,372,936	0.7‡	5.3‡	3.5‡
1930	3,376,438	0.1	3.3‡	3.3‡
1931	3,341,913	1.0‡	6.3‡	6.1‡
1932	3,236,913	2.9‡	....	15.6‡
1933	....	....	....	21.7‡

* Computed by the writer from the enrolment in the Chicago grade schools.
† See Table XLIV.   ‡ Percentage decrease.

cent from 1916 to 1919 (see Fig. 100 on p. 412), Chicago office rents had advanced but 7 per cent and dwelling rents but 8 per cent in that period. It is significant to note that the rents began to advance more rapidly at the very time that the rate of population growth increased.[5]

2. *Net rents rise even more rapidly.*—Thus as a result of, or coincident with, the rapid increase in the rate of population growth of Chicago from 1918 to 1921, gross dwelling and office rents rose sharply. Since interest on mortgages is fixed for several years in advance and since the

[5] See Table LI.

expenses of operating buildings contain many items that are slow to advance, the net income remaining to holders of equities in improved real estate increases even faster, as Figures 34 and 35[6] on pages 239 and 240 and Table LII show.

Thus while office rents increased 90 per cent from 1918 to 1926, operating expenses rose but 31 per cent, so that net income advanced 300

TABLE LII*

GROSS INCOME, TOTAL EXPENSE (INCLUDING TAXES AND DEPRECIATION), AND NET INCOME OF A CHICAGO OFFICE BUILDING, 1918–32

YEAR	ABSOLUTE AMOUNTS			RELATIVE NUMBERS 1918=100		
	Gross Income	Operating Expenses, Taxes, and Depreciation	Net Income	Gross Income	Operating Expenses	Net Income
1918	$387,375	$304,075	$ 83,299	100	100	100
1919	390,446	289,848	100,598	101	95	121
1920	410,803	322,062	88,740	106	106	107
1921	478,206	356,559	121,647	123	117	146
1922	529,818	365,724	164,093	137	120	197
1923	609,840	392,123	217,817	157	129	261
1924	627,126	386,435	240,691	162	127	289
1925	688,082	400,505	287,577	178	132	345
1926	734,234	399,699	334,535	189	131	402
1927	754,655	474,455	280,211	195	156	336
1928	764,022	448,822	315,199	197	148	378
1929	757,400	417,418	339,982	195	137	408
1930	728,656	426,394	302,262	190	140	364
1931	675,218	422,976	252,243	174	139	328
1932	564,504	482,700	81,804	146	159	98

* John P. Hooker, "Financial History of a Chicago Property," *Journal of the American Institute of Real Estate Appraisers*, July, 1933, p. 347. Relative numbers computed by the writer.

per cent. The same situation prevailed in apartment buildings, even of the "walk-up" variety, because expenses for heat, janitor service, decorating, etc., which form a considerable proposition of the gross rent, do not rise as fast as the increase in rents, as Figure 92 shows. In the case of kitchenette-apartment buildings, where charges for elevator service, the use of furniture and linen, free gas and electricity, and maid service are included in the gross rent, the increase in net incomes was even greater than in the case of the ordinary unfurnished-apartment buildings.

[6] See above, p. 239–40.

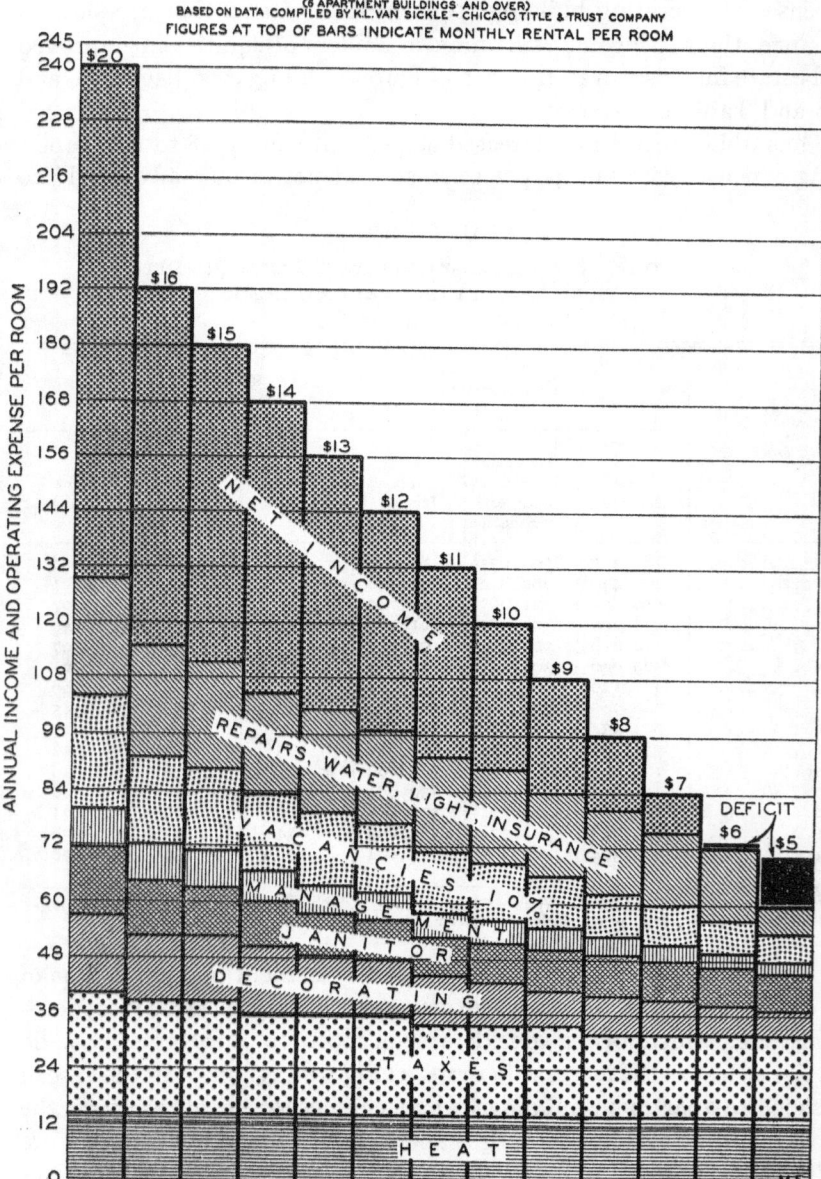

Fig. 92

3. *As a result of the rise in rents, selling prices of existing buildings advance sharply.*—The great bulge in the profits to be derived from the ownership of old buildings would naturally cause their selling price to advance unless there was a prospect for the curtailment of this gain by the supply of new buildings which contractors would hasten to construct to take advantage of this opportunity. It so happened, however, that prior to the Chicago land booms culminating in 1836, 1856, 1873, and 1926 there had been a rise in wholesale prices in the United States. Even though the general level of commodity prices had fallen after the Civil War and the World War, within five years after both of these wars the money wages of unskilled labor were double the pre-war figures.[7] Nearly half of the cost of erecting a building consists of wage payments, and a large part of the cost of manufacturing brick out of clay, of making cement out of rock, and of sawing lumber out of trees in a forest is made up of labor outlays.[8] Therefore, building costs tend to rise with wages and to hold the increase, even after the wholesale prices of commodities have declined. From 1914 to 1920 Chicago building costs, according to the Holabird and Root Index, advanced 60 per cent, and even after a sharp decline from 1920 to 1922, they remained 30 per cent above the pre-war level.[9] Thus notwithstanding rising rents, building contractors find that they cannot erect new buildings on the same cost level as those already in existence, and, fearful of the stability of the higher-cost building level, they hesitate to make the long-term commitments involved in the erection of a building. Old buildings are consequently worth more not only because of their higher net incomes, but because of the higher reproduction costs which prevent this income from being reduced by an increase of the supply of buildings at the old cost level. The first phase of activity in the real estate market is thus the sale of improved properties at advancing prices due to the capitalization of their higher net incomes. This feature of the Chicago market

[7] Fig. 98.

[8] *National Association of Building Trades Employers Bulletin*, March, April, May, 1933, p. 2: "The chart of the American Construction Council indicates that 76.17 per cent of the construction dollar goes into the workingmen's pockets. This labor hire is divided as follows: at site, 44.36 per cent; shop, mill, dealer, 20.69 per cent; at source, 7.33 per cent; transportation, 4.09 per cent."

[9] From an unpublished index of building costs in Chicago prepared by Holabird and Root for the type of buildings constructed by them. It covers the period 1888–1932 and has costs for the year 1888 as the base.

began in early stages of the major cycles, or in 1832, 1848, 1863, 1887, and 1920, and continued until the culmination of the boom.

4. *It pays to erect new buildings.*—The rise in gross and net building rents continues under the pressure of the rapidly expanding population

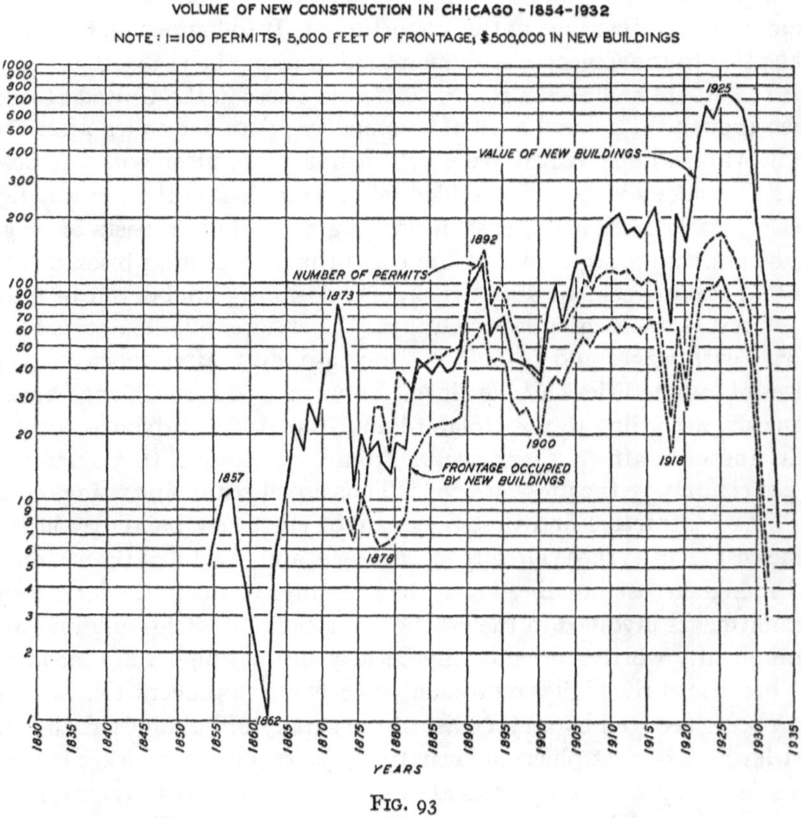

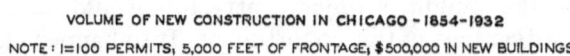

Fig. 93

until it becomes profitable to erect new buildings. The first step in speculative building is the acquisition of a site, so that during or even before the building boom gets under way there is a rise in the volume of vacant lot purchases and in the number of lots subdivided. Notwithstanding the higher production costs of new structures, which may be partially offset by the increased use of machinery or labor-saving devices, the first crop of new buildings proves to be very profitable for the following reasons: Because they are new, because they are in the latest architectural style, because they are in new neighborhoods, and because they contain the most modern conveniences of the time, these new quarters command higher rents than do old buildings. Furthermore, as the new buildings are adjusted to the prevailing size of family or type of use, there is less waste space and a larger proportion of net rentable area so that the returns per cubic foot of building space are even greater. Economy in the use of land may also be secured by those who first erect skyscraper or tall buildings in an area as they pay a price for the ground on the basis of its use for low buildings and thus virtually acquire the space above the old building heights for nothing. Thus by producing residential or office units of higher quality in better locations, the builder obtains sufficiently high returns, taken in conjunction with economies in the use of land and labor, to obtain a profit notwithstanding the higher level of building costs. Or as in the cases of factories, banks, stores, and theaters during periods of expanding activity, the cost of the building may be so small a proportion of the total cost of producing or selling goods that the structures are erected notwithstanding a high cost level.

5. *The volume of new construction rises.*—The impulse from an increase in the rate of population growth having thus communicated itself to the rent cycle, the upswing in that cycle in turn stimulates the cycle of new construction and causes it to expand rapidly. The volume of building mounts very fast from the low point of the depression. The volume of new houses, stores, and factories erected in Chicago in the forty most active building years since 1854 was five times as great as the amount reared in the thirty-nine least active years. Tables LIV and LV show the extent of the rise in new building in the last two cycles.

6. *The volume of building is stimulated by easy credit.*—The building boom is stimulated and sustained by a liberal supply of capital made available by the expansion of credit institutions and attracted into new construction by the high profits made in such projects and by the high net yields of existing buildings. Financial institutions play an important rôle in this mania for building. In 1836 the Chicago branch of the Bank of Illinois and the state banks of issue were lavish in their grants of loans to real estate speculators and to builders. In the period prior to 1856 the new state banks of Illinois supported the building boom. In the great rebuilding of Chicago after the fire of 1871, eastern insurance

companies readily loaned money for Chicago building operations. In the skyscraper and World's Fair boom of 1889 to 1892, funds were se-

TABLE LIII*

SEVENTY-NINE YEARS OF BUILDING IN CHICAGO, 1854–1932

No. Years	40 Most Active Years	Total Value	No. Years	39 Least Active Years	Total Value
4........	1854–57	$ 18,306,306	6........	1858–63	$ 10,281,500
10........	1864–73	152,083,600	8........	1874–81	205,356,626
4........	1889–92	189,852,800	7........	1882–88	
12........	1905–16	1,014,854,917	12........	1893–1904	354,249,215
1 }	{ 1919	2,671,847,462	2........	1917–18	99,036,650
9 }........	{ 1921–29		1........	1920	79,102,560
			3........	1930–32	126,053,530
40........	....	$4,046,945,085	39........	....	$ 834,080,071

* $4,046,945,085 built in 40 active years; 83 per cent built in 40 active years, nearly five times as much built in the half-period that was most active. The physical volume of building in the 40 active years is exaggerated to some extent by the value figures because building costs were higher in these years. Computed from the annual figures for the cost of new buildings as shown by permits from the records of the Building Department of the city of Chicago.

TABLE LIV*

INDEX NUMBERS OF POPULATION, OFFICE RENTS, NEW CONSTRUCTION, NUMBER OF LOTS SUBDIVIDED, AND AGGREGATE LAND VALUES IN CHICAGO, 1918–27

(Relative Numbers, 1918 = 100)

Year	Population	Gross Income	Net Rents†	Value of New Construction	Lots Subdivided in Chicago Metropolitan Area	No. of Transfer	Land Value
1918..........	100	100	100	100	100	100	100
1919..........	102	101	121	300	311	144	100
1920..........	106	106	107	227	480	171	100
1921..........	111	123	146	360	544	168	100
1922..........	114	137	197	655	888	204	125
1923..........	118	157	261	946	1,233	243	150
1924..........	124	160	289	861	2,033	245	175
1925..........	128	180	345	1,034	2,444	262	225
1926..........	130	190	402	1,054	2,777	260	250
1927..........	134	195	336	1,014	2,000	233	250

* See Table LXIII for figures for 1928–33, inclusive.
† Figures from Table LII.

cured from banks, the sale of stock, and mortgage obligations to finance the office and apartment buildings. In the last boom that culminated in 1929, a vast supply fund for building projects was tapped by the sale of real estate bonds because the public had become familiar with bonds as a result of the Liberty Loan campaigns in the World War and because the splitting of a large mortgage into bonds of denominations as low as $100 vastly widened the market. This supply of capital mobilized by real estate mortgage houses and by the outlying state and national banks of Chicago whose growth had been extremely rapid from 1900 to 1929 was poured into the building field.[10] Table LVI shows the

TABLE LV

INDEX NUMBERS OF POPULATION, BUILDING, NUMBER OF LOTS SUBDIVIDED, AND LAND VALUES IN CHICAGO, 1885–93

Year	Population*	New Building†	Lots Subdivided in Chicago Metropolitan Area	Aggregate Land Values	Consideration in Deeds
1885	100	100	100	100	100
1886	106	109	244	100	151
1887	111	100	422	120	165
1888	118	104	633	140	180
1889	126	127	1,090	160	236
1890	135	242	1,800	240	414
1891	146	270	2,600	255	316
1892	156	324	1,422	273	314
1893	158	151	800	240	225

* In 1933 corporate limits of Chicago.
† Figures before 1890 did not include rapidly growing annexed territory which increased in population from 53,000 in 1880 to over 200,000 in 1890.

increase in the amount of money loaned on mortgages and trust deeds in Cook County from 1918 to 1929.

7. *"Shoestring" financing swells the number of new structures.*—The ease of financing new buildings attracted many subcontractors and even building mechanics into the construction industry. It became possible to erect buildings with a very small outlay of capital on the

[10] "A particularly ominous development was the expansion of the banking system itself for the specific purpose of financing real estate promotion and development. Real estate interests dominated the policies of many banks, and thousands of new banks were organized and chartered for the specific purpose of providing the credit facilities for proposed real estate promotions. The greater proportion of these were state banks and trust companies, many of them were located in the outlying sections of the larger cities or in suburban regions not fully occupied by older and more established banking institutions" (Herbert D. Simpson, "Real Estate Speculation and the Depression," *American Economic Review*, XXIII, No. 1 [March, 1933], 164).

part of these entrepreneurs, for almost the whole amount required to erect the building and even to buy the lot could be secured in the heyday of these booms by loans on first and second mortgages.[11] Contractors in the last boom in Chicago sometimes made an agreement to purchase a lot, put up a small deposit on the purchase price, drew plans for an elaborate structure, and on this basis secured a loan large enough

TABLE LVI*

THE AMOUNT OF MONEY LOANED ON MORTGAGES AND TRUST DEEDS IN COOK COUNTY, ILLINOIS, 1918–32

Year	Aggregate Amount of Stated Consideration	Relative Numbers 1918 = 100
1918	$ 163,687,177	100
1919	241,177,840	148
1920	305,587,870	187
1921	361,925,299	221
1922	550,914,192	337
1923	696,882,247	426
1924	746,795,339	456
1925	986,960,148	603
1926	1,033,864,243	632
1927	1,045,997,413	639
1928	1,039,432,235	635
1929	759,395,774	464
1930	425,164,215	260
1931	264,584,983	162
1932	143,309,644	87

* From the annual reviews of the *Economist* (Chicago, 1919–32). The foregoing figures include renewal of old loans and new loans on existing buildings as well as loans on new construction projects.

to pay the balance due on the lot and to complete the building.[12] Again several large Loop office buildings, such as the one at the southwest corner of Clark and Madison streets[13] and other structures, were erected by parties who secured a ground lease and who virtually without any capital succeeded in securing a loan on a bond issue sufficient to erect a skyscraper. The increase in the volume of long-term leases during these boom periods is a material factor promoting rapid speculative advances in land values, for it makes possible "shoestring"

[11] Walter Kuehnle, an unpublished study in the county assessor's office.

[12] From cases reported to the writer by real estate brokers and also from cases the details of which are known by him.

[13] Statements of Loop real estate brokers to the writer.

financing in the case of ground sites, whose outright purchase would require a large sum of money. The lessee under the terms of a long-term lease, after satisfying the lessor as to his ability to meet the terms of the lease, is required to pay only the annual rent instead of a capitalized sum of from ten to twenty times that amount. If the lessee, after obtaining a lease for ninety-nine years[14] in this manner, could float a bond issue to erect a skyscraper on the mere security of the leasehold, it is readily observable that little capital was required by some of the promoters of huge structures. When such financing methods prevailed, it is little wonder that there was such a rush to erect new buildings, regardless of the cost of the land, labor, or materials, for the promoter who engineered the affair did not risk much of his own wealth. Thus a great many men worked secretly and independently on a great variety of structures in many sections of the city. There was no central clearing house to correlate the impending supply of buildings with the probable demand, so that when all these plans came to fruition an astonishing number of new structures had been erected.

8. *The new buildings absorb vacant land: the land boom.*—A building boom absorbs a considerable amount of vacant land and thus suddenly gives an earning power to certain tracts that have long been dormant. The 97,511 buildings erected in Chicago in the seven years from 1922 to 1928, inclusive, required 3,060,111 front feet, or 580 miles of street frontage.[15] As a result of this demand for vacant lots, the prices of tracts adjoining the settled area that have street improvements which make them "ripe for building" advance rapidly. Speculators who have acquired these lots from owners who did not foresee this movement and those who held their property are in a position to make large profits. The news of the fortunes made in their very back yards or in their own neighborhoods spreads like wildfire through the members of the community. At such times the possibility of making more money by buy-

[14] In Chicago the wharf sites along the Chicago River were leased for nominal rentals for nine-hundred and ninety-nine years by 1835. A survey of the records of the Chicago Title and Trust Co. indicates that many leases for twenty years and a few for as long as fifty years were made in the central business district of Chicago prior to the panic of 1873. Some ninety-nine-year leases were noted in 1887, and in the boom of 1890 and the years following these ninety-nine-year leases increased in number until by 1933 a considerable proportion of the property in the Loop was tied up by such leases. There is no legal reason for the ninety-nine-year period, save for an early belief, which had no basis in court decisions, that a lease for a longer period would violate the rule against perpetuities. See Table XCVI.

[15] Records of the Building Department of the city of Chicago.

ing and selling a few vacant lots than by lifetime of hard labor proves an irresistible temptation to many persons.[16]

9. *Optimistic population forecasts during the boom.*—At this phase of the real estate cycle, the rapid rate of increase in the population of the city that has recently taken place is projected far into the future in the rosy calculations that are broadcast by real estate men. A city that will surpass in size any metropolis the world has ever known before is erected in these speculative dreams, and facts and figures are collected by business men of the community and by "distinguished scholars" to buttress these "castles in Spain" and to make them seem tangible to the lay mind. Thus Charles H. Wacker in 1924 estimated that Chicago would have a population of 18,000,000 by 1974[17] and Professor J. Paul Goode predicted in 1926 a total of 15,000,000 for the city at an indeterminate future date when it might be the greatest city the world has ever known.[18] Other far more conservative forecasts, such as that of Helen Jeter in 1927 which indicated a population of only 5,100,000 for Chicago by 1960,[19] would have been lightly passed over in the heyday of the boom of 1925 and 1926.

At such a period the imagination of the community conjures up the picture of an endless stream of population increase concentrating about Chicago. This undiminished flow of people will require homes; it will cause the vacant prairies for miles and miles to be filled with new dwellings and new shopping centers to spring up in cornfields. Such a constant population pressure will sustain apartment rents at constantly advancing levels and will produce astounding increases in store rents, for there is never the slightest doubt but that all these people will be employed fully at ever advancing wages.

10. *The vision of new cities in cornfields: the methods of some subdividers.*—As deceptive as a mirage in the desert is this vision of new cities that seems to be about to rise on the outskirts of the old city, and many

[16] A Greek physician who came to Chicago about 1915 acquired with a small original investment a number of vacant business corners until by 1928 he owned eighty-seven such corners, subject to mortgages with an estimated equity of $6,000,000. Blocks along Seventy-ninth Street that sold for as little as $14,000 in 1905 brought over $1,000,000 in 1926. Thousands of stories of sudden profits accruing to the owners of land could be cited for this period.

[17] *Chicago Journal*, April 22, 1924.

[18] J. Paul Goode, *The Economic Background of Chicago* (1926), p. 69.

[19] Helen R. Jeter, *Trends of Population in the Region of Chicago* (Chicago: University of Chicago Press, 1927).

members of the community, fascinated by the picture, are filled with a longing to acquire a plot of land that will so speedily rise in value as a result of this population pressure. Some professional subdividers take advantage of this situation.[20] They know that the mechanics of the

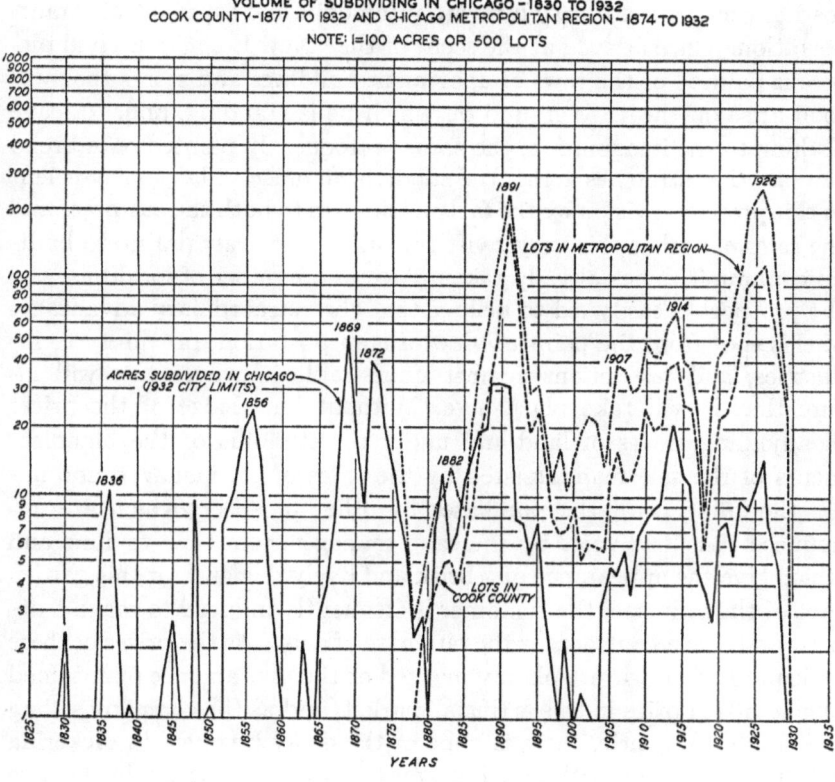

FIG. 94

real estate market are a mystery to a layman and that there is no device like the stock ticker for broadcasting land prices. Accordingly, they subdivide large tracts of land in all directions; develop large sales forces

[20] The following account applies particularly to subdividers who entered the business or enlarged the scope of their operations in boom periods. A number of conservative real estate firms who subdivided tracts and sold lots in the period from 1895 to 1920 stopped subdividing before 1924. The large profits made by many investors who purchased lots from these conservative firms in the period from 1895 to 1920 stimulated the sale of lots by the reckless subdivision operators of 1925 and 1926.

who get into contact with "prospects" through advertisements and telephone "leads"; enlist amateur salesmen called "bird dogs" for the main purpose of securing introductions to their circle of acquaintances; and work through house-to-house canvasses. An appointment once secured with a prospective lot-buyer, he is induced to visit the "property," the road to which is made easy by swift automobile and express-train transportation. Once arrived at the scene of the "New Eden,"[21] a vivid picture is painted of the rows of apartment buildings and stores that will soon arise on the very ground on which he is standing, and, to leave nothing to the imagination, the scene is frequently painted on a broad canvass that stretches across the subdivision office. Plausibility is lent to this prophetic vision by the fact well known to both the customer and the salesman, that this very swift transition from raw prairie to built-up communities has already taken place in a number of localities, and the prospect is easily led to believe that the extraordinary advantages of this spot from the point of view of transportation, proximity to industries, and restrictions against undesirable improvements will insure that it will take place here. Without knowledge of the prices of adjoining tracts of land and under the stimulus of the blandishments of the salesman, assisted by the wiles of his manager, and under the influence of the purchases by other prospects which are announced in a loud voice by the sales manager from time to time and which give the appearance of a brisk and lively demand for this garden spot of the universe, the customer is frequently induced to make a deposit and sign a contract for the purchase of a lot. As the prices of these little plots of prairie are plainly marked on the plat and are maintained at a standard price in this artificial market, and as the company selling the lots has the title, there is none of the delay involved in dickering with the owner and with higgling over the price that occurs in the case of transactions made in a broker's office. Thus the "prospect" has become the owner of an equity in a lot which he is told will save him from the poorhouse in his old age. If he later repents of his zeal and wonders if he was not mistaken, the fact that he will lose his deposit deters him from withdrawing or a second visit of the salesman restores his confidence. He soon finds, however, that he has a continuing obligation, for the monthly payments which he must make to preserve his equity

[21] "New Eden" was the name of the townsite described in Charles Dickens' novel, *Martin Chuzzlewit*.

THE CHICAGO REAL ESTATE CYCLE 391

and to prevent the forfeiture of his contract make a constant drain upon his resources. In most of the land booms a great many lot-buyers stop making payments or abandon their holdings before receiving their deeds, so that in the end they have not even a narrow strip of vacant land to show for their outlays, and not even a cemetery lot in which finally they can be interred with their hopes.[22]

Such is the nature of the subdivision boom which has occurred at the most hectic phase of all the five major real estate cycles in Chicago, as Figure 94 on page 389 indicates. In 1836, in 1856, in 1872, in 1890, and in 1925 the same story was repeated with some variations in the mode of transportation to the subdivision and of communication with the prospect but with little change in the nature of the sales arguments. The assumption at all such times is that population and new building will continue to grow indefinitely at the same rapid rate and that vacant land will continue to be absorbed at least as rapidly in the future as it has been in the immediate past. Close or careful calculations are not even made on the basis of the prevailing rapid rate of absorption, and the territory subdivided into lots exceeds any possible demand for years to come. Figures 5, 10, 19, and 41, showing the area subdivided in the various boom periods compared with the maps of the settled area for those periods, indicate how far beyond the built-up area the subdividers extended their activities in every cycle. When the town of Chicago was confined to the banks of the river, subdivisions south of Roosevelt Road or near Chicago Avenue were extremely remote. Again when in 1856 Chicago did extend to Roosevelt Road and Chicago Avenue, subdivisions in Hyde Park and Lake View townships were far beyond the fringe of the city. Again, prior to 1873 great numbers of lots were subdivided southwest along the Rock Island Railroad and northwest along the North Western Railroad, although these sections were very thinly settled. Prior to 1893 not only were wide areas subdivided within the corporate limits of Chicago, but thousands of lots were offered for sale in outlying suburban towns and in proposed manufacturing centers. In the last boom, vacant lots were being sold in a belt of land three miles wide along the lake shore for forty miles north

---

[22] For an excellent account of subdivision operations see Ernest M. Fisher, "Speculation in Suburban Lands," *American Economic Review*, XXIII, No. 1 (March, 1933), 158-61. See also Herbert D. Simpson and John E. Burton, *The Valuation of Vacant Land in Suburban Areas* (Chicago, 1931).

of Chicago, in another belt south along the lake shore to Michigan City, and beyond and in still another belt stretching westward along Roosevelt Road and Twenty-second Street to Wheaton and LaGrange. There were also numerous other subdivisions stretching northwest along the North Western Railroad to Barrington and Palatine and southwest to One Hundred and Eleventh and Harlem Avenue. Regardless of how rapidly Chicago has grown, the new subdivisions have grown faster.[23] Tables LIV and LV show the extreme speed with which the subdivision business gained momentum and how its rate of growth outstripped that of all other factors in the real estate cycle in the land booms culminating in 1890 and 1926.

11. *Lavish expenditures for public improvements.*—During this building and subdivision boom, there are lavish expenditures for public improvements in some localities. The cost of these is financed either by bond issues, which are readily passed by popular vote at such times, or by special assessments payable in five or ten annual instalments, which are likewise cheerfully assumed by landowners in the belief that it will enhance the value of their land still more.[24] Consequently, new bridges are built or streets are widened in old neighborhoods, and miles of pavements, sidewalks, and sewers are constructed in outlying subdivisions. Thus the public authorities not only do not limit the output of subdivided lots, but they encourage the rapid increase in their supply by enabling sewers, sidewalks, and pavements to be installed on vacant prairies without cost to the subdivider. The sight of newly installed sidewalks in a tract that would otherwise be only a farm or cow pasture gives the misleading impression that it is the first step in the growth of a new community, the other steps of which are to follow shortly. If in addition to these sidewalks, which are so cheap in proportion to the selling effect they produce that they are frequently installed by the subdividers themselves, paved streets are laid down at community expense, and a few houses or apartment buildings are erected as decoys, this seems to be a positive guaranty to gullible lot-buyers in boom periods that the

[23] In Cook County outside of Chicago there were 335,000 vacant lots in 1928, which according to the estimates of population increase by Helen R. Jeter will not be entirely absorbed even by 1960 (Simpson, *op. cit.*, p. 164).

[24] In some cases the improvements were paid for by the subdividers and added to the lot prices, but this method of financing was usually applied only to sidewalks in the Chicago area.

entire district will soon be built solidly with homes, apartments, and stores. The contractors who have constructed the "frame" of pavements and sidewalks for this beautiful picture which usually does not become a reality for years afterward, if ever, frequently reap large profits from lucrative contracts and after cashing in their bonds or warrants withdraw from the scene. The community is left with the problem of abandoned subdivisions for years afterward—lots overgrown with weeds, wasted capital in unused streets and sewers, defaulted improvement obligations, unpaid taxes and special assessments, a few houses in disrepair or occupied at low rentals by the few persons who care to live in such lonely places, and discouraged lot-buyers who have their funds tied up in a manner that can yield them no return for years to come. Such areas cannot be turned back into farms, for after a number of lots have been sold, it is usually impossible to assemble the parcels under one ownership so that streets and alleys can be vacated and fields large enough for farming pieced together, and the sidewalks and pavements likewise are an obstacle to agricultural use. Hence such subdivided districts forcibly withdraw land from any kind of use for a long period of time, for they are not "ripe" for full utilization as homesites and they cannot be used as farms except in the limited form of garden spots. By the time these areas are actually needed for residential development, the old street improvements have usually fallen into disrepair and have to be replaced, while a straggling collection of old houses frequently occupied by disreputable elements that sometimes live on the fringe of a city, and a lot and block plan that may have become archaic, make such districts less desirable for new homes than adjoining farm lands that have not been marred by such premature promotion.

Tables LVII, LVIII, and LVIX and Figure 98 show the rapid rise in the amount of money spent in public improvements in the boom periods prior to 1873, 1893, and 1929 as well as the subsequent decline.

Summarizing the various phases of the real estate cycle up to this point, Tables LIV and LV show how increased demand for buildings as a result of improved business conditions and population increase produce an even greater increase in gross rents, how that in turn causes a still greater rise in net rents, how that leads to an even higher percentage of increase in building operations, and how that finally produces an even more extraordinary rate of increase in the number of lots sub-

TABLE LVII*

INCREASE IN ANNUAL COST OF SPECIAL ASSESSMENTS IN CHICAGO, 1862–71, FOR YEARS ENDING APRIL 1

Year	Aggregate Amount	Index Numbers (1862=100) Amount
1862	$ 46,635	100
1863	46,493	100
1864	89,169	191
1865	103,576	222
1866	802,575	1,721
1867	317,206	680
1868	1,354,436	2,907
1869	2,395,683	5,142
1870	2,836,852	6,088
1871	2,359,836	5,063

* *Report of the Board of Local Improvements of Chicago* (1901–2), p. 141.

TABLE LVIII*

INCREASE IN ANNUAL COST OF SPECIAL ASSESSMENTS IN CHICAGO, 1877–92

(For Years Ending April 1 Prior to 1876, and for Years Ending December 31 Thereafter)

Year	Aggregate Amount	Index Numbers (1877=100) Amount
1877	$ 124,498	100
1878	284,900	229
1879	588,936	473
1880	980,896	796
1881	1,227,170	989
1882	1,395,373	1,120
1883	2,232,757	1,793
1884	2,857,905	2,293
1885	2,889,545	2,320
1886	3,307,568	2,660
1887	3,160,474	2,540
1888	3,655,957	2,936
1889	4,220,870	3,400
1890	6,987,155	5,612
1891	8,790,443	7,060
1892	14,505,702	11,650

* *Report of the Board of Local Improvements of Chicago* (1901–2), p. 141.

THE CHICAGO REAL ESTATE CYCLE

TABLE LIX*
RISE IN ANNUAL AMOUNTS OF SPECIAL ASSESSMENTS IN CHICAGO, 1919–27

Year	Aggregate Amount	Relative Numbers 1919=100
1919	$ 6,521,691	100
1920	7,417,431	113
1921	8,183,549	125
1922	19,305,363	299
1923	16,151,344	248
1924	34,472,824	528
1925	20,940,415	320
1926	31,065,812	477
1927	56,980,268	874

* Includes cost of sidewalks, paving, sewers, drains, water-service pipes, water-supply pipes, and street openings and widening installed both by public authorities and under private contract. See Table LXII for figures for 1927–32.

TABLE LX
DECREASE IN ANNUAL COST OF SPECIAL ASSESSMENTS IN CHICAGO, 1870–77

Year	Aggregate Amount	Index Numbers 1870=100
1870	$ 2,836,852	100
1871	2,359,836	83
1874	749,460	26
1875	723,254	25
1876	1,516,081	53
1877	124,498	4

TABLE LXI
DECREASE IN ANNUAL COST OF SPECIAL ASSESSMENTS IN CHICAGO, 1892–97

Year	Aggregate Amount	Index Numbers 1892=100
1892	$14,505,702	100
1893	6,001,446	41
1894	2,903,814	20
1895	4,387,214	30
1896	4,037,320	28
1897	2,102,951	15

divided, accompanied by a rapid growth in the amount spent for public improvements.

12. *All the real estate factors at full tide: the peak.*—The point is then reached in the Chicago real estate cycle when all the various factors

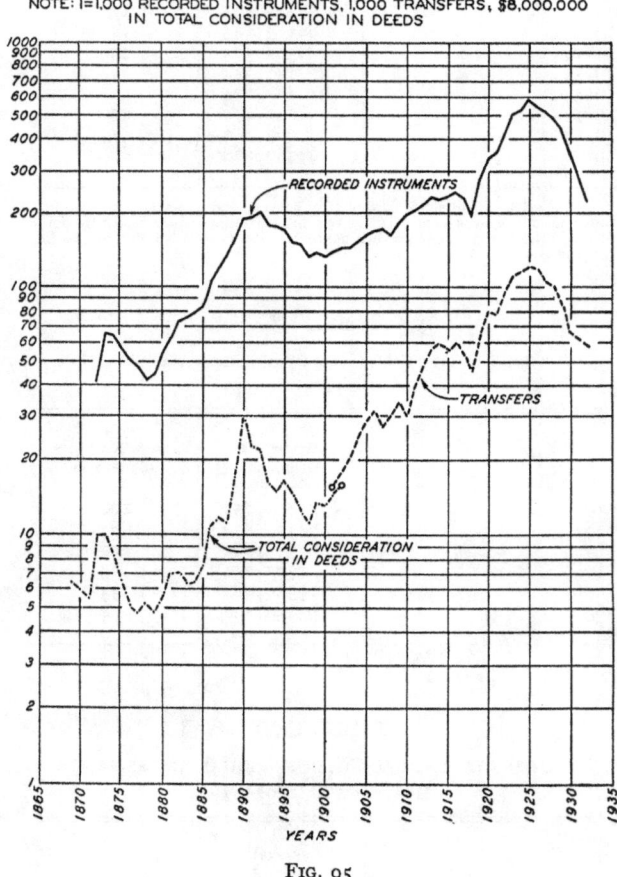

Fig. 95

combine to produce their maximum effect and when all the forces pull together in the same direction to bring the real estate market to its apex of activity. Such a point is indicated by the maximum volume of real estate transfers shown in Figure 95, and it occurred in 1836, 1853–55,

1869, 1872, 1890, and 1925. The volume of building and the number of lots subdivided may not reach their high points at the same time that the market is most active in all its phases. Plans for buildings that were formulated and financed at the height of the boom may not come to

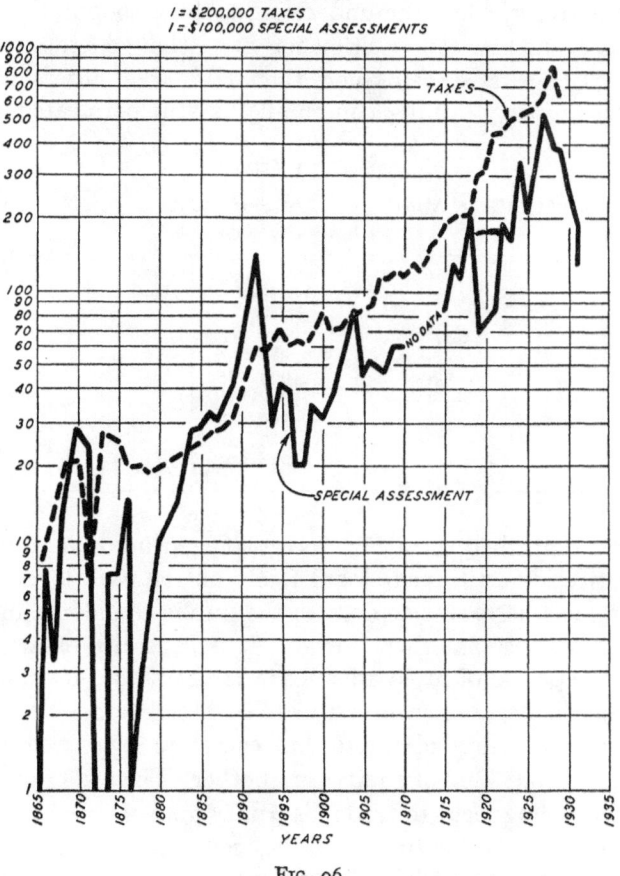

Fig. 96

fruition until the following year. A heavy sale of subdivision lots in the heyday of the market may result in extensive new subdivisions in the following year, the lots in which, however, are not so extensively sold.

Thus in some cycles, even before the real estate market has reached its peak, and in all cases before the beginning of the depression, the rate of population growth of Chicago has fallen off. As the supply of building space has greatly increased at the same time, the rise in rents slackens and the number of vacancies increases. Table LXIII shows the factors operating in the downsweep of the last cycle.

13. *The reverse movement begins: the lull.*—Soon after the peak of real estate activity, while the underlying factors—population growth, rent increases, and new construction activity—that generated the boom are preparing to reverse their trend, the land market enters into a dull phase. The property-owning community is still permeated with the

TABLE LXII

Decrease in Annual Cost of Special Assessments in Chicago, 1927–32

Year	Aggregate Amount	Index Numbers 1927=100
1927	$56,980,268	100
1928	39,989,835	70
1929	27,672,576	48
1930	26,768,512	47
1931	12,829,030	23
1932	2,038,209	4

rosy dreams that filled the air on the great upswing in land values, financial institutions still make loans freely on the peak level of prices, and nothing has happened to disturb the public confidence in the stability of the values that then prevail. It is generally observed, however, that the period of rapid advance in land prices is over, and there is no rush on the part of new investors to buy land before it rises higher. Asking prices are being advanced, but there are fewer cash sales and more trading of one kind of equity for another. The owner of a heavily mortgaged building seeks to trade his equity for a clear lot or farm and is sometimes even willing to take mortgaged vacant land for his interest. The possessors of equities in subdivision contracts find no market for their interests except from other subdividers, who while regarding such contracts as of no value, induce their holders to trade them in for other subdivision lots at a higher price in order to secure an additional cash down payment or monthly cash instalments. Such was the situation that prevailed in the latter parts of 1836, 1856, 1873, and throughout most of the entire year in 1891, 1892, 1927, 1928, and 1929.

14. *Foreclosures increase.*—Meanwhile, the foreclosure rate has begun to increase. The holders of heavily mortgaged properties, who find themselves called upon to meet prepayments upon both first and second

TABLE LXIII

Rents, Value of New Buildings, Transfers, Number of Lots Subdivided, Number of Foreclosures, Vacancies in the Central Business District, Land Values in Chicago, 1926–33

(Relative Numbers, 1926 = 100)

Year	Gross Office Rents*	Rents Working-men's Dwellings†	Net Office Rents*	Value New Buildings	No. Acres Subdivided in Chicago†	No. Foreclosures in Cook County	Occupancy of Offices in Central Business District‡	Land Values	Transfers
1926	100	100	100	100	100	100	100	100	100
1927	103	96.8	84	96	50	153	101	100	90
1928	104	93.3	94	86	31	220	95	100	84
1929	103	90.2	101	55	9	270	92	95	69
1930	99	87.5	90	22	0	400	91	80	56
1931	90	82.2	76	13	0	700	89	62	51
1932	77	69.4	24	1	0	1,060	86	50	49
1933		54.3					81	40	

* John P. Hooker, *op. cit.*, p. 347. The following figures for 90 properties in the central business district of Chicago, which represented one-fourth of the value of the land and buildings in the Loop and which were in an exceptionally strong financial position, are as follows

	Gross Income	Net Income
1928	100	100
1931	82.5	66.7
1932	69	45.9

† U.S. Department of Labor, *Retail Prices and Cost of Living* (December, 1932), p. 16. The figures are for June of each year. The figures of the National Industrial Conference Board indicate a decline of 50 per cent in certain classes of workingmen's dwellings in Chicago from 1923 to 1933.

‡ Figures are for January 1 of each year (*Report of Office Building Managers' Association of Chicago*).

mortgages as well as the interest charges, begin to get into difficulties with the holders of the junior incumbrances as soon as the peak income declines slightly or a heavy prepayment falls due. For example, the holders of second mortgages began to foreclose in increasing numbers in 1927, 1928, and 1929, but there was as yet no doubt as to the safety of the underlying first mortgages.

15. *The stock-market débâcle and the onset of the depression in general business.*—Up to this time there has been no major recession in general

business activity, and real estate has grown dull because of reasons peculiar to itself. The end of the general period of prosperity in all lines is approaching, however, and on some red-letter day in 1837, 1857, 1873, 1893, or 1929 a crash on the stock market rudely shatters the dream of never ending profits. At first this fact has no great effect upon real estate value. No overnight call for more margin forces the liquidation of land, and there is no short selling. Mortgages or trust deeds usually have five years to run, and even when they fall due, about eighteen months is required in Illinois for the holder of a trust deed to gain title by foreclosure. Hence the equity holders of real estate, unlike those of stocks, are not panic-stricken when the first financial storm breaks over the country. In fact, they frequently contrast their favorable position with that of the fate of stock-buyers and secretly rejoice in the misfortunes of the public in the security field, hoping that the stock *débâcle* will turn the people back to land-buying.

16. *The process of attrition.*—The general slackening of industrial activity which continues after the stock-market crash, however, begins to wear down land values by a process of attrition. Within a year after the onset of the depression, increasing unemployment and reduced wages have sapped the public buying power. Many men leave the urban centers and return to the farm or the small town where they can live more cheaply. The result is that the population of the great centers remains stationary or declines, and many of those who are left are forced to "double up" or to contract their living quarters in order to save money.[25] Thus the supply of vacant houses or apartments increases and in order to secure occupants the agents cut rents. This decline in gross rents causes an even greater decline in net rents, because the same elements in operating expenses that are fixed or slow to change that helped the landlord on the upswing of the cycle now work against him. The reduction in the margin between income and operating expenses has now proceeded to the point where there is not even enough left to pay the interest charges on the first mortgages. The second-mortgage holders, who were the first to foreclose, are themselves wiped out in the flood of foreclosures of first mortgages, such as that which began in 1930. All the factors now operate to depress real estate values

[25] In 1857 Colbert and Chamberlin (*Chicago and the Great Conflagration*, p. 96) state: "Great numbers of workers left the city for want of employment and those who remained were obliged to go into narrowed quarters to reduce expenses."

as they operated to elevate them before. As more buildings go into the hands of receivers, rents are cut more drastically than they were by the owners, for these court officers do not hestitate to make reductions that will fill their buildings at the expense of owners who are struggling to keep their rents high enough to meet their fixed charges. The progressive lowering of rents forces more buildings into the hands of receivers. Meanwhile, the tax burden has not been reduced in proportion to the decline in net incomes, and it now amounts to a higher proportion of the aggregate rent roll. The owners of many small homes who in many cases have used all their savings as well as their surplus earnings in the attempt to save their mortgaged dwellings now find they can keep up the struggle no longer and the bungalow goes through the foreclosure mill with the twenty-story office building or apartment hotel.

17. *The banks reverse their boom policy on real estate loans.*—In this situation the financial institutions reverse their liberal lending policy of the earlier period. In most cases the banking power is badly crippled, as it was in 1837 when the state banks of Illinois were being forced into liquidation, or in 1861 and 1862 when the state banks of issue were compelled to close, or in 1877 when most of the Chicago savings banks failed, or in 1893 when several Chicago banks failed, or from 1930 to 1933 when 163 out of 200 Chicago banks were compelled to suspend operations. As real estate investment was one of the principal means by which the assets of the banks had become frozen and as liquidity is of extreme importance during an epidemic of bank runs, the banks that remain open are extremely cautious.[26] With part of their assets already tied up in real estate obligations, they will hardly loan money on mortgages on any basis. In the case of one Loop building, for which a $3,500,000 construction loan was readily obtained in 1928, a first-mortgage loan of $350,000 could be secured only with difficulty in 1932.

18. *The period of stagnation and foreclosures.*—Nearly all phases of real estate activity are now virtually suspended. Subdividing had come to a stop with the advent of the dull market even before the *débâcle* in general business. New building operations which were maintained at

[26] "But it would seem that we can safely say this much: that real estate, real estate securities, and real estate affiliations in some form have been the largest single factor in the failure of the 4,800 banks that have closed their doors in the last three years and in the "frozen" conditions of a large proportion of the banks that still remain open" (Simpson, *op. cit.*, p. 165).

full volume to the very eve of the business depression have dwindled away to a negligible amount. Gross rents have declined 50 per cent and net rents of the best properties are not enough to pay interest charges on conservative mortgages, and in most cases they are no more than sufficient to pay operating expenses and taxes. Normal sales of real estate have ceased. There is a considerable number of "transfers," but these are mostly conveyances to relatives to avoid judgments, quit-claim deeds of equity holders to the mortgage holders to avoid foreclosure, transfers involving a trade of other properties, and masters' deeds disposing of the title of foreclosed properties. Most vacant land is unsalable at any price, for there is no immediate prospect of its profitable utilization. Improved property, incumbered with mortgages, is not in shape to be delivered to buyers or to be sold conveniently because most of the mortgages are in default or in process of going through the foreclosure mill. A buyer would have to acquire not only the title of the owner, but he would be compelled to pay off or renew also the maturing or past-due mortgage obligation. A large number of properties are being disposed of at foreclosure sales, but since an absolute title is not transferred, and since all cash payment would be required, few attend the sales except the holder of the mortgage who bids in the property at his own price. If the title holder signed the mortgage and is financially responsible, the mortgagee will bid far less than the face amount of the mortgage and secure a deficiency judgment for the balance; but if the title holder has no other known assets, the mortgagee will bid up the property to the full amount of the mortgage and costs to prevent creditors of the defaulting owner to secure the property for a smaller amount. The amount of such sales consequently has little bearing on the value of real estate. In the recent depression, the cheapest way to acquire properties was to acquire the mortgage bonds from discouraged holders at a great discount and then to foreclose upon the title holder and freeze out the remaining bondholders at the foreclosure sale. While this was going on, there would naturally be few buyers for properties from title holders. Foreclosures must run their course and old obligations be wiped out before the real estate market is in a position to revive.

19. *The wreckage is cleared away.*—In time, however, usually four or five years, the wreckage of the collapse of the previous boom is cleared away. Property that was heavily incumbered comes into the hands of

mortgage holders, and the past obligations are thereby wiped out. A new start can be made, as the mortgage holders are frequently willing to accept the amount of their mortgage or less for their holdings. Meanwhile, the beginnings of industrial recovery or a rise in the stock market has given funds to certain groups to invest in real estate. These shrewd individuals begin to pick up the best bargains to be found, until these are taken off the market. During this period in which there has been little if any building, population has been increasing slowly until most of the vacant space has been absorbed. Rents begin to rise once more, and as construction costs have been hammered down somewhat by the depression, it becomes profitable to build again. The long real estate cycle has come back again to the starting-point.

20. *Ready for another boom which does not come automatically.*—From this account it might be inferred that the real estate cycle automatically repeats itself. Such is by no means the case. According to the view presented, the cycle has been generated largely by a sudden and unexpected increase in population which was in turn due to a rush to take advantage of economic opportunities. If this theory is correct, then the recurrence of land booms in Chicago in the future will depend on the expansion of industrial opportunities which attract a sudden accession of population.

E. MINOR MOVEMENTS OF THE INDIVIDUAL REAL ESTATE FACTORS

In the foregoing description of a typical sequence of events in the Chicago real estate cycle, there is a danger of oversimplification. As Figures 99, 100, 101, and 102 show, there has been no definite time interval between land booms in Chicago, and, as they also indicate, the various factors in the real estate cycle sometimes trace independent cycles of their own, which do not coincide or follow each other in exactly the same order in different cycles. In the period from 1879 to 1882 a rise of building activity above normal was accompanied by a rapid rise of land values in the Board of Trade quarters of Chicago, but there was no widespread land boom throughout the city. From 1910 to 1916 building and subdivision activity rose above the trend line, but the rate of increase in land values did not carry it above normal. Thus some of the factors in the real estate cycle may have abnormal periods of activity without communicating their effect to all the other forces. When all the real estate forces are stimulated to activity far above normal, however, the phenomenon of the real estate or land boom is produced.

TABLE LXIV

THE PERCENTAGE INCREASE OF FACTORS AFFECTING CHICAGO REAL ESTATE IN BOOM PERIODS

FACTORS	AGGREGATE PERCENTAGE INCREASE FOR LAST YEAR OVER FIRST YEAR					AVERAGE INCREASE IN PER CENT PER ANNUM				
	1833–36	1842–56	1861–72	1885–92	1918–26	1833–36	1842–56	1861–72	1885–92	1918–26
Population*	1,100	1,400	206	56	30	275	93	17	7	3.3
Land values†	4,000	8,900	900	210	150	1,000	593	75	26	17
Consideration in deeds‡	....	....	....	214	160	....	....	....	24	18
New construction§	150	....	4,900	224	954	37	....	408	28	106
Lots subdivided‖	....	1,300¶	1,800**	1,322	2,677	....	100	180	167	297
Manufactures††	....	....	1,290‡‡	85	dec. 13	....	....	100	11	−1.5
Bank clearings§§	....	....	....	118	40	....	....	....	15	4.5
Wholesale trade‖ ‖	....	....	....	51	34	....	....	....	6	4
Amount of new trust deeds¶¶	....	....	....	....	530	....	..	....	....	59
Gross office rents***	....	....	....	....	90	....	....	....	....	10
Net office rents***	....	....	....	....	301	....	....	....	....	45
Rents of workingmen's dwellings†††	....	....	....	....	80	....	....	....	....	9

* Annual population estimates from city, state, and school censuses and local estimates. Population figures from 1880 to 1933 estimated by the writer largely on the basis of the grade-school enrolment.
† Computations of the writer.
‡ Consideration in deeds reported in the annual reviews of the *Tribune* and the *Economist* prior to 1901. Number of transfers, 1901–32, from the county recorder's office.
§ Value of new construction as shown by permits from the records of the Building Department of the city of Chicago.
‖ Area subdivided in 1933 limits of Chicago from 1830 to 1932 computed by the writer from the original plats in the office of the Chicago Title and Trust Co. Lots subdivided in Chicago Metropolitan Region from an unpublished study.
¶ From 1844 to 1856.
** From 1863 to 1872.
†† From annual reviews of the *Chicago Tribune* and U.S.Census of Manufactures.
‡‡ From 1860 to 1872.
§§ From a typewritten statement furnished by the Chicago Clearing House Association.
‖ ‖ From annual reviews of the *Chicago Tribune*.
¶¶ From annual reviews of the *Economist*.
*** From a study by James P. Hooker, "Biography of an Office Building," *Real Estate*, July, 1933.
††† U.S. Bureau of Labor Statistics, *op. cit.*, see Table LXXXVIII for full reference.

It must also be borne in mind that the curves of aggregate land values for the entire city smooth out the great differences between individual sections that were discussed in chapter vi, and that the aggregate building curve for the city lumps together all types of buildings for all parts of the city. There are many individual variations from the main trend of values for different areas in the city and for different types of uses, but the tracing of these neighborhood cycles would require a voluminous treatment that would far transcend the scope of this work.

F. STATISTICAL SUMMARY OF SEQUENCE OF FACTORS IN THE CHICAGO REAL ESTATE CYCLE

Since practically all of the data for the Chicago real estate cycle are aggregate annual figures, the time intervals between the movements of the different factors cannot be measured as closely as in the case of

TABLE LXV

THE PERCENTAGE DECREASE OF FACTORS AFFECTING CHICAGO REAL ESTATE IN DEPRESSION PERIODS

FACTORS	AGGREGATE PERCENTAGE DECREASE FOR LAST YEAR OVER FIRST YEAR					AVERAGE DECREASE IN PER CENT PER ANNUM				
	1836–41	1857–61	1873–78	1892–98	1926–32	1836–41	1857–61	1873–78	1892–98	1926–32
Land value............	86	50.0	56.0	33.0	60.0	17	12.5	11.0	8.0	10.0
Consideration in deeds	.....	.....	51.4	65.0	51.5	.....	.....	10.3	13.0	8.6
New construction.....	56	91.8	83.2	69.7	99.0	11	22.7	16.6	11.6	16.5
Lots subdivided......	100	100.0	95.6	97.0	100.0	20	25.0	19.1	16.1	16.6
Public improvements..	.....	.....	95.6	85.3	82.6	.....	.....	19.1	14.2	13.8
Population (increase)..	31	30.0	15.0	20.0	5 dec.	6.2	7.5	3.0	4.0	−1.25
Foreclosures (increase).	.....	.....	70.0	220.0	900.0	.....	.....	14.0	37.0	150.0

monthly data. If the year in which each of the real estate forces made a significant turn is set down as in Table LXVI, it is important to note that in every cycle the curve for population increase is the first to begin its rise from the low point, and in three of the five cycles it was the first to turn down. The beginning of the upturn in real estate transfers, lots subdivided, and new construction takes place from one to four years after the first acceleration in population growth, but still within ample time to enable land-buyers to accumulate holdings for the boom, which is still eight to ten years away. The danger signal of the approach to a falling market is the rise in the number of lots subdivided to a point far above normal for the second or third year in succession. It is almost necessary for the real estate investor, who desires to avoid the possibility of loss or of a long waiting period, to sell out a number of months before the peak is reached, because when the land market first slackens its pace and enters that "Saragossa Sea" known as "the dull period," it is very difficult to make a cash sale. When the decline in the real

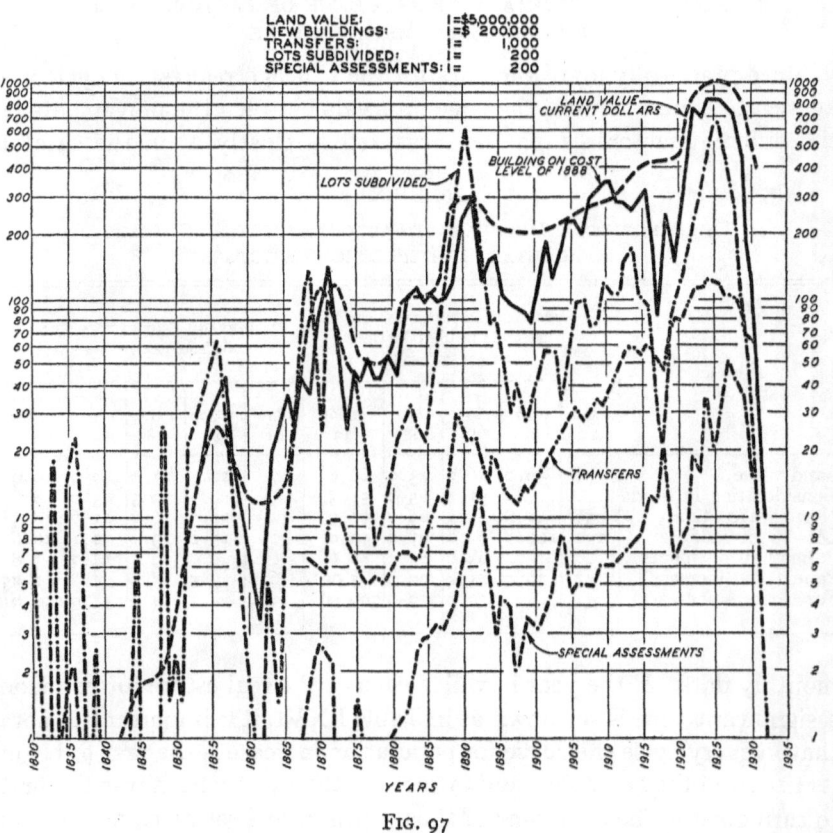

Fig. 97

estate factors begins, it drags out its course on the average from five and a half to eight and one-fifth years before it hits bottom. The lack of short selling, the tenacity with which owners cling to their mortgaged homes or apartments, and the slow and cumbersome process of foreclosure, which requires about two years in Illinois, prolong the agony far beyond the short shift allowed margin holders of stocks. After the liquidation is completed, there is usually no quick rebound as in the case of stocks or commodities. While there may be a mild recovery in income-producing property, it may require a lapse of from eight to thirty years before the way is prepared for another land boom. The experience of the Chicago real estate cycle, showing the probable expectancy of life of each of the factors in their various phases, is presented in Tables LXVI and LXVII.

So far the Chicago real estate cycle has been considered as a phenomenon isolated from the rest of the United States. No satisfactory comparison can be made between the real estate cycle of Chicago and the cycles of other cities, because comparable data on all aspects of the cycle do not exist.[27] If the phases of the real estate cycle depend largely upon the acceleration in the rate of population growth, as herein contended, then since the rate of growth of different cities between decennial periods varies greatly, marked local differences in these cycles may be expected. Only careful studies of population growth between census years and land values in other cities could furnish the evidence for such a comparison.

G. THE CHICAGO REAL ESTATE CYCLE COMPARED WITH THE GENERAL BUSINESS CYCLE IN THE UNITED STATES

1. *The magnitude of the oscillations.*—The range of fluctuations in Chicago land values has on the average been considerably greater than that of wholesale commodity or rail-stock prices.[28] The great rises in wholesale prices during the Civil and the World wars; the rail-stock booms culminating in 1853, 1881, and 1906; and the industrial stock upturn ending in 1929 have alone been comparable in magnitude to the

[27] For a general journalistic account of land speculation in other cities in the United States from colonial times to the present see A. M. Sakolski, *The Great American Land Bubble* (New York, 1932). For a study of land values in New York City from 1905 to 1929 see Edwin H. Spengler, *Land Values in New York in Relation to Transit Facilities* (New York: Columbia University Press, 1930). For a description of the real estate cycle in St. Louis in which statistics on rent and marriage rates are presented see Delbert A. Wentzlick, *Journal of the American Institute of Appraisers*, January, 1933. For a description of some phases of the real estate cycle in San Francisco see Lewis A. Maverick, "Cycles in Real Estate Activity," *Journal of Land and Public Utility Economics*, IV, No. 4 (November, 1928), 405. For a study of subdivision activity in other American cities see Ernest M. Fisher, *Subdivision Activity in Nine Suburban Areas* ("University of Michigan Business Studies," Vol. I); see also Fisher, "Speculation in Suburban Lands," *op. cit.*, p. 153.

[28] See Table LXVIII.

TABLE LXVI
Sequence of Factors in the Chicago Real Estate Cycle, as Indicated by Deviations Above and Below the Normal Trend

Factors	Rise Begins	Peak or Year of Maximum Deviation above Normal	Decline Begins	Cross Normal Line on Way Down	The Bottom or Year of Maximum Deviation below Normal*
Cycle I, 1830–42					
Population..............	1831	1834	1835	1837	1838
Lots subdivided, Chicago, 1933 limits............	1830	1836	1837	1838	1838–44
Land values.............	1832	1836	1837	1840	1842
Cycle II, 1842–61					
Population..............	1839	1853	1854	1856	1858
New construction.........	1854†	1857	1858	1859	1862
Lots subdivided, Chicago, 1933 limits............	1844, 1851	1856	1857	1858	1861
Land values.............	1843	1856	1857	1858	1865
Cycle III, 1861–79					
Population..............	1858	1872	1873	1873	1875
Lots subdivided, Chicago, 1933 limits............	1863	1869	1870	1876	1880
Real estate transfers‡.....	....	1872	1873	1875	1879
New construction.........	1863	1872	1873	1874	1874
Land values.............	1866	1869	1872	1875	1878
Cycle IV, 1877–97					
Population..............	1877	1882, 1891	1892	1893	1896
Lots subdivided, Chicago, 1933 limits............	1881	1890	1891	1892	1900
Lots subdivided in Chicago Metropolitan Area......	1878	1891	1892	1893	1899
Real estate transfers.......	1880	1890	1891	1896	1898
New construction.........	1882	1892	1893	1893	1900
Land values.............	1879	1891	1892	1895	1897

* Present depression not over in 1933.
† No data before 1854.
‡ Data begins in 1869.

THE CHICAGO REAL ESTATE CYCLE

TABLE LXVI—Continued

Factors	Rise Begins	Peak or Year of Maximum Deviation above Normal	Decline Begins	Cross Normal Line on Way Down	The Bottom or Year of Maximum Deviation below Normal*
		Cycle V, 1917–33			
Population	1918	1924	1925	1926	1932
Lots subdivided, Chicago, 1933 limits	1920	1926	1927	1927	1930
Lots subdivided in Chicago Metropolitan Area	1919	1926	1927	1929	1931
New construction	1919	1925	1926	1930	1932
Land values	1920	1925	1926	1931	1933
Real estate transfers	1918	1925	1926	1929	1932

Summary: Time Sequence of Factors in Real Estate Cycle; Number of Years Each Factor Follows the Movement of Population

Factors					
Real estate transfers	2.67	0.5	1.0	2.67	2.0
New construction	3.67	1.5	1.5	2.0	1.5
Land values	3.6	1.2	1.5	2.8	3.2
Lots subdivided in Chicago Metropolitan Area	1.0	1.0	1.5	2.5	2.67
Lots subdivided, Chicago, 1933 limits	4.5	2.0	2.0	1.2	2.6

TABLE LXVII

AVERAGE TIME INTERVALS IN THE CHICAGO REAL ESTATE CYCLE (YEARS)

Factors	From Beginning of Rise to Peak	From Peak to Crossing Normal Line on Way Down	From Peak to Bottom
Population	12.0	2.2	4.8
Lots subdivided, Chicago, 1933 limits	8.0	2.8	8.2
Lots subdivided in Chicago Metropolitan Area	10.0	2.5	6.5
Real estate transfers	8.5	4.3	7.5
New construction	8.3	2.5	5.5
Land values	7.4	4.4	7.6

land booms.[29] The differences between the oscillations of the indices of Chicago real estate activity and those of other forms of local and of general American business movements are far more extreme. In an entire century there has been no single year in which general American business activity, according to the Ayres chart, has averaged more than 16 per cent above normal. In the last sixty-seven years the extreme rise of Chicago bank clearings has carried the curve only 28 per cent

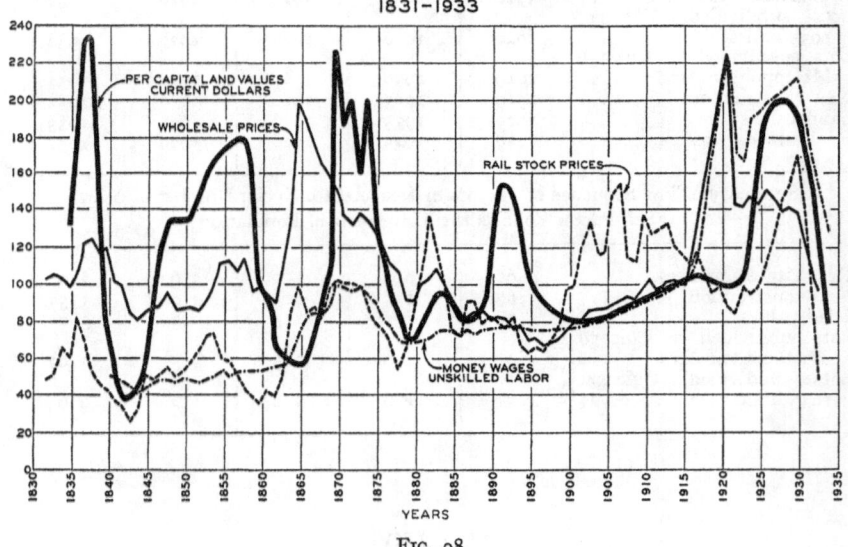

FIG. 98

above the trend line, and in the period from 1875 to the present the high point of Chicago manufactures has been only 20 per cent above normal.[30] These rises appear moderate, indeed, when compared with the advances in the factors that measure real estate activity. Even the index of real estate transfers, which fails to register the full volume of sales at the peak, has attained a maximum of 131 per cent above nor-

[29] See Fig. 102. In this figure the wholesale commodity price cycle has been computed from the indices of Professors G. F. Warren and F. A. Pearson. The canal-rail stock index is the one used by Leonard P. Ayres, in his chart, "American Business Activity and Four Price Series." Industrial stock prices are from Warren M. Persons, *Forecasting Business*, and are brought down to date by the Dow-Jones figures.

[30] See Table LXVIII and Figs. 99, 100, and 101.

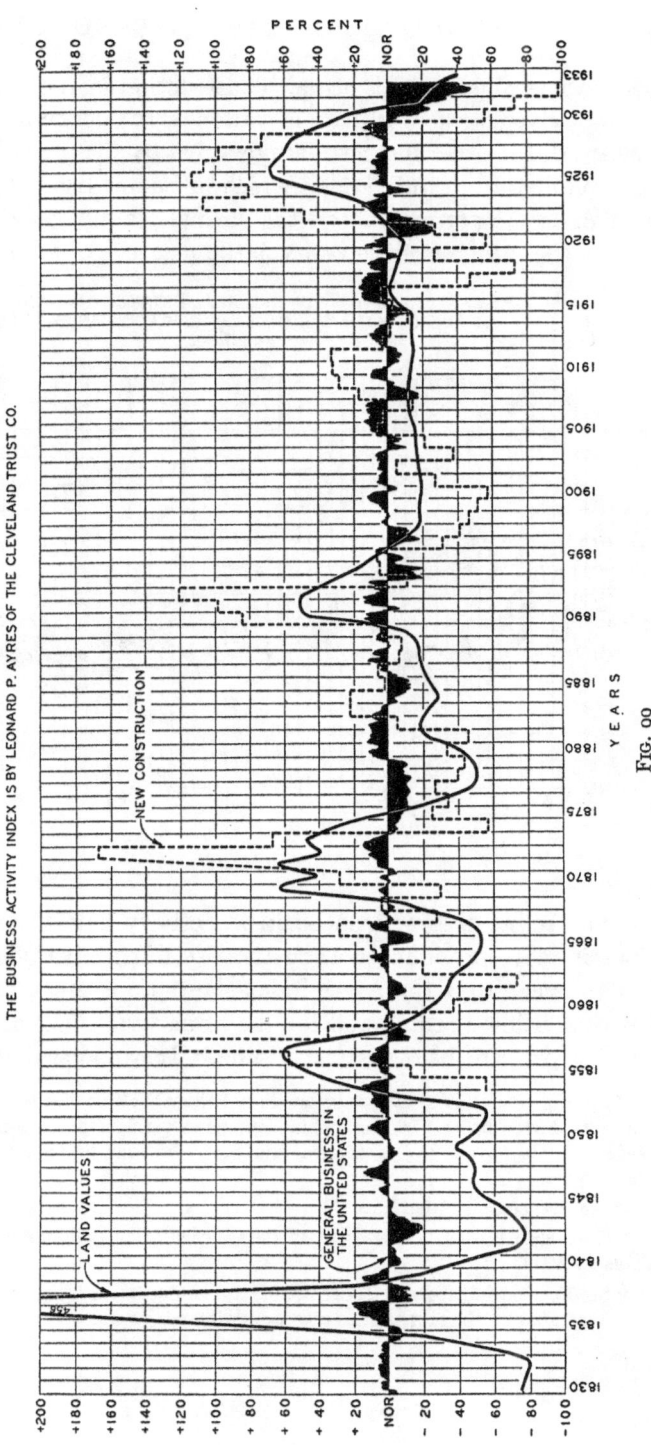

Fig. 99

mal.[31] The highest peak of new construction in the period since 1854 looms above transfers with an elevation of 167 per cent above the trend line.[32] All the other increases are dwarfed by the precipitous ascents in the volume of lots subdivided which in booms have reached altitudes as high as 540 per cent above the normal plain.[33] Subdivision activity is thus the most sensitive and volatile measure of a land boom.

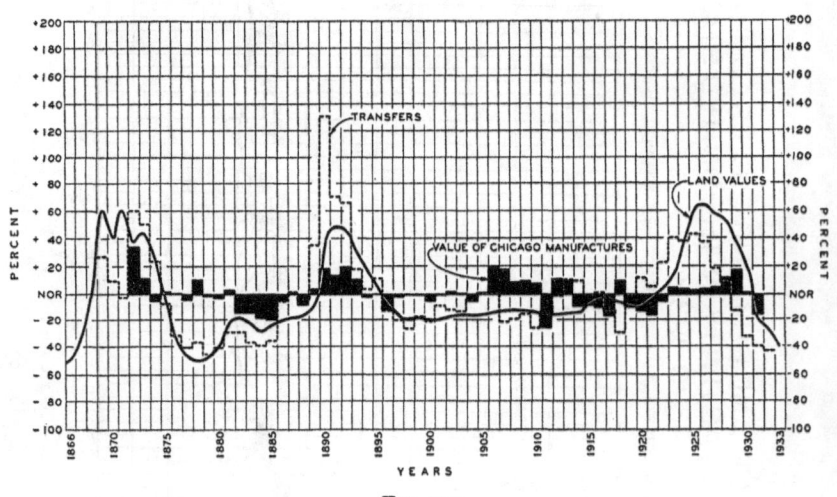

THE CHICAGO LAND VALUE AND REAL ESTATE TRANSFER CYCLES COMPARED WITH THE CYCLE OF CHICAGO MANUFACTURING 1866-1933

FIG. 100

The decline of American business activity below normal in depressions is more pronounced than the rise during periods of prosperity. For the year 1932 the Ayres index shows an average recession of 41.6 per cent below normal, and for the same year Chicago bank clearings were 52 per cent below the trend line.[34] It would seem that dips as ex-

[31] See Fig. 100. Real estate transfers do not show the heavy sales of lots on instalment contracts during boom periods, and in depression periods they are padded by master's deeds to avoid foreclosure, exchanges, and deeds recorded on transactions made several years before.

[32] See Fig. 99 and Table LXVIII.

[33] This figure is for lots subdivided in the Chicago Metropolitan Area. See Fig. 101 and Table LXVIII.

[34] See Figs. 99 and 101 and Table LXVIII. The decline in Chicago bank clearings may be exaggerated by the fact that so many outlying banks closed from 1929 to 1933.

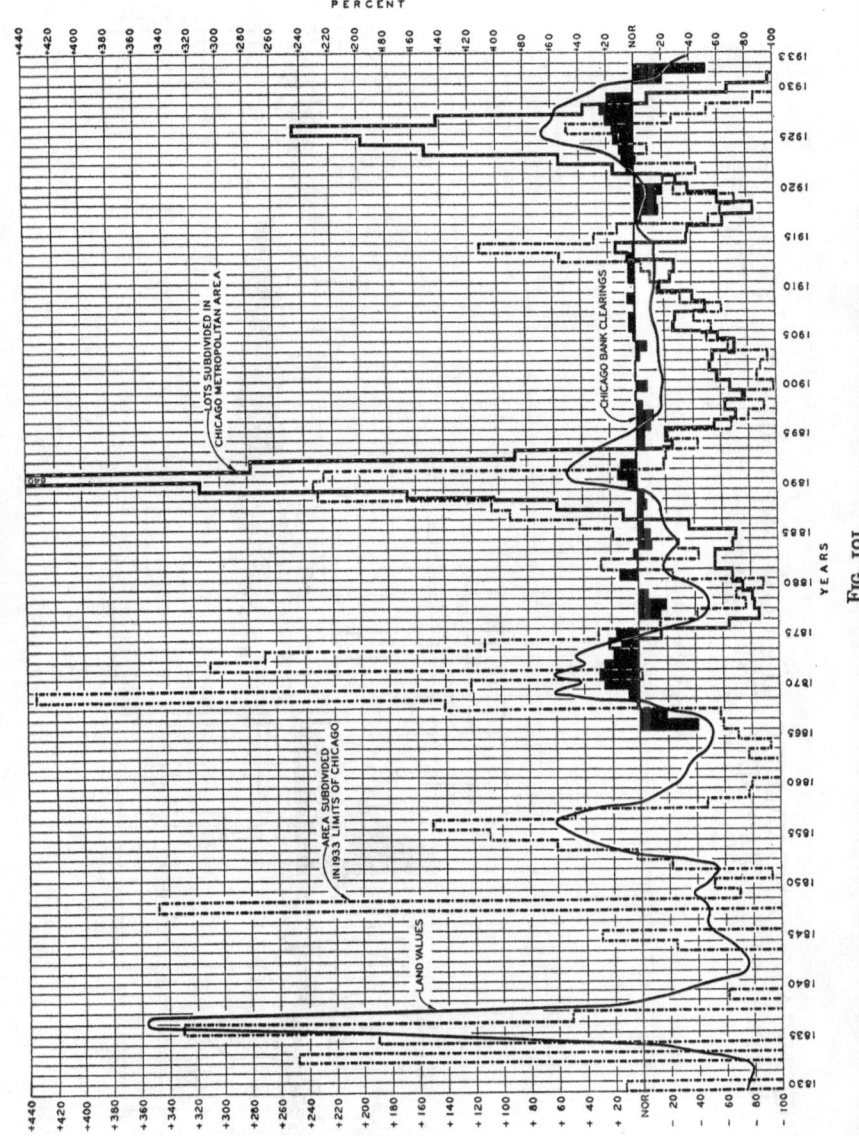

Fig. 101

THE CHICAGO LAND VALUE AND SUBDIVISION CYCLES COMPARED WITH THE CYCLE OF CHICAGO BANK CLEARINGS
1830–1933

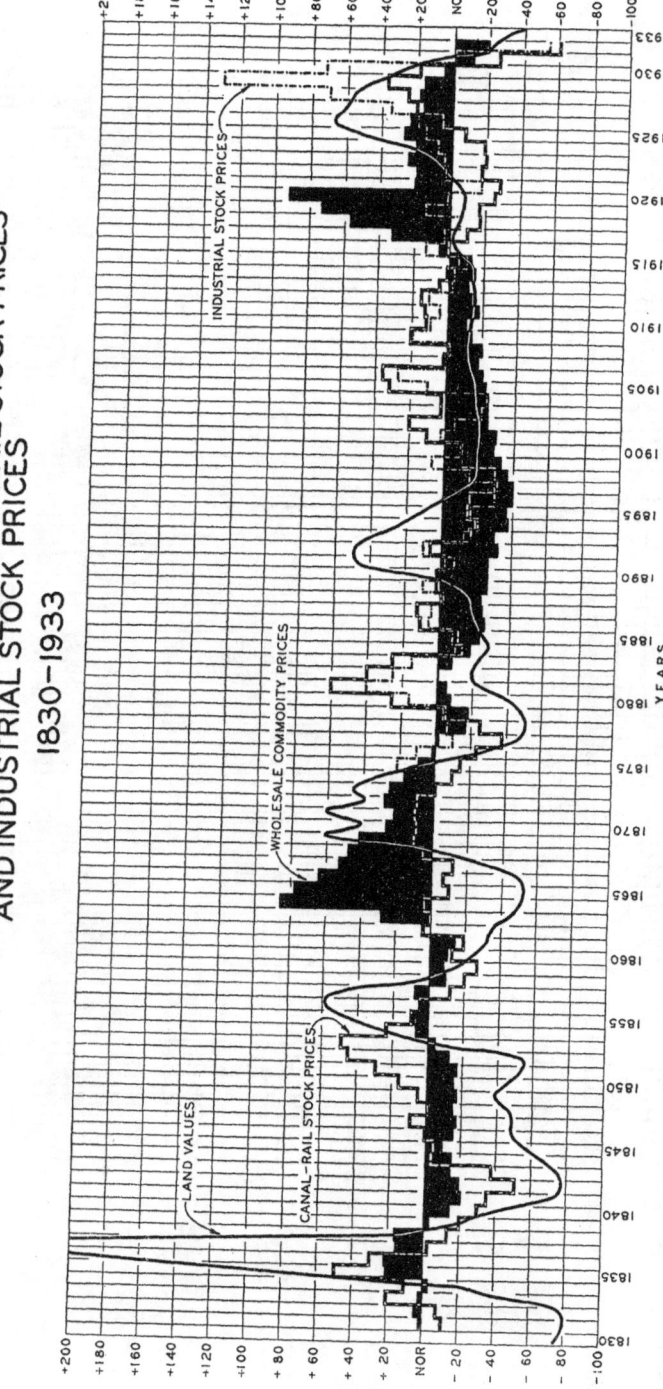

THE CHICAGO LAND VALUE CYCLE COMPARED WITH THE CYCLES OF WHOLESALE COMMODITY PRICES, CANAL-RAIL STOCK PRICES AND INDUSTRIAL STOCK PRICES

1830–1933

FIG. 102

treme as these would not be exceeded by the fall in real estate activity. Ruling out of consideration real estate transfers for the reasons already given, the indices of real estate activity do manage to decline even more

TABLE LXVIII

A Comparison of Fluctuations of Chicago Real Estate Factors Above and Below Normal with Fluctuations in General Business Factors

Factors	Percentage Maximum Deviation		Percentage Average Deviation		Maximum Length of Period (Years)		Average Length of Period (Years)		Per Cent of Entire Period Above Normal
	Above Normal	Below Normal	At or above Normal	Below Normal	At or above Normal	Below Normal	At or above Normal	Below Normal†	
Business activity in U.S., 1830–1932,* monthly..........	21	47.2	6.2	8.5	3.5	5.83	1.73	1.65	57.0
Business activity in U.S. annually*.....	16	41.6	5.1	7.5	7	6	3.0	2.0	58.8
Chicago value of manufactures, 1872–1931.	35	19	8.7	8.5	8	5	3.2	2.55	53.3
Chicago bank clearings, 1866–1932....	28	52	8.5	12.3	12	6	5.4	3.8	60.0
Canal-rail stock prices, 1831–1932.........	60	60	16.4	17.0	8	9	3.8	4.3	48.5
U.S. wholesale commodity prices, 1831–1932..............	92	40	26.0	18.1	15	39	10.0	16.2	42.1
Chicago real estate transfers, 1872–1932	131	43	29.0	21.8	9	12	3.6	6.1	41.0
Chicago new construction, 1854–1932....	167	98	45.5	34.6	8	9	3.4	3.7	46.2
Chicago land values, 1830–1933.........	456	80	58.4	30.0	9	26	6.0	16.3	29.0
Area subdivided in Chicago, 1830–1933	330	100	128.5	62.0	9	18	3.9	7.8	32.3
Area subdivided in Chicago Metropolitan Area, 1874–1933	540	100	134.9	55.6	7	19	5.3	12.7	28.3

* Chart of Leonard Ayres of the Cleveland Trust Co. The annual figures are annual averages of the Ayres figures.

† Periods below normal at the beginning or end of each series of data omitted, because the full length of the subnormal period was not determined.

precipitously than those measuring the general volume of business, for they fall 98 per cent below normal in the case of new construction and to absolute zero in the case of lots subdivided. In a depression a certain minimum of industrial activity is necessary to supply the population with food, some restricted requirements of clothing and luxury articles, and to maintain a skeleton organization for plants with no immediate business. Hence it is not possible for all American industrial activity to be suspended even in the worst business years. Nor can all forms of real estate activity be closed down even for a short time. People must rent houses and apartments; properties must be managed, decorated, heated, and supplied with janitor service; and roofs must be kept from leaking. It is possible, however, to stop building any new structures for a time and to cease making any additional investments in vacant lots. All speculation in real estate can come virtually to a standstill when the foreclosure mill is grinding away. Even then courts, lawyers, and receivers are busy, but their activity is of a nature that profoundly discourages people from acquiring more real estate. Short selling might maintain some semblance of a market, if it were possible to group real estate lots into standard units, with a sufficiently large supply of each grade to insure the probability that someone would always be willing to sell a lot at a reasonable price. As any such development is extremely unlikely because of the diversified nature of real estate, it would seem that the land and buildings which comprise over half of our national wealth are commodities of such a nature that in a few brief intervals can be sold at extravagant figures and that in other long periods cannot be converted into cash at all save at a tremendous sacrifice. While the lack of a stable and continuous market is particularly noticeable in the case of vacant lots on the fringe of a city, the same situation with respect to marketability applies to a less degree to properties even in the heart of central business districts of large cities. This defect could be remedied to a large extent in the case of income-producing holdings by a more stable and consistent lending policy on the part of banks and financial institutions. If money could be borrowed at all times on a conservative basis, or valuations established by earnings over a long period of years, instead of upon the vagaries of booms and depressions, a powerful stabilizing force would be exerted upon the real estate market. It is true that the rapid shifts in population that have occurred not only within the United States but within American cities, and the revolutionary shifts in the character and the intensity of land utilization, have made the calculation of long-run trends of earnings extremely difficult, if not impossible. The problem of the lack of stable markets for real estate may be solved by a slackening of population migrations and of the rate of population increase in the United States.

THE CHICAGO REAL ESTATE CYCLE 417

2. *Duration of the Chicago real estate and general business cycles.*—
From 1830 to 1933 there have been only five land booms in Chicago,
but, on the other hand, there have been only two great rises in commodity price levels and only about five extraordinary booms in rail and
industrial stocks in that period of a little over a century.[35] There have
been more numerous minor movements in stocks and commodities than
in the fluctuations of aggregate Chicago land values, but there have
been local and neighborhood movements in Chicago that are smoothed
out by the general average for the whole city. The exceptional speculative movements in land, commodities, and stocks are separated by
long intervals of time, and there is no definite period of years between
one boom and the next. Chicago land booms have occurred less frequently since 1873 than before, until thirty-five years elapsed from the
hectic land market of 1890 to that of 1925. If it be considered that the
speculation of 1890 was chiefly confined to the central business district
and the South Side and that the North Side was but little affected by it,
then in some sections a valley of the fifty-three years from 1872 to 1925
intervened from one peak to the next. Of course, there was a steady
rise in land values on the North Side from 1900 to 1920, even before the
last exuberant wave of buying that carried all Chicago land values to
their all-time peak. In fact, the length of the ensuing depression seems
to be measured by the shadow of the preceding peak. After the wild
speculation south of the World's Fair grounds in Chicago, from 1890 to
1893, there was no widespread upturn in values for thirty years,[36] while
at the same time the people on the North Side, which was suffering
from no such aftermath, were witnessing a slowly rising land market.

a) The long periods of depression in Chicago real estate.—The periods
of activity above normal for Chicago real estate factors are much shorter than the periods of depression. The very fact that the peaks go so
far above the normal line when they do occur necessarily requires either
deep valleys or long intervals of slightly below normal activity or both
combined. Chicago land values have remained below normal for as
long as twenty-six years in a stretch, and the minimum period under
the trend line was ten years. In fact, Chicago land values and Chicago

---

[35] See Fig. 102.

[36] In the vicinity of Eighty-seventh and Jeffery Avenue, there were in some cases no
transfers between 1890 and 1922.

subdivision activity have been above normal only about 29 per cent of the time.[37] New construction activities make a better showing, but still the volume of new building is depressed over half the time.[38]

The long periods of depression in real estate are in sharp contrast with the situation in general business. The longest period of subnormal activity, that in the seventies, lasted only six years, according to the Ayres chart, and the average period below normal lasted only three and a half years even when the data are computed on an annual basis. If monthly variations in business be considered, the average duration of a subnormal business period was only one and sixty-five one-hundredths years. American business activity, Chicago bank clearings, and Chicago manufactures have been above normal 59.60 and 53 per cent, respectively, of the time.[39]

General American business activity dips much more frequently above and below the normal line than Chicago land values or subdivision activity. Whereas in the period from 1830 to 1933 American business rose above normal approximately thirty times, land values advanced above this line only five times and lots subdivided twelve times. Since 1875 American business activity has had fifteen separate periods of prosperity interrupted by recessions below normal, but since that time there have been only two periods when land values, four times when lots subdivided, five times when real estate transfers, and six times when new construction were above normal.[40] The long periods of subnormal activity in the case of the real estate factors again illustrates the lack of a continuously active land market.

3. *The relationship of wage and interest rates to the land-value cycle.*— In considering the relationship of land values to other general price movements in the United States, it is important to consider the course of wages and of interest rates.[41] Wage rates affect construction costs to a far greater extent than commodity prices, for a considerable proportion of the cost of a building is in the form of direct wage outlays for the work at the site or for the production of the building materials. A rise in commodity prices, however, does lead to a delayed advance in wage rates, which gain is mostly retained even after the decline in the

---

[37] See Table LXVIII.

[38] The percentage of time below normal is 53.8 per cent.

[39] See Table LXVIII.   [40] See Figs. 99, 100, and 101.

[41] See Figs. 78 and 98 on pp. 349 and 410.

price level. As a result, construction costs are permanently higher after an upheaval in commodity prices, and there is an appreciation in the value of old buildings which gives rise to speculation. A decline in interest rates affects land values through the capitalization rate. A fall in the rate of interest on mortgages in the central business district of Chicago from 10 to 4 per cent between 1856 and 1896, which in turn reflected the effect of the declining yield on bonds, was one of the most important factors in the rise in land values in the business center of Chicago in that period.

4. *The sequence of the real estate and the commodity and stock cycles:*
 a) *The valleys coincide but the peaks do not.*—A comparison of the Chicago land-value cycle with the cycles for wholesale commodity prices in the United States, canal-rail stock prices and industrial stock prices, as shown by Figure 102 and Tables LXIX and LXX, indicates that peaks for these series occur at widely divergent points but that the points of maximum depression for all of them come almost at the same time. Thus if Chicago land values be compared with wholesale commodity prices, the land values rose during two periods of rising prices, two periods of falling prices, and one period of stationary prices. The peak in land values was attained five years after the great peaks of wholesale commodity prices in 1864 and 1920. If the comparison be made between Chicago land values and canal-rail or industrial stock prices, it is to be observed that stock prices reached their peak one year before the land-value peak of 1836, three years before the land-value top of 1856, and four years after the land-value maximum of 1925. In other periods there was no agreement between speculative movements in land and stocks. There was no Chicago land boom in 1881 and 1906 that corresponded with the rise in stocks; there was no upturn in stocks from 1869 to 1873 or from 1889 to 1892 that corresponded in magnitude with the sharp advance in land values.

On the other hand, while the peak points of the speculative indices rarely coincide, their maximum depression points show a far greater degree of agreement. The trough of the depression for Chicago land values, stock prices, and wholesale commodity prices came in the periods 1841–42, 1859–61,[42] 1877–79, 1896–98, 1920–21, and 1932 or 1933. It requires varying periods of time for each set of factors to reach new

[42] Chicago land values were at their absolute low points in 1861, although the maximum low point according to the deviation from the normal trend came in 1865.

peaks after each valley, but in certain major depressions they all reach bottom at about the same time.

b) Commodity, land, and stock speculations do not come together but alternate.—It is a striking fact that the greatest speculative movements in wholesale commodity prices, Chicago land values, and rail and industrial stocks have not concurred but have alternated, in point of

TABLE LXIX

YEAR IN WHICH MAJOR PEAKS OCCURRED IN CHICAGO LAND VALUES COMPARED WITH MAJOR PEAKS IN WHOLESALE PRICES, CANAL-RAIL STOCK PRICES, AND INDUSTRIAL STOCK PRICES

	1830–42	1842–61	1861–79	1879–98	1898–1917	1917–33
Chicago land values........	1836	1856	1869	1891	*	1925
Canal-rail stock prices	1835	1853	1869†	1881	1906	1929
Industrial stock prices......	‡	‡	‡	1881	1906	1929
Wholesale commodity prices	1836†	1855, 1857†	1864	§	§	1920

* No major peak.   † Not a predominant peak.   ‡ No data.   § No peaks.

TABLE LXX

YEAR IN WHICH THE MAXIMUM POINT OF DEPRESSION OCCURRED FOR CHICAGO LAND VALUES COMPARED WITH MAXIMUM DEPRESSION POINTS FOR WHOLESALE PRICES, CANAL-RAIL STOCK PRICES, AND INDUSTRIAL STOCK PRICES

	1830–43	1843–66	1866–79	1879–99	1899–1921	1921–33
Land values...............	1842	1865	1878	1898	1920	1933
Canal-rail stock prices......	1842	1859	1877	1897	1921	1932
Industrial stock prices......			1877	1897	1921	1932
Wholesale commodity prices	1841	1861	1879	1896–97	1899, 1921	1932

time, since the Civil War.[43] In both the Civil and the World wars, there was an extraordinary demand from Europe for American foodstuffs and for American mineral products that was added to the civilian and military requirements of the United States. This exceptional demand caused a rapid rise in many of the components of the commodity price index and it also caused labor and capital to be concentrated on the production of the kind of goods for which there was such imperative need. The demand for housing and for comfort or luxury articles was

[43] See Fig. 102.

held abnormally low during these war periods. With the cessation of war and the return of normal agricultural production in Europe, the abnormal demand for American farm products declined and the wholesale commodity price index fell. The return of soldiers and sailors to their homes and the influx of the rural population into the industrial centers, however, created in turn an abnormal need for the residential accommodations, whose increased supply had been held back by the war-time regulations of industry and by the high profits of war industries. This led to a rise in rents and to a land boom. Finally, when the housing shortage was made good, the demand for automobiles, radios, and manufactured articles supplying the comforts of life or luxurious tastes increased the profits of industrial plants and led to booms in the common stocks of these companies.

Thus the lack of a balanced demand for foodstuffs, housing, and other manufactured articles has alternately speeded up prices and production in farm products and agricultural land, in the construction industry and urban land, and in manufacturing plant and capital goods. While one part of the economic system was stressed, other parts were neglected, so instead of an even and equal flow of production, there was an alternation of booms and depressions.

c) The advantage of a source of liquid capital for real estate operators.—The fact that speculation alternates from commodities to urban lands and to stocks suggests that the movement of each may be enhanced by the concentration of funds upon each in turn instead of the diffusion of capital over all of them at the same time. Speculators who have reaped large profits in the rise or fall of commodity prices may do as Potter Palmer did and invest in land. It is significant to note that some of the largest fortunes in real estate have been made by men who were not primarily real estate operators. John Jacob Astor acquired his liquid capital in the fur trade, Marshall Field accumulated large savings from wholesale and retail trade, and Potter Palmer had interests in trade and in his hotel that furnished him with ready funds. Real estate is not a liquid asset in a depression, and in these recurring periods of subnormal business activity it is almost impossible to refinance even a conservative loan upon land and buildings. Hence some of the largest real estate owners, who had no other business or fund of capital to draw upon, lost all their holdings by foreclosure because of their inability to renew the mortgages upon their properties.

d) Speculators tend to stick to the game they know best.—Switching back and forth from real estate investments to those in commodities and in stocks or bonds is probably not a common practice, however, because investments in real estate are difficult to liquidate and because the methods of buying and selling land are of such an altogether different nature from trading in stocks, bonds, or commodities that speculators familiar with the technique of one kind of market are utterly lost in the other. Some land speculators confine their activities entirely to one neighborhood or section of one city, or to one type of property in that city, and while some speculators follow land booms from city to city, there are probably not very many who alternately trade in commodities, land, and stocks.

e) The public is swayed by the prevailing crowd psychology.—If the same persons do not change from one type of speculation to another, there are always newcomers or members of the general public who are ready to embark upon any form of enterprise that promises quick profits. When agricultural land speculation or commodity speculation is rife, they enter that field, but if an urban land boom is sweeping their city when they have funds to invest, they will buy lots. If stock speculation is uppermost in the public mind, these same people will buy stocks on margin. Sometimes the same persons may enter the different speculative fields in turn, but frequently the field first entered is their last, for they either lose their money and are deterred from all speculative ventures of any kind thereafter or make profits and are inclined to stick to the same form of speculation with which they have become familiar. In all events, the concentration of speculative capital upon each of these fields in turn causes them to reach greater heights than if the same funds were distributed among several forms of speculation.

f) The delayed effects of a great war.—The interrelationships between the various parts of the economic mechanism are thus illustrated by the delayed reaction of commodity-price upheavals upon land booms. The emphasis which the economic system put upon the production of foodstuffs and war materials from 1914 to 1919 with the consequent worldwide rise in commodity prices caused an abnormal curtailment of construction work, which in due course led to a stressing of the production of housing facilities and to excessive activity in that direction. It seems that the dislocations of the normal flow of economic activity caused by great wars produce a series of speculative tidal waves that do not subside until years after the echo of the last cannon shot has died away. There are, of course, many other causes that disturb the balanced distribution of productive effort, and it is possible that the economic system would generate a wavelike motion within itself if such cataclysmic influences such as wars were ruled out of consideration. In actual historic surveys, however, the ordinary course of events is intermingled with extraordinary occurrences that interact violently upon the other elements, so that the actual fluctuations reflect the combined influence of both the normal and the abnormal events. Two great land booms in Chicago occurred during post-war booms, but three others took place without such a stimulus, so that no catastrophic theory of business fluctuations is sought to be propounded here.

H. REAL ESTATE CYCLES MAY BE A PASSING PHASE

The real estate cycle itself may be a phenomenon that is confined chiefly to young or rapidly growing cities. An ancient city may have a land boom if it becomes like Warsaw, the political capital of a new state, but if rapid rises or declines in land values become of rare occurrence in older or more stable societies, the sequence of events just described may in the future be of interest only to historians delving in the habits and customs of "early machine age culture in the United States," and the knowledge of the mode of behavior of forces in the real estate cycle will have no value in forecasting the trend of future events. The long and uncertain duration of the cycles described in this book in itself makes practical application of any of the precepts that may have been disclosed herein difficult, for one must live long and be gifted with extraordinary patience to wait for an opportunity that knocks on the door not oftener than once every twenty or thirty years.

APPENDIXES

APPENDIX I

THE CHICAGO LAND MARKET

A. THE LACK OF HOMOGENEITY OF CHICAGO LOTS

In the main body of this study, aggregate land values of the entire city or large sections have been the principal subject matter. The methods by which total values for each square-mile area were determined were not discussed and the difficulties in the summation process were therefore not revealed. If the lots in each section were of a homogeneous character, the sample sales of a few might establish the value of all, but it is well known that no two urban lots are exactly alike, and in the case of Chicago the differences are extreme. Of the 740,512 lots within the city limits in 1928, the range in values was from $5.00 to $50,000 a front foot.

This lack of uniformity between Chicago lots not only imposes limitations upon computations of land values in a given year, but it causes even greater difficulties in determining the trends of values through a series of years. There are not enough land units of the same kind and character to establish a continuous market, and sales in many sections are at times infrequent and far between. As a result of this, interpolations and estimates must be made, even when all the sales data are available.

In this appendix, not merely the differences but the causes or the kinds of differences between Chicago lots will be considered. If each lot were as unique as an old painting or the last remaining specimen of an issue of postage stamps, there would be no common or general market at all, but each lot would be *sui generis*, or a law unto itself. It is the fact that the individual parcels, notwithstanding their unique qualities, are linked together by certain differentials that makes it possible to form the concept of a Chicago land market as an entity. The differences in lots according to the purpose for which they are used have already been discussed, but three main groups of factors causing variation in individual lot values remain to be treated. These are, first, differences in lot and block size and location with respect to corners as determined by the layout of the original subdivision; second, differences in title caused by acts of the owner; and, third, differences caused by variations in control by community and governmental units.

1. *Layout of the original subdivision lot and block size: depth-rule and corner-influence factors.*—The size of the block, and also to a large extent the depth and width of individual lots within the block, are often irrevocably determined by the subdivider who first plats a raw acre tract or farm into town lots. It is true that if few or none of the original lots are sold, and if no development in the form of buildings or street improvements takes place, the entire subdivision may be "vacated" or turned back into farm land. Thus the early subdivisions in Chicago, such as Canalport, Calumet, George, and Cottage Grove, that were laid out in 1836 with

their lots oriented toward the lake or the Chicago River were thus vacated and an entirely different pattern of streets later superimposed over the old plan. When some part of a subdivision is sold and a few houses are built in it, however, it becomes extremely difficult to consolidate the tract again under one ownership and to lay out the streets and the blocks in a different way. After the street improvements are installed, it would also be very expensive to alter the original plan. Thus the original block measurements of the Chicago "Loop" and the near North and West sides of Chicago have never been materially changed.

Since, as will be noted later, urban lots do not necessarily have a uniform square-foot value regardless of their width, depth, and shape, the maximum aggregate lot value that can be derived from a given acre tract varies with the lot and block plan. As the size of lot that may yield the maximum value at one time may cease to represent the best layout for the highest land utilization of another period of time, some sections of the city may lose part of their land value because the size of

TABLE LXXI

LOT AND BLOCK DIMENSIONS OF ORIGINAL SUBDIVISIONS IN OR NEAR THE PRESENT LOOP

Name of Subdivision	Typical Block Size (Feet)	Lot Width (Feet)	Lot Depth (Feet)	Street Width (Feet)
Original Town.........	320×360	80	180	80
Kinzie................	218×300	50	100	74
Carpenter.............	250×341	50	150	66

their land units has become obsolete and cannot readily be changed. Therefore it becomes important to consider briefly the history of lot and block plans in Chicago.

The Chicago plain, in common with most of the Western United States, was surveyed in mile-square sections, which in turn were cut into four square quarter-sections and thus sold to settlers. Subdividers found it convenient to adopt a rectangular block plan in cutting up these quarter-sections, and such a layout was virtually forced upon them when the one-hundred-and-sixty-acre tracts were divided into four square "forties," or into sixteen square ten-acre parcels. Except for the circular plan of Norwood, practically the only deviations from the rectangular lot and block plan of Chicago are caused by the radial and axial highways which cut across section lines at oblique angles and create many triangular and truncated lots along their route.

The first Chicago subdivisions from 1830 to 1837 provided mostly short, almost square, blocks, which meant as many as fourteen to eighteen streets to the mile in both directions. Table LXXI shows the plan of part of the present Loop and part of the near North and West sides which has persisted to this day. Some of the other subdivisions of 1836–37 that were later vacated provided blocks with a length of twice the width, as Table LXXII shows. The typical lot width of 50 feet of that period was considered necessary to provide for a "garden home."

In the subdivisions in the next boom, or from 1848 to 1858, the typical lot width was still 50 feet, with a depth of 150–160 feet, as shown by the subdivision of Hyde Park. Extreme lot depth was absolutely necessary for an aristocratic residential development at this time, for the carriage and servant's quarters were in the rear of the mansion itself. Hence the 600-foot square blocks of Kenwood allowed lot depths of 300 feet. In the subdivisions from 1866 to 1873 also, the districts intended for fashionable occupancy, such as Ashland and Drexel boulevards, were provided with wide streets and deep lots.

In the boom from 1866 to 1873 the block size that has since become the typical block unit for Chicago made its appearance. This was the 600-by-266-foot block with a 66-foot street and a 16-foot alley, which made possible lot depths of 124 or 125 feet. The long sides of these blocks usually ran north and south, so that there are generally eight blocks to the mile going north and south in Chicago and sixteen blocks to the mile going east and west. At the same time the width of the typical

TABLE LXXII

LOT AND BLOCK DIMENSIONS OF OUTLYING SUBDIVISIONS OF 1836–37

Name of Subdivision	Typical Block Size (Feet)	Lot Width (Feet)	Lot Depth (Feet)	Width of Street (Feet)
Calumet-George	200×400	50	100	60
Canalport	200×400	50	100	66
Cottage Grove	200×400	50	100	66
Duncan's	266×600	50	125	66

lot was reduced from 50 to 25 feet, so that a lot 25 by 125 feet was the usual unit in the subdivisions from 1868 to 1900. Beginning about 1910, the ordinance requiring windows to be set back 3 feet from the lot line and the increasing construction of two-flat buildings that were three or four rooms deep made necessary a greater lot width to provide for sufficient light and air. Residential lots in new subdivisions after 1910 had a width of 30 feet, and old subdivisions not built up were frequently resubdivided into lots of the new width. The prevailing depth of 125 feet and the width of 25 feet for business lots were not changed, however. Because of the new requirements, a residential lot with a width of only 25 feet had a value of less than one-half that of a 30-foot lot in a similar location, because it could be used only with difficulty.

Having thus considered the historical development of Chicago lot and block plan, the question now arises as to how the variation in these plans affects the aggregate value of a given quarter-section of land. This involves a discussion of depth rules and corner-influence tables.

In the matter of depth rules, it was recognized by Hoffman as early as 1866 that the front half of an urban lot was worth more than the rear half. Nearly every city has a different rule to express this difference, however, and the front half of the lot is valued at from 57.5 to 72.5 per cent, depending on whether the lot is in Los

Angeles, Cleveland, Baltimore, Chicago, or London.[1] These rules, based on experience or observation in the different cities, are themselves subject to change with changing conditions or with more detailed and accurate analyses. For Chicago a separate rule has been devised by Harry Cutmore and Walter Kuehnle for tax-assessment purposes, which is based on thousands of Chicago appraisals and which takes into account not merely general conditions peculiar to Chicago but also the different uses of Chicago land. It is commonly known in Chicago that a front half of a business lot contains a greater percentage of the total lot value than the front half of an apartment lot because most modern stores require no greater depth than

TABLE LXXIII

AGGREGATE LAND VALUE UNDER DIFFERENT SUBDIVISION PLANS AND DEPTH RULES

SUBDIVISION PLAN	TOTAL FRONTAGE	LOT DEPTH	DEPTH FACTORS UNDER RULE NO.			
			I	II	III	IV
A	4,800	289	1.2	1.52	1.31	2.33
B	7,200	179	1.08	1.2	1.12	1.44
C	9,600	124	1.0	1.0	1.0	1.0
D	14,400	69	0.65	0.65	0.74	0.56

SUBDIVISION PLAN	TOTAL FRONTAGE	LOT DEPTH	AGGREGATE VALUE UNDER RULE NO.			
			I	II	III	IV
A	4,800	289	$5,760	$7,296	$6,288	$11,184
B	7,200	179	7,769	8,640	8,050	10,368
C	9,600	124	9,600	9,600	9,600	9,600
D	14,400	69	9,360	9,360	10,656	6,384

50 or 60 feet, while an apartment building can be extended to the full depth of the lot. Accordingly, the rules developed for Chicago tax-assessment purposes allow the front half of a business lot to be valued at 70 per cent of the total, while the front half of an apartment lot is valued at only 60 per cent of the total lot value.[2]

To illustrate by a concrete example, the differences in aggregate land values under different lot and block plans and under different uses consider the various modes of subdividing forty acres of land as shown by Figure 103.

The four different lot and block plans, A, B, C, and D yield the aggregate street frontage shown in Table LXXIII, and the aggregate land value in each case is shown by multiplying the frontage by the depth factor. There are four different depth factors, I, II, III, and IV, Rule 1 being that used for residential and small

---

[1] Walter R. Kuehnle, *Real Estate Magazine* (Chicago), August, 6 1932.

[2] *Real Estate Assessment Manual, Cook County, Illinois* (February, 1933), pp. 21–22.

apartment property, Rule II for multiple-apartment or high-grade business land, Rule III for ordinary business property, and Rule IV being a factor that would regard every square foot of equal importance and which would nullify the depth factor. The first three rules are those applied by Harry Cutmore and Walter Kuehnle in the assessment of Chicago land for 1931.

Thus, under the foregoing rules, Subdivision Plan A would yield the greatest aggregate value if each square foot was of equal importance, because in that plan the smallest percentage is taken for streets and alleys; Plan C would yield the

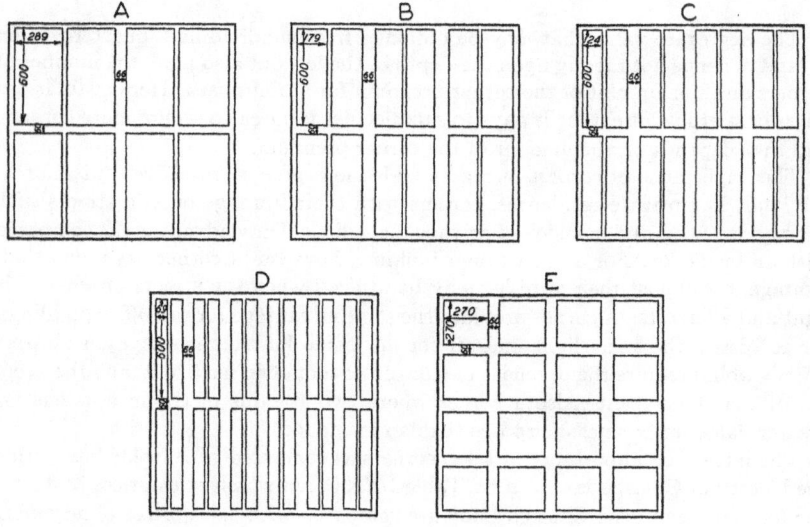

FIG. 103

maximum value for residential or apartment use; and Plan D, with the highest amount of street frontage, would produce the greatest value for commercial use. Since no entire subdivision is expected to be devoted to commercial use, but only a small part of it, Plan D would seldom be the best arrangement, as more would be lost on the shallow residential lots than would be gained on the shallow business lots. Of the four subdivision plans considered, Plan C, or the one most commonly in use today, would yield the maximum advantage to the subdivider under present conditions.

In the subdivision of land for industrial use, the dedication of any streets and alleys to public use is considered a serious disadvantage, as switch tracks can be laid across public streets only by securing consent of the City Council. Therefore the streets necessary for ingress are retained as private thoroughfares, so that switch tracks may be placed across them or their route may be changed if industrial needs require a different plant layout. The lots used for industrial purposes should be deep enough to permit a switch track with a radius of at least 250 feet or else shaped to permit the entry of a switch track on an angle, as the accompanying diagram shows.

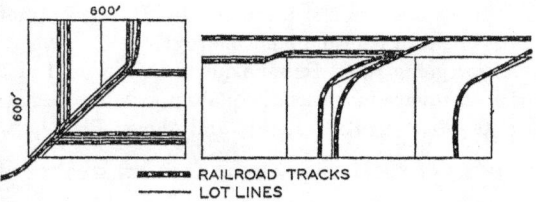

RAILROAD TRACKS
LOT LINES

The aggregate value that may be obtained from subdividing a quarter-section of land depends not merely upon the depth of the lot, but also upon the number of corners and the amount of the corner premium for various uses. Here again it is a question as to what extent it pays to sacrifice net lot area to secure more corners, and that depends on the amount of the corner premium.

The importance of corners increases with the degree of intensive utilization of the land. For private residences, corners with their frontage on two streets with their added noise and invasion of privacy, have little if any advantage as compared with an inside lot. For an apartment building, however, a corner has a great advantage, for almost the entire lot may be utilized when the streets provide wide light and air shafts. A corner provides the same advantage for tall office buildings, for to obtain the same light and air for an inside lot that frontage on a street affords would require the purchase of a 60- or 80-foot strip next to it, and the keeping of that lot vacant. Also a corner where two streams of traffic flow has far greater value for business purposes than an inside lot.

The increasing importance of Loop corners as compared with inside lots during the history of Chicago is shown by Table LXXIV, in which sales prices of 80-by-180-foot corners in the Chicago Loop are compared with sales prices of adjoining 80-by-180-foot inside lots.[3]

Similarly, prior to 1900 there were few outlying business corners that had a special value much higher than inside lots or other corners on the same street. In 1926 not only were ordinary business corners considered to be worth 25 per cent more than adjoining inside lots, but there were also several hundred double section or transfer corners where neighborhood land values reached value peaks that were determined by special rules. Land values dropped downward from these corners. Thus in the 1931 assessment the average front-foot value of eighty-six such corners was over double the value of the average inside lots on the best street within 300 feet, triple the value of the average inside lots on the best street from 300 to 600 feet away, and quadruple the value of the best inside lots 600 feet away.

The extent to which it pays to provide extra corners in a subdivision depends

[3] These premiums include much more than the ordinary corner premium, for an 80-by-180-foot corner whose long side is on State Street, for instance, includes frontage on State Street in addition to the ordinary corner. In view of the lack of data on small corners, this is the only method that can be applied throughout.

upon the amount of the corner premium. Thus in Plan C, suppose that the number of corners be doubled by increasing the number of cross-streets, as Plan E in Figure 103 shows. The amount of corner and inside frontage and the aggregate value of the tract, depending on different corner premiums, are shown by Table LXXV. Thus, if corners are worth over 50 per cent more than inside lots, or at least as much

TABLE LXXIV

ESTIMATED CORNER PREMIUMS OF LOTS IN THE CENTRAL BUSINESS DISTRICT OF CHICAGO

Year	Average Corner Premium (Per Cent)
1836	20
1856	25
1873	25
1896	60
1926–32	100–300*

* Using the corner influence and depth tables of Cook County Assessors for 1928 and 1932, the premium is 100 per cent where both intersecting streets are of equal value and proportionately higher where the most valuable frontage is on the long side of the lot.

as 75 per cent more, then it pays to use Subdivision Plan E. For ordinary residential, apartment, or commercial use, where the corner premium is less than 50 per cent, such a subdivision plan would not be the most profitable, but for the Loop or

TABLE LXXV

EFFECT OF DOUBLING THE NUMBER OF CORNERS UPON AGGREGATE LAND VALUES

Subdivision Plan	Inside Frontage	Corner Frontage (50 Ft. Cor.)	Corner Premiums					Aggregate Value				
			I	II	III	IV	V	I	II	III	IV	V
C	8,000	1,600	0.1	0.25	0.50	0.75	1.0	$9,760	$10,000	$10,400	$10,800	$11,200
E	5,440	3,200	0.1	0.25	0.50	0.75	1.0	8,960	9,440	10,240	11,040	11,840

central business area, numerous cross-streets and numerous corners add to the aggregate land value. Hence the original mode of Loop subdivision turned out to be most advantageous in the long run.

2. *Differences in the owner's title.*—Title to real estate, unlike that to stocks, bonds, and negotiable securities, varies with the status of the owners with respect to judgments, marital status, interests of adverse holders, and contractual capacity. A deed conveys only the title that the grantor has, and this is subject not only to

any defects in the title of the immediate owner, but to all the defects in his predecessors' titles that have not been cured by adverse possession or suits to quiet title. Hence title to real estate is ordinarily not conveyed without an examination as to the state of the title, and the submission of a report to the prospective buyer which is called an "abstract" and which is a digest of all prior conveyances and all judgments or matters of record affecting the title. This abstract is submitted to the buyer's lawyer, and if in his opinion it discloses nothing that will seriously impair the seller's title, the deal is ready for consummation. Frequently, however, a minute examination will reveal some faint flaw in the title, which some lawyers will pass over and other punctilious lawyers will not, so that when abstracts are used exclusively the buyer who wants to withdraw from a deal may cause his lawyer to search for such faint flaws. Defective titles are seldom sold, so that the seller usually takes steps to remove all judgments against him or clouds against his title until it is made merchantable. Sometimes, however, men who are willing to take long speculative chances pay for deeds from land claimants whose titles are open to

TABLE LXXVI

NUMBER OF GUARANTY ORDERS TAKEN BY THE CHICAGO TITLE
AND TRUST COMPANY, 1911–33

1911	16,696	1917	23,936	1923	71,919	1929	83,557
1912	19,869	1918	18,373	1924	80,948	1930	61,912
1913	23,589	1919	31,477	1925	98,018	1931	47,298
1914	23,966	1920	34,878	1926	103,496	1932	37,536
1915	26,426	1921	40,240	1927	107,432	1933*	32,695
1916	28,235	1922	53,507	1928	104,283		

* First ten months.

serious doubt or are the subject of litigation. Captain Streeter thus gave deeds to land in Streeterville on the strength of various claims preferred by him which were later held by the courts to be without validity.

a) Guaranty policies of the Chicago Title and Trust Company.—In Chicago and the adjacent territory, transfer of real estate on examination of abstracts alone has been supplanted to a considerable extent since 1900 by use of Chicago Title and Trust guaranty policies as evidences of title. In the great fire of October 9, 1871, all the records of deeds in the County Building upon which the evidence of title depended were destroyed. The private abstract companies managed to save copies of these records, so that they alone had the knowledge of the state of the early titles. Beginning in 1887 with the organization of the Title Guaranty and Trust Company and continuing in 1891 with the formation of the Cook County Abstract Company the practice was started of not merely showing an abstract and giving an opinion as to the state of the title, but of guaranteeing for a consideration the validity of the title. In 1901 all of the abstract and guaranty companies were consolidated in the Chicago Title and Trust Company, which acquired all the original records of the abstract companies, such as Chase Brothers (1847–73), Shortall and Hoard (1852–73), Handy and Company (1873–1901), and which thus having the only original ante-fire title records, proceeded to issue title guaranty policies in increasing numbers, as Table LXXVI shows.

APPENDIXES 435

The declining importance of abstracts is indicated by Table LXXVII, showing orders taken by the Chicago Title and Trust Company for abstracts as well as for guaranty policies.

In securing a title guaranty policy, the company first renders a preliminary report showing all objections to the title. The owner then takes steps by affidavits and other means to remove these objections if it is possible. If the objections are slight, the company may waive them and guarantee against them, whereupon the subse-

TABLE LXXVII

GUARANTY ORDERS OF THE CHICAGO TITLE AND TRUST COMPANY COMPARED WITH ABSTRACT ORDERS

Year	Guaranty Orders	Abstract Orders	Per Cent Guaranty Orders to Abstract Orders
1911	16,696	36,989	43.3
1912	19,869	41,340	48.3
1913	23,589	46,947	50.2
1914	23,966	41,807	57.0
1915	26,426	39,832	61.3
1916	28,235	39,564	71.2
1917	23,936	30,433	79.7
1918	19,373	24,825	74.0
1919	31,477	44,319	71.0
1920	34,878	53,687	65.0
1921	40,240	51,656	77.8
1922	58,617	53,507	109.6
1923	71,919	68,080	105.7
1924	80,948	56,466	143.5
1925	98,017	53,300	183.9
1926	103,496	45,830	226.0
1927	107,432	38,897	276.2
1928	104,283	32,737	319.0
1929	83,557	27,325	306.0
1930	61,912	20,509	302.0
1931	47,298	15,797	300.0
1932	37,536	11,544	325.2
1933*	32,695	7,755	421.6

* First ten months.

quent owners are relieved of further anxiety on that score. If the objections are of a more serious nature but are still capable of being classified as insurable risks, or if it is a case of an impediment to transferring the title that can be covered by a bond, the company will still issue its policy. Title guaranty policies have been favored also because they are issued in the amount of the purchase price of the property, whatever may be its amount, and they are also issued to guarantee the validity of large mortgages and bond issues, thus assuring purchasers of the bonds that they will suffer no loss from defects in the title. One of the important protection features of these policies is their insurance against the possibility of a forged deed in the chain of conveyance, which would transfer no title of any kind; another is that the company undertakes the burden of defending a title which is assailed.

b) The Torrens system.—In 1900 the Torrens system was adopted in Cook County. By this method the property goes through a judicial process, to remove all clouds or possible defects. The growth of the Torrens system since 1900 has been steady, but it still enjoys only a small minority of the total title business.

c) Differences in mortgages and leasehold interests.—In boom periods, when many lots have been recently sold on partial payments, with a mortgage or trust deed given back for the balance of the purchase price, lots are resold subject to mortgages maturing within from one to three years or longer. As these obligations come due, the prospective buyer at such a time must deal with both the owner of the fee title and the holder of the mortgage, for unless the mortgage can be extended, the buyer must pay the equivalent of all cash for the property. Later, when these mortgages have been paid off or foreclosed upon, the property can be sold on any terms the holder of the clear property and the buyer may agree upon, regardless of any mortgage interests. It is a disadvantage for any property to be incumbered by a mortgage that soon falls due, and hence prospective buyers are careful to inquire into maturity dates of mortgages on the property. Heavy prepayments required to be made by the terms of the mortgage are also regarded as objectionable from the buyer's standpoint, as they lessen the income he can enjoy from the property in the immediate future.

The growth of the practice of ninety-nine-year leases after 1890 divided the ownership interests in most of the Loop real estate in two. The owner of the fee received a fixed ground rent, and the value of his interest was determined by capitalizing the ground rent, which varied only with the interest rate. The holder of the leasehold interest, on the other hand, was in position to reap a larger profit if the market rentals increased over that he agreed to pay under the terms of his lease. On the other hand, many leases made at the peak of booms were later forfeited for non-payment of the ground rent.

d) Differences in financial necessities of the owner.—The price for which an owner will sell his lot frequently depends on the past history of the prices of the lot. If the owner bought during a boom, he will often hold tenaciously for a price that will enable him to recover the principal invested. A large number of lots in the blighted area have been so held for years in the hope that some big industry will eventually need the lot and enable the owner to recoup his loss. If, however, the original purchaser dies, and it comes into the hands of heirs who regard it as a windfall, the same lot may be sold for whatever it will bring. Again, if an owner is suddenly pressed for money, he may sell a lot below the market value in order to raise cash to meet the emergency. Sometimes the necessity of expanding a growing business forces the owner of the business to pay an excessive price for an adjoining parcel.

e) Differences in ownership units.—It frequently happens that the value per square foot of a large tract is greater than the value per square foot of a smaller parcel in the same tract. For instance, it is not economical to build a tower office building on a small lot because the space taken up by walls, elevators, and halls forms so large a percentage of the total building area that the percentage of the rentable area to the total area is abnormally small. The Mather Tower, on the

Wacker Drive, is an example of such a tower building on a small lot. If, however, it is proposed to erect a huge building covering a block or several blocks, like the Merchandise Mart, it is difficult, if not impossible, to acquire sufficient ground in the heart of the Loop, for most of the blocks are partly improved already with tall buildings, and the blocks occupied by old structures are frequently in the hands of a number of owners, some of whom are not willing to sell at a reasonable price. The builders of the Merchandise Mart were forced to acquire the air rights over the railroad tracks on the north bank of the Chicago River in order to acquire a site large enough for their purpose. Thus a single large holding under one ownership has a greater value for purposes requiring a tract of such size than the same holding in the hands of a number of owners, because all of the difficulties of assembling the property have been met.

Again in the rebuilding of the so-called blighted areas one of the greatest problems is to acquire a single solid block of land. The blocks are nearly all split up into many ownership units, and if an attempt were made to buy all the parcels in the block, before all the lots were acquired the owners of the remaining lots, feeling that something big was in the wind, would raise their prices to prohibitive figures and defeat the project. Therefore, a solid block under one ownership would have a greater value per square foot than the individual lots in the block for one who needed the entire block for his projected housing development.

There are other interesting examples of how the mere fact of division of ownership lessens the aggregate land value. Thus at the northwest corner of Michigan and Austin the corner holding fronting along Michigan is only 25 feet deep, and the building erected on it is too small for the most economical operation. Yet this building shuts off entirely from Michigan Avenue the rest of the block, and thereby deprives it of most of its value. It is estimated that under a divided ownership the two holdings have an average value of $16.67 a square foot, but that if united in one ownership, so that the west part of the block had an outlet on Michigan Avenue, the average value of the entire holding would be $30 a square foot. Again the air rights over an alley entering Wacker Drive would be almost as valuable as the fee, if the lot on each side of the alley was owned by the same person, because a large building could be constructed economically over the alley. Divided in two, the air rights are far less valuable; because, since no pillars or foundations can be placed in the alley and since the space over the alley could not be spanned, expensive cantilever construction would have to be employed to secure the advantages of the air rights and this added expense would greatly lessen their value.

Thus in many cases a loss of utility results from the dividing of land into small ownership units. The efficient and economical development of an entire block or tract is frequently not possible until all the individual lots are acquired by a single owner, and to merge these scattered holdings is sometimes a matter which requires great finesse and long negotiations.

f) Differences in the effectiveness of propaganda.—The owner of a tract of land may by his own efforts create a value for it that it would not otherwise have. He may take a tract of raw acres, subdivide it, give it a beautiful name, and induce a number of his friends and clients to settle there. Although there are a number of other tracts equally suitable and desirable, if not more so, than this one, the mere fact that he has induced a restless swarm of people to settle there like a hive of bees has given it value. A large number of people are led to select their homesite by the persuasive talk of a real estate salesman; but, once having selected it, they become attached to it, and persuade in turn some of their friends to follow them. Houses are built, street improvements are installed, and railroad stations are built at certain locations rather than at other places only because of the energetic actions of some promoters or landowners. Similarly, the action of some local banker or real estate man may "make" some new business at one point because a new theater, a new bank, a drug store, and a block of new stores is financed and built at that spot.[4]

3. *Differences in land values due to actions of the community or the state.*—There is another group of forces that are not under the control of the individual landowner or the succession of owners of a tract of land, except in so far as they can control or modify public opinion or persuade the legislature to pass new laws. This group includes ordinances of the City Council affecting land values, local union rules, and laws of the state of Illinois. First are the conditions affecting the tax rate levied on different tracts of land, second are the laws relating to foreclosure and the sale of land for non-payment of taxes, third are local zoning laws, fourth are local building codes, and fifth are local union wage scales.

a) Differences in tax rates and exemptions.—There is a slight difference in the tax rates in the different townships constituting Chicago as a result of the differences in expenditures of local taxing units. A very marked difference in the tax rate exists between land just inside and that just outside the city limits, and in sections where the land within the city limits is undeveloped and possesses no advantages over that outside the city limits, as on the Southwest Side, the difference in the tax rates causes the land just inside the city limits to be worth less than that just outside. Frontage on Howard Street on the Evanston side is worth less than land across the street on the Chicago side, on account of higher telephone, water, electric-light, and gas rates.

A greater basis of differentiation in taxation has been the extra-legal underassessment of certain townships and districts as compared with others. In 1927 Calumet was assessed at 13.1 per cent of its sales average as compared with a general average of 35.9 per cent for the entire city.[5] When this discrimination prevails for years, it is reflected in higher land values in the favored districts. Even in the 1931 assessment Calumet has been assessed at 76 per cent of sample spot appraisals as compared with an average of 95 per cent for the city and 105 per cent for the West Side, although the unusual discrimination that existed before has been greatly lessened.[6] Similarly, certain favored interests in the past have been assessed at as little as 1–10 per cent of the sales value of their property, while others were assessed as high as 90 and 100 per cent.

[4] Blake Snyder and Ralph West Roby, *Fundamentals of Real Estate* (New York: Harper & Bros., 1927), pp. 121–24.

[5] Herbert D. Simpson, *Tax Racket and Tax Reform in Chicago* (1930), p. 170.

[6] Writer's own computation.

Property actually used for religious, educational, or burial purposes is exempt from taxation by law, and all the real estate of Northwestern University, whether used for educational purposes or not, is by special charter under which the University was incorporated, exempt from taxation, provided the amount held does not exceed two thousand acres.

b) Differences in foreclosure and other laws relating to land titles.—Chicago lots differ from those in other states, but not as between themselves in state foreclosure, tax laws, and in other laws affecting land titles. In some states, e.g., Missouri, a short and summary method of foreclosure enables a mortgage holder to obtain title in case of default within sixty days without great expense, but in Illinois the owner of the equity has a period of a year and his creditors three months more to redeem after his real estate has been sold to satisfy the mortgage. The owner of the mortgage or trust deed can only acquire the title by filing a bill to foreclose through his attorney, by filing his evidence before a master in chancery, and thereby incurring expenses, including attorney's fee, master's fee, and court costs, which usually amount to 10 or 15 per cent of the value of the property. Hence it usually pays a mortgage holder to give the title holder a substantial sum for a quit-claim deed, even if the property is worth less than the amount of the mortgage. Although this lengthy and cumbersome method of foreclosure is held to be beneficial in protecting the title holder from losing his property, it causes loss to everyone except attorneys in periods of depression and is said to hinder capitalists from investing in Chicago mortgages.

The tax laws of Illinois also differ from those of other states, in that a tax deed which is granted after two years' non-payment of taxes to private buyers of tax liens does not convey a title to the tax-buyer which cannot be defeated, but only a claim which can be removed as a cloud on the title at any time thereafter on payment of the amount of the taxes and penalties. This fact partly accounts for the large percentage of tax delinquencies in periods of depression, for owners are not faced with a loss of their property but only an accumulation of penalties. It is true that the Illinois statutes provide for a foreclosure of land for non-payment of taxes, but this law has seldom, if ever, been enforced.[7]

Another feature of Illinois law before July, 1933, was the prohibition or refusal to allow corporations to be formed for the purpose of dealing in real estate. Hence until 1933 a means of obtaining standard units that could be bought and sold in a market through the issuance of stock in corporations owning tracts of land was rendered unavailable. The Calumet and Chicago Canal and Dock, however, did own large tracts of land in the Calumet region and the sale of its stock did reflect rising land values.

Differences in state and local laws affecting title to real estate is another obstacle in the way of the organization of a national real estate market.

c) Differences in building codes and fire limits.—Each city has its own building code, and to the extent that the requirements of these codes exceed the needs of

[7] The Skarda bill, which became a law in 1933, provides for the appointment of receivers to collect income for past due taxes, but this does not cause a forfeiture of title.

safety, they add to building costs and detract from land values. It is charged that the present Chicago code stipulates the materials to be used under certain conditions and refuses to allow the substitution of cheaper materials of equal strength, thereby adding to building costs and lessening land values.

The establishment of fire limits after the fire of 1871, within which frame structures could not be erected, temporarily lessened the value of some of the land within the fire limits in 1872, as the best use of some urban land at that time was for cheap frame dwellings. The extension of the fire limits since that time to cover almost the entire city has now been looked on as an advantage, preventing, as it does, the erection of cheap frame houses that would lower property values.

Finally, the local zoning ordinance passed in 1923 limits the height, the volume of use, and the kind of use, whether residential, business, or industrial. This zoning law does not impose a very serious limit on the use of land, for if all the land in Chicago were built to the limit allowed by the zoning law, the entire population of the United States could be housed in the city. The 5,000,000 feet zoned for business is enough for the needs of a population of 10,000,000 people, or three times the present population. Moreover, whenever there is any possibility of a higher use for any block or parcel of land than the one for which it is zoned, it is not very difficult to have it zoned for the higher use, as the five thousand amendments to the zoning law testify. Private restrictive agreements that have already been considered are far more effective barriers to land utilization than the zoning law.

The foregoing categories have listed causes of differentiation between Chicago lots, but the actual combinations of these factors that occur in the case of individual lots are so diverse that no lot of land can be properly appraised without a personal inspection of its location and that of the surrounding neighborhood, a study of the character of the people living near it, a knowledge of the history of the community, and an acquaintance with all the facts pertaining to rents, taxes, and operating costs. With all this information as to value, the title to no lot can be safely purchased without an examination of the records of ownership and a search of judgment records, tax and special assessment rolls, marriage and divorce records, the copies of deeds, mortgages, and contracts affecting the title; a survey of the lot to determine its exact location; and an inspection to make certain there are no squatters on the land who are claiming title by adverse possession.

With all the possibilities of variation which makes each lot a distinct entity, there are, nevertheless, certain factors that link them together in a market, even though it be an imperfect one. The majority of Chicago lots have the common depth of 125 feet, and for those that differ from this standard there are depth tables for computing their values in terms of the common unit. Similarly, the value of corners is expressed in terms of ratios to the value of inside lots. Again, wide areas of residential land of substantially the same character have about the same value. When values differ widely, it is usually on the basis of some gradient, by which the values slope up toward a transfer corner, or toward a fast transportation line, or toward the lake, or a park, or by which values slope downward toward an objectionable section, such as a colored district, the Stock Yards, the drainage canal, or the railroad yards. Moreover, differences in ownership records have been standardized by the Chicago Title and Trust Company, which by their guaranty make all titles equally merchantable and of the same grade as to title. Finally, money rents and capitalization rates reduce diverse factors to a common pecuniary basis, showing the composite result of all the multiple permutations and combinations.

B. THE MECHANISM OF THE CHICAGO LAND MARKET

Such being the nature of the units bought and sold in the Chicago land market, it now remains to discuss the mechanism of that market. This subject will be considered in the following order: (1) the character of the buyers and sellers, (2) the method of bringing buyers and sellers together, (3) the making of the contract, (4) terms of sale and financing purchases, (5) sources of price information, (6) relations between the parties after the deal is closed, and (7) seasonal elements in the Chicago market.

1. *Buyers and sellers.*—Since every real estate transaction is a matter of public record, the identity of the present or past title holders of any tract of land can be determined by examination. Persons who are subject to judgments, or who do not want other real estate operators to know what they are doing, frequently take title through "dummies" who pose as the ostensible owners, or through a trust company which holds title under a trust agreement.

Buyers may be classified according to their degree of knowledge of land values, according to their residence and occupation, according to the purpose for which they are buying, and according to their race.

a) Degree of knowledge of land values.—The "lambs" in the real estate market are those who during the height of a boom buy from subdividers at prices that are usually from three to ten times the current market price for acre tracts. The professional operators are the brokers who have acquainted themselves with the asking prices of all the land in their vicinity or the speculators who have had considerable experience in buying and selling. The "insiders" are traction magnates or officials of transportation lines who buy land in advance of a proposed extension, as in the case of the building of new street-car lines by Yerkes before 1900[8] and the construction of the rapid transit lines to Niles Center and Westchester in 1925 and 1927. Within the same category also fall those who have special knowledge in advance that a motion-picture palace or a branch of a big department store is about to be erected in a certain locality. Of a similar nature is the case of politicians who buy tracts or lots and resell them to the city or county for use as parks, school sites, or fire stations.

b) Purpose of buying land.—In addition to purchase by the city for public uses, the demand for land comes from at least four types of buyers. The first is the home-buyer, who either buys land with a house, bungalow, two-apartment building

---

[8] Alonzo H. Hill, who became a director in the Yerkes traction companies for the purpose of learning when and where new lines would be built, according to a statement made by him to the writer in September, 1933, received advance information that the Ravenswood elevated line would be constructed to Kimball Avenue. He thereupon bought the 41-by-125-foot northwest corner of Lawrence and Kimball for $3,300 and later sold it for $52,000.

already on it, or else buys a lot for the purpose of building a home. This demand is perhaps the most stable of all and continues even during periods of depression. The second source of demand for land comes from builders and contractors who erect houses and apartments for the purpose of resale, and finance their operations on borrowed money as much as possible. This demand is very strong during booms, but almost ceases in a depression. The third class of land-buyers are the speculators, who purchase for the sole purpose of reselling the land without further improvements to home-buyers, contractors, the general public, or other speculators. Demand from this group rises high during the boom and stops altogether in the depression. A fourth type of demand comes from institutions like the Marshall Field estate which are required by the terms of a trust or will to invest in Chicago real estate. The foregoing list is not exhaustive, but it will serve to suggest the variety in the sources of the demand for land.

c) Residence or occupation of the buyer.—In the boom of 1836 Chicago lots were sold at auction-rooms of New York City, and in 1889 and 1890 the publicity attending the World's Fair attracted buyers from many other cities. In the last boom, however, buyers have usually restricted their purchases to the locality in which they live. In the boom of 1926 North Side residents bought lots chiefly on the North Side and South Side residents chiefly on the South Side. Moreover, buyers tend to confine themselves to the type of land with which they have been familiarized by their occupation. Storekeepers buy business lots; apartment-owners, builders, tenants, or janitors invest in apartment lots; and manufacturers in industrial land.

d) Race or nationality.—The racial factor is also important in the Chicago land market. The Greeks were noted for their desire to acquire double-section corners as sites for candy stores, and they formed syndicates among themselves to make such purchases. The Jews exercised a marked influence in stimulating the speculative boom on certain business streets such as Lawrence Avenue. The foreign-born in general were more eager than native Americans to attain the prestige of land-ownership, which was frequently impossible for them in Europe. Prior to the shutting-off of the main current of immigration, there was a steady business in the older sections of the city in selling the poorer grade of houses to the newest immigrants, and of immediately making another sale to the seller of a house in a newer neighborhood.

Sellers as well as buyers differ in their degrees of knowledge. On the one hand are "sleepers" who live out of the city, and are unaware of a sudden boom that has made their dormant landholdings valuable. Some real estate operators work like detectives to discover the whereabouts of such persons and to secure an option on their land before they learn the facts. At the other extreme are the subdividers who sell with full cognizance of the inflated values of their properties, but who engineer an organized system of propaganda to sell their lots to persons ignorant of land values.

Sellers also differ as to their plan of selling their land. Some speculators have made a mistake in holding a large tract in the line of development out of use by seeking very high prices for it, which may cause the development to go around them or in another direction. Thus the attempt by the Pullman Land Company to create a business center in the old part of Pullman caused merchants to acquire cheap land on Michigan Avenue and to start the main business center there. So also the attempt of West Randolph Street landowners to secure high prices from the South Water Street merchants caused them to jump to a new location entirely. Again, when the owners on South Clark Street raised the rents to Chinese merchants, they migrated in a body to Twenty-second and Wentworth Avenue. Some sellers in disposing of a tract of land, therefore, adhere to a policy of selling part for whatever it will bring and reserving only part of it to hold for the rise in values made possible by the developing community. Sometimes, however, tracts held out of use until ripe for their highest and best use have attained higher values than tracts sold piecemeal, for they are not marred by any cheap buildings or residences of varying age and styles of architecture.

2. *Methods of bringing buyers and sellers together.*—A prospective buyer may get in contact with landowners by (1) reading advertisements of land listed for sale in the newspapers, (2) through a telephone or personal call or advertisement of a subdivision company maintaining a sales force, (3) through a neighborhood broker who has listings of lots in his neighborhood offered for sale, (4) through "For Sale" signs on the lot, (5) by acquiring from the county deed and tax records the names and addresses of all the owners of land in a given neighborhood and by writing to all of such owners and thereby ascertaining which lot is for sale at the lowest price. The last method is that frequently employed by the brokers themselves, who, in addition to maintaining an office to receive listings, often send out hundreds of letters to obtain listings, with the hope of obtaining one or two bargains they can buy and resell at a substantial profit.

The means of spreading information as to land values has changed with the growth of Chicago. In the boom of 1836, when the town was huddled along the banks of the Chicago River, riders on horseback shouted the news of land sales through the streets, and crowds thronged auction-rooms to keep in touch with prices in the land market. Buyers were taken to suburban tracts in omnibuses as early as 1853, and in the boom of 1890 excursion trains carried large crowds to new subdivisions. With the increasing size of the city, other methods were devised by subdividers to get in touch with prospective customers. Canvassers or agents as well as handbills and newspaper advertising were employed in 1890. In the boom of 1925 and 1926 the widespread distribution of telephones caused some firms to employ men to call up nearly everyone whose name was in the telephone directory for the purpose of making appointments with salesmen.[9] The auction method of selling fell into disuse in Chicago after 1873 partly because the fact that owners were allowed to withdraw their offerings if the bids were not satisfactory discouraged buyers and partly because buyers did not come in sufficient numbers to insure a market satisfactory to the sellers. Market information was obtained thereafter mainly through brokers' offices. There was a marked sectional separation in the market as between the North, South, and West sides, those living in the respective sections usually buying lots only in their own part of the city. Markets were split

[9] According to investigations made by the writer.

into neighborhoods or tracts, with the buyer's knowledge of land values frequently confined to that of the scale of values shown on the subdivider's plats. This was frequently true of the customers of the subdividers who after being taken to the sales office on the property had little opportunity to see or learn the sales prices of other properties. In the first two decades of the twentieth century, however, most of the lots developed and sold were reasonably valued, enabling buyers to resell at substantial profits with the subsequent rise in land values. The widespread success that had accrued to average lot-buyers from 1900 to 1920 was taken advantage of in the boom of 1925 and 1926 by less scrupulous subdividers who sold large tracts of outlying land at prices higher than those justified by its possibilities or utilization.

3. *Signing the contract.*—Because of the Statute of Frauds, originally enacted in England and subsequently adopted in every American state, no agreement for the sale of land is valid, unless there is a memorandum signed by the party selling the land agreeing to the terms of sale. Hence the quick dispatch of the stock market in which sales of millions of dollars are made by a broker nodding or holding up a finger is impossible. The requirement of writing imposes delay, for the contract must state the location or technical legal description of the property, the consideration and the terms of sale, and a party who has orally agreed to a sale may change his mind before the formal contract can be drawn up and signed. If the contract is once signed and recorded in the recorder's office, no other conveyance of the land can be made until the contract is disposed of, and if the contract is legal and binding, the owner will be forced to convey the property by a Chancery Court on a bill for specific performance. Even in such a case, however, the title is not immediately transferred and there may be a delay of a year or more before the court proceedings are instituted and brought to a conclusion.

4. *Terms of sale and methods of financing purchases.*—The general practice of buying Chicago real estate on partial payments dates back to 1836 when the Canal Commissioners offered lots for sale at one-fourth down and the balance in one, two, and three years, with interest at 6 per cent. These famous "canal terms" were adopted in private transactions for many decades thereafter. Subdividers in selling lots set their terms at from one-fifth to one-third down, with the balance payable in monthly instalments for three to four years, and on such a basis of sale they do not give a deed until all the payments are completed. In cases where a deed is given to the property, usually one-half of the purchase price is paid at the time of the conveyance and the payment of the balance is secured by a mortgage on the property itself. In still other cases where a broker or prospective buyer secures an option or an exclusive sales contract for a period of from sixty to ninety days, very little, if any, cash is paid down, and the holder of the option has an opportunity to reap a large speculative profit on a small cash investment. Thus in the case of the majority of real estate transactions, credit is extended by the seller to the buyer. This is one of the important factors tending to inflation of real estate prices during booms, for the proportion of cash required for purchases usually declines as values rise. In periods of depression, sales are made at low prices for all cash or for heavy cash payments, but as the speculative rise gets under way, sellers are induced by the prospect of selling at large profits to accept smaller cash down-payments.

The banks further aid in the process of inflation during booms, as they also accelerate the liquidation in the depression. The boom of 1836 was financed on a flood of "wild-cat" money, and Chicago real estate was skyrocketed by the note issues of the State Bank of Illinois and the issues of Michigan banks that were issued against wild land. The collapse of these banks with the forced liquidation of their holdings intensified the gloom of the depression in 1841 and 1843. The rise of the new state banks of issue in Illinois in 1852 accelerated the rise to the new peaks of 1857, and their *débâcle* on the outbreak of the Civil War enhanced the gloom in real estate circles in 1861 and 1862. The advent of the new national banks in 1863, and the loans of eastern life insurance companies on Chicago real estate were factors in the rise in land values finally culminating in 1873. The suspension of some of the banks and the closing of the savings banks in Chicago featured the intense depression of 1877. The national banks again aided the rise in land values up to 1890, and their refusal to make further loans for real estate on so extensive a scale put a damper on real estate activity in the fall of 1890. The sensational rise of the deposits of outlying state and national banks from $30,000,000 in 1890 to $800,000,000 in 1928 was accompanied by an equally sensational rise in the value of outlying Chicago real estate. These banks contributed to the rise in land values in many and devious ways. The rise in the number of outlying state and national banks from 8 in 1890 to 203 in 1928 created a considerable demand for sites for banking quarters. Of far more importance than this was the fact that these banks invested most of their funds in local real estate in one form or another. They gathered the savings of their communities, which amounted in 1928 to more than the savings deposits of the Loop banks, and put them at the disposal of contractors, builders, storekeepers, etc., for the purpose of building stores, apartments, or theaters. Many of the bank presidents were also real estate operators, and in some cases real estate loans were the largest items on their balance sheet. But the percentage of real estate loans to total loans by no means shows the total extent of these real estate operations, large as this item was. Loans were made on personal notes or on financial statements to men whose assets consisted chiefly of real estate. Loans were also made on the security of real estate mortgages as collateral. Neither of these types of loans appeared as "real estate loans" although they were such in essence. Furthermore, the banks sold large issues of real estate bonds on local real estate.

The sale of real estate bonds in huge volume was one of the features of the postwar bond market. The war had popularized the sale of bonds to the public through the drives to sell Liberty Bonds. Finding that the public could be induced to buy real estate bonds in large quantity, corps of salesmen were trained to canvass the field. The public response was so great that opportunities for selling bonds were created. Contractors were encouraged to plan large buildings, stores, office buildings, kitchenette apartments, and loans were offered sufficient to pay for 100 per cent of their cost or more. These loans were justified on appraisals that capitalized the boom rents.

The ease of obtaining credit for buying land or for building purposes from the banks and the mortgage houses stimulated the real estate boom prior to 1928, as did also the sale of lots on small down-payments. The movement could not have gone so far had a large amount of cash been required of the speculators. But the possibility of shoestring financing encouraged them to extend their operations to the limit. Erecting buildings entirely on borrowed money in many cases, contractors borrowed an additional amount on second mortgages and proceeded to continue the process.

Thus the point was reached in 1928 where 100 per cent loans were made on first mortgages in many cases, and where an additional 20 per cent was obtained on a second mortgage. These junior issues had hitherto enabled an owner to raise 80 per cent of the conservative value of his property on the basis of mortgages. A first mortgage of from 50 to 60 per cent of the value of improved holdings could be secured at normal interest rates, and an additional 20–30 per cent on a second mortgage at a premium of from 3 to 6 per cent additional per year. In the inflated market of 1927 and 1928, however, the two mortgages frequently exceeded 100 per cent of the cost value of the property even at boom levels.

The contraction of credit began with the failure of owners to meet second-mortgage charges which began in 1928. As rents declined, owners began to fail to meet even the charges on the first mortgages, which usually called for heavy prepayments, and, as the first mortgages were foreclosed, the second mortgages were wiped out. After 1929 the outlying banks with their assets, including savings deposits largely in real estate, were unable to liquidate on the dull and declining market, and the failure of 155 banks from October, 1929, to July, 1932, reduced their number to 45. These failures absorbed community savings, paralyzed business initiative in the vicinity, and rendered money for even conservative real estate financing unavailable. The banks and insurance companies still solvent passed from one extreme to another. Whereas in 1928 first-mortgage bonds were made for as high as four and five times the inflated annual income, in 1932 a first-mortgage loan could scarcely be made for over double the depressed income of a building in a good location.

Thus the credit operations of banks have tended to exaggerate the extravagances of real estate booms and depressions rather than to counteract them.

5. *Sources of price information.*—Compared with the facility of the stock ticker, which flashes the prices of stocks to all parts of the United States within a few minutes after the sale is made on the floor of the New York Exchange, real estate prices stand at almost the opposite extreme. Moreover, instead of the trend in Chicago being toward greater publicity of real estate sales, it has been toward greater secrecy. In 1836, and even as late as 1873, auction sales, with the results published in the local papers, gave a reliable index as to values. From 1830 down to 1890 or later, the true consideration was usually given in the deed, which became a matter of public record, so that within a month or so after the contract was signed, the true price information became available. In the nineties, however, fictitious considerations became more common, and finally the practice was adopted of giving the consideration as "ten dollars and other good and valuable considerations." The real purchase price could be ascertained only by examining the sales contract, which was seldom recorded and which was usually kept secret. During the periods in which revenue stamps were required, from 1898 to 1901, from 1917 to 1926, and beginning again in 1932, the reputed sales price could be ascertained

by counting the stamps on the deeds, but in some instances a number of stamps were added for the purpose of creating the appearance of high value when a bond issue was being floated. Another indirect method of arriving at sales values is to take the amount of the trust deed or mortgage and to assume that it bears a certain relation to the sales price.

To obtain price information as to land transactions, buyers and sellers are forced to rely chiefly on the asking or listed prices given in brokers' offices, or by asking or advertised prices which appear in the newspapers in large numbers during booms. In the case of subdivider's property, the prices of the lots are fixed by the subdivider and are marked on each lot. The greater ease of ascertaining subdivider's prices as compared with the prices of other lots is one of the reasons for their volume of sales. Another method of ascertaining the price is from a sign posted on the property, though these signs seldom give the asking price but only the owner's name and address. To secure all the asking prices of all lots in a neighborhood, it would be necessary to secure all the names of the owners from the tax records and to write or telephone to them, which is what the local brokers do in periods of activity.

In view of the difficulty in securing information as to land values from sales records, George C. Olcott has performed a valuable service in his *Land Values Blue Book of Chicago*, which is published annually. These valuations, giving a front-foot land value for every block in the city and adjacent suburbs, lag behind actual values for from one to three years, but with allowance for this factor, they give a good approximation of Chicago land values.

Because of the great diversity of lots in the Chicago land market and the long periods of inactivity, there is really no active and continuous market for all types of property.[10] Deals are seldom made without a good deal of higgling, and the first bid and offer is seldom the final one. As a result of the infrequency of sales and the many factors involved, land values do not advance or decline by minute gradations as in the case of stocks. In a boom land values that have remained dormant for thirty years may double, triple, and quadruple in a month. On the other hand, as a period of dulness sets in, offering land at slight or even fairly drastic concessions as against peak prices will not necessarily induce purchases. The beginning of a decline is concealed by the trading of one type of inflated equities for another, so that the parties are able to console themselves with the belief that they have suffered no loss. Real estate owners are the last to admit that their property has declined in value.

The sales price of a tract of land covers a number of elements which are included in the sales contract. The usual terms call for the transfer of the property on the date the deed is passed, with all obligations paid up by the former owner to that moment, and with all income credited to him up to that moment. This is called "prorating." Thus the seller normally is debited with past due taxes and taxes for

[10] Harry Cutmore (*Journal of American Institute of Real Estate Appraisers*, October, 1932, pp. 17–18) says: "Sales of high type properties are few and scattering and the diversity between the sites of several fine stores or commercial buildings is so great as to limit seriously the usefulness of any sale as evidence of the value of every other site."

the current year up to the time of conveyance, with mortgage interest accruing up to the date of conveyance, with janitor's salaries due or accrued, with accrued water or light expense, and he is credited with accrued rents, unused coal, and advance payments for salaries, water, and light. The balance between these items is added or subtracted from the cash down-payment. Thus there is a great difference, in many cases, from taking a deed to property "as it is" subject to unpaid taxes, interest on mortgages, etc., and taking property with all these obligations paid up to date. The fact that Chicago taxes for 1931 had not been in process of collection even in 1932 would mean that any transaction closed in 1932 would involve an allowance for the estimated 1931 tax and the pro rata share of the 1932 tax.

6. *Future relations of the parties.*—The relations between a buyer and the seller of real estate are frequently not terminated by the transaction as in the case of stocks where the seller receives all his cash for his equity. The seller usually takes a mortgage back from the buyer to secure the payment of part of the purchase price. Sometimes he sells this mortgage to a bank, but in many instances he retains it himself and collects interest and prepayments from the purchaser. If the buyer fails to meet the obligations of the mortgage, the holder of the mortgage note may file a bill to foreclose, have a receiver appointed to collect the rents, and in the course of eighteen months or two years regain title to the property. As a foreclosure is an expensive and lengthy proceeding, the mortgage holder frequently prefers to pay the owner of the equity for a quit-claim deed. In the case of a real estate bond issue, however, the holders of the bonds are scattered, so that the owner of the equity can seldom deal with them directly. The bond house that sold the bonds is the only one that possesses a list of their names, so they find it necessary to form protective committees which proceed to file foreclosure proceedings and appoint receivers whose charges come ahead of everything else. Complicated foreclosure laws necessitate expensive receivership and legal expenses that add to the bondholder's burden. Thus even the holders of first mortgage obligations on real estate frequently suffer serious losses in a depression.

Thus contrasted with the quick and summary fashion in which the accounts of margin holders of stock are closed out in a few minutes on the stock exchange, the equity holders of real estate may hold on for several years and their interest can only be closed out at considerable expense. This is one of the reasons for the relatively slow decline in land values in the first part of a depression as compared with the sharp breaks that occur on the stock market.

7. *Seasonal elements in the land market.*—Because of the necessity of inspecting land and the surrounding neighborhood, the land market is affected to an unusual degree by the weather. Land sales reach peak in the spring and in the fall, when weather conditions are most favorable, and are almost suspended in summer and in winter when it is too hot, too cold, or too wet for outdoor operations. The long-prevailing custom of Chicago families in moving just before either the first of May or the first of October also caused contractors to buy their land for building purposes so that their new buildings would be ready for fall or spring occupancy. This

[11] Cf. Dickens' *Bleak House.*

necessitated acquiring land in the spring for fall buildings, and land in the early autumn for buildings that were to be finished as far as the outer walls before winter set in. A further seasonal influence was the effect of summer vacations in taking some large buyers away from the city.

The slackening of real estate operations with the approach of winter is a factor that has hastened the end of many land booms in Chicago. Land transactions were most active in the spring and early summer of 1836, 1873, 1890, and 1925, and the market failed to regain the old pitch of activity after the seasonal lull imposed by the winter.

C. THE FUNDAMENTAL BASIS OF LAND VALUES: CAPITALIZATION OF NET INCOME

So far we have considered the blend of factors that have produced the sequence of market values in the history of Chicago land values. At times, the sales value of large tracts has born little relation to present or prospective income, and speculators have bought land merely because they have believed that they could sell the land at a higher price to some other speculator. There is, of course, a fundamental and well-known basis on which land value rests. The value of land is the sum of all the net land incomes that will accrue in perpetuity discounted for the period of time that will elapse before they are received. Since incomes due one hundred years in the future have only a negligible value today, the valuation of land involves a prophecy as to the net income of the land for the next thirty or forty years. Such is a simple statement of a principle whose application is extremely difficult.

1. *Necessity of a building to produce income.*—In the first place, to obtain an income from urban land it is necessary for most purposes, except parking automobiles and advertising signs, to erect a building upon it. The income received from the property so improved is a joint land and building income, and it is only after the expenses of operating the building, the taxes, and the interest and depreciation on the building are deducted that the residual land income is determined. Manifestly, the amount of the total income depends upon the character and size of the building erected and upon its suitability to its location. The total income may be increased by multiplying the number of stories, but unless the site is "ripe" for this higher use, the income may not increase in proportion to the operating expenses and to the higher interest charges on the more expensive building. There is for every site a theoretical building which will be the highest and best use of a given site at the given time. A lot improved with a four-story building might yield better returns if it were improved by a skyscraper of forty stories, or vice versa.

The suitability of a building to its location depends upon the consideration of those factors which we have already noted in describing the influences that determine the character of a neighborhood. A fine apartment building erected in the slums will probably fail to pay operating expenses. A big department store constructed on a prairie would represent a capital loss. The net land income cannot be increased by such overimprovements. The builder should locate either in the midst of the trend of growth or perhaps somewhat in advance of it.

2. *Suitability of building to location.*—In the dynamic society of Chicago, however, neighborhoods have changed so that buildings that were once suited to their

environment have been left behind as derelicts. In other cases promoters have overshot their mark and developed apartment buildings too far in advance of the main settled area. In the constant shifting of uses in the Chicago area it thus happens that many tracts of land do not yield the maximum net income because the buildings upon them do not represent the highest and best use of the site. Before making a calculation of the net income that might be derived from such a higher use, however, it is necessary to ascertain whether there is any demand for such use at the time, and, if not, to estimate how many years must elapse before there will be a demand for the lot for this purpose.[12]

A building designed to yield the maximum net income at the time it is erected may fail to accomplish its object because of the inefficiency of its design or the layout of its rooms. A skyscraper, erected on a lot too small in size or of unusual shape, may have an unduly small percentage of rentable area, because of the higher proportion of the total space required for hallways and elevator shafts.

Given, finally, a building which represents the most efficient development of a location, the net income from the land will vary with the amount of the operating expenses and the cost of the building.[13] If an old frame store, for which the tenant provides the heat and janitor service, yields a rent of $500 a month, the net land income is manifestly far greater than that in the case of a new steam-heated store four stories high rented for the same amount. To secure the rent from stove-heated or arcola-heated stores, the least deductions from the gross rents are made, since the owner has only taxes and insurance to pay. In the case of steam-heated, unfurnished, walk-up apartments, the owner's expenses increase by the amount of the coal, the janitor's wages, and decorating costs. If the building is a tall kitchenette-apartment building, to these items must be added the cost of maid service, elevator service, mechanical refrigeration, furniture upkeep, linen, gas, electricity, and the salaries of an engineer and resident manager. In the past century, services provided by the owner constantly have tended to increase. In the first office buildings the tenant provided his own heat, did his own cleaning, and walked up several flights of stairs to his office, but now all these services are included in his rent. Since the cost of these operating expenses usually does not decline as fast as gross rents in a depression, it follows that net incomes and net land rents decline faster in the case of buildings with heavy operating expenses than they do in the case of those with lighter charges.

Once the net land income is finally determined for a past interval of time, this income is not necessarily to be capitalized to determine the land value. The only bearing the past income has upon the present land value is its indication as to what the probable future net income will be. It is frequently assumed that the future will be like the past and that a given income will continue indefinitely. Such assumptions have been proved false in the case of peak incomes in boom periods, in

[12] H. A. Babcock, "On the Valuation of Land Awaiting Conversion to a Higher Use," *American Mathematical Monthly*, March, 1933.

[13] In the case of land that is overdeveloped with a large building that is unsuited to the site, nothing might be left for the land. The land has at least as great a value as it would earn in a less intensive use.

the case of changing neighborhoods or in the transition from higher to lower uses, in the unexpected obsolescence of a building due to improvements in new buildings just erected, in the decline of an industry for which the building is especially constructed, and other dynamic factors. The possibility of a change in the income level must be carefully weighed in the light of trends of neighborhood growth, of the type of building, of the position in the business cycle, and of the possibility of obsolescence of the building in an unexpected manner. Adverse factors affecting income will manifest themselves in the form of lower rents, higher vacancies, heavier collection losses, and less desirable tenants who cause greater physical wear and tear on the building. Another set of adverse factors tend to increase operating expenses and show themselves in the form of higher taxes, higher wage rates, less efficient labor, and the necessity of providing extra and additional services to retain tenants at the same rents. Buildings have been successively provided with water in the kitchen, bath tubs, gas, steam heat, electric light, and mechanical refrigeration without rents increasing in many cases to cover the expense of these added features. The owners of older buildings find it necessary to incur these added costs in order to hold their tenants.

A given net income, at the present time, may be the same for a number of different lots of land, and yet the value of those lots may vary widely. In one case the appraiser judges that this income will be stable and permanent for years to come, because of his observation of the stable character of the surrounding property, and accordingly he makes a low allowance out of the income for future vacancies, and capitalizes the income at the lowest rate. In another case the valuator may feel that the property is on the downgrade, that the income will soon decline and vacancies increase, and so he makes a large allowance for vacancies and capitalizes the income at a high rate. Or, again, there may be a very good prospect for a rapid enhancement of the income due to a conversion to a higher and better use in a short time, in which case a higher value than that justified by the present income will be attributed to the lot.

3. *The residual income.*—Thus the net income of urban land which is capitalized to determine its value is the residual amount remaining out of the joint land and building income after the income attributed to the building is subtracted. Since the building can be reproduced at current labor and material costs, it normally can have no greater value than its reproduction cost less depreciation, and therefore any surplus return on the land and building above that necessary to pay operating expenses, taxes, interest, and depreciation on the building is properly assigned to the non-reproducible element in the combination—the land. To this general principle, however, there are certain exceptions. While the income of ordinary apartment or commercial property is not materially affected by the character of the management, the income derived from hotels depends to a considerable extent upon the ability of the men operating them, and consequently the entire return cannot be attributed to the land and building alone. Even in the case of ordinary store and apartment property, selling prices of completed buildings in boom times are higher than the current cost of the building and the current value of similar land. At such times there is a profit to the entrepreneur or promoter who creates out of raw land and

bricks and mortar an income-producing property. Conversely, in times of depression lots improved with buildings are sometimes sold for less than the current reproduction cost of the buildings alone. Thus in the one case the land value derived from capitalizing the residual income left after deducting expenses attributable to the building would be higher than the selling value of adjoining lots, and in the other case the land value derived in the same manner would be zero or less than zero. The difficult question as to how much should be attributed to the land and how much to the building in cases where the combined earning or sales value of the land and building is less than the reproduction cost of the building alone is usually answered by computing the residual income that would be earned by the land if improved by a cheaper building exactly suited to the location. It would seem, however, that where a modern skyscraper with a physical life of a century or more is constructed upon a lot, that the land is so irrevocably bound up with the use to which it is devoted that no hypothetical use is worth considering. If the land under such a building is valued as high as an adjoining and similar piece of land that is improved by a smaller building that allows a greater residual return to the land, then the value of the skyscraper must be depreciated to the point where its value as a building added to the value ascribed to the land is no greater than the capitalized income value of the entire property. This method would correctly penalize the investors in the brick and mortar in the building for their overdevelopment of the lot, and for carrying their applications of capital to it too far past the point of diminishing returns.

The net income of the land thus cannot always be derived by subtracting from the joint land and building income the operating expenses and the interest on the reproduction cost of the building. Even if this method be conceded to be correct as a normal method of procedure subject to corrections for the factors just discussed, its application to concrete cases is fraught with great difficulties. For it is necessary to calculate the probable trend for thirty years in the future of each of the following factors, if we are to calculate the present value of a vacant lot or of a lot improved with a building.

4. *Forecasting future incomes*.—Factors determining the future ground rent of an Urban Lot and its present value are as follows:

A. Factors determining the gross combined land and building income
    I. The type of improvement best suited to the site
        A. Character of the neighborhood at present
        B. Trend of growth
        C. Restrictive agreements contained in deeds
        D. Present zoning laws and the possibility of change in such laws
    II. The estimate as to the number of years that must elapse before the land will be in demand for utilization in its highest and best manner, if it is not now so used
    III. The aggregate amount of rents that can be derived from the property when improved in its highest and best manner
        A. The total number of apartments, stores, or rentable units
        B. The rent that may be expected for each unit when the building is new, with allowances for a decline from this level as the building grows older
        C. The estimate of the loss resulting from vacancies
        D. The estimate of the loss resulting from bad debts

B. Factors affecting the net combined land and building income
   A. Operating expenses
      1. Janitor's wages as affected by unions
      2. The cost of coal
      3. The cost of water and electricity
      4. The cost of decorating, repairs, and ash removal
      5. The cost of elevator and maid service where provided
      6. The cost of furniture where provided
      7. Agent's commission and manager's salary
      8. Fire-insurance rates
      9. The cost of new services that may be required in the future
   B. Taxes
      1. The cost of local government—the total tax levy
         a) Increase in governmental functions
         b) Waste and duplication of governmental agencies
         c) Salaries for teachers and other employees
      2. The proportion of the burden borne by real estate as compared with personal property
C. Factors affecting the net ground rent
   A. The amount deducted for cost of developing the land
      1. Cost of sewers, pavements, and sidewalks
      2. Interest rate during the period of development
   B. The amount deducted for the interest on the building cost
      1. Rates of building labor and the efficiency of labor
      2. Mechanical devices in constructing buildings
      3. The prices of building materials
      4. Architects' fees and financing costs
      5. The rate of interest on investment in building
   C. The amount deducted for depreciation on the building
      1. Estimated useful life of the building
      2. Type of structure
D. Factors affecting the interest rate for capitalizing the net ground rent

5. *Factors in determining future ground rent.*—The range of possible variation of all these items is very great. Considering the intensity of the use of land alone, the net income justifies a value of from $31 to $12,550 a front foot, depending on whether the land is used for a bungalow or an eighteen-story kitchenette apartment, as Table LXXIX shows. Yet a decline in rent levels and an increase in vacancies in fact reduced this apparent great land income to zero by 1932, for operating expenses did not decline in the same proportion as rents. Consequently, actual land values neither reach such heights nor go to such depths as the fluctuations in net land income for single years.

One of the major causes of booms and depressions in real estate is that a rise in gross rents usually gives a disproportionate rise to the net rent left the owner, because operating expenses do not rise in the same proportion. The greater the percentage of operating expenses to gross income, the greater the rise or fall in net rents, as Table LXXVIII shows. Similarly, in a period of depression a fall in gross rents means a greater fall in net incomes left the owners, for operating expenses do not fall as rapidly. This is shown by the report of the Central Committee to the

Assessor showing the gross income of ninety properties in the Loop from 1928 to 1932. While the gross income declined only 31 per cent, the net income declined 54 per cent because operating costs declined only 9 per cent.

So far it is seen that there is a bewildering variety of possible net income resultants even under conditions where it is assumed that land has been put to its highest and best use. Present land values depend upon future and not past land incomes, and the valuation of land therefore depends upon the ability to forecast the future. Usually it is assumed that present incomes, operating costs, and interest rates will be permanent and calculations are made on that basis. The grievous error of such assumptions need scarcely be alluded to in the light of the history of the Chicago land market, in which every factor in the calculations has been subject to great change. Gross rents have fluctuated with changes in the national income and

TABLE LXXVIII*

RELATION BETWEEN THE RISE AND FALL OF GROSS AND NET RENTS

Percentage Expenses to Gross	Gross Rents, Rise or Fall	Net Rents, Rise or Fall	Gross Rents, Rise or Fall	Net Rents, Rise or Fall	Gross Rents, Rise or Fall	Net Rents, Rise or Fall
10	20	22	40	44	60	66
20	20	25	40	50	60	75
30	20	29	40	56	60	85
40	20	33	40	66	60	100
50	20	40	40	80	60	120
60	20	50	40	100	60	150

* Richard M. Hurd, *Principles of City Land Value* (4th ed.); *Record and Guide* (New York, 1924), p. 129.

mass purchasing power, as well as with local conditions in the city. The total amount of rent derived from a plot of land has varied with the height of buildings, and these in turn with new inventions which raised the economical height from six or eight to forty stories. Rent from store property has also varied with the flow of traffic and its sudden shifting with population movements and with the attractions of new business centers. Net income has been affected by the lag of operating costs such as wages, coal, taxes, decorating expense, which has reduced net incomes from land faster than gross incomes in the depression. Net land income again is affected by the amount of vacancies, falling in the period of prosperity until overbuilding provides extra space, and rising in the period of depression as families double up. Finally, the capitalized land value varies with the long-term rate of interest and with special capitalization rates set up for different types of property.

Notwithstanding all these causes of variation, the determination of the value of land by income analysis is the best method of approach for determining what its normal value ought to be. Actual market or sales value fluctuates above and below this "normal" standard, which is, as we have seen, far from a stable or unvarying quantity. In periods of high speculation, however, land values are higher than warranted even by the high incomes of the time, for a still further increase in rents

TABLE LXXIX*
LAND VALUE DEVELOPED ON A 50-BY-150-FOOT LOT IN CHICAGO BY DIFFERENT TYPES OF RESIDENTIAL USES, 1926

No. and Type of Buildings†	Size of Ground Floor	No. Sq.Ft. in Bldg.	No. Cu.Ft. in Bldg.	1926 Cu.Ft. Cost‡	Total Bldg. Cost, 1926	Furn. Cost	No. Apts.	Rent per Apt.	Total Income, 1926	Allow. Vacancies	Oper. Expense, 1926§	Int. on Bldg. and Furn.‖	Land Income	Land Value per Fr.Ft.¶
1 bungalow	25×52	1,300	13,000	42¢	$ 5,500	....	1	$85	$ 920	$ 74	$ 442	$ 330	$ 72	$ 31
2 bungalows	50×52	2,600	26,000	42	11,000	....	2	85	1,840	148	884	660	145	62
1–2 flats	25×52	2,600	36,300	30	10,500	....	2	85	1,840	148	972	630	88	35
2–2 flats	50×52	5,200	72,600	31	21,000	....	4	85	3,680	292	1,944	1,260	176	70
1–3 flats	25×52	3,900	49,500	31	16,000	....	3	85	3,060	244	1,610	960	240	80
2–3 flats	25×52	7,800	99,000	31	32,000	....	6	85	6,120	488	3,220	1,920	480	160
Six flats	44×55	7,260	100,000	35	35,000	....	6	85	6,120	488	2,888	2,450	290	97
12 flats	35×135	14,175	189,000	31	59,000	....	12	85	12,240	976	4,874	4,400	930	232
18 flats	42×135	17,010	227,000	31	72,000	....	18	70	15,120	1,210	7,497	5,760	1,359	340
Kitchenette apartments:														
3-story	44×120	15,740	228,000	42	95,760	$10,000	42	60	30,000	2,400	11,000	10,000	6,600	1,650
7-story	44×120	36,960	550,000	45	250,000	25,000	84	75	75,600	6,048	26,000	26,000	17,000	4,250
12-story	44×120	63,360	860,000	50	430,000	45,000	144	75	129,600	10,368	44,422	45,000	29,600	7,400
18-story	44×120	85,040	1,280,000	50	640,000	67,500	216	75	194,400	15,600	59,500	67,800	51,000	12,550

* Computed by the writer from data furnished by contractors and real estate operators.
† Number of rooms per apartment in each building.
‡ Includes financing costs, interest during construction, and architects' fees.
§ Includes taxes, insurance, coal, janitor, decorating, light, ashes, repairs, and depreciation.
‖ Eight per cent on building, 25 per cent on furniture.
¶ Capitalized at 6 per cent for bungalow; two- and three-apartment use; 7 per cent for six-apartment use and 8 per cent for higher uses.

is expected. This statement should be qualified in the case of kitchenette-apartment buildings in the boom of 1926 and 1927, for the theoretical income left to the land was far higher than the market price, because there was a greater supply of lots available for tall buildings than could immediately be utilized. In the case of store property, land values rose higher after 1925 than net earnings would justify, and hence conservative appraisers, such as those of the Chicago Title and Trust Company, valued land frequently at from 25 to 30 per cent less than it was selling for on the market. In the depression, on the other hand, sales are infrequent, and at prices usually below conservative appraisals based on capitalization of normal income.

In the historical method of this study we have looked at land values through the eyes of former generations, who did not know what the future would bring forth. From our present knowledge it is possible to point out the errors in their calculations as to the future which influenced past sales and conservative appraisals.

D. SPECULATIVE ERRORS IN CALCULATING FUTURE CHICAGO LAND INCOME

1. *Errors in estimating long-run forces of supply and demand:*

a) Demand: Population—The close relationship between the increase in the population of the city and the land values of the city has been recognized from the beginning. Hence estimates as to the future population of Chicago had an important effect on speculation. Land-buyers in 1836 had visions of a teeming population at the mouth of the Chicago River, but hopes had sunken low in 1843 and the speech of Balestier predicting a population of 200,000 for Chicago within the lifetime of children then living was greeted with derisive laughter. In 1856, when the railroad had poured hundreds of thousands into Chicago, more optimistic estimates again prevailed. Even in 1861, Wright's prediction of a ten-fold increase in the population of Chicago by 1886 slightly surpassed the actual rate of growth, rapid as it was. John Paul Goode in 1926 forecasted a future population of at least 15,000,000 for Chicago, and Charles H. Wacker in 1924 estimated that Chicago would have a population of 18,000,000 by 1974.[14]

Purchasing power.—Since the value of land occupied by cheap homes or apartments is limited, speculation in land is frequently based on optimistic estimates as to the amount of land that will be used for aristocratic homes or for intensive uses. Thus in the boom culminating in 1873 there was an overestimate of the amount of land required for homesites by the rich or moderately wealthy, for miles of boulevard and park frontage were sold at prices that precluded use by the poor. In the boom of 1925–28 there was an overestimate of the number of people who could afford to pay high rents for kitchenette apartments. Large tracts of land near the lake and the parks acquired a high speculative value on account of the projection of hypothetical high buildings rented at a high rate per room.

Similarly, in the booms of 1890 and 1926 there were overestimates as to the number of hotels, office buildings, and bank floors required for Chicago, and not only were more of these types of structures erected than required, but a large

[14] *Chicago Journal*, April 22, 1924.

amount of land acquired a high value on the prospect of a still further extension of such structures. In 1925–28 there was also an overspeculation in stores and commercial property in Chicago, stimulated by the high profits of merchants, the spread of chain stores and their competition for choice locations, the shift of population to outlying centers with the growth of new neighborhoods, the promotion of new business centers by real estate men and bankers, and the reports of profits made by earlier investors in business property. In Chicago over 5,000,000 feet were zoned for business, while only 1,500,000 feet were used for it, leaving enough unused for 7,000,000 people. In Niles Center, with a population of 5,200, 55 miles of frontage were zoned for business, enough for 580,000 people.

In the boom of 1890 there was an overestimate of the amount of land required for manufacturing sites, for railroad use, for World's Fair hotels, and for homesites on the South Side.

Further errors are made in estimating the trend of growth. Russell Sage once predicted that the center of Chicago would be at Madison and Ashland Avenue, and before 1873 and even later there were hopes by West Side residents that the business center would shift westward from State to Halsted Street. Senator Stephen A. Douglas predicted that the center of Chicago would some day be at the mouth of the Calumet River.[15] In the first decade of the nineteenth century there was considerable speculation in land south of the present Loop on the theory that the Loop would spread southward. Again from 1920 to 1928 there was heavy speculation on the northward expansion of the Loop on North Michigan Avenue and the Wacker Drive. Similarly, from 1868 to 1893 the growth of the fashionable residential district southward along Prairie, Calumet, and Michigan avenues was anticipated.

Also there are underestimates of the obsolescence of neighborhoods due to the aging of buildings, the intrusion of undesirable racial elements, and the advent of new buildings of a superior type. The effect of the expansion of the colored section of the South Side was not foreseen in the days of that section's fashionable development.

Sometimes the underestimates are on the side of conservatism. When buildings were limited to six or eight stories by elevators and massive masonry, the possibility of twenty- and forty-story buildings made possible by steel-frame construction and steam or electric elevators was not conceived.

Again, the shift of population to a given area and the flow of a great tide of traffic past a point that was a vacant prairie seemed impossible to truck farmers who had occupied the land.

b) Supply.—In computing the need for certain tracts of land as the city grows, the effect of new transportation lines that will make available distant areas and will cause people to pass by more accessible land is lost sight of. Nor is it always remembered that the supply of land increases as the square of the distance from the city and hence the amount of land increases with widening concentric circles from the city. Furthermore, it is forgotten that the more intensive the use of land and

---

[15] Statement made to Paul Cornell, founder of Hyde Park, according to his son, John Cornell.

the higher the buildings, the less land will be required. Thus the vertical expansion of the Loop lessened its lateral expansion.

c) Capitalization rate.—The fall in the capitalization rate on Chicago real estate in the central business district from 10 per cent in 1836 to 8 per cent in 1873 and finally to 4 per cent in 1900 meant a corresponding increase in land values on the same income, but such a decline was not foreseen in early days.

d) Wage rates.—The rise in wage rates for building labor from one dollar a day in 1833 to fifteen dollars a day in 1926 would have seemed impossible in 1833.

e) Movement of a leader: human and catastrophic elements.—The sudden shift of the business center from Clark and Lake to State Street in 1867, partly as a result of the move of Marshall Field, the southward shift of the financial district in 1868 and 1880 following the Board of Trade, the shift of the wholesale district west of Wells when the fire of 1871 had leveled the old vice district there, the development of Prairie Avenue from the fashionable home of Clark, of Ashland Boulevard from the mansions directed by Walker, and of the frog pond on the Lake Shore Drive from the start made by Potter Palmer, as well as hundreds of other minor shifts, seem as much directed by human caprice as any other factor and would be hard to predict in advance.

2. *Errors due to the business cycle.*—The foregoing errors have been due to failure to foresee dynamic shifts, new inventions, and long-run changes in customs, habits, or population group. A new series of errors arises in connection with the business cycle.

The first set of errors arises from bank inflation in the boom, due to liberal extension of credit for the purchase of real estate with the resultant feeling that it is a secure, safe, and salable investment, because loans can readily be obtained for most of its value. The reverse of this takes place in the depression, when the liberal policy is reversed and loans can hardly be obtained at all, creating the impression that land has no value and is an unsalable commodity.[16]

The second set of errors arises out of the assumption that the peak purchasing power of tenants, consumers, etc., will not decline but will remain constant or advance so that the peak rentals can always be obtained. The fact that net rentals have increased faster than gross rentals, because operating expenses have lagged behind the rise in rents, causes a building boom because of the seeming profit in building operations. The rapid absorption of land by new buildings leads to the expectation that this rapid rate of utilization will continue, and leads to great speculation in vacant land. Far more land is subdivided than can be used for several generations. Meanwhile, municipal extravagance leads to a rise in the tax rate so that taxes are higher than ever before. A falling-off in employment curtails purchasing power and rents fall, and as operating expenses do not fall as fast as gross rents, net rents decline to a point where there is no surplus above operating expenses.

---

[16] Thus during 1928, a first mortgage of $3,500,000 was easily sold on a Loop building. In 1932, it was with difficulty that a first mortgage loan of $350,000 was obtained on the same property.

Buildings erected at peak level of costs in the booms of 1836, 1856, 1872–73, 1890–93, and 1925–28 can be reproduced for much less in the ensuing depressions. Incomes fail to meet interest on mortgages, and there is a heavy wave of foreclosures, which in the course of two or three years wipe out equities and enable the properties to be sold for the old mortgage. At such times there are errors on the pessimistic side. It is not foreseen that a rise in gross rents will cause a disproportionate rise in net income, because operating expenses will not go up in proportion. With no new construction, vacancies are gradually filled and rents rise slowly with increasing population. Finally, there is a building shortage, but lack of confidence in the stability of the level of construction costs may deter new building until the shortage is acute.

APPENDIX II

METHODS EMPLOYED IN DETERMINING CHICAGO LAND VALUES, 1830–1933

A. THE MAIN METHODS EMPLOYED IN DETERMINING THE VALUE OF CHICAGO LAND

There are two main methods of computing land value, one based on sales or market price, the other on the capitalization of expected future net income. Theoretically the two methods should coincide, for sales value over a long run should approximate the capitalized income. It is found, however, that in practice the value of land based on sales exceeds its capitalized earning power in booms and falls below it in depressions. Appraisals based on net earnings are, however, not immune from the optimistic view of the future prevailing at the heyday of prosperity and may exceed sales value.

The two methods have both advantages and disadvantages. The computation of land value on the basis of sales during booms is said to be a false guide of true cash or sound value because it includes "sucker" sales, or purchases by persons ignorant of real estate values. In times of depression, as in 1932, few sales of land are available, and computations of land value that rely on sales alone must necessarily fail at such times.

On the other hand, appraisals based on income analysis that show land value lower than it will actually sell for in the market during the boom or higher than it will sell for during a depression iron out the speculative facts of the market. The construction of such normal standards are desirable, however, for the purpose of long-term investments in real estate or for taxation. It is undesirable to seize upon boom peak levels for taxation, because the assessment is often made for four years at a time and is not readily adjustable. It is equally unwise to base long-term calculations on the speculative caprices of a few years.

In this study, which is mainly concerned with the historic facts of the Chicago land market, and in which so-called speculative "crazes" are part of its very essence, the computation of land values is based mainly on sales. Sales are definite and objective facts which can be obtained from the records for a hundred years. It would be difficult, if not impossible, to obtain sufficient rental and income data, operating costs, etc., for a hundred years to construct a theoretical table of what land ought to have been worth. Moreover, certain large classes of property have never been susceptible to appraisal on an income basis. Residences occupied by the wealthy and the poor frequently cannot be rented for a sum sufficient to yield a normal return on the land and building cost, being regarded as consumption goods for conspicuous display or as a necessary cost of family rearing. The value of vacant land, which is derived from its expected future income, similarly cannot be closely estimated on the basis of earnings, for its future earnings and the period of time that will elapse before it will come into use are frequently both uncertain.

The computation of land value on sales must, however, be subject to some limitations. As already noted, there are not sales enough during periods of dulness and depression to establish a general level of land values, and at such times appraisals based on expected future income must be used to supplement the scanty sales data. Some heed must also be paid to the argument against using "sucker" sales. In boom periods sales are made, usually by subdividers, which are higher than the asking prices of adjoining and similar land. In 1928 leases were made in the Chicago Loop for the purpose of floating bond issues in which the appraised values were known to be far above the inflated market of the time. Therefore, while such extreme sales and leases should be noted as a feature of the aberrations of the times, they should be disregarded in computing the value of surrounding land, and in arriving at estimates of total value for the entire city even in boom periods. Similarly, there may be sales in a depression at foreclosure proceedings in which no buyers appear except the mortgage holders and in which any bid, however low, takes the property. Such transactions also are not indicative of the average level of land values even in a depression, although they are a striking commentary on the nature of the real estate market. In making the computations of land value in this study, such extremes have been avoided in determining the total land value of the entire city, although the speculative excesses of booms and depressions enter otherwise into all the computations.

1. *Sources of land-value data—assessments for taxation purposes.*—The first source of information on land values may be obtained from the tax assessment. If these values had been accurately and honestly computed in Chicago for the last one hundred years, the study of Chicago land values would be vastly simplified. A number of insuperable obstacles prevent the use of such data for the whole period, however, although some of the earliest and the most recent assessments have furnished valuable material for single years. The first objection is the lack of records on the separate valuations for land and buildings, for most of the years prior to the 1928 reassessment. The second objection is the lack of records for small districts or areas, the totals only being published for whole townships. The third and most important objection is the capricious variation of the rates of assessed value to market value for most of the period of Chicago's history. It was in the limbo of confusion and uncertainty that tax fixers flourished prior to 1928. Before 1866 assessed values were supposed to be 25 per cent; in 1866, $33\frac{1}{3}$ per cent; and in 1867, 100 per cent of market values.

By 1871 the nominal 100 per cent of market value had slipped back to an actual 60 per cent. Soon after 1873 the whole basis of assessment was unofficially lowered, and it kept falling until in 1896 assessed values averaged one-ninth of market values in the central business district, but it varied in individual cases from 1 to 100 per cent of market value.[1] The theoretically full market value as a standard for assessments was changed in 1898, when the facts of actual practice were recognized and the assessed values were placed at one-fifth of full value. This was raised in 1909 to one-third, in 1919 to one-half, and finally in 1927 it was changed

[1] *Report of the Tax Commission* (1896).

to full value.² Nevertheless, prior to 1928 there were great variations in the full value established for assessment purposes and the full value established by sales. In 1926 the average rate of assessment was 31.3 per cent of full market value, but it varied from 6.2 to 78.3 per cent between different sections of the city, from 19.7 to 53.8 per cent for different types of property, and from 1 to 100 per cent for different individuals.³

Assessments in Chicago for most of the city outside of the Loop came to be based on customary or conventional values from 1873 to 1926, which bore no fixed or constant relation either to sales or to any other basis of market or income value. The careful report of the Swift Tax Commission in 1896 on the market value of the land north of Roosevelt Road to the Chicago River led to a thorough revision of Loop land values and thereafter they were more nearly in accordance with sales and leases.

The reassessment of Chicago land and buildings in 1928 attempted to raise all Chicago land to full value. Thousands of actual sales and leases were studied and analyzed. The final figure of $3,700,000,000 was 25 per cent lower than the estimates based on actual sales by Herbert D. Simpson, and also 25 per cent lower than the valuations of George C. Olcott's *Blue Book* of 1929. Both of these authorities would indicate that the full sales value of Chicago land in 1928 was approximately $5,000,000,000. The assessors, however, were justified in taking a more conservative view and in discounting the sales of the boom period. In the reassessment of 1931, made in 1932, the assessor was confronted with an almost total absence of sales data and was compelled to rely on appraisals or on the opinions of real estate "experts." The valuation established for the city land of $2,400,000,000 represented a decline of 35 per cent from the assessed value of 1928 and a decline of 50 per cent from the market value of 1928. There was a maximum variation of from 75 to 105 per cent of full value as between different sections of the city due to slightly different assessment standards, but nevertheless it was probably the most accurate assessment ever made in Chicago. The values, theoretically based on those of April 1, 1931, really reflected the materially lower level prevailing in 1932.

2. *Advertised or listed prices.*—The use of prices listed in brokers' offices was recommended in a recent study as a means of ascertaining the trend of the market.⁴ In an active market when there is little difference between the bid and asking prices, such data might be a very reliable guide, but at such times there is also usually abundant data on actual sales. Since buyers commonly ask more than they will take, asking prices are not very close indices of the market even in a boom period. These listings are not frequently revised, so that unless they were procured immediately after their submittal by owners, they would lag behind the market in a boom and remain far above it in the ensuing lull. When sales are very infrequent in the depression, asking prices representing some holdovers from prosperous times,

---

² In 1928 the fall value for assessment purposes was first determined and then 37 per cent of this was taken as the assessed value to which the tax rate applied.

³ Herbert D. Simpson, *Tax Racket and Tax Reform in Chicago* (Evanston: Northwestern University, 1931), pp. 44–45.

⁴ Herman Wyngarten, *An Index of Local Real Estate Prices* (Ann Arbor: University of Michigan, 1927)

intermingled with the prices submitted by those in desperate need of cash, present an extremely varied and chaotic picture. Moreover, it is difficult to obtain such listings from brokers. When they are recent, they are regarded as confidential, and when they are old, they are destroyed. Such listings, as well as advertised asking prices in newspapers, are useful at times when there are no other sources of information, and they tend to fix an upper limit to values. Thus George C. Olcott used advertised prices in arriving at values from 1900 to 1910 and in supplementing his other sources of information from 1910 to 1932.

3. *Appraisals and opinions of experts.*—A third source of information in regard to land values is the opinions of real estate men. These vary from those based on customary levels or neighborhood gossip to those based on a careful analysis of sales and all the factors relating to the gross income and operating expenses of the land. Since real estate values are affected by a multitude of local factors and vary from block to block, opinions of neighborhood brokers may represent a correct composite judgment of many diverse elements which may be superior to a careful analysis that overlooks some important element. Nevertheless, the buyer who desires to form his judgment without being duly influenced by the neighborhood horizon and by the psychology of the moment may well employ a real estate expert to analyze all the elements affecting the future value of the site in question. The difficulty in expert opinion, here as elsewhere, is the lack of external standards by which it can be judged. Frequently, too great reliance has been placed on the authority, prestige, and reputation of the individual appraiser. It has usually been found that real estate appraisers could be found who would testify for either side of a case and who would demonstrate either a high or a low value, according to the interest of the party paying their fee. Such was the great evil of the boom days before 1929 when bond issues of 100 per cent or more of the entire value of the property were floated on the appraisals of "convenience" appraisers who valued the property for the purpose of the bond issue as high as 150 per cent of its market value even in boom times.

Even if the appraisers are honest, there are differences in method that makes possible a wide variation in results as to final value. One difference of result in determining land values depends on how the value of the building is computed. Some appraisers deduct from the joint land and building value the reproduction cost of the building with allowances only for physical depreciation and not for lack of earning power. The land is worth only what remains after the full physical value of the building is deducted. By this method the larger the building on a lot, the greater the land value, and if there were bungalows, six-flat buildings, and twelve-flat buildings in the same block, the land under each would have a different value. To avoid this paradoxical situation, other groups of appraisers adopt a conventional unit of land value for the block, and make the building the variable element in the joint land and building factor by charging off failure to earn on original cost against the building. Appraisers also differ in judgment, as to capitalization rates, as to percentage to be allowed for vacancies, as to the rate of future rents, and as to operating costs.

The method of appraisal by experts is therefore not an infallible test of land value taken alone. Nevertheless, real estate men and writers whose reputation for veracity and sound judgment has long endured, and who were actually on the ground at the time and knew the intimate details surrounding the sales, perform the same function as a jury. Their opinion, sustaining the considerations given in the records, corroborates them and strongly indicates that the sales themselves were bona fide and not fictitious. The records of sales used by the writer have accordingly been fortified by the opinions of William B. Ogden, first mayor of Chicago, expressed in letters written from 1836 to 1841; by the printed statements of John S. Wright, one of the early speculators and boosters of Chicago for the period from 1835 to 1861; by the opinions of Elias Colbert and Everett Chamberlin in their books covering the period from 1860 to 1873; by the written opinions of real estate editors of the *Chicago Tribune*, from 1868 to 1932; by the opinions of the editor of the *Real Estate and Building Journal* for the years from 1872 to 1897; and by the opinions of the editor of the *Economist* from 1889 to the present. The record of sales is further corroborated by statements of William H. Kerfoot, pioneer real estate dealer; by the estimates of land value from 1876 to 1894 made by Frank C. Chandler, oldest member of the Chicago Real Estate Board; by the estimates of land value in Chicago in 1883 made by J. G. Couzins, secretary of the Citizens' Committee; by the appraisal of the central business district by the Swift Tax Commission in 1896; by the appraisals of William A. Bond, 1890–1910; by the estimate of land values for Chicago for 1928 by Professor Herbert D. Simpson on the basis of 6,445 actual sales; and by studies made in connection with the assessment of land in Cook County for 1928 and 1931 by Harry S. Cutmore and J. L. Jacobs.

Finally, special mention must be made of George C. Olcott's annual books of land valuations covering the value of every block in Chicago, for every year from 1910 to the present, with the exception of 1917 and 1918. These valuations have been based on sales, on advertised prices, on leases, and on the opinion of neighborhood brokers, and on any other source of land value data that could be obtained. Mr. Olcott's books are widely used in Chicago by real estate brokers, bankers, and real estate owners as reference books for determining the value of land in any section, and they have been used as authoritative in studies of land values. They are, however, subject to certain criticisms. In a few cases values were influenced by real estate subdividers desiring to create a favorable impression. In the main, the land values have not been subject to bias or manipulation. The chief fault has been the failure to adjust the values quickly to changes in market conditions. It has been a conscious and deliberate policy of Mr. Olcott to lag behind the actual market. Thus, it was not until 1929 or 1930 that he caught up with peak prices reached in many cases in 1926. His valuations, regarded as ultra-conservative in 1926, became excessive by 1930 and 1931. His valuations for 1932, reduced 30 per cent from the peak, were still higher than warranted by the prevailing conditions. In spite of these objections, in view of the lack of sales information on deeds from 1910 to 1932, the use of Mr. Olcott's work is indispensable. Without such a painstaking and pioneer effort, which has systematically registered and preserved sales data and neighborhood-value opinions, that would otherwise have been lost, and which harmonized and brought them into proper relationship with each other, a study of this kind would have been impossible in any reasonable length of time.

4. *Sales.*—The main method used in this study for computing land values in the

hundred years of Chicago history has been that based on actual sales or the market price, supplemented and fortified whenever possible by appraisals and opinions of real estate "experts." Notwithstanding criticisms already enumerated against this method, mostly relating to exceptional transactions in which advantage was taken of a buyer's ignorance, it is believed that for a long-run study designed to show fluctuations of land value in the business cycle it is the best method available.

B. SOURCES OF SALES DATA

The evidence of the amount for which land is sold in actual transactions may be obtained in several ways: by a knowledge of the details of the transfer obtained from the principals direct or from records in brokers' offices; by the amount of stamp taxes on the deed; from the prices on subdividers' plats; by recorded contracts or agreements to purchase; by estimates based on the amount of recorded mortgage indebtedness; by the public reports of auction sales; and by the actual amount specified on the face of the deed.

Direct knowledge of the details of a deal, unless preserved in written form, soon fades out of the memory of even the principals, and for transactions of many years ago cannot be obtained. Even the written records have in most cases been destroyed, as has already been noted. The method of ascertaining sales values by the amount of the stamp taxes can only be used during the limited periods when stamp taxes are imposed, and for such periods their use requires very intensive work to establish the land values for a small section for a brief period of time. The method of using subdividers' plat prices, which do usually indicate the actual selling price of that type of property, although such selling prices are controlled by an artificial market, are of some utility for recent transactions, but it is difficult to secure many of such plats for the period prior to 1915. The records of contracts or agreements to purchase usually state the real consideration of the transfer, even when the deed of conveyance recites only a nominal consideration. In the past, however, the same information was given in the deeds and was more easily accessible in that form, but since 1900 deeds giving the purported actual consideration have been too few in number and too difficult to analyze to be used in an extensive investigation like the present one. Estimates of total value based on the known amount of the mortgage would form only a rough index, unless in the case of the type of property studied the mortgage bore a fixed and definite ratio to the total selling price of the property. That would not be true in the case of the present study. The published reports of the amounts realized at auction sales is one of the best possible methods of securing actual sales value, if the sale was made openly without reserve and without secret bidders. It was a reliable index of sales values at the time of its extensive use by the Canal Commissioners from 1830 to 1857, and by other noted auctioneers of that period such as Clark, Leighton and Company. For this period and even up to 1873 this method furnished considerable data for the present study. Later the auction method fell into disuse and has ceased to be an important factor in the Chicago market. Finally, there is the method of using the actual consideration shown on the face of the deed. For this period from 1830 to 1890 this was the chief source of the land-value data used by the writer. In view of the fact that within the last few decades nearly all deeds recite only the conventional "ten dollars and other good and value considerations," it may seem surprising that this method has been so extensively used. The writer has found, however, that in the opinions of the real estate editor of the *Chicago Tribune*, of the editor of the *Real Estate and Building Journal*, and of numerous other writers and real estate authorities the consideration then stated in the deed was at least until 1891 usually the real and true consideration. The amounts expressed in thousands of deeds have been examined and they are consistent with each other, with published opinions as to real estate values, with reports of auction sales, and with computations made on the basis of assessed values where there was any basis for making such comparison. Furthermore, sales amounts taken from the recorded deeds were cited and extensively used by such real estate writers as Chamberlin, Putney, Smyers, the editors of the *Chicago Tribune*, and other publications to show the real trend of land values. There was no impelling reason, such as would be afforded by the present Federal Income Tax Law, for concealing the real consideration, and when fictitious considerations were given, they were likely to draw forth critical comment from those familiar with the general level of values. Finally, the very number of sales available is a check on their accuracy, for wilful misrepresentation would seldom be expected to distort every case in the same manner and degree.

Beginning in 1891, an increasing number of cases of fictitious considerations were reported, as a result of trades at inflated figures, of attempts to conceal the fact that demand at the peak prices of 1890 had fallen off, of conveyance to avoid foreclosure, so that the considerations given in the deeds ceased to be trustworthy in many cases. The fact that the practice of inflating the consideration really deceived many people, including real estate reporters, indicates that the abuse had not been common before 1891.

Accepting the considerations stated in the deeds as the best means of ascertaining actual sales for Chicago land for the period before 1891, the question arises as to the best source of procuring this information. All of the deeds recorded since the great fire of October 9, 1871, are on file in the county recorder's office, but the task of tracing thousands of records for an extensive survey such as the present one would require a large staff of workers. Fortunately, the *Chicago Tribune*, beginning in 1868, published daily a list of the conveyances by street locations, and arduous as the task is of examining each daily paper from 1868 to 1891 or 1897, it is far simpler than going through the files of the recorder's office, where the legal description and not the street address is given. Furthermore, classified compilations of sales for peak prices have been made by Everett Chamberlin for 1871 to 1873 and by M. H. Putney for 1890 to 1893. For the period prior to 1868 when the *Chicago Tribune* began to publish complete lists of sales, there are sporadic references to sales in the early Chicago newspapers such as the *Chicago American*, the *Chicago Journal*, and the *Chicago Democrat*. The main source of information for this period used by the writer was the ante-fire abstracts of the Chicago Title and Trust Company, the use of which was obtained through the courtesy of J. Frank Graf, vice-president of the Company. Several thousand of these abstracts were examined to obtain sales data on the period from 1830 to 1868.

From the foregoing records of deeds, including in the aggregate several hundred thousand transactions, the sales were compiled of all large acre tracts, of all sales in the central business district, of all sales on the most valuable residential and outlying business streets, and of sample sales for cheap residential and business streets for the period from 1830 to 1891. From this mass of data, sales were discarded where the property was obviously improved except in the central business district, and the question as to whether the property was improved or not was determined by reference to current descriptions of the extent of the built-up area, by current comments on the sale as to whether it was vacant land or not, by the amount of the consideration, and by the comparison with opinions of land values by current observers. In many cases the improvements were known to be of negligible value and were disregarded. In still other cases where the land was partly built up, a comparison was made between a number of sales in the same vicinity, and the sales at the lowest figures were assumed to be sales of vacant land. Where the property was entirely built up, it was necessary to rely chiefly on opinions of land value by current observers. In the central business district, which was covered with buildings during the greater part of the period of the study, except just after the great fire of 1871, it was not difficult to secure estimates of the value of the ground apart from the buildings, because being the most valuable part of the city, it attracted the greatest attention and drew forth the most comments.

C. METHOD OF COMPUTING TOTAL VALUE OF CHICAGO LAND
FROM SAMPLE SALES

Notwithstanding the large quantity of sales data for the period from 1830 to 1891, it has been, of course, impossible to secure sales for every block in the city for every year in the study. In fact, for some of the years, particularly in the dull periods following a boom, the data are quite meager. Even for those years in the peak of the boom when the activity is most intense, sales data are lacking at certain points. Since the attempt has been made to compute a fairly accurate index of values for the land in Chicago for the peak periods, the question arises as to whether enough sales have been secured to make this computation. Obviously, there must be a fairly wide distribution of sample sales, but these samples need not, and in fact should not, be uniformly distributed over the entire area of Chicago. In sections where the value of the land is very high and there are sharp changes in values from one block to another, there should be sample sales for each side of every block or the equivalent of over two hundred and fifty to the square mile, but where the land is a homogeneous residential area of low or medium land value, four or five sample sales would be sufficient to indicate the average value of the entire section, and in the case of outlying suburban acres, one sale might be sufficient to establish the value of several square miles in the vicinity. The sales data in this study correspond as nearly as possible in their frequency to the case just cited. For the central business district, where the land values are highest, there are sales and valuations for almost every block in every peak period, and, similarly, there are sales for nearly every block for the high-grade business and residential streets. For the cheaper residential areas a few samples have been taken to establish the value of the entire section. For unsubdivided land, where instead of sixty-four hundred 25-foot lots in a square mile with that many possibilities of sale there may be only from one to sixteen holdings with no transfers for many years, the sales in such acre tracts are altogether missing, it is necessary to interpolate values according to sales of contiguous tracts, making allowances for distances from the city according to the scale that is established by current sales.

The land value of the city may thus be determined for peak periods like 1836, 1856, 1873, 1890, and 1926 with a close approximation to values current at the time; but since the sales data for the corresponding troughs of 1841, 1861, 1877, and 1897 are far less abundant than for the peak periods, a partial computation can be made from the sales data available for these low points, but this involves many interpolations. There is, however, another method available, and that is to deduct a percentage from the values of the preceding peak that in the opinion of current observers correctly measures the fall that has taken place. Both methods have been used here.

If it is difficult to determine aggregate values of Chicago land at the bottom of a depression, what may be said of the problem of arriving at land values in those dull periods when such few sales as are made are at widely different levels for the same type of property at the same time? Manifestly, a curve through this period can be only conjectural, for the market has virtually been suspended, as in those periods when the Stock Exchange has closed. There are other problems of the greatest importance, such as determining the slope of the upward or downward curve of land values. This can be done by taking the trend of the available sales, and, after giving them the proper weight for the value of the territory they represent, calculating a trend for the entire city. It can also be done by translating statements into figures. For if it is reported that throughout a certain period of thirty years land values in a certain section of the city have been stationary, sales data at any point of time in this period would establish the value for the entire period. If again it is said that most of the upward movement in land values took place in a certain year, and if the value at the high and low points of the entire cycle are known, this statement that gives no numbers or price data would fix the position of the curve.

The determination of the course of land values for the entire period of the study requires the use of several methods spliced together, and while checks can be made at several points between different methods, the different series of data do not parallel each other for a sufficiently long period to form an independent check on each other. Moreover, all the types of data are not independent but interrelated, and they all purport to show the same thing—the true cash value of the land. Having used sales considerations expressed in deeds as the main basis for the period from 1830 to 1891, and appraisals, sales, advertised prices and opinions, and capitalized incomes for the period from 1891 to 1910, George C. Olcott's *Land Values Maps of Chicago* have been the main source of data for the period from 1910 to 1929. As already indicated, various other methods have also been employed to check the other data from time to time.

Another problem is raised by the terms of credit on which the land is sold in the reported sales. The customary terms were the celebrated canal terms of one-third down and the balance in one, two, and three years, and it is assumed that some such basis of credit was allowed in the case of most transactions and that the sales are not all for cash. If sales had been made on an all-cash basis, the market would have been entirely different from what it actually was, because it would not have been possible to carry on speculation to such an extreme degree. To attempt to reduce all transactions to an all-cash basis would require some hypothetical computations that would be extremely difficult to make, for in many cases purchase money mortgages could not be discounted at the banks with any degree of facility. It is true that sales for all cash should not be placed in the same category as sales on easy payments, but to secure the data to make this distinction over a long period of time would be almost impossible, and it is believed that the bulk of sales were approximately on the foregoing canal terms.

A further question may arise as to the method of determining the total value of a square-mile section after the sales value of an adequate number of samples is obtained. In some cases, as for the central business district for 1836 and 1896, computations or valuations for every tract of land or every lot in a section are made. In that event the aggregate value is determined merely by the addition of the separate items. Again, where a representative twenty-acre tract is sold in a section, the price per acre is multiplied by 640 to give the value of the entire section. Again, if the section is homogeneous and the lots are of a normal depth of 125 feet—there are 153,600 front feet to the acre, after allowing for streets and alleys, and the total value of the section is determined by multiplying the average front-foot value of the sample sales by 153,600 and adding a premium for corner values according to the character of the use of the land. If the residential and business portions of the section have different values, separate computations are made for each. If the lots are of abnormal depth, such as 200 feet, the total number of front feet in the section is computed by actual measurement, and this figure is multiplied by the front-foot value of lots of that depth. In the downtown area, where Olcott shows land values only for lots of 100 feet deep, in making computations from his valuations it is necessary to add a percentage determined by the depth rule to this figure as well as to add a premium for corners.

In making this study of Chicago land values the writer has endeavored to marshal the evidence available for demonstrating the behavior of prices of land in Chicago. It is not contended that the formula for arriving at the sound or true values of land have been discovered, because the record demonstrates that the character of the subject matter is itself unstable. For the extreme and baffling fluctuations in land values that respond to whims of fashion and speculative rumors are not eternal verities to be measured by mechanical exactitude but states of mind that are regarded as either hallucinations of grandeur or fits of melancholia after they have swept past. Those who solemnly weigh all the attributes of a tract of land on their scales and send forth from their cloisters, like Delphic oracles, the results of their deliberations—pronouncing that the land has a certain value, no more and no less, frequently impress the public who have not watched the gyrations of land values. Some students search for that will-o'-the-wisp, true cash value of land, and accept the statements of appraisers and tax assessors as gospel. It is more important to see the limitations in all land-value data than it is to set up a standard of artificial accuracy—when no superfine accuracy in fact exists.

APPENDIX III

STATISTICAL TABLES

TABLE LXXX

Aggregate Value of the 211 Square Miles of Land in the 1933 Corporate Limits of Chicago

Year	Aggregate Value	Year	Aggregate Value
1833	$ 168,800	1883	$ 485,000,000
1836	10,500,000	1892	1,500,000,000
1842	1,400,000	1897	1,000,000,000
1856	125,000,000	1910	1,500,000,000
1861	60,000,000	1915	2,000,000,000
1873	575,000,000	1926	5,000,000,000
1879	250,000,000	1933	2,000,000,000

TABLE LXXXI*

Number of Instruments Recorded in Cook County, 1872–1932
(Includes Warranty Deeds, Quit-Claim Deeds, Master's Deeds, Trust Deeds, Mortgages, Contracts, Recorded Notices, and Chattel Mortgages)

Year	No. of Instruments	Increase	Decrease	Percentage Increase	Percentage Decrease
1872	41,053				
1873	66,827	25,774		62.7	
1874	64,599		2,228		3.3
1875	57,638		6,961		10.7
1876	50,883		6,755		11.7
1877	47,860		3,023		5.9
1878	42,101		5,759		12.0
1879	44,824	2,723		6.4	
1880	52,947	8,123		18.1	
1881	63,332	10,375		19.6	
1882	73,876	10,554		16.6	
1883	75,968	2,092		2.8	
1884	79,663	3,695		4.8	
1885	84,202	4,539		5.7	
1886	105,496	21,224		25.1	
1887	123,502	18,006		17.1	
1888	135,974	12,472		11.4	
1889	158,691	22,717		16.7	
1890	191,750	33,059		20.8	
1891	194,897	3,147		1.6	
1892	203,061	8,164		4.1	

* Chicago Title and Trust Co. Compiled by J. Frank Graf and Kenneth E. Rice, vice-presidents.

APPENDIXES

TABLE LXXXI—*Continued*

YEAR	No. of Instruments	INCREASE	DECREASE	PERCENTAGE Increase	PERCENTAGE Decrease
1893	180,675		22,386		11.0
1894	179,827		848		0.4
1895	173,485		6,342		3.5
1896	153,696		19,789		11.4
1897	151,164		2,532		1.6
1898	137,092		14,072		9.3
1899	140,308	3,216		2.3	
1900	138,664		1,644		1.1
1901	141,883	3,219		2.3	
1902	146,444	4,561		3.2	
1903	147,424	980		0.6	
1904	153,913	6,489		4.4	
1905	163,323	9,410		6.1	
1906	172,230	8,907		5.5	
1907	173,206	976		0.6	
1908	168,136		5,070		2.9
1909	184,877	16,741		10.0	
1910	200,021	15,144		8.1	
1911	209,490	9,469		4.7	
1912	218,968	9,478		4.5	
1913	233,499	14,531		6.6	
1914	232,911		588		0.2
1915	234,911	2,000		0.9	
1916	254,814	19,007		8.1	
1917	245,582		9,232		3.6
1918	198,200		47,382		19.2
1919	280,271	82,071		41.4	
1920	341,467	61,196		21.8	
1921	355,509	14,042		4.1	
1922	422,235	66,726		18.7	
1923	507,520	85,285		20.2	
1924	524,598	17,078		3.3	
1925	580,714	56,116		10.7	
1926	553,609		27,105		4.6
1927	523,357		30,252		5.4
1928	489,527		33,830		6.4
1929	434,934		54,593		11.1
1930	355,370		79,564		18.3
1931	308,526		46,844		13.0
1932	240,515		68,011		20.0

TABLE LXXXII*

TOTAL CONSIDERATION IN DEEDS RECORDED IN COOK COUNTY, 1868–1902

Year	Amount	Year	Amount
1868†	$29,669,961	1886	$ 86,900,000
1869	50,487,731	1887	95,000,000
1870	47,078,561	1888	93,000,000
1871	44,682,906	1889	135,800,000
1872	78,183,500	1890	237,831,600
1873	78,428,000	1891	181,522,269
1874	67,871,700	1892	180,862,364
1875	53,149,850	1893	129,614,572
1876	42,153,000	1894	120,177,305
1877	38,123,900	1895	132,225,170
1878	42,126,800	1896	105,475,557
1879	38,123,900	1897	99,556,147
1880	43,682,900	1898	93,100,276
1881	54,859,190	1899	108,210,111
1882	56,510,539	1900	105,324,550
1883	51,924,700	1901	114,556,952
1884	51,900,000	1902	126,536,745
1885	57,482,321		

* Files of the *Chicago Tribune*. † Five months.

TABLE LXXXIII*

NUMBER OF TRANSFERS IN COOK COUNTY, 1901–33
(Including Torrens Transfers)

Year	Number	Year	Number
1901	15,871	1918	46,883
1902	18,063	1919	67,530
1903	19,880	1920	80,260
1904	24,450	1921	78,693
1905	28,940	1922	95,949
1906	31,562	1923	113,865
1907	27,256	1924	114,708
1908	30,327	1925	122,900
1909	34,074	1926	121,818
1910	31,847	1927	109,129
1911	39,629	1928	102,399
1912	48,524	1929	84,453
1913	57,489	1930	67,770
1914	59,660	1931	63,022
1915	56,882	1932	59,668
1916	60,520	1933†	43,635
1917	54,647		

* *Annual Reports of the Recorder of Deeds, Cook County, Illinois.* † First ten months.

APPENDIXES

TABLE LXXXIV*
NEW MORTGAGES AND TRUST DEEDS, COOK COUNTY, ILLINOIS, 1896–1933
(Including Torrens Trust Deeds since 1907)

Year	Amount of Stated Consideration	Year	Amount of Stated Consideration	Number
1896	$ 88,999,723	1915	$ 251,395,189	....
1897	100,579,458†	1916	950,750,498	....
1898	196,519,070	1917	389,023,601	....
1899	60,877,917†	1918	163,687,177	....
1900	282,959,882	1919	241,177,840	....
1901	132,195,132	1920	305,587,870	....
1902	151,689,383	1921	361,925,299	....
1903	84,265,276	1922	550,914,192	80,249
1904	323,920,126	1923	696,882,247	97,484
1905	151,604,890	1924	746,795,339	100,586
1906	147,857,419	1925	986,960,148	120,276
1907	337,583,140	1926	1,033,864,243	123,723
1908	512,226,963	1927	1,045,997,413	126,389
1909	497,333,159	1928	1,039,432,235	120,346
1910	243,292,120	1929	759,395,774	94,671
1911	262,119,879	1930	425,164,215	68,161
1912	407,365,536	1931	264,584,983	48,159
1913	202,745,276	1932	143,309,644	23,043
1914	293,453,798	1933‡	73,971,629	11,630

* *Annual Report of the Recorder of Deeds of Cook County, Illinois* (1931) and the *Economist* (Chicago, 1896–1931).
† Exclusive of large railroad mortgages.   ‡ First ten months.

TABLE LXXXV*
CONSIDERATION STATED IN DEEDS FOR TRANSFERS OF PROPERTY MORE THAN SEVEN MILES FROM THE COURTHOUSE COMPARED WITH THE TOTAL CONSIDERATION IN ALL DEEDS IN COOK COUNTY

Year	Consideration beyond Seven Miles	Total for County	Percentage of Outside to Total
1889	$25,267,238	$133,374,949	19.0
1890	43,608,498	227,486,959	19.2
1891	36,270,802	181,522,269	20.0
1892	26,488,451	180,892,364	14.4
1893	20,797,689	129,614,572	16.0
1894	15,174,362	120,177,305	12.5
1895	16,291,023	133,546,172	12.1
1896	11,528,012	103,970,720	11.0
1897	13,517,539	108,012,138	12.5
1898	10,886,359	100,622,436	10.9
1899	11,916,899	111,884,223	10.7
1900	10,328,868	105,180,670	9.6
1901	10,521,553	114,158,722	9.2

* *Economist* (Chicago, 1889–1901).

TABLE LXXXVI*

Annual Amount of New Construction in Chicago, 1854–1933

Year	No. of Buildings	Frontage	Value
1832	18		
1833	150		
1834 1835 1836	270		
1837	66		
1838–42	845		
1843			
1844	600		
1845	871		
1846–51	1,966		
1851–53	3,414		
1854			$ 2,438,910
1855			3,735,254
1856			5,708,624
1857			6,423,518
1858	1,872		3,246,400
1859	2,400		2,044,000
1860			1,188,300
1861			797,800
1862			525,000
1863	7,000		2,500,000
1864	8,000		4,700,000
1865	9,000		6,950,000
1866	9,000		11,000,000
1867	12,000		8,500,000
1868	4,410		14,000,000
1869			11,000,000
1870			20,000,000
1871 (Oct. 9–Oct. 9, 1872)			40,133,600
1873	1,000	42,300	25,500,000
1874	757	33,065	5,785,541
1875	875	55,479	9,778,080
1876	1,636	43,222	8,270,300
1877	2,698	35,033	9,071,050
1878	2,709	31,118	7,419,100
1879	1,624	33,000	6,745,000
1880	3,868	35,200	9,071,850
1881	3,493	40,096	8,832,305
1882	3,113	73,161	16,286,700
1883	4,086	85,588	22,162,000
1884	4,169	98,782	20,857,300
1885	4,638	108,850	19,624,100
1886	4,654	112,302	21,324,400
1887	4,833	115,500	19,778,100
1888	4,958	116,419	20,350,800
1889	4,931	119,573	25,065,500
1890	11,608	266,284	47,322,100
1891	11,805	282,672	54,001,800

* *Chicago Tribune*, *Chicago Daily News Almanac*, and reports of the Building Department of Chicago.

TABLE LXXXVI—Continued

Year	No. of Buildings	Frontage	Value
1892	13,118	326,232	$ 63,463,400
1893	8,265	214,427	28,517,700
1894	9,736	221,100	33,805,565
1895	8,724	217,923	34,920,643
1896	6,438	158,650	22,711,115
1897	5,279	128,886	21,690,030
1898	4,067	133,603	21,294,325
1899	3,794	112,469	20,857,570
1900	3,554	100,056	19,100,050
1901	6,035	170,644	34,911,755
1902	6,074	186,609	48,070,390
1903	6,135	174,932	33,645,025
1904	7,132	203,785	44,724,790
1905	8,337	243,485	63,455,020
1906	10,447	276,770	64,298,330
1907	9,353	254,440	54,093,080
1908	10,771	291,655	68,204,080
1909	11,241	309,351	90,558,580
1910	11,406	327,250	96,932,700
1911	11,106	299,032	105,269,700
1912	11,325	320,008	88,786,960
1913	10,792	318,329	89,668,427
1914	9,938	289,263	83,261,710
1915	10,340	317,161	97,291,480
1916	10,277	327,496	112,835,150
1917	4,938	161,675	64,244,450
1918	2,529	85,628	34,792,200
1919	6,589	209,807	104,198,850
1920	3,745	135,440	79,102,650
1921	7,800	233,025	125,004,510
1922	12,581	395,478	227,742,010
1923	15,494	474,143	329,604,312
1924	16,253	479,712	296,893,990
1925	17,501	534,256	360,794,250
1926	14,263	442,388	366,586,400
1927	12,025	397,096	352,936,400
1928	9,394	337,038	315,800,000
1929	6,146	215,507	202,286,800
1930	2,434	86,344	79,613,400
1931	725	43,150	46,440,130
1932	467	14,364	3,824,500
1933†	412	11,045	3,407,100

† First ten months.

TABLE LXXXVII*
NUMBER OF DIFFERENT TYPES OF BUILDINGS ERECTED ANNUALLY, 1912–1933

Year	No. of Business Buildings	No. of Hotels and Offices	No. of Single Houses	No. of Apartment Buildings†
1912	1,614	65	3,827	4,341
1913	1,355	99	4,015	4,475
1914	976	64	3,865	4,401
1915	1,077	67	3,954	4,525
1916	1,399	107	3,789	4,293
1917	1,366	57	2,074	1,174
1918	971	64	1,082	326
1919	1,339	48	4,596	457
1920	1,426	56	2,058	103
1921	1,306	49	4,645	1,466
1922	1,801	79	6,340	3,693
1923	1,726	126	7,852	5,179
1924	1,610	81	8,768	5,235
1925	1,853	114	9,371	5,397
1926	1,560	130	7,415	4,523
1927	1,538	133	5,655	4,101
1928	1,402	100	4,299	2,962
1929	1,191	81	2,931	1,579
1930	844	43	1,076	330
1931	450	20	625	130
1932	219	13	197	17
1933‡	235	16	132	13

* Department of Buildings, city of Chicago. † Does not include apartments over stores.
‡ First ten months.

TABLE LXXXVIII*
INDEX NUMBERS OF RENTS OF WORKINGMEN'S DWELLINGS IN CHICAGO
(Rents for December, 1914 = 100)

Dec., 1914	100.0	June, 1925	205.6
Dec., 1915	99.9	Dec., 1925	204.4
Dec., 1916	100.7	June, 1926	199.5
Dec., 1917	101.4	Dec., 1926	196.7
Dec., 1918	102.6	June, 1927	193.9
June, 1919	108.0	Dec., 1927	190.0
Dec., 1919	114.0	June, 1928	186.8
June, 1920	135.1	Dec., 1928	183.6
Dec., 1920	148.9	June, 1929	180.3
May, 1921	178.2	Dec., 1929	177.2
Dec., 1921	183.9	June, 1930	175.1
June, 1922	187.4	Dec., 1930	171.1
Dec., 1922	188.9	June, 1931	164.4
June, 1923	192.1	Dec., 1931	156.5
Dec., 1923	195.4	June, 1932	138.8
June, 1924	204.4	Dec., 1932	124.9
Dec., 1924	205.8	June, 1933	108.7

* U.S. Department of Labor, *Monthly Labor Review*, XXIX, No. 2 (August, 1929), 20; XXXVI, No. 2 (February, 1933), 433.

TABLE LXXXIX

NUMBER OF LOTS SUBDIVIDED ANNUALLY IN COOK COUNTY AND THE CHICAGO METROPOLITAN AREA, 1874–1930

Year	Lots in Cook County	Lots in Metropolitan Area*
1874	4,523	11,235
1875	1,829	8,067
1876	643	3,555
1877	425	1,382
1878	437	1,909
1879	1,060	2,128
1880	1,730	3,143
1881	1,942	4,085
1882	1,908	6,003
1883	2,668	6,208
1884	1,829	4,555
1885	3,210	4,402
1886	4,135	10,243
1887	13,714	17,671
1888	18,813	26,101
1889	39,997	45,225
1890	54,674	72,939
1891	79,803	115,892
1892	38,968	65,380
1893	17,691	35,494
1894	9,860	14,524
1895	11,652	15,969
1896	6,538	9,104
1897	3,763	6,022
1898	3,459	8,015
1899	3,463	5,190
1900	4,800	7,599
1901	2,909	9,846
1902	3,047	11,312
1903	3,015	11,034
1904	2,866	7,085
1905	5,731	10,338
1906	7,656	18,868
1907	5,845	19,073
1908	5,560	13,812
1909	7,601	16,234
1910	11,870	23,634
1911	9,844	21,351
1912	10,235	20,965
1913	19,173	31,326
1914	20,231	34,241
1915	12,705	19,253
1916	12,937	19,392
1917	6,962	11,573
1918	2,939	5,220
1919	6,931	13,376
1920	10,334	21,430
1921	11,395	23,765

* The counties included in the Metropolitan Area are Cook, Lake, and DuPage counties in Illinois and Lake and Laporte counties in Indiana.

TABLE LXXXIX—*Continued*

Year	Lots in Cook County	Lots in Metropolitan Area*
1922	15,570	39,309
1923	24,828	53,607
1924	45,759	88,713
1925	48,070	106,513
1926	61,243	125,956
1927	31,432	89,243
1928	14,081	51,176
1929	17,081	34,141
1930	2,874	12,128

* The counties included in the Metropolitan Area are Cook, Lake, and DuPage counties in Illinois and Lake and Laporte counties in Indiana.

APPENDIXES

TABLE XC

APPROXIMATE NUMBER OF ACRES SUBDIVIDED ANNUALLY IN THE
1931 CITY LIMITS OF CHICAGO, 1830–1932

Year	Total*	No. of Acres North of Madison Street	No. of Acres South of Madison Street
1830	240	240	0
1831	0	0	0
1832	0	0	0
1833	742	102	640
1834	0	0	0
1835	620	220	400
1836	920	240	680
1837	320	0	320
1838	0	0	0
1839	100	100	0
1840	0	0	0
1841	0	0	0
1842	0	0	0
1843	0	0	0
1844	160	160	0
1845	275	275	0
1846	0	0	0
1847	0	0	0
1848	960 (2,640)	0	960
1849	60	10	50
1850	100	10	90
1851	60 (160)	20	40
1852	755 (160)	95	660
1853	1,015 (960)	510	505
1854	1,565 (320)	305	1,100
1855	2,060 (1,420)	1,350	710
1856	2,450 (1,160)	1,110	1,340
1857	1,450 (800)	915	535
1858	510	80	430
1859	220 (360)	10	210
1860	190 (160)	110	80
1861	0	0	0
1862	0	0	0
1863	220	0	220
1864	60	5	55
1865	290	150	140
1866	395	145	250
1867	815	90	725
1868	2,365 (160)	300	2,065
1869	5,270 (320)	1,520	3,750
1870	2,180 (160)	355	1,825
1871	955	265	690
1872	4,025	1,545	2,480
1873	3,635 (640)	2,295	1,340
1874	2,080	505	1,575
1875	1,270 (160)	465	805
1876	830 (220)	220	570
1877	575	345	230
1878	230	190	40

*Figures in parentheses are number of acres divided into 5- and 10-acre tracts.

TABLE XC—*Continued*

Year	Total	No. of Acres North of Madison Street	No. of Acres South of Madison Street
1879	295	160	135
1880	110	20	90
1881	735	350	425
1882	1,255	615	640
1883	565	340	225
1884	700	295	405
1885	1,165	315	850
1886	1,400	690	710
1887	1,895	545	1,350
1888	2,015	645	1,370
1889	3,255	695	2,560
1890	3,280	1,115	2,165
1891	3,215	1,570	1,745
1892	800	360	440
1893	780	410	370
1894	560	300	260
1895	770	520	250
1896	320	240	80
1897	190	170	20
1898	80	30	50
1899	220	180	40
1900	20	20	0
1901	130	70	60
1902	110	60	50
1903	60	60	0
1904	330	200	130
1905	480	170	310
1906	455	355	100
1907	570	110	400
1908	375	165	210
1909	665	435	230
1910	825	425	400
1911	880	390	490
1912	950	430	520
1913	1,520	420	1,100
1914	2,090	750	1,340
1915	1,270	680	590
1916	1,110	470	640
1917	460	100	360
1918	380	140	240
1919	280	140	140
1920	710	460	250
1921	775	330	445
1922	550	370	180
1923	980	160	820
1924	885	525	360
1925	1,090	245	845
1926	1,460	310	1,150
1927	720	80	640
1928	460	40	420
1929	130	100	30
1930	0	0	0
1931	0	0	0
1932	0	0	0

APPENDIXES

TABLE XCI*

VALUE OF MANUFACTURES, WHOLESALE TRADE, PRODUCE TRADE, TOTAL TRADE OF CHICAGO (GOLD), 1850–1931

Year	Manufactures	Wholesale	Produce	Total Trade†
1850	$ 2,562,583			$ 20,000,000
1856	15,513,063			
1860	13,555,671‡			97,000,000
1868				310,000,000
1869				336,000,000
1870	76,848,120§			377,000,000
1871–72	179,831,000			437,000,000
1873	176,000,000			514,000,000
1874	163,634,000			575,000,000
1875	191,009,000	$ 250,000,000	$200,000,000	566,000,000
1876	200,493,000	254,000,000	211,000,000	587,000,000
1877	202,115,000	264,000,000	203,000,000	595,000,000
1878	227,560,000		218,000,000	650,000,000
1879	223,809,000		253,000,000	764,000,000
1880	269,050,000		312,000,000	900,000,000
1881	317,000,000		367,000,000	1,015,000,000
1882	305,000,000	432,000,000	382,000,000	1,045,000,000
1883	307,000,000	412,000,000	400,000,000	1,050,000,000
1884	292,237,000	370,000,000	356,000,000	933,000,000
1885	316,900,000	380,000,000	337,000,000	959,000,000
1886	349,679,000	408,000,000	322,000,000	997,000,000
1887	403,109,000	449,000,000	350,000,000	1,103,000,000
1888	401,161,000	437,500,000	371,000,000	1,125,000,000
1889	452,223,000	448,165,000	388,000,000	1,177,000,000
1890	664,568,000‖	486,806,000	471,385,000	1,380,000,000
1891	567,012,000	517,166,000	499,600,000	1,459,000,000
1892	586,335,000	573,000,000	507,000,000	1,538,000,000
1893	574,420,000	519,350,000	469,973,000	1,435,000,000
1894	501,175,000	464,000,000	427,275,000	1,280,000,000
1895	532,235,000	504,675,000	394,193,000	1,316,700,000
1896	483,325,000	469,000,000	368,401,000	1,216,400,000
1897	547,550,000	543,000,000	419,300,000	1,400,517,000
1898	613,085,000	618,000,000	469,302,000	1,577,085,000
1899	687,725,000	731,075,000	492,690,000	1,770,485,000
1900	741,079,000	786,205,000		
1901	803,925,000	892,800,000		
1902	911,750,000	1,007,405,000		
1903	950,650,000	1,249,140,000		
1904	1,034,790,000	1,314,525,000		
1905	1,290,874,000	1,521,937,000		
1906	1,642,000,000	1,744,750,000		
1907	1,732,879,100	1,847,821,000		
1908	1,598,147,500	1,685,057,000		
1909	1,782,935,000	1,892,949,000		
1910	1,867,329,000	2,046,172,000		
1911	1,212,813,600	2,027,195,000		

* *Chicago Tribune* and U.S. Census.
† An aggregate of manufactures, wholesale trade, and produce trade with elimination of duplicated items.
‡ U.S. Census.
§ Local census. U.S. Census gave $62,736,228.
‖ U.S. Census, which included many small firms not included in local census of 1889 or 1891.

TABLE XCI—*Continued*

Year	Manufactures	Wholesale	Produce	Total Trade
1912	$1,978,404,000	$2,295,680,000		
1913	1,998,713,000	2,333,700,000		
1914	1,660,202,000 ¶	2,121,619,000		
1915	1,723,700,000	2,283,119,000		
1916	2,111,609,000	2,841,299,000		
1917	2,483,176,850	3,199,584,000		
1918	3,943,535,713	3,338,175,100		
1919	3,657,424,000**			
1921	2,485,819,000**			
1923	3,323,341,000**			
1925	3,439,163,000**			
1926		4,484,761,000		
1927	3,478,754,000**			
1929	3,884,675,000**			
1931	2,200,000,000††			

¶ Local census. U.S. Census gave $1,483,498,000.
** U.S. Census.
†† This is an estimate derived from U.S. Census figures for Cook County.

TABLE XCII*

PERCENTAGE OF VACANCIES IN CHICAGO OFFICE BUILDINGS

Date	Percentage of Total Space Vacant	Date	Percentage of Total Space Vacant
Jan. 1, 1926	6.3	Jan. 1, 1930	14.5
Jan. 1, 1927	5.3	Jan. 1, 1931	17.5
Jan. 1, 1928	11.0	Jan. 1, 1932	20.4
Jan. 1, 1929	14.0	May 1, 1933	27.8

* Association of Building Managers of Chicago.

TABLE XCIII
POPULATION OF CHICAGO (PRESENT CITY LIMITS)

YEAR	Current City Limits	1933 City Limits	YEAR	Current City Limits	1933 City Limits||
1830	50		1882	560,693	671,099
1831	100		1883	590,000	729,725
1832	200		1884	629,985	785,926
1833	350		1885	700,000	831,422
1834	2,000		1886	825,880	884,768
1835	3,265		1887	850,000	922,894
1836	3,820		1888	875,500	983,644
1837	4,170*		1889	900,000	1,048,894
1838	4,000		1890	1,098,570†	1,112,575
1839	4,200		1891	1,215,000	
1840	4,479†		1892	1,295,000	
1841	5,000		1893	1,315,000	
1842	6,000		1894	1,400,000	
1843	7,589*		1895	1,425,000	
1844	8,000		1896	1,440,000	
1845	12,088‡		1897	1,535,000	
1846	14,169*		1898	1,641,000	
1847	16,859*		1899	1,652,000	
1848	20,023*		1900	1,698,575†	
1849	23,047*		1901	1,700,610	
1850	29,963†	32,949	1902	1,702,856	
1851	34,000		1903	1,708,500	
1852	38,754		1904	1,714,144§	
1853	59,130*		1905	1,740,411	
1854	65,872		1906	1,801,702	
1855	80,023‡		1907	1,875,000	
1856	84,113*		1908	1,924,060	
1857	93,000		1909	2,074,000	
1858	91,000		1910	2,185,283†	
1859	95,000		1911	2,199,380	
1860	109,206†	117,387	1912	2,210,351	
1861	120,000		1913	2,265,019	
1862	138,186*		1914	2,369,023	
1863	150,000		1915	2,448,426	
1864	160,353*		1916	2,492,000	
1865	178,492‡		1917	2,492,204	
1866	200,418*		1918	2,546,144	
1867	220,000		1919	2,599,502	
1868	252,054*		1920	2,701,705†	
1869	272,043		1921	2,820,992	
1870	298,977†	309,635	1922	2,901,507	
1871	325,000		1923	3,010,850	
1872	367,396*		1924	3,155,843	
1873	380,000		1925	3,263,196	
1874	395,408		1926	3,296,679	
1875	400,000		1927	3,402,296	
1876	407,661		1928	3,397,067	
1877	420,000		1929	3,372,936	
1878	436,731		1930	3,376,438†	
1879	465,000		1931	3,341,913	
1880	503,298†	553,834	1932	3,236,913	
1881	530,000	605,384			

* City census.   ‡ State census.
† U.S. Census.   § School census.
|| From 1900 to 1932 there was a very slight difference between the population in the current city limits and the 1933 city limits, as annexations in that period included only small and sparsely settled areas.

TABLE XCIV*

DISTRIBUTION OF CHICAGO POPULATION BY MILE ZONES, 1860–1916

Mile Zone	1860	1870	1880	1890	1900	1910	1916
	Number of Persons in Mile Zones Measured from State and Madison Streets						
0– 1	30,000	70,000	70,000	80,000	80,000	75,000	75,000
1– 2	49,000	115,000	170,000	250,000	250,000	255,000	255,000
2– 3	25,000	70,000	140,000	303,000	400,000	377,000	335,000
3– 4	8,000	35,000	87,000	175,000	295,000	351,000	351,000
4– 5		20,000	50,000	100,000	180,000	350,000	416,000
5– 6		1,000	10,000	70,000	175,000	250,000	370,000
6– 7			2,000	48,000	105,000	175,000	290,000
7– 8			1,000	30,000	95,000	100,000	150,000
8– 9				25,000	55,000	83,000	107,000
9–10				15,000	30,000	70,000	75,000
10–11				5,000	20,000	30,000	35,000
11–12				2,000	10,000	10,000	12,000
12–13					5,000	10,000	12,000
13–14						7,000	8,000
14–15						2,000	5,000
	Population Densities (per Square Mile) in Mile Belts from State and Madison Streets						
0– 1	15,000	34,000	37,500	37,500	37,500	42,000	42,000
1– 2	10,000	24,000	35,000	51,000	52,000	53,000	55,000
2– 3	7,000	10,000	20,000	43,000	47,000	53,000	57,000
3– 4	1,000	4,000	10,000	20,000	30,000	36,000	37,000
4– 5		1,000	4,000	7,000	15,000	27,000	34,000
5– 6			1,000	4,000	11,000	15,000	23,000
6– 7				3,000	5,500	9,000	15,000
7– 8				2,000	5,000	5,000	8,000

* *Report of the Chicago Traction and Subway Commission* (1916), p. 73.

TABLE XCV*
NUMBER OF PASSENGER AUTOMOBILES, MOTOR TRUCKS, AND HORSE-DRAWN VEHICLES REGISTERED IN CHICAGO, 1910–33

Year	Passenger Automobiles	Motor Trucks	Horse-drawn Vehicles
1910	12,926	799	58,114
1911	15,144	1,679	55,785
1912	21,512	3,195	55,502
1913	27,729	4,207	50,429
1914	32,258	5,075	52,021
1915	39,916	6,996	49,541
1916	53,852	11,098	46,666
1917	64,132	15,398	39,639
1918	62,129	16,378	33,331
1919	78,883	19,869	29,339
1920	89,973	22,833	20,391†
1921	141,916	29,239	26,535
1922	176,508	34,508	24,992
1923	222,557	40,052	22,904
1924	264,405	44,931	21,071
1925	293,206	48,262	17,965
1926	323,769	51,080	15,276
1927	340,864	52,063	13,209
1928	367,073	54,428	11,886
1929	408,260	57,596	11,027
1930	409,878	56,751	9,351
1931	425,294	56,629	7,869
1932	398,376	52,309	6,095
1933‡	367,763	48,881	4,816

* Records of the License Department of the city of Chicago.
† Eight months.
‡ To November 4.

TABLE XCVI*

VALUE OF PROPERTY PLACED UNDER LONG-TERM LEASES AND SOLD AT JUDICIAL SALE AT THE CHICAGO REAL ESTATE BOARD ANNUALLY, 1890–1928

(Leases Capitalized at 5 Per Cent, 1890–97, and at 4 Per Cent Thereafter)

Year	Long-Term Leases	Judicial Sales
1890	$10,000,000	
1891	8,700,000	
1892	12,000,000	
1893	5,000,000	$ 4,182,603
1894	4,000,000	6,967,192
1895	4,900,000	8,256,527
1896	3,000,000	10,697,288
1897	2,600,000	13,380,240
1898	5,200,000	13,609,858
1899	3,150,000	11,821,711
1900	2,500,000	9,923,090
1901	2,381,500	10,078,070
1902	6,750,000	6,986,402
1903	6,608,000	6,911,775
1904	4,630,000	5,586,267
1905	10,000,000	5,400,032
1906	9,750,000	5,263,821
1907	4,300,000	7,099,155
1908	7,400,000	4,728,812
1909	16,600,000	6,192,896
1910	9,800,000	4,179,104
1911	31,000,000	4,347,701
1912	15,000,000	5,265,245
1913	13,690,000	5,265,245
1914	8,649,800	5,431,731
1915	3,230,000	5,194,402
1916	9,051,350	5,502,624
1917	5,892,200	5,011,924
1918	3,414,000	5,686,745
1919	6,250,000	8,146,692
1920	14,234,150	6,801,411
1921	6,250,000	5,883,665
1922	19,201,700	5,867,838
1923	18,950,000	6,066,250
1924	15,948,800	5,498,243
1925	36,934,000	6,772,285
1926	33,562,000	9,262,262
1927		11,864,288
1928		14,404,843

* *Economist.*

APPENDIXES

TABLE XCVII*
ASSESSMENT OF REAL ESTATE IN CHICAGO, 1837–1932
(Land and Buildings Combined)

Year	Assessment	Year	Assessment
1837	$ 236,842†	1885	$ 107,146,881
1838	235,996†	1886	122,980,123
1839	94,803†	1887	123,169,455
1840	94,437†	1888	123,292,358
1841	127,024	1889	127,372,618
1842	108,757	1890	170,553,854
1843	962,221	1891	203,353,791
1844	1,992,085	1892	190,614,636
1845	2,273,171	1893	189,299,120
1846	3,664,425	1894	190,960,897
1847	4,995,466	1895	192,498,842
1848	4,998,266	1896	195,684,875
1849	5,181,637	1897	184,632,905
1850	5,685,965	1898	178,801,172‡
1851	6,804,262	1899	260,265,058‡
1852	8,190,769	1900	202,884,012‡
1853	13,130,677	1901	259,254,598‡
1854	18,990,744	1902	276,509,730‡
1855	21,637,500	1903	289,371,249‡
1856	25,892,308	1904	291,329,703‡
1857	29,307,628	1905	295,514,443‡
1858	30,175,325	1906	303,033,228‡
1859	30,732,313	1907	346,843,590‡
1860	31,198,135	1908	344,499,927‡
1861	31,314,749	1909	586,253,655§
1862	31,587,545	1910	603,022,875§
1863	35,143,252	1911	663,376,027§
1864	37,148,023	1912	670,652,219§
1865	44,065,499	1913	688,387,352§
1866	66,495,116	1914	707,366,379§
1867	141,445,920	1915	749,905,059§
1868	174,490,660	1916	742,695,603§
1869	211,371,240	1917	753,321,967§
1870	223,643,600	1918	757,914,948§
1871	236,898,650	1919	1,174,655,872‖
1872	239,154,890	1920	1,166,211,873‖
1873	262,969,820	1921	1,178,965,784‖
1874	258,549,310	1922	1,176,570,644‖
1875	125,468,605	1923	1,297,355,021‖
1876	128,832,403	1924	1,293,019,838‖
1877	116,082,533	1925	1,356,608,934‖
1878	104,420,053	1926	1,403,963,316‖
1879	91,152,229	1927	3,247,359,299¶
1880	89,032,038	1928	2,753,318,047**
1881	90,099,045	1929	2,830,506,884**
1882	95,881,714	1930	2,750,237,800**
1883	101,596,795	1931	2,098,003,781**
1884	105,606,743	1932	1,573,500,000**

* *Chicago Daily News Almanac.*
† Includes personal property.
‡ 20 per cent of full assessed value.
§ 33⅓ per cent of full assessed value.
‖ 50 per cent of full assessed value.
¶ Full assessed value.
** 37 per cent of full assessed value.

TABLE XCVIII*

CHICAGO TAX LEVY, 1837–1931
(For Corporate and School Purposes)

Year	Levy	Year	Levy
1837	$ 5,905	1885	$ 5,152,366
1838	8,850	1886	5,368,410
1839	4,665	1887	5,602,715
1840	4,722	1888	5,723,067
1841	10,005	1889	6,326,561
1842	9,181	1890	9,558,335
1843	8,648	1891	10,453,270
1844	17,166	1892	12,142,449
1845	11,078	1893	11,810,970
1846	15,826	1894	12,267,644
1847	18,159	1895	14,239,685
1848	22,052	1896	12,290,145
1849	30,045	1897	12,939,333
1850	25,271	1898	12,207,907
1851	63,386	1899	13,359,271
1852	76,949	1900	17,086,408
1853	135,663	1901	14,245,294
1854	199,082	1902	14,039,030
1855	206,209	1903	14,815,388
1856	396,652	1904	15,994,411
1857	572,046	1905	16,845,974
1858	430,190	1906	17,434,169
1859	513,164	1907	22,605,709
1860	373,315	1908	22,666,544
1861	559,968	1909	24,078,061
1862	564,038	1910	23,485,538
1863	853,346	1911	27,311,842
1864	974,656	1912	24,733,839
1865	1,294,184	1913	31,122,666
1866	1,719,064	1914	32,225,665
1867	2,518,472	1915	37,816,929
1868	3,223,458	1916	39,662,464
1869	3,990,373	1917	40,923,952
1870	4,139,799	1918	39,087,772
1871	2,897,465	1919	60,671,389
1872	4,262,961	1920	64,703,260
1873	5,617,314	1921	92,905,279
1874	5,466,693	1922	92,809,667
1875	5,108,981	1923	100,880,727
1876	4,046,806	1924	105,329,426
1877	4,013,410	1925	112,810,090
1878	3,777,757	1926	114,994,301
1879	3,776,451	1927	133,888,791
1880	3,899,127	1928	119,731,517
1881	4,136,608	1929	148,888,298
1882	4,227,403	1930	168,606,720
1883	4,540,506	1931	156,751,219
1884	4,872,457		

* *Report of the Comptroller of the City of Chicago for the Year 1931*, p. 173; figures for 1931 from unpublished records in the City Comptroller's office.

APPENDIXES

TABLE XCIX
BANK CLEARINGS IN CHICAGO BY YEARS FROM 1865 TO 1932, INCLUSIVE

Year	Amount	Year	Amount
1865*	$ 309,606,229	1900	$ 6,799,535,598
1866	453,798,648	1901	7,756,372,455
1867	580,727,331	1902	8,394,872,351
1868	723,293,445	1903	8,755,553,649
1869	734,661,950	1904	8,989,983,764
1870	810,676,036	1905	10,141,765,732
1871	868,936,755	1906	11,047,311,894
1872	993,060,503	1907	12,087,647,870
1873	1,047,027,828	1908	11,853,814,945
1874	1,101,347,918	1909	13,781,843,612
1875	1,212,817,208	1910	13,939,689,984
1876	1,110,093,624	1911	13,925,709,803
1877	1,044,678,476	1912	15,380,795,542
1878	967,184,093	1913	16,073,130,524
1879	1,257,756,124	1914	15,692,828,997
1880	1,725,684,895	1915	16,198,985,175
1881	2,249,329,925	1916	20,541,943,206
1882	2,393,437,874	1917	24,974,974,479
1883	2,517,371,581	1918	25,930,200,368
1884	2,259,680,392	1919	29,685,973,092
1885	2,318,579,003	1920	32,669,233,536
1886	2,604,762,912	1921	25,974,692,057
1887	2,969,216,211	1922	28,036,204,345
1888	3,163,774,463	1923	31,112,845,762
1889	3,379,925,189	1924	31,653,583,955
1890	4,093,145,904	1925	35,391,593,572
1891	4,456,885,230	1926	34,907,132,946
1892	5,135,771,188	1927	35,958,215,640
1893	4,676,960,968	1928	37,842,393,664
1894	4,315,440,477	1929	36,713,580,967
1895	4,614,979,203	1930	28,707,627,137
1896	4,413,054,109	1931	19,201,221,287
1897	4,575,693,341	1932	10,936,884,811
1898	5,517,335,477	1933†	8,292,004,951
1899	6,612,313,611		

* Nine months.   † To November 13.

TABLE C
ILLINOIS BELL TELEPHONE COMPANY STATIONS IN CHICAGO AT END OF EACH YEAR, 1882–1933

End of Year	Stations	End of Year	Stations
1882	2,610	1908	181,533
1883	2,957	1909	207,719
1884	3,331	1910	239,083
1885	3,802	1911	268,383
1886	4,197	1912	308,177
1887	4,694	1913	348,417
1888	4,667	1914	382,133
1889	5,556	1915	411,680
1890	6,518	1916	458,598
1891	7,598	1917	487,481
1892	9,202	1918	504,428
1893	10,218	1919	554,114
1894	10,505	1920	575,840
1895	11,680	1921	605,495
1896	12,576	1922	638,694
1897	13,682	1923	691,545
1898	16,315	1924	741,936
1899	20,412	1925	790,764
1900	26,661	1926	848,070
1901	40,889	1927	903,460
1902	60,395	1928	942,015
1903	76,147	1929	987,891
1904	86,744	1930	981,325
1905	104,388	1931	939,481
1906	123,177	1932	831,679
1907	156,079	1933*	799,234

* September 30.

APPENDIXES

TABLE CI
Number of Passengers Carried by Chicago Rapid Transit Company for Years Ending on December 31, 1892–1932

Year	Metropolitan Division	Northwestern Division	South Side Division	Lake St. Division	Total
1892			5,738,372		5,738,372
1893			30,055,747		30,055,747
1894			13,587,791	8,206,304	21,794,095
1895	8,224,952		14,218,004	9,936,450	32,379,406
1896	15,339,179		13,442,266	11,025,977	39,807,422
1897	16,982,718		12,237,727	11,229,245	40,449,690
1898	23,915,542		18,898,538	12,390,856	55,204,936
1899	28,564,487		22,628,074	13,635,312	64,827,873
1900	31,481,276	10,185,141	24,990,878	14,617,363	81,274,658
1901	33,573,964	20,327,005	26,320,189	15,394,038	95,615,196
1902	38,653,857	23,362,883	28,676,569	15,849,411	106,542,720
1903	41,180,853	24,937,500	32,587,206	16,176,682	114,882,241
1904	41,643,349	25,766,604	30,468,424	16,005,333	113,883,710
1905	45,358,843	28,239,609	32,959,752	17,097,216	123,655,420
1906	49,771,812	30,309,050	34,424,270	17,453,473	131,958,605
1907	54,280,888	35,097,533	40,438,620	17,446,944	147,263,985
1908	51,587,667	39,235,878	42,994,610	16,553,800	150,371,955
1909	52,519,609	41,559,004	42,722,624	15,635,963	152,437,200
1910	57,229,886	44,369,249	46,875,642	16,401,197	164,875,974
1911	55,360,839	44,271,102	46,540,681	16,693,494	162,866,116
1912	55,448,146	44,913,255	47,368,074	16,585,049	164,314,524
1913	54,748,564	44,814,561	48,067,355	16,533,745	164,164,225
1914	54,518,720	46,458,012	48,381,097	16,412,332	165,770,161
1915	51,855,495	48,454,964	48,151,164	16,211,893	164,673,516
1916	56,599,284	53,753,178	52,852,277	17,449,893	180,654,632
1917	60,917,343	57,176,321	56,840,439	18,186,070	193,120,173
1918	61,071,287	58,816,568	59,291,835	18,260,417	197,440,107
1919	56,570,076	55,727,761	55,063,960	17,301,228	184,663,025
1920	59,023,126	56,923,354	56,285,536	18,406,929	190,638,945
1921	55,325,272	55,111,280	52,560,577	17,632,153	180,629,282
1922	54,701,387	56,966,991	51,933,043	17,679,333	181,280,754
1923	62,369,432	64,428,869	56,980,513	20,174,760	203,953,574
1924	65,158,427	69,006,684	57,830,285	20,905,628	212,901,024
1925	66,136,055	71,317,843	57,455,225	21,136,452	216,045,575
1926	69,897,338	76,088,865	60,395,369	22,431,194	228,812,766
1927	69,737,972	76,157,505	57,932,586	22,384,109	226,212,172
1928	64,100,745	70,935,223	52,119,123	20,709,147	207,864,238
1929	60,546,610	67,907,811	48,539,192	19,780,782	196,774,395
1930	55,587,848	64,249,167	44,638,199	18,479,632	182,954,846
1931	45,427,249	55,152,325	36,236,783	15,597,891	152,414,248
1932					126,989,541

TABLE CII*

Annual Cost of Special Assessments, 1862–1932
(Including Pavements, Sewers, Sidewalks, Water Pipes, and Street Openings)

Year	Amount	Year	Amount
Ending:		Ending:	
April 1, 1862	$ 42,635.49	Dec. 31, 1894	$ 2,903,814.16
April 1, 1863	46,493.67	Dec. 31, 1895	4,387,214.44
April 1, 1864	89,169.31	Dec. 31, 1896	4,037,319.96
April 1, 1865	103,576.35	Dec. 31, 1897	2,102,951.45
April 1, 1866	802,574.56	Dec. 31, 1898	2,122,757.35
April 1, 1867	317,206.18	Dec. 31, 1899	3,685,400.36
April 1, 1868	1,354,436.48	Dec. 31, 1900	3,255,989.75
April 1, 1869	2,395,683.03	Dec. 31, 1901	3,722,569.17
April 1, 1870	2,836,852.48	Dec. 31, 1902	5,082,647.86
April 1, 1871	2,359,835.89	Dec. 31, 1903	7,000,000.00
April 1, 1872	62,222.25	Dec. 31, 1904	8,350,000.00
April 1, 1873	....	Dec. 31, 1905	5,100,000.00
April 1, 1874	749,460.27	Dec. 31, 1906	4,380,000.00
April 1, 1875	723,254.42	Dec. 31, 1907	4,800,000.00
		Dec. 31, 1908	4,600,000.00
Nine months ending:		Dec. 31, 1909	6,100,000.00
Dec. 31, 1875	60,585.72	Dec. 31, 1910	6,100,000.00
		Dec. 31, 1911–14	No data
Ending:		Dec. 31, 1915	8,479,293.00
Dec. 31, 1876	1,516,081.07	Dec. 31, 1916	12,983,137.00
Dec. 31, 1877	124,498.48	Dec. 31, 1917	11,123,955.00
Dec. 31, 1878	284,900.45	Dec. 31, 1918	20,164,794.00
Dec. 31, 1879	588,963.44	Dec. 31, 1919	6,521,691.00
Dec. 31, 1880	980,895.50	Dec. 31, 1920	7,417,431.00
Dec. 31, 1881	1,227,169.71	Dec. 31, 1921	8,183,549.00
Dec. 31, 1882	1,395,372.98	Dec. 31, 1922	19,305,363.00
Dec. 31, 1883	2,232,757.04	Dec. 31, 1923	16,151,344.00
Dec. 31, 1884	2,857,905.28	Dec. 31, 1924	34,472,824.00
Dec. 31, 1885	2,889,544.80	Dec. 31, 1925	20,940,415.00
Dec. 31, 1886	3,307,567.99	Dec. 31, 1926	31,065,812.00
Dec. 31, 1887	3,160,474.67	Dec. 31, 1927	56,980,268.00
Dec. 31, 1888	3,655,956.78	Dec. 31, 1928	39,989,835.00
Dec. 31, 1889	4,220,869.93	Dec. 31, 1929	27,672,576.00
Dec. 31, 1890	6,987,155.48	Dec. 31, 1930	26,768,512.00
Dec. 31, 1891	8,790,443.29	Dec. 31, 1931	12,829,030.00
Dec. 31, 1892	14,505,701.79	Dec. 31, 1932	2,038,209.00
Dec. 31, 1893	6,001,445.65		

* *Report of the Board of Local Improvements* (1901–2), p. 141, and unpublished records of Board of Local Improvements.

TABLE CIII

ELECTRICITY GENERATED AND SOLD IN CHICAGO BY THE COMMONWEALTH EDISON COMPANY, 1893–1931

Year	K.W.H. Generated and Purchased for Use of Customers in Chicago	Kilowatt-Hours Sold
1893	10,320,000	....
1895	13,720,000	....
1900	39,080,000	....
1905	131,200,000	....
1910	614,610,000	544,315,000
1915	1,189,369,000	1,065,215,000
1920	1,831,628,000	1,610,741,000
1925	2,943,148,000	2,619,844,000
1928	3,851,106,000	3,464,692,000
1929	4,276,181,000	3,821,694,000
1930	4,191,296,000*	3,717,360,000*
1931	4,023,855,000	3,526,955,150

* The sales of kilowatt-hours are always less than the amount generated and purchased. The Company uses some electricity itself and there are considerable losses in transmission, distribution, through meters, and in other ways.

BIBLIOGRAPHY

BIBLIOGRAPHY

The principal sources for the material in this book have been the ante-fire abstracts in the files of the Chicago Title and Trust Company, the records of the county assessor's office, the files of the *Chicago Tribune* from 1868 to 1933, the files of the *Economist* from 1888 to 1933, George C. Olcott's *Land Values Blue Books* from 1910 to 1933, the files of the *Real Estate and Building Journal* from 1872 to 1900, Chicago city directories (particularly for 1844, 1856, and 1872), the subdivision plats of the Chicago Title and Trust Company, Sanborn's *Insurance Atlas of Chicago*, unpublished studies of the Chicago Regional Planning Association and the Chicago Plan Commission, and letters and personal interviews with old residents of Chicago and real estate brokers and appraisers. Consequently, much of the source material is available only in Chicago. The books that have been most useful have been the *History of Chicago*, by Captain A. T. Andreas, and *Chicago and Its Suburbs*, by Everett Chamberlin.

BOOKS

ANDREAS, ALFRED THEODORE. *History of Chicago*. 3 vols. Chicago: A. T. Andreas, 1884–86.

———. *History of Cook County, Illinois*. Chicago: A. T. Andreas, 1884.

BROSS, WILLIAM. *History of Chicago*. Chicago: Jansen, McClurg & Co. 1876.

BURGESS, ERNEST W., and NEWCOMB, CHARLES. *Census Data of the City of Chicago, 1920, 1930*. Chicago: University of Chicago Press, 1931, 1933.

CHAMBERLIN, EVERETT. *Chicago and Its Suburbs*. Chicago: T. A. Hungerford & Co., 1874.

Chicago and Its Makers. Chicago: Felix Mendelsohn, 1929.

Chicago Traction and Subway Commission Report. Chicago, 1916.

COLBERT, ELIAS, and CHAMBERLIN, EVERETT. *Chicago and the Great Conflagration*. Chicago: J. S. Goodman & Co., 1871.

COOK, FREDERICK FRANCIS. *Bygone Days in Chicago*. Chicago: A. C. McClurg & Co., 1910.

Edwards' Merchants' Chicago Census Report. Chicago, 1871.

GAGER. *Chicago City Directory, 1856–57*. Chicago, 1857.

GALE, EDWIN OSCAR. *Reminiscences of Early Chicago and Vicinity*. Chicago and London, etc.: F. H. Revell Co., 1902.

GANIWARIS (FRANK CHANDLER). *Chicago*. Chicago: Faithorn Co., 1924.

GOODSPEED, WESTON A., and HEALY, DANIEL D. *History of Cook County, Illinois*. 2 vols. Chicago, 1909.

JETER, HELEN RANKIN. *Trends of Population in the Region of Chicago*. Chicago: University of Chicago Press, 1927.

LEWIS, LLOYD, and SMITH, HENRY JUSTIN. *Chicago, a History of Its Reputation*. New York: Harcourt, Brace & Co., 1929.

MCILVAINE, MABEL. *Reminiscences of Chicago during the Forties and Fifties.* Chicago: R. R. Donnelley & Sons Co., 1913.
———. *Reminiscences of Early Chicago.* Chicago: R. R. Donnelley & Sons Co., 1912.
MOSES, JOHN and KIRKLAND. *History of Chicago, Illinois.* Chicago and New York: Munsell & Co., 1895.
NORRIS, J. W. *General Directory and Business Advertiser for the City of Chicago for the Year 1844.* Chicago: Ellis & Fergus, 1844.
OLCOTT, GEORGE C. *Land Values Blue Book of Chicago.* Annual vols., 1910–33.
PIERCE, BESSIE LOUISE. *As Others See Chicago.* Chicago: University of Chicago Press, 1933.
PUTNEY, MARK HERBERT. *Real Estate Values and Historical Notes of Chicago.* Chicago, 1900.
QUAIFE, MILO MILTON. *Chicago's Highways, Old and New.* Chicago: D. F. Keller & Co., 1923.
SHEAHAN, JAMES W., and UPTON, GEORGE P. *History of the Great Conflagration.* Chicago: Union Publishing Co., 1871.
SIMPSON, HERBERT D. *Tax Racket and Tax Reform in Chicago.* Evanston: Northwestern University, 1930.
SIMPSON, HERBERT D., and BURTON, JOHN E. *The Valuation of Vacant Land in Suburban Areas: Chicago Area.* Evanston: Institute for Economic Research, Northwestern University, 1931.
SULLIVAN, GERALD E. (ed.). *Story of Englewood, The.* Chicago, 1924.
WIRTH, LOUIS. *The Ghetto.* Chicago: University of Chicago Press, 1928.
WRIGHT, JOHN STEPHEN. *Chicago, Past, Present, Future.* Chicago: Horton & Leonard, 1870.
ZORBAUGH, HARVEY WARREN. *The Gold Coast and the Slum.* Chicago: University of Chicago Press, 1929.

BOOKS ON LAND VALUES AND URBAN USES IN GENERAL OR IN OTHER CITIES

BABCOCK, FREDERICK MORRISON. *The Valuation of Real Estate.* New York and London: McGraw-Hill Book Co., 1932.
BARTHOLOMEW, HARLAND. *Urban Land Uses.* "Harvard City Planning Studies," Vol. IV. Cambridge: Harvard University Press, 1932.
HURD, RICHARD M. *Principles of City Land Values.* New York: Record and Guide, 1924.
MCKENZIE, RODERICK D. *The Metropolitan Community.* New York and London: McGraw-Hill Book Co., 1933.
PARK, ROBERT E., BURGESS, ERNEST W., MCKENZIE, RODERICK D. *The City.* Chicago: University of Chicago Press, 1925.
SAKOLSKI, A. M. *The Great American Land Bubble.* New York, 1932.
SHAW, CLIFFORD R. *Delinquency Areas.* Chicago: University of Chicago Press, 1929.
SPENGLER, EDWIN H. *Land Values in New York in Relation to Transit Facilities.* New York: Columbia University Press, 1930.

TAN, PEI-LIN. "The Belt and Switching Railroads of Chicago's Terminal Area, 1931." Typewritten thesis (Ph.D.), University of Chicago.
THOMAS, ROLLIN GEORGE. "The Development of State Banks in Chicago, 1930." Typewritten thesis (Ph.D.), University of Chicago.

PLATS, MAPS, ABSTRACTS

ASSESSOR OF COOK COUNTY. *Assessor's Manual* (1930).
———. *Ibid.* (1931).
———. *Land-value maps* (1928, 1931).
———. Property-record cards.
CHICAGO TITLE AND TRUST CO. Abstracts.
———. Numbered documents.
———. Plats of subdivisions.
———. *Shorthall and Hoard's Abstracts.*
CHICAGO PLAN COMMISSION. Maps of blighted areas.
CHICAGO REGIONAL PLANNING ASSOCIATION. Regional maps.
ROBINSON. *Insurance Atlas* (1886).
SANBORN. *Insurance maps* (1933).
U.S. Quadrangular Survey Map of Chicago (1899, 1926-27).

NEWSPAPERS AND PERIODICALS

Chicago Daily News Almanac and Year Book (1933).
Chicago Tribune (file daily, 1868-1933).
Economist (Chicago; file weekly, October, 1888-1933).
Real Estate and Building Journal (Chicago).

UNPUBLISHED MATERIAL

CHICAGO HISTORICAL SOCIETY. Maps, photographs.
———. William B. Ogden letters.
JOHNSON, EARL. "Ecological Studies of Chicago."
LEGLER LIBRARY. Photographs; accounts of settlers at Madison and Crawford.
PALMER, VIVIAN. "Chicago Community Studies" (typewritten notes).

INDEX

INDEX

Abstracts, orders of Chicago Title and Trust Co., 435
Accretions of land, along the lake front, 296–97
Accuracy of land values, vii, 468
Acre tracts: speculation in, *1889*, 163–64; rise in value of, *1879–92*, 193; low prices of, *1905*, 218; comparative values of, *1890–1910*, 228; speculation in, *1925*, 255–56
Acres, subdivided in Chicago, *1830–1932*, 479–80
Adams Street, land values on, Michigan to Market streets, *1830–1931*, 340–42
Advertised prices, as a basis of estimating values, 461
Advertisements, newspaper: as a means of bringing buyers and sellers together, 442; means of giving price information, 446
Aftermath: of panic of *1837*, 42; of World's Fair, 210
Age, of buildings in Loop, 335.
Agricultural land in the United States: value of, *1900–1926*, 233–34; causes for decline in value of, *1920–26*, 234–35
Air, extension into, 296
Air rights, 241; effect of, on supply of land, 297
Air space: tables showing the same, 331; chart of, occupied by buildings in central business district, 332
Airplane: effect of, on real estate, 199; effect of, on supply of land, 296
Aldis, Graham, x
Alleys: pavement of, 199; lack of pavements on Northwest Side, 203
Alternations of speculative activities, 420–21
Andreas, A. T., x
Annexations to Chicago: map showing, 154; of Hyde Park, Lake, Lakeview, and Jefferson, 155
Apartment areas, land values in, *1910–28*, 246
Apartments: the first, 127; rapid growth in, *1881–83*, 133; "the flat craze," 133; along the South Side elevated, *1898*, 208; rush to build, *1897–1903*, 215; number built, *1910–15*, 231; in Chicago and other cities, 292; table of, 307

Appearance of Chicago: in *1832*, 17; in *1833*, 18; in *1834*, 19; in *1835–36*, 19–20; at close of *1836*, 21; in *1837*, 21; in *1842*, 23; in *1844*, 49; in *1846*, 50; in *1848*, 51; in *1849*, 61; in *1853*, 62; in *1854*, 62–3; in *1867*, 87–8; in the eighties, 4; in *1900*, 200–205; in *1933*, 4
Appleyard, Roger E., ix
Appraisals of real estate, value of, 462–63
Ashland Avenue: fashionable West Side residential avenue by *1871*, 94; decline of, 230; growth along, 302; value of, *1870–1933*, 305
Assessed land values, *1871*, 116
Assessments, special, annual cost of, *1862–1932*, 492
Assessments of land for taxation: defects of those before *1928*, vii, 461–62; real estate by years, *1837–1932*, 487
Astor Street, values of, in *1915*, 229
Atlantic and Pacific Tea Co., establishes chain stores, *1910*, 226
Attrition, process of: *1873–76*, 122; in real estate cycle, 400
Auction sales of real estate, 31–32, 108, 446, 464
Auditorium Building, finished, *1889*, 151
Austin: land values, *1830–1933*, 306; high-grade residential land, 310
Automobiles in Chicago: effect of, 199; growth of number of, *1908–20*, 205; first shop leased, *1902*, 212; sales-center growth of, *1909*, 223; showrooms for, on Michigan Avenue, 225; increase of, *1920–30*, 237; registration of, by years, *1910–33*, 485
Avalon highlands, growth of: in *1911–15*, 227–28; in *1921–26*, 245
Avenues, the, on the fashionable South Side, 93
Ayres, Lennard P., chart on general business activity, *1830–1933*, 411

Bailey, E. L., ix
Baltimore and Ohio Railroad shops, 134
Baltzer, Benjamin, ix
Band concerts, used in selling subdivision lots, 167
Bank clearings, Chicago: in *1878–81*, 128–29; in *1898–1915*, 205; in *1908–18*, 222;

503

in *1921–26*, 237; cycle of, 413; by years, *1865–1932*, 489
Bank moratorium, in March, *1933*, 272, 275
Bank notes, state: and land speculation, *1835*, 27–28; specie circular, 38; secured by bonds of southern states, 60; chaotic condition of, *1863*, 76
Bankruptcy, of lessees, 184
Banks: State Bank of Illinois chartered, *1835*, 27; failure of, *1842*, 41; real estate holdings of, 41; banking law of *1851*, 59; collapse of state banks of issue, *1861–63*, 76; National Banking Act, *1863*, 77; new national banks, 82; savings-bank failures, *1877*, 123; outlying or neighborhood, growth of, to *1915*, 226; growth of, after World War, 249; *débâcle* of, *1931–33*, 268; map showing decline of, *1929–33*, 271; easy credit of, 383; financing real estate developments, 385; reverse liberal lending policy, 401; summary of policies of, in regard to real estate, 445
Bargains, in real estate, *1878–79*, 125, 133
Baring Brothers: report of committee on canal, 45; failure of, *1890*, 173
Bartlett, Frederick H., sales of, *1910*, 229
Basements, area of, in Loop, 296
Bechtel, Clifford R., x, 294
Belt-line railroads, *1886–87*, 143
Beverly Hills, 310
"Bird dogs," 390
Blighted area: in *1900*, 201–2; reclamation of, 317, 350, 355–56, 361–63
Block and lot sizes, 427–29
Blue Island Avenue, *1868–73*, 108
Board of Trade: formation of, *1848*, 60; moves from LaSalle and South Water streets to Washington and LaSalle streets, *1865*, 89; moves to Jackson and LaSalle streets, *1881*, 135
Board of Trade Quarter: boom in *1881–83*, 135; total rise in values in, *1881–85*, 136
Boarding-houses, on the near North Side, 310
Bond, William A., x; valuation of sixty-seven parcels, *1898–99*, 217
Bond, William Scott, x; data on interest rates, 386
Bond-secured bank notes, 60
Bonney, W. L., statement of, as to land values, *1909*, 219
Boom: in land values, *1835–36*, 28–33; in Board of Trade Quarter, 135–36; in *1889*, 161; culmination of, *1890*, 170;

in the real estate cycle, 387; subdivision, 391. *See also* Speculation, land
Bottom, of land values: in *1841–42*, 40–41; in *1877–79*, 125–26; in *1933*, 272
Bridgeport, 97
Bridges: in *1857*, 64; in *1865–71*, 87; map of, in *1873*, 92; delay caused by, *1867*, 93, 300
Bringing buyers and sellers together, 442
Britigan, William, sales methods, *1917*, 229
Building: codes, differences in, 439–40; necessity of, to produce land income, 449
Building, new: in *1844–45*, 50; in *1842–57*, 63; decline of, in *1857–58*, 74; in *1858–59*, 75; in *1859–60*, 75; in *1862–64*, 82; in *1873–74*, 119; in *1889–92*, 177; in *1908–18*, 222; decline of, in *1928–33*, 266; by years, *1854–1932* (chart), 382; seventy-nine years of, 384; index numbers of, *1918–27*, 384; in *1885–93*, 385; cycle of, *1854–1932*, 411; by years, *1832–1933* (table), 474–75
Building space: increase in volume of, 286–87; factors determining, 287–88
Buildings: increase in number of, *1830–1928*, 285–86; principal types of, in Cook County, 291; age, number, and cubic content of, in central business district, 335; number of different types of, erected annually, *1912–33*, 476. *See also* Height of buildings
Bungalow areas: growth of, after World War, 245; utilization of ground in, 294; land values in, *1910–28*, 246; new, 317
Burgess, E. W., x
Burnt area: map showing area burnt by fire of *1871*, 105
Burton, John E., x
Business centers, outlying: at Twenty-second Street and Michigan Avenue, *1868–71*, 98; values of, on car-line streets, *1865–71*, 98; in *1880–90*, 191; affected by downtown stores, 195; growth of, *1908–15*, 225–27; land values of principal corners, *1910–29*, 252; maps showing values of principal corners, *1910* and *1928*, 253–54; table of average value of 425 street intersections, *1910* and *1928*, 255; origin and development of, 320, 322; amount zoned for, 457
Business cycle, general: compared with Chicago real estate, 407; chart showing American, *1830–1933*, 411; fluctuations above and below normal, 412, 415; duration of, 417
Buyers of real estate: knowledge of values, 441; lambs, insiders, politicians

INDEX

as, 441; race or nationality, 442; residences or occupations of, 442

Cable lines: on South Side, *1882*, 137; on South Side, 144; rise in values along, 146; on North Side, *1888*, 147; on West Side, *1890*, 147

Calumet Canal and Dock Co., *1873*, 108

Calumet region, growth of, 213–14

Calumet River, growth of commerce on, *1889–1916*, 213–14

Canal, at Chicago (Illinois and Michigan Canal): Joliet discusses possibility of, 7; early importance of, 10; organization of a company to build, 11; purchasing and surveying the route of, 11; federal land grant for, 12; anticipated effect of, on Chicago, 12–13; loan to start, 27; Baring Brothers' committee reports on, 45; work stopped on, 41; new start on, 45; work on, resumed, 46; completion of, 53; effect of completion of, 53

Capitalization, of net income: as affected by racial groups, 314; fundamental basis of land values, 449; rate of, 458; as a method of determining land values, 460

Car-repair shops (railroad), *1856*, 65

Carpenter, Philo, losses in panic of *1837*, 42

Carriages, fashionable, parade of, on boulevards, 133

Carville, *1857*, 66

Cash sales, in depression, 444

Cass Street, in forties and fifties, 302

Cause and effect, in history of Chicago, 5

Center of population of the United States, 198

Central business district: land values, *1877–98*, 185; expands vertically and laterally, 241; maps showing sales and leases in, *1830*, *1836*, *1856*, *1873*, *1896*, *1913*, *1928*, *1931*, 338–39; maps of land values in, *1830*, *1836*, *1856*, *1873*, *1894*, *1910*, *1928*, *1931*, 340–42; tables of land values in, 345–46

Central manufacturing district: in *1904–6*, 213, rise in values of, *1900–1915*, 230; growth in, after war, 246; values in, *1910–29*, 249

Chadwick, Stanley C., ix

Chain-store leases, cancellation of, *1932–33*, 275

Chamberlin, Everett, x, 464, 466

Chandler, Frank R.: files of, x; valuations of, *1879–91*, 174–75

Chatham Fields: sales in, *1914*, 229; growth of, *1921–26*, 245

Cheap residential areas: origin and growth of, 311–12; land values in, *1890–1932*, 313; land values in old settled areas, *1830–1933*, 318

Chicago, University of, effect of founding on adjacent land, 178.

Chicago American, the: first appearance of, *1833*, 19; sales from, 338, 466

Chicago and Alton Railroad, reaches Chicago, *1857*, 58

Chicago, Burlington and Quincy Railroad, origin of, 55

Chicago and Eastern Illinois Railroad, 134

Chicago and Northwestern Railroad, beginnings of system of, 58

Chicago Rapid Transit Co., passengers carried on, *1892–1932*, 491. See also Elevated lines

Chicago real estate cycle. See Real estate cycle, Chicago

Chicago Rock Island Railroad, beginnings of, 55

Chicago Title and Trust Co.: records and maps of, used, viii; growth of, number of guaranty policies, *1911–32*, 434; method used by, of removing objections to title, 435, table of guaranty and abstract orders of, 435

Chicago Tribune, the: real estate editors of, x, list of conveyances in, 466; opinions of, 466

Chicago and Western Indiana Railroad, 134

Chinese: on South Clark Street, 201; shift of, to Twenty-second Street and Wentworth Avenue, 443

Cicero, population of, *1900–1930*, 282

Cicero Avenue: Eighty-seventh Street to Seventy-ninth Street and, land values of, *1833–1933*, 306; land values on Fifty-fifth Street to One Hundred and Eleventh Street, 328

Civic Opera Building, 241

Clark and Lake: value of, *1842*, 42; financial center, *1848*, 60; beginning of shift from, 89; best business corner, 89

Clark and Madison corner, 89

Clark Street: bridge in *1840*, 23; land values on, Roosevelt to Lawrence avenues, *1873*, *1910*, *1928*, 326; land values in central business district, *1830–1931*, 340–42, 345

Clarke residence, *1836*, 21

Clearing manufacturing district: growth of, by *1915*, 230; growth of, after World War, 246; values of, *1910–29*, 248

Cleaverville, *1857*, 66

Coal, in Illinois, 83, 197
Colored race: area occupied by, before and after *1874*, 97; location of, in *1900*, 201; expansion of, by *1908*, 216; increase of, in numbers, 284; movement of, 313-14; map showing location of, 315; rents paid by, 316
Commercial Street: corner at Ninety-second Street, in *1891*, 192; value of, *1910-29*, 252; traffic counts and store rents on, Eighty-ninth to Ninety-second streets, *1932*, 327
Commodity-price speculation, 421
Commonwealth Edison Co., electricity generated by, 205-6, 493
Compound interest: growth of money at, compared with rise of Chicago land values, 351; map showing, 352; table showing, 354
Congested living quarters: in *1834-37*, 21-22; in *1854*, 62-63; in *1900*, 201
Consideration in deeds: index numbers of, *1885-93*, 385; accuracy of, 465; table of, *1868-92*, 472; for property more than seven miles from the courthouse, *1889-1901*, 473
Construction, new: costs of, *1919-21*, 236; number of buildings, *1832-1932*, frontage, *1873-1933*, value, *1854-1933*, 474-75. *See also* Building, new
Contract, written, necessity of, in real estate, 443
Conveyances, volume of real estate: from *1873* to *1932* (chart), 396; real estate transfer cycle, 412; instruments recorded, 470-71; transfers, *1901-33*, 472
Cook County, *1836*, 22
Corn Products Co., buys plant in Summit, *1906*, 213
Cornell, John E., x
Cornell, Paul: starts movement for south parks, 99; profits on land at Grand Crossing, *1873*, 108; statement of, 457
Corner-lot premiums: private residences as, 431; in loop, 432
Cornfields, new cities in, 388-89
Corporations to hold real estate, 439
Corrections of land values for changes in wholesale prices, wages, and interest, 344-45
Corruption, *1868-69*, 88
Cottage Grove Avenue, chart of land values, Fifty-fifth to Ninety-fifth streets, *1928*, 328
Cottages, 311

Counts, traffic: steamboat and stagecoach arrivals, *1845*, 48; wagon traffic, *1847*, 48; at bridges, *1854*, 63; at bridges, *1871*, 87; hourly on State Street, *1890*, 172; pedestrian, *1932*, 327
Cox, Garfield V., viii
Credit in land deals: summary of, 444-45; effect of, on prices, 468-69
Crisis. *See* Panic
Cross-sections of land values, 308-9
Cummings, E. A., real estate sales methods, 167
Cumulative growth of a city, 6
Cutmore, Harry: depth rules of, 431; on sales as evidence of value, 447
Cycle, Chicago real estate. *See* Real estate cycle, Chicago
Cycles, charts on: Chicago real estate, 406; real estate in other cities, 407; business activity in the United States, 411; Chicago land value, 411-14; Chicago manufacturing, 412; real estate transfers, 412; Chicago subdivision, 413; canal-rail and industrial stocks, 414; wholesale commodity prices in the United States, 414
Czechoslovakians, 313; map showing residences of, 315; effect of, on land values, 316

Daly, Alice, xi
Davis, Abel, viii
Davis-Orrington business section (in Evanston), *1929*, 258; competition of, with Chicago business centers, 275
Dearborn Street: bridge, *1839*, 23; skyscrapers on, 153; boom of, *1889*, 188; value of, near Goethe, *1865-1933*, 305; value of, in central business district, *1930-1931*, 340-42, 345
Debt, internal, increase of, in the United States, *1914-31*, 199
Decline, in land values: in *1839*, 39; in *1857-61*, 75-76; after *1873*, 119-22; after *1893*, 180-81; in *1931*, 266
Decorating, as item in operating expenses, 380
Deficiency judgments: *1877*, 123-24; in real estate cycle, 402
Delay in real estate deals, 444
Density of population, in Chicago, 293-94
Department stores, rise of, 158, 201
Depression: forces of, *1837*, 37-38; in *1858*, 74; after *1873*, 117-24; after *1893*, 179-81; after *1929*, 266, 268-72
Depth rules for lots, 343; Hoffman on, *1866*,

429; Walter Kuehnle and Harry Cutmore on, 431
Devon and Western avenues: value of, *1913*, 227; growth of area of, 245
Differences in lots, due to: actions of community or state, 438; foreclosure laws, 438; tax rates and exemptions, 438
Double-section corners. See Business corners, outlying
Doubling the radius, effect of, on area of land, 296
Douglas, Stephen A., 457
Douglas Park: bill authorizing, passed in *1869*, 99; rise in land values near, *1867–73*, 107; elevated line, 182
Downtown area, *1900–1907*, 212. See also Loop and Central business district
Drexel Boulevard: in *1879–93*, 190; in *1900–1908*, 215, 304
Dulness in real estate, 37, 119, 174, 265. See also Lull

East Chicago: Forsythe tract, 143; boom of *1903*, 214; population of, *1900–1930*, 282
Edgewater: telephones in, *1906–16*, 228; land values and population of, *1910–30*, 271
Electric light, invention of, 127
Electric surface lines: Cicero and Proviso line, *1890*, 147; conversion of horsecar to electric line, by *1897*, 182
Electricity generated by Commonwealth Edison Co.: in *1895–1920*, 205–6; in *1893–1931*, 493
Elevated lines: South Side, *1890–93*, 146; projected, *1889–90*, 149; progress of, on Lake Street, and the Metropolitan, *1893–95*, 181–82; survey of Northwestern, *1893*, 182; effect of, on central business district, *1895*, 182; in the Loop, 183; traffic, *1898–1918*, 205; consolidation of, *1911*, 225; traffic into Loop, 225; map of extensions to *1903–32*, 264; passengers carried annually by, *1892–1932*, 491
Elevators, in office buildings, 149–50
Employment: in gainful occupations in Chicago, *1910–30*, 200; decline in, Chicago manufacturing industries, *1927–33*, 269
Englewood: in embryo, *1857*, 66; begins to grow rapidly, 100; houses in, *1873*, 111; growth of, *1879–83*, 138; as fashionable area, 190; extension of elevated line to, *1907*, 216; high-grade residences in, 310
Equity in a lot, 390

Erie Canal, effect of, on growth of Chicago, 17
Errors in estimating demand for land, due to: dynamic changes, 456; business cycle, 458
Evanston, 203; population of, *1900–1930*, 282
Exchanges, of equities, 119–20, 176, 265, 398, 447. See Inflated equities
Excursion trains to real estate developments, 108, 171, 257, 390
Exclusive sales contract, 444

Failure of banks, 41, 76, 123, 268, 271, 445–46. See also Banks
Farm land: value of, in twenty-three American states, 3; value of, in the United States, *1900–1926*, 233–35
Fashionable residential areas: first fashionable homes, 21; on North Side in the forties, 43; on Wabash and Michigan near Congress, *1854*, 65; values of, *1856*, 67; development of, before *1873*, 90–91; paved streets and sewers in, *1873*, 92; on the South Side, 93; on the West Side, 94; advance in values of, by *1873*, 113; from *1877* to *1895*, 189; in different sections, *1900–1908*, 214–15; location of, in different periods, 302–4; charts of fluctuations of values of, 305–6
Field, Marshall, moves from Lake Street to State Street, 90
Field, Leiter & Co., sales of, *1872*, 84
Financial center: at Clark and Lake streets, 60; at LaSalle and Washington streets, after *1865*, 89; at Jackson and LaSalle streets, 135
Fire, the great, of October 9, 1871: buildings destroyed and property loss in, 101; description of, 101; ends residential use, 102; rebuilding after, 102; map of burnt area and fire limits, *1872*, 105; effect of, on suburban growth, 107
Fire limits, 105, 439–40
Flats, *1881–83*, 133. See Apartments
Florida boom, collapse of, *1926*, 258
Flossmoor, subdivision at, 257
"For Sale" signs: as a means of attracting buyers, 442; use of, in giving price information, 446
Forecasting: of population, 365–66, 388, 456; of land values, 367; of future incomes, 452
Foreclosure laws, differences in, 439
Foreclosures: in *1860*, 76 n.; increase of, *1874–77*, 120; in *1877*, 123; in *1879*, 131;

in *1893–98*, 181; in *1930–31*, 269; in *1931–32*, 270; chart of, *1926–32*, 270; in real estate cycle, 399
Fort, at Chicago, 9, 10
Fort Dearborn, 10: massacre at, *1812*, 10; Addition, 39
"Forty-niners," 61
Franklin Street, land values, from the river to Van Buren, *1830–1931*, 340–42, 345
Furniture center, at Sixteenth Street and Indiana Avenue, 212
Full assessed value, 461
Futures, dealing in grain, inaugurated, 84

Gainful occupations, persons employed in, in Chicago, *1910–30*, 200
Galena and Chicago Union Railroad, first railroad from Chicago, *1848*, 55
Garfield Park: land near, *1871*, 95; bill authorizing, passed in *1869*, 99; rise in land values near, *1867–73*, 107; elevated line, 181
Gary: founded, *1906*, 214; population, *1910–30*, 282
Gas lights: growth of, to *1856*, 64; introduced, *1850*, 64
General business conditions in the United States: in *1878–84*, 128; in *1919–33*, 232; Ayres chart of, 411
Germans: immigration of, *1848*, 62; at Wells Street and North Avenue, 97
Ghetto: in *1900*, 201; expands westward, 215
Gilded Age, era before *1873*, 88
Glaciers, create strategic position of Chicago, 7
Gold Coast: rises into prominence, 190; effect of Michigan Avenue bridge on, 242; as social capital, 304; rents on, 308; after *1900*, 333
Goode, John Paul, forecasts of population by, 388, 456
Graf, J. Frank, viii, 470
Grain elevators: in *1870*, 84; in South Chicago, *1907*, 214
Grain trade: in Chicago, *1850–56*, 58; in Calumet area, *1907*, 214
Grand Boulevard: in *1873–93*, 190; in *1900–1908*, 215, 304
Grand Crossing, 66
Gross and net rents, 452–53
Growth of Chicago: in *1830–37*, 15–23; in *1837–57*, 46–47; *1857–62*, 77–78; in *1863–65*, 81–88; in *1865–71*, 88–101;

in *1872–73*, 102–7; in *1873–77*, 127; in *1878–84*, 128, 133–38; in *1884–93*, 143–59; in *1894–98*, 181–84, 195; survey of, in *1830–1933*, 195–207; in *1898–1908*, 207–19; in *1909–18*, 222–31; in *1919–29*, 237–64; in *1929–33*, 265–76
Guaranty policies, of Chicago Title and Trust Co., 434, 435

Halbwachs, Maurice, cited, 279, 294, 314 n
Halsted Street: land values on, Fifty-fifth to One Hundred and Eleventh streets, *1928*, 328; anticipated shift from State Street to, 457; and Madison (*see* Madison and Halsted corners); and Sixty-third Street (*see* Sixty-third and Halsted streets)
Harmon, William E.: statement of, as to values, *1909*, 219; selling prices of real estate and real value of, 223
Healy manufacturing district: growth of, after the World War, 246; land values in, *1918–29*, 249
Heat, as factor in operating expenses, 380
Hegewisch: founded in *1883*, 135; in 1900, 203
Height of buildings: in central business district, *1871*, 104; height of first skyscrapers, 153; height of tallest buildings, 285; average height in Cook County, 289, 293; space at various height levels in Cook County, 293; average, in Loop, 294; air space at different height levels in Loop occupied by buildings, *1836*, *1873*, *1893*, *1923*, *1933*, 331–32; method of computation of, 333; forecast of, 457
Height limit, for buildings: 130 feet, *1893*, 153; by ordinance, in central business district raised from 130 to 260 feet, *1902*, 211; limited to 200 feet, *1911*, 224; towers permitted, *1923*, 241; zoning law of 1923, restrictions as to, 440
Higgling in real estate deals, 447
High-grade residential areas, map of, 303. *See also* Fashionable residential areas
Highest and best use: valuation on basis of, *1889*, 152–53; discussion of, 450
Hill, Alonzo H., 322, 441
Holstein, *1857*, 66
Home Insurance Building, first skyscraper, 134, 150
Homogeneity, lack of, in Chicago lots, 427
Hooker, John P., x
Horse railways: the first systems, *1859–66*, 77; map of, *1880*, 126; give way to electric power, 208

INDEX

Horseback, riders on, spread news of land sales, 443
Horse-drawn vehicles, registration of, *1910–32*, 483
Hotels: projects for, *1890*, 171; space occupied by, 336
Howard Avenue, business section of: Howard and Paulina corner, value of, *1910–29*, 252; competition of, with Davis-Orrington section, 275
"Hubbard's Folly," 19
Humboldt Park: bill authorizing, passed in *1869*, 99; rise in land values near, *1865–73*, 107
Hyde Park: first suburban railroad service, *1856*, 56; in embryo, *1857*, 66; growth of, by *1871*, 94; begins to grow rapidly, 100; rise in land values of, *1865–73*, 107; population of township of, *1870*, 111; annexation of, to Chicago, *1889*, 155; population growth of, *1880–90*, 195

Illinois, state of: formed to include Chicago area, 11; program of internal improvements in, *1837*, 37; state banks and state bonds of, 38; relief of land-buyers by legislature, 41; value of state bonds in, *1842*, 41; credit of, improves, 46
Illinois Bell Telephone Co., stations of, in Chicago, *1882–1932*, 490
Illinois Central Railroad: first plan for, 54; building of, down lake front, 56; land grant for, from Congress, 56; suburban service of, to Hyde Park, 56; assigns for benefit of creditors of, 74; air rights over tracks of, 241; electrification of, 256–57
Immigration, from Europe: Irish and German, after *1846–48*, 62; increase of, *1877–82*, 128; of Italians, Poles, Russian Jews, 201; increase of, in foreign-born population of Chicago, by decades, *1860–1930*, 284; of Russian, Polish, Italian, and Czechoslovakian, 312–13; map showing residences of, 315; effect of, on land values and rents paid by foreign-born, 316
Immoral resorts. *See* Vice area
Improvements, street or public: in *1848–57*, 63–64; extravagance in, before *1873*, 117; extravagance in, *1890–92*, 180; extravagance in, during real estate boom, 392–93; expenditures for, *1862–71*, *1877–92*, 394; in *1870–77*, *1892–97*, 395; in *1919–27*, 395; city taxes and special assessments for, *1865–1931* (chart), 397; table showing annual cost of special assessments for, *1862–1932*, 492.
Indiana Harbor, boom of, *1903*, 214. *See also* East Chicago
Indians, Pottawatomie, land sale to government, *1833*, 24
Industrial areas: in *1833*, 19; in *1847*, 49–50; in *1848–57*, 65; in *1863–71*, 95–96; in *1879–83*, 134–35; in *1886–94*, 142–44; in *1899–1908*, 213–14; value of different locations in, *1904–7*, 214; land values in, *1910–29*, 246; movement of, 226; in *1919–29*, 246–48; direction of growth in, 318, 320; map of location of, 319; land values in, *1931*, 321
Industrial land values, 214, 246, 321
Infant industries of Chicago, 59
Inflated equities: trading in, *1874–75*, 119–20; in *1891*, 176; in *1927–28*, 265; in real estate cycle, 398, 446
Insull, Samuel, 232
Instruments, recorded in Cook County, number of, *1872–1932*, 470–71
Insurance companies, eastern, loans of, in Chicago, 131
Interest, compound, and rise of Chicago land values, 351–52, 354
Interest rates, on Chicago Real Estate: decline of, *1873–78*, 127, 130; in *1881*, 139; in *1898–99*, 208; in *1910*, 224; chart showing annual, *1830–1933*, 349; relation of, to land-value cycle, 419
Internal improvements, in Illinois, *1837*, 37–38
Interpolating methods, in determining land values, 427, 467–68
Irish: immigration of, *1845–46*, 62; at Bridgeport, 97
Iron ore: Chicago's position as to, 83; development of Mesabi Range, 197
Irving Park: suburb of, *1869*, 100; in *1900*, 203; telephones in, 228
Italians: immigration of, 201, 313; map showing residences of, 315; rank of, as to effect on land values, 316
Ivanhoe, subdivision at, 257

Jackson Boulevard: in *1900*, 202; growth along, 302; land values on, in central business district, 340–42
Jackson Park: extension of elevated line to, 146; sale of acres south of, *1890*, 171; in *1905*, 218; area south of, builds up, 228, 307
Jacobs, J. L., ix

Jefferson Township, annexation of, 155
Jeter, Helen R., Chicago, population forecasts of, 388, 392 n.
Jews: location of, 313; map showing residences of, 315; rank as to effect on land values, 316
Johnson, Earl, x
Joliet, 7
Judicial sales: value of property sold at, *1892–99*, 181; in *1893–1928*, 486. See also Foreclosures

Kensington, 203
Kenwood: as fashionable residential area, *1871*, 94; as fashionable center, 190; growth of, *1900–1918*, 215; growth of, *1909*, 224, 304
Kenwood manufacturing district: established, 230; growth of, after *1919*, 246; land values in, *1919–29*, 249
Kerfoot, W. D., statement of, *1907*, 218
Kilgubbin, *1858*, 65
Kitchenette apartments, 231, 287
Kuehnle, Walter R., ix; depth rules of, 430

Labor, wages of unskilled: land values deflated by, 346, 349; chart of, *1831–1933*, 410
Labor riots, *1877*, 123
Laissez faire, Chicago an example of, 276
Lake, the (Michigan), effect of, on land values, 299–300
Lake Forest, 203
Lake front, growth of, in importance, 304
Lake Street: as business center, 49; as main retail street, *1856*, 65; decline in values of, *1856–73*, 113; land values on, in central business district, *1830–1931*, 340–42
Lake and Marion streets: business section in Oak Park develops at, *1930*, 258; competition of, with Chicago centers, 275
Lake Shore Drive: start of, *1882*, 134; rise of, in value, 189–90; center of fashion after *1900*, 214; rise of, 304; value of, *1874–1933*, 305
Lake Township: population of, *1870*, 111; annexation of, 155; population growth of, *1880–90*, 195
Lake vessels, entering Chicago: in *1831–33*, 19; in *1860–69*, 84
Lamp posts: in *1865–71*, 87; in swamps of Calumet region, 180

Land Office, United States Government, sales of, in Chicago, 38
Land values: in *1830*, 23–24; in *1832*, 24; in *1833*, 24–25; in *1834*, 26–27; in *1835*, 28–29; at summit of *1836*, 33; map, by square miles for *1836*, 34; map, sales of acre tracts, *1836*, 35; in *1839–42*, 39–42; map, sales of acre tracts, *1841–43*, 43; in *1844–48*, 52; in *1848–57*, 67, 69–70; map, per front foot, *1856*, 71; map, by square miles, *1857*, 72; map, sales by acre tracts, *1856–57*, 73; in *1862*, 78; map, sales of acre tracts, *1860–63*, 79; outlying, *1865–73*, 107; map, per front foot, *1873*, 112; in Chicago, compared with London, Boston, and New York, *1873*, 113; map, by square miles, *1873*, 114; map, sales of acre tracts, *1870–73*, 115; full assessed value, *1871*, 116; by mile zones from State and Madison streets, *1836–79*, 116; in *1878–83*, 138; by principal uses, *1879–91*, 175; summary of, *1877–98*, 184–85; map, per front foot, *1892*, 186; map, by square miles, *1892*, 187; map, sales of acre tracts, *1890–92*, 194; on State Street, *1906–7*, 211; industrial tracts, *1904–7*, 214; acre tracts, *1905–7*, 218; map, residential, per front foot, *1910*, 220; map, by square miles, *1910*, 221; Michigan Avenue near Congress Street, *1916*, 225; Michigan Avenue near Twenty-second Street, *1911*, 225; outlying business corners, *1912–16*, 226–27; acres tracts, *1890*, *1910*, 228; Lake Shore Drive and Prairie Avenue, *1915*, 229–30; central manufacturing district, *1900–1915*, 230; of all farms in the United States, *1900–1926*, 233–35; of all urban land, *1920–26*, 234; maps of, by blocks in central business district, *1830*, *1836*, *1856*, *1873*, *1894*, *1910*, *1928*, *1931*, 240–42; in the Loop, *1910–28*, 242; on the near North Side, *1920–26*, 242; Tables of, 245–46; in apartment areas, *1910–28*, 246; in bungalow areas, *1910–28*, 246; table of, in old settled areas, *1890*, *1910*, *1915*, *1929*, *1931*, 247–48; in industrial areas, *1910–29*, 249; on Seventy-ninth Street, *1910*, *1928*, *1931*, 250; on Lawrence Avenue, *1910*, *1928*, *1931*, 251; at forty-five principal outlying business corners, *1910–29*, 252; maps of, at principal outlying corners, *1910* and *1928*, 253–54; at 425 street intersections, *1910–29*, 255; in Niles Center, *1925*, 255; aggregate of, at the peak, *1928*, 258; map, residential areas per front foot, *1928*, 259; map, by square miles, *1928*, 260; by principal areas and types of uses, *1910* and *1928*, 261; map, increase in, *1918–28*, 263;

INDEX

map, residential area per front foot, *1931*, 267; at the bottom, *1932-33*, 272-74; reduction in, *1928-31*, by types and value classes, 274; contour map of, 297-98; chart, fashionable residential, *1865-1933*, 305; chart, in outlying high-grade areas developed after *1900*, 306; chart, residential, one block north of Division Street, *1920* and *1928*, 308; chart, residential South Side between Fifty-fifth and Fifty-sixth streets, *1910* and *1928*, 309; chart, fluctuations in cheap residential, *1890-1931*, 313; chart, in old areas settled before *1873*, *1830-1933*, 318; map, industrial, 321; chart, State Street, *1873*, *1910*, *1928*, 323; chart, Madison Street, *1873*, *1910*, *1928*, 324; chart, Michigan Avenue, *1873*, *1910*, *1928*, 325; chart, North Clark Street, *1873*, *1910*, *1928*, 326; chart, Cottage Grove, Halsted, and Cicero avenues, *1928*, 328; chart, Milwaukee Avenue, *1910* and *1928*, 329; chart, Sixty-third and Seventy-ninth streets, *1928*, 330; developed by tall buildings, 336; in central business district and entire city, 337; maps, individual lots in Original Town showing sales and leases, *1830*, *1836*, *1854-56*, *1870-73*, *1896*, *1909-13*, *1925-28*, *1931*, 338-39; by principal uses of, *1910-33*, 347; chart, trend of, population and manufactures, 348; chart, in current dollars and corrected for changes in wholesale prices, wages, and interest rates, 349; chart, rate of increase of, and growth of money at compound interest, 352; for zone of land along the lake, *1836*, *1856*, *1873*, *1892*, *1910*, *1928* (map), 361; chart of aggregate for entire city, inner city, outer city, and Loop, *1830-1933*, on semi-log. scale, 362; same on natural scale, 363; chart of, with population curve for four sections of city, *1900-1933*, 371; index numbers of, *1918-27*, 384; in *1885-93*, 385; chart, per capita, *1830-1933*, 410; chart of, and building cycle, *1830-1933*, 411; chart of, and real estate transfer cycle, 412; chart of, and subdivision cycle, 413; chart of, and commodity and industrial-stock cycle, 414; developed on fifty-foot lot by different types of buildings, *1928*, 455; Table of aggregate of, 470

LaSalle Street: on North Side, *1871*, 95; replacement of buildings on, 335; land values of, in central business district, *1830-1931*, 340-42, 345

Lawrence Avenue: sale of at the lake, *1847*, 52; runs through zone of maximum population increase, *1919-27*, 250; land values on, *1910*, *1928*, *1931*, 251

Lawrence and Kedzie corners: sales of, *1911-15*, 227; land values of, *1910-29*, 252

Lawrence and Kimball corners: in *1908*, 216-17; value of, *1909-18*, 227; growth of, *1921-26*, 245; value of, *1910-29*, 252; example of buying with "inside" knowledge, 441

Layout of subdivision, 427-31

Leader, movement of, 457-58

Leadville mining stocks, 130

Leases: speculation in, *1897*, 184; long term, *1908-18*, 222; and office-building activity, 224; bond issues on, 267, 386-87; cancellation of chain store, 275; value of long-term, *1890-1926*, 486

Leland, Simeon E., viii

Lesch, Lyndon, x

Liberty bonds, 237, 445

Limitations on land-value data, viii, 376-77, 468-69

Lincoln Park: northward extension of, *1869*, 99; fire burns to, 101; land values north of, *1868-72*, 108

Listed prices, as a means of estimating values, 462-63

Listings with brokers, 443

Loans, real estate: in *1874*, 119; in *1874-76*, 120; interest rates on, *1830-1933* (chart), 349; amount of, *1918-32*, 386; of 100 per cent, 445; amount of, *1896-1932*, 473

London, land values of, compared with Chicago land values, *1873*, 113

Loop: of elevated lines; opened, *1897*, 183; in *1900*, 208

Loop, the, the central business district of Chicago: origin of the term, 208; retail district of, *1900-1906*, 211; vertical expansion of, 332-33; corner-lot premiums of, 432. *See* Central business district

Lot and block dimensions, in Chicago, 427-31

Lots subdivided: in *1835-36*, 31; maps of subdivisions, *1830-43*, 32; in *1844-62*, 68; in *1856*, 70; in *1868-73*, 110; in *1863-79*, 110, in *1885-87*, 159-60, in *1887-88*, 161; in *1889*, 171; in *1891*, 177; in *1891-98*, 180; in *1908-18*, 222; in *1918-26*, 237; in *1880-1932*, 256; in *1926-33*, 399; table of, *1874-1930*, 477-78

Ludlow, E. H., statement of, on real estate cycle in *1881*, 132

Lull, the: in *1836*, 37; in *1858*, 75; in *1873*, 119; in *1891*, 174; in *1927-28*, 265; in business cycle, 398

ONE HUNDRED YEARS OF LAND VALUES

Lumber trade: beginning of, 48; in *1843–56*, 58; decline of, *1857–58*, 74; in *1868*, 84; waning of, 198

Lumber yards, location of: in *1848*, 50; in *1871*, 95

McCormick Reaper Works: on north bank of river, 65, 95; after *1871*, 103–4

McKenzie, R. D., x

Madison Street: "way out in the country," *1837*, 21; horse-car lines on 77–78; traffic on, 89; values near Halsted Street, *1873*, 98; cable line on, *1890*, 192; land values on, *1873*, *1910*, *1928*, 324; land values of, in central business district, *1830–1931*, 340–42

Madison and Crawford corners: value of, *1913*, 227; land value of, *1910–29*, 252; in *1927–28*, 258; competition of, with Lake-Marion district, 275

Madison and Dearborn corner, sale of, *1889*, 162

Madison and Halsted corners, value of, *1873*, 98

Mail-order houses, 199; move to new locations, 213

Manufactures: value of, in Chicago, in *1850* and *1856*, 59; chart, *1870–1929*, 84; in *1877–83*, 129; in *1884–93*, 144; in *1896* and *1915*, 205; in *1908–18*, 222; cycle of, 412; table, *1850–1931*, 481–82

Manufacturing districts, map showing location of, 318. *See also* Industrial districts

Manufacturing industries, Chicago, employment in: in *1850* and *1856*, 59; in *1873*, 86; in *1879–83*, 129; in *1884–93*, 144; in *1910*, *1920*, *1930*, 200; index numbers of, *1927–33*, 269; pay-rolls among October, *1929*—September, *1933*, monthly, 268

Manufacturing industries, Chicago, growth of: in *1833*, 19; in *1850–56*, 59; in *1867*, 84; in *1856–73*, 85–86; in *1884–93*, 143–44; in *1890–1930*, 198–200; long-run trend in, 317, 319–20

Manufacturing towns, near Chicago, 176

Market Street, land values on, from the river to Van Buren, *1830–1931*, 340–42, 345

Market value and normal value: William E. Harmon on, 223; 367

Masonic Temple (Capital Building), 153

Maxwell Street, near Halsted, description of a slum in, *1873*, 97

Merchandise Mart, 241

Mexicans, 314, 357

Michigan Avenue or Boulevard: fashionable homes near Congress Street, *1854*, 65; value of, in *1856*, 70; wholesale trade, on, 90; fashionable homes on, 93; decline of, south of Twenty-second Street as fashionable center, *1908*, 215; booms near Congress Street by *1916*, 225; rises as automobile center, *1911*, 225; bridge in *1920*, 242; land value at Eighteenth Street, *1865–1933*, 305; auto showrooms on, 310; land values on, *1873*, *1910*, *1928*, 325; store rents and traffic counts on, One Hundred and Tenth to One Hundred and Fourteenth streets (chart), 327; land values in central business district, 340–42; 345

Michigan Central Railroad: enters Chicago from East, *1852*, 56; assignment for creditors of, *1857*, 74

Michigan City, subdivision near, 257

Michigan and One Hundred and Eleventh Street, land values, *1910–29*, 252

Michigan Southern Railroad: enters Chicago from the East, *1852*, 56; assignment for creditors of, *1857*, 74; fall in price of stock of, *1856–57*, 74

Millis, H. A., viii

Milwaukee Avenue: plank road on, *1848*, 54; main axis of Northwest Side, *1871*, 98; cable line on, 192; poles expand along, *1900*, 202; triple intersections on, 227; value of corners on, *1910–29*, 252; in *1900–1933*, 313; land values on, *1910*, *1928*, 329

Minor movements of real estate factors, 403–4

Monroe Street, land values on, in central business district, *1830–1931*, 340–42, 345

Montgomery Ward & Co., 199; move in *1906*, 213

Mortgages. *See* Trust deeds, loans, real estate

Motor trucks: effect of, on location of factories, 320; registration of, *1910–32*, 485

Murphy, Carroll Dean, ix

Murray, Janet, xi

Near North Side, and Michigan Avenue bridge, 242

Negro districts: first location, before *1874*, 97; expansion of, *1900–1908*, 215–16; expansion of, 313–14; map showing location of, *1933*, 315

Net income: of apartment building, *1905–32*, 239; of office building, *1905–32*, 240

New Eden, 390

INDEX

New era, after World War, 232
New immigration. *See* Immigration
New residential areas, *1908*, 216–17. *See* Residential areas
New York City: Chicago land sales in, *1835–36*, 27; time in transit to Chicago, *1836*, *1849*, *1852*, 61–62; land values of, compared with Chicago, 113; decline in land values of, in central park district, *1873–77*, 127; land boom, 207; growth of, aided by Chicago, 280–81; population of, compared with Chicago, 281–82; land values in, 407 n.
Newcomb, Charles, x
Niles Center: speculation at, *1925*, 255; land zoned for business, 457
Ninety-nine-year leases: in *1892*, 178; history of, 387 n. *See also* Leases, long-term
North Avenue and Austin, growth of adjacent area of, *1921–26*, 245
North and California avenues: in *1895*, 192; value of land at, *1910–1929*, 252
North Side: growth in, *1835*, 20; in *1837–40*, 22–23; horse-car lines, 78; bridge difficulties on, 91; fire destroys, 101; setback caused by fire on, 103; growth of, in twentieth century, 210; summary as to, 301; residential land values of, 308
Northwest Side: in *1900*, 203; growth of, in twentieth century, 210
Northwestern University, tax exempt by special charter, 439
Norwood Park, 203

Oak Park, 203
Office buildings: in *1885–94*, 150–53; rents reduced, *1893–97*, 184; rise in rents of, *1902–3*, 210–11; new, *1908–15*, 224; income and operating expenses of, *1905–32*, 240; number of, *1928*, 291; cubic feet of space in Loop, *1933*, 336; index numbers of rents, *1915–31*, 377; operating expenses, net income of, *1918–32*, 379; growth of services provided for, 450
Ogden, William B., letters of, 23, 37, 38, 39, 40, 42
Olcott, George C.: accuracy of values of, ix, 447, 464; valuations of sixty-seven parcels by, *1910*, 217
Old residential areas, in *1897–1908*, 215–16
Old Settled areas, land values in, *1830–1933*, 318
Omnibus lines, in *1856*, 64
Operating expenses: in *1875*, 119; of apartments, *1920–29*, 239; chart of, of an office building, *1905–32*, 240; table of, of an office building, *1918–32*, 379; of apartments at different rents, 380; vary with amount of services provided, 450
Option, 444
Original Town of Chicago: sale of first lots in, *1830*, 12; map of, 25; sales and leases in part of, *1830–1931*, 338–39
Outlying business corners. *See* Business corners, outlying
Ownership units, differences in, 436–37

Packing industry, meat: Dole's, *1832*, 19; at Bull's Head and at Twenty-ninth Street and Cottage Grove Avenue, *1856*, 65; Chicago the leading pork-packing center by *1862*, 81; chart of hogs packed, *1851–70*, 85; concentrated at Thirty-ninth and Halsted streets, *1865*, 85–86; refrigerator cars, 127
Palmer, Potter, buys on State Street, 89–90
Panic: of *1837*, 37–38; of *1857*, 74; of *1873*, 117, 119; of *1893*, 178
Paris, France: boulevard system of, 99; compared with Chicago, 276, 279
Park, Robert D., x
Parks: establishment of south and west park systems, *1865–71*, 99–100; land speculation near, *1873*, 117; effect of, on development of fashionable areas, 302. *See also* Jackson, Garfield, Humboldt, Douglas, and Lincoln parks
Passengers: carried by steamboat and stagecoach to Chicago, *1845*, 48; carried by railroads into Chicago, *1853–57*, 62; chart of, on surface and elevated lines, *1895–1932*, 206; going into Loop, *1911*, 225; table giving annual figures on elevated lines by divisions, *1892–1932*, 491
Paved streets: lack of, *1844*, 49; in *1848*, 51; plank roads, 53–54, 64; macadam, cobblestones, and wooden blocks, *1856–57*, 64; wooden-block, *1865–71*, 87; effect of, on fashionable residential development before *1873*, 91; map of, *1873*, 92; lack of, on Northwest Side, *1900*, 203; aggregate cost of, 348
Pavements, new, miles of, constructed annually, *1855–92* (chart), 350
Pay-rolls, in Chicago manufacturing industries, October, *1929*—September, *1933*, 268
Peaks, in land values: in *1836*, 29–32; in *1857*, 70; in *1873*, 111; in *1890*, 173, 185; in *1926–28*, 258–59
Pedestrian traffic counts and store rents, 327

Personal service, gain in number of persons in, *1910–30*, 200
Pettibone, Holman D., ix
Pittsburgh, Fort Wayne, and Chicago Railroad, *1859*, 58
Plain, the (Chicago), effect of, on land values, 300–301
Plank roads, 53–54; in business center, 64
Poles: immigration of, 201; on Milwaukee Avenue, 202; movement of, 313; map showing residences of, 314; rank as to effect on land values, 316
Policies, guaranty of Chicago Title and Trust Co., 434–35
Population: in *1833–36*, 19; distribution of, *1837*, 21; in *1844–46*, 50; by wards, *1837–45*, 51; growth of, *1847–48*, 61; in *1845–55*, 62; North and South sides, *1853–56*, 66; West Side, *1848–57*, 66; suburban, 66–67; in *1877–83*, 129; growth of Hyde Park, Lake, and Lakeview, *1880–90*, 195; growth of, in Illinois, *1830–50*, 196; of North Central states, *1830–90*, 196–98; center of, in the United States, 198; congestion of, on Halsted, Ashland, Roosevelt, and Twenty-second streets, *1900*, 201; growth of, *1900–1920*, 205; in *1918–26*, 237; increase of, in outer belt, *1917–27*, 238; growth of, in Chicago, compared with other American cities, 279–92; sources of, in Chicago, 282, 284; causes of growth of, in Chicago, 283–84; density of, in Chicago, 293–94; growth of, by two-mile zones, *1830–1930* (chart), 356; areas of increasing and declining, *1920–30* (map), 357; chart of, per square mile, Ashland to Halsted streets, Fullerton Avenue to Pershing Road, *1850–80*, 358; chart of, per square mile in sections from Ashland to Halsted streets, Touhy to One Hundred and Twenty-seventh streets, *1890, 1910, 1930*, 359; density of, per square mile along the lake, *1840–1930*, 360; estimates of future of, in the United States, 365–66; tide of, 368; predictions of, 369; chart of, increase above average growth, 370; and residential land values (four charts), 371; effect of growth of, on real estate cycle, 372–73; spurt in growth of, 373–74; qualifications as to influence of, on real estate cycle, 375–76; rate of increase of, compared with rents, *1915–33*, 378; optimistic forecasts of, during boom, 388; of Chicago, *1830–1932* (table), 483; distribution of, by mile zones, *1860–1916*, 484
Portage at Chicago, 7; LaSalle discusses, 9

Prairie Avenue: rise of values on, *1856*, 70; as fashionable center, 93; in its heyday, 134; at the peak, *1889*, 189; in decline, *1900–1908*, 214; decline of, 304; chart of land values on, *1865–1933*, 305
Produce trade in Chicago, table showing value of, annually, *1875–1899*, 481
Production, index of, in the United States, *1908–18*, 222
Profit margins of landlords, 233
Profits in building, *1919–26*, 239–40
Propaganda: of subdividers, 166; differences in effectiveness of, 437
Prorating, 447
Prospects, 390
Price information as to land values, 446
Prices of land. *See* Land values
Psychology, crowd, 422
Public improvements. *See* Improvements, public or street
Public participation in real estate market: in *1868–71*, 100–101; in *1889–90*, 164, 167–68; in *1925–26*, 257; in real estate cycle, 389–90
Pullen, Paul P., x
Pullman: the site acquired, *1880*, 135; growth of, *1900–1906*, 213; causes of shift in business center in, 443
Putney, Mark L., x, 466

Qualifications as to influence of population on land values, 375–76

Railroads: map of, entering Chicago, *1854*, 57; Chicago as a center of, 58; earnings of Chicago, *1851–57*, 58; decline in earnings of, *1857–58*, 74; earnings of, *1860–69*, 83; mileage of, *1860–69*, 83; mileage of, in the United States, increases, *1879–83*, 128; new trunk lines enter Chicago, *1880–82*, 134; belt-line projects, 143; growth of, *1870–90*, 197. *See also* Names of individual railroads
Raising the level of the city, *1856–60*, 64, 75
Randolph Street, land values on, in central business district, *1830–1932*, 340–42
Real estate bonds: in *1889–90*, 151; increase of, in popularity, *1919–27*, 237; overissue of, in *1927–28*, 265
Real estate cycle, Chicago: population growth of, 272–73; definition of, 369; supply of houses cannot be increased immediately, 374; gross rents rise, 378; net rents rise more, 378–79; selling prices of old buildings, 381; new building profitable, 382; easy credit, 383;

INDEX

new construction increases, 383; shoestring financing, 385–86; new building absorbs land, 387; optimistic population forecasts, 388; visions of cities in cornfields, 388–89; lavish public improvements, 392–95; all the factors at full tide, 396; reverse movement begins, 396; foreclosures increase, 399; stock-market, *débacle*, 399–400; attrition, 400; banks reverse boom loan policy, 401; stagnation and foreclosures, 402; wreckage is cleared away, 402–3; ready for another boom, 403; table showing increase in factors on upswing, 404; table showing factors on downswing, 405; chart of, *1830–1930*, 406; Chicago, compared with the United States general business cycle, 406; tables showing sequence of factors, 408–9; time intervals in, 409; fluctuation of factors in, 415; duration of, 417; may be a passing phase, 423

Real estate excursion trains: in *1872*, 108; in *1889–90*, 167, 171; in *1925–26*, 257; in real estate cycle, 390

Receivers: in *1898*, 207; in *1931–32*, 272; rent policies of, 401

"Red light" district, 201; abolished, *1912*, 230. *See* Vice area

Refrigerator cars, begin to develop, 127

Rents: of stores, *1836*, 36; in *1848*, 52; of stores on Lake Street, *1856*, 70; in *1864*, 82; decline in, *1873*, 118; in *1875*, 119; in *1876–77*, 120; rise in, *1878–79*, 130; of offices, *1899*, 208; in *1902*, 210; old residential areas, *1892–1908*, 216; house, in the United States, *1914–18*, 233; of apartments in the United States, *1919–24*, 236; of offices, *1919–24*, 238; of stores, *1919–24*, 238; competition in, for corners, 249; in outlying business centers, 249; decline of, in stores, *1928–33*, 272; paid by native white, foreign-born, and colored, *1932*, 316; store and traffic counts, 327; index numbers of, of office buildings, *1915–32*, 377; of workingmen's dwellings, *1915–33*, 377; gross, rise rapidly, 378; net, rise even more rapidly, 379; and operating expenses of walk-up apartments, 380; factors in determining future ground, 453; relation between rise and fall of gross and net, 454

Residential districts: in *1856*, 21; in *1848*, 51; slums, *1857*, 65–66; suburbs, *1857*, 66; the avenues, *1867*, 87–88; marble-front dwellings, on South Side, *1871*, 88; fashionable districts, before *1873*, 90–91, 93–95; slums, vice areas, and workingman's quarters, *1865–71*, 96–98; suburbs, *1868–69*, 100; belt of workingmen's homes after fire of *1871*, 104, 107; Michigan Boulevard, *1880*, 133–34; flat buildings, 136–37; fashionable areas, *1877–95*, 189–90; in *1900*, 201–3; fashionable areas, *1900–1908*, 214–15; apartments in, 215; old areas, of 215–16, 230; new areas in, 216–17; new neighborhoods in, *1908–15*, 227–28; fashionable areas in, 229; tall apartments in, 244; bungalows in, 245; two-flat areas of, 245; old areas of, 246; summary of fashionable areas in, 302–10; map of, 303; summary of cheap areas in, 311–17; shift of, to outer city, 355–58; new and blighted areas in, compared, 361–64; shifting uses of, 364; speculation in, 365

Residential land values: best sites, *1857*, 67–70; cheap homesites, *1857*, 69; in fashionable centers, *1864–73*, 93–94; table showing, *1876–83*, 140; in old West Side residential areas, *1890*, 170–71; on Grand and Drexel boulevards, *1895*, 180; fashionable areas, *1877–95*, 189–90; map of, per front foot, *1910*, 220; in apartment and bungalow areas, *1910–28*, 246; in old areas, *1890–1931*, 247–48; map of, per front foot, *1926*, 259; map of, per front foot, *1931*, 267; decline of, *1928–31*, by value classes, 274; chart of, fashionable land, *1865–1933*, 305; chart of, high-grade areas, *1830–1933*, 306; chart of, one block north of Division Street, *1910* and *1928*, 308; chart of, South Side, Fifty-fifth to Fifty-sixth streets, 309; chart of, cheap land, *1890–1931*, 313; chart of, in old areas, *1830–1933*, 318; total, *1910*, *1926*, *1933*, 347; per acre along the lake, *1836*, *1856*, *1873*, *1892*, *1910*, *1928* (chart), 361

Retail business: stores, *1837*, 22; prior to *1848*, 48; effect on, of opening canal, 60; on Lake Street, 89; moves to State Street, 89–90; on secondary business streets, 98; department stores in, 158; expanding in, in the Loop, *1907*, 211–12; outlying, *1908–15*, 226–27; in *1919–27*, 248–50; origin and development of outlying, 320, 322; amount zoned for, 457. *See also* Business centers, outlying

Reversing flow of Chicago River, 86

Rice, Kenneth E., ix

River and Harbor Convention, *1847*, 50

Riverdale, 109, 203

Rogers Park: telephones in, *1906–16*, 228; land values of, *1830–1933*, 306

Rosenthal, H. S., ix

Rudolph, Emil, x

Rush Street in forties and fifties, 302

Sales: as method of land valuation, vii, 459–60; canal terms of, 444; options, exclusive, 444; sample of, method of using, 467–68

Saloon Building, *1836*, 21

Saloons: *1900*, 205; exclusion from residential areas, 304

Sands, the, raided, *1857*, 65, 307

Santa Fe Railroad, enters Chicago, 159–60

Scalping, *1890*, 173

Schepler, F. A., ix

Schiffman, Mae, x

School Section: first sale of, *1833*, 26; sales in, *1835*, 29

Schwengel, Frank R., ix

Sears Roebuck & Co., 199; moves, *1904*, 213

Seasonal elements, in land market, 448

Second mortgages, holders of, forced out, 266

Section-line streets. See Business centers, outlying

Sections, the three, of the city, 13–14, 301

Sellers of real estate, "sleepers" and subdividers, 442

Sequence of factors in Chicago real estate cycle, 405

Settled area: map showing extent of, *1834*, *1844*, *1857*, *1873*, 103; map showing extent of, *1873* and *1899*, 204; map showing extent of, *1899* and *1926*, 262

Seventy-ninth Street: chart showing land values on, *1910*, *1928*, *1931*, 250; zone of maximum population increase on, 250–51; value of, *1916–23*, 252; and Ashland Avenue, 310; chart of land values on, *1928*, 330

Seventy-ninth and Halsted street corners, value of: in *1911–12*, 227; in *1910–29*, 252

Sewers, first, *1851*, 64; map of, *1873*, 92

Sheridan Road, 307

Shifting land uses, 364

Shoestring financing, 265, 386–87, 446

Shultz, Earle, x

Sidewalks: of plank, *1854*, 64; in outlying subdivisions, 180, 392

Simpson, Herbert D.: cited, x, 258, 391, 401, 438, 462, 463; estimate of, of Chicago land value, *1928*, 462

Sixty-third Street: growth of, begins *1880*, 191; land values on, *1928*, 330

Sixty-third Street and Cottage Grove Avenue: sale, *1847*, 52; in *1906–12*, 226–27; land values on, *1910–29*, 252

Sixty-third and Halsted streets: sale, *1847*, 52; land values on, *1878*, 125; growth of, 216; in *1910–13*, 227; values on, *1910–29*, 252; rise in values on, *1928*, 258

Sixty-third Street and Kedzie Avenue: values on, *1913*, 227; values on, *1910–29*, 252

Sixty-third Street and Western Avenue: sales on, *1912*, 229; values on, *1910–29*, 252

Skindzier, Edward G., x

Skyscrapers: Home Insurance Building, *1885*, 136, 150; growth of, *1885–94*, 149–51; Tacoma Building, 150; financing, 151

Slums: first, 51; Kilgubbin, 65; sands, 65; in *1863–71*, 96–97; Halsted and Maxwell, *1873*, 97; in *1900*, 201–3; land values in, *1890–1931*, 247–48; cheap residential areas, 311–17; blighted areas, 361–64; capitalization of income in, 451

Smith, George, money of, 59

Smyth, John Usher, x

South Chicago: subdivision of Calumet, *1836*, 31; harbor and docks at, *1873*, 96; southern expansion toward, 107; Calumet Canal and Dock Co., 108; "resurrection" of, *1879–83*, 134; belt-line railroads near, 143; acre tracts at, 176; business center, *1891*, 192; description of, *1900*, 203; growth of commerce on Calumet River, *1889–1916*, 213–14

South Shore, 171, 218, 228, 231, 307; land values in, *1830–1933* (chart), 306

South Side: land trails through, 14–15; in *1836*, 19; population, *1837–40*, 22–23; fashionable residences on, 51; in *1848–57*, 66; land values on fashionable avenues of, *1855*, 74; horse-car lines, 77; fashionable avenues of, *1871*, 88; trend to, 91; development of the avenues on, *1871*, 93–94; manufacturing areas on, *1871*, 96; slums of, 97; secondary business streets on, 98; parks on, *1865–71*, 99; suburbs on, 100; recovery in land values on, after fire, 107; population of, *1870*, 111; boulevards on, *1880*, 133; manufacturing areas of, *1880*, 134–35; marked growth of, after *1880*, 137; belt lines in, 143; leads in transportation, *1887–94*, 144–46; transfer corners in, 146–47; cable lines on, 148; projected elevated lines on, 149; annexation of Hyde Park and Lake on, *1889*, 155; as site of World's Fair, 156; speculation in land and buildings near Fair grounds, 157; new areas building up on, 161; as center of speculation in acres, 164; con-

INDEX

struction of "Alley Elevated," 171; boom and collapse at Washington Park, *1890*, 173; erection of hotels and apartments for World's Fair on, 177; University of Chicago founded on, 177; lack of guests to fill hotels on, 178; receiverships on, *1893*, 179; transportation lines change from horse to electric power on, 182; aggregate rise and fall of land values on, *1877–98*, 184–85; fashionable areas on, *1877–95*, 189–90; outlying business centers on, 191–92; population growth of Hyde Park and Lake on, *1880–90*, 195; in *1900*, 202–3; in decline, 210; fashionable residential areas on, *1900–1908*, 214–15; expansion of colored race on, 216; new residential areas on, *1907–8*, 216; outlying business centers on, *1908–15*, 226–27; lot sales on, 229; manufacturing areas on, 230; values of land in old areas on, *1890–1931*, 247; summary of growth of fashionable areas on, 302–4; chart, with cross-section of residential land values on, *1910* and *1928*, 309; cheap residential areas on, 312; expansion of colored race on, 313–14; store rents and traffic counts on, 327

South Water Street: wholesale street by *1856*, 65; decline of, in values, *1856–73*, 113; congested produce market on, *1915*, 225; land values on, *1830–1931*, 340–42

Special assessments, in Chicago, *1862–1932*, 492

Speculation, land: in *1833–36*, 26–33; in *1848–57*, 67–70; in *1865–71*, 89–90, 100, 101; in *1865–73*, 107–9; in *1880–82*, 135, 136; in *1889–90*, 161–73; in *1925–26*, 255–58; in real estate cycle, 383–97. *See also* Boom, in land values

Speculation, in stocks and commodities, 407

Speed, of horse cars, cable cars, and elevated lines, 146

Spikings, William H., x

Stability in real estate values, *1880*, 139

Stagnation in real estate: in *1841*, 44; in *1861*, 78; in *1877*, 124; in *1896–97*, 180–81; in *1933*, 272; in real estate cycle, 401–2

Start, the, of the Rise of land values in Chicago: in *1830*, 23; prices at first sale, 24

State Street: development of, begins, 89; Potter Palmer and Marshall Field on, 90; shift to, 90; rebuilt after fire of *1871*, 103; land values on, *1873*, 111; sale of corner of Madison and, *1879*, 133;

hourly traffic on, *1890*, 172; at new peak, *1896*, 188; still higher peaks, *1906*, 211; south of Van Buren, *1911*, 225; chart of land values on, *1873*, *1910*, *1928*, 323; land values on, *1830*, *1836*, *1856*, *1873*, *1894*, *1910*, *1928*, *1931* (maps and tables), 340–42, 345

Statute of Frauds, 443

Stevens Hotel, 241

Stickney tract: purchase of, 160; in ill repute, 176. *See also* Clearing manufacturing district

Stock-market crash: of October 24, *1929*, 258; in real estate cycle, 400

Stock prices, canal, railroad, and industrial: railroad stocks, *1856–57*, 74; in *1883*, 141; chart of, *1830–1933*, 414; table of peaks and valleys in, 420; price information on, compared with land, 446

Stock Yards: Dole's *1832*, 19; at Bull's Head and at Twenty-ninth Street and Cottage Grove Avenue, *1856*, 65; concentrated at Thirty-ninth and Halsted streets, *1865*, 85–86; land sales near, *1872–73*, 108

Stores, in Chicago, *1837*, 22. *See also* Retail business

Street-car intersections, land value at, *1910–29*, 255. *See also* Business centers, outlying

Street-car lines, surface: in *1859–65*, 77–78; map of horse-car lines, *1880*, 126; extensions of, *1870–78*, 127; South Side cable lines, *1882*, 137; in *1887–94*, 144–49; map of, *1891*, 145; new lines, *1894–98*, 181–82; electric power on cable lines, 208; map of, *1902*, 209; map of extensions to, *1903–32*, 264; effect of, on supply of urban land, 295; advance information as to location of, 441

Street improvements, allowance for cost of, 348. *See also* Improvements, street or public

Streeter, Captain, 307, 433

Streets, condition of, 49, 51, 62. *See also* Paved streets

Subcenters, business. *See* Business streets, outlying

Subdividers, sales methods of: in *1836*, 30–31; in *1872*, 108; in *1889–90*, 163–69; in *1917*, 229; in *1925–26*, 255, 257; in the real estate cycle, 389–91, 444

Subdivision activity: in *1835–36*, 31; in *1856*, 70; in *1868–73*, 110; in *1885–88*, 159–61; in *1889*, 171; in *1891*, 177; in *1891–98*, 180; in *1908–18*, 222; in *1918–26*, 237; in *1926–33*, 399; cycle of (chart),

413; layout, 427–30; table showing lots subdivided, *1874–1930*, 477–78; table showing acres subdivided in Chicago, *1830–1932*, 479–80
Subdivisions, maps of original: in *1830–43*, 32; in *1844–62*, 68; in *1863–79*, 110; in *1880–1932*, 256
Suburbs: embryonic, *1857*, 66; growth of, after *1868*, 100; growth of, to *1873*, 108; in *1880*, 137; in *1900*, 203; population of, 282; North Shore towns, 307
Suffering, due to collapsing of booms, 122–23
Suitability of building to location, 449
Sullivan, J. V., ix
Supply of urban land in Chicago and the United States, 295
Surface lines. *See* Cable lines, Electric surface lines, Horse-car lines, and Street-car lines

Tall apartments, 307
Taverns at Wolf's Point, 17
Tax assessments. *See* Assessment of land for taxation
Taxes: delinquent, *1877–79*, 131; burden of, *1930*, 268–69; city, *1924–31*, compared with ninety-three years, *1830–1922*, 351–52; effect of future, 367; chart of, and special assessments, *1865–1931*, 397; inequalities in, 438, 461–62; table of Chicago city tax levy, *1837–1931*, 488
Telegraph, completion of first lines, *1848*, 53
Telephone: invention of, *1876*, 127; growth of, *1890–1930*, 198; increase in, *1895–1920*, 205; chart of number of, in Chicago, *1890–1932*, 206; growth in number of, by districts of city, *1906–16*, 228; use of, in selling real estate, *1917*, *1925–26*, 229, 257; increase in number of, *1921–26*, 237; as a means of bringing buyers and sellers together, 442; in real estate cycle, 390, 442–43; number of stations in Chicago, *1882–1933* (table), 490
Theaters: in Loop, in *1900*, 201; growth of outlying by *1915*, 226; space occupied by, 336; motion picture, 355
Time required to go from New York to Chicago, *1836–52*, 61–62
Time intervals, between factors in real estate cycle, 408–9
Title, differences in owner's, 434
Torrens system, 436
Tower buildings, space occupied by, 241, 330, 333
Townsites: new towns platted, *1835–36*, 28; speculation in, 30–31

Trading equities, 119–20, 176, 265, 338, 446
Traffic counts. *See* Counts, traffic
Trails, land: Indian, 13; map of, 14; described, 15
Transfer corners: in *1890*, 146; rise of, *1909–13*, 231. *See also* Business centers, outlying
Transfers, real estate: in *1874–77*, 120; in *1890*, 173; in *1908–18*, 222; in *1927–30*, 266; cycle of, 412; number of, in Cook County, *1901–33*, 472. *See also* Conveyances, real estate
Trust deeds and mortgages: amount of, *1918–32*, 386; in Cook County, annually, *1896–1933*, 473
Tunnels, under Chicago River: traffic, through Washington Street, *1871*, 87; at Washington and LaSalle streets, 147
Two-flat apartment buildings, in Chicago, 245, 292

Union Pacific Railroad, completion of, *1869*, 83
Union Park: land near, 94; first park, 99
United Cigar stores, establish chains, *1910*, 226
University of Chicago. *See* Chicago, University of
Unskilled labor: amount of, required to purchase site of Chicago, 346; charts showing, 348–49; chart showing wages of, *1830–1933*, 410
Urban land in the United States: condition of, in the World War, 233; rise of, *1920–26*, 234–35
Urbs in horto, 288
Utilization of land in Chicago, *1850*, *1870*, *1890*, *1911*, *1923*, 290

Vacancies in buildings: on West Side, *1890*, 172, 189; in apartments, *1898–99*, 208; in apartments, *1902*, 215; on South Side, *1926–33*, 270; as factor in operating expenses, 380, 451–52; in office buildings, *1926–33*, 482
Vacant lots, 180, 217–18. *See also* Lots subdivided
Valleys of depression coincide, 419
Value, land. *See* Land value
Van Buren Street, land values on, in central business district, *1830–1931*, 340–42
Vice area: in *1871*, 97; after fire of *1871*, 103; in *1900*, 201–2; abolished, *1912*, 230; west of Wells, 312

Wabash Avenue: fashionable homes near Congress Street, *1854*, 65; wholesale

INDEX

trade on, 90; fashionable homes on, 93; boom of, after fire, 102; decline of, 103; center of musical-instrument trade, *1892*, 189; retail trades expand to, *1902*, 211; land values on, in central business district, *1830–1931*, 340–42, 345

Wacker, Charles H., estimate of population by, 388, 456

Wacker Drive (South Water St.), land values on, *1830–1931*, 340–42

Wages: in *1858*, 75; in *1872–73*, 118; in *1874*, 119; in *1899*, 208; of unskilled labor, *1831–1933* (chart), 410

Wagon traffic: in *1837–48*, 46–47; estimate of, entering Chicago, *1847*, 48; estimate of, crossing bridges, 63, 87

Walgreen drug stores, 249

War, effect of, on speculation, 422

Washington Heights: speculation in, *1868–73*, 108; culmination of boom in land values in, *1873*, 117

Washington Park: boom of, *1890*, 173; area south of, builds up, *1908–12*, 227

Washington Street: churches move on, *1856*, 65; banks on, *1872*, 103; high-grade residential area, 302, 304; as boulevard on West Side, 191, 310; land values on, in central business district, *1830–1931*, 340–42

Waterways systems: the Great Lakes and Mississippi Valley, 7; map of, 8

Waterworks: crib, *1853*, 64; new tunnel, *1867*, 86

Wells Street (Fifth Avenue), land values on, in central business district, *1830–1931*, 340–42, 345

West Side: in *1838*, 20; growth of, as manufacturing center, 50; growth of, *1848–57*, 66; horse-car lines on, 77–78; growth of, after fire, 102; transportation lines on, *1890–91*, 147; vacant houses on, *1890*, 172, 189; transportation lines on, by *1897*, 182; in *1900*, 201–2; growth of manufacturing on, *1900–1907*, 213; land values of cheap residential areas on, *1890–1931* (table), 247–48; land values of business corners on, 252; summary of growth of, 301; fashionable areas on, 302; chart of, 313; expansion of racial groups on, 313

Westchester, speculation at, 255

Western Electric Co., moves, *1903*, 213

Wheat trade, start of the, 47. See also Grain trade

Wheeler, George S., xi

Wholesale area or district, 37; on South Water Street, *1856*, 65; expansion of, *1865*, 89; new district west of Wells after fire of *1871*, 103; value of land in, *1876–83*, 140; in *1900–1908*, 212–13; decline of, in area west of Wells Street, *1929–33*, 274, 334; land values in area west of Wells Street, *1830–1931* (maps), 340–42

Wholesale prices: decline in, after Civil War, 82; decline in, *1877*, 123; in *1900–1915*, 205; in *1908–18*, 222; land values deflated for changes in, 344; chart of, 349; allowance for changes in, in forecasts, 367; chart of, *1831–1933*, 410

Wholesale trade: after *1848*, 60; growth of, *1860–68*, 83; "drummers" sent out, 83; in *1877–81*, 129; value of, *1875–1926*, 481–82

Wilmette, 303; population of, *1900–1930*, 289

Wilson Avenue district: in *1900*, 202; extension of elevated lines to, *1908*, 216; population of, *1908*, 216; competition of Davis-Orrington section, 275

Windsor Park golf course, growth of, *1921–26*, 245

Winnetka, 203; population of, *1900–1930*, 282

Wirth, Louis, x

Wolf's Point, 17

Wooden-block pavement, *1871*, 87

Woodlawn, *1880*, 138

Woolworth stores, 249

Workingmen's cottages, after fire of *1871*, 104

World's Fair, *1893*; Chicago, the choice, 155; first proposed, *1887*, 155; Jackson Park, site selected, 156; effect of, on land values in vicinity, 157; fantastic projects suggested by, 157; blamed for depression, 158; effect of closing of, 179

Wright, Chester Whitney, viii

Wright, John S.: losses of, *1837*, 42; estimate of, on decline in land values, *1856–61*, 75, 76, 80; population forecast of, 456; opinion of, as to land values, 464

"Y," configuration of Chicago land made by river, 299

Yields, on central business property, 130, 131, 161, 212

Young, Hugh E., ix

Zoning law: height limits of, 241, 440; restrictions on towers, 296; business use, 324, 457

[PRINTED IN U·S·A·]

www.ingramcontent.com/pod-product-compliance
Lightning Source LLC
Chambersburg PA
CBHW020630230426
43665CB00008B/110